OUT OF THE SHADOWS

Out OF THE Shadows

A Biographical History of African American Athletes

EDITED BY
DAVID K. WIGGINS

The University of Arkansas Press
Fayetteville 2006

Manufactured in the United States of America

10 09 08 07 06 5 4 3 2 1

Designed by Liz Lester

♾ The paper used in this publication meets the minimum requirements of the American National Standard for Permanence of Paper for Printed Library Materials Z39.48-1984.

LIBRARY OF CONGRESS CATALOGING-IN-PUBLICATION DATA

Wiggins, David Kenneth, 1951–
Out of the shadows : a biographical history of African American athletes / edited by David K. Wiggins.
p. cm.
Includes bibliographical references and index.
ISBN 1-55728-826-7 (casebound : alk. paper)
1. African American athletes—Biography. 2. African American athletes—Portraits. 3. African American athletes—History. 4. Sports—United States—History. I. Title.
GV697.A1W534 2006
796.092'396073—dc22
[B]

2006019218

For Brenda, Jordan, and Spencer

CONTENTS

PREFACE

This book chronicles the lives of twenty prominent African American athletes who competed either behind segregated walls or in predominantly white organized sport or, in some cases, at both levels of sport. Written by noted academicians with long lists of major publications on various aspects of sport, each biography describes the respective athletes' various sporting successes and disappointments as well as struggles encountered in a society marred by deep-seated stereotypes and history of racial discrimination. Taken as a whole, the biographies are intended to furnish perspectives on the changing status of African American athletes over the past two centuries and how those changes mirrored the transformation of sport, American society, and civil rights legislation. The biographies are intended, moreover, to provide a better understanding of such processes as assimilation, the interconnection between sport and race, and the simultaneous quest to establish individual identities and group loyalty.

The athletes I have chosen for this volume represent a variety of sports, different personalities, and diverse approaches to civil rights and the institution of sport. Some of them came from very humble backgrounds while others were more privileged, some of them were reticent about speaking out on racial issues while others were more vocal about protesting discriminatory practices, and some were not always popular among Americans while others were admired by many in both the black and white communities. All of them, however, realized great success as athletes, garnering prestigious honors and awards and numerous individual and team championships. These athletes were considered some of the best, if not the best, at their particular sport, during the time in which they competed and at whatever level of participation they found themselves.

Though several of the athletes in this volume have been written about in great detail elsewhere, I have elected to include them since any one volume work on the experiences of African Americans in sport would be incomplete without them. Those individuals are Jack Johnson, Jesse Owens, Joe Louis, Jackie Robinson, and Muhammad Ali. In addition to these individuals, I include athletes from the late nineteenth century who realized enormous success in sport, but who are largely unknown except to specialists in sport history. Those individuals are Jimmy Winkfield, Marshall "Major" Taylor, and William Henry Lewis. I also include athletes who spent much of their careers behind segregated walls and whose lives have largely been told either through general histories or children's literature rather than through specialized scholarly studies. Those individuals are Ora Washington, Satchel Paige, Alice Coachman, Althea Gibson, and Wilma Rudolph. I also include athletes, in addition to Muhammad Ali, who enjoyed outstanding careers in sport and were part of the civil rights struggle of the tumultuous decade of the 1960s and early 1970s. Those individuals are Bill Russell, Jim Brown, and Arthur Ashe. Lastly, I include noted contemporary athletes who have become intertwined with the new celebrity age and marketing-driven popular culture. Those individuals are Michael Jordan, Tiger Woods, and Venus and Serena Williams. In essence, the choices of biographies reflect my desire to introduce readers to relatively little known yet extremely gifted athletes while at once providing insights into the lives of athletes who have seemingly always been part of our collective historical memory.

I owe a debt of gratitude to a number of people who assisted me in the completion of this project. Patrick Miller, my friend and colleague from Northeastern Illinois University who collaborated with me on two previous works dealing with African American participation in sport, offered sage advice and cogent comments that improved the overall quality of this book. Lisa Reeves of George Mason University was indispensable in the completion of this book, spending an enormous amount of time making editorial changes, formatting materials, and typing all introductions. Ellen Rodgers took time away from her own scholarly endeavors and her multitude of other responsibilities at George Mason University to assist with the completion of this project. Larry Malley, as he has done with a countless number of historical studies during his long and distinguished career in publishing, guided me through this project with much care and great insight. Finally, I am indebted, as always, to my wife, Brenda, and two boys, Jordan and Spencer, for their constant support, encouragement, and patience. The three provide perspective on what is important and most meaningful.

I Striving for Athletic Success in a Jim Crow Society

The first two African Americans to achieve fame and international notoriety in sport were Bill Richmond and Tom Molineaux. Richmond, born a free black on Staten Island, New York, in 1763, moved to England at the age of fourteen with the British commander Lord Percy. In London, he established a reputation as an outstanding boxer and trainer of other boxers. In 1800, with the help of friends and wealthy patrons, Richmond opened his very successful Horse and Dolphin Tavern where he sold spirits and taught the finer points of pugilism to up-and-coming fighters. Five years later he made history by becoming the first African American to compete for the heavyweight title when he fought the great English boxer Tom Crib. Unfortunately, Richmond lost to the heavily favored Crib in a relatively short bout.

Molineaux came from a different background than Richmond, but the two will forever be bound together in history. Legend has it that Molineaux grew up a slave on either a Virginia or Maryland plantation and eventually gained his freedom after winning several boxing matches for his master. Although there is no primary evidence to support this legend, we do know that Molineaux traveled to England in 1809 and began to train under the tutelage of Richmond at his Horse and Dolphin Tavern. In 1810 and 1811 "the Tremendous Man of Colour," as Molineaux came to be known, lost heavyweight championship bouts to Crib. The first bout was a controversial one, with Crib declared the winner after the forty-fourth round.

A telling fact about both Molineaux and Richmond is that the information we do have about their careers derives from British rather than American sources. This is evidence, as the historian Elliott Gorn has pointed out, of the apparent indifference of the American public at that time to boxing. It was also probably a reflection of the limited popularity and lack of organizational structure in American sport more generally during this period. Sport in this country was still essentially an informal, unorganized activity with horse racing being the only pursuit with a national following and consistent press coverage. The large majority of African Americans were confined to southern plantations where they participated in various recreational activities in the slavequarter community or were utilized by slaveholders in such visible athletic roles as boxers and trainers and jockeys in horse racing. There were also a smaller number of free blacks in America during the first half of the nineteenth century who fashioned their own recreational and sporting life, but we know very little about that life, either in regards to individual athletic performances or the types of clubs or organizations formed.

In the mid-nineteenth century, sport in America would evolve from an unorganized activity to a more highly structured and organized phenomenon. The influence of various immigrant groups and the rise of industrialization and urbanization would combine with a host of other societal factors to transform sport into a culturally significant institution characterized by an increasing number of teams, leagues, and bureaucracies. This transformation in sport would be beneficial to African American athletes just as it would be to their white counterparts. In the latter half of the nineteenth century and early part of the twentieth century, African Americans established separate sports organizations behind segregated walls that helped to satisfy their competitive impulses, contributed to a much-needed sense of community, and served as visible examples of business acumen and self-reliance. In addition to separate sports organizations, there were a select number of outstanding African American athletes who achieved success in predominantly white organized sport, even at the turn of the twentieth century when Jim Crow laws had sanctioned rigid racial segregation and relegated many African Americans to a life marred by poverty and limited opportunities for success. Through talent, force of will, and often with the help of white benefactors and friends, these athletes realized much fame and became household names in this country and sometimes even internationally when they competed in their respective sports in foreign lands because of the lack of competition or deteriorating racial conditions in the United States.

One of those sports in which African American athletes found fame was horse racing. Used as jockeys by southern slave owners during the antebellum period, African Americans continued to ride horses with great success in the most prestigious races throughout much of the nineteenth century. Included among these African American riders were Billy Walker, Isaac Murphy, Pike Barnes, Tony Hamilton, Alonzo Clayton, Chippie Ray, Willie Simms, Jimmy Lee, Isaac Lewis, Kid Stoval, Spider Anderson, Monk Overton, and Jimmy Winkfield. Of these riders, it was Winkfield who perhaps enjoyed the most intriguing and remarkable career. Often dubbed the "last great black jockey," Winkfield was the winning rider in a number of prestigious races, including the Kentucky Derby in 1901 and 1902.

In 1903 Winkfield took his riding skills to Europe, the result of a contract dispute with a disgruntled owner and the deteriorating racial conditions in the horse racing industry specifically and America more generally. As Susan Hamburger makes clear in "Jimmy Winkfield: The 'Black Maestro' of the Racetrack," Winkfield enjoyed a great many successes on tracks in Russia, Poland, Germany, Austria, Hungary, and France before retiring from riding in 1930 and becoming a full-time trainer of racehorses. Tellingly, Winkfield's outstanding career on the track and his personal life, which included failed marriages and illicit relationships with several white women, went largely unnoticed in the United States. The "insularity of sports reporting" combined with Winkfield's reticence to speak out about himself, notes Hamburger, helped contribute to the relatively little attention he received from the American public. Fortunately, Winkfield's outstanding career in horse racing has recently been acknowledged through different honors and awards he has received posthumously. In 2003 an exhibit honoring his last ride at the Kentucky Derby was held at the Kentucky Derby Museum at Churchill Downs. He was inducted into the National Thoroughbred Racing Hall of Fame in Saratoga Springs, New York, in 2004. Finally, in 2005 Winkfield had a race named after him at the aqueduct racetrack in New York.

The career of Marshall "Major" Taylor, the outstanding African American bicyclist, was similar to Winkfield's in that it involved travels outside the United States in an effort to achieve success in his chosen sport. Like the "last great black jockey," American racism combined with a flourishing culture of sport and seemingly more racial tolerance evident in many foreign countries enticed Taylor to ply his trade away from his home country. As Andrew Ritchie writes in "Marshall 'Major' Taylor: The Fastest Bicycle Rider in the World," Taylor achieved enormous success on the oval in his native America, but also found fame in such places as Australia, Canada, and France. During his career, Taylor set many world records in time trials against the clock. In 1899 he captured the International Cycling Association one-mile World Sprint Championship in Montreal, a significant event because it was the second world title won by an African American athlete (bantamweight boxer George "Little Chocolate" Dixon became the first African American world titleholder when he defeated English champion Nunc Wallace in 1890). As was the case for many African American expatriate writers and artists, it was Paris where Taylor seemingly found much hospitality and unparalleled acceptance and racial tolerance. The city allowed him a sense of freedom while at once furnishing him untold opportunities to race against some of the world's best riders. Upon his arrival in Paris for the first time in 1901, claims Ritchie, Taylor realized hero status, with the daily press recounting in great detail almost every move he made while in the city.

The select number of African Americans who achieved success in intercollegiate athletics on predominantly white university campuses during this period were generally different than Winkfield, Taylor, and many other professional athletes in regards to family backgrounds, educational attainments, and post-sport careers. Typically from middle- to upper-middle-class families who placed a decided emphasis on academics and service to their race, these individuals usually attended either a private academy in New England, a prominent public school, or a historically black college in the South before matriculating to one of the more racially liberal institutions in the northern half of the United States where they could participate in sport while receiving the education necessary to prepare for careers in various professions and to assume their place among the African American elite. Certainly one of the most notable of these individuals was William Henry Lewis, the son of freed slaves from Berkeley, Virginia, who fashioned a great career as a center and captain of the football teams at Amherst and Harvard Colleges. Gregory Bond points out in his essay "The Strange Career of William Henry Lewis" that Lewis's play was so extraordinary that he was selected to Casper Whitney's All-American football team in both 1892 and 1893. Following his playing days, Lewis spent some ten years as an assistant coach at Harvard, an important event in that it made him the first African American coach at a predominantly white college. He added to his fame by eventually becoming the United States attorney for Boston and assistant attorney general of the United States under President William Taft. Lewis's success in the political arena, however, seemingly came at a price. Bond explains that in order for Lewis to climb the political ladder he had to abandon the frontal assault on racial inequality that marked his early career and adopt the accommodationist strategy of Booker T. Washington and utilize "the power of the Tuskegee machine." This personal transformation came amid the "rapidly deteriorating race relations" in American society during the early part of the twentieth century.

The most controversial athlete of this period, and perhaps of any period in American history for that matter, was Jack Johnson, the great black boxer from Galveston, Texas, who was heavyweight champion of the world from 1908 to 1915. Refusing to acquiesce to the white power structure and seemingly without fear of death or danger, Johnson lived life on his own terms and played on the racial fears of many Americans by marrying three white women and having intimate relationships with many others. His relationships with white women and brash and uncompromising lifestyle, explains Gerald Gems in "Jack Johnson and the Quest for Racial Respect," was abhorred by a large majority of white Americans, but viewed in a far more complicated fashion by those in the African American community. To some in the African American community, including the great intellectual W. E. B. Du Bois, Johnson realized much respect because of his victories in the ring and the fact he insisted on living his life as a proud black man without any apparent regard for the power wielded by white Americans. To others in the African American community, including the "wizard" himself, Booker T. Washington, Johnson was a poor representative of the race because he was unwilling to adhere to the racial restrictions of American culture and assume the subservient role deemed essential to the future success of all blacks.

Jimmy Winkfield, photographed here in his racing silks, is considered the last of the great black jockeys. *(Keeneland-Cook, Keeneland Library)*

1 Jimmy Winkfield

The "Black Maestro" of the Racetrack

SUSAN HAMBURGER

In many respects, Jimmy Winkfield's career as a jockey mirrored that of many other outstanding African American athletes of the late nineteenth and early twentieth centuries in that he was grudgingly acknowledged at home in the United States, while revered as a champion in Europe. He managed to enjoy a long racing career, first as a jockey then later as a trainer, well beyond the age when most jockeys retire. Through two world wars and the Great Depression, Winkfield survived and succeeded—because of, despite, and regardless of his race.

Horse racing in America enjoyed a long history parallel with the young country. Brought over from England with the colonists, the sport appealed to all classes and races while participation at various levels sorted out among these selfsame divisions. Eighteenth- and nineteenth-century racing saw owners and breeders of racehorses come from the moneyed upper classes. During the era of racing as a gentleman's sport, some owners also trained their own horses. As the sport moved from an avocation to a business, the ranks of trainers arose from the lower classes—farm boys with minimal formal education or opportunity to better themselves. As a predominantly rural sport transplanted to the fringes of urban areas, horse racing attracted farm youth to the track in search of jobs in a milieu with which they were familiar.

The primary theory, still accepted today, is that the jockey's weight is a major factor in slowing a horse's speed and endurance. The early race riders—sometimes the full-size adult owner, sometimes a young stable boy—soon demonstrated that the smaller and lighter-weight jockeys won more races than their larger, heavier counterparts. To gain a competitive edge, owners and trainers started using smaller men and young boys to ride their racehorses.

As the breeding industry developed in the southern states of Maryland, Virginia, and Kentucky with limestone-enhanced water and grass to develop strong bones in young horses, so too did the apprenticeship of jockeys. Prior to the American Civil War, most of the southern jockeys were slaves. After the war, these same men continued in the profession as successful riders at tracks in the border and northern states before the southern economy recovered enough for racetracks to flourish there again. From New Orleans to Cincinnati, black jockeys dominated the sport. But with the rise of Jim Crow and the competition for rapidly increasing paychecks from winning races, white riders insinuated themselves into the black-dominated profession and, by fear and intimidation, began to squeeze out African American jockeys until the only black faces seen on the track were either in the grandstand betting on the horses or working at menial jobs tending horses on the backstretch.

At a time when African American jockeys reigned supreme on the American turf, Jimmy Winkfield (1880–1974) began his rise to racing stardom only to be stymied by racism and the decline of horse racing in the early 1900s. His determination to continue riding sent him to Czarist Russia, Poland, and France as a jockey, then to the United States and back to France as a trainer of thoroughbreds. Throughout his long life and rollercoaster career, Winkfield exhibited the perseverance of an indomitable will to survive and to succeed.

The youngest of seventeen children, Winkfield learned to ride saddle horses on the farms near where his parents sharecropped tobacco and hemp in Chilesburg, Kentucky. Orphaned at ten, Winkfield left his home and went to live with his older sister in Lexington, Kentucky, the center of the state's—and the nation's—horse racing and breeding. Surrounded by successful black jockeys such as James "Soup" Perkins and three-time Kentucky Derby winner Isaac "Ike" Murphy, Winkfield saw much to admire as he worked his first job shining shoes. The supportive environment reinforced a strong sense of self-worth and pride. Winkfield respected Murphy's honesty and integrity and learned a valuable lesson about a strategy for making money in the profession. Murphy, considered a "money rider," accepted mounts in stakes races rather than the cheaper claiming races. Instead of going for the greatest number of wins in a season, he focused on riding quality horses with better than average chances of winning to give him an unusually high percentage of wins. Murphy theorized that a jockey who won in big stakes races gave him a good reputation and the opportunity to ride better horses with excellent chances of winning the stakes races—money follows money—rather than racking up wins in a hundred minor races for low pay.[1] Winkfield emulated this example and sought the better-paying races instead of frequent wins.

During the evenings Winkfield attended school but daytime found him driving carriages throughout Lexington as the horsemen conducted their business. He observed and absorbed how these white men interacted. On Saturdays, he and his friends played marbles and watched the horses at the historic Kentucky Association racetrack, nicknamed Chittlin' Switch, at Sixth and Race Streets abutting the black neighborhood where they lived. When the opportunity arose at age seventeen, Winkfield began working at the track as a stable hand. In later years he remembered, "I galloped an old mare that year that won five races, and each time she win the owner give me $5 and the jockey $5. Next spring, Bub May hired me for $10 a month and board. His daddy was mayor of Lexington, and in the summer of '98 they took some horses to Chicago."[2] Winkfield progressed to race riding as a jockey in 1898, with an inauspicious debut, being disqualified—too eager to win—for bumping another horse. His one-year suspension gave Winkfield the time to hone his craft in morning workouts and illegal races outside the official sanctions of the Jockey Club in New York. The Mays traveled the then-western circuit from Chicago to New Orleans, where Winkfield won his first race a year later.[3] In 1902 Winkfield signed with the more prominent trainer Patrick Dunne, son-in-law of the powerful Chicago stable owner Edward Corrigan. As early as 1900 Corrigan also raced his horses in England.[4] Horseman Phil Chinn remarked, "May brought him up, but May never had to teach that boy how to ride. He was a natural from the start. He had no particular style; he just sat up there like a piece of gold."[5] Winkfield learned his lessons well from Ike Murphy and other black jockeys who dominated the sport.

Paralleling the white paternalism so common to the sports world, Winkfield had a string of white patrons who first acted as surrogate fathers and one was later his father-in-law. One would almost think he was more comfortable in white society since for most of his life he lived with white women in Europe. The strictures of race are an artificial construct. With a white grandfather and unknown antecedents on his mother's side, it is possible that only Winkfield's skin color assigned him to the category of black while his personhood inwardly gravitated toward his white paternity. In any event, the superficiality of Winkfield's blackness is what people saw and those in the United States treated him as black. In Europe, however, even though his skin color was a novelty, Winkfield transcended racial barriers to live, love, and work unfettered by the constraints of racist negativity. One European horseman commented that "on the ground Winkfield was a perfect gentleman. But in the saddle he was a demon."[6] Winkfield's skin color made him easily identifiable among the pale Europeans, but it was his skill with horses that distinguished "the black maestro" from the other jockeys.

Expatriate African Americans such as Josephine Baker and James Baldwin, and other celebrated figures like Paul Robeson, experienced not only the adulation of European audiences but acceptance as human beings—a comfortableness among people lacking the baggage of hundreds of years of institutionalized racism. Ironically, in Europe, the novelty of blackness made these expatriates sought-after rather than discriminated against. Baker remembered that a waiter once told an American who had insulted her, "You are in France, and here we treat all races the same."[7] In this milieu Jimmy Winkfield thrived and prospered.

As a young black man living in the segregated South, Winkfield learned early that politeness and deference to white folks kept you alive. He had to carefully balance this off-track public demeanor with his competitive spirit to win on the racetrack. Described as courageous and confident in the saddle, well mannered, smart, quick minded, and fun, Winkfield never shied away from hard work as long as it paid. Over the years, Winkfield honed the skill of promoting himself to be hired while not appearing boastful or arrogant. By the time he lost the 1900 Kentucky Derby, Winkfield had already learned to quickly weigh out after a race to be the first jockey interviewed. Typical of the time, the newspaper rendered black speech in dialect while an equally country-boy white's answers were printed with perfect grammar and diction. Winkfield never seemed bothered by this affront, perhaps adhering to the adage, "any publicity is good publicity." While he knew the benefits of talking himself up to the press to garner recognition for his feats and thus attract owners and trainers to hire him for stakes races, he treaded lightly in the path of Murphy toward whom the press had turned hostile after badly losing a race. A few well-placed interviews kept his name in the paper, but Winkfield did not court notoriety just to see his name in print.

Unlike current horse racing with months' long or year-round racing at one track, early-twentieth-century racing consisted of three or four days at one venue with constant traveling necessary to make a living wage. His first mentors, white trainer Bub May and his father, stable owner W. H. May, took care of the teenaged Winkfield, but their cold, remote businesslike approach to him set an example for the jockey that remained with him for life. Winkfield's lack of stability in his family life and his mentors' unaffectionate stance imprinted on him and informed his relationships with women throughout his life. The nomadic life of a jockey also strained any attempt at a normal home life.

The racing climate at the turn of the twentieth century began to change from predominantly black jockeys to only white riders as purses became more lucrative. Fewer blacks were growing up on farms and black migration to northern cities to escape the Ku Klux Klan and lynchings combined to supply fewer riders. As one of only four back-to-back winners of the Kentucky Derby, in 1901 on His Eminence and in 1902 on Alan-a-Dale, Winkfield would seem to be able to command the racing world's respect as a journeyman rider and consummate professional. However, even the prestigious racing publication, *Goodwin's Annual Official Turf Guide,* omitted Winkfield from its annual rankings in 1899, 1900, and 1901 despite being the fifth leading rider and Kentucky Derby winner in 1901, while listing a few of the other black jockeys with worse records.[8] The *Louisville Courier-Journal* acknowledged him as "a colored boy but one of the great race riders of the world" in 1903.[9] Perhaps Winkfield was too good at a time when collective white amnesia erased black accomplishments from the written record of the sport. The racism embedded in society coupled with the fierce competition among all jockeys for a dwindling number of mounts just to make a living pitted riders viciously against one another up and down the circuit while antigambling forces closed racetracks across the country. Winkfield once explained the subterfuge he used to ride the better horse in the 1902 Kentucky Derby. The horse's owner, Thomas Clay McDowell, had contracted Nash Turner to ride one of his two horses and Winkfield would ride the other. While exercising both horses, Winkfield held back Alan-a-Dale in workouts so it appeared The Rival was faster. "Nash was a good jockey, pretty famous by then, and he was a white boy, so he was goin' to get his pick. So when Nash come down on the mornin' of the race, naturally he pick The Rival."[10] Even though Winkfield won, McDowell gave each jockey one thousand dollars apiece. Competing with white jockeys for riding assignments, Winkfield, already with back-to-back Kentucky Derby wins, accepted mounts at the third-rate Queen City track outside Cincinnati when he should have been riding for the premiere stables at the New York racetracks.[11]

Coupled with the decline in the number of racetracks, the scramble for jobs created a tension-filled and often-hostile environment for African American riders. The primitive racing conditions—predating starting gates, film patrols, and racing judges stationed around the racecourse—allowed cutthroat riding tactics among the jockeys. Racing, dangerous enough in a clean race, became life-threatening as white riders bumped, squeezed, and struck black jockeys during a race. At Chicago's Harlem track in August 1900, white riders crowded Winkfield and his horse into a fence, injuring both.[12] The *Thoroughbred Record* reported that "a race war is on between the jockeys at the local tracks. Jealous because of the success of so many colored riders, the white boys . . . have taken desperate measures to put their rivals out of business. . . . The officials, who are aware of the jealousy, have done all they can to adjust matters and keep peace among the boys but have not yet succeeded in preventing accidents."[13] While not banning blacks from being jockeys, the racing establishment turned a blind eye to the white jockeys' intimidation tactics —neither condoning nor reproaching them. Because of both the hierarchical nature of the sport with rich white owners at the top of the pyramid and jockeys at the bottom, and the expense of running a stable, jockeys—black and white—were at the mercy of owners and trainers for their livelihood. Jockeys could not walk off easily and start their own rival business; it takes a lot of financial capital to operate a stable. Horses eat whether they win or lose. Racing could not sustain a separate and parallel black league as in baseball. When the gang mentality surfaced and the white riders injured their black rivals during a race, the owners and trainers acceded to the implied threat. If they wanted their horses to run and win—and even survive because the rough riding hurt not only the jockey but the horse if it fell—owners and trainers would have to hire only white riders. Roscoe Goose, a white jockey, said the owners and trainers did not want their horses at a disadvantage. "People got to thinking that if they had a colored boy up, he'd have the worst of it." African American trainer Nate Cantrell believed it was not only the money but also the winning reputation the whites coveted.[14] Rather than forcing horse racing to treat the African American jockeys fairly, white stable owners quit hiring them. In the face of this unstated boycott of black jockeys, their number quickly diminished on the racetracks. As the older jockeys disappeared, no young ones took their place. The top black jockeys left the sport altogether, turned to riding steeplechasers, or were relegated to minor bush league tracks where they faded into obscurity. Some became trainers or assistant trainers, while others ended up doing menial labor caring for the horses on the backstretch just to have a job. The overt hostility on the track mirrored the behavior toward blacks in society at large.[15]

Facing the declining job offers and threats not only to his employment but also to his person, Winkfield entertained the notion of leaving the United States to ride in Europe. Racing enjoyed a higher status and prestige among the European and British nobility, and they appreciated American riders' skills in winning races with the "American seat," also known as the "monkey seat," introduced by black jockey Willie Simms but credited to white rider Tod Sloan. Initially skeptical of this crouched-over position, the Europeans soon came to acknowledge the aerodynamic style as far superior to their traditional upright, straight-backed seat, which hindered rather than helped the horse. The lure of money, better riding conditions, steady employment, and adoration from racing fans sent the best riders across the Atlantic Ocean in the first mass exodus of American athletes. American jockeys returned from England and Europe with fantastic tales of big money and easy lifestyles. Others never returned, preferring to stay abroad.

Ever mindful of hedging his bets, Winkfield reneged on a contract with the powerful trainer John E. Madden in the 1903 Futurity Stakes to ride instead for his old friend and mentor Bub May. When both horses lost, the enraged Madden threatened to have Winkfield banned from racing. To escape the trainer's anger, the hostility of white jockeys at the Chicago and New York tracks, and the scarcity of riding opportunities,

Winkfield signed a contract—although still not as lucrative or beneficial as ones received by his white cohorts who moved to Europe at the same time—with Mikhail Lazareff, the leading Russian stable owner, to ride for him in Poland and Russia.[16] By 1908, American racing reeled from the antigambling backlash as the pressure closed racetracks across the country, diminishing their number from 314 to 25 and collapsing the purse structure by one-third in a two-year period.[17] The antigambling laws in New York State drove the best stable owners, trainers, and jockeys to Europe and England to make a living. By this time, Winkfield was the leading rider in Russia. While he thrilled the European racing fans, earned accolades for his skills, and won riding titles, these achievements went unnoticed in America outside his native Kentucky. In one of his rare interviews with the *Courier-Journal,* Winkfield talked about his good year in Russia.[18] Neither whites nor blacks, on or off the turf, knew of Winkfield's European victories or riding titles. He had disappeared from the American sports scene. Before the days of global television coverage and Internet access to international news and sporting events, the insularity of sports reporting confined itself to the newspapers' immediate location except for the annual major events such as the Kentucky Derby. News of European racing did not filter through the wire services to the United States unless it involved the social elite of a Whitney or Belmont.[19]

Life in Poland during the spring training season and in Russia during the summer race meets brought Winkfield consistent reinforcement of his decision to leave the United States, winning 51 percent of his races and the 1904 Russian National Riding Championship. He won the Emperor's Purse, the Moscow Derby twice, the Poland Derby twice, and the Russian Derby three times.[20] Although he made his living in Europe, during the first several years Winkfield returned to the United States each winter during the off-racing season to visit his family in Kentucky, and never renounced his American citizenship. He knew the reaction to his white Russian mistress would be hostile so he left her behind. A practical and reticent man, Winkfield kept his private life private and, unlike boxer Jack Johnson, did not flaunt his relationships with white women for American bigots to attack him over.

He expanded his racing sphere into Austria, Germany, and Hungary between 1910 and 1912, and rode full-time for the Armenian oil tycoon Leon Mantacheff by late in 1913, winning the Grand Prix de Baden.

Mantacheff paid the jockey 25,000 rubles a year plus 10 percent of all purses. Winkfield never rode for Czar Nicholas, who, he claimed, "never paid his jockeys nothin'."[21] World War I had no effect on Russian racing; it continued as war ravaged the rest of Europe. The racing elite were oblivious. As a financial precaution, Winkfield branched out as an owner of an ice skating rink in Moscow.[22] Had he continued along this path uninterrupted, Winkfield's life and career may have brought him even more acclaim, riding titles, plus money, and perhaps recognition in the United States. However, the Russian Revolution intervened. In a later interview, Winkfield remembered that "before the Revolution that was a good country. And I never had to pay no income tax."[23] The racing aristocracy could ignore the first world war, but revolutionaries denouncing the czar and his imperialist circle, among whom Winkfield counted employers, friends, and lovers, threatened not only his livelihood but also his very life.

Riding for the wealthy Russian bourgeoisie imperiled Winkfield with the revolutionaries. The natty dresser attired himself in workers' clothes to avoid being murdered by the anti-aristocracy mobs rioting in the streets. To save himself and the thoroughbreds, he fled Moscow to Odessa, the last refuge of Polish and Russian racing in 1917 and 1918. Winkfield traveled in 1919 with a coterie of 260 horses, owners, trainers, jockeys, and stable hands on a three-month, eleven-hundred-mile circuitous route—often without food and through hostile territory—to safety in Poland. The 252 surviving horses became the foundation of a new Polish breeding program, and Winkfield was soon to embark on the next phase of his life; Mantacheff summoned him to Paris to ride.[24]

In Europe, Winkfield's name was a drawing card to the races. Similar to the early racing in the United States, Europeans staged multiday events in one place. When Winkfield moved to the outskirts of Paris, he could travel easily from home to any one of the several racecourses in the countryside surrounding the city. Fans flocked to watch him ride and the French daily newspaper, *Le Figaro,* reported on each race won by "le blackman."

Winkfield finally appeared to settle down in Maisons-Laffitte. But his love life continued along a tumultuous path. His childhood and career affected his relationships with women. An early marriage was marked by frequent absences on the racing circuit. Although his African American wife, Edna, accompanied him to Russia in 1906 where they adopted a girl in 1907, she soon returned to the United States to raise the child alone, eventually divorcing Winkfield in the summer of 1911 for desertion. In the meantime, his Russian mistress, Alexandra Yalovicina, gave birth to their son George in January of that same year.[25] Dapper and well spoken, Winkfield attracted the attention of women wherever he traveled in Europe. Liaisons with several white women produced children, both in and out of wedlock. As in Russia, Winkfield enjoyed the celebrity of a winning career in France. He either began or renewed a friendship with Lydie de Minkwitz, daughter of a Russian baron, in 1921; they married in 1922 and had a son, Robert, in 1923, and daughter, Liliane, in 1924. His former mistress, Alexandra, and their son, George, moved to France in 1926 and lived near the Winkfields in Maisons-Laffitte. Reportedly, a Hungarian woman, Clara-Beatrice Haiman, who claimed to be Winkfield's mistress and mother of his twins, shot and wounded him after an argument in 1931. At age sixty, Winkfield had yet one more affair with an English woman.[26] A pattern of distancing himself from his wives, lovers, and children was seemingly the result of a lack of a parental role model during his early orphaned years. Winkfield did not know how to relate to his young children and treated them as sternly as he had been dealt with by his gruff racing-stable mentor.

Success in France continued in the same vein as in Russia with a big win in the Prix du Président de la République. Winkfield rode winning horses for Mantacheff and, after a falling-out, as a freelance rider. While he never made the kind of money in France that he earned in Russia, Winkfield saved enough to buy the property at Maisons-Laffitte twelve miles northwest of Paris. His father-in-law designed and built a house as a wedding gift there and, in 1924, Winkfield started training racehorses, first for his mother-in-law and then for himself and other owners, winning the Grand Prix de Paris. As he increased his training duties, Winkfield gradually decreased his race riding, finally retiring from riding at age fifty in 1930. Having ridden more than twenty-three hundred winners in the United States, Poland, Russia, Germany, Austria, Hungary, and France, Winkfield had forged a brilliant international career. Americans in Paris who attended the races and invariably lost sought out Winkfield for dinner money. Phil Chinn remarked that Winkfield "fed an average of ten Americans a day over there. He was a man with a heart."[27]

Phase three of his remarkable life would soon come to a close with the advent of World War II.[28]

Acutely aware of Hitler's anti-black, anti-miscegenation ideology, Winkfield realized the danger facing his mixed-race fourteen-year-old daughter's life. Winkfield sent his daughter Liliane to live with relatives in Cincinnati, Ohio, in 1939 to escape Nazism. He carried on with training until racing was banned in France in May 1940. The French army took over his stables, and quartered their two hundred horses and soldiers there until just prior to the Nazi invasion of France; the Nazis then occupied the stables. As a United States' citizen, Winkfield obtained an exit visa for himself, his wife Lydie, and son Robert and they journeyed to Portugal where, with eight hundred dollars borrowed from the American Consulate, they sailed for New York City and safety. Friends in Harlem initially took them in but the family soon moved to Jamaica, Queens. Long forgotten by most of the New York horsemen, the only job Winkfield could find was jackhammering the streets of Jamaica for the Works Progress Administration. Robert, an experienced jockey in France, quickly found a job as a steeplechase rider for the Bostwicks, a noted steeplechasing family. He helped his father get a job, first as a groom then exercise rider in New York and then at the Bostwicks' winter stable and training track in Aiken, South Carolina, where Pete Bostwick recognized him. Leaving his white wife, Lydie, working in a New York glove factory to avoid bringing her to the segregated South, Winkfield trained horses for the Bostwicks and began adding other owners within a few years. Training on the Maryland-Delaware-West Virginia circuit brought Winkfield back into the winner's circle and he helped start the riding career of Racing Hall of Fame jockey Bill Hartack. The success Winkfield had training Little Rocket, coupled with Lydie's shrewd bets on him, afforded the family the chance to return to France. Lydie went back first, and Winkfield followed a year later; Robert joined them in 1953, leaving behind his new wife and child—an old Winkfield family pattern. Jimmy and Robert Winkfield reestablished their racing stable at Maisons-Laffitte; Jimmy, at age seventy-six, turned over the stable's ownership to Robert in 1956, but as Robert noted, "I do most of the work. He just tells me all the things I'm doing wrong."[29] After Lydie died in 1958, Winkfield began spending the winters in Cincinnati with daughter Liliane and her physician husband and their three daughters.[30]

Expediency seemed to run through many of Winkfield's actions. As an older man seeking any kind of work during the second world war, he recognized that age discrimination would handicap his chances and therefore applied shoe polish to his graying hair so he would appear younger; it worked. Winkfield also shaved years off his birth date to stretch his riding career beyond when most jockeys retired.[31]

Thanks to an interview with him in *Sports Illustrated,* the National Turf Writers Association invited Winkfield to attend their annual banquet a few days before the 1961 Kentucky Derby. With Liliane by his side, Winkfield again faced down the indignity of initially being refused entrance through the front door of the whites-only Brown Hotel in Louisville on the night of the dinner. Of all the people in attendance only Roscoe Goose bothered to speak to Winkfield during the entire evening. Three days later the two old jockeys sat together in the stands at Churchill Downs for their last Kentucky Derby. Winkfield lived the remainder of his life in Maisons-Laffitte, dying in his sleep at age ninety-three on March 23, 1974.[32] The sole American obituary in the *New York Times* attested to his obscurity in the United States when it noted, "Only turf historians, or perhaps those who heard stories told by their grandfathers, would have recognized Winkfield's name in the United States in this decade."[33]

Jimmy Winkfield was never a black activist. He concentrated on his racing career to the exclusion of outside activities or social causes, living his life among horses and horse people. His struggles were personal ones—the fight back to a semblance of the comfortable life he led in Europe prior to World War II. Despite the adversity of starting again from scratch as a stable hand and exercise rider in his sixties, Winkfield climbed back to a modicum of success as a trainer in the United States. By returning to France for the last years of his life and resuming his training operations, Winkfield lived out the remainder of his life on his own terms as a respected trainer in France. He never really retired even though he turned over daily operations of the stable to his son. Fortunate to practice his craft long after most men his age, Winkfield transitioned into a second career as a trainer and thus kept his hand in the racing game. Resilient and persistent, Winkfield met adversity head-on and triumphed.

Winkfield finally received recognition in the United States for his lifetime accomplishments. In 2003 the Kentucky Derby Museum at

Churchill Downs racetrack in Louisville mounted a nine-month exhibit of his life in honor of the 100th anniversary of his last Derby ride.[34] He was inducted into the National Thoroughbred Racing Hall of Fame in Saratoga Springs, New York, on August 9, 2004. His daughter, Liliane Winkfield Casey, accepted the plaque in his honor that day, remarking, "He was a little man, but he had a huge heart for his love of horses. He had his ups and downs, but he had a beautiful life."[35] Finally, Aqueduct Racetrack in New York honored him in 2005 by naming a race the Jimmy Winkfield Stakes.

Marshall "Major" Taylor standing next to manager Victor Breyer in a 1901 photograph in Paris. This was at the height of Taylor's fame. *(Andrew Ritchie)*

2 Marshall "Major" Taylor

The Fastest Bicycle Rider in the World

ANDREW RITCHIE

"Major Taylor is a stern reality. He is here in flesh and blood, and he must be dealt with as a human being, entitled to every human right."[1]

The presence of black or "colored" athletes in every sport does not seem remarkable today. African Americans, West Indians, Ethiopians, Kenyans, Brazilians, Cubans, and Indians star in baseball, boxing, soccer, golf, tennis, and track and field. Ultra-traditional bastions of sporting privilege, such as the elitist Wimbledon tennis championship or cricket Test Matches have been permanently breached. Athletes of all races, from every country of the world, compete against one another in an atmosphere of sustainable and amicable cooperation. In the United States, athletic prowess, like show business, is much admired among African Americans and recognized as a well-defined route for young people to advance themselves, socially and financially.

But the right for black athletes to compete, like every other civil right, has had to be won in a long, hard struggle. Before World War II, those blacks, mostly black Americans or British colonials, who had succeeded in arriving at the top of their chosen sports were few. Boxers, jockeys, and pedestrians, their activities patronized by an affluent spectator class, stood as isolated, individual exceptions rather than giving proof that wider opportunity existed. Against the odds, they had slipped through the net of racism and succeeded in the white world, but that did not mean that the general condition of their people improved. The vast majority of black Americans and British "coloureds" still had limited social horizons and few athletic or professional possibilities outside the confines of their communities.

Marshall "Major" Taylor (1878–1932) was a unique and extraordinary pioneer of American sports at the turn of the century.[2] Determined, fit, and agile as a fox, Taylor overcame the constraints of a society bounded by the racial hypocrisy of "Jim Crow" and the "separate but equal" *ad hoc* segregation of *Plessy v. Ferguson* to establish himself as a uniquely controversial figure in one of the most popular sports of his day.[3] Before the famous names of later black athletic ascendancy, those who are traditionally recognized as having "broken the color barrier," such as the baseball player Jackie Robinson, the boxer Joe Louis, and the runner and jumper Jesse Owens, earlier even than the notorious rabble-rousing boxer Jack Johnson, the modest young cyclist also broke the color barrier and defied the uncomfortable but habitual order of post-slavery America. His success was adroitly timed and was made possible by the commercial bicycle boom of the mid-1890s. One might say that he had the luck to have been born at the right moment, but the talent, skill, and persistence with which he grasped the opportunities he was presented with certainly had nothing to do with luck.

Supported by liberal promoters, and especially by Birdie Munger, the white "father figure" who housed, trained, and advised him, the young Taylor insisted on his right to compete in America in the face of systematic and ferocious racist opposition. His presence in cycling was, for fifteen years, a crucial test of racial attitudes within sport and society. The fact that he was black made everything he did in his sport exceptional. An almost naïve, fragile, and innocent figure, he sat quietly and tenuously in the eye of racial hurricanes. Controversy and tension swirled around him while he single-mindedly thrilled and entertained the spectators. By 1901, when he was still only twenty-two years old, Taylor had become a superstar in professional bicycle racing on the tracks of America and Europe, making a fortune at the very highest level of international competition. Bicycle racing had existed as a competitive sport in America for only about twenty years (since 1877–78), and there had been official world championships for only six years, when Taylor took his first and only world title in Montreal in 1899.

But it was impossible, at the turn of the century, for a black man to be accepted and openly honored as a champion in the United States. His exploits were widely reported, his dominance grudgingly conceded, but he was never acclaimed, and once he had retired he was quickly forgotten. Only by leaving the United States for Europe was Taylor able to sustain and prolong his career as one of the three or four best sprinters of his generation. For ten years, he was probably the most famous black American athlete, and briefly, in Paris in 1901, he was probably the best-known, most extensively publicized black American in the world.

Taylor was raised in the 1880s in semi-rural Indianapolis, Indiana, where a black boy was expected to doff his cap and step aside to let a white man pass in the street. He first learned the tastes and habits of the white world when he lived, for several formative years, in the Indianapolis suburbs, as the "companion" to Dan Southard, the young son of a wealthy white family for whom his father, Gilbert Taylor, worked as coachman. Here he was given his first bicycle. Here, also, Taylor learned who he was when Dan was allowed to join the Indianapolis YMCA while he was turned away at the door.

Later, working in bicycle shops in Indianapolis during the bicycle boom of the early 1890s, Taylor met former high-wheel champion Birdie Munger, a white bicycle maker, who hired him as his houseboy and quickly recognized his precocious, natural cycling talent. One of his first bosses, Tom Hay, discovering that Taylor was a skillful trick cyclist, dressed him in a military uniform, with a peaked cap, and had him perform his routine on the sidewalk outside the shop to attract customers. Thus, Taylor fulfilled his first engagements as a professional cyclist. He also became the little "Major," a nickname that stuck to him and helped to define his professional identity throughout his cycling career. His wife, Daisy, later expressed her dislike of the nickname and insisted on addressing him with the more proper and, as she saw it, respectable "Marshall." A cyclist, as an entertainer, was not quite an honorable occupation in upper-middle-class black society.

By the age of fifteen, Taylor had already won numerous road and track races in Indianapolis and Chicago, particularly in those segregated races promoted for blacks only. He was encouraged, trained, and supported by Munger, who became in effect his father and advisor. The trust Munger had put in the youngster, including keeping him supplied with expensive bicycle equipment, was meticulously repaid as Taylor worked faithfully for him in various capacities. In the face of concerted opposition to his attempts to integrate himself into amateur racing in the Midwest, Taylor and Munger moved, in 1895, to Worcester,

Massachusetts, where a more liberal racial climate allowed the young prodigy to prove himself very quickly as "colored champion of America" and one of the fastest American sprinters.

Taylor turned professional in 1896, at the age of eighteen, and his debut was a sensational six-day race held before wild and raucous crowds at Madison Square Garden in New York.[4] Through the seasons of 1897, 1898, 1899, and 1900, Taylor made a rapid ascent to stardom within American cycling. It was both shocking and thrilling when Taylor took his place on the starting line, posing a public sporting challenge to the assumption of white exclusivity and superiority. The press was alert to the drama of his presence and reported his races openly and fairly. Spectators admired his audacity, and the animosity his presence generated among often hostile white riders made for a dramatic sporting spectacle. He was good for the sport, and promoters were quick to recognize his drawing power at the box office. But many of his white competitors detested him and his victories were unacceptable to some promoters, managers, and bureaucrats, especially those with a controlling interest, within the sport.

Slavery had been abolished in Reconstruction America, but segregation had intensified by the 1890s in many societal institutions. The League of American Wheelmen, the governing body of amateur cycling (whose Racing Board attempted only partially successfully to control both amateur and professional competition), had introduced legislation in 1894 excluding blacks from membership, thus creating and encouraging a *de facto* apartheid within cycling institutions.[5] At the local, amateur level, blacks had their own cycling clubs which sponsored their own races. As a professional, Taylor was of course free to compete against his fellow African American cyclists, but there was fierce opposition to his attempts to integrate himself into the highest level of competition in the national racing scene, particularly into the American championship circuit, in which championship points were earned in a series of important race meetings held in different locations throughout the racing season, and where the big money prizes were to be won. With persistence, and against a great deal of resistance and hostility, Taylor succeeded in establishing his right to compete on the East Coast and in the Midwest, but when the national circuit went into the South, it was life threatening for him to compete. The dilemma was summarized as follows in an Indiana newspaper report from April 1898, entitled "The Color Line":

> An interesting question has arisen over the decision of the L.A.W. Racing Board (that racing men must register), in regard to the Board's treatment of colored racers. Negroes are excluded from the L.A.W. and it is argued that the League cannot accept the registration of a colored racer in consequence. There are not many negro racers on the track, but the effect of the Board's decision will be especially interesting if it only touches the case of Major Taylor, the fast colored lad, whose course was attended with so many difficulties last season, owing to the aversion of his white competitors to racing with him.[6]

The newspaper article discussed alternative courses of action, suggesting that Taylor might ask to be licensed by the Canadian Wheelmen's Association, which had no "color line," or that he might simply move to Europe.

During his first few years as a professional in the United States (1896 to 1900), Taylor aroused an intense hatred among some white riders as he began to challenge them for the best prizes—hefty purses of gold coins. A first place in an important regional race could easily be worth one hundred dollars, equivalent to perhaps ten times that amount in today's values. Some riders, especially on the East Coast, accepted him with good grace and even openly praised his exceptional abilities. In Boston, in July 1897, he was accepted by four white riders as a member of a five-man team that defeated a Philadelphia team in a five-mile pursuit race.[7] But other competitors, from Kentucky, Ohio, and California, found his presence on the starting line intolerable and were personally outraged when he won, which he sometimes did with what seemed an almost insulting ease. Short-distance bicycle racing on the track was then, as now, a fast and dangerous sport. Jostling and elbowing were part of the excitement the crowd paid to see. A conspiracy grew among white riders to exclude Taylor from victory. They ganged up against him and tried to block him, forcing him to ride from the front (the hardest way to win) and pull victory out of seemingly impossible situations. They were verbally abusive and physically hostile to him both on and off the track.

"Taylor rides in all his big races in deadly fear of his racing companions," reported the *New York Sun* in September 1897. "Taylor was recently thrown at Worcester and badly bruised in a race . . . The situation calls for prompt action on the part of the Racing Board. Taylor now ranks among the fastest men in the country, but the racing men, envious of his success and prejudiced against his color, aim to injure his chances whenever he competes."[8] Taylor himself confirmed this fear: "I have a dread of injury every time I start in a race with the men who have been on the circuit this year. They have threatened to injure me and I expect that before the season is finished they will do so," he told the *Worcester Telegram,* his hometown newspaper.[9]

At Taunton, Massachusetts, Taylor was physically attacked and choked into unconsciousness by a white rider, William Becker, after Taylor had beaten him in a one-mile sprint race. The crowd, agitated and angry at Becker's attack, threatened him, and only the police presence prevented an already ugly incident from becoming even uglier. Becker was not arrested, and the incident was a sharp reminder of the aggressive feelings aroused by Taylor's challenge within a sport dominated by whites. *Bicycling World* called the Becker attack "one of the deplorable features of the racing season of 1897 . . . It is such incidents as these that bring discredit on a sport whose promoters have strenuously endeavoured to keep it clean and honest."[10]

When Taylor went south to Savannah, Georgia, at the beginning of 1898, to put in some early-season training in the warm climate, he was threatened following a training encounter on nearby public roads by local white riders who sent him a letter with a crude drawing of a skull and crossbones: "Mister Taylor," it read, "if you don't leave here before 24 hours, you will be sorry. We mean business. Clear out if you value your life. Signed—White Riders." An intelligent black person did not argue with such a threat in the racial climate of the day, and Taylor left.[11] That season, 1898, he told the reporter from the *Worcester Telegram:* "I am riding faster this year than I was last, and that has saved me a good many times. I simply ride away from the rest of the bunch and do not give them a chance to pocket me . . . It always falls to my lot to set the pace and it is not always pleasant to have to push out in the lead . . . That is the way I have won all my races this season."[12]

A conspiracy grew to exclude Taylor from the sport. The white riders ganged up against him, blocked him, jostled him. Racist bureaucrats within the sport sought constantly for ways to interfere with his career.

The *Worcester Telegram* in 1897 printed a dramatic headline: MAJOR TAYLOR'S LIFE IN DANGER. NEW YORK PAPER SAYS THERE IS A COMBINATION AGAINST HIM. CONDUCT OF RACING MEN SHOULD BE INVESTIGATED. SUBJECTED TO CONSTANT THREATS OF INJURY.[13] In the context of a prolonged dispute for control of professional racing between the L.A.W. and its rival, the National Cycling Association, Taylor was duped and threatened with exclusion from both licensing authorities. He had continual problems when he was out on the road, finding hotels and restaurants willing to serve him; promoters made promises to him about accommodations only to break them. The editor of the *New York Morning Telegraph,* under the headline "The boycott against Taylor was too long delayed," was "pleased to see this emphatic assertion of the superiority of the Caucasian over the Ethiopian," although he wished that the white riders had boycotted Taylor before "the black whirlwind" had defeated them all. "It is, of course, a degradation for a white man to contest any points with a negro," he thought. "It is worse than that, and becomes an absolute grief and social disaster when a negro persistently wins in the competition."[14] The polarization of attitudes stimulated by the presence of the black cyclist within the sport could not be more strongly illustrated than this.

But backed by liberal New Englanders, the New York, Boston, and Philadelphia press and honestly opportunistic business promoters and managers, Taylor and Birdie Munger persevered and refused to be intimidated, defending Taylor's right to compete as a licensed professional. He won his mostly short-distance races by outmaneuvering his opponents tactically, frequently riding from the front of the bunch with superb displays of speed, to keep out of the way of the threats from white riders who tried to work together against him. Even his most aggressive opponents and his worst enemies were forced to concede that he was an astonishing athlete.

Those, like the New York editor quoted above, who saw it as degrading for whites to be challenged in open sports competition *on a regular basis* by a black man (an unprecedented and innovative situation) were opposed by strong anti-racist currents in the press, whose positive influence upon Taylor's dramatic career was of critical importance. Many East Coast newspapers published editorials and reportage on Taylor's struggles, aware of the importance that these events within the narrow world of cycling had for the larger society. "The condition of the colored man in America is one of the great questions for us to handle," wrote the *Syracuse Telegram* in 1898. "All intelligent people know that we can't benefit the state of the colored man by denying him the privileges we enjoy . . . If he fulfils all the requirements, his color should not weigh against him. If he can ride a bicycle or a horse as well as a white man, he should not be denied the privilege of displaying his abilities."[15]

The press thus followed Taylor throughout the years of his personal and professional difficulties in the United States, greeting his constant victories with sometimes breathless surprise, referring to him as "the colored cyclone," or "the dusky wonder," or the inevitable "black whirlwind." Journalists from the large and energetic cycling press reported every detail of Taylor's squabbles with the cycling authorities, frequently taking sides with him. The press was, in fact, his most ardent and reliable fan and supporter. The fact that he was fighting such an uphill struggle was in itself a story. Few black American's lives were so extensively documented or interrogated at that moment in time, or their interactions with the white world recorded in so much detail. "Within the past five years there probably has been no bicycle rider who has been more in the public mind and the public eye than the colored whirlwind from Worcester," said an 1898 article in a Boston newspaper which was headlined, "How the colored whirlwind forced his way to the front rank of cycle riders despite obstacles."[16]

Following one particularly striking victory, a reporter summed up the mixture of strength and weakness in Taylor's situation, and the reasons why he generated such waves of emotion within the sport. "Coming as it has after the successful efforts of certain race meet managers to debar Taylor from their tracks, the colored boy's victory is especially fortunate," he wrote:

> He may now be counted by promoters among the best, if not the best, drawing card among the racing men of the country . . . As for those riders who have given him the cold shoulder and sought by unfair methods to defeat him . . . they will now do well to get on a match with him without delay. Their mere success in arranging a contest with the colored boy will bring most of them greater notoriety than they have enjoyed in their entire careers, while to defeat him will make them famous.[17]

One of the fortunate ironies of Taylor's situation was that he could also make money in the sport without even competing against white cyclists in person, for once his superb speed had been recognized, his paced world records could be made against the clock and needed only a sympathetic promoter interested in publicity and willing to foot the bill for his record attempts.

One article written by cyclist Howard Freeman, a white rival and friend of Taylor's, showed with alarming frankness the entrenched and sometimes naïve racism that he was up against. "The boys willingly acknowledge that Taylor is the fastest man on the track, and also that he is a 'good fellow,' but on account of his color they cannot bear to see him win. If it was possible to make him white all the boys would gladly assist in the job. But try as they may, I think it will be nearly impossible to keep this little negro from winning the championship."[18]

Black people, of course, admired and loved Taylor's victories. To them, he was a hero, an example of black courage and strength in the face of adversity, a person who had found a way to hit back and prove he was superior. His victories helped the black community to reinforce its own sense of self-worth, and he was a regular guest at winter social events, at one of which he met his future wife, Daisy Morris. Taylor, an ardent Baptist, insisted on the importance of regular training, clean living, hard work, moral uprightness, fair play, and faith in God—values widely shared by black Americans, and his own behavior remained exemplary in the face of provocation. He proved that it was possible to succeed with talent and hard work. But such success led elements within white society to fear that it might escalate and be repeated. Taylor was suspected of being that dreaded figure, the "uppity nigger," who took a little and would soon be demanding a lot more, bringing a lowering of moral standards, undermining the order and respectability of society. In fact, Taylor's behavior was carefully cultivated not to be "uppity": he was soft-spoken, nonaggressive, tactful, and polite, determined not to give offense.

Taylor's victories were, however, especially threatening because they were won in cycling, a sport in which speed, tactical skill, and intelligence were more important than physical force or brute strength. Bicycle racing on the track was a rough and dangerous sport, where a certain amount of jostling and elbowing was accepted, but it was not a contest of direct physical contact. The success of a black boxer might be dismissed with the observation that the ability to fight was expected from a brute. But when Taylor, a finely built, smallish man, with the muscular, lithe, and supple legs of a dancer, outsmarted his rivals and shot by them on the final banking, his athletic superiority was impossible to dismiss.

Racist opposition prevented Taylor from winning the League of American Wheelmen's championships of 1897, 1898, and 1899, but he finally succeeded in 1900. In 1898 and 1899, he established numerous world records in time trials against the clock, a type of racing where he could demonstrate his enormous athletic skills without the possibility of racist interference. He was handsomely paid by bicycle and tire manufacturers to publicize their products. In 1899, when he won the International Cycling Association's one-mile world sprint championship in Montreal, he became the second black athlete ever to win a world title (the first was boxer George Dixon, nicknamed "Little Chocolate," bantamweight champion in 1890). This victory cemented his claim to being a world-class athlete, one who was about to win much greater fame in Europe.

After this world championship, Taylor rejected an offer of fifteen thousand dollars to cross the Atlantic for a season's racing. The French promoters had at first insisted that he agree to race on Sundays, but he had refused. The press was astonished that he could turn down such an offer. But the promoters were so anxious to have Taylor race in Europe that they were forced to concede that there would be no Sunday racing. In March 1901, when Taylor crossed the Atlantic for the first time, he was, according to the *Worcester Spy,* "the most universally admired passenger on the big ocean liner."[19] In France, wrote Robert Coquelle (one of Taylor's French managers) in the cycling daily, *Le Vélo,* Taylor was "awaited like the Messiah."[20]

When he arrived in Paris, Taylor was a celebrity and was instantly transformed into an athletic superstar. The exhausting and triumphant tour of the summer of 1901 established him as black America's unofficial ambassador to Europe. His fame was consolidated and sustained by extensive coverage in the sporting and general interest press and by the publicity machine of the promoters. It was a press-generated fame of a totally modern kind, with sport as the selling point and a dramatic, idiosyncratic personality to give it spice and meaning. The press met Taylor at Boulogne and followed him everywhere. In hundreds of daily reports, they wrote about what he looked like, how he dressed, what he did, what he said, what he ate, and how his training and racing were progressing. The sporting establishment, the newly prominent automobile manufacturers, and the Parisian aristocracy competed to entertain him. Letters from America addressed simply to "Major Taylor, Paris, France" arrived safely at his hotel. People followed him in the street just to touch him and paid entry fees to the tracks just to watch him train.

For probably the first time in modern sport history, a black athlete was marketed as a star and seen by thousands of people in a short space of time, in France, Germany, Italy, Austria, Denmark, and Holland. On one occasion, when a race meeting was cancelled because of rain, the disappointed Belgian crowd refused a refund and marched instead to Taylor's hotel, demanding that he appear at a window so that *"le nègre volant"* ("the flying negro") could, like visiting royalty, simply be seen. Many in the crowd had never before seen a black man.

Recognition was now showered upon him. His races, in all the European capitals, were sold out, with crowds of twenty thousand not unusual. Thousands of people lined the streets to see him as he drove from the railway station to the track. The European champions, against whom he successfully competed, accepted him as their social equal and were astonished by his performances. At Taylor's much-heralded races in Paris against Edmond Jacquelin, the then-current world champion and champion of France, twenty-five thousand spectators paid double-money and many more were turned away. Victor Breyer, one of Taylor's managers, reported that he saw people turn pale with anxiety, bite their lips, and clutch themselves with excitement, so great was the tension during the matches.[21] The crowd was reported as the biggest ever known for a sporting event of any kind in Paris.

In Bordeaux, *Le Vélo* reported, Taylor was examined by a group of famous physicians, who pronounced him "an absolute masterpiece of the human form. He might have been absolutely perfect if his thighs had not become a little over-developed."[22] One French journalist wrote to a friend in Chicago that he had not believed all of the claims made for Taylor, but that he was convinced after seeing him perform. He was also impressed by Taylor's character. "Not one among the many riders who have visited us during the last five years may be compared with him in the manner of politeness and good behavior," he wrote:

> We were literally amazed to find him better educated than the average foreigner who comes over and possessed of far better manners than our own riders. When we think of some of the harsh treatment to which this man has been subjected on account of his color, we cannot refrain from uttering the strongest words of disapprobation of such acts, nor from thinking that some parts of your country must be in a state of savagery.[23]

La Vie au Grand Air (Open Air Life), an important French weekly sporting paper, published an article ostensibly written by Taylor himself, with a dozen photographs depicting him not just as an athlete, but as a human being who liked to play the piano and mandolin, who was interested in art and driving the new-fangled automobiles, and who had a fiancée in America. Such a human and generous portrait of him had never been, and never would be, published in the United States. One photo showing off Major Taylor's superb physique showed him standing dressed only in briefs, a photo impossible to have been shown in America![24]

Like famous black American musicians, dancers, and show business personalities after him, Taylor was able to experience a new identity and freedom in Europe. There, he could concentrate on the business of racing and making money in his chosen sport without having to cope constantly with hostility and racism. He was thrust into a totally different world, where he was lionized and acclaimed not only as a champion bicycle racer, but as the underdog who had triumphed over adversity in America. His reception in Europe in 1901 allowed him to refocus his career and to redefine his identity.

Upon his return to the United States in the summer of 1901, in spite of initial praise in the daily press, there was barely a glimmer of recognition from American cycling authorities of his extraordinary European successes and his huge status in world bicycle racing, and he was immediately embroiled in new bureaucratic squabbles. Fatigued and sick from his travels, Taylor was unable to meet prearranged contractual obligations to race at certain events. The chairman of the National Cycling Association, Batchelder, worried that Taylor's absence would have a negative effect on gate receipts, and he refused to accept Taylor's apology and his doctor's letter of medical evidence. "Sick or well," he told Taylor, "you must ride at each National Circuit meet . . . a champion being under greater obligation to promoter and public than any other rider is always expected to keep faith and appear when advertised unless prevented by the most urgent reasons," and he proceeded to fine the returning black star one hundred dollars for each occasion on which he failed to appear.[25] Ironically, Taylor was now needed by the same sport establishment that had abused him so frequently.

Taylor was incensed and threatened to quit racing altogether, but in the end paid the fines. The editor of *Cycle Age* reminded his readers that when the great American sprinter, Arthur Zimmerman, had returned to the States from Europe several years before, "there was nothing in the country good enough for him. He had nobly represented the United States in Europe. He had demonstrated that the Yankee cyclist led the world in the matter of speed. And he was rewarded as he deserved." But Taylor had been rewarded with insulting fines. "Who would have dared to treat the mighty Zimmerman as the N.C.A. has treated Taylor? The wrath of the whole cycling world would have fallen on the head of anyone who dared suggest such a thing . . . Zimmerman was a white man. But Taylor . . . ? Oh well, he's only a negro."[26]

From 1901 on, Taylor's athletic ambitions were directed away from the United States. Even the annual National Cycling Association's professional sprint championships, the ultimate accolade in American cycling, won for many years after 1900 by the great Frank Kramer, did not tempt Taylor, so intense was the feeling against him still, and so intense the effort needed to be out on the circuit, finding food and lodging, just getting on with the business of being a professional bicycle racer. In effect, Taylor was lost to American cycling because the sport had rejected him and had made it nearly impossible for him to compete at home. He returned to Europe for two more seasons (1902, 1903) and in 1902 and 1903 went to Australia for what proved to be two athletically taxing and very lucrative winter seasons. His daughter, Sydney, who, at the time of this writing, was one hundred years old, was born there in 1904. After a brief retirement (1904, 1905), Taylor returned to Paris for the European seasons of 1907, 1908, and 1909, before finally retiring in 1910.

Upon retirement, Taylor was thirty-two years old and a wealthy man. He owned a fine house and several other properties in Worcester, and reportedly had thirty-five thousand dollars in the bank. But he did not adjust easily to retirement. Because of his color, he was refused entry to study engineering at the Worcester Polytechnic Institute. He launched a number of automobile-related enterprises, none of them very successful. In one abortive project, he apparently invested and lost ten thousand dollars. But there were no opportunities for him to parlay his world champion status in cycling into a new career, as, for example, a trainer, manager, or journalist, or even a manufacturer's representative.

Well respected in Worcester, an active member and financial supporter of the Baptist church and of the needy in his community, Taylor gradually exhausted his savings as he struggled to maintain his comfortable lifestyle. Illness took a severe toll on his resources and he was forced gradually to sell his properties. From 1923 to 1928, afraid that his pioneering sporting exploits would be forgotten, Taylor labored on his autobiography, *The Fastest Bicycle Rider in the World: The Story of a Colored Boy's Indomitable Courage and Success against Great Odds.* He dedicated the book to his "true friend and advisor," Birdie Munger, and self-published it, selling it from door to door. He was, he wrote, writing it "not for any personal glory . . . but rather to perpetuate my achievements on the bicycle tracks of the world, for the benefit of all youths aspiring to an athletic career, and especially for boys of my own group as they strive for fame and glory in the athletic world."[27]

Taylor separated from his wife in about 1929–30, left his home in Worcester, and set off for Chicago with boxes of his book in his car. Possibly, he also stopped in Indianapolis, his home city. In Chicago, at the height of the depression, in a suffering black community, he found himself destitute, dependent on the YMCA for food and lodging. Ill with heart problems and hypertension, he died alone and forgotten in 1932 in the Cook County Hospital and was buried in an unmarked pauper's grave when no one, neither family nor Chicago friends or associates, stepped forward to claim his body. Among major American newspapers, only the *Chicago Defender* immediately honored him with an obituary: "In the field of professional athletics, Major Taylor is the only member of his Race, outside the field of boxing, who ever held a world title. He won fame and reknown throughout the world. He practically blazed and made the trail single-handed."[28] In 1948, former cycling colleagues and industry representatives, including Frank Schwinn of the Schwinn Bicycle Company, professing to have been shocked and surprised when they learned of the manner in which Taylor had died, organized his reburial and placed a bronze plaque on the new grave belatedly honoring the "God-fearing, clean-living, gentlemanly athlete, a credit to his race, who came up the hard way without hatred in his heart."[29] Thirty years later, the city of Indianapolis named its new velodrome after him, and Taylor's more recent historical rehabilitation had begun.

Taylor's life and career is thus strangely lopsided. His greatest athletic feats had all been accomplished by 1904, when he returned to the United States from the second of his winter racing tours in Australia in a state of mental and physical collapse and with a new baby to care for. By 1904, when he was still only twenty-five years old, the pinnacle of his lifetime achievements in cycling had been reached; there were to be no further records or championships, although he continued to race in Paris between 1907 and 1910. In eight solid years of professional bicycle racing, and constant traveling, from 1896 to 1904, he had surged to the highest level of the newly affluent and popular sport of track cycling, and had maintained his position as one of the three or four best professional sprinters in the world for about five years, from 1899 to 1904. From 1907 to 1910, although not at his athletic best, he was still competitive in world-class sprinting, and was a popular personality, a box-office draw who enjoyed star billing. In doing so, he had challenged and overturned every American and European assumption about what a black athlete could achieve, and in the process showed high moral stature and tolerance in the face of great provocation. But his successes in Europe had always been at the expense of recognition at home.

After retirement, Taylor relapsed into a personal life that did not demand such a prodigious output of physical energy and courage. But his cycling career was always on his mind. His autobiography makes clear that he worked on the project with the intention of proving to the world "that there are positively no mental, physical, moral or other attainments too lofty for a Negro to accomplish if granted a fair and equal opportunity." He was, he added, writing his memoirs "in a spirit calculated to solicit simple justice, equal rights and a square deal for the posterity of my down-trodden but brave people, not only in athletic sports, but in every honorable game of human endeavor."[30]

But Taylor's personal qualities had never fitted him comfortably for the role of black activist. He had been an activist on the bicycle track, and his victory over the entrenched racism within American society and within his sport had been symbolically reenacted every time he beat his white opponents. Yet he had never attempted to be a political spokesman for black aspirations, and to have adopted the outspoken stance of an activist during his cycling career might have been literally fatal in America when his right to compete in the sport hung by a thread and depended on the support of Munger and white liberal promoters. It is hardly surprising that after retirement he did not choose to take on a role that had always been unfamiliar to him. He was an athlete, an entertainer, not a thinker, a politician, or a social reformer.

In his retirement, Taylor was not given a second chance to assert himself and to excel. He remained confined in his early fame. In Worcester, Massachusetts, he became a kind of fossil, famous in the past, but not able to fulfill himself in the present. His eclipse showed the fragility of athletic achievement as a means for a black person to advance socially. He was doomed to remain locally famous, but of marginal significance.

Thus, in later life, Taylor sought refuge in a morally upright, Christian family and community life, conforming to the ideals of the bourgeois and respectable black middle class. He appears to have been a man stranded, almost tragically, between the white world that had given him so much and his own black community—not quite belonging entirely in either. Between 1910 and 1930, he was also evidently haunted by introspection, by the memories of his past extraordinary fame and guilt and shame for the anonymity and financial difficulties into which he had fallen. He became a severe father to his daughter Sydney and a difficult and fastidious husband.

Taylor's last two years, in bad health, his financial resources exhausted, separated from his wife and daughter, homeless except for the YMCA, and his death in the charity ward and near-anonymous burial in a pauper's grave, was a return to the world of his roots, the urban equivalent of the semi-rural poverty into which he had been born. They are hard to contemplate and difficult to accept. The circumstances of his end were further proof of how unique and unprecedented his rise to fame had been. For a brief moment, in Paris, the sporting, artistic, and cultural capital of the modern world, he had enjoyed his moment of glory, but he was just one individual who had managed to escape, for a short period, by means of his athletic talent and success, from the struggle and racism millions had to endure.

Had Taylor stayed in France, or perhaps turned his hand to road racing, he would certainly have continued to enjoy the status of a cycling celebrity. By returning to his own country, he pursued a path that led to his gradual descent into anonymity. It was a progression that, for this proud and motivated man, used to the stress of competition and the glare of publicity, was a journey into physical and spiritual distress. To be historically accurate, we do not know what Taylor's state of mind was when he lived in the Chicago YMCA during his final two years. Did he take refuge comfortably in his lifelong Christian beliefs, resigned to his predicament? We do not know. One of the last glimpses we have of him is from Christopher Sinsabaugh, a Chicago automobile pioneer, who wrote, "The last time I heard of Major Taylor was when a wizened colored man, looking not unlike a minister and wearing glasses, called on Jim Levy, veteran Buick dealer in Chicago who used to race with Taylor. It was Taylor himself and he sold Jim one of his books."[31]

According to the evidence of his autobiography, Taylor was not, in the end, consumed by bitterness, and he struggled to forgive those he knew had wronged him. "Notwithstanding the bitterness and cruel practices of the white bicycle riders, their friends and sympathizers, against me," he wrote:

> I hold no animosity toward any man. This includes those who so bitterly opposed me and did everything possible to injure me and prevent my success . . . When I am called home I shall rest easy, knowing that I always played the game fairly and tried my hardest, although I was not always given a square deal or anything like it . . . Life is too short for a man to hold bitterness in his heart, and that is why I have no feeling against anybody. I always gave the best that was in me . . . In fact, I have never hated any rider I competed against . . . As the late Booker T. Washington, the great negro educator, so beautifully expressed it—"I shall allow no man to narrow my soul and drag me down, by making me hate him."[32]

This photograph of William Henry Lewis originally appeared in his 1896 instructional book, *Primer of College Football*.

3 The Strange Career of William Henry Lewis

GREGORY BOND

Today, William Henry Lewis is most famous as the answer to trivia questions about numerous African American "firsts," but in the early twentieth century he was one of the most well known and newsworthy blacks in the country. Lewis was a true Renaissance man who achieved remarkable success in each of his chosen avocations, and his career demonstrated both the integrationist possibilities for successful and respectable blacks and the very real limitations that these members of W. E. B. Du Bois's "talented tenth" faced in an increasingly segregated United States. A native of Virginia, Lewis lived most of his life in Massachusetts, and he came to embrace his adopted state for its relatively liberal racial atmosphere that afforded him uncommon—and at times unparalleled—opportunities in intercollegiate football, the legal profession, and the political arena.

The son of former slaves, Lewis rose through the American educational system from the all-black campus of the Virginia Normal and Collegiate Institute to the integrated halls of Amherst College and Harvard University. Lewis first garnered national attention for his athletic accomplishments, impressing the Eastern sports establishment with his powerful, quick, and agile play at the centre rush position. On the field, he earned considerable respect and numerous accolades that culminated with positions on two of Casper Whitney's prestigious All-American squads. After his playing days, he continued to find opportunities in the Ivory Tower and moved to the sidelines to help coach the Harvard football team for more than a decade.

Lewis's achievements as a public figure were also impressive. An able politician, he represented his mostly white neighbors on the Cambridge

City Council and in the Massachusetts Statehouse. Drawing on his positive experiences at integrated colleges, he also became a strong advocate for civil rights and fought hard for African American equal opportunity. Early in his career, he used his considerable legal and oratorical skills to confront segregationists, but Lewis slowly abandoned his radical agenda in the face of increased white resistance and rapidly deteriorating race relations. When his electoral success ended, he relied on patronage positions from influential friends like Theodore Roosevelt and Booker T. Washington for the continuance of his political career. He received numerous powerful federal appointments in the years before World War I, but, in return, he had to forsake the confrontational politics of his youth. To the chagrin of some black leaders, Lewis adopted Washington's accommodationist strategy and harnessed the power of the Tuskegee machine to rise through the federal bureaucracy to the rank of United States assistant attorney general. Despite his success, Lewis was forcefully reminded of the limitations of Jim Crow when the American Bar Association tried to draw the color line and expel him from the organization.

William Henry Lewis was born on November 28, 1868, in Berkeley, Virginia, a small town near the city of Norfolk. His parents, Ashley Henry Lewis and the former Josephine Baker, were ex-slaves who had received their freedom prior to the Civil War. Lewis's father fought briefly with the Union army and received his first education in an army camp. He would become a prominent Baptist minister in the Norfolk area, but the 1870 census found the twenty-six-year-old Ashley listed as a laborer supporting his wife and one-year-old William. Fifteen years later, the elder Lewis had received his pulpit, and his family had welcomed two daughters and two more sons.[1]

From an early age, William showed an interest in learning, and, years later, Booker T. Washington related the genesis of his friend's intellectual curiosity: "Mr. Lewis has told me that he received many a good thrashing for running away at night to attend the trial of some of the cases that were once famous in the annals of Portsmouth courts." Washington accurately surmised that "a murder trial is not, perhaps, the best sort of amusement for a boy," but, he just as rightly observed, "the excitement of these murder trials, in which some of the keenest minds in the state were pitted against each other, provided a kind of stuff to kindle the imagination of an impressionable boy."[2] Spurred by courtroom dramas, young William eagerly took to his studies at local segregated public schools.

In 1884, Lewis enrolled in the preparatory department of the all-black Virginia Normal and Collegiate Institute. Chartered a year before as a political favor to Virginia blacks who had supported the independent Readjusters in state elections, the Petersburg institution was one of the few southern public black colleges to offer a full-fledged collegiate course.[3] The fifteen-year-old Lewis had limited monetary support from his family, and he financed his education by working as an errand boy in the United States Congress and by doing odd jobs at local hotels. Although he took classes at Virginia Normal for the next four years, Lewis did not receive a degree. Few records remain from his tenure on campus, but the young scholar cultivated two important relationships while in Petersburg —with the school president and with a fellow classmate.

John Mercer Langston, a versatile and storied black leader, presided over Virginia Normal in the 1880s and had a profound impact on the future course of Lewis's life. The biracial son of a wealthy plantation owner, Langston was the fifth black graduate of Oberlin College and was a radical civil rights agitator before, during, and after the Civil War. Prior to coming to Petersburg, he had founded the law school at Howard University and had served as the United States consul general to Haiti. A nationally known orator and savvy politician, Langston was an early role model for Lewis, who fondly recalled his mentor later in life.[4] Also on campus in the mid-1880s was William Tecumseh Sherman Jackson a student from tiny Glencairn, Virginia. Although Jackson was four years older than Lewis, the two classmates quickly became friends.[5]

Lewis and Jackson admired the school president and his record as a politician and activist. By the mid-1880s, however, the Democratic Party had reestablished control over Virginia politics, and the Redeemers did not approve of a black agitator at the Petersburg school. The white board of directors harassed and interfered until they forced Langston to resign in 1887. Lewis and Jackson led a group of students who visited the governor to protest Langston's departure. The governor declined to intervene, and when the student protesters returned to campus the faculty suspended them for "disorderly conduct."[6] Langston responded to the affront and attracted considerable attention by winning election to the United States House of Representatives as an independent candidate from a nearby heavily black district. He did not forsake his student allies, however, and it was Langston's introduction of Lewis and Jackson to Massachusetts senator George Hoar that brought the two pioneers to New England. Hoar reportedly encouraged both students to continue their educations at Amherst College, and he probably aided their enrollment at the elite private school.[7]

In the fall of 1888, Lewis and Jackson continued their education in western Massachusetts. A third black student, George Washington Forbes, who had come to the Berkshires from Ohio's Wilberforce University, joined the two Virginians at Amherst. The three African Americans were among the school's first black students, but they generally received a warm reception on campus. Lewis, in particular, always remembered his alma mater with great fondness. "Life opened its gates for me at Amherst," he later recalled, while commending the school for "incorporat[ing] . . . the principles of true democracy . . . into the life of the College." As a recent graduate in 1892, Lewis similarly praised his peers and professors for forging an environment in which there was "no snobbery, no caste, no invidious social distinction. Every man is a fellow," he declared, "[and] a member of the true college fraternity."[8]

At Amherst, Lewis availed himself of numerous activities but still worked part-time. One morning while Lewis groomed horses, the college president Julius Seelye entered the stables and handed the young student tuition money. When asked the source of the funds, the president said merely that it had come from God, and, in later years, Lewis joked that "the Lord sent me through Amherst."[9] With his finances settled, he focused on his studies and extracurricular activities, and, while attentive to schoolwork, he made his mark on campus in other areas. Lewis represented his class in the college senate for two years, and his classmates tabbed him to compete in the prestigious Hardy Debate and Hardy Oratory prize competitions. He was also a member—and in his senior year the president—of the Hitchcock Society of Inquiry, a social and literary organization that competed with traditional Greek letter fraternities.[10]

Lewis found his greatest fame, however, on the football field. It is unclear when he first took up the sport, but in the fall of 1889 at the beginning of his sophomore year, Lewis—along with Sherman Jackson

—went out for the Lord Jeffs's varsity. Both black athletes immediately found positions in the starting lineup with Lewis at centre rush and Jackson in the backfield.[11] The two Amherst stars, along with Thomas James Fisher of Wisconsin's Beloit College, made history that season as the first known African Americans to compete for predominantly white college football teams.[12] Lewis remained on the varsity during the rest of his time in school, while Jackson played sporadically after 1889. Both players, though, received frequent plaudits from the press. After a game at Harvard in 1891, for example, the *New York Times* gushed: "Jackson, a young colored fellow, played halfback for Amherst and was by all odds the best man on the field . . . Lewis, the colored centre, also played a phenomenal game."[13]

Lewis starred for Amherst throughout his career, impressing knowledgeable observers on and off campus. He repeatedly drew rave reviews in the press, doing, for example, "the best work" against Yale in 1889 and again versus Dartmouth the next year. As a senior, he so dominated his counterpart from Yale that the Eli coaching staff was forced to send in a substitute.[14] His teammates, too, recognized his athletic ability and strong leadership by electing him to the team captaincy for his final season. Captains represented and spoke for their teammates, and, in these days before permanent coaching staffs, they also helped to devise and implement the squad's strategies and tactics. Despite the powerful responsibilities invested in the position, Lewis's colleagues showed no qualms about elevating him to be the first African American to captain an integrated college team. Soon after the election, the *New York Times* reported approvingly: "the election of Lewis '92, a colored man, to the football captaincy for the next year does not cause much comment owing to the democratic spirit of Amherst."[15]

Amherst was not the only college with such a "democratic spirit." After Reconstruction, many northern schools took it as part of their mission to educate the most talented members of the African American community. Although a handful of blacks had graduated from predominantly white schools before the Civil War, not until the end of the nineteenth century did the elite keepers of northern colleges and universities open their doors to African Americans in any significant numbers. These upper-class integrationists hoped to develop a biracial alliance among the "best men" of each race based upon ideas of education, behavior, culture, and common citizenship. David Gerber, a leading historian of race relations in the north during the Gilded Age, has explained that "with black citizenship firmly established in the law, the restraints which had kept higher-status whites from recognizing a basis for solidarity with their black counterparts had somewhat lessened. After all," he continues, "these blacks and whites shared social and moral values . . . [and] aspired to the same lifestyle." Some white integrationists, he asserts, "were sincere enough in their egalitarian beliefs to act against the color line, [because] they believed society should aspire to be more open to educated, accomplished, and conventionally refined Negroes." Such whites were, no doubt, "limited by class and cultural factors," but Gerber concludes "the ethos of the new era . . . creat[ed] a receptive atmosphere which inspired and would be inspired by the efforts of black leaders to seek . . . a color blind . . . society."[16]

There were very real restraints to this upper-class integrationist ethos, and northern colleges did not intend to educate the mass of African Americans—this role they reserved for historically black schools. The president of Harvard recognized this reality in 1907, declaring, "Harvard has about five thousand white students and about thirty of the colored races. The latter are hidden in the great mass . . . If they were equal in numbers or in a majority," he emphasized, "we might deem a separation necessary."[17] Within the limitations of this elitist philosophy, however, white colleges enrolled some of the best black scholars and produced the vanguard of twentieth-century African American leadership. The collegiate integrationist ethos also allowed Lewis and other pioneering amateurs to remain on the field while their professional counterparts like Major Taylor and Jimmy Winkfield were systematically forced from competition.

Lewis embraced this nascent biracial philosophy. At Amherst's graduation ceremonies in 1892, he gave his class oration and elaborated on his beliefs. "A College," the senior class spokesman explained, should train the "many-sided man" and not the "narrow-contracted specialist." A "full-minded man," he argued, "with all his powers and faculties finely trained . . . is ready to enter the race of life." Not surprisingly, he recommended that "nothing gives more real strength of character, decision, and purpose of will than honest athletics." More importantly, though, Lewis argued that the well-rounded college man heeded "the principles of true democracy" and believed that "a man's a man for all that." "Merit," he insisted—and not wealth or color—"is the test of influence and honor." At colleges like Amherst "liberty, fraternity and equality . . . have been accomplished," and he concluded optimistically: "preparation for citizenship [has] produced equality."[18] In the audience for Lewis's talk was a group of black students from the Boston area who had come to see the graduation of Amherst's three African Americans. Among the visitors were Harvard undergraduate William Monroe Trotter and Wellesley's Elizabeth Baker, both of whom would figure prominently in Lewis's life.

After graduation, Lewis moved east and enrolled in Harvard Law School. Years later, he told a reporter that "from the start" he had intended to study law, and Cambridge seemed a natural fit.[19] Once in school, he joined the likes of Trotter and W. E. B. Du Bois in the small but vibrant contingent of African Americans on campus. Lewis's arrival at Harvard, however, attracted more notice than most new students—black or white—enjoyed. His considerable reputation as a football player had preceded him, and, because of the lax rules governing intercollegiate athletics, the Crimson faithful had high hopes for him. Lewis quickly cracked the lineup in 1892 and remained an integral part of the Harvard football program until 1906.

Though small for his position, the five-feet-eleven, 170-pound lineman claimed the starting centre rush position midway through his first year on campus. As at Amherst, Lewis blazed a trail as the first African American athlete at Harvard and the first black football player in the future Ivy League. He also drew rave reviews on the gridiron. The *Harvard Crimson* explained his value after one game in which he had come off of the bench. "When Lewis again came to the centre," the paper commented, "the eleven pulled together once more and began scoring."[20] One national football correspondent similarly praised Harvard's star lineman. "Lewis," he analyzed, "is a man thoroughly versed in all the fine points of the position . . . and, being very quick . . . he is able to not only play his position but to get out and into almost every play, and to do a surprising amount of tackling."[21] The black press, too, noticed Lewis's exploits and took pride in his accomplishments. A correspondent to the *Cleveland Gazette* penned a column, praising "Harvard's great rusher." "Mr. Lewis," the writer noted approvingly, "is the most talked of Afro-American in New England." In addition to being an "exemplary student" and an "all-round good fellow," he asserted, "the Herald, Globe, and Journal of this city [Boston newspapers] give him the palm as the greatest rusher on the line."[22] His performances impressed others as well. In particular, Casper Whitney, the influential editor of *Harper's Weekly*, placed Lewis—the first black player to be so honored—on his All-American team.[23]

Harvard's centre rush occasionally faced prejudicial treatment during his tenure with the Crimson eleven. At a banquet following the Yale game in 1892, for instance, an Eli lineman balked at dining with "any damn nigger," and Lewis "with the massive dignity that would subsequently characterize his conduct" simply moved to another seat.[24] On the gridiron, some opposing players similarly resented his participation, and they sometimes treated Harvard's black player roughly and violently. Later in life, Lewis recalled that such obstacles simply had emboldened him. "I played for Harvard with all I had, because Harvard had done all it could for me," he said in 1948. "There, I learned to regard with indifference trifling insults; [and] there, I learned to consider even severe physical hurts but slight wounds to be endured."[25]

Lewis returned to the Crimson eleven for his second year in law school in 1893, and he garnered even more accolades for his dominant defensive play. Against Dartmouth, he "broke through [the] lineman opposite [him] with ease," while against Brown, "Lewis was a host in himself; his cool, steady work was all that could be desired."[26] In the annual game against Yale later that season, he was up to his old tricks "tackling like a Fiji Islander, [whom] the Yale center found . . . impossible to stop." The Elis eventually won the game 6–0 on a late touchdown, but the Crimson centre had given his all: "Lewis the Harvard centre rush," wrote the *Boston Globe*, "was left silent and motionless on the sod like a dead log thrown shoreward in a storm."[27]

Although the Crimson lost to Yale in 1893, Lewis's college football career ended on a high note. Less than a week later, Harvard closed its season with a Thanksgiving Day game against the University of Pennsylvania. The Crimsons' injured captain missed the game, and, in his place, Harvard chose its centre rush to act as captain. Under Lewis's leadership the home team convincingly won 26 to 4. In recognition of his strong play throughout the season, Casper Whitney once again tabbed Lewis as the centre rush on his prestigious all-star team. "There can be no two opinions as to the choice of centre for the All-America team," he enthused. "Lewis has proved himself to be not only the best centre of this year, but the best all-around centre that has ever put on a college jacket." Whitney then paid the ultimate compliment to the Harvard centre: "I should also make Lewis the captain of the All-America team, both from his position in line, and, from the fact that I have always considered him eminently fitted for such a position."[28]

His fame as a football player did not fade quickly. In 1904, no less of an authority than Walter Camp—the father of American football—selected Lewis as the centre for his mythical team of "the eleven greatest football players."[29] Twenty-five years later, the *Boston Globe* called Lewis "the first great Harvard center"; and, as late as 1951, Crimson athletic authorities listed him as one of the school's "great" players and complained that he had been unfairly left off a recent Associated Press "All-Time Football Team."[30]

Lewis's playing career came to an end after the 1893 season, because Harvard, along with several other colleges, adopted stricter athletic eligibility requirements that disqualified the All-American.[31] The indefatigable Lewis, though, refused to let this setback end his association with intercollegiate football. Before the new regulations took effect, Harvard's football team had been poised to name Lewis as its captain, but, undeterred, he simply took his leadership skills from the gridiron to the sidelines and began a thirteen-year stint as one of Harvard's top assistant coaches.[32] In the late nineteenth century, most college football teams did not employ professional coaching staffs, but, instead, engaged groups of former players, known as alumni coaches. As a testament to the sincerity of Harvard's integrationist ethos, nobody thought it odd that the African American ex-centre would coach his former teammates. Lewis, however, had actually begun his coaching career the previous year. In the fall of 1893, he split his time between Cambridge and Amherst, where he helped to organize and direct the varsity at his first alma mater. Lewis lent his coaching expertise to Amherst again at the beginning of the 1894 season, and, as late as 1900, the busy ex-All-American still found time to assist the Lord Jeffs.[33]

His notoriety as a coach, though, came through his lengthy association with Harvard, and he quickly developed a considerable reputation as a strategic mastermind, who "was a wizard at fathoming plays."[34] Lewis, who specialized in training linemen, remained an instrumental part of the Crimson coaching staff until 1906. For several seasons, in fact, he "was in complete charge of the defense."[35] The sporting community widely respected his football acumen and often solicited his advice. In 1896 he published one of the first books on football strategy, and in 1903, he wrote the section on line play for Walter Camp's *Football Guide.* At about the same time, *Outing*'s Casper Whitney, who had commissioned him to write an article on assembling a successful football team, described Lewis as "one of Harvard's most brainy coaches."[36]

As his reputation grew other schools sought his services. Cornell University recruited Lewis and another Harvard coach to take charge of its football team in 1899. Lewis worked with the Cornell eleven in September, but he was back on the Harvard sidelines later that season.[37] He had apparently impressed Cornell's athletic administrators, though, because, at some point, they attempted to hire Lewis as a full-time professional coach. Cornell reportedly sweetened the deal by offering him a joint appointment as the head football coach and as a professor in the law school. He eventually declined the position, because his family was comfortable in Cambridge and because he was not eager to give up his private legal practice.[38]

Cornell's interest encouraged Harvard to formalize its relationship with Lewis. The Crimson broke with tradition in 1901 and hired its first full-time professional football coach. Although Lewis was in the running for the job, Harvard opted to hire William T. Reid, another former player. At least one observer alleged that the Crimson had discriminated against its former All-American. In headline form, the *Brooklyn Eagle* asked, "Did the color line work against the great center rush?" The newspaper insinuated that "although Harvard will accord a colored man equal privileges as a student, such a person is not desired at the head of any department in athletics." Despite these suspicions, no other commentators doubted the school's motives. Lewis never complained about the situation, and he remained on Harvard's coaching staff—working for Reid—for several more seasons. The Crimson athletic authorities did, however, reward Lewis for his years of loyalty and service. Probably to counter the overtures from Cornell and to placate Lewis for passing him over for the top job, the Harvard Athletic Board voted to compensate him with an annual salary, thus making him the first African American professional college coach in the country. The former centre rush continued to man the Crimson sidelines and to lead Harvard's defense until 1906.[39]

Inspired by the possibilities of the elite integrationist ethos, African American commentators praised Lewis's accomplishments. After he helped Harvard to an upset victory over Penn in 1900, one observer exulted that he was "the most famous football strategist in America." "Our race is proud of him," the author continued, "because in all his success he stands for us, and the higher he goes in the physical field of athletics or the mental field of law or literature, he must necessarily open the way for others, and lift us all up at the same time."[40] The *Cleveland Gazette* was similarly hopeful. "When there is a niche in the old university that a black man can fill better than a white one," the newspaper asserted," he is pretty sure to be invited to fill it. They don't draw a color line against true merit at Harvard."[41]

Although time consuming, coaching was a diversion from Lewis's primary careers. After graduating from Harvard, he readily passed the Massachusetts bar exam and also took an active interest in politics. Locally, he worked with the Republican Party and enjoyed rare electoral success in Cambridge. He also involved himself in African American politics, and, influenced by his experiences at Amherst and Harvard, he associated himself with militant integrationists. During the 1890s, Lewis established himself as a leader of the "Boston Radicals," a group of young, college-educated blacks who eschewed Booker T. Washington's accommodationist philosophy and advocated confrontational tactics to advance the cause of civil rights.

His career as an activist, though, had begun before his graduation. In May 1893, Lewis let his hair grow long for spring football practice, but, before final exam period, he decided to clean up his appearance. He twice visited a Cambridge barbershop for a trim, but each time the proprietor drew the color line. Upon learning of the incident, a group of campus leaders, including the captain of the football team and several other top athletes, wrote a letter to the school newspaper "expressing [their] unqualified indignation" at the event. The *Crimson,* too, denounced this "contemptible spirit of snobbishness" and argued that "such a man . . . whose character has always been borne out by his conduct . . . deserves . . . impartial treatment."[42] The Boston press also rallied to Lewis's defense. The *Post* commended the "refreshing" attitude of the students and thought that "an aristocracy of muscle and pluck is entirely permissible in a pure democracy." In a similar vein, the *Record* argued that "a colored student at Harvard is apt to be socially the peer of even a Cambridge barber."[43]

With public sentiment behind him, Lewis capitalized on the

situation. Using his Harvard contacts, he arranged a meeting with the governor. Democrat William E. Russell "expressed unqualified condemnation of the act" and pledged his support for a legislative remedy.[44] Along with Butler Wilson, the leading black lawyer in Boston, Lewis visited the statehouse, where sympathetic legislators pushed through a new civil rights bill that outlawed racial discrimination at "all private establishments open to public patronage."[45]

Emboldened by his experiences at Amherst and Harvard and heartened by such interracial support for his civil rights, Lewis continued to agitate for black equality. He joined former classmates George Washington Forbes and William Monroe Trotter as the leading spokesmen for Boston's contingent of radical integrationists. Some of Lewis's earliest activism, however, was personal. After graduating from law school, his two younger brothers had come to live with him in Boston, and, in 1895, a Cambridge barbershop refused service to one of Lewis's brothers. In response to the slight, the elder Lewis successfully sued the barber, who had to pay a fifteen-dollar fine, under the terms of the two-year-old civil rights law.[46]

As the decade progressed, Lewis and his allies watched the national ascent of Booker T. Washington with horror. The "Boston Radicals" vigorously disagreed with the Wizard of Tuskegee's strategy of accommodation and with his endorsement of industrial education to the exclusion of a traditional collegiate course. In 1898, Washington visited Boston to resolve his differences with the radicals over dinner at a local hotel. In a series of speeches, the integrationists refused to compromise and strongly condemned Washington's tactics. Lewis was the last to speak, and he advised his adversary to go "back to the South [and] leave to us the matters political affecting the race."[47] A year later, Lewis mocked Washington's "gospel of industrial education" and wondered by what "mysterious process" the Tuskegee plan proposed to "give the negro all his rights as a man and a citizen."[48]

In addition to his activism, Lewis also embarked on a mainstream political career. In 1899, he won the first of three consecutive one-year terms to represent his predominantly white neighborhood as a Republican on the Cambridge city council. In 1902, his neighbors elected him to the Massachusetts state legislature where he served on the prestigious Judiciary Committee. He failed to win reelection, however, and for many years he held the dubious distinction of being the last African American to serve in the Massachusetts Statehouse.

Lewis's political philosophy underwent a profound transformation at the turn of the century. Particularly when his electoral success ended, he reevaluated the nature of his activism and affected a rapprochement with Booker T. Washington. For a variety of reasons—not the least of which was political expediency—Lewis drastically tempered his radical views. Once he adopted a more conservative racial outlook, he benefited from the considerable power of the Tuskegee machine, and, with Washington's endorsement, he secured a series of increasingly powerful federal patronage positions.

As the state of race relations deteriorated and support for African American rights became a political liability, many of Lewis's powerful white allies encouraged him to reconsider what they believed was his embarrassing radicalism. Amherst president Seelye counseled him that "your race will never get its rights by dwelling upon its wrongs," and he advised Lewis to "preach . . . not of condemnation [but] . . . with a lively hope of . . . redemption."[49] In 1900, Lewis exchanged letters with President Theodore Roosevelt, whom he knew through their mutual support of Harvard football. In one letter, the Cambridge city councilman criticized the current racial order and advocated a more vigorous defense of civil rights. In response, Roosevelt told Lewis that "your letter puzzles and troubles me." The president confided that "I am at my wits end to know what to advise" and then urged Lewis to meet with Booker T. Washington, who, Roosevelt said, "is a man for whom I have the highest regard."[50] One last important individual urged Lewis to switch his allegiances. His wife, former Wellesley student Elizabeth Baker, whom he had married in 1896, also reportedly encouraged him to abandon his confrontational philosophy.[51]

Faced with such increasing resistance to his radicalism, Lewis reconsidered his politics and his attitude toward the Wizard of Tuskegee. In 1901, the two leaders exchanged cordial letters, and Washington informed his erstwhile rival, "I believe that both you and I are going to be in a position in the future to serve the race effectually . . . and I am sure that in our anxiety to better the condition of the race there is no difference between us."[52] As the two race spokesmen drifted closer together philosophically, Washington made it clear that he could assist

Lewis's political ambitions, and letters between the two men make frequent references to potential appointive positions.[53] In 1903, when Lewis lost his reelection bid to the state legislature, Roosevelt, upon the recommendation of Washington, appointed the Cambridge lawyer to a position as an assistant United States attorney for Massachusetts.

Lewis's final break with his radical allies came later that year when Washington traveled north to address a meeting of Boston's black leadership. William Monroe Trotter, George W. Forbes, and other strident integrationists infiltrated the gathering. Lewis chaired the meeting and informed the audience that disruptive behavior and disorderly conduct would not be tolerated. When Trotter and other radicals ignored the warnings and interrupted the proceedings, Lewis called in several police officers to restore order. In the ensuing melee, the police arrested Trotter, his sister, and two other radicals. The incident, known by the sensational name of the "Boston Riot," further polarized the black community and alienated radical integrationists from mainstream white public opinion. The Bookerites pressed their advantage and refused to drop criminal charges against the arrested radicals. Lewis, in fact, was the star witness at the trial that sentenced his former Harvard classmate Trotter to thirty days in jail.[54]

In subsequent years, Lewis occasionally discussed his transformation. In 1909, he explained that "our old time methods of agitation, denunciation and exposition have fallen on deaf ears . . . and will accomplish nothing." "The educated colored men," he concluded, "have failed to realize that . . . the field of diplomacy has scarcely been touched in the solution of race problems."[55] Several years later, he admitted that "for a time after leaving the Law School I was counted as one of the radicals and agitators," but, he recalled, "I began to ask myself if they [the Bookerites] were wholly wrong and myself wholly right." Concluding that "they were more right than I . . . I decided that I should not make the business of my life . . . slinging mud at a real worker."[56] In another speech, he put it more succinctly: "I thought, as a young man, that Latin conquered everything. Washington read it right," he affirmed, "labor conquers all. I saw the form. He saw the substance."[57]

The Boston radicals were incensed at the defection. Using their weekly newspaper, the *Boston Guardian,* as a forum, Trotter and Forbes angrily attacked their former ally. Trotter called Lewis "the dirtiest cur" involved with the "Boston Riot," and the *Guardian,* which took to calling him "Football Lewis" and "Bre'r Lewis," insinuated that "his is a real case of being colored for leadership and revenue only."[58] Earlier, when he had addressed a pro-Washington banquet, the radical newspaper wrote disgustedly that "there is not a true and tried well-wisher of Lewis who would not a thousand times rather have seen flowers heaped around his coffin than around his [dinner] plate for such a service."[59]

Despite his critics, Lewis remained a loyal Republican and Tuskegee man, and his patrons rewarded him well. In 1907, to quell dissension among black supporters, President Roosevelt elevated Lewis to assistant United States attorney for the New England states in charge of immigration proceedings. Trotter remained unimpressed and scornfully wrote that Lewis "has repeatedly and flagrantly sold his honor and sold out his race in order to get a political position with a salary which he has seemed unable to earn at the law."[60] A year later, Lewis demonstrated his loyalty by defending Roosevelt's discharge of the soldiers involved in the Brownsville affair—something, he admitted, "no other colored Federal office-holder" had done.[61] In response, the *Guardian* called him simply "the Worst Traitor to [the] race in its history."[62] His willingness to stand by unpopular decisions, however, finally brought him the plum appointment he coveted. President William Taft, responding to criticisms that he had forsaken the African American community, appointed Lewis an assistant attorney general of the United States in 1911. Lewis had been agitating for the position for several years, and the promotion made him the highest-ranking African American federal appointee until the 1950s.[63]

Lewis occasionally justified his decision to work within the system. After breaking with the radicals, for example, he had defended Washington's strategy by arguing that his new ally was simply "trying to bring the wooden horse inside the walls of Troy." He later elaborated on this philosophy in a letter to the Wizard of Tuskegee. "If I could get a chance in Washington in the Department of Justice," Lewis wrote, "I feel certain that I could 'make good' and put race prejudice to flight in that department."[64]

Lewis would ultimately be disappointed by his ability to put "race prejudice to flight." After his appointment, numerous southern senators delayed his official confirmation by eight months, and, in a more personal slight, several clerks at the Justice Department requested transfers when he arrived in Washington.[65] The most embarrassing rebuke, however, came later. Before Lewis left for D.C., a group of Boston attorneys had nominated him for membership in the American Bar Association. The ABA approved his membership, but when the organization realized it had enrolled an African American, the leadership threatened to expel Lewis.

The ABA took up the issue at its 1912 convention, and United States attorney general George W. Wickersham threatened to resign if the organization revoked Lewis's membership. Wickersham condemned the idea of catering to "a race prejudice entertained by some," and the *Nation,* an influential political journal, derided such "astounding and indefensible . . . lawlessness," accusing the segregationists of "shaming themselves and the body for which they speak."[66] In the face of mounting criticism and bad press, the ABA opted not to draw the color line officially, but it adopted a new regulation requiring all future candidates to indicate clearly their racial heritage. The organization consistently used the new stipulation to deny membership to African Americans and did not revise its Jim Crow policy until the 1940s. That a highly educated, well-respected, politically connected man could not escape the restraints of his race even in a learned organization like the American Bar Association must surely have disillusioned Lewis.[67] Others, though, were not so surprised. As far back as 1902, William Monroe Trotter had predicted just such an outcome as a result of Lewis's accommodationist politics, when he wrote poetically: "The thorns which I have reaped are off the tree I planted; they have torn me, and I bleed. I should have known what fruit would spring from such seed."[68]

Soon after the ABA controversy, Democrat Woodrow Wilson won the presidency, and the assistant attorney general, along with most other patronage appointments, lost his position. A tired and frustrated Lewis left politics and retired to a private law practice back in Boston. He quickly established a reputation as one of the best defense lawyers in the city and took on many high-profile cases. During prohibition, he became rich defending bootleggers, and, in the 1930 census, he appraised the value of his house at $12,000. He maintained an interest in civil rights, though, and, in 1926 he assisted lawyers from the NAACP in arguing the case of *Corrigan v. Buckley* before the United States Supreme Court in which they unsuccessfully challenged the use of racially restrictive covenants in real estate transactions.[69]

Although he mostly avoided politics to concentrate on his legal career,

Lewis occasionally resurfaced as a racial leader. In 1915, he assisted Trotter in an unsuccessful campaign to ban D. W. Griffith's film *Birth of a Nation* in Boston. The former rivals affected a reconciliation a year later when Lewis attended the *Guardian's* fifteenth anniversary banquet.[70] In the early 1920s, he used his influence with Calvin Coolidge, an old Amherst classmate, to secure the appointment of another former foe, W. E. B. Du Bois, as a special minister to Liberia's presidential inauguration. In 1924, though, he broke with Coolidge and the Republican Party—his longtime political home—when he perceived that the GOP was not forceful enough in condemning the resurgent Ku Klux Klan. Lewis endorsed Democrat John W. Davis for president, but Coolidge won in a landslide, and Lewis was back in the Republican fold by 1928.[71]

Despite these political setbacks, Lewis remained optimistic about the future of race relations, and he continued to hope for the realization of the merit-based integrationist ideal of his college days. In 1911, for example, he counseled his fellow African Americans that "ye shall overcome the world by character, by conduct, by achievement; ye shall overcome it by suffering, by sacrifice, and by service." "The Negro at this day," he then told his white audience, "does not ask for special laws made for him alone. All that he asks is for just and equal laws applicable to all men." In the end, Lewis proclaimed hopefully: "I believe that our country will yet show to the world how people of many races, aye, of totally dissimilar races, may live together on the same soil under just . . . laws." Two years later he presciently predicted that "within the next 50 years all these discriminations, disfranchisements, and segregation will pass away."[72]

After Lewis's retirement from the Harvard coaching staff in 1906, the former All-American did not take an active interest in intercollegiate athletics and instead directed most of his energy to his political and legal careers. He did, however, look out for other African American athletes who competed at New England colleges. In 1908, for example, he befriended Leslie Pollard, a Chicago schoolboy star, who played football at Dartmouth. Several years later, Pollard's younger brother, Fritz, traveled east to play football but had trouble deciding on a school. After briefly attending several colleges, Pollard visited Lewis's Boston law office where the ex-assistant attorney general lectured his young charge on the danger of becoming a "tramp athlete" and warned him not to "disgrace" his family. Lewis arranged for Pollard to improve his academic record at nearby Springfield (Massachusetts) High School after which he enrolled at Brown University.[73] Pollard led the Providence school to football fame, and, in 1916, he earned recognition as the first black All-American since William Henry Lewis in 1893. Aside from such personal interests, however, Lewis grew apart from the game as he aged. He seems to have attended some Harvard home games, but, like many ex-athletes, he criticized the changes in the sport. Shortly before his death, for example, he condemned the contemporary rules. "Free substitution is ridiculous," he exclaimed, "it's [just] not fair to use four, five, or six elevens!"[74]

As a new generation of African American leaders emerged, he also faded from the national political scene and concentrated on his law firm, which his son William Jr. joined after graduating from Harvard Law School. The elder Lewis tried cases until 1948 when heart problems forced him into retirement. William Henry Lewis died on January 1, 1949, at the age of eighty, leaving behind his son and a daughter who lived in Paris. Most Boston papers prominently noted his passing, and his obituary appeared in *Time* magazine and the *New York Times*. The latter called him simply "one of the most eloquent pleaders before the Massachusetts Bar."[75]

In his ground-breaking book, *The Strange Career of Jim Crow*, the eminent historian C. Vann Woodward described a "twilight zone" at the turn of the twentieth century during which "there was a great deal of variety and inconsistency . . . in race relations." "It was a time of experiment, testing, and uncertainty," he wrote, "quite different from the time of repression and rigid uniformity that was to come . . . Alternatives were still open," Woodward emphasized, "and real choices had to be made."[76] Although he was specifically writing about the post-Reconstruction South, his analysis also applies to the racial situation in the north during these years as Americans in all sections of the country were struggling to replace the racial order destroyed by the Civil War and Reconstruction.

The "strange career" of William Henry Lewis embodied many of the tantalizing possibilities of this uncertain era, as well as the ultimate frustration of African American hopes. One of the racial alternatives available to contemporary Americans was the integrationist ethos of elite northern colleges and universities. In the late nineteenth and early twentieth centuries, some northern whites sincerely believed in and worked toward a biracial conception of citizenship that afforded equal opportunities to competent and gentlemanly African Americans. In this atmosphere, white students at Amherst College chose to elect a black football captain, and Harvard University chose to employ an African American football coach. Certainly, not all whites were so progressive, and a Cambridge barber could choose not to cut the hair of a black Harvard football player. In response, however, sympathetic whites discredited and embarrassed such segregationists by overwhelmingly championing civil rights and by choosing to pass a new law banning such discrimination. Lewis succeeded spectacularly on his merits in this world and rose to the highest pinnacles of athletic achievement by earning All-American recognition and landing a spot on the Harvard coaching staff.

Outside of college athletics, however, he never found such unqualified success. As race relations deteriorated throughout the nation and as his career took him farther from the Ivory Tower, the options available to even a highly skilled and impeccably credentialed African American dwindled. An increasing number of northern whites chose to default on their promises of a biracial standard of citizenship, and successful blacks like Lewis found themselves with few allies. By eschewing the activism of his youth, he was able to rise in the ranks of the federal bureaucracy, but he encountered resistance every step of the way. To segregationists who advocated "the rigid uniformity" of Jim Crow, Lewis's law degree, political success, intellectual achievement, and athletic exploits were irrelevant. By the time the American Bar Association attempted to draw the color line against him, the captaincy of the Amherst football team and the boycott of a Cambridge barbershop were distant memories, because too many whites had chosen to abandon any notion of biracial equal opportunity.

The eventual success of Jim Crow has obscured the fact that many whites chose publicly and strongly to support successful and gentlemanly African Americans. The all-encompassing racial segregation of the early twentieth century was but one alternative available to American society, and many northern whites and blacks chose instead to support a biracial notion of citizenship. The "strange career" of William Henry Lewis, therefore, is more than a series of trivia questions; it is a vivid reminder of this integrationist alternative that allowed some African Americans to flourish in mainstream society.

Jack Johnson enjoyed the finer things in life, including large automobiles which he liked to drive very fast and use as showpieces. *(University of Notre Dame)*

4 Jack Johnson and the Quest for Racial Respect

GERALD R. GEMS

The Progressive Era proved a misnomer for African Americans. Lynchings occurred on a regular basis. Jim Crow laws separated society and the United States Supreme Court affirmed racial segregation in the *Plessy v. Ferguson* case in 1896. Miscegenation laws prohibited interracial unions in many states. The Ku Klux Klan rose to power in the South, spread into northern states, and terrorized black families with violent retributions for any transgressions upon white authority. A popular 1915 movie entitled *The Birth of a Nation* glorified the Klan for approving white audiences. Black resistance to white dominance in the form of race riots met with brutal and forceful subjugation. Booker T. Washington, a national leader of African Americans, advocated a slow and gradual accommodation between the races, as he emphasized vocational training as a means to economic progress.

Sport seemingly offered African Americans more rapid opportunities for advancement. Isaac Murphy, the great black jockey, won three Kentucky Derbies and earned a lavish salary for his exploits on the track. Marshall "Major" Taylor garnered the world cycling championship in 1899 and earned similar remuneration. By 1900 however, African Americans faced exclusion from horse racing, and jealous white rivals colluded to force Taylor to seek his sustenance in Europe by 1901. Within that context Jack Johnson, a flamboyant, proud, and arrogant African American boxer, emerged to stun white Americans. He compelled whites to reevaluate their Social Darwinian beliefs in white superiority and their assumptions of white privilege. Unlike Booker T. Washington, Johnson forced a rapid change in American society.

Jack Johnson was born on March 31, 1878, the fifth of six children of Henry, a school janitor, and Tina ("Tiny") Johnson in Galveston, Texas. Johnson faced a difficult childhood.[1] He received an elementary school education, but had little interest in studying. Forced into battle royals at a young age, Johnson discovered his fighting abilities. In such affairs white townsmen formed a ring around black youths, who were sometimes blindfolded, and forced them to fight each other until only one emerged. The winner might be rewarded with spare change.[2] Johnson worked a series of odd jobs during his early years, but his earnings failed to match the losses resulting from his gambling habit. As a Galveston dockworker forced to confront a local bully, Johnson won a victory that established his local reputation and he soon embarked on a ring career. As a teenager he traveled to Dallas and other points around the country, learning his trade as a sparring partner and engaging in minor professional bouts.[3]

By 1900 Johnson gained greater public notice and his complex, troubled life began to assume greater national importance. In his own words, Johnson stated that "my life, almost from its very start, has been filled with tragedy and romance, failure and success, poverty and wealth, misery and happiness."[4] Johnson's early romances apparently set the stage for much of his future notoriety. Mary Austin, a common law wife, left him after three years in 1901. He met another black paramour, Clara Kerr, the following year, but she eventually ran off with another man. In his remorse, Johnson turned to white women for solace and status. The conquest of a white woman by a black man threatened white men in particular and reinforced the mystique of black sexual powers.[5]

In 1901 the inexperienced Johnson was knocked out by Joe Choynski, a fighter with a national reputation, in a Galveston bout. Both spent nearly a month in jail for violating Texas laws that prohibited prizefights. The event signaled a lifelong pattern of conflict with white authorities for Johnson.[6]

Boxing provided blacks with one means to exhibit their physical prowess, gain a measure of social mobility, and earn a limited degree of respect. George Dixon, a transplanted Canadian, won the featherweight title by a knockout in 1890. Two years later he brutally pummeled the white boxer Jack Skully in the New Orleans Carnival of Champions. Skully's mauling engendered a crusade to ban interracial bouts, lest blacks assume physical equality with whites.[7] Joe Walcott gained the welterweight title in 1901 and Joe Gans wore the lightweight crown a year later. Nevertheless, only at the heavyweight level did whites enact an unofficial ban on black fighters. Symbolizing the notion of Social Darwinian masculinity, the heavyweight title proved too sacred to chance. John L. Sullivan imposed a color ban after winning the title from Paddy Ryan in 1882. A succession of heavyweight champions, James J. Corbett, Bob Fitzsimmons, and Jim Jeffries, reinforced the prohibition.[8]

Despite this obstacle, Johnson persisted in his quest for the heavyweight title. In 1903 he defeated Denver Ed Martin in a twenty-round match in Los Angeles. The decision earned him the unofficial claim to the Negro heavyweight championship of America. Johnson's laurels rested largely on his quickness, a splendid defense, effective counter punching, and a devastating right uppercut. As his purses enhanced his lifestyle, Johnson began to assume a public persona that forced Americans, and eventually Europeans as well, to take notice. Inside the ring he wore colorful tights; outside of it he changed clothes as often as four times a day. Sartorial splendor marked the remainder of his days. A bon vivant, raconteur, and spendthrift, Johnson later carried a roll of large bills to entertain his entourage in lavish fashion. He often disdained the payment of his bills, rebelled against any form of authority, and lived recklessly, particularly when behind the wheel of his automobiles. During fights, Johnson engaged in a repartee with his opponents and the fans. At times comical or antagonistic, the tactic often proved disconcerting to his white adversaries.[9]

Jim Jeffries retired as the undisputed heavyweight champion in 1905, leaving the division in confusion. Tommy Burns, a Canadian of middleweight stature, eventually succeeded in capturing the title from an undistinguished Marvin Hart in 1906, while Johnson toiled against lesser whites and tough blacks like Joe Jeanette and Sam Langford. The top black fighters often labored against each other, unable to get matches that might embarrass whites. In his public life, however, Johnson began to openly flaunt his conquests of white women.

With few American opponents of note available to him, Johnson traveled to Australia in 1907, where he easily defeated the local combatants. That same year he returned to the United States to face the aged former champion, Bob Fitzsimmons. Impoverished, Fitzsimmons needed a big pay day, even if it meant a bout with an African American. Johnson had little pity on the ex-champ, whom he knocked out in only two rounds. Johnson celebrated in the arms of yet another white woman, a prostitute named Hattie McClay, who became his companion over the next four years.[10]

In 1908 Johnson followed Tommy Burns to England, but could not arrange a title fight. While there, Johnson impressed the British with his abilities by pounding several English heavyweights, but he offended the kingdom with his decided lack of deference to whites. Johnson then chased Burns to Australia, where he succeeded in arranging a title fight by allowing the white man to keep $30,000 of the $35,000 purse and agreeing to let Burns's manager serve as the referee. The tactic failed to help the diminutive Burns, who at 5' 7" struggled against the 6' 0" African American giant. Johnson taunted, badgered, and toyed with Burns, letting the white champion hit him in the stomach to dispel the myth of black intestinal vulnerability. Johnson then battered Burns as retaliation for the latter's racial slurs, finally stopping the champion in the fourteenth round. Johnson now ruled the boxing world, much to the chagrin and horror of whites. He embarked on a theatrical tour of Australia, glorying in his new celebrity.[11]

When Galveston balked at his homecoming celebration, fearing the ramifications of his white female companion, Johnson adopted Chicago as his hometown. He had spent some time there in his early career, and by 1908 the city claimed a large and growing African American population. For many African Americans, Johnson represented retribution for centuries of slavery and oppression. His white women represented the ultimate conquest for the black man and the greatest insult to white notions of security and dominance in race relations. It signified the inability of white men to protect their most precious treasure.

Throughout 1909 white promoters searched for a "Great White Hope" who might return the crown to its rightful place and remove the black scourge on Anglo pride. Johnson easily disposed of each contender, five in all. His most noticeable battle occurred with Stanley Ketchel, the ferocious middleweight champion of the world. Johnson outweighed Ketchel by more than thirty pounds, but by the end of the year Ketchel was the best white fighter available. Ketchel fought gamely, even knocking the black champion to the canvas in the twelfth round. The blow enraged Johnson, who retaliated with a crushing uppercut that not only rendered Ketchel unconscious, but tore the front teeth from his mouth.[12]

By that time Johnson had taken up with yet another white woman, a young prostitute named Belle Schreiber. She became the favorite in his bevy of mistresses, at least temporarily. When jilted, her jealousy eventually accomplished more than any white hope in the toppling of Jack Johnson. Meanwhile, Johnson assumed the trappings of royalty. The African American prince reversed social and economic roles by hiring white managers, chauffeurs, valets, and women who waited upon him and served his needs. In Chicago he sported a grandiose house where he eventually installed his mother and sisters. He sped throughout the city and around the country in racing cars, oblivious to the laws. In 1910 he even challenged Barney Oldfield, one of the premier professional auto racers of the era. Oldfield vanquished Johnson, something white fighters couldn't do.[13]

That contest proved of little consequence, for Johnson had already won his greatest victory. Finally bowing to the public clamor that he restore the Social Darwinian order and put Johnson in his proper place, the undefeated champion, Jim Jeffries, emerged from retirement. Hounded by fans and sportswriters for a year, many of whom still believed him to be the true holder of the heavyweight title, Jeffries reluctantly acquiesced. Although he had never tasted defeat, he was now thirty-five years of age and at least three hundred pounds. Still, the $101,000 purse and movie rights proved an added inducement, and Jeffries managed to shed more than seventy pounds by the appointed date.

Originally scheduled for forty-five rounds in San Francisco, that site was abandoned for Reno, Nevada, for the Fourth of July, 1910, when the governor of California surrendered to the national campaign efforts of moral reformers. Tex Rickard offered the winner 75 percent of the astronomical purse. He designated himself as the referee to ensure a fair outcome for his investment. Twenty thousand fans trekked to the sweltering Nevada desert, doubling the population of Reno. Among them hundreds of journalists traveled from around the world, some from as far away as Europe and Australia to witness the grand spectacle. Newspapers lionized Jeffries, and betting odds favored him right up to the opening bell. He outweighed the black champion by twenty pounds. Despite his achievements, the media featured Johnson in Sambo cartoons that denigrated his considerable intelligence and physical prowess. Writers referred to "the big spade" as a "childlike," cowardly loafer, and reported that black churches were praying for his deliverance.[14]

Before the start of the contest Jeffries made an announcement that left no doubt as to the racial ramifications of the pugilistic war. The white warrior asserted that "that portion of the white race that has been looking to me to defend its athletic superiority may feel assured that I am fit to do my very best." Johnson proved more magnanimous by stating,

> Every fighter on the eve of his fight declares that he hopes the best man wins. I am quite sincere when I say that I do. If Mr. Jeffries knocks me out or gains a decision over me I will go into the corner and congratulate him as soon as I am able. My congratulations will be no fake. I mean it. If Mr. Jeffries has it in him to defeat me I think that I can modestly say he is entitled to all the congratulations he may receive.[15]

Johnson had little to fear. He counterpunched effectively as he verbally provoked Jeffries and his corner man, former champion James J. Corbett. Corbett had predicted a knockout for his white colleague and bet $5,000 on the outcome. He claimed that blacks harbored an innate fear of white men. An avowed racist, Corbett shouted racial epithets at Johnson throughout the fight, but the latter answered with his fists. Johnson bloodied the Great White Hope for fifteen rounds, even breaking his nose. In the fifteenth round Johnson pounded Jeffries to the canvas, the first time the latter had ever been knocked down. To the amazement of whites, he repeated the assault with the same outcome. Each time Jeffries barely managed to beat the count. Johnson then knocked the lumbering giant through the ropes, but those at ringside pushed him back into the fray. Jeffries's corner and Rickard had seen enough, however. A black man had beaten the seemingly invincible white champion, and the Social Darwinian belief system in white superiority crumbled.[16]

Although whites had to accept the physical outcome, most offered only grudging respect. Novelist Rex Beach lamented, "Today we saw a tragedy. A tremendous, crushing anti-climax had happened and we are dazed. . . . He (Johnson) demonstrated further that his race has acquired full stature as men; whether they will ever breed brains to match his muscle is yet to be seen."[17]

Throughout the United States, African Americans rose in jubilation despite the remonstronces of some middle-class black clergy who railed against Johnson's lifestyle. In Pittsburgh the police banned a planned celebration for fear of white reprisals. In Chicago blacks and whites fought each other in a mixed crowd of ten thousand that listened to the report of the championship encounter. In numerous other locales, whites did retaliate, killing and lynching African Americans who reveled in the symbolic reversal of the racial hierarchy. Among the worst incidents, a newspaper headline screamed that "New York Roughs Burn Tenement of Colored People and Try to Cremate Occupants." Riots ensued throughout the land, brutally suppressed by police or white vigilantes. Proud African Americans no longer felt the need to defer to whites. To stem the violence, authorities banned the showing of the fight films in some communities. On the national level, moral reformers campaigned for a general prohibition of the entire sport.[18]

Jack Johnson presented a dilemma for the top black leaders in America. He challenged the notion of Booker T. Washington, who favored passive assimilation. Johnson's loud, defiant, rebellious behavior defied Washington's image of the model African American and risked alienation for all blacks. Washington's rival within the black community, W. E. B. Du Bois, disliked boxing but characteristically took a contrary stand. Perhaps feeling an empathy with his own rebelliousness and a strong race consciousness, he lauded Johnson's achievement and his ability to overturn the stereotypes of black debility. Du Bois continually made the same case for the black intellect.[19]

In Chicago, however, Johnson returned to a hero's welcome and a day-long festival. A lengthy ceremony honored his triumph and his new stature as a black messiah. In New York a crowd of ten thousand African Americans greeted him at the railroad station. By the end of the month, a company offered eighteen-inch bronze statues "as an ornament for the home of every negro [*sic*] for he is the first negro [*sic*] to be admitted the best man in the world." Johnson earned a lucrative payday for the Jeffries affair. His winner's share, a bonus, and the movie rights amounted to $140,000, and he soon embarked on a vaudeville tour through the Midwest, East, and Canada. Despite his fame, he continued to suffer racial indignities, denied access to dressing rooms in theaters and rooms at the better hotels. Theater operators feared his association with white women, and Johnson characteristically fulfilled their trepidations. He soon faced myriad legal suits over real and imagined offenses, and worse, even assassination attempts. He further infuriated whites by actually marrying Etta Terry Duryea, a previously wed white woman with whom he had been cohabitating. He enraged his new wife by maintaining his dalliance with Belle Schreiber. Eighteen months later, Etta Johnson committed suicide.[20]

While promoters searched for a new White Hope in 1911, Johnson embarked on a theatrical tour in London, but the government refused to allow any boxing matches. By this time Johnson had reached the status of international celebrity. The European press reported his adventures and characterized boxing as a "war" between blacks and whites. The German government restricted public showings of the Jeffries fight film, while journalists denigrated Johnson's successes.[21]

On July 4, 1912, Johnson met yet another white hope, "Fireman" Jim Flynn in Las Vegas, New Mexico. The desolate site had little to recommend it other than the fact it had no laws preventing a boxing match. Flynn's only claim to fame rested upon his defeat of other white hopefuls, for Johnson had previously beaten him by a knockout. Flynn lasted nine rounds before being disqualified for illegal tactics. Chicago blacks had another victory celebration, but Congress moved to ban the fight films. The federal government had already indicted Johnson for smuggling because he had failed to pay customs tax on a diamond necklace he had purchased for his wife in England.[22]

His wife's death hardly slowed Johnson's frenetic pace. He had already opened the Café de Champion, a swanky Chicago black and tan cabaret complete with orchestra, just south of the vice district. For African Americans Johnson's new entrepreneurial nature represented a mark of further black ascendance and material success. The mixed crowds drawn to the establishment fostered a greater sense of integration in American society; but whites viewed such intermingling as a dangerous sign, and white journalists even criticized the lavishness of the décor.[23]

Barely two months after his wife's death, Johnson married another young white woman, Lucille Cameron. Still a teenager, the Minneapolis native worked at Johnson's cabaret. She represented another white conquest for the champion. To her mother, however, she represented a victim. Mrs. Cameron-Falconet allegedly stated that "I would rather see my daughter spend the rest of her life in an insane asylum than see her the plaything of a nigger."[24] She charged Johnson with abduction and white slavery, a violation of the Mann Act, which forbade the transport of women across state lines for immoral purposes. The racial nature of the charge quickly escalated. The Appomattox Club, an association of elite African American businessmen in Chicago, admonished white newspapers for condemning all blacks for the sins of Johnson. They called upon the champion to retract his alleged statement that he could have any white woman that he wanted. Johnson met with the black leaders and cast his defense, not as a question of morality, but of basic human rights. He denied uttering such a claim.

> But I do want to say that I have the right to choose who my mate shall be without the dictation of any man. . . . So long as I do not interfere with any other man's wife I shall claim the right to select the woman of my choice. Nobody else can do that for me. That is where the trouble lies.[25]

The case quickly disintegrated and Johnson won exoneration when Lucille admitted to practicing prostitution before she had ever met her employer. She and Johnson sealed their union, to the chagrin of many whites, with a formal marriage on December 4, 1912. The government, however, persisted in its efforts at conviction on Mann Act charges by recruiting the jealous Belle Schreiber to testify against her former lover. In addition, the local government in Chicago effectively closed Johnson's cabaret when it refused to renew his license. Realizing his predicament, the champion fled to Canada on board a train on the night of January 14, 1913. He got as far as Battle Creek, Michigan, where authorities arrested him the next morning.[26]

In April 1913 Johnson paid an exorbitant penalty in a smuggling case when he failed to report a diamond necklace bought in England, then faced the trumped-up Mann Act charges the following month. A white male jury quickly convicted the proud black champion, and the judge imposed not only a one-thousand-dollar fine, but also a prison sentence of 366 days. Johnson, indomitable in the ring, lost by a decision in the courts. True to his defiant nature, he refused to obey the verdict. Under mysterious circumstances, probably through well-placed bribes, Johnson's second flight proved successful. He arrived safely in Montreal, and then set sail for France. Throughout the remainder of the year and the next he engaged in stage shows, boxing exhibitions, and even wrestling matches in Europe, London, and Russia in order to replenish his coffers and fund his extravagant lifestyle.[27]

By midyear in 1914 Johnson had succeeded in defending his title three times in Paris, but he made little money against relatively unknown fighters. With the eruption of World War I in Europe that summer Johnson faced dim prospects of any employment. In early 1915 he left the continent for South America, landing in Buenos Aires, Argentina, where his theatrical performance and a bout with a little-known American fighter garnered little interest. From there, he traveled to Barbados and Cuba. In Cuba he arranged to meet yet another white hope, the six-feet-six, 238-pound "Pottawatomie Giant" Jess Willard.[28]

Other than his size, Willard possessed limited distinction as a contender. The fight, however, proved one of the most controversial in ring history. The combatants met on April 5, 1915, near Havana. A reporter stated that

> From the moment the two entered the ring it was more than a battle between prize fighters in the eyes of those who saw the contest. To them it was a struggle between the white and black races and an opportunity to reassert the superiority of the Caucasian over the African. . . . such a wild, hysterically shrieking enthusiastic crowd . . . men and women who begged Willard to yipe [*sic*] out the stigma they and hundreds of thousands of others, especially in the south, believed rested on the white race through the negro [*sic*] holding the championship.[29]

In a contest scheduled for forty-five rounds, the champion spent the first twenty toying with, then pounding the challenger. A white sportswriter acknowledged that "the fight was all Johnson's during the first twenty rounds . . . on occasions Johnson played with him, once standing with guard down and letting Willard swing at him, only to dodge and laugh at the awkwardness of his opponent."[30] But in the twenty-sixth round Willard landed a big right hand that sent Johnson to the canvas, where he lay with his knees bent and his right arm shielding his eyes from the glaring sun. The Associated Press correspondent stated: "There is much discussion tonight and probably will be for a long time, among the followers of the fighting game as to whether Johnson was really knocked out. In the sense of being smashed into unconsciousness he certainly was not put out. . . . A second or two after Jack Welsh, the referee, had counted ten, Johnson quickly got up."[31]

Even some whites had doubts, as stated by a reporter, "he [Willard] has a lot to learn. This is the opinion held by the experts about the ring. Certainly we have had no champion since Corbett to set a new mark in fighting who has so little in his equipment."[32] Although most historians doubt his veracity, Johnson later maintained that he had thrown the fight for a large sum of money and the expectation of a lenient return to the United States. If so, the federal government betrayed him by refusing to grant him a passport.[33]

There is no doubt as to the racial importance of the outcome. Willard announced: "Naturally I am jubilant at having brought the title back to the white race. I shall do all in my power to hold it." Fair or foul, whites rejoiced in the outcome. The same day the *Chicago Tribune* ran a racist cartoon depicting Johnson as a burning building and Willard as the fireman who put out the "Big Smoke."[34] With the heavyweight crown returned to a white head, Jess Willard promptly reinstated the color ban. Jack Dempsey, Willard's conqueror, adhered to the prohibition, effectively ensuring that Johnson, or any of the other prominent black heavyweights of the era, would not gain another opportunity for the title.

Left without an option in the United States, Johnson returned to England. No longer the champion and with British losses in World War I a national concern, Johnson's theatrical tour held very limited interest. Compounding his problems, court cases over bill payments caused him to lose money on the venture. Intemperate, pro-German remarks further alienated the British government, which expelled him from the country in February 1916. With the war raging in France, he opted for a sojourn in Spain.[35]

There he waited out the war and engaged in a few uneventful boxing matches, the most notable against the eccentric poet Arthur Craven. Johnson knocked out the bohemian in less than a minute; but no longer the champion, neither he nor boxing held great interest for Spaniards. To amuse himself Johnson took up bullfighting and briefly operated a failed advertising agency. After the United States entered World War I, Johnson offered his services in return for a pardon but to no avail. By 1919 he had been forced to pawn his wife's jewelry and he no longer enjoyed the same limelight or celebrity status. With no prospects in Spain he turned his attention to Mexico, where he hoped to revive his chances under the sympathetic government of Venustiano Carranza.[36]

Carranza, no admirer of the United States, received Johnson warmly. In Mexico Johnson arranged several boxing matches, but none against top-ranked contenders. He pursued his new avocation, bullfighting, and publicly chastised the United States for its racially oppressive policies, and African Americans listened. In 1919 his adopted hometown of Chicago had erupted in a race riot that lasted two weeks and cost thirty-eight lives as blacks fought back in a departure from the passive resistance of the past. Johnson's fortunes improved, and he clearly enjoyed his popularity in Mexico, as well as his notoriety in the United States. He opened a prosperous saloon in Tijuana, just across the border from California. His luck lasted only as long as his patron, however; and in 1920 Carranza was ousted and murdered by oppositional forces.[37]

With the new Mexican leadership more amenable to better relations with the United States, Johnson soon lost his saloon and his boxing opportunities. After seven years in exile the proud warrior decided to return to the United States and accept his punishment. On July 20, 1920, he presented himself at the California border, where a U.S. marshal took him into custody. He served one year in the federal prison at Leavenworth, Kansas, where he worked as an instructor of physical activities and organizer of athletic events. He maintained a level of fitness while incarcerated by boxing exhibition matches. Upon his release throngs of African Americans met him in Chicago, and in New York Harlem residents held a parade in his honor. He returned to the ring and continued to fight regularly until 1928, but he never got the opportunity for another championship bout.[38]

In 1924 his wife divorced him, but Johnson wasted little time in taking a third white wife. He married Irene Pineau in August 1925. With the promise of big paydays long gone after his release from prison, Johnson turned to a variety of entrepreneurial ventures and incongruous roles. He served as a boxing promoter, a preacher, a representative of a brewery, a stockbroker, a museum lecturer, and a nightclub owner. In 1931 he returned to the ring at age fifty-three, recording a win over Dynamite Jackson, another black boxer reputed to be the heavyweight champion of the Pacific Coast. Five years later Johnson still sought the spotlight, appearing as a slave in a production of the opera Aida. He fought yet another exhibition in 1945 at the age of sixty-seven as part of a fundraising campaign during World War II. A year later, on June 10, 1946, his life ended in an auto accident while speeding in North Carolina. His death mirrored his life, for Johnson had led a fast and provocative existence, challenging all obstacles in his path. The funeral was held in Chicago; twenty-five hundred crowded into the church auditorium. In death Johnson achieved what he so sought in life—equality with whites. He was buried in Graceland Cemetery, the final resting place of Chicago's elite and wealthy residents.[39]

Jack Johnson left an enduring legacy. As a boxer some ring historians considered him to be the best of all-time. He wore the heavyweight crown longer than any of his predecessors in the gloved era. His social impact far surpassed his boxing exploits, however. Eldridge Cleaver, a political activist and leader of the Black Panther Party, asserted that "the boxing ring is the ultimate focus of masculinity in America, the two-fisted testing ground of manhood and the heavyweight champion, as a symbol, is the real Mr. America."[40] In that sense, Johnson proved a social force. A complex, proud, and provocative figure, he forced issues that probably sped the pace of racial integration in American society. He made white Americans take notice. He forced people to question the Social Darwinian belief in racial and physical superiority. He confronted and helped dispel the prevalent racial stereotypes. In so doing he gave millions of African Americans hope, pride, and self-esteem. Historian Jeffrey Sammons even claims that Johnson paved the way for the "New Negro" of the Harlem Renaissance by instilling a sense of dignity, black pride, and a newfound militancy.[41] Certainly one can see the self-confidence of contemporary young black males of that era such as Fritz Pollard and Paul Robeson, pioneers in early pro football. Pollard eventually pursued entrepreneurial ventures in the African American community, breaking racial barriers in the process. Robeson achieved great fame as a singer and actor. His defiant radical political stances, relationships with white women, and conflicts with the United States government paralleled, in some ways, those of Jack Johnson.[42]

Joe Louis assumed a decidedly different tact in his quest for the heavyweight championship. He met with success and a measure of acceptance in white America because his docile, humble, unpretentious demeanor did not represent the threat posed by Jack Johnson.

The Black Power Movement of the 1960s, however, resurrected the ghost of Jack Johnson in the form of Muhammad Ali. Loud, brash, and defiant, Ali challenged white America like no black athlete since Johnson. Like Johnson he represented years of oppression, pent-up black emotions, and a quest for respect harbored by millions of African Americans. Ali eventually achieved that respect and even gained heroic status in white America—but the groundwork for such stature had been founded by Jack Johnson.

II Fashioning a World of Sport behind Segregated Walls and on the International Stage

The lives of African Americans during the first half of the twentieth century were characterized by many changes and filled with both important successes and bitter disappointments. The northern migration of southern blacks, depression of the 1930s, world conflict, and a host of other societal factors would dramatically alter the economic position and status of African Americans in a society still beset with stifling racial discrimination and prejudice. In regards to sport, African Americans were still largely excluded from intercollegiate athletics on predominantly white university campuses, denied the opportunity to participate in Amateur Athletic Union (AAU) sponsored events in the south, and not allowed to engage in white organized professional baseball, football, and basketball, among others. In spite of these constraints and racially discriminatory practices, a number of African American athletes during this period realized enormous success and much notoriety in sport, both in selected white organized competitions and in separate black organizations established behind segregated walls.

Two athletes who achieved enormous success behind segregated walls were Ora Washington and Satchel Paige. Pamela Grundy explains in her essay "Ora Washington: The First Black Female Athletic Star" that Washington came from a working-class background and took advantage of the opportunity created by the northern migration of southern blacks to fashion an outstanding athletic career. Through force of will and extraordinary physical talent, Washington realized great success in both tennis and basketball. She was the American Tennis Association's national singles champion eight times and was a standout player on the famous Philadelphia Tribune girls' basketball team which dominated the sport during the early 1930s.

Unfortunately, notes Grundy, Washington's career ended at about the same time that many racial barriers were being shattered in American sport. The result was that the African American community focused on such racial pioneers as Jackie Robinson while at once losing sight of the accomplishments of Washington and other black athletes who competed in relative obscurity during the Jim Crow era. The relative obscurity of Washington was in direct contrast to Satchel Paige, the extremely talented and flamboyant pitcher who was Negro League baseball's most famous showman and biggest gate attraction. Combining great pitching talent with extreme confidence and a gift for bravado, Paige was, according to Donald Spivey in his essay "Satchel Paige's Struggle for Selfhood in the Era of Jim Crow," an enormous drawing card who parlayed "his celebrity status for a fee at every opportunity." He sold his services to the highest bidders, playing for more than forty different teams, including "squads of Negro League stars in well-attended matches with major league All-Star teams led by Dizzy Dean and Bob Feller." When not playing in the United States, Paige was plying his trade for teams in Venezuela, Cuba, Mexico, and the Dominican Republic. In 1948, Paige broke into major league baseball with Bill Veeck's Cleveland Indians, registering a 6–1 record for that year's American League and World Series champion. He garnered the American League Rookie of the Year Award for his performance, and attendance at Indian games tripled because of his presence. In 1965, he became, at the age of fifty-nine, the oldest player in major league history when he pitched three innings for the Kansas City A's. In 1971, Paige became the first Negro League player elected to the National Baseball Hall of Fame.

The athletic career of Jesse Owens was decidedly shorter than that of either Ora Washington or Satchel Paige. His name still resonates, however, with people around the world, even those with a limited knowledge of sport or the history of African American athletes. This name recognition stems largely from Owens's four gold medal winning performance in the 1936 Berlin Olympics. Immortalized in Leni Riefenstahl's documentary, *Olympia,* Owens's victories in Berlin were of symbolic importance in that they were accomplished by an African American on the world's largest sporting stage and in a country whose government espoused the belief in Aryan racial superiority. Although not changing the course of events and preventing world conflict, Owens's victories on the track served as examples of possibility for the African American community while at once casting doubt on the notion of biological determinism and the supremacy of one race over another.

Owens's life after Berlin, however, was not always easy and was characterized by major disappointments intermingled with periods of financial success and much adulation. As Mark Dyreson makes plain in his essay "Jesse Owens: Leading Man in Modern American Tales of Racial Progress and Limits," Owens never did receive his college degree and was forced to run stunt races, tour with black softball and baseball teams, front for a swing band, and participate in other forms of entertainment to make a living in the racially divided and financially depressed America of the late 1930s and early 1940s. He eventually secured more substantive professional employment, involved himself in politics, served as an ambassador for the State Department, acted as a corporate pitchman for a number of corporations, and represented the United States at several Olympiads. He also continued to espouse through his public appearances and various writings, notes Dyreson, that sport offered a way "out of poverty for oppressed minorities" and was "a bastion of American egalitarianism." This idealized conception of sport brought rebukes from the more radical members of the African American community, including young athletes, who believed the path to equal rights and freedom of opportunity could result only through active protests and political action.

An athlete who has frequently been juxtaposed with Owens in textbooks and other scholarly writings is the great boxer, Joe Louis. Like Owens, Louis was a native of Alabama who moved north with his family at a relatively young age. Like Owens, many of Louis's victories were of great symbolic importance in the United States because they came during the tumultuous late 1930s against opponents representing dictatorial regimes and political and cultural ideologies that fostered genocide and world conflict. And like Owens, his triumphs engendered enormous pride in the African American community during a time of rampant and debilitating forms of racial discrimination and inequality in the United States. The "Brown Bomber," who generally had a positive image among whites because of his gentlemanly behavior and the fact that his carefully constructed lifestyle was seemingly the antithesis of the controversial Jack Johnson, realized near mythical status among African Americans for his victories in the squared circle, especially against white opponents. His level of popularity, notes Anthony Edmonds in his essay "Joe Louis, Boxing, and American Culture," is reflected in the many songs written in celebration of his ring exploits, the enormous amount of attention paid to him in the black press, and the wild celebrations that took place in black neighborhoods across the country following his victories. His level of popularity is also poignantly reflected in the reminiscences of Richard Wright, Malcolm X, and Martin Luther King, among others. These reminiscences address the hero-worship of Louis and how the African American community realized enormous satisfaction and pleasure from Louis's ring triumphs. Edmonds recounts the story of a black convict on death row in 1935 who "wrote to Louis that the photograph of the Brown Bomber he had hanging on [my cell] wall will make me feel better as I wait for the electric chair."

The attention and notoriety garnered by Alice Coachman was far less than that realized by Louis and many other African American athletes of the twentieth century. The relatively less attention and notoriety had little to do with Coachman's athletic skills, argues Jennifer Lansbury in her essay "Alice Coachman: Quiet Champion of the 1940s," and more to do with the circumstances of her career and the status of women athletes. Coachman has been lost from the public memory because of the male-dominated world of sport and the fact she participated in track and field, which has never realized continual widespread popularity in America.

Irrespective of why she has faded from the American consciousness, Lansbury provides little-known information about Coachman's life and career, convinced that her athletic exploits on the track "helped pave the way for other African American women to continue using sports to bring down race and gender barriers." A native of Albany, Georgia, Coachman competed for the legendary Tuskegee Institute women's track and field team and would establish a reputation as one of this country's great sprinters and high jumpers. She captured several AAU championships in the fifty-meter dash and for ten consecutive years was the national outdoor high jump champion. Most importantly, Coachman became the first African American woman to win a gold medal in Olympic competition when she defeated Dorothy Tyler in the high jump at the 1948 Games in London. Unfortunately, Coachman, like so many other gifted athletes, lost out on other opportunities for gold medals because of World War II and the cancellation of both the 1940 and 1944 Olympic Games. This did not prevent her from eventually doing promotional ads for Coca-Cola and serving as a physical education teacher in Albany.

Ironically, while World War II prohibited athletes such as Coachman from realizing more Olympic glory, it also served to inspire African Americans to reexamine their position in American society and be more aggressive in exposing racial inequities and discrimination. This was certainly true for organized baseball. The democratic ideology and rhetoric with which the war was waged provided black sportswriters and other concerned citizens with a unique opportunity to protest racial discrimination in the National Game. These protests, along with his own self-interest, prompted Branch Rickey to sign Jackie Robinson to a contract with the Brooklyn Dodgers in 1945. In 1946 Robinson played for the Dodgers top minor league team in Montreal and then the following year was brought up to the parent club to become the first African American to play in the major leagues since Moses Fleetwood Walker in the late nineteenth century.

In "Jackie Robinson: Racial Pioneer and Athlete Extraordinaire in an Era of Change," Michael Lomax provides an overview of Robinson's extraordinary life, both within and outside of baseball. He offers information on Robinson's early life and family background, athletic accomplishments in college sport and professional baseball, and involvement in politics and social activism. Lomax also makes clear the complex nature of Robinson, pointing out that the great Brooklyn Dodger player's approach to civil rights issues and fight for equality was often contradictory. He took an assimilationist approach on some social issues, and more of a black nationalist approach on others. All told, writes Lomax, "Robinson was a complex figure, admirable in many ways and paradoxical in others. This is what makes him so interesting to study, because his strengths and weaknesses exemplified the age that produced him."

Ora Washington pictured here, second from left, at the 1947 American Tennis Association Championships. To her right is George Stewart, and to her left are Walter Johnson and Althea Gibson. *(Courtesy of Tuskegee University)*

5 Ora Washington

The First Black Female Athletic Star

PAMELA GRUNDY

On a now-forgotten day in the mid-1910s, a young African American woman stepped off a train car, and on to the bustling streets of Philadelphia, Pennsylvania. As Ora Washington gathered her belongings and set off to stay at an aunt's home, she likely attracted little notice. The Great Migration was underway, and black southerners had become a dime a dozen in Philadelphia, pouring into the city by the tens of thousands in search of work and of some respite from rising racial oppression. Washington, arriving from rural Virginia, was just one more.

But there was far more to Ora Washington than met the eye. In Philadelphia, she found not only a job, but an outlet for an extraordinary set of athletic gifts. By the mid-1920s, the young Virginian had become one of the brightest stars on a growing African American tennis circuit. By the 1930s, she was the nation's first full-fledged black female sports star, dominating not only black women's tennis, but basketball as well. No African American woman had ever played the way she did. Black newspapers across the country dubbed her "Queen Ora," describing her as "brilliant," "peerless," and "inimitable."[1]

"No one who ever saw her play could forget her," recalled one admirer, "nor could anyone who met her."[2]

Washington's fame, however, proved short-lived. Her career stretched from the mid-1920s into the mid-1940s, ending just as many racial barriers in American sports began to crumble. After World War II, a hopeful black public focused much of its attention on a new generation of racial pioneers, barrier breakers such as Jackie Robinson, Althea Gibson, and Wilma Rudolph. Stars of the Jim Crow era faded out of view. In 1963, when veteran sportswriter A. S. "Doc" Young profiled Washington for his book *Negro Firsts in Sports,* he termed her "virtually an unknown name." A private person, Washington herself rarely talked about her achievements. "She wasn't a person to tell you too much," recalled nephew Bernard Childs. "She would tell you some things, some parts of her career. . . . Older people might have known a little bit, but we didn't." When she passed away, in May 1971, her death attracted little notice.[3]

In many ways, Ora Washington remains an enigma. Photographs show a tall, light-skinned woman with a square jaw, a quietly serious expression, and a sharply incised set of muscles. Descriptions of her play make clear that she possessed enormous natural talent, backed by a keen sense of strategy and a fierce competitive drive. But she left no memoir. The friends and family who knew her best have passed away. The reporters who rhapsodized over points scored and games won rarely dipped below the surface to chronicle what she thought of her life and accomplishments.

Still, even in fragmentary, enigmatic form, hers is an emblematic story. Washington belonged to a remarkable group of working-class black women who seized on the opportunities created by the Great Migration, traveling from the rural south to the urban north and pioneering careers as businesswomen, evangelists, blues and gospel singers, even airplane pilots. Her triumphs point to the remarkable fortitude these women possessed and to the family and community resources on which they drew. The obstacles she faced make clear how taxing these struggles were. Together, they tell a story at once sobering and inspiring, about human potential both thwarted and achieved.

Ora Washington blazed her own trail. She was born at the close of the nineteenth century, into a world where female athletic stardom was not even a far-fetched dream. Her parents—James Thomas "Tommy" Washington and Laura Young Washington—lived on a family farm amid the gentle hills of Virginia's Caroline County, about halfway between Richmond and Washington, D.C. In the small, rural community of File, farming was the main occupation, and the Washington's nine children—Ora was number five—lived lives focused on home and family, moving between the fields, the two-room File school, and Jerusalem Baptist Church, which had been founded by former slaves in 1866.

The Washingtons had escaped the fate of most of the South's African Americans, who were forced to eke out a meager living as sharecroppers, laboring for others in the region's massive and debilitating cotton economy. File was home to a cluster of black families who owned their own farms, their good fortune likely due to the Richmond, Fredericksburg and Potomac Railroad, which laid a trunk line through the county in 1836. In the years after the Civil War, a local historian once noted, the railroad proved a ready customer for cordwood and railroad ties, and newly freed slaves seized eagerly on the chance to earn money, which many spent on land.[4]

The Washingtons raised corn, wheat, vegetables, and hogs, as well as some tobacco for cash. There was plenty of work—tobacco was a labor-intensive crop, with tasks for small hands as well as large. But there was playtime, too. Community baseball was a popular summer pastime, and the children developed a lifelong love of sport and games. Decades later, whenever family members visited Caroline County, competition was fierce. "They all used to love to play croquet," Childs recalled. "On Saturdays, the yard would be full of croquet players, playing against each other."[5]

The family also faced its share of challenges. Agricultural depression plagued much of the nation from the late nineteenth century into the twentieth, pressing landowners as well as sharecroppers. The Civil War had wreaked havoc on Virginia's finances—the cash-strapped state did not even issue birth certificates from 1896 to 1912, making Ora's exact date of birth yet another mystery. Educational opportunities were scant; the area's only black high school was in the county seat of Bowling Green, too far away for rural students to attend unless they boarded in town. Even as black farmers struggled to make ends meet, a rising tide of white supremacy augured a darker era. Although Virginia saw few of the violent lynchings that terrorized black communities further south, the state's African Americans watched their rights slip away. In 1900 state legislators rewrote the state's election laws in ways that robbed African Americans of the vote. Other measures began to enforce strict racial segregation, steadily pushing African Americans into second-class citizenship.[6]

In addition, the large, close Washington family suffered its share of tragedy. In 1908, Laura Washington died while giving birth to her ninth child. Although Tommy Washington supplemented the farm income with work as a house plasterer, such jobs were scarce. At the time of the

1910 census he had been out of work for months, and the family farm had been mortgaged.[7]

Like many of their peers, the Washingtons began to look north for opportunity. They set their sights on Philadelphia, a five-hour train ride away. Ora's aunt, Mattie Washington, was the first to leave. Philadelphia apparently suited her—she married, settled in the up-and-coming suburb of Germantown, and then offered to help her nieces establish themselves in the city. Ora made the trip sometime in the mid-1910s, and may have attended high school in Germantown. In January 1920, a Philadelphia census taker found her working as a live-in servant in a home on Springfield Avenue. By then, other family members had made their way to the city as well—Washingtons would travel back and forth between Philadelphia and Caroline County for decades.[8]

Moving to Philadelphia did not liberate the Washingtons from racial struggle. The city's African Americans were generally confined to the bottom rungs of the economic ladder—most men worked as laborers, and most women as maids or housekeepers. Philadelphia saw its African American population grow from 84,000 in 1910 to 134,000 in 1920, and the new arrivals crowded black neighborhoods to bursting, overwhelmed social services, and heightened racial tensions. Unofficial segregation also spread through civic institutions, as organizations that provided housing, medical care, and cultural activities barred African Americans from their programs. Black citizens fought long battles over growing segregation in the city's public schools. The Ku Klux Klan enjoyed a brief heyday in the early 1920s, gaining 30,000 members by 1922. Philadelphia also became known for the many white, working-class neighborhoods where young black men ventured at their peril.[9]

Such setbacks, however, were balanced by opportunities. As in black communities across the country, Philadelphia's African Americans responded to a hostile racial climate by turning inward. Southern migrants proved avid entrepreneurs, filling the city's black neighborhoods with restaurants, beauty parlors, churches, and nightclubs. A black-owned bank, the Citizens and Southern, became one of Philadelphia's most stable financial institutions. The city's black theaters showcased nationally renowned performers such as Bessie Smith, Duke Ellington, Louis Armstrong, and Marian Anderson. At the Royal Grand movie palace, lucky moviegoers could sometimes find jazz great Fats Waller manning the organ.[10]

Migration proved a particular boon to black sports, swelling the ranks of players and spectators throughout the country. Growing enthusiasm for black men's basketball led to the formation of several professional teams, including Chicago's Harlem Globetrotters and New York's Harlem Renaissance. Black tennis enthusiasts, shut out of the United States Lawn Tennis Association (USLTA), formed the alternative American Tennis Association, which sponsored local and national black championships. Philadelphia's Hilldale baseball team was a key player in the Eastern Colored League, the eastern counterpart of the midwest-based Negro National League. Black colleges, churches, YMCAs, YWCAs, and other organizations all expanded their athletic offerings.[11]

The institution that would mean the most to Ora Washington opened in Germantown in 1918. The "colored" branch of the Germantown YWCA, formed in response to the rapid growth of Germantown's black community, combined cultural programs with classes and activities designed to meet the needs of single working women such as Washington. It sponsored classes in shorthand, bookkeeping, mathematics, dressmaking, and domestic science, as well as black history, literature, and music. It ran rooming and employment agencies that helped find lodgings and positions for new arrivals, and offered afternoon and evening entertainments designed to be "so attractive that the girls will want to come to the Association instead of going in town." Lecture programs, often held on Thursdays to coincide with the traditional maid's day off, featured leading black intellectuals such as W. E. B. Du Bois, Alain Locke, and James Weldon Johnson. True to the YWCA emphasis on mind, body, and spirit, the Y also organized a broad range of sports programs. From the start, administrators were particularly proud of the facility's tennis courts.[12]

The Y's surviving records do not indicate when Ora Washington became a member. Nor do they record the day she first stepped on a tennis court. Still, she likely started playing some time in the early 1920s. A. S. Young's account, the most detailed available, suggests that she took up the game in an attempt to distract herself from the deep grief she felt over the death of a sister. Uncertain as that story is (many details in

Young's descriptions are inaccurate) it does coincide with the death of Washington's older sister, Georgia, who succumbed to tuberculosis early in the decade.[13]

However she began, her rise was swift. She loved the game from the start, immersing herself in the challenges of strokes and strategy. In September 1924, she entered the city championships in nearby Wilmington, Delaware, and swept the singles, doubles, and mixed-doubles titles. In 1925, she upset the reigning national singles champion, Chicago's Isadore Channels. She also captured her first national title, pairing with fellow Philadelphian Lula Ballard to win the women's doubles competition at the American Tennis Association national tournament.[14]

The ATA tennis championships, begun in 1916, were a major social event in black America, and Ballard and Washington returned to Philadelphia as celebrities. The Germantown Y held a reception for the newly crowned champions and presented each with a gift of expense money (although tennis was technically an amateur endeavor during the era, for whites as well as blacks, top competitors regularly had travel and other expenses paid by tournaments or other sponsors). "If our courts had done nothing more than make this possible, I am sure the Health Education Committee would think that its worries of nets, wiring and repair of courts had not been in vain," the Y's branch secretary happily reported.[15]

For her part, Washington was likely less satisfied. She was a focused, no-nonsense individual, unafraid of hard work and eager to succeed. On the court, she believed in getting down to business. "I didn't believe in long warm-ups," she was once quoted as saying. "I'd rather play from scratch and warm up as I went along." Rather than resting on her doubles laurels, she set her sights on the singles crown.[16]

It would take some time to reach that goal. Observers quickly pegged Washington as a potential title contender, noting her year-by-year growth in strength and confidence. She became a perennial doubles champion, winning twelve straight titles from 1925 to 1936. But for several years she faltered in the singles bracket. In 1926, Isadore Channels retook the title. Lula Ballard then won again in 1927 and 1928.

In the spring of 1929, perhaps to escape Ballard's shadow, Washington moved briefly to Chicago, where she worked as a hotel maid, and no doubt joined in the Windy City's thriving tennis culture. The change seems to have done her good. In August 1929, "after six lean years of toil," she "finally crashed through . . . to the supreme honor of National Women's Singles Champion," defeating Frances Gittens 4–6, 6–4, 6–2 to win the title.[17]

Her goal achieved, Washington became almost unbeatable, dominating the competition with powerful strokes and an intimidating intensity. "She had the strategy and was dynamic to watch," one fan later recalled, adding that "her overhead game was terrific." Opponents struggled to cope. "She was so strong," recalled Amaleta Moore, whose sister competed against Washington. "It was hard for you to fight against her with the talent she had." She also had a winner's drive. Off the court, family members described her as a kind, caring person, who was always looking out for others. But her competitive zeal was fierce. "If you made her mad," noted nephew Lewis Hill, "you had a tiger on your hands." Opponents often feared her. "She was intimidating," Moore noted. "The way she looked at you: 'You've got no business in my way.'" The *Chicago Defender* concurred, noting in 1931 that "her superiority is so evident that her competitors are frequently beaten before the first ball crosses the net."[18]

With no serious black rivals, Washington was apparently eager to try her skills in the white tennis world, then dominated by international sensation Helen Wills Moody. But segregation remained firmly entrenched across the country throughout the 1930s, and there was little a black woman—no matter how talented—could do about it. Although ATA officials constantly pressed the USLTA to admit black players to its tournaments, the national organization maintained its unwritten ban on African Americans until 1948, too late for Washington to make her mark.[19]

Barred from expanding her tennis ambitions, Washington instead cemented her position as the nation's dominant black female athlete by taking up basketball. Women's basketball had become a popular sport in working-class communities during the 1920s, sparking interest in high schools, athletic clubs, colleges, and other organizations. African Americans were especially enthusiastic. Concerns about health and propriety prompted many white teams to play with a modified set of half-court "girls' rules," and most predominantly white colleges limited their female students to intramural play. In African American communities, where women's work was the norm and female strength a necessity, teams often met fewer restrictions. Black women's squads frequently competed with full-court "boys' rules," and many historically black colleges fielded highly competitive varsity teams.[20]

Washington entered the fray in the fall of 1930, when she moved back to Philadelphia and began playing center for the Germantown Hornets, based at the Germantown Y and coached by Lincoln University track coach Joseph Rainey. From 1930 into 1931, the Hornets traveled up and down the Eastern seaboard, playing teams from New York, Baltimore, Pittsburgh, New Jersey, and Washington, D.C., as well as Philadelphia. At the end of the season, they boasted a 22–1 record, and proclaimed themselves black national champions (in the absence of a national tournament, the team with the top record generally claimed the national title). Washington had lived up to her championship billing, averaging almost thirteen points a game. When the *Philadelphia Tribune* summed up the season's action, it placed Washington "in a class by herself."[21]

The Hornets' achievement set the stage for one of the most exciting basketball seasons Philadelphians had ever seen. Capitalizing on their popularity, the Hornets parted ways with the Y and became a full-fledged professional squad. Rising to challenge them was a new rival—the newspaper-sponsored Philadelphia Tribune Girls. The *Tribune's* entrepreneurial circulation manager, former Negro League baseball star Otto Briggs, had organized a men's basketball team in 1931. The Hornets' success convinced him that there was money in women's ball as well. In the fall of 1931 he agreed to sponsor the city's second-best women's team, Inez Patterson's "Quick Steppers." Their name was changed, and the Tribune Girls were born.[22]

Inez Patterson was already a Philadelphia legend—she had won city high school championships in several sports and gone on to excel at then-predominantly white Temple University. Aided by several other strong competitors, including Hampton Institute veteran Rose Wilson and the multitalented Helen "Midge" Davis, the Tribunes began to match the Hornets victory for victory. Spiced by enthusiastic *Tribune* coverage, interest in the teams mounted, and the women's games began to outdraw those played by the Tribune's male squad, teams from nearby Lincoln University, and even the professional Harlem Renaissance. By January, the two teams launched into prolonged public negotiations over the details of a championship series, aimed, as Joseph Rainey put it, at "giving the public what it wants while it wants it."[23]

The teams finally settled on a five-game series, which got off to a rousing start on February 3. "From the opening 'til the closing whistle the fans stood en masse and amid the most rabid and demonstrative exhibition of partisanship, yelled themselves so hoarse that on one occasion a halt had to be placed on hostilities to put a quietus on the pandemonious gathering," wrote the *Tribune* sports editor Randy Dixon. For their part, "the players went stark berserk in their quest for victory. Every conceivable shot was attempted. Many found their mark for precious markers but more circled the rims and then rolled off to inject additional cause for delirium." Near the end of the game, with the Tribunes leading, Washington went into action, executing "a foul goal then a left-handed stab on the run, and another heart-winger made on the left side of the basket over her left shoulder." The Hornets triumphed, 20–15.[24]

The series stretched on for almost two months, tensions building all the while. Three weeks after the Hornets' initial triumph, the Tribunes rallied to win the second game, 33–24, handing the Hornets their first defeat in more than forty games. The Hornets returned to win the third, 22–18, and the Tribunes took the fourth, 33–27.[25]

The fifth and deciding game, played on Easter Monday, again showcased Washington's talents. At the end of the third quarter, with the Tribunes ahead, Washington "let go a humdinger from way back beyond the center of the court." The ball fell straight into the basket. "It was an awe provoking effort," Randy Dixon noted, "and gave the Hornets the necessary impetus to inaugurate a rally. Ora came right back to dribble down the left side of the court, stop abruptly to shake off two men, pivot, and sink a heart-twister off balance that cut the cords clean as a whistle." Two clutch free throws by Tribune forward Helen "Midge" Davis sent the game into overtime. When the Tribunes scored eight unanswered points in the overtime period, triumphing 31–23, the crowd exploded with delirium.[26]

"It was fully ten minutes before order could be restored," Dixon reported. "The cash customers fanned to fever heat by the ardor and closeness of combat gave outlet to all kinds of riotous impulses. They stood on chairs and hollered. Others hoisted members of the winning team upon their shoulders and paraded them around the hall. They jigged and danced, and readers believe me, they were justified. It was just that kind of a game."

Her team may have lost the title, but Washington remained the sport's top star. When Randy Dixon picked the year's all-star team, he called her "the greatest girl player of the age." While Washington was "lacking the perfection of smoothness that goes with the finished product," he concluded, she "can do everything required of a basketball player. She passes and shoots with either hand. She is a ball hawk. She has stamina and speed that make many male players blush with envy. And despite . . . elaborate defenses especially mapped out to stop her she has averaged 16 points per game with a high total of 38 points in one game."[27]

Washington's skills were not lost on Otto Briggs. When basketball season opened the next fall, Washington was sporting a Tribunes uniform. The Tribune Girls would be an integral part of Philadelphia's vibrant black sporting scene for the rest of the 1930s, laying an undisputed claim to the black national championship at the end of every season. The team received regular coverage in the national black press, and spectators flocked eagerly to their games, which often included dancing or other entertainment. "Start saving 25c now so you can attend on Thanksgiving Nite the TRIBUNE Girls big opening BASKETBALL Game and DANCE," a 1932 ad suggested, noting that the dance would be conducted by "the Peppiest Orchestra this Side of Hades." The copy continued: "Don't miss seeing ORA WASHINGTON and INEZ PATTERSON in action. They are two of the greatest girl players in the world. They make you forget the Depression."[28]

The combination of promotion and high-level play proved enormously successful. The team drew well at home and on the road—in 1933 so many spectators showed up for one New Jersey contest that the playing floor had to be roped off. By 1934, the players had become so popular that Briggs scheduled an extended tour of the South and Midwest, with an eye toward profit as well as publicity.[29]

The Tribunes' widespread appeal showed clearly at the tour's first stop, in Greensboro, North Carolina. A game against historically black Bennett College had been booked in Greensboro's spacious city arena, where black teams rarely played. More than a thousand fans showed up to see what a local newspaper called "the fastest girls' team in the world," paced by "the indomitable, internationally famed and stellar performer, Ora Washington."[30]

The Tribunes opened the game dressed in red and white, their sleeveless tops cut low in back, and their socks chosen to match. At halftime they changed into a second set of uniforms, these in gold and purple. The outfits read "Tribune" in script on the front, and had no numbers—a touch that conveniently threw the referees off guard. They played at a level few in Greensboro had ever seen. Decades later, Bennett star Ruth Glover spoke of them with unabashed admiration. "They just had it all together," she recalled. "They could dribble, and keep the ball and make fast moves into the basket which you couldn't stop." Washington scored thirteen points as the Tribunes defeated Bennett, 31 to 22.[31]

Washington's intensity set the tone for the team. "She was one of those strong players," Glover explained. "She wasn't a huge person, or very tall. But she was so fast. And see, they fed her the ball. . . . The team was built up around her." She also knew how to use her elbows. As she faced off against Washington, Bennett center Lucille Townsend recalled, she heard a whispered warning: "Don't outjump me." Townsend disregarded the admonition at her peril. "I never saw her when she hit me, but she did it so quick it would knock the breath out of me, and I doubled over," she explained. "She could hit, and she told me that she had played a set of tennis on her knees and won it."[32]

Even as she built her basketball career, Washington stayed atop the tennis world, winning seven of eight singles titles from 1929 to 1937 and maintaining her reputation as a singular athletic talent. When the Tribunes launched a second southern tour in 1938, the *Atlanta Daily World* reported that the team's Atlanta appearance would be "a double feature in itself," as it included "the famous Ora Washington, national tennis champion for seven consecutive years." Washington, the article continued, "moves as sprightly in the hard wood court as she does on the clay court and those who have never seen her manipulate on either court, will have this rare treat . . . when she appears here in company with her fellow national cagers."[33]

By 1938, however, Washington was in her late thirties, and her athletic career was winding down. She had gone full tilt for almost a decade, playing basketball in the winter and tennis in the spring and summer.

During most of that time, she also worked as a housekeeper—neither tennis expense money nor her Tribune salary was enough to pay the bills. The first sign of a slowdown came in 1936, when she lost the national singles title for the first time since 1929. Supporters blamed the loss—an 8–6, 6–1 defeat by Lula Ballard—on sunstroke, and Washington regained her crown in 1937. But in the spring of 1938, she announced her retirement from singles competition.[34]

The reason for her decision was not entirely clear. She was still an avid player—she would continue to compete in doubles and mixed doubles for more than a decade. But her long reign as women's tennis queen had clearly sparked some consternation, and the criticism may have taken its toll. "It does not pay to be national champion too long," she told the *Baltimore Afro-American* in the summer of 1939. "It's the struggle to be one that counts. Once arrived everybody wants to take it away from you and you are the object of many criticisms." The subject was far from new. As early as 1934, the *Tribune* reported that Washington's five-year reign had "been the subject of talk for many years," with some in the sport questioning whether her dominance had "proved more harmful than helpful to the game."[35]

On the surface, those questions focused on whether Washington's overwhelming skill discouraged potential champions from pursuing the sport. But they may also have reflected unease with the degree to which her powerful strokes and forthright demeanor clashed with prevailing notions of femininity. Although African American women often won support for athletic endeavors, this job always proved easier when they tempered their skill with the trappings of conventional ladyhood. Ruth Glover summed up the fine line many female athletes walked. "We were ladies," she explained. "We just played basketball like boys." Refined manners, fashionable dress and conventionally feminine demeanor met community expectations, and also won acclaim as a challenge to racial stereotypes. It did not hurt if an athlete was also pretty. When A. S. Young lauded the achievements of Olympic track champion Wilma Rudolph, he noted that not only did Rudolph dazzle with her skills, she was *"the first Negro woman athlete to draw world-wide praise for her beauty,"* a recognition he called "indisputable proof that 'things are getting better' for Negroes!"[36]

Washington, in contrast, made her reputation solely on the quality of her play. She dressed and spoke plainly, and rarely downplayed her strength. She never married, living instead with family members, and with a series of female companions. Her rural roots and working-class demeanor seem to have made her an uneasy fit within African American tennis circles, which were dominated by the educators and professionals that made up the nation's black elite. Shortly after her retirement, Randy Dixon lamented that "the land at large has never bowed at Ora's shrine of accomplishment in the proper tempo." To him, the reason was simple: "She committed the unpardonable sin of being a plain person with no flair whatever for what folks love to call society."[37]

Washington returned to singles one last time, in 1939. She had a point to make. The 1938 championship had been won by Detroit-based Flora Lomax, who was cut from a far more conventional mold than Washington. Dubbed "the glamour girl of tennis," Lomax credited her husband with teaching her to play, and gave black sportswriters plenty of copy with her trademark white pleated shorts, her love of dancing, and her penchant for hobnobbing with stars such as Joe Louis. Lomax had plenty of ardent supporters, and when Washington stayed out of the 1938 tournament, rumors began to circulate that she had retired rather than risk losing to the up-and-coming star.[38]

In the summer of 1939, Washington responded. She entered a tournament in Buffalo, New York, defeated Lomax 6–2, 1–6, 6–2, and promptly retired again. She made no secret of her motive. "Certain people said certain things last year," she told a reporter. "They said Ora was not so good any more. I had not planned to enter singles this year, but I just had to go up to Buffalo to prove somebody was wrong. I lost the second set to her but this was the first and only set she ever won from me."[39]

Washington continued to play with the Tribunes until 1943, when Otto Briggs died of a sudden heart attack. That blow proved fatal to the team as well. Interest in black womens' basketball was at an ebb. Newspaper coverage of the sport had plummeted. Many colleges had disbanded their women's varsities in favor of intramural play, and the constraints of wartime limited games and travel. As with tennis, there were few opportunities outside of segregated circles. The Tribunes regularly played against a handful of independent white women's teams, winning some games and losing others. But the Amateur Athletic Union, the major sponsor of top-level women's basketball, did not admit professional squads such as the Tribunes. Most of the country's most prominent white teams were in the south, and had no interest in meeting black competitors. Although Washington and her teammates tried to find another sponsor, their search proved fruitless, and the team was forced to disband.[40]

Washington won her last national title in 1947, when she and partner George Stewart defeated R. Walter Johnson and an up-and-coming teenager named Althea Gibson to win the ATA mixed doubles crown. By then, the athletic era she had dominated was drawing to a close. Newspaper columns were filling with stories of athletes who were finally getting their chance to compete against top white talent. Shortly after losing the mixed doubles match to Washington (and following careful grooming of her manners as well as her game) Althea Gibson would take on the role of tennis pioneer, winning enduring respect by becoming both Wimbledon and U.S. champion in 1957 and 1958.

Washington, in contrast, slipped out of sight, into a quiet life marked by family and work. "She was a person, she worked all the time," Bernard Childs recalled. "She was always home on Saturdays and Sundays. In fact she was home every night." She stayed close to her family and a few friends from her athletic days. She maintained her love of sports, and when she visited Caroline County she was a fierce croquet player. "She was out there mostly with somebody, about every day," Childs said. "They would go there just about every afternoon."[41]

Late in her life, she fell ill, gave up the apartment she had shared with another woman, and moved in with Childs and his sister. She died on May 28, 1971, and was buried back in Caroline County.

Hers had not been an easy life. But she had made the most of it, traveling farther and achieving more than anyone could have imagined for a black farm girl making her own way at the inauspicious start of the twentieth century. Accounts of her life frequently credit her with a ringing assessment of her career: "Courage and determination were the biggest assets I had." It is impossible to know if those were in fact her words. But they ring unmistakably, inspiringly true.[42]

6 Satchel Paige's Struggle for Selfhood in the Era of Jim Crow

DONALD SPIVEY

Leroy Paige would rise from the humblest beginnings imaginable to become one of the most famous and acclaimed athletes in the world, black or white, and he accomplished this feat in a period synonymous with Jim Crow, the color line, grandfather clauses, literacy tests, poll taxes, white citizens councils, nightriders, and lynchings. Baseball would become not only his ticket out of poverty but also a platform for self expression as he entertained throngs of thousands throughout the United States, Latin America, and the Caribbean.

Leroy Paige (the spelling of the family name was "Page" until changed years later) was born on July 7, 1906 in Mobile, Alabama. The alleged uncertainty of his actual date of birth was a controversy that Paige himself fueled when, years past the usual prime in an athletic career, he turned reporters' questions about his age into a game of hide-and-seek, to the delight of fans and sport pundits. Ironically, although Paige was purposefully deceiving and toying with the media regarding his date of birth, his actual birthday was at best an approximation. His mother, Lula Paige, had not recorded it in the family Bible. Indeed, the Paiges were so impoverished they did not possess a quality family Bible. Leroy, like countless other African Americans in the South, was delivered by a midwife. It was also fairly common for state authorities to neglect to officially document black births, with many remaining unrecorded or uncertified until employment or other personal needs necessitated it. The document that would be used to "authenticate" Leroy Paige's date of birth was issued as the result of a formal request for proof made decades after his birth. The Office of Vital Statistics in Mobile received the request and, after its investigation, which typically

Satchel Paige was one of the most-photographed players in Negro League baseball. Here he is pictured in his Kansas City Monarchs uniform. *(National Baseball Hall of Fame Library, Cooperstown, New York)*

meant asking questions and taking into consideration whatever evidence, including character witnesses, issued a "verification of birth"—not a birth certificate—in 1954. Whether born on July 7, 1906, or a few days earlier or later, or off by a year or two, that date was in all likelihood just a reasonably close approximation.[1]

The debate regarding the authentication of the date of Leroy Paige's birth paled in significance to the raw conditions into which he was born. The Paige family home, which lay literally across the tracks at 754 South Franklin Street in Mobile, was more a home in theory than in function and reality. It was indeed the place where the family, headed by Lula and John Paige, came in out of the rain, slept, and took their meals. It was, however, a far cry from being a home. The tiny four-room shotgun house could simply not accommodate a family of twelve. The well that fed the pump outside provided the only "running" water and the odor from their too-close outhouse had become so familiar that it went unnoticed. John Paige's work as a common laborer and Lula Paige's work as a domestic were not enough to guarantee that there would be food on the table. The finer things of life were at best a distant dream for the ten siblings and perhaps no longer even a memory for John and Lula. Poverty necessitated that every member of the family work. Young Leroy began scavenging for discarded refundable bottles when he was barely five years of age. As soon as he was big enough, he graduated to hustling luggage at the L&N train station. The more bags you could tote, the more you earned in tips. By the time Leroy was nine he had established himself as a freelance master porter. Carrying as many satchels as his youthful strength humanly permitted—sometimes as many as four or five strapped to a pole—his fellow young porters soon dubbed him with the nickname that became his personalized moniker for the rest of his life: "Satchel."

His nickname legacy was born out of poverty as was the athletic skill that would eventually hoist him out of impoverishment and make his name known throughout the sports world. It would have been equally accurate to give him the name "Deadeye" as this tag was often used to describe his marksmanship with rocks. Young Paige hunted small game with nothing more than a pocket full of pebbles. His rock throwing acumen enabled him to bring home squirrels, rabbits, and birds to be added to the dinner table. On more than one occasion the game he brought home made up that evening's meal or constituted the only meat in the stew. That skill in hurling stones proved to be transferable to the baseball diamond.

At ten years of age Paige attended the W. H. Council School where he made pitcher on the baseball team. Lanky, with long arms, he was a phenomenal pitcher for his age. Leroy was a rapidly growing boy. Already a mid-five-footer, he would eventually grow to six feet three and a half inches tall. The height and arm length afforded him a velocity on his pitches that, when combined with his pinpoint accuracy, spelled doom for any would-be hitter. The early success Paige achieved on the baseball mound, however, did not endear him to the school nor inspire him to attend classes on a regular basis.

Truancy and other disciplinary problems plagued his pre-teen years. The number of his youthful indiscretions was large but the seriousness of the incidents was relatively minor, until he was caught shoplifting several toy trinkets from a local five-and-dime store. Frightened to the point of tears, young Leroy was held at the local sheriff's office while his mother was summoned. When distraught and tearful Lula Paige arrived to take custody of her son, she was informed that further action might be taken and that she and the boy would have to appear before a magistrate the following day. July 24, 1918, would forever be imprinted in Leroy Paige's mind as the ultimate day of infamy in his life. Barely twelve years old, and with his mother sobbing at his side, Leroy was sentenced to serve five years in reform school. The major crime, Leroy Paige reminisced many years later, was that "I was a nigger kid."[2]

The Reform School for Negro Children lay just outside of Montgomery, one hundred and eighty miles from Leroy's hometown of Mobile and a lifetime removed from his family and friends. During the next five years in reform school he obtained more of an education than he received (or took advantage of) back home, engaged in a structured environment of sorts, and honed the skills to what would become his most important asset—how to play the game of baseball. Paige obeyed the institution's rules and regulations. There were virtually no reports of him causing any disciplinary problems. He relished the cultural activities and excelled as a member of the choir, becoming a soloist in several performances hosted at the school. The school's drum and bugle corps was upgraded with Paige's rapid mastery of drums. Singing in the choir and playing drums in the band harnessed his creative energy, but it was the playing of baseball that captured his soul. The three P's of prayer, plowing, and planting were the first chores of the day; followed later in the afternoon by the three R's of reading, 'riting, and 'rithmetic. Despite the daily work in the fields, coupled with classroom lessons, Paige and the other boys managed time at the end of the long day for a quick game of baseball. When not engaged in a structured game of ball, Paige was throwing and catching with someone. You could count on one of the other boys to grab a bat and try for a hit against him. The results were predictable until Paige decided to throw easy ones with which the batter might connect. He rarely, however, gave the batter a chance. Generosity of spirit was something he had yet to learn. Throwing an un-hittable baseball was a skill he performed far better than any other boy. He was not about to relinquish his source of greatest accomplishment and pride for the sake of making someone else happy. The result was that Leroy made no lasting friendships with any of the other boys during his stay in reform school. Subsequent accounts of his life are correctly void of any names of boys with which Leroy Paige became friends with in reform school or with whom he continued contact with after his release in 1923.

He returned to a home condition that was relatively unchanged in his five-year absence. Life was still a daily struggle to make ends meet and to put food on the table, although there were a few changes to the Paige household while he was away. There was a bit more space in the old shotgun house owing to the departure of three siblings who were now married but living nearby. Everyone, however, was older now. Some of the girls and boys were now young women and young men and desired a tad of privacy.

After a few days of taking it easy and reacquainting himself with some of his neighborhood chums, Leroy turned his attention to finding a job. The efforts and results were painful reminders of black life in the Deep South. Leroy had no interest in returning to scavenging for bottles for pennies or to toting satchels for tips at the train depot. There were few employment opportunities for a young black man or woman in Mobile except for the traditional Negro work of sharecropping, or as a common laborer, or domestic. Leroy eventually found work picking up the trash and sweeping the stands of the small stadium where the local white semi-pro baseball team, the Mobile Bears, played. On occasion he caught the tail end of a game before he began cleaning. It had to be extremely difficult for him to watch the games, knowing that he was as good and, indeed, a better player than those he observed.

Leroy's opportunity came in 1924 when his older brother, Wilson, arranged for him to tryout with the Mobile Tigers, a black semi-pro baseball team. At the tryout Paige awed the team's manager and players with his display of pitching prowess. He proved in his first game, and in every game thereafter as a Mobile Tiger, that his performance at the tryout was no fluke. Word of his success on the mound spread rapidly and other teams sought his assistance. After one year Paige was still receiving only a few dollars per week from the Tigers. That could have been enough money for a nineteen-year-old black male in the South, but that and much more was needed to help carry the difficult load of the Paige family. Since there was no written contract with the Tigers, Leroy simply did what necessity dictated and tradition permitted. The result was that he began engaging in a practice that he would continue through the rest of his career and life: "jumping." Leroy was not the first good player to jump from one team to another. This was common practice, especially for good pitchers and excellent hitters. Exceptionally good pitchers, however, were especially hard to come by and thus usually engaged in more movement between teams than did players of other positions. Another black semi-pro team, the Mobile Bay Boys, needed some pitching help and they sought Paige's assistance. Leroy jumped for several games with the Bay Boys and other area teams for a few dollars per game. He then jumped back to the Tigers without missing a game.

While pitching a game for the Bay Boys, Paige pulled a stunt that colored his baseball career from that day forward. The team played dreadfully that day. The outfield seemed unable to catch a ball and a routine single easily became a double or triple because of inept fielding, throwing, and catching. In short, the Bay Boys were an awful squad. The only hope that they had was that the pitching might shut down the opposing team. When Paige realized that the entire game was on his shoulders and he had no support from his untalented teammates, he literally called the outfield in and had them sit behind the pitching mound. It meant that any hit off of him would have resulted in a score. Spectators went wild over the stunt. They marveled in utter delight at Paige's bravado and showmanship and watched him completely shut down the opposing team. No one got another hit that day. Fans broke into pandemonium at the end of the game, and a legend was born.

The showmanship on the mound, and the talent to back it up, gained Paige a rapidly growing reputation among baseball fans in Mobile. Blacks were starting to call him by his nickname, as if they knew him personally. He was becoming simply "Satchel." Many whites had heard of him too. Leroy "Satchel" Paige would have one of the greatest moments in his young life when, working one late afternoon cleaning up the stadium grounds after a game between the white Mobile Bears and a visiting team, four of the players from the Bears approached him. They wanted to know if he was the Negro pitcher boy they had been hearing about. Paige confirmed that he was a pitcher for the Tigers semi-pro team. They wanted to know if he was as good as they had heard. Paige, in a cockiness dangerous for the Jim Crow South, assured them that he was that good and better. The white players challenged him to a wager of one dollar that they could hit his pitching. Paige accepted the wager. Whether he actually had a dollar to cover the bet is doubtful. He was confident that he was not the one who would be paying. After warming up a bit, and with one of the boys catching, one of them grabbed a bat and starting walking to the plate. Paige remembered the incident very well: "'No need for you to tote that wood up there,' I yelled at him. 'It's just weight. You ain't gonna need it 'cause I'm gonna throw you nothin' but my trouble ball.'" In rapid succession, Paige struck out all three hitters. He never forgot the remarks of one of the white ball players after striking them all out. The player said, "We sure could use you [on our team]. If you were only white."[3]

He was not. No matter how outstanding his abilities, he was a young black man in a place and time that judged him solely on the color of his skin. Despite the environment, the legend of Leroy "Satchel" Paige was growing rapidly. When his first season with the Tigers ended, Paige had accumulated the incredible number of at least thirty wins. He was clearly the best pitcher in Mobile and in the semi-pro league. The second season with the Tigers saw him skyrocket to twenty-five wins with enough games remaining that it was a cinch that he would easily exceed the thirty-game victories of his rookie year. In a showdown contest against a very strong visiting nine from Gulfport, Mississippi, Paige gave a dazzling pitching performance while chalking up another win. He struck out seventeen that day in front of his growing legion of hometown fans. One of the spectators in the stands was Alex Herman, manager of the Chattanooga Black Lookouts of the Negro Southern Baseball League. Herman had come back home to Mobile to relax for a few days after a long road trip. He decided to take in a local ball game, which featured a young pitcher about whom he had been hearing. He was extremely pleased that he took in the game and had the opportunity to see "Satchel" for himself. Impressed with the youngster's overpowering fastball and pinpoint accuracy, Herman approached him with an offer to play professional baseball. The offer included considerably better pay than the few dollars he received every now and then with the Tigers. Paige would receive fifty dollars per month. More importantly, a portion of the money, Herman promised, would be mailed home to Lula Paige to help the family. Lula gave her consent, though not needed since her son was nineteen years of age and legally grown. Leroy was on his way to Tennessee. Herman kept his word and a portion of Paige's salary was mailed home to his mother each month.

Baseball offered Leroy "Satchel" Paige a chance for a life without poverty. It was also an economic lifeline for the Paige family. The money that he would be paid for playing professional baseball and the portion that was mailed home were far more than he could possibly earn and contribute to the family coffer playing with the semi-pro Mobile Tigers and doing odd jobs around town. In short order, Paige's value to the Lookouts grew with each new victory on the mound. In two months he was earning double the fifty-dollar-a-month mark. By the time that his first season with the Lookouts came to an end in 1926, Paige's salary had reached the munificent amount of two hundred dollars per month.

The rapid ascendancy Paige achieved at Chattanooga was due to his superior pitching ability and, contrary to popular belief, his hard work in perfecting his craft. Paige put in long hours under Herman's tutelage, fine tuning his throwing motion and control. In just one season he became the standout pitcher of the Lookouts, and the entire Negro Southern League. The Lookouts reached an all-time high leaping from their usual ranking in the cellar to first place in the league for the first time in the team's history. It was the quintessential example of the premise that a winning baseball team begins with superior pitching, and no one was more supreme at it than Satchel Paige. Paige had a perfect string of twenty-five wins during the 1926 season, ending the year with an incredible total of thirty victories on the mound.

Accomplishment off the mound was a different kind of success story for the new star hurler. Paige was a young man who now had money in his pocket and rising celebrity status to go with it. This translated into long evenings and nights out on the town. Acting first as a chaperone, manager Herman quickly became a friend and running buddy. He and Paige forayed together in the nightclub scene of Chattanooga and Memphis. Good times and women were the objective and they found plenty of both. Whenever the Lookouts traveled to New Orleans to play the Black Pelicans, Paige was offered the pleasure of experiencing first hand the spectacular night life of the Crescent City with its rich array of music, food, and more women. The young man was quickly coming of age.

Away games would give Paige ample opportunity to sample the night life of different locales and provide an advanced education in the ways of black ball. First-hand knowledge of the true world of black ball was important for his professional development. That world was not always pretty. The bus the Lookouts traveled in was a patchwork jalopy that provided little comfort and even less in terms of safety and reliability. It was never a small matter for the team to make it to the next game on time or at all. Along the way the players routinely suffered the indignities of travel for black folk in the Jim Crow South. Restaurants refused them service, public toilets were off limits to them, and overnight lodging was an impossibility unless Alex Herman could arrange enough accommodations for his players in homes in the black community. Such a scenario was unlikely since the Lookouts' travel budget was so small. More often than not, the players slept on the bus or under the stars at the ball park where they would be playing. Paige found the conditions utterly disappointing, even for one coming from a background steeped in poverty. He had envisioned a life for professional ball players that included glamorous road trips with quality transportation, good food, and lodging at a first-rate Negro hotel or a respectable black boardinghouse. The accommodations quickly improved for Paige as his status rose on the team. Before the end of the first season he was often housed with some family that Herman knew in the town where the team was playing.

Paige and the Lookouts did a great deal of traveling as did the rest of the teams of the Negro Southern League and black baseball in general. They made their best money on the road, particularly by barnstorming. Moving from town to town, playing team after team, barnstorming games generated income during the regular season and spring training, and came in especially handy during parts of the winter off-season in the South and eventually in Latin America and the Caribbean. Barnstorming gave Paige great exposure and put him in demand from other teams that needed better pitching. During the last month of his first season Paige jumped from the Lookouts to the Black Pelicans in New Orleans. The most important incentive that the Pelicans provided was the added bonus of an automobile. It was just an old Model-T but it opened up the world to Paige. His stay with New Orleans was only a month but he kept the little jalopy. In his second season he jumped for a brief stay with the Memphis Red Sox and then other teams before joining the premier team of the Negro Southern League. The white-owned Birmingham Black Barons sought his pitching services on a more permanent basis at the princely salary of $450.00 per month as the Barons entered the jewel of black ball, the Negro National League. Paige was spectacular on every team. In 1929, while playing with the Barons, he set a strikeout record for black ball that would hold forever: 184 strikeouts in 196 innings. William Dismukes, writing for the *Pittsburgh Courier,* suggested at the end of the 1928 season that an "all star Negro National League club" be formed. Included in his list of the twelve players he thought should be on the team was Leroy Satchel Paige as pitcher.[4]

Paige, however, had his off days. During the 1929 season he nicked several of the St. Louis Stars' batters with fastballs that missed their marks. On this occasion his reputation for accuracy worked against him. St. Louis hitters never considered that the fabulous Satchel could be having a bad game. Instead, they concluded that what had begun as an effort on his part to brush back a few hitters from the plate had degenerated into a deliberate decision to throw at the head of several players. One St. Louis player took the beanball personally. He left the plate and went after Paige with his bat. Paige demonstrated superior speed in staying ahead of the outraged player who finally flung the bat in a tiring effort to hit him. Paige retrieved the bat and then repaid the compliment by lending chase after his former pursuer. The incident received coverage in both black and white sport columns throughout the nation.[5]

It would take more than superior foot speed, however, to stay ahead of the coming crisis at the end of 1929 and throughout the 1930s. The onslaught of the Great Depression negatively impacted every arena of life, including sport. If not nimble in regards to foot speed, Paige demonstrated a jumping ability second to none in his effort to survive the depression years. Survive he did by jumping from one team to another. While still under contract with the Black Barons he managed to jump to the Nashville Elite Giants, back to the Barons, and then to the Cleveland Bears, and back to the Barons before making his biggest jump thus far and finally leaving Birmingham and the Barons for good. In 1932 he signed with the Pittsburgh Crawfords, which numbers racketeer Gus Greenlee had purchased two years earlier. Greenlee was interested in better positioning himself and his "underground" activities under the cloak of respectability that came with owning a baseball club. That ownership helped him in laundering money and staying ahead of the Internal Revenue Service. Just as important, it gained him new political respectability as the Crawfords grew into one of the greatest teams in Negro League history. Every politician, black or white, mayor or alderman, fire chief or police superintendent wanted to be associated with the winning enterprise and the high visibility afforded those identified as friendly to the team and, by inference, a friend to black voters. The Crawfords' next-door neighbor had long been one of the strongest teams in black ball, the Homestead Grays. The Grays were a perennial powerhouse with a stable of long-ball hitters, including the most heralded run-producer in all of black ball, the incomparable Josh Gibson. Defeating them was an immediate goal of Greenlee in his effort to establish his baseball preeminence. Their first meeting as the 1930s began was a 9–0 thrashing of the Crawfords at the hands of the Grays. The third meeting of the two teams would tell a very different story. The difference in the game was the new ultimate weapon that Greenlee had added to the Crawfords roster: Leroy "Satchel" Paige. "And I'll tell you," Harold Tinker, a former Crawfords' team member, recalled, "The Grays had one of the best shooting teams in the sandlot, but they hardly hit a foul ball off of Satchel the rest of the game. He was mowing those guys down like mad. Throwing nothing but aspirin tablets—fastballs. He hadn't developed all that fancy stuff then. So we beat the Grays." Paige's signing with the Crawfords made him one of the highest paid players in all of black baseball at seven hundred dollars per month. The following year the Crawfords also acquired none other than the "black Babe Ruth" Josh Gibson. Indeed, many blacks touted the reverse, that Babe Ruth was the "white Josh Gibson." At any rate, the Crawfords now had him. The combination of Paige pitching and Gibson hitting, along with the supporting cast of extraordinarily talented team members, garnered five Negro League championships for the Crawfords during the 1930s. The team's payroll was the highest in black ball and its star players, including the likes of Cool Papa Bell, Judy Johnson, Ted "Double-Duty" Radcliff, Oscar Charleston, Josh, and Satchel, seemed well positioned to even stave off the Great Depression, at least temporarily.[6]

Surviving the Great Depression, however, was not that simple even for the best of the black players and teams. The task was made more difficult with the death in 1930 of Rube Foster, the father of the National Negro League. It was Gus Greenlee who reconstituted the National Negro League in 1932 and gave black ball a new lease on life with the establishment of the East-West All-Star Game the following year. The East-West Game quickly emerged as the pinnacle of black ball, its most successful economic event, despite the hardship of the times. It was dubbed an "economic boom." Somehow blacks in the thousands came up with the price of a ticket to attend the event each year at Comiskey Park in Chicago.[7]

Satchel Paige's first appearance came in the 1934 East-West All-Star Game in a perfect setting for baseball immortality before a record crowd of thirty thousand screaming fans, probably more. In the sixth inning with a man on second and nobody out and the East pitcher tiring fast, Satchel Paige took the mound in relief. He put on a brilliant pitching display, retiring the side and shutting down the opponents for the rest of the contest to win the game. The black press reported that there was "No Greater Pitcher" and that "Satchel Paige Stole the Show." The *Pittsburgh Courier* trumpeted that Paige gave "one of the greatest mound exhibitions modern baseball has ever seen as he twirled three more scoreless innings to enable the East to chalk up their first victory." Paige had won a special place in the baseball community, and he knew it. The fans showered him with affection and repeatedly voted him on the All-Star Team. In the coming years he was the unquestioned top attraction in the annual All-Star Game. With his celebrity status as top vote getter, Paige sought higher fees for his services. He may have been from the country but he understood his worth and wanted the compensation commensurate with his preeminence. This action put him at odds with the Crawfords' ownership and completely on the outs with Gus Greenlee after missing the 1937 East-West All-Star Game on account of a salary dispute and a much more lucrative offer abroad.[8]

The Great Depression of the 1930s was not easily surmounted, and Paige took advantage of each and every economic opportunity that came his way. Even Gus Greenlee had difficulties during the period meeting the salaries of his players, which were the highest overall in the Negro Leagues. His bookmaking and numbers-running activities felt the pinch of the depression as did his famous Crawfords Grill, the most popular restaurant and club in black Pennsylvania. Many of his star players jumped back and forth or were loaned out to other teams. Paige was a frequent jumper or loaner with fees often being paid to Greenlee as well for Satchel's pitching services. Paige jumped or was loaned to a semi-pro team in Bismarck, North Dakota, to help them win their league championship. That stint netted Paige a few extra hundred dollars per week and a new Chrysler automobile.

Satchel Paige redeemed his celebrity status for a fee at every opportunity. He barnstormed with the best of them, did solo jumps to more than forty different teams, often for just one or two days of pitching, and headlined squads of Negro League stars in well-attended matches with major league All-Star teams led by Dizzy Dean and Bob Feller. White pro players like Dean and Feller and others also needed to supplement their incomes during the lean years of the 1930s and 1940s and appreciated the opportunity to step across the color line and reap the mutual economic gain from these barnstorming matches. The stands were usually packed at these interracial showdowns, with the Negro League stars winning the vast majority of the contests. Dean would later say that Satchel Paige was one of the best pitchers he had ever seen, and could make it in the Majors or any other league.[9]

Leroy "Satchel" Paige was increasingly becoming more his own person and demanding a larger share of black baseball's economic pie. Paige had become not only the major gate attraction at the East-West All-Star Game by the mid-1930s; he also had become the biggest draw in all of Negro League baseball. He entertained the fans by shuffling to the mound, doing tricks with the ball, performing wildly exaggerated windups and other crowd-pleasing antics. But when the ball left his hand, it was all business. He showboated and boasted on the mound and backed it up with sterling pitching. Spectators adored him. Negro League stars had a national and international following that made them invited guests everywhere and especially highly coveted additions to teams throughout the Americas. The star of the stars, Satchel Paige, was welcomed and sought after throughout the baseball-crazed Latin hemisphere and the Caribbean. Paige and teammate Josh Gibson went to Puerto Rico to play ball during the winter. From Puerto Rico to Venezuela, from Cuba to Mexico, Paige sold his baseball skills to the highest bidder. He understood that baseball was a business and that his growing superstar status had cash value.[10]

Cashing in on the value had its downside as well. Following the money had near disastrous results in 1937 when Paige and several other Negro League stars sold their services to Dominican Republic dictator Rafael Trujillo. Paige received a "satchel full of cash" to lead the Trujillo All-Star Team to victory over the team of Trujillo's arch political opponent. The series, however, was a tense and dangerous affair. After losing the first game of the contest, Paige and teammates were visually reminded of the expectations with some of Trujillo's machine-gun-totting soldiers lining the stadium for the rest of the series. Losing was not an option for Paige and his fellow highly compensated teammates from the States. Fortunately, their skills proved superior and they won the championship for Trujillo. After safely escaping that situation, however, Paige put himself in harm's way the following year pitching in Mexico where he injured his arm and nearly brought his baseball career to an end.[11]

The injury would be an ongoing problem for Paige for nearly four years from 1937 to the end of 1940, but he still managed to survive in baseball. He also did battle with the Negro League and Gus Greenlee, who, after the league failed to honor its own suspension of Paige for the Dominican jump, traded him to the Newark Eagles, to which Paige refused to report. In 1939, the Kansas City Monarchs were able to acquire Paige. With or without a viable pitching arm, Satchel had the name recognition and persona that continued to put fans in the seats. This translated into a bonanza for Monarch's owner, J. L. Wilkinson, who funded a barnstorming squad dubbed Satchel Paige's All-Stars, to the delight of fans everywhere and to the enrichment of his and Paige's coffers. The contests between Paige's All-Stars from the Negro League and Bob Feller's All-Stars from the major league routinely drew crowds from six thousand to as many as fifty thousand from the late 1930s into the 1940s and throughout the years immediately following World War II.

The rejuvenation of Paige's pitching arm in 1941 only enhanced the mystique surrounding the man, fueled debates about his age and athletic longevity, and made him an even hotter sport commodity. Paige understood this and nurtured it for all it was worth. His fee went up. He made as much as $2,500 for one evening of pitching against Feller's All-Stars. He missed several East-West All-Star Games because they failed to meet his appearance fee and other special demands. The games he missed suffered in attendance and thus revenues. More than once in the late 1930s and the 1940s Paige earned approximately $40,000 a year—a princely amount for the times. The youngster from Alabama had risen to become an American black icon with national and international name recognition as one of the highest paid athletes of the era, black or white.[12]

Little wonder then that as World War II raged and talk of integrating the major leagues gained new fervor, Paige seemed lukewarm to the idea. He was rapidly approaching what for most was the typical sunset of athletic prime, yet commanding a salary and appearance fees that provided an exceptional living. The signing of a black to a major league contract meant to Satchel Paige that finally a member of his race would gain admittance to the pinnacle of baseball, but it would not be him or his generation of greats who had made the Negro Leagues. When questioned in 1942 about the eventual integration of baseball, Paige's response sounded understandably reserved. He acknowledged that the big show was the white majors. But Paige believed that the integration of the Majors would mean the demise of black baseball and a likely end to his own gate appeal. In his response to the press he sounded a note of caution about the consequences of integration of the majors, which elicited such an angry outcry in the black press that Paige was forced to respond. At the "Satchel Paige Appreciation Day Game" at Wrigley Field in Chicago in 1942 and at the East-West All-Star Game that same year at Comiskey Park, he took the microphone to say that he had been misquoted and did, indeed, support the integration of major league baseball. When Jackie Robinson signed with the Brooklyn Dodgers three years later, Paige had little to say about it except that he would not have signed for the mere five-thousand-dollar salary that Robinson accepted. It is true that when Satchel Paige finally made his debut in the major leagues, taking the field with the Cleveland Indians in 1948, he was forty-two years of age. What is usually forgotten or missed is that Cleveland was paying him the salary he demanded of forty thousand dollars a year to do so. He was certainly worth every penny. Attendance virtually tripled at Cleveland games, and Paige performed magnificently in helping the Indians win the pennant. Defying all odds he earned the American League Rookie of the Year Award for 1948. Even once doubting pundits were left wondering what old Satchel might have achieved had he been admitted into the Majors ten or fifteen years earlier when still in his prime.[13]

Leroy "Satchel" Paige's climb up the racial mountain of baseball did not end with his admittance into the major leagues, the 1948 American League Pennant, or with the Rookie of the Year Award. He remained in baseball, in one capacity or another, with one team or another, throughout the 1950s, and finally ending with a brief stint in 1965 with the Kansas City Athletics and an even briefer stint in 1969 with the Atlanta Braves. He became famous enough to have his life story featured on the television show *This Is Your Life* and to appear in a Hollywood motion picture. The pinnacle seemed finally at hand when it was announced that Satchel Paige would be the first player from the Negro Leagues to be inducted into the Baseball Hall of Fame at Cooperstown in 1971. But the climb was still not over. The Hall of Fame committee had decided to establish a separate wing to hang the portraits and plaques of Negro League players rather than to house them in the main hall with all major league players.

The public outcry against this continued segregation in major league baseball caused the committee to finally change its mind and to place the likeness of Paige, and all future inductees from the Negro Leagues, in the main hall. Perhaps he had finally reached the mountaintop. Leroy "Satchel" Paige died in his adopted hometown of Kansas City in June 1982 at the age of seventy-five.[14]

Jesse Owens taking an early morning run in London with some of his admirers in 1936. Owens four gold medal winning performances that year in the Berlin Olympic Games would garner him instant celebrity status. *(Getty Images)*

7 Jesse Owens

Leading Man in Modern American Tales of Racial Progress and Limits

MARK DYRESON

Captured in motion by Leni Riefenstahl's cameras at Berlin in 1936, Jesse Owens has ever after embodied the story of human speed.[1] Owens also embodied other stories. His life served as an American epic about triumph over racism and poverty. He symbolized American hopes that the nation's venerated ideals might be realized. His life was also told as a tragic tale of American hypocrisy. The man who beat Adolf Hitler and Nazi racial theories to become an American hero returned to a nation gripped by an awful apartheid that condemned him to second-class citizenship. This alternative narrative cast Owens as a victim of racial exploitation condemned to eke out a meager living running humiliating races against horses. In still another version of the Jesse Owens story, the sprinter became the most important specimen in scientific studies of racial difference. The awesome acceleration captured in the frames of Riefenstahl's movie became evidence in popular mythologies of African athletic "genes."[2]

Decades after the 1936 Olympic Games Owens continued to play a central character in American tales. Some later twentieth-century chroniclers portrayed him as a key figure in the story of the civil rights struggle, a racial pioneer who stood with such luminaries as A. Phillip Randolph, W. E. B. Du Bois, and Marian Anderson in the pantheon of heroes who paved the way for future victories in the war for equality. A related rendering of Jesse Owens made him an international ambassador for American goodwill during the cold war and the globe's leading apostle of modern sport as the great reconciler of peoples, races, and nations. In an altogether different interpretation Owens was cast in the role of "Uncle Tom," chastising the revolutionary prophets of black power in his role as overseer of the "athletic plantation" run by white America.[3]

Reading athletes and their feats as texts has become a popular strategy for scholars interested in deciphering the meanings of sport in modern cultures.[4] The Owens text, in its many translations, resides at the heart of twentieth-century American discourses about color lines and the limits of opportunity. Jesse Owens became a canonical text in the history of American race relations in part because he constantly told stories about himself and his victories. In part, the storytellers of modern society molded Owens into a racial icon. Newspapers, magazines, radio shows, newsreels, television, film, adolescent literature, and history books spun his life story into a rich set of parables that ranged in tone and meaning from boundless optimism to unreconstructed cynicism.[5] As a *New York Times* reporter marveled nearly thirty years after Owens, as legend proclaims, beat Adolf Hitler in Berlin, the sprinter "remains one of the most magnetic of all sports heroes." In the same article Owens himself testified that "'I came along at a time when the Negro in America needed an image.'"[6]

The structure of this *New York Times* story reveals a crucial detail about the many American narratives that swirled about Owens. If "the Negro" needed an image then Owens and the American media were willing to supply it. Both he and his chroniclers crafted these stories. While he hardly possessed complete power over how his life was rendered, he constantly provided his own translations of the Jesse Owens story. As Owens's most insightful biographer, the historian William J. Baker, amply demonstrates, Owens continually told and retold his life story in public forums. The media and the public were captivated by his stories and fashioned and refashioned them for their own purposes.[7] Since the 1930s the Jesse Owens story has been required "reading" for grappling with the complexities of twentieth-century American culture.[8]

His story began in 1913 in Alabama. James Cleveland Owens was born in the hamlet of Oakville, the youngest of ten surviving children of Henry Cleveland Owens and Mary Emma Fitzgerald. Henry Owens was the son of freed slaves who sharecropped the meager Alabama soil and struggled to support his family. Poverty plagued not only the relatively small number of black families who lived in the area but also many of the white families who shared the sharecropping grind with their black neighbors. Common labor, however, did not produce a commonweal. Racial boundaries were starkly drawn. Poor and wealthier whites in the Oakville region policed Jim Crow lines vigorously. At a very young age Jesse Owens learned a survival strategy that many southern blacks adopted—a ready smile and pleasant deference made them less threatening to their white neighbors. Owens also learned the cadences of black southern evangelical oratory at Oakville Missionary Baptist Church, one of his family's Alabama anchors. His facility with spoken language would serve him well in his life as an American icon.[9]

Owens attended a segregated school in Oakville. On the playground he earned an early reputation as the fastest child around. His father was reconciled to the harsh realities of the Jim Crow South, but his mother was the source of hopes and dreams for a better life. During the First World War one of Owens's sisters joined the great migration of southern blacks to the North. In Cleveland, Ohio, she found a job and a husband. She frequently wrote her family about the better prospects available in her new home. Sometime between 1919 and 1924, the precise date is uncertain, Mary Owens convinced her husband to join the black exodus out of the South. The Owens family moved to Cleveland. Jesse Owens's childhood journey across the Mason-Dixon line was an archetypal experience for a generation of great African American athletes born in the early twentieth century. As a child the boxing champion Joe Louis moved from Alabama to Detroit, Michigan. A young Jackie Robinson along with his older brother Mack Robinson, who ran with Jesse Owens on the American team at the 1936 Olympic Games, left Georgia and landed in Pasadena, California. The list of black athletes who moved north or west during the great migration, including track rivals and teammates of Owens such as Eulace Peacock, Ralph Metcalfe, David Albritton, goes on and on. The great migration fundamentally transformed American society and American sport.[10]

The Owens family moved into a house on Cleveland's East Side, the city's working-class ghetto which provided homes for the numerous Eastern and Southern European immigrants as well as African Americans. Most of the East Siders toiled in Cleveland's booming factories. Henry Owens and three of his older sons found work in a steel mill. The family's material fortunes improved considerably. Jesse Owens, the youngest in the family, went to Bolton Elementary School with the sons and daughters of the neighborhood Italian, Polish, and Slavic families. Cleveland had a reputation among African American migrants as a relatively open and welcoming city. However, as the black population doubled during the 1920s, de facto segregation descended on the city's theaters, restaurants, hotels, and housing. The Ku Klux Klan developed a large local chapter. While voting rights, access to schools, and public transportation remained the legal property of Cleveland's black population, a perceptible chilling of the racial climate created severe strains in the city.[11]

In this tense environment Jesse Owens attended a school system that stressed vocational training and citizenship instruction rather than college preparatory education for its immigrant and black students. Owens did not struggle against this system. He adopted the accommodationist philosophy of Booker T. Washington and thrived as a class leader and an athlete if not as a scholar. At Fairmount Junior High School he found the perfect tutor for his talents, a physical education teacher and coach named Charles Riley. The white Riley became Owens most influential mentor, a surrogate father who nurtured Owens's athletic talents and taught him social graces. Owens's warm and familiar relationship with Riley shaped the budding track star's lifelong view that harmonious and integrated race relations were not only possible but natural–given proper conditions.[12]

In the 1930s, as the Great Depression set in, the Owens's family economy took a serious blow. His father, severely injured when he was hit by a car in 1929, lost his steel mill position. Henry Owens would never again hold a steady job. One by one his older brothers were laid off of their factory positions and scrambled for work. His other siblings dropped out of school in search of jobs to keep the family afloat. Jesse Owens would be the only member of his family to finish high school. With an eye on his family travails, the pragmatic Owens enrolled at East Technical High School in 1930, determined to get a vocational education that would guarantee him a decent job. This was a typical path for African American athletes in the 1930s. His friend and fellow track star David Albritton attended East Tech. Olympic sprinters Eddie Tolan, Ralph Metcalfe, and Mack Robinson also went to vocational high schools. At East Tech Owens learned the trades but did not develop his reading skills. Mostly, he polished his athletic talents. He dabbled briefly in football and basketball but quickly gave them up for track.[13]

In the sprints and the long jump Owens quickly set records and developed a national reputation as a rising star. As a high school junior he tried out for the 1932 Olympic team but failed to advance beyond the regional trials. His older rivals, Tolan and Metcalfe, won glory in the sprints at the Los Angeles Olympic Games.[14] During his senior year at East Tech Owens dominated Ohio interscholastic track and field. His classmates elected him as the captain of the team, the first African American to earn that honor in his high school. By the summer of 1933 Owens was challenging Ralph Metcalfe and other world-class sprinters in the AAU national championships. Several colleges sought Owens's services. In that era scholarships were generally not available to college athletes but schools found decent-paying, short-hour "jobs" to recruit prospective stars. Metcalfe urged Owens to attend the 1932 Olympic star's school, Marquette University. Owens also briefly considered Indiana University. Owens really had his eyes on the University of Michigan, an institution with a strong lineage in the 1920s and 1930s of African American track stars, including DeHart Hubbard and Eddie Tolan. Michigan boosters arranged for full-time employment of Owens's father, Henry. But when the elder Owens balked at the low salary for the custodial position, Michigan withdrew from the chase.[15]

Owens turned to Ohio State University where a Cleveland sporting goods magnate and Buckeye booster arranged a job for Owens as a freight elevator operator in the state government office complex. Ohio State had a well-deserved reputation during the 1930s for being less than hospitable toward African American students. The black press warned Owens away from Ohio State, and Owens himself at one point declared that he would not venture to Columbus. But with Michigan out of the picture, Owens did not perceive that he had other options and so he changed his position and enrolled at Ohio State. On campus he found himself barred from the dormitories by the color line and kept out of public view in his state job. In the pattern typical of his lifelong reactions to discrimination, Owens ignored the racial slights and tried to fit himself into Columbus. Owens was less than a stellar student, no surprise given that his education before Ohio State had focused on vocational training and not on a college preparatory curriculum. While he floundered in the classroom, he flourished on the public relations circuit. Ohio State's athletic department sent him to local schools to market their program. Owens was a hit in the schools, earning excellent "expense money" for his talks.[16]

In an era of freshman ineligibility for varsity competition, Ohio State track coach Larry Snyder used Owens in special exhibitions to draw fans to track meets. Owens also dominated the freshmen Big Ten track competitions. As a sophomore Owens became a national star. He challenged Metcalfe for the title of top intercollegiate sprinter on both the indoor and outdoor circuits. In May 1935, at the Big Ten Championships in Ann Arbor, Michigan, Owens set three world records and tied another in the span of one hour. Track cognoscenti consider that performance the greatest in the history of the sport.[17]

After his record-breaking season Owens spent the summer running on the national track circuit. On a tour of California he met an alluring young Los Angeles woman who was the daughter of a prominent family. Their budding romance made national news in the African American press. In Cleveland, his longtime girlfriend and the mother of his child, Ruth Solomon, decided it was time to get married. Solomon pressed Owens for a commitment. A Cleveland newspaper threatened Owens with the publication of a picture of their daughter if the track star did not do the right thing and marry Solomon.[18] Owens and Solomon were married on July 5, 1935. The next day he went back on tour.[19] Shortly after the nuptials a scandal broke over the job that Ohio State had secured for their track star as a page in the state legislature. An AAU investigation revealed that Owens had been paid by the state government for time when he was actually running track meets. Reluctant to disqualify one of the drawing cards for AAU events, the organization slapped Owens with minor sanctions. The AAU also removed Owens's name from the 1935 Sullivan Award list—the annual prize given to the top amateur athlete in the United States.[20] *Chicago Defender* sports columnist William Penn blasted the AAU's treatment of Owens. "Nazi Germany never pulled a smarter trick on the Jews than the sanctimonious A.A.U. handed Jesse Owens in the disposition of the 1935 Sullivan Memorial Award," Penn reproved.[21]

Penn's reference to Nazi Germany underscored a major controversy swirling around the upcoming Berlin Olympic Games.[22] With revelations of Nazi oppression of various religious and political opponents in

Germany, in particular their antipathy toward Jews, a powerful boycott movement emerged in the United States. Both the pro-Olympic and anti-Olympic organizers in the United States sought to recruit famous black athletes for their cause, especially gold-medal favorite Owens. Owens initially voiced support for the boycott but his Ohio State coach, Larry Snyder, stepped in and changed the Buckeye sprint star's public position.[23] The African American community and the black press were divided over the boycott.[24] Some voices urged blacks to support the boycott to oppose German racism and religious bigotry. Walter White, the secretary of the nation's leading civil rights organization, the National Association for the Advancement of Colored People (NAACP) penned a letter to Owens urging the sprinter to join the boycott. White never sent his powerful missive to Owens.[25] The *Amsterdam News,* one of the leading voices of the black press, made its opposition public, publishing an open letter in an effort to "beg" Owens and other black athletes to join the Berlin boycott.[26]

Other voices urged black athletes to go to Berlin and prove that Nazi racial theories were false. Much of the black press also pointed to the hypocrisy of a boycott effort which vociferously targeted German racism but remained silent on American racism. Some of the white press joined that argument. *Scholastic Magazine* told millions of schoolchildren that "Americans, in whose country Negro athletes from the South are compelled to go North to participate in open athletic meets, are not in the best position to act alone and independently of the International Committee." In the absence of International Olympic Committee (IOC) support for barring Berlin from hosting the games, *Scholastic* urged American athletes to strike a blow against the Nazis by beating them in athletic competitions.[27]

In the 1930s, an era in which the vast majority of white Americans paid more attention to the track exploits of Jesse Owens and the boxing feats of Joe Louis than to any other accomplishments by African Americans, boycotting an immensely popular world event such as the Olympic Games, which provided blacks with an opportunity to prove their equality against whites was not a particularly appealing option. Indeed, in a 1935 study that sought to survey "Negro Self-Respect," one of the questions measured how the exploits of Owens and other African

American athletes had substantially raised black self-esteem.[28] The editors of the *Crisis*, the public voice of the NAACP, understood that reality better than NAACP leader Walter White. The *Crisis* contended that while African American intellectuals and artists might be more important in many arenas than athletes it would be "foolish" to think that academics and writers had more influence on the general public, and especially on whites, than sports heroes and heroines. The editors stressed that "it is not the infinitesimal intellectual America which needs conversion on the race problem; it is the rank and file." This "rank and file" appreciated athletic accomplishment far more than intellectual genius. "For these millions, who hold the solution of the race problem in their hands, the beautiful breasting of a tape by Jesse Owens and the thud of a glove on the hand of Joe Louis carry more 'interracial education' than all the erudite philosophy ever written on race," testified the *Crisis*.[29]

Owens became a symbol of "interracial education" even before he ran in the Berlin Olympics. During his junior year in college Owens was elected by his teammates as the captain of the track team, the first African American to win that honor at Ohio State.[30] That season Owens began to lose consistently to a new rival, Eulace Peacock of Temple University. As frontrunners for the Olympic squad, Peacock and Owens, along with 1932 veteran Ralph Metcalfe, signed a list of American athletes who supported U.S. participation at Berlin.[31] At the 1936 Penn Relays Peacock snapped his hamstring, removing a major obstacle in Owens's march to Olympic glory in the summer of that year. Owens made sure that his part in the "interracial education" of his nation would have a Berlin chapter by qualifying for the 1936 American Olympic team in the 100-meters, 200-meters, and long jump. He joined nine other African American men and two African American women on the track team, the largest black delegation to that date in American history. Shortly before the trials African American prizefighter Joe Louis lost to German boxer Max Schmeling in a match steeped in racial and national symbolism. Louis's defeat left the burden of "interracial education" squarely on the shoulders of Owens and his "black auxiliaries," as the German press dubbed the African American Olympians.[32]

At Olympic Stadium in Berlin Owens dominated the track and field contests. He won gold medals in the 100-meters, the 200-meters, the long jump, and the 4x100-meter relay. The latter event sparked controversy when two Jewish sprinters on the American team, Sam Stoller from the University of Michigan and Marty Glickman from Syracuse University, were replaced on the final roster.[33] Another controversy arose over Adolf Hitler's "snub" of Owens. The American media created a firestorm of sensation by reporting that the German leader pointedly refused to congratulate Owens and the other "black auxiliaries" after their victories.[34] The reality of the "snub" was more complex than the American press revealed. Hitler had publicly congratulated winners on opening day, retreating from the stadium with rain and darkness descending, just before African American high jumper Cornelius Johnson leapt to gold. Whether Hitler would have saluted Johnson remains uncertain. After opening day IOC president Henri Baillet-Latour warned Hitler that as host the *fuehrer* was not allowed to demonstrate any favoritism through public demonstrations. Hitler publicly snubbed neither Owens nor any other Olympic champion. During the Berlin Games Owens denied to a skeptical American press that Hitler had in fact spurned him. But eventually, as the tale became American folklore, Owens made the alleged snub a standard highlight in his many retellings of his Olympic experiences.[35]

The swirling controversies enhanced Owens's Berlin feats. *Time* anointed Owens as the "No. 1 hero" of the Olympics.[36] *News Week* proclaimed "that the ebony shoulders of Jesse Owens tower above any other individual who competed."[37] His victories were regarded then and for the rest of the century as the greatest sprinting and jumping performance in Olympic history under the most adverse conditions imaginable.[38] Preserved in cinematographic grandeur in Leni Riefenstahl's famous film of the Berlin Games, Owens remained in the public mind for decades thereafter as the embodiment of human speed, the undisputed fastest human on earth. The outbreak of the Second World War and the subsequent cancellation of the 1940 and 1944 Olympic Games kept Owens in the spotlight as the reigning Olympic champion far longer than would otherwise have been the case.

Owens returned to the United States as a national hero. Not even his refusal to complete the European fund-raising tour of racing exhibitions demanded of the American Olympic stars by the AAU and his subsequent suspension from amateur competition could sully his golden reputation. Offers poured in from the movies, musicians, and nightclubs.

Many of the deals turned out to be bogus attempts to generate publicity by floating rumors of lucrative contracts in the press without intentions of making good on the proposals. Among the hoaxes were a few real offers. Wilberforce College, a historically black institution in Ohio, offered him an excellent depression-era salary of $2,800 a year to serve as track coach, provided that Owens finished his degree at Ohio State.[39] Ohio State athletic officials hoped Owens would return to campus so that they could cash in on his celebrity. Track coach Larry Snyder dissented from his institution's official stance and counseled Owens to turn professional while he was still a hot commodity.[40]

Huge parades honored home state hero Owens in Cleveland and Columbus.[41] He also starred in the traditional ticker-tape march through Manhattan to honor the returning Olympic team.[42] Owens received a cooler than expected reception when the American Olympians motored through Harlem, in part because he rode with former heavyweight champion Jack Dempsey, a fighter notorious in the African American community for his refusal to fight black challengers.[43] After the parade New York mayor Fiorello La Guardia paid homage to Owens. "We are all Americans here; we have no auxiliaries in this country," La Guardia proclaimed. After La Guardia's speech Owens turned to Bill "Bojangles" Robinson and presented the famous entertainer with the first gold medal the Ohio State runner had won in the Olympics. "An Olympic medal is the highest honor an athlete can win and I treasure mine above all my other possessions, but I want to make a presentation to Bill Robinson, the mayor of Harlem, for all he has done for me, for all of us," proclaimed Owens in paying tribute to the famous show business entrepreneur whom Owens hoped would help the sprinter cash in on his newfound celebrity.[44]

Certainly a variety of activists and interest groups were at that very moment employing Owens's fame to further their own causes. The leading critics of American racism made Owens's story into a parable highlighting the mendacity of national claims of equality. Oswald Garrison Villard, the grandson of the old abolitionist crusader William Lloyd Garrison and editor of the influential political journal the *Nation*, made the case that Owens and the "black auxiliaries" personified the long history of noble black struggles against white bigotry. Villard blasted those who cheered African American Olympians for exposing Nazi racism while remaining blind to the virulence of the homegrown strain of the disease. While their brethren were being lynched in their homeland, cried Villard, "they win the greatest honors at the Olympics–to share them with us white Americans!"[45] The *Nation*'s civil rights stalwart admitted that he was heartened by the fact that even southerners had begun to acknowledge Owens's patriotic service. Conveniently, a southerner writing in the *North American Review* confessed that Owens was indeed changing southern minds. "We pick up our daily papers to see that Jesse Owens has piled up the largest number of points at the Olympics," noted the observer. "Our orthodox answers leave us unable to account for a Negro's being the outstanding athlete at Berlin," he concluded.[46]

The NAACP president J. E. Spingarn contended that Owens and the "black auxiliaries" had proved two things to "fair minded" observers. "First, that the American Negro does not belong to an inherently inferior race," Spingarn proclaimed. Indeed, in "at least one important human activity," blacks had proved themselves "if anything, superior to the white race." The second axiom that Spingarn derived from the Berlin Olympics was that "the theory that miscegenation inevitably produces an inferior stock has been knocked into a cocked hat." He noted that many of the black Olympians had racially mixed genes and that the mixture of white and black blood produced "a highly superior strain" of athlete.[47]

Spingarn's speculations about heredity, race, and performance represented one of a multitude of claims about whether biology or culture produced athletic champions. In the aftermath of Owens's brilliant Berlin performance, supposedly "scientific" stories about the racial distribution of athletic talents would swirl through American culture for the rest of the twentieth century. Indeed, this quest to discover "athletic genes" shows no signs of abating in the twenty-first century.[48] Owens became the central specimen in early versions of these stories. Supporters of the notion that people of African descent had somehow been favored by evolution for superior athletic performance made Owens into the foremost example of their theories. Opponents of the new pseudoscience of athletic genes such as the African American anthropologist and physiologist W. Montague Cobb used Owens's anatomy to argue against simplistic biological determinism. In the decades following Owens's Olympian runs and jumps, the idea of a biological explanation for black athletic prowess evolved into the dominant public paradigm. Owens became the primary embodiment of these modern fables.[49]

Owens embodied not only the new narrative of African athletic genes but more traditional American allegories of the perils of success as well. Just one month after his triumphant performances in Berlin, Owens discovered that most of the deals that had been dangled in front of him were not firm proposals. The rumored big-money offers from the movie industry, the vaudeville tours, and nightclub circuit proved either cynical efforts to garner a little publicity or unfulfilled schemes. Owens confessed to his hometown press that he was "a sadder but wiser man."[50]

Owens decided that to cash in on his celebrity he had to return to the track. He first tried the openly professional route. Rumors swirled that promoters planned to match Owens against 1932 Olympic sprint champion Eddie Tolan in a series of races for $50,000 in prize money.[51] This big-money series fizzled. Owens then attempted to regain his amateur status in order to earn a living by collecting "expenses" for running in amateur meets. Given his enormous fame such a career would have been a lucrative endeavor, as it was for many other Olympic and intercollegiate track and field stars. In autumn of 1936 the New York Caledonian Club invited Owens to headline their Yankee Stadium extravaganza. To cash in he needed the permission of the AAU. While his Cleveland allies supported his petition to regain amateur status, Avery Brundage and the New York City power brokers in the AAU denied his application.[52]

Locked out of running for a living, stymied in his efforts to find well-paying entertainment gigs, Owens turned to politics to improve his fortunes.[53] Both the Republican and Democratic Parties eagerly sought African American support in the 1936 election, believing that the "Negro vote" could determine the outcome of the presidential election. The 1930s marked the beginning of a shift in African American voting patterns as blacks migrated from their old home in the "Party of Lincoln" to a new relationship with Democrats.[54] Owens, the most famous African American in the United States during the election season of 1936, was a prize recruit coveted by both parties. The Democrats initially seemed to have the inside track on his loyalty. Owens told the press he thought Franklin Delano Roosevelt was a "swell" president. *News-Week* magazine revealed that "the Democrats now want him to run for office."[55]

Spurning early Democratic dalliances, Owens decided to back Republican presidential candidate Alf Landon, the governor of Kansas. The track star took to the campaign trail to stump for Landon, receiving a considerable sum of money for his support, probably $10,000. He drew adoring crowds in many cities, mixing Olympic anecdotes with Lincolnian rhetoric on American opportunities in his speeches supporting Landon. The African American press, deeply divided itself but increasingly moving toward the Democrats, sometimes described Owens as an effective advocate. On other occasions black columnists and reporters were less than impressed with the performance of the Olympic hero and advised Owens to abandon politics and stick to athletics. Owens's support for Landon failed to stem a landslide for Roosevelt. Overall, Roosevelt garnered three-quarters of the northern African American ballots.[56]

While his campaign orations for Landon had not put his candidate into the White House, Owens began to polish his public storytelling skills during the election of 1936, mixing autobiographical tales with patriotic vignettes. Those skills would serve Owens well in the marketplace. He earned large sums through a variety of other endorsements of products and appearances at public events. How much money he actually made is unknown but he earned enough to spend profligately and to end up in serious tax trouble for failing to report more than $20,000 in income for his post-Olympic promotions. In the winter of 1936 Owens earned the Associated Press award as athlete of the year, beating out baseball players Carl Hubbell, Joe DiMaggio, and Dizzy Dean, boxers Max Schmeling and Joe Louis, college football star Larry Kelley, tennis champion Fred Perry, and fellow Olympians Forrest Towns and Glenn Morris.[57] In the balloting for the Sullivan Award, the AAU's annual prize for the top amateur athlete of the year, Owens lost to Olympic decathlon champion Morris.[58]

Owens's refusal to finish the AAU's post-Olympic moneymaking tour and his conversion to professionalism no doubt impacted the AAU voters. One of the nation's leading sportswriters, John Tunis, claimed that the vote for Morris over Owens also revealed the depth of the AAU's racism. Tunis asserted that "Owens was good enough to win the Olympics for us, but as a Negro not good enough to receive the obvious award he had earned." Tunis cynically argued that "when we need him to prevent German Aryan supremacy from asserting itself in sports in which we formerly triumphed, the Negro is an American." Tunis then cited one of his fellow sportswriters: "At other times, as Paul Gallico put it: 'He remains just plain nigger and we'd rather he weren't around because he represents a problem.'"[59]

The controversy over the Sullivan Award and the racial divisions it revealed added another layer to the Jesse Owens story. The frequency with which Owens ran up against a bewildering array of color lines in his post-Olympic life stung even the idealistic sprinter. As Owens wove the public narrative of his life in the decades after the 1936 Olympic Games, he returned over and over to the fact American society had not allowed him to take monetary advantage of his feats and fame in the immediate aftermath of his athletic service to his beloved nation. All he had wanted as a reward for all of his sacrifices, he insisted, was a solid, decent-paying job. In his memories the nation he returned to in 1936, depression-ridden and racially segregated, had no opportunities for its black patriot. In fact, in the absence of a professional track and field league, neither white nor black athletes could directly cash in on their fame by running and jumping. The amateur realm, with all of its pitfalls and secretive remuneration schemes, was the only place track and field athletes could compete. That province had been effectively closed to Owens right after the Olympics by a combination of his career choices and the actions of the AAU. For athletes who had retired from amateur competition, a variety of opportunities beckoned. Owens, in spite of his later claims, had offers from an assortment of suitors. The doors that opened for him, and those that remained closed, revealed both the contours of American racism and limited range of possibilities available to those, like Owens, who did not finish college.[60]

Owens's fellow "black auxiliaries" who finished their degrees such as Ralph Metcalfe, James LuValle, and John Woodruff earned decent jobs as respected professionals in coaching, law, the professorate, and politics. Those who did not complete college often slipped quickly to the margins of the economy, the route that Eddie Tolan and Mack Robinson unfortunately descended. Owens had an opening to the professional middle classes waiting in the coaching position at Wilberforce but he did not initially return to Ohio State. When, several years later, he did make a second try at completing his degree, he failed.[61]

The same pattern generally held for white athletes. Those who completed degrees frequently enjoyed professional careers. Those who did not often tried to cash in as entertainers. Ice capades, aquacades, and Hollywood turned Olympic fame into box office payoffs. Johnny Weissmuller, Buster Crabbe, and even Glenn Morris, the decathlete who beat Owens for the 1936 Sullivan Award, appeared in the movies.[62] Racism certainly limited Owens's ability to exploit himself as an entertainer. His movie offers turned out to be mirages. Although Hawaiian native and Olympic swimming champion Duke Kahanamoku played bit parts as Indians in "B" Westerns, Hollywood had no roles for a black Tarzan that Owens could fill.[63]

Owens found roles in other entertainment arenas that catered mainly to black audiences. He was offered not just one job in the 1930s but many. He fronted for a swing band, in spite of a self-confessed absence of even a hint of musical ability, touring the nation for months and earning a healthy salary. He created a barnstorming basketball team, the Cleveland Olympics, performing pregame and halftime running stunts to bring fans to their games. He toured with black softball and baseball teams, especially baseball's version of the Harlem Globetrotters, the Indianapolis Clowns. He ran stunt races against handicaps or other celebrities or, frequently, against horses, at carnivals, county fairs, and other venues. He later recalled his contests against equestrian rivals as humiliations he had to endure to support his family. At the time, however, he claimed he enjoyed the lucrative entertainment stunts.[64] While racism certainly played a role in his runs against animals, white Olympians engaged in similar practices in the entertainment arena as Johnny Weissmuller's swims with alligators in aqua shows and the movies reveal.[65]

Owens made good money, by depression-era standards, in his various entertainment pursuits. He spent or squandered much of it. By the beginning of the 1940s he had little to show for his constant touring and performing.[66] World War II marked a turning point in Owens's fortunes. It also marked a turning point in the struggle for civil rights and integration of American society. Early in the war Owens took a job with the federal government as the head liaison to the black community of a national fitness program. He traveled the United States giving physical fitness demonstrations and patriotic speeches. While in Detroit for an appearance he met with old friends, including former University of Michigan rival Willis Ward, who worked for Ford Motor Company. They recruited Owens to work for Ford in overseeing corporate relations with black workers. When Ward was called to active duty in the military, Owens took over leadership of the office. After the infamous 1943 race riot in Detroit, Ford began to use Owens as its public relations face with Detroit's black community. Owens's initial stint in the corporate world ended when he was let go in a major reshuffling of the company's managers.[67]

After a failed effort to start a Detroit sporting goods store, Owens went back on tour, running stunts against horses and his old Olympic teammate, Helen Stephens. He relocated to Chicago and opened several businesses. His political contacts also began to pay off when the Illinois Republican establishment tabbed him as the secretary for the state's athletic commission. He soon moved up in the ranks of state bureaucrats when he was selected to run the Illinois Youth Commission.[68]

In 1950 Owens beat out Jim Thorpe and Paavo Nurmi to win the Associated Press title as the greatest track athlete in the first half of the twentieth century.[69] The honor moved him back into the public spotlight at an opportune moment. The long history of racial discrimination in the United States did not serve the nation well in the propaganda battles with the Soviet Union raging during the cold war. The United States needed a symbol to reinvigorate the national myths of freedom and social mobility, someone who could "prove" that self-reliance could triumph over the nation's history of racism. Owens fit the role perfectly, offering himself as flesh and blood testimony that even a poor black kid could make it in the legendary land of opportunity. To so-called radicals such as the African American actor, former athlete, and activist Paul Robeson who proclaimed that the black community had no reason to support the United States in the cold war given the enormity and pervasiveness of American racism, Owens responded by offering his life story as testimony that anyone could succeed in American society if they worked hard and persevered.[70]

Owens played the role of self-made hero in his 1951 world tour "selling America" that he starred in with the Harlem Globetrotters. Returning to Olympic Stadium in Berlin where he had been "snubbed by Hitler," Owens urged a cheering German crowd to stand fast with the West in the cold war.[71] The Republican administration of Dwight D. Eisenhower took notice of Owens's ambassadorial potential. In 1955 the State Department sent the Olympic hero on a goodwill tour of the Far East. *Life* did a major photo-story on how he dazzled crowds in India with his demonstrations of athletic prowess and his promotions of American ideals.[72] In 1956 President Eisenhower selected Owens to represent the White House at the Melbourne Olympic Games. Once again, Owens impressed the world as an ambassador of goodwill. At the same time his old enemy Avery Brundage, elevated to the presidency of the IOC, reconciled with Owens and authorized the former sprinter to serve as the leading American apostle of Olympism.[73]

He continued his diplomatic tours, and his support of the GOP, through the 1960s and 1970s. During the summer of 1960 he performed goodwill duties at the Rome Olympic Games. During the fall he campaigned for Richard Nixon in the contest with John F. Kennedy. The Republican defeat in that election, both nationally and in Illinois, cost Owens his job as the head of the Illinois Youth Commission. Owens hardly missed the income from his government gig since by then he had migrated to a prosperous new career as a corporate pitchman for a variety of companies, including Quaker Oats, Sears, United Fruit, U.S. Rubber, Johnson & Johnson, Atlantic Richfield, and even the corporation that had fired him in 1945, Ford. Personal setbacks, from whispered rumors of his marital infidelities to a well-publicized conviction on tax evasion charges, failed to erode his public appeal.[74]

Throughout the 1960s Owens continued to tout athletic egalitarianism and American exceptionalism in his public appearances, in his trips to the Olympic Games in Tokyo and Mexico City, and in his participation in films such as Bud Greenspan's documentary, *Jesse Owens Returns to Berlin.*[75] The turbulent social changes of the 1960s, however, challenged his status as the leading American icon of race relations. While ceaselessly promoting racial reconciliation and integration, Owens had since the 1930s remained aloof from the center of the civil rights movement. He did not join the NAACP or the Congress of Racial Equality, two organizations that actively pushed for equal treatment of African Americans in all walks of American life. He spoke admiringly of Dr. Martin Luther King Jr., but did not enlist in the nonviolent army of activists that King headed. As the civil rights movement gained momentum during the 1950s Owens was increasingly invoked as one of the crusade's trailblazers. Rufus Clement, the president of Atlanta University, made Owens the leading character in the war to integrate American sport.[76] The *New York Times,* heralding a federal court decision that struck down a Louisiana law that attempted to enforce segregation in athletic competitions, agreed that "the world of sport" was indebted to Jesse Owens. "But the world of philosophy and morals also has its debt," to Owens and other great black champions the editors maintained, because their struggles "have helped us to get and keep straight our basic sense of values, no less than have the great Negro artists of other fields."[77]

As the 1950s gave way to the more turbulent 1960s, Owens contended that recognition of his role desegregating America from the white mainstream media such as the *New York Times* indicated that his strategy was the best corrective to racism. He continued to endorse the old gradualism and individualism espoused by his longtime hero, Booker T. Washington, a position that appealed to many in the white mainstream but was perceived as hopelessly näive by the civil rights leadership and as sniveling "Uncle Tom"–style collaboration by the more radical elements in the burgeoning black power movement.[78] Owens responded that although "I'm old enough to be their uncle. . . . I'm not their Tom."[79]

Owens had always perceived sport as a route out of poverty for oppressed minorities. He consistently idealized sport as a bastion of American egalitarianism. Running Olympic races was a political act in that it created opportunities for blacks to become "credits to their race" in the eyes of the white masses–as the *Crisis* had long ago observed. The new concept of using sport to foment a revolt against "the establishment," articulated most forcefully by the sociologist Harry Edwards and embraced by a growing cohort of young African American athletes, struck Owens as anathema to all he stood for and all he believed in.

When Edwards organized the Olympic Project for Human Rights (OPHR) and first threatened a boycott of the 1968 Olympic Games and then organized protests to symbolize the plight of African Americans, Owens led the charge against the plan. Joined by his old teammate Ralph Metcalfe and another prominent African American Olympic champion, 1960 decathlon gold medalist Rafer Johnson, the elder statesmen of black athletes chastised their young rivals for politicizing sport.[80] "There is no place in the athletic world for politics," proclaimed Owens in defense of the Olympic movement.[81] That was a strange claim from a man who ran in Berlin in 1936 when politics, in its most nationalistic form, transformed his athletic accomplishments into American legend.

The supporters of the much-ballyhooed "athletic revolution" dismissed Owens's concerns. At the headquarters of Edwards's OPHR hung a sign identifying the "Traitor (Negro) of the Week," with a picture of Jesse Owens underneath.[82] When Owens sought apologies from the rebels after their black-gloved protests on Mexico City victory stands, they publicly repudiated the American legend as, at best, a dupe of the white establishment. Owens went home and penned, with his longtime collaborator Paul Neimark, an angry diatribe against the black power movement. *Blackthink,* which previewed in abridged form in *Reader's Digest,*[83] claimed the firebrands did not speak for a huge "silent black majority."[84] Owens's invocation of Richard Nixon's phraseology and perspectives might have comforted many white Americans but it angered much of the black community. While President Nixon sent him on a goodwill tour of Africa and network television made him the narrator of a documentary on *The Black Athlete,* many African Americans criticized Owens for downplaying the pervasive racism which still limited black opportunity even after the changes wrought by the civil rights movement.

In the furor over his book and the mounting criticisms over his intransigence in challenging racism more directly, Owens retreated from the position that he had staked out in *Blackthink.* Writing again in tandem with Neimark, Owens produced a new commentary entitled *I Have Changed.* In the new book he toned down his earlier criticisms of the black power movement and conceded that the raging social cancer of racism limited possibilities for far too many African Americans. In spite of his concessions he remained, ultimately, an optimist, predicting that true equality resided in the near rather than distant future. He continued to preach the old verities of perseverance, responsibility, and opportunity.[85]

In the final decade of his life Owens continued to tell stories about his life and collected honors. He joined the senior leadership of the U.S. Olympic Committee. He lectured constantly for considerable fees about his athletic experiences, his recipes for success, and his faith in the American dream. Ohio State presented him with an honorary Doctor of Athletic Arts. The NCAA gave him its highest tribute, the Theodore Roosevelt Award. President Jimmy Carter conferred the Living Legends Award on Owens. The state of Arizona, where he had relocated from Chicago in the 1970s, celebrated a Jesse Owens Day. Even his old hometown of Decatur, Alabama, honored him with an award for patriotism. In 1980 he succumbed to lung cancer.[86]

In memoriam, as in life, Jesse Owens served American culture as a text which generally evoked hope on the climb up the "racial mountain." Tributes to Owens celebrate the beneficent possibilities of racial integration, promote the idea that the determined individual can triumph over all obstacles, and glorify the dream of social mobility. While Owens has sometimes been read in other ways, as a victim of racism, a specimen of science, or a saboteur of black power, his most prominent role, and the one he chose for himself, was as a twentieth-century prophet of Abraham Lincoln's sweeping moral egalitarianism.[87] Like Lincoln, Owens believed that prudent if penniless commoners could make their own life stories. They could rise from poverty to prosperity. They could defeat tyrannies. They could build a nation to match the boasts of American mythology. Owens was much more certain than Lincoln had ever been that black as well as white people could participate in making America, having leavened Lincoln's often melancholy view of race with the sunny faith of Booker T. Washington. As Washington had commanded his people to rise up from slavery, Owens tried to command his people to rise up from the shackles of segregation.[88]

In defining himself and being defined as his life story, Owens created a new genre in American literature. Autobiographies of African American athletes, some brilliantly insightful and others less illuminating, litter the late-twentieth-century literary landscape.[89] In the last three decades of Owens's life his appeal endured most passionately with the generations born before the Second World War. His ideas seemed more comfortable for many white Americans than many black Americans. A younger generation, the "baby boomers" born a decade or more after Owens beat Hitler in 1936, discovered a new text for deciphering the complexities of race in American life. His name had been Cassius Clay. As Muhammad Ali he opened, like Jesse Owens before him, a multiplicity of new ways to read the arduous climb up the "racial mountain."[90]

Joe Louis striking a pose during one of his training sessions. Perhaps no athlete has ever meant so much to the African American community as the great heavyweight champion from Detroit. *(University of Notre Dame)*

8 Joe Louis, Boxing, and American Culture

ANTHONY O. EDMONDS

Early in the professional prizefighting career of Joe Louis, former heavyweight champion Jack Johnson consistently dismissed the rising young star. Johnson picked Louis's opponents to win throughout 1935–36. Papa Jack, as Johnson was called, assumed that former champs Primo Carnera and Max Baer would outfight the twenty-one-year-old. (Louis KOed both of them.) He certainly felt vindicated when German Max Schmeling knocked out Louis in the twelfth round of their June 1936 bout. He even predicted a victory by lightly regarded Jack Sharkey in Louis's next fight in August. (Sharkey went in three.) When Louis took on Al Ettore in September, Johnson offered to be in Ettore's corner. Prior to Louis's championship fight against James Braddock in June 1937, Johnson pontificated: "I'd like to say Louis was a great fighter because he is one of my race, but if I did I'd be kidding myself and anybody else who might be interested. Louis not only has marked mechanical flaws, but he's not a bright boy."[1] Braddock, Johnson believed, was sure to win. He didn't.

A quarter century later, Joe Louis, the most successful heavyweight champion in history, was saying much the same thing about Muhammad Ali, aka Cassius Clay, another youngster who had garnered significant public attention when he upset Sonny Liston for the championship that Louis had held for twelve years. Joe not only condemned Ali for his conversion to the Nation of Islam, he made light of the new champ's fighting skills: "Clay has a million dollars' worth of confidence and a dime's worth of courage." Louis claimed that Clay (as he insisted on calling him) "can't punch [and] can't hurt you." Louis placed him in the same league as Max Baer, Johnny Paycheck, and Abe Simon, all fighters Louis had easily defeated.[2] Cassius Clay was no Joe Louis.

If Jack Johnson and Muhammad Ali were bookends, then Joe Louis clearly wrote the book. Arguably, these three black men were the greatest heavyweight champions of the twentieth century. More important, they all transcended their sport to become important cultural symbols. In the context of his times, however, none was more important and influential than Joe Louis.

There are a number of possible takes on Louis. We could focus on his boxing skill, which, according to many observers, made him the greatest heavyweight of all time.[3] Or we could examine him as a tragic figure who fell from grace because of all-too-human flaws, especially involving trust, generosity, and terrible financial handlers. These approaches, while no doubt of interest to sports fanatics and lovers of soap opera, miss the central historical importance of Louis. As I wrote more than thirty years ago, "Joe Louis is much more crucial in terms of what people thought of him than of what he in fact accomplished" either as an athlete or a person. In other words, "Joe Louis as a public symbol is more meaningful than Joe Louis as a fact."[4] Nowhere was this symbolism more vibrant than at the intersection of race and national identity, especially in the 1930s and early 1940s. No black American was more discussed and revered than this prizefighter from rural Alabama—both by whites and blacks, although, as we shall see, for very different and revealing reasons.

There was little in Joe Louis's early life to indicate that he would someday become a transcendent figure. He was born on May 13, 1914, just outside Lafayette, Alabama, the seventh of eight children born to Munn and Lillie Barrow. His father, a strapping six-feet-three, two-hundred-pound man, suffered intermittently from mental illness, perhaps brought on by the stress of keeping a large family fed on the meager results of sharecropping in the early-twentieth-century South. Two years after Joe's birth, his father was permanently institutionalized. Louis recalls that Munn died at age fifty-eight, never knowing that his son was heavyweight champion of the world. Lillie tried sharecropping on her own for eight years until in 1924 she married Pat Brooks, another farmer and a widow with nine children of his own. Failing to make a decent living, in 1926 the Brooks clan, like many other southern blacks, moved north, to Detroit.

Significantly, Joe had no memories of any sort of racial conflict during his twelve years in the South, at least none he shared publicly. In fact, he told the journalist Meyer Berger that "in all those years in Alabama I never knew anything about race. . . . If there was lynch talk, it never got to me or my folks."[5] Perhaps he had repressed a frightening incident that did happen to his mother and stepfather. According to Joe's sister Vunies, Lillie and Pat were returning from a visit to a sick friend late one night when they were stopped by Ku Klux Klansmen. Only the fact that one of the marauders recognized Pat Brooks as "a good nigger" prevented a tragedy. Brooks "made up his mind that night he was leaving Alabama."[6]

Initially, the Brooks family lived with friends, but Pat finally found work at Ford, but was laid off early in the depression. Joe went to Bronson Trade School where he was an indifferent student but developed a taste for boxing, taking his first lesson at sixteen. He became so fascinated with the sport that he began skipping the violin lessons his mother had foisted on him—she thought he would be good with his hands—and hanging around Brewster Center Gym, whose manager thought he saw a raw talent that could be developed. (He dropped the "Barrow" from his name in hopes of hiding his newfound passion from his mother.) Over the next few months, Joe trained, then was pummeled by one Johnny Miler in his first amateur bout. After a hiatus when he worked at a Ford plant to help his family, Joe went back to boxing, ultimately winning the 1934 AAU heavyweight championship. He had come to the attention of John Roxborough, a local black lawyer and boxing aficionado (who also happened to dabble in the numbers racket in the Motor City). He agreed to manage Louis, with the financial assistance of Julian Black, another Detroit businessman and gambler. Jack "Chappie" Blackburn, a former fighter himself, became Joe's trainer, completing the triumvirate of African Americans who would bring the young fighter to prominence. Joe turned professional in June 1934 and in the next twelve months won twenty-two fights, all but four by knockouts.

In March 1935, Louis's managers agreed to allow New York sports impresario Mike Jacobs to promote the young fighter's bouts. Key to the deal was Jacobs's promise to secure a fight with an internationally recognized figure—Italian Primo Carnera, a former heavyweight champion. Louis demolished Carnera in six rounds. Then over the next fourteen years he compiled perhaps the most astonishing record of any heavyweight fighter in history. He lost only one bout—to Max Schmeling in 1936—became heavyweight champion in 1937, revenged the Schmeling loss in 1938, and had defended his championship twenty-five times by the time he officially retired in 1949, a record that will probably never be broken.

Louis's years after 1949 were marked by severe financial and emotional challenges. In order to pay back taxes, he unsuccessfully launched a comeback. He tried professional wrestling, a career that ended when his chest was crushed by an opponent, one Rocky Lee. He spent his final few years serving as a professional greeter at Caesar's Palace, a Las Vegas Casino, while spending time off and on in mental institutions. He died on April 12, 1981.

From the beginning of his career, the fact that he was black dominated the public discourse about Joe Louis. The race issue was certainly uppermost in the minds of Louis's management and trainer. They knew how far the shadow of Jack Johnson spread. Johnson's behavior inside and outside the ring in the early twentieth century had made it impossible for black heavyweights to fight for the championship, as boxing's white establishment had effectively erected a color line. Louis recalls that Blackburn made it very clear that breaking through this barrier would be extraordinarily difficult:

> The boxing game is a tough one, son. . . . There's no easy way to the top. And for a colored fighter, it's even tougher. You've got to be good—lots better than the other man. The surest way to win is to knock your man out. You've got to fight clean and be on the level always if you want to go places.[7]

John Roxborough affirmed the need for Louis to conduct himself with dignity in the ring. Recalling the fact that Jack Johnson would verbally abuse white opponents, much to the dismay of most white Americans, he told his charge "never to gloat over a fallen opponent." Moreover, he insisted that there would be no "soft" or "fixed" fights. But most important, Joe had to overcome Jack Johnson's legacy of sexual association with white women—the ultimate vision of the *bete noire* in the minds of most whites. Roxborough told Louis not to even "have his picture taken along with a white woman," much less consort with one. In sum, to succeed in the lily-white world of prizefighting, Joe Louis would have "to live and fight clean."[8]

Certainly the issue of race was uppermost in the minds and words of the white journalists who would mould the image of Joe Louis for most white Americans. Biographer Chris Mead rightly contends that "to white sportswriters and their readers, the color of Louis's skin was his most salient characteristic."[9] From the perspective of the vast majority of white observers, Louis succeeded in overcoming the stigma of Johnson, for which he was roundly praised. We must be careful to note, however, that Louis's positive image among whites, especially during the early stages of his career, was grounded in deeply held stereotypes about blacks. The two dominant images that whites used to define blacks were the "angry bestial" and the "docile childlike," or, more bluntly, the "bad nigger" and the "good Negro." Clearly Louis was a powerful fighter who was often described as a beast in the ring. Journalist Bill Corum, for example, talked about the "animal" in Louis that made him the "killer supreme."[10] But, crucially, the animal in Louis stayed in the ring and within its proper parameters: using skill to win contests. The public relations machinery put in place by the Louis team worked. White reporters spoke in glowing terms about Louis's demeanor, placing him firmly in the docility category. He was, first of all, "clean living," according to reporter Richard Vidmer, as well as "God-fearing and Bible-reading."[11] As an anonymous poem, quoted approvingly in the *New York World Telegram,* asserted:

> He don't smoke
>
> Amen
>
> He don't pour red hot likker down his throat.
>
> Amen.[12]

Louis was also perceived as modest and unassuming. When he defeated Bob Pastor in 1939, for example, a reporter for the *Charleston* (South Carolina) *Daily Mail* complimented Louis on his restrained behavior: "He didn't jump up in the air in the ring and yell and clap his hands over his head or in any way make a play for the crowd. He is, once the job is done, the most mild-mannered champion we have ever had."[13] In his 1940 biography of Louis, journalist John Van Duesen generalized this point when he noted that Louis never "antagonized his audience by seeming to gloat over a fallen white man," a clear allusion to the vital perception that Joe Louis was the antithesis of Jack Johnson.

These images clearly show Louis resonating with the "good Negro" stereotype; in the words of sportswriter Bruce Dudley: "The colored boy is clean, fine and superb, modest and unassuming as a chauffeur or as the man who cuts and rakes the lawn once a week."[14] We understandably shudder today at such clearly patronizing racial profiling. But in the context of the 1930s, such a comment is hardly out of line. Many white Americans praised Joe Louis precisely because his modest persona reminded them of the ideal characteristics of a "good Negro" menial laborer. In spite of his celebrity and growing wealth, Joe did not rise above his psychological station but remained a nice "colored boy."

And, of course, there was never a whisper of any Johnsonesque association with white women. Interestingly, the issue was seldom specifically mentioned in the press. When Louis won the title in 1937, the columnist Arch Ward reminded his readers of the other black champion: "Jack Johnson['s] antics are still bitter memories," especially "his record outside the ring."[15] Of course, the lion's share of these "antics outside the ring" involved his dalliances with white women. Journalists were well aware that Louis's handlers wanted to make sure that no hint of such behavior attached itself to Joe. Reporter J. V. McCree observed that any white woman who hoped to consort with their fighter "would have to conquer Blackburn, Black, and Roxborough in the preliminary engagements." Such risk-taking white women, he concluded, "were few and far between."[16]

In sum, the white response to the Joe Louis persona so carefully crafted by his managers and trainer was largely positive. Louis was not a danger. In most ways he was a comforting confirmation that successful blacks need not be a threat to the structure of racial custom and etiquette. Blacks perhaps could be mobile, if, paradoxically, they also stayed in their place. Joe was all right. Indeed, as one white minister wrote to him in 1936, a year before he took the title from Braddock, Joe Louis was, well, darn near white: "Some day I feel you will be the champion," the churchman accurately predicted. "Try always to be the champion of your people, so that when you are no longer the champion, the world will say of you—he was a black man outside, but a white man inside—most of all in his heart."[17]

Most of Joe's "people" had an equally positive if more richly layered and textured response to his career. For many black Americans in the 1930s and early 1940s, Joe Louis was the most important public figure in their lives. His story dominated the black press. As sociologists St. Clair Drake and Horace Cayton observe in their study of Chicago, "Joe Louis, between 1933 and 1938, received more front page exposure in the [black] *Chicago Defender* than any other Negro. Three times as much as Hailie Selassie, four times as much as [Chicagoan] Oscar DePriest, 1st black Congressman since 1901."[18] Similarly, the *Baltimore Afro-American* devoted its entire front page to Louis's victory over Braddock and added five inside pages of photographs.

Every Louis victory, especially the major ones, led to huge celebrations in black neighborhoods, especially outside the South. According to the *New York Amsterdam News,* after Louis won the crown in 1937, "Harlem went crazily wild," as "thousands poured into the streets . . . and marched to the staccato screams of horns and improvised drums." According to Drake and Cayton, the main excuses for blacks to throw parties in Chicago were "Christmas, Thanksgiving, Easter, birthdays, or a Joe Louis victory." Lucille Johnson, a domestic living in Harlem, summed up the feeling of many blacks about Louis when she said, quite simply, "I am so glad to have a Negro champion after so long."[19]

The views of some black observers mirrored those of most whites. Louis succeeded in large part because of his "good" behavior. Walter White, executive director of the National Association for the Advancement of Colored People, claimed that because of his "clean living" as well as his prowess, he had "done more than any other individual toward raising the standards of the prizefighting game." Similarly, in 1936 the director of a black insurance company praised Louis for his "exemplary character," which was an "inspiration to the Negro youth of America," then named him to its board of directors. And in a somewhat florid poem of praise in the *Chicago Defender* that same year, one Ruth Olga May Davis commended Louis for putting his "trust / In the Monarch of all things" as well as for eschewing "Poor sportsmanship." She concluded that "to taunt the loser is a beastly thing."[20] Of course, Louis studiously avoided this kind of behavior.

Far more common among black observers was the sense that Louis's success would potentially help blacks gain increased social and economic mobility. Phillip Crutchfield, a black employee of the Wyoming State

Liquor Commission, thought that the championship would prove to other African Americans that they too "had the capabilities of climbing to the top of [their] professions as well," while columnist Roi Ottley believed that Louis's success had "been phenomenal and inspiring," especially to "the younger members of his race." The *Amsterdam News* concluded that the championship would have a "positive value to Negroes" because the "average white" would respect a sports champion.[21]

Purveyors of African American popular culture chimed in as well. Musicologist Rena Kosersky has found forty-three songs about Louis, almost all of them written by African Americans in the 1930s and early 1940s. Several themes emerge which reinforce various images of mobility and vicarious gratification generated in the black press. First of all, Louis is a winner, a black man who succeeded. Lil Johnson in her "Winner Joe" (sung to the tune of "Franky and Johnnie") extolled a black man whose violence was channeled in a legitimate activity. In the Max Baer fight in 1935, Joe "left him layin'" on the canvas, saying, "'Take it Joe / You got the best blow.'"[22] As Carl Martin summarized the Brown Bomber's career in "Joe Louis Blues," also recorded a few days after the Max Baer bout, "Now he's won all his fights / Twenty three or four / And left twenty of his opponents / Lying on the floor."[23] Moreover, he was able to overcome adversity. His revenge in the second Schmeling contest in 1938 inspired singer Bill Gaither (who had seen the bout) to write, "Schmeling went down like the Titanic" and he wound up "down on his knees" looking "like he was praying to the good Lord / To 'Have mercy on me please.'"[24] Blues artist Memphis Minnie expanded this image by suggesting that Louis represented the fantasy of escape from the poverty that resulted largely, no doubt, from racial discrimination. In "He's in the Ring" (1935), she asserted that she would bet all her meager funds on Joe if he said "Take a chance with me, / I'm going to put you on your feet." She wouldn't even "buy me nothing to eat" in the hopes of seeing another Louis victory and financial security because of her wise wager.[25]

These songs echo the idea that somehow Louis's triumphs were good for blacks if only in a psychological sense. The dream of American mobility was played out in the drama of black success, even superiority in the ring. But none of these focused directly on race, on the fact that all but two of Louis's victims between 1935 and 1949 were white. For many black observers, the most crucial affect of Louis's exploits was the enhancement of racial pride among millions of African Americans. After all, it was a black man who had risen to the top of a profession that for years had excluded members of his race. Malcolm X, for example, vividly recalled the outpouring of joy in his hometown when Joe became champion: "All the Negroes in Lansing . . . went wildly happy with the greatest celebration of race pride our generation has ever known." Certainly, much of this pride, according to the black psychologist Kenneth Clarke, lay in the fact that through Louis "it was possible for the masses of Negroes to obtain vicarious satisfaction and release."[26] One of the most poignant cases of black hero-worship of Louis came in 1935 when a young African American convict on death row in a southern penitentiary wrote to Louis that the photograph of the Brown Bomber he had "hanging on [my cell] wall will make me feel better as I wait for the electric chair."[27]

For some black observers, the racial component of the Louis legend went beyond hero-worship and race pride. Joe's victories were, of course, sweet because a black man was winning. But even sweeter, the overwhelming majority of his victims were white. Writing in 1941, the black sociologist Charles Johnson, like many others, claimed that black superiority in athletics, led by Louis's success in boxing, had "contributed more to race pride than any other single factor in recent years." He added that black youngsters "who cannot resent insults, or pit their strength fairly with that of white youth" must feel a special thrill when they hear that Joe Louis has demolished another white man. They see their "special racial handicap . . . removed" as "a Negro reveals his superior physical quality." The noted black writer Richard Wright agreed. As early as the Max Baer fight in 1935, Wright exulted that Louis had become "the concentrated essence of black triumph over white," as "from the symbol of Joe Louis's strength [blacks] took strength." Indeed, claimed Wright, because of Louis black Americans had "stepped out of the mire of hesitation and irresolution and were free."[28]

Of course, not all African Americans felt this way; Wright was exaggerating in the way that novelists sometimes do. In fact, there was always a certain ambivalence about Louis among blacks, especially those straining to achieve at least a modicum of middle-class respectability. As Chris Mead rightly points out, although they might be thrilled by Louis's victories, they also realized that he was "just a boxer," and not a very intelligent one at that. One black teenager, interviewed by the sociologist Franklin Frazier, admitted that "outside of fighting, I think he is a laughing stock. It's too bad he is so ignorant." Even the black press sometimes wondered about the full implications of the impact he seemed to have. When the Pennsylvania state athletic commissioner said that he had "never been so proud of the fact that I am a Negro" after the Carnera bout, the *New York Amsterdam News* took him to task for seeming to ignore such African American luminaries as Carter Woodson and W. E. B. Du Bois. Their accomplishments, claimed the *News,* should give blacks "greater pride in achievement than a victory in any sporting event."[29] That said, for the mass of black Americans, Joe Louis was by far more important than any black lawyer or doctor or, perhaps especially, historian. While doing research for *An American Dilemma,* his magisterial work on race in America, Gunnar Myrdal visited a one-room black school in Georgia. The children could not identify the NAACP or W. E. B. Du Bois or even the president of the United States. But they sure recognized the name of Joe Louis.[30]

No doubt those school children were also very much aware of the Brown Bomber's greatest triumph. In June 1938, he defeated the only man who had ever beaten him in a professional fight in a bout that combined the strands of racial and national identity. Such national and international overlays had occurred in other Louis bouts. In 1935, some observers saw the Carnera fight as a symbolic battle between black Ethiopia, represented by Louis, and white Italy—the invader of Ethiopia—represented by native son Primo Carnera. Even more pundits made similar observations about the first Louis-Schmeling fight in 1936. When Louis lost, most Americans bitterly resented the way in which Germany used the victory to "confirm the claim of the Nazi government that the German race is superior to all other races," as reporter Joe Williams put it.[31] The return bout, however, saw even more America versus Germany hype. Commentators were especially critical of Schmeling. Journalist Wilfrid Diamond claimed that Max believed he "was fighting . . . to prove the superiority of German manhood over decadent Americans." The sport historian Edwin Henderson concurred that "all of Aryan conscious Europe" was pulling for Schmeling.[32]

When Louis knocked out his German opponent in the first round, public attention focused on Joe striking a blow for America. The great celebrations triggered by the Louis victory had all the trappings of political rallies, especially in the black community. According to a report in the *Milwaukee Journal,* the festivities in Harlem featured "placards denouncing Nazism and fascism. . . . They proclaimed the knockout 'a victory for democracy.' 'Louis wins, Hitler weeps,' one sign said."[33] Contemporary white observers were also quick to see the victory as a blow against the pernicious doctrine of Aryan supremacy. According to the *Dallas Morning News,* Louis was a symbol whether he realized the role or not: "His pile-driving blows to Schmeling's head . . . were sending a message to the fairy story of Nazi Aryanism."[34] One unidentified correspondent saw the victory as a devastating blow to the German propaganda machine created by Joseph Goebels: "The Aryan idol has been beaten, the bright, shining, shimmering symbol of [Nazi] race glory has been thumped into the dust."[35] Even in the heart of segregationist America—Biloxi, Mississippi—a young white matron recalled hugging her black maid after the fight, yelling at the top of her lungs, "We won! We won."[36]

In his finest hour as a fighter, then, Joe Louis managed to fuse racial and national identity, as he transcended the mere boxing ring. If there was American guilt over its reluctance to commit military power to stop the German juggernaut, this prizefight provided at least temporary relief. And ironically, it was a black man, whose people still suffered the enormous burdens of racial discrimination, who temporarily unified the nation in opposition to an even greater horror. Even if unfair to Max Schmeling, it is not surprising that four years after that stunning one-round victory, when the United States was at war with Germany and Joe Louis had joined the army to help in the battle, he was introduced to a crowd of fellow soldiers as "the first American to K.O. a Nazi."[37]

Louis continued his fight against America's enemies when he joined the U.S. Army in 1942, even though he was exempt from the draft. He refused a commission because he feared it would distance him from common soldiers, and he spent most of his time in the service touring army bases and giving boxing exhibitions. One ex-soldier confirmed that a Louis appearance was "always one of the biggest events at the camp, especially for the colored soldiers."[38] He did more than just appear, however. Having clearly ended the color line in heavyweight boxing, he quietly spoke out against white racism. He protested against rules that prevented blacks from attending officer training school and the custom that required black soldiers to sit in the back of buses in southern military camps. In 1944, he was quoted in the *Baltimore Afro-American:* "The world is not meant to be ruled by one color."[39] The tortured history of race relations during the next six decades proved Joe Louis right.

That Joe Louis climbed the racial mountain is beyond dispute. That he made the journey easier for others, especially in the field of sports, is also clear.[40] In one sense, he did so by following a carefully crafted script that made him acceptable to whites and therefore "worthy" of fighting for the championship. In another sense, his accomplishments and the publicity surrounding them inevitably made him a hero to his fellow African Americans. He became a kind of world historical figure with the combination of athletic prowess and public persona that clearly resonated with the times. His career provided a sense of security for most whites and a sense of pride for most blacks as America suffered through the twin traumas of depression and war. He was, in the words of Louis scholars Dominic Capeci and Martha Wilkerson, a "multifarious hero" and "genuinely the people's choice."[41] As a race hero, Joe Louis was a man for the ages, who could be all things for all people. And that, not the trials, tribulations, and sadness of his final years is what we should all remember.

Ultimately Joe Louis sort of came around to respect Muhammad Ali. He still believed he would have beaten the brash young champ had both met in their primes, but he also "recognized Ali's skills as a fighter."[42] And Ali learned to appreciate again the virtues of his childhood hero. In 1976 while training for a bout with Ken Norton, Ali invited Louis to his camp for ten days and even offered him a gift of $30,000 to help the financially strapped ex-champ. Later, the two appeared on television together, after which Ali revealed to Louis that he had dreamed that he had knocked Louis out. Joe gave him a classic deadpan look and mock growl, "Don't you even dream it."[43] And in late 1980, a few months before he died, Joe showed up in a wheelchair at an Ali press conference. Ali promised when he fought Larry Holmes to copy the techniques that Louis had used against Max Schmeling in 1938. He also promised to visit Joe in his house.

Louis died in April 1981 before Ali could pay that visit. And shortly after Joe's death, when reminded by a reporter that he had once called Louis an Uncle Tom, Ali reacted angrily:

> I never said that, not that way, anyhow. That's demeaning. Look at Joe's life. Everybody loved Joe. . . . From black folks to redneck Mississippi crackers, loved him. They're all crying. That shows you. Howard Hughes dies, with all his billions, not a tear. Joe Louis, everybody cried.[44]

A rhetorical exaggeration, no doubt. But metaphorically, symbolically, how true, how true.

Alice Coachman with her teammates from Tuskegee. She is kneeling on the far right in the first row. *(Tuskegee University)*

9 Alice Coachman

Quiet Champion of the 1940s

JENNIFER H. LANSBURY

America revels in its sports lore. From the first in this to the most in that, from football to track and field, from the World Series to the Olympics—Americans have long loved to keep track of their sports stars. Names such as Jesse Owens, Babe Ruth, Hank Aaron, Althea Gibson, Johnny Unitas, Wilt Chamberlin, Joe Louis, Arnold Palmer, Wilma Rudolph, Muhammad Ali, Martina Navritalova, and countless more, evoke a sense of sports greatness and achievement. While none but the most avid of sports fans may remember the specifics of what made each of these athletes memorable, many Americans would nonetheless recognize the names and be able to associate the athlete with his or her sport.

At least one name, however, has faded somewhat from the American public memory. On August 8, 1948, in a track and field stadium in London, high jumper Alice Coachman leapt 5 feet, 6⅛ inches to become the first African American woman to win an Olympic gold medal. She achieved this distinction at the end of a ten-year career in which she amassed a total of thirty-six track and field national championships—twenty-six individual and ten team titles—a remarkable record.[1] From 1939 when she first won the national championship for her signature event, the high jump, no one else owned the title until after she retired ten years later. She was a member of the first All-American Women's Track and Field Team in 1943, as well as every year thereafter through 1948, her last year of competition. In the early 1950s, she was one of the first African American sports celebrities that Coca-Cola used to endorse their soft drink. She has been inducted into nine halls of fame throughout the country, including the National Track and Field Hall of Fame, and, most recently in 2004, the U.S. Olympic Hall of Fame. Yet mention her name, and many Americans will say they have never heard it.

In part, the loss of Coachman from the public memory speaks to the gender constructions in the culture of American sport. Indeed, the word *athlete* in and of itself is gendered male in American society. While the list of sports greats includes some females, it has overwhelmingly been a male domain during the twentieth century, particularly in terms of those athletes that have become part of the American cultural memory. Yet, Coachman's accomplishments have also faded because of the sport in which she participated. While track and field certainly has its share of statistics, Americans are not "assaulted" with it in the way we are baseball, football, and basketball. National championships simply do not get the media coverage of team sports, and the media-saturated Olympic Games come around only once every four years. As such, who can tell whether the Jackie Joyner-Kersees and Marion Joneses of today will become the Alice Coachmans of tomorrow, or whether we will even remember Carl Lewis in the same way we remember Jesse Owens. Not every Olympic gold medalist becomes part of the national cultural memory, nor do we hallow every sport's "first." If Alice Coachman has been lost to America's sports lore, is there a reason to resurrect her? Is there, in short, a value to remembering this particular sports' first?

Within the last few years, historians have begun to argue for an expanded time frame for the African American civil rights movement. Rather than confine the movement to the important activism of the 1960s, scholars are recognizing how the contributions of individuals from the 1930s through the 1950s were critical antecedents to bringing the 1960s and 1970s to fruition.[2] Harry T. Moore was recruiting for the NAACP in Florida as early as the mid-1930s; fifteen years of bold activism on his part led to his death in 1951.[3] In response to a segregated armed forces, the Tuskegee airmen used their status as successful World War II pilots to stage two nonviolent protests in 1945, ten years before the Montgomery bus boycotts.[4]

Yet another type of activism occurred during these years. A whole cadre of individual African Americans used whatever personal talent they possessed to push against the racial boundaries that American society had constructed. Alice Coachman was one of these quiet, less visible, activists. Some would argue that to call her an *activist* pushes the limits of the word's meaning. She did not march, recruit, or protest. She was not an orator or writer. Indeed, Coachman probably did not think of herself in such a way. But she could run and jump, faster and higher than other

American women of her era. By doing just that, persistently and determinedly for ten years, she forced even white Americans to take notice. Her goodwill and doggedness contributed to, if not the deconstruction of the masculinity of track and field, the beginning of changes in American society regarding women's participation in the sport. Using her athletic prowess to reach beyond the circumstances of her race, Coachman's efforts helped pave the way for other African American women to continue using sports to bring down race and gender barriers.

Raised in the rural outskirts of the southwest Georgia town of Albany, Alice Coachman was the fifth of ten children born to Evelyn and Fred Coachman. Memories of growing up in the 1920s were punctuated with a firm and religious mother, a conservative father that was the unquestioned head of the household, and a desire to be outside running and jumping most of the day. Reality included picking cotton and sleeping three to four in a bed. But Coachman could also be found outside racing the boys since the girls offered little competition against her blazing speed. And early on, it became clear that she could jump over just about anything, although generally it was a bamboo fishing pole or timber and rags tied together to fashion a rope.[5]

Unfortunately, 1930s American society did not consider most sport an appropriate feminine activity. Track and field, in particular, held little promise for women. A relatively new sport for women in the 1920s, it did not take long for the jarring movements of track and field to upset certain white middle-class notions of propriety. Physical education instructors began positing that women's femininity and reproductive capabilities suffered from the rigors of track and field and, as such, recommended that white women withdraw from the sport.[6]

As many white middle-class women left track and field, African American and white working-class women stepped in to fill the void. Such a composition of women track and field athletes caused the sport to become even more marginalized in American society. Yet these athletes discovered travel and educational opportunities that might otherwise have been unavailable to them, as well as the opportunity to accomplish something for themselves, their gender, and their race. Such opportunities were open to few others in American society.[7]

Evelyn and Fred Coachman were sensitive to the masculine associations of women's track and field and wanted their daughter to adopt more ladylike pursuits. Years later, Coachman remembered the stigma of being different: "It was a rough time in my life. It was a time when it wasn't fashionable for women to become athletes, and my life was wrapped up in sports."[8] However, there were other ways that Coachman's parents provided her with a foundation that helped her succeed. From her father, a man who firmly ruled his house and had little patience for tears, she learned inward strength and self-reliance. "Papa taught us to be strong," she recalled, "and this fed my competitiveness and desire to be the first and best."[9] Her mother set before her, both in words and example, a humbleness of spirit and respect for others. After Coachman had won her first national championship in 1939, her mother reminded her that people might be looking up to her for what she had done, but she would pass the same people on the way back down the ladder.[10]

Despite her parents' hesitation, Coachman found adult support for her love of athletics elsewhere. Her fifth-grade teacher, Cora Bailey, recognized that Coachman had a natural talent. Moreover, Bailey understood that personal and racial advancement could be achieved in many ways and so encouraged her young student to look for an opportunity to hone her skills by joining a track team. That opportunity came at Madison High School under the direction of Coach Harry Lash. It was that association with Coach Lash and Madison High that opened a door for Coachman and changed her life. It was that association that led Coachman to Tuskegee, Alabama.[11]

In 1939, Coachman traveled with the Madison High team to the May Day Track Carnival held in Tuskegee, Alabama. The carnival, hosted each year by Tuskegee Institute, provided a venue for area African American high schools and colleges to participate in a track meet. The high school participants competed against one another for the junior championships while the college athletes competed for the senior titles. Coachman was asked to go because Coach Lash needed points for the field events, which included the high jump, broad jump, shot put, and discus, javelin, and baseball throws. He had plenty of fast girls to run, she remembered, but needed her for the high jump. Coachman won the junior high jump event decisively by breaking the record for both the junior and senior levels.[12]

Such a performance caught the interest of Tuskegee coach Cleve Abbot. After Coachman had returned to Albany, the Tuskegee coaching staff visited her parents, requesting that Coachman be allowed to attend Tuskegee to finish her high school education and compete with the women's track team, the Tigerettes, while there. Coachman remembered years later how she was ready to go:

> I was tired of picking cotton, so I said to myself, if I'm going to spend the summer picking cotton, I can spend the summer learning. And then have a bed to sleep in by myself, and have three meals a day, and not have to do anything but work in the gym or out on the track. It was kind of fun, but it was hard work.[13]

So it was that Coachman left her family at age sixteen to begin one of the most important and transforming periods of her life. Her natural talent, hard work, and association with the Tuskegee coaches propelled her to the national and international stage of women's track and field. Her immersion into the Tuskegee culture helped her understand what was possible for a young African American woman, even in the 1940s.

When Coachman joined the Tuskegee Tigerettes she became part of an already nationally ranked team. For two consecutive years, the Tigerettes had come away with the team title at the Amateur Athletic Union (AAU) National Outdoor Championship. Coachman's first national meet was in the summer of 1939 before she officially started high school classes there, and Tuskegee once again came away with the team trophy. Coachman's contribution to the team championship was to bring home the individual title for the high jump, something she would do every year until she retired in 1948.

While at Tuskegee, Coachman raced and jumped herself into track and field history. During her high school years, she added several sprinting titles to her consecutive high jump victories. Coachman recalled when the Tuskegee coaches discovered that she could run as well as jump:

> When Coach found out I could run, good God Almighty! He started running me in that 50-[meter] and that [400-meter] relay and of course I had the high jump. I'd just stop when I'd won [the high jump, instead of going for a record] so I would have the energy to run that 50 and relay.[14]

By the time she graduated in 1943, she had become the team's leader in many respects, including running anchor for the 400-meter relay team. Following her graduation from the Tuskegee high school program, Coachman entered the Tuskegee Institute College to pursue a trade degree in dressmaking. It was during these years that the maturing athlete reached her peak. Following its first loss of a national title in seven years at the 1943 nationals, Tuskegee came back in 1944 to completely dominate its opponents and win the team championship by a landslide. At the 1945 nationals, headlines on the sports page of the *Baltimore Afro-American* read, "Alice Coachman Crowned National Sprint Queen," as she scored a triple win by capturing the 50- and 100-meter sprints as well as the high jump. Reaching "the acme of her brilliant career," she dethroned previous sprint champion Stella Walsh to win the all-around trophy awarded to the athlete scoring the most points.[15] In 1946, her last year to compete with the Tuskegee team, she repeated her triple win. By the time she graduated from Tuskegee Institute in 1946, Coachman had amassed twenty-three national titles.[16]

Some of Coachman's success came from her personal drive to succeed. Several of her Tuskegee teammates found her "peculiar" because she refused to talk to anyone, teammate or competitor, during meets. She thought that talking robbed her of energy she needed to perform her best and retain her titles, and she simply refused to do it. "I would talk to you all you wanted after the meet," she recalled, "but I knew what it was doing to my body," to waste energy on being social during the middle of a competition.[17] Today we would refer to such discipline as an athlete's *focus*. But at the time, the other athletes often mistook such discipline for aloofness and a sense of superiority.

Yet Tuskegee could not have captured fourteen national titles during this period with Coachman alone. Tuskegee's program attracted many talented athletes during these powerhouse years. When Coachman joined the team in 1939, most of the athletes were in college and raced for the senior titles. Coachman and the few high school girls there looked up to athletes like Lula Hymes and Jessie Abbot, who had been with the team since 1937. The older girls, in turn, took the "babies" under their wings and brought them along in the Tuskegee way. "We were family," Coachman remembers.[18] By the time Hymes and Abbot graduated, Coachman was a seasoned Tigerette who began mentoring the younger girls who looked up to her. In this way, Tuskegee maintained their powerhouse stature in the world of women's track and field. From 1937 to 1951, the Tuskegee Tigerettes held the national outdoor team title all but one year.[19]

The training, conditioning, and hard work demanded by the coaching staff were also factors in Tuskegee's success. "Coach" always referred to Cleve Abbot, head coach of the men's and women's track teams, who was respected in the track and field world for his strong program at Tuskegee. The athletes followed his instructions inviolately. The women's coach, Christine Evans Petty, made sure her girls lived up to the expectations set by the more famous Abbot. Petite and lithe, Petty nonetheless was not to be dismissed. In short, Coachman may have recognized from the days under her father's roof someone who liked to rule her domain with an iron hand. Coach Petty also thought that allowing the girls' team to compete against the boys' during practice sessions, coupled with a strict training regimen, helped better prepare the Tuskegee women for the nationals. Coachman remembers running against the men in preparation for the meets because there were no women around who could give the Tuskegee women any competition.[20]

So stunning was the women's team performance during these years that the black press even looked for a "secret" to their success. One *Baltimore Afro-American* sportswriter, Levi Jolley, devoted an entire article to discovering the secret to the Tigerettes' success—the use of George Washington Carver's peanut oil as a rubbing liniment. There may have been something to Coach Petty's insistence that consistent use of the oil prevented strained muscles and charlie-horses during their rigorous workouts. However, the entire article suggests a scoop, a discovery of the "secret" behind the athletes' success, as if training, talent, and hard work weren't enough.

The "peanut oil" story also suggests that these athletes were regarded predominately as women rather than athletes. In addition to preventing muscle cramps, the sportswriter noted, "the girls like to use it because of the smoothness it gives their skin—oftimes they request rubdowns with the oil to obtain relaxation, as it has a very soothing effect."[21] Indeed, this attitude speaks to the marginalized status women's track and field occupied in the 1930s and 1940s, even in the black community. While the white press virtually ignored Tuskegee's success, the black press, reporting extensively about their accomplishments, nonetheless found ways to feminize the athletes through articles such as the peanut oil story.[22]

Coachman's days at Tuskegee were not confined entirely to track and field, however. Music had always been an important part of her life, so Coachman balanced her track and field pursuits by also participating in the Tuskegee Choir under the direction of the famed conductor William L. Dawson. Participation in the choir "kept her sane" while at

Tuskegee, she remembered. She also played on the Tuskegee women's basketball team, making All-American, and helping Tuskegee secure three conference titles. Moreover, there were practical aspects to her Tuskegee experience. Coachman's parents could not afford the tuition, so Tuskegee arranged for her enrollment under its work-study program. As a member of the women's track team, Coachman's work involved extra duties around the gym and various athletic fields.[23]

But the most memorable part of Coachman's Tuskegee years was the culture that dated back to the school's inception. Booker T. Washington began Tuskegee Normal and Industrial Institute in 1881 to provide African Americans with the means to lift themselves out of economic and educational despair. The school taught practical trades as well as self-reliance and determination. The community of Tuskegee introduced its students to a middle-class way of life that contrasted sharply from the rural, economically depressed backgrounds in which many of them were raised. Tuskegee's influence went beyond the school and community, however. In what came to be known as the Tuskegee Machine, Washington and other Tuskegeeans recruited black allies throughout the United States. Tuskegee Institute alumni, both in and around the campus but also those who relocated elsewhere in the country, spread the network even further. When the Tigerettes traveled north for the nationals, Coach Abbot easily found housing for the athletes by placing them in the homes of Tuskegee alumni.[24]

Coachman remembers initially having difficulties in making the transition from the economically depressed environment in Albany. There was more to adjust to at Tuskegee than just the school, and newcomers felt the palpable difference in culture and class. A little time to adapt, however, transformed this southwest Georgia native into a true believer of the Tuskegee culture. So much so, that she eventually returned to make her home there, suggesting that once you become a part of it, it's hard to leave.[25]

The atmosphere surrounding Tuskegee did more than transform the individual lives of African Americans, however. Washington's accommodationist position toward whites was criticized by other black leaders, most notably black intellectuals like W. E. B. Du Bois, who favored a more outspoken form of protest.[26] Yet there were quiet, less obvious ways that the culture surrounding the Tuskegee Machine was positively affecting race relations. During Coachman's high school years there, a white woman visiting the area from the North asked her for directions to the Catholic Church. The young track and field athlete decided to walk the visitor to the church instead of just giving her directions because "that was how we were taught at Tuskegee." Shortly after the woman returned to New York, she sent Coachman a box of clothes to thank her for the assistance. While such an act may seem somewhat condescending, Coachman did not interpret it that way. The only way she could afford to be at Tuskegee was through its work-study program, and her parents rarely had money to send for any "extras." Coachman was grateful for the woman's generosity. The clothes, she later remembered, lasted her for several years. The relationship did not end there, however. When the Tigerettes would travel north for a meet, Coachman's new "friend" would sometimes show up to watch her compete.[27]

This story is not meant to suggest that the Tuskegee culture and African Americans like Coachman were making great strides in race relations, particularly in the South. What it does argue, however, is that activists like Coachman were making positive contributions even in the 1940s by quietly and politely, yet repeatedly, pushing against the race and gender boundaries of American society. While the short-term result may have been the uplift of thousands of individual African American men and women, the longer-term accomplishment was the collective gradual erosion against the notion that blacks were different and inferior.

When Coachman graduated from the Tuskegee trade program in 1946, she was at her peak as an athlete. Looking beyond her athletic career, however, she was also interested in teaching; she returned to Albany to work on a teaching degree at Albany State Teacher's College. While there, she became a member of their track and field team and continued her domination of the high jump and the 50-meter dash. She also began to train seriously for the upcoming 1948 Olympic Games. The 1940 and 1944 games had both been canceled because of World War II, so the upcoming games in London would be Coachman's only opportunity to compete on an international scale. She stood a very good chance of taking home at least one medal.

During her training for the Olympics, Coachman, along with her Albany State coach, Chris Roulhac, returned to Tuskegee. Albany State's facilities at the time were inadequate for Coachman to prepare for her Olympic bid, so Coachman and Roulhac spent a month of intensive training at the Tuskegee Institute track and field to prepare her for the

Olympic trials scheduled for July 1948.[28] The return to Tuskegee for training paid off. At the Olympic trials, Coachman bettered the old record to easily qualify for the U.S. Olympic team in the high jump. She also qualified for the 50-meter dash. Of the twelve-member team that set sail for London, nine were African American.[29] Of those nine, Tuskegee Institute claimed three plus one alumnae.

Such an overwhelming majority of black athletes on the U.S. team made news in the African American community.[30] Indeed, these same track and field athletes had long been a subject of interest to the black press. For almost a decade, however, white newspapers had basically shunned women's track and field. While the men's national meets headlined the sports pages with one- to two-page spreads that included several photographs, the comparable women's meet often received only one short column. Photographs of the women cinder stars were rare. When a photograph did appear, a white woman was usually given precedence over an African American, despite the fact that Coachman or a teammate had often decidedly outperformed their white competitors.[31] Black women athletes of the 1930s and 1940s were fighting the cultural constraints of both their gender and race. Coachman's response was to quietly yet decisively keep winning national championships. Such determination and success caused at least one white newspaper to take notice in a fairly dramatic way.

Coachman's hometown paper, the *Albany Herald,* had reported on her success as a track and field athlete since the mid-1940s. The coverage, typical of the white press for a woman track and field athlete, consisted of short, one-column articles in the sports section.[32] With her qualification at the Olympic trials, however, Coachman jumped to the sports page headlines with a feature article that discussed the trials and the composition of the women's Olympic team. A week and a half later, the *Herald* devoted an entire article to Coachman's Olympic bid. Calling Coachman one of the most outstanding stars on the American team, the sportswriter reported that she had "surpassed all, with the exception of the fabulous Stella Walsh, in the field of women's track."[33] Such praise was not completely unheard of in the white press for Coachman, who had come to be known by black and white sportswriters alike as "the Tuskegee flash" for her sprinting prowess.[34] The exceptional thing about this article, in addition to its dedication solely to Coachman, was that it included a photograph of her lined up for a training sprint. In short, a white newspaper in the Deep South crossed both gender and race barriers that had been inviolate for nearly a decade in women's track and field reporting.

Certainly, the *Albany Herald* was interested in promoting Coachman as a "hometown hero." There had been only one other Georgia native who had won Olympic gold.[35] Coachman's win at the Olympics would be huge. Yet, this article appeared two weeks before Coachman would compete in the high jump, not after she was a bonafide Olympic champion.[36] Moreover, despite the fact that this was Coachman's hometown paper, it was all the more remarkable given its location deep in the Jim Crow South of the 1940s. In short, Coachman had advanced both her race and gender through her outstanding track career.

Once in London, Coachman made an important decision. She chose to concentrate solely on the high jump rather than dividing her training time between the jump and the 50-yard sprint that she had also qualified for. In part, this decision came as a result of back pain she had been experiencing in the months leading up to the Olympics. "I knew I had won that high jump, both indoor and outdoor, for 10 years," she remembered years later. "Now here I come up at the peak of my training, and get this backache, and I didn't know what was going to happen. So my best bet was to stick with what I had gone through with all these years and see what I could do there."[37]

As the track and field competition progressed, however, Coachman also felt an increasing amount of pressure to perform well. There had been high expectations for the women's track and field team in this first Olympics following the war. However, one by one, the United States' hopes were eliminated as the Europeans, particularly Dutch sensation Fanny Blankers-Koen, bested the American women.[38] The United States and Canada had only each other to compete against since the 1936 Olympics. Despite the fact that the United States had sent the fastest women from North America over to the Olympic Games, they had no idea of the strength of track and field on the other side of the Atlantic. Coachman recalled being sick over it: "I was sitting in the stands, and I just watched these fast girls out of Chicago, out of Tuskegee, out of Mississippi, out of Louisiana, everywhere, all over the United States, so fast—just fade away. It was just embarrassing, and you felt sorry." Coach Catherine Meyer had arrived thinking that the American team would come away with at least three gold medals. By the time the competition ended eight days later, the only other medal won by the American women was a bronze in the 200-meter distance by seventeen-year-old Tennessee student Audrey Patterson.[39]

Coachman's high jump competition came in the late afternoon of the last day that the Olympic track and field events were contested. Resting the day before, she felt ready for what would be her final high jump competition. Slowly, the other qualifying competitors started dropping out, leaving Micheline Ostermeyer of France, Dorothy Tyler of England, and Coachman. In the end the contest came down to Tyler and Coachman, both clearing the bar at 5 feet, 6⅛ inches, but unable to go any higher. The *Chicago Tribune* caught the drama of Coachman's victory:

> Alice Coachman, student at Albany (Ga.) Teachers college, saved the United States girls from a shutout when she won the high jump, setting an Olympic record of 5 feet 6⅛ inches. Sixty thousand of the crowd remained in the arena as the track games drew to a close in darkness and a drizzling rain. . . . Coachman and Mrs. Richard Tyler, mother of two boys, cleared the same height but Coachman was awarded the title for the least number of attempts at all heights.[40]

Coachman's victory came not only through hard work, athletic prowess, and desire, but also through some excellent coaching. Coachman and Tyler and Ostermeyer approached the bar from opposite sides, Coachman from the left and Tyler and Ostermeyer from the right. Coachman was consistently hitting her jumps, while the Europeans would miss here and there. She remembered how her two competitors began coming over to her side to see how she approached the bar. At that point, Coachman employed a strategy that Coach Chris Roulhac had given her at the Olympic trials. Before getting to her takeoff point where she would leap over the bar, Roulhac told Coachman to take a lot of steps during her run. Her competitors observed this, and in trying to imitate the preparation and thereby reduce their number of missed jumps, they threw off their own rhythm and ended up with more missed attempts. Years later, Coachman recalled how she had "got 'um," at least in part, due to a good coach.[41]

Upon her return to the States, Coachman was greeted with a round of celebrations. Legendary jazz musician Count Basie threw a party to honor the new Olympic champion, and Coachman joined the other gold medal winners to meet with President Truman at the White House. Once back in Georgia, seven towns between Atlanta and Albany hosted receptions for her during the 180-mile road trip. In Albany, the city celebrated Coachman with a "giant parade, an official greeting, and a college reception" that had been planned for almost a month.[42] As an Olympic hero, Coachman garnered front-page status in the *Albany Herald*. Coverage included six front-page articles, detailing not only Coachman's win but also the planning and execution of the celebrations in Albany to honor their new international sports star.[43]

The realities of life in southwest Georgia contrasted sharply to such apparent racial harmony, however. Coachman remembered the segregated seating at the municipal auditorium as well as the refusal by certain city officials to shake her hand. But the culmination of Coachman's ten-year athletic career resulted not only in a gold medal but also in recognition beyond anything she might have imagined ten years earlier. White and black Albanians alike had come together to honor a young African American woman—one of their own who had achieved something on the world stage. To realize that her accomplishment stemmed from track and field reflected how much had changed for black women track athletes since Coachman had won her first national title in 1939.

Clearly, momentum was building in American society for some radical changes in the treatment of African Americans. The black press had pushed the "Double V" campaign during the war that called for a double victory over tyranny—abroad for all Americans and at home for African Americans. Returning servicemen refused to succumb to the same fate of their fathers and grandfathers whose return from the Great War met with racial conditions in the United States unchanged.[44] Moreover, the cold war began to have an impact. The American government experienced heightened sensitivity regarding its own race relations in light of the negative press it received in the communist regimes of the Soviet Union and China.[45] Some of this awareness was even making itself felt during Coachman's Olympic bid. With a byline of "U.S. Girl Wins," the *Chicago Tribune* concluded their report of the women's Olympic high jump competition with the following: "Thus the track meet started as begun eight days ago, with victory for an American and the Star Spangled Banner of the United States providing the closing music."[46] Far from being ignored by the white press, Coachman was lifted up as an American hero who saved the U.S. women's team from a shutout.

The work of numerous African Americans from the 1930s and 1940s helped lay the groundwork for this important change in American society. Some of these men and women, like Harry T. Moore, chose to take a more outspoken approach—perhaps even bordering on militant for the period—in agitating for civil rights. Many others, like Coachman, combined their natural talent with hard work and determination to prove to themselves and the country that they could achieve things beyond what even many white Americans achieved. Athletes, artists, writers, musicians, actors, doctors, lawyers, business persons—individual achievement that together not only served as examples of what was possible but also slowly chipped away at racial, and in Coachman's case, gender barriers.

Following her Olympic victory, Coachman resumed her senior year at Albany State. She graduated from the teacher's college in the spring of 1949, with a degree in home economics and a minor in science, and prepared to settle down to a life absent most of the media attention that surrounds today's sports stars. By the early 1950s, however, Coachman was offered another opportunity to push against the race and gender hierarchies of American society. Coca-Cola, in a company campaign to incorporate more African Americans in advertising, approached Coachman with an offer to use her status as a former gold-medal Olympian to endorse the soft drink.[47] Coachman appeared in several print ads for Coca-Cola, both alone and with the former Olympic track and field great Jesse Owens. The two former Olympians were among the first African American celebrities to be featured in company ads in a campaign that included several other well-known African American athletes and musicians of the 1950s. While these paled in comparison to the lucrative endorsement contracts that athletes sign today, Coachman was again at the forefront of change. Indeed, in considering the status of women's track and field at the outset of Coachman's career, inclusion in such a campaign represented a remarkable transition in American society.[48]

As the years passed, the "first" that Coachman had achieved in 1948 began to fade from even the public memory of those in Albany. The former Olympian understood this in all too real a way while teaching physical education in Albany during the 1970s. Prior to the start of their unit on track and field, Coachman gave her pupils an assignment to read and report on the history of the sport. The students returned with a book that stated that Wilma Rudolph, who had won three gold medals at the 1960 Rome Olympics, had been the first African American woman to win Olympic gold. The only way Coachman could convince her students that the information in the book was wrong was to bring her gold medal to class the following day.[49]

Although African American women continued to fight both racism and sexism, much had changed since Alice Coachman captured her first high jump title. A team of African American athletes had dominated women's track and field for twelve years. A sport that had once been considered "too masculine" for women began offering up the successes of its female athletes as American "heroes" in the fight against communism. And a young African American woman made the black *and* white inhabitants of a southwest Georgia town take notice of her in 1948. The landmark *Brown* decision was still six years away.

One wonders why it is, then, that Jesse Owens and Wilma Rudolph have become so firmly imbedded into America's cultural memory while Alice Coachman has not. Perhaps for Owens it was a combination of world events, his athletic showdown with Hitler's Aryan sports specimen, and his multiple golds. For Rudolph, maybe her battle with childhood polio, the winning of three gold medals in front of a television audience, the influence of the cold war, and the progress of the African American civil rights movement helped keep her name in the public consciousness.

Yet the individual contributions of the Alice Coachmans of the 1930s and 1940s laid the groundwork for the later success of what we traditionally think of as the African American civil rights movement.[50] Coachman's was a different kind of agitation, one that was born of consistently doing what she knew how to do best—run and jump. Her quiet, yet steady, dedication to being the best she could be coupled with an African American culture that fostered things like determination, graciousness, and individual achievement took her from a small southwest Georgia city to the top of the medal stand in London. Coachman became, although unwittingly, a quiet champion for her race and gender as well. For along the way, a white press that had virtually ignored women's track and field for years was forced to acknowledge the accomplishments of this track and field phenomenon. Coachman made it possible for athletes like Rudolph, Jackie Joyner-Kersee, Florence Griffith Joyner, and Marion Jones to follow in her wake. Indeed, by refusing to accept society's condemnation of women's track and field and steadily climbing to the pinnacle of her sport, Coachman not only transformed life for herself, but she also became one of the unsung civil rights activists of the 1940s.

Jackie Robinson poses at the door of the Brooklyn Dodgers Club House at Ebbetts Field in April 1947, just prior to his historic integration of Major League baseball. *(National Baseball Hall of Fame Library, Cooperstown, New York)*

10 Jackie Robinson

Racial Pioneer and Athlete Extraordinaire in an Era of Change

MICHAEL E. LOMAX

Few athletes in the history of professional sports have made such a dramatic political, economic, and social impact as Brooklyn Dodgers hall of famer Jackie Robinson. Certainly no other athlete defined the era of the late 1940s and 1950s like Robinson, a period that gave us the early stages of expansion and the initial challenge to the reserve clause in major league baseball, witnessed the rise of professional football as a television spectacle, and experienced the emergence of the National Collegiate Athletic Association into a cartel organization. Various individual sports stars emerged during these decades, from Willie Mays and Mickey Mantle to Jim Brown and Johnny Unitas, from George Mikan and Althea Gibson to Bob Petit and Ted Williams. Yet in many ways Jackie Robinson towered over all other sports figures of the era. In the tumultuous period of the cold war that spawned the nuclear arms race, the early years of the civil rights movement and the white response to the *Brown v. Board of Education* decision, and the emergence of rock and roll in the popular consciousness, Jackie Robinson influenced several of the political, economic, and social changes that occurred during his young adulthood as he also seemed to be a product of them.

Jack Roosevelt Robinson was born on January 31, 1919, in Cairo, Georgia. He was the youngest of four brothers and one sister. His father, Jerry Robinson, was a sharecropper and his mother, Mallie Robinson, was a domestic. In 1920, after separating from her husband, Mallie Robinson moved her family to Pasadena, California, where Jackie spent his childhood. From the outset, Jackie Robinson would be characterized by today's standard as an at-risk youngster. He was a product of a broken home and by his own admission a "full-fledged delinquent." Robinson became a member of the Pepper Street gang, and he was constantly in trouble.

Several mentors would begin to have a positive influence on Robinson, however. Carl Anderson, a mechanic whose automobile shop was close to where the Pepper Street gang hung out, offered Jackie some sound advice. He told Robinson if he continued with the gang it would hurt his mother as well as him: Anderson made Robinson confront the fact that he didn't have to be in a gang, and peer pressure was the reason he was a member. The Reverend Karl Downs also had a profound influence upon young Jackie's life. Reverend Downs proposed radical changes in the church Robinson attended, many of which were designed to win favor with young people. This sense of belonging resulted in these young people planning dances at the church and playing on a new badminton court that the minister installed. These recreational activities served as an alternative to hanging out on street corners.

Robinson developed a love for sports at an early age, which undoubtedly helped him cope with the traps of racism. Jackie also developed a burning desire to win at everything he competed in. As his sister remembered, "He was a special little boy . . . and ever since I can remember, he always had a ball in his hand." Regardless of the activity, Robinson wanted to win, and he usually did. He earned letters in football, basketball, and track at John Muir Technical High School. In Pasadena, Robinson competed against other gifted young athletes—black, white, or Asian American—without allowing race to produce conflict or resentment among them. No doubt these early experiences in Robinson's life convinced him that Jim Crow in any sport, or in any other facet of American society, was not right or natural.[1]

Robinson went on to excel in sports at Pasadena Junior College (PJC). He earned a spot on the baseball team, which played in the Western Division of the Southern California Junior College Athletic Association. Robinson's excellent fielding, timely hitting, and aggressive base running made him one of the favorites of Bulldog coach John Thurman. Thurman had helped Jackie develop his skills the previous summer in a city-sponsored baseball school in Brookside Park. Robinson also established himself as the school's second-best broad jumper, behind his brother "Iron Man" Mack Robinson.

Football was the sport Robinson excelled in, despite an early season injury. On September 13, 1937, at the first scrimmage Robinson chipped a bone in his right leg that required a cast; he missed a month of the season. When he returned he dazzled the PJC fans with his athletic prowess. In a game against Loyola University, Jackie intercepted a pass and returned it ninety-two yards for a touchdown. He ran back a punt for eighty yards and a touchdown against Chaffey Junior College, and in the final game of the season against Caltech Robinson scored one touchdown and ran for another.

Robinson's athletic achievements at Pasadena Junior College sparked interest among several colleges and universities to recruit him. He ultimately decided to attend UCLA and emerged as the school's first four-letter man, starring in football, basketball, track, and baseball. In basketball, Robinson led the Pacific Coast Conference in scoring twice, leading one coach to call him "the best basketball player in the United States." In his junior year, Jackie teamed with All-American Kenny Washington and averaged eleven yards a carry on the gridiron. Although baseball was considered one of Robinson's lesser sports, Ned Cronin reported in 1940, "Had it not been for the policy prohibiting Negroes in organized baseball, he would have been sought by half a dozen major league scouts."[2]

At UCLA, Robinson displayed his versatility in several other sports. He competed in golf and won the Pacific Coast intercollegiate golf championship. Jackie also won tennis championships at UCLA. He reached the semifinals in tennis at the national Negro tournament. Undoubtedly no other athlete, including Jim Thorpe, competed as effectively in as broad a range of sports.

Academically, Robinson was an average student. In his first semester, for example, he earned C's in courses in education, geology, and history. He earned C's in two more history courses, in Spanish, and in military science in his second semester. Robinson also earned two A's in physical education.

It was at UCLA that Jackie Robinson met the love of his life. Rachel Annetta Isum had just turned seventeen and recently graduated from Manuel Arts High School. She lived at home with her parents and her brother Raymond. Her father, Charles Raymond Isum, had worked as a bookbinder with the *Los Angeles Times* for over twenty years. Rachel's mother, Zellee Isum, was a self-employed caterer, with clients in Beverly Hills and Hollywood. Rachel's charm and drive was a product of the way her parents raised her. She had become indispensable to her father due to his illness. Rachel assumed many of the tasks in the house including cleaning, cooking, and shopping. Although she characterized herself as a very shy child, Rachel added that she was "happy and loved, and self-confident in many ways."[3]

At first, Robinson admired Rachel from afar and he did not act upon his feelings. He finally confided his feelings to his best friend, Ray Bartlett, who was more comfortable talking with women. Bartlett recalled: "He talked about this girl and how nice she seemed . . . And one day I said, 'Haven't you met her yet? No? Well, come on! You'd better meet her before classes really get going and she disappears.' And I introduced him to her."[4]

Rachel knew who Jackie Robinson was. She had seen him play football in high school. Her first impression of Robinson was that he was conceited because he stood in the backfield with his hands on his hips, all too unemotional awaiting the impending violence of the next play. Later, she found out that was the way Jackie carried himself on the field; it was not reflective of his character. She never forgot their first meeting when Bartlett introduced them to each other. "I remember the awkwardness of the moment," Rachel recalled. "What I like about Jack was his smile, and a kind of confident air he had about him, without being a cocky person." She also noticed that Jack almost exclusively wore white shirts. "I thought to myself, now why would he do that." She added: "Why would anybody that dark wear a white shirt? It's terrible!" Robinson appeared ambivalent about his apparel, however. "He wore his color with such dignity and pride and confidence that after a little while I didn't even think about it. He wouldn't let me. He was never, ever, ashamed of his color."[5]

Despite his athletic brilliance on the field, Robinson decided to leave UCLA, due to financial difficulties and a desire to support his mother. He was convinced that "no amount of education would help a black man get a job." Most of his coaches, along with Rachel, his mother and Reverend Karl Downs, attempted to persuade Jackie from leaving the university. But as Robinson stated: "Despite all this, I could see no future in staying at college, no real future in athletics, and I wanted to do the next best thing—become an athletic director." Whereas such logic appears naïve by today's standards, Robinson's rationale was not without foundation. Opportunities were limited for African Americans to pursue professional sports careers in 1940s America. The color line was drawn tight in organized baseball and in professional golf. Professional football was a minor sport, and no blacks had played in the National Football League since 1932. Basketball was also a minor sport, and its doors were closed to blacks. The few offers Robinson did receive came from semiprofessional clubs, like the Broadway Clowns, a basketball team.[6]

Through the assistance of Pat Ahearn, athletic director for the National Youth Administration (NYA), Robinson was offered a job as an assistant athletic director at a work camp in Atascadero, California. The job involved working with youngsters, many of them who came from poor or broken homes. The thought of working with youngsters in the sports field excited the former UCLA star. Robinson also supplemented his income playing for the Los Angeles Bulldogs, a barnstorming football team.

Robinson's experience with the NYA was short lived. In the spring of 1942, he was drafted into the U.S. Army. No other period in his life exemplified Robinson's defiance of racism and segregation as did his brief military career. He experienced several confrontations with the Jim Crow military. At Fort Riley, for example, officials denied him entry to Officers' Candidate School (OCS) despite his college background. Robinson protested to heavyweight champion Joe Louis, who was also stationed there. Louis informed Truman Gibson, a black advisor to the Department of War, who forced a reversal of the Fort Riley policy.

Controversy continued to plague Robinson during his military stint. As morale officer for the black troops at Fort Riley, Robinson sought to increase the number of seats provided for black soldiers at the segregated Post Exchange. Soldiers complained bitterly to him about the conditions at the PX, where they often waited for long periods of time for the few seats assigned to blacks while "white" seats went unused. Robinson telephoned the provost marshal, a Major Haffner, to voice the black soldiers' complaint. Haffner was unaware that Robinson was black, as the young lieutenant made his case for the black soldiers. Finally, Major Haffner came to the point: "Lieutenant, let me put it to you this way. How would you like to have your wife sitting next to a nigger?" Robinson exploded. He raged on the phone for several more minutes. He then took the grievance to the battalion commander, who led Robinson to believe that he was sympathetic to his plight. Robinson did succeed in getting additional seats for blacks at the PX. However, one constant of African American life remained: segregation.[7]

On April 13, 1944, a dozen black officers received orders to proceed immediately to Camp Hood, Texas, and report to the 761st Tank Battalion. From the outset, Robinson found out that his lieutenant's bars meant little at Camp Hood. Running short of cash one night, he stopped by the white officers' club to cash a check. He was barred from entering the club; the episode infuriated Robinson. On July 6, 1944, Robinson became involved in a controversy that almost ended his military career. He boarded a city bus that took him from McCloskey Hospital in Temple, Texas, to Camp Hood. Robinson obeyed Texas law requiring Jim Crow seating on the bus, but he also knew that the army now prohibited segregation on its military bases. After driving approximately six blocks, the bus driver, Milton N. Renegar, ordered Robinson to move to the back of the bus. The young lieutenant refused. The driver threatened to make trouble for him when the bus reached the station. The conversation between Renegar and Robinson grew more intense. When the bus reached the station, another passenger, Mrs. Elizabeth Poitevint, let Robinson know that she intended to press charges against him.

Captain Gerald M. Bear, an assistant provost marshal, conducted an investigation of the event. Upon completion, Captain Bear filed three separate charges against Robinson for a general court marshal. In response, Robinson made several calls and wrote some letters: he contacted Joe Louis and several members of the black press. He wrote a letter to Truman Gibson, outlining what had happened, and reminding him—and the Pentagon—that because he was a prominent athlete his case was almost certain to receive substantial media attention. Robinson also wrote a letter to the NAACP asking for advice and legal help.

On August 2, 1944, Jackie Robinson's case went to trial. The trial lasted more than four hours. An able defense lawyer, the plethora of pretrial publicity, and the weakness of the case against him led the army judges to rule that he had acted within his rights in his refusal to bow to southern tradition. Robinson secured the two-thirds votes necessary for his acquittal and was found not guilty on all charges. Robinson's exoneration contributed to the legend of his brutality and suffering. David Williams, a white fellow officer, wrote about witnessing Robinson restrained in a manner Jack never discussed previously: "He was handcuffed, and there were shackles on his legs. Robinson's face was angry, the muscles on his face tight, his eyes half closed."[8] Variations of the story leading up to Robinson's court marshal began to circulate. They characterized Jackie as a man with a quick temper and much pride who fought back at any signs of racial oppression. For example, he supposedly roughed up the bus driver for letting black passengers off the bus short of their destination. These stories only added to the legend that portrayed Jackie Robinson as a violent man.

In 1945, Robinson signed with the Kansas City Monarchs and spent an unhappy season barnstorming the nation. Robinson never quite adjusted to the boisterous life of the Negro Leagues. The loose play and erratic scheduling appalled the young Monarch, who was accustomed to the discipline and structure of intercollegiate athletics. Whereas most black ballplayers resigned themselves to their Jim Crow status, Robinson often spoke of impending integration. Teammate Othello Renfroe remembered: "We'd ride miles and miles on the bus and his whole talk was 'Well you guys better get ready pretty soon baseball's going to sign one of us.'"[9]

Whereas many Negro League players viewed Robinson as an unlikely racial pioneer, others saw the Monarchs' shortstop as the perfect candidate to cross the color line. Quincy Trouppe declared: "With Jackie's temper being the way it was, it didn't seem likely that a major league team would be willing to take the chance with him." However, black sportswriters Wendell Smith and Sam Lacy argued that Robinson could succeed in the majors. In an article written in *Negro Baseball* Lacy named several black ballplayers with major league potential; he called Robinson the "ideal man to pace the experiment," and noted that his college experience made him no stranger to interracial competition. Lacy added: "He would have neither the inferiority complex we should steer away from, nor would he have the cocky bulldozing attitude we likewise must avoid."[10]

By August 1945, Brooklyn Dodgers president Branch Rickey also believed that Robinson was the ideal candidate to cross the color line. Robinson possessed the qualifications that Rickey deemed essential for baseball integration. In addition to his athletic ability, Jack was college educated, articulate, and intelligent, and he had played with white teammates. His service as a military officer made his claim to equality on the baseball diamond persuasive and, as his actions in the service had proven, he possessed the courage and the conviction necessary for the endeavor. Robinson's off-field behavior appealed to Rickey. Jack was a Methodist who neither drank nor smoke. Robinson's temperament remained the sole question mark. Rickey could only hope that Jack would understand the need for self-control and the necessity to exercise it.

On October 23, 1945, President Hector Racine of the International League Montreal Royals called a press conference at the team's home ball park, the Delormier Downs. Racine stated that the Royals would make "a very important announcement" that would dramatically impact the baseball world. Over two dozen newspaper and radio men jammed into the Royals' offices. Racine entered the room along with Lieutenant Colonel Romeo Gavreau, the Royals' vice president, Branch Rickey Jr., the director of the Dodgers farm system, and an unidentified African American gentleman. Racine introduced Jackie Robinson to the press and announced that the Royals had signed him to a contract. A moment of "stunned silence" resonated throughout the room before the members of the press dashed for telephones to relay the news-breaking event to their newspapers and radio stations.

The signing of Jackie Robinson marked the start of what became known as baseball's "noble experiment." Agreeing to abide by a proscribed set of behaviors devised by Branch Rickey, combined with his on-field performance, Robinson would attempt to shatter organized baseball's color line. Rickey held to the belief that the players themselves would embrace Robinson. He would not force Jack on the players, the public, or the press. Furthermore, Rickey wanted the players to make their own decision after watching him play. More important, the success or failure of the experiment rested on Robinson's shoulders.

Jackie Robinson's resolve was tested early in spring training. Segregation, law, and custom resulted in Robinson living separate from the rest of his teammates. Being segregated from the team during spring training would continue to irritate Robinson throughout his baseball career. Several early exhibition games were canceled due to Robinson's presence on the Royals. On March 25, 1946, the Royals were scheduled to play in Deland, Florida. Upon their arrival they learned that the game had been canceled due to a malfunction in the lighting system, although the contest was scheduled for the afternoon. In a game against the St.

Paul Saints at Sanford, Robinson started the game and beat out an infield hit in his first at-bat. When Jack was about to step on to the field for the start of the third inning, the local chief of police ordered Montreal manager Clay Hopper to remove his second baseman or risk prosecution. Hopper replaced him.

Clearly, Robinson and his black teammate Johnny Wright recognized that this chaotic spring training was a direct result of their presence, undoubtedly causing insurmountable pressure on both of them. Their experience was further exacerbated by the fact that they still had to make the ball club. Despite these obstacles, Robinson and Wright persevered, keeping to themselves and speaking only when spoken to. More important, Branch Rickey remained committed to the overall experiment.

On April 18, 1946, Jackie Robinson made his debut in the International League against the Jersey City Giants. In his first at-bat, Robinson hit a weak ground ball to the shortstop, who threw him out at first. In the third inning, Robinson hit a chest-high fastball into the left field stands for a home run, his first hit in professional white baseball. He proceeded to hit safely three more times, stole second twice, and scored four runs, leading his Montreal Royals to a 14 to 1 victory. Neither Rickey nor Robinson could have scripted a better opening game.

Whereas Robinson was well received by the Montreal fans, road trips could be precarious. Syracuse, New York, and Baltimore, Maryland, proved to be the most inhospitable of cities. Fans booed Robinson when he appeared at the plate, and Syracuse players heckled him mercilessly from the dugout. When Robinson knelt in the on-deck circle waiting to hit, a Syracuse player pushed a black cat in his direction and yelled, "Hey Jackie, there's your cousin clowning on the field." The umpire stopped the game and ordered the Syracuse manager to silence Robinson's assailants. In Baltimore, a little over three thousand fans attended the first game of a three-game series, where Rachel sat horrified in the stands as a man behind her shouted that "nigger son of a bitch," Jackie Robinson. The following day, over twenty-five thousand fans attended a doubleheader, with roughly ten thousand blacks packed into the segregated and inferior seating. Again Robinson was subjected to abuse from white fans. The presence of thousands of blacks, who watched his every move, both elated and weighed on him. He later wrote, "It put a heavy burden of responsibility on me, but it was a glorious challenge."[11]

Despite the antagonism he endured in Syracuse and Baltimore, Robinson had a spectacular rookie season. He became the first Royal to win the International League batting title. His .349 batting average also eclipsed the Royals' record set in 1930. Whereas he hit only 3 home runs and drove in 66 runs, Robinson led the league in runs scored with 113. More important, Robinson was instrumental in leading the Montreal Royals to the International League pennant and the Little World Series championship.

By the same token, abiding by the objectives of the noble experiment left some emotional scars on Robinson. Opposing pitchers repeatedly threw at his head. According to teammate Al Campanis and others, several base runners aimed their spikes at his flesh whenever they could. Robinson did not complain about the treatment, but Royals' general manager Mel Jones knew different. Jones stated: "He came into the office more than once and he'd say, 'Nobody knows what I'm going through.'" At the end of the season, one Montreal journalist reflected: "Because of his dark pigmentation Robbie could never protest. If there was a rhubarb on the field . . . he had to stay out of it. Otherwise, there might have been a riot."[12]

As the 1947 season approached, Branch Rickey made a series of moves to facilitate a smooth elevation of Jackie Robinson into the major leagues. Rickey moved the Dodgers' spring training base from Florida to Cuba, scheduling additional games in Panama. He kept Robinson on the Montreal roster and scheduled a series of games between the Royals and the Dodgers to allow him to showcase his talents. In addition to Robinson, three black players were assigned to the Montreal club: Roy Campanella, Don Newcombe, and Roy Partlow. When Robinson reported to spring training camp, he was stunned to learn that the black players would be segregated from not only the Dodgers, but also from the Royals. At first, Robinson blasted the Cuban government for insisting on these Jim Crow arrangements. However, it was Rickey's idea. The ever-cautious Dodgers' president wanted to avoid any disruptive racial incident that might occur.

Robinson's plight was further exacerbated by the efforts of several Dodgers veterans who sought to prohibit his promotion to the club. Rickey and Dodgers manager Leo Durocher attempted to quell the uprising by threatening to trade any player who persisted in their opposition. One player, pitcher Kirby Higbe, was traded, while the others rescinded their protest. Robinson sensed this aversion toward his promotion to the Dodgers and resented it. He sharply pointed out in an interview with a sportswriter that Montreal in the previous year "did not suffer from his presence." Robinson also stated that the pennant had come from high team morale. "No sir," he said, "moral is important. If the Dodgers don't want me there would be no point in forcing myself on them. I am in the Dodger organization and naturally I want to see them win. I wouldn't want to feel that I was doing anything that would keep them from winning."[13]

Nevertheless, on April 15, 1947, Jackie Robinson made his debut in the major leagues. Unfortunately for him, there would be no repeat of his storybook opening in 1946 in Jersey City. He went hitless in three at-bats and was taken out late in the game for defensive purposes. He continued to struggle at the plate throughout the remainder of April. Due to his 0-for-20 hitting slump, Robinson was, according to Arthur Mann, "within a single day of being benched."[14]

To add to Robinson's woes, on April 22, the Dodgers returned to Ebbets Field for a three-game series with the Philadelphia Phillies. Phillies manager Ben Chapman ordered his players to challenge Robinson with a barrage of racial derisions "to see if he can take it." No topic was out of bounds for Chapman and his Phillies. According to Harold Parrott, "Chapman mentioned everything from thick lips to the supposedly extra thick Negro skull . . . [and] the repulsive sores and diseases he said Robinson's teammates would become infected with if they touched the towels he used." The assault continued throughout the series.[15]

Chapman's crusades had a devastating effect on Robinson. "I felt tortured and I tried just to play ball and ignore the insults," he recalled. Jack pondered what the Phillies wanted from him, and what Branch Rickey expected from him. "For one wild and raged-crazed moment I thought, 'To hell with Mr. Rickey's noble experiment' . . . To hell with the image of the patient black freak I was supposed to create." Despite his desire to retaliate, Robinson held his peace. He remembered his pact with Rickey that he would have "to bear indignities and humiliations without complaint."[16]

Robinson's misfortune was about to change, however. He began to improve at the plate, hitting safely in the first ten games in May, and batting .395 over that span. By June he had erased all doubts about his playing abilities. Jack's relationship with his Dodgers teammates began to improve. He continued a policy he had pursued in Montreal regarding his interactions with teammates. Robinson didn't sit with any white players unless he was asked to. This practice was consistent with his personality. "I sort of keep to myself by habit," he recalled. "Even in the colored leagues I was that way."[17]

Jackie Robinson went on to have an excellent rookie season. He finished with a .297 batting average, ranked second in the league in runs scored, and led the league in stolen bases. Robinson led the Dodgers in home runs, and he appeared in 151 of 154 games, despite his reputation for being injury prone. This was more games than anyone else on the club played.

From 1948 to 1956, freed from the restraints of the noble experiment, Jackie Robinson was instrumental in the Brooklyn Dodgers' phenomenal success on the diamond. The Dodgers never finished below third place, and they won five National League pennants and one World Series championship. They won consecutive pennants in 1952–53 and 1955–56. In 1948, Robinson had his best season in major league baseball. He led the National League with a .342 batting average and twenty-nine stolen bases. By 1955 and 1956, his performance on the field faltered after eight seasons in which he never batted below .296. Robinson played in only 105 games during the Dodgers' world championship season of 1955, batting only .256. He rebounded somewhat the following year, appearing in 117 games, hitting .275, and delivering a memorable game-winning hit in the World Series against the New York Yankees.

Robinson was still embroiled in controversy both on and off the field. In 1949, Robinson appeared before the House Un-American Activities Committee (HUAC) in response to statements made by former All-American football player, actor, and activist Paul Robeson in a speech he made in Paris, France. At first, Jack had been encouraged not to appear before the committee but, out of "a sense of responsibility," decided to "stick my neck out." He stated that he believed black Americans had legitimate grievances and "the fact that it is a Communist who denounces injustice in the courts, police brutality, and lynching when it happens doesn't change the truth of his charges." Racial discrimination in America was not "a creation of Communist imagination." Prior to his appearance before the HUAC, Robeson had written to Robinson to warn him that the press had "badly distorted" his remarks in Paris. Robinson explained that "if Mr. Robeson actually made" the statement attributed to him about American blacks refusing to fight in a war against Russia, it "sounds very silly to me . . . He has a right to his personal views, and if he wants to sound silly when he expresses them in public, that is his business not mine." From Robinson's perspective, however, as "a religious man" he cherished America as a place "where I am free to worship as I please"; "that doesn't mean that we're going to stop fighting race discrimination in this country until we've got it licked," but it did mean "we can win our fight without the Communists and we don't want their help." Three members of the committee joined in complementing Robinson on his "splendid statement."[18]

The appearance before the HUAC illustrated the paradoxical character of Jackie Robinson. Robinson became more active in the civil rights struggle after he retired from baseball in 1956, but he also campaigned actively for Richard Nixon in 1960. He became active in Republican politics at a time when the party was split between the liberal wing headed by New York governor Nelson Rockefeller and the conservative wing led by Arizona senator Barry Goldwater. In his last autobiography, *I Never Had It Made,* Robinson declared that he had no regrets regarding the statements he made before HUAC. But in fact he did. Disillusioned over both the conservative leadership of the NAACP and the apparent impasse over improving the plight of the average black person, he wrote in his autobiography:

> In those days I had much more faith in the ultimate justice of the American white man than I have today. I would reject such an invitation if offered now . . . I have grown wiser and closer to painful truths about America's destructiveness. And I do have increased respect for Paul Robeson who, over a span of twenty years, sacrificed himself, his career, and the wealth and comfort he once enjoyed because, I believe, he was sincerely trying to help his people.[19]

In the 1990s, scholars began to reexamine Jackie Robinson's life, as a myriad of studies emerged, many of which commemorated the fiftieth anniversary of his pioneering effort to break the color barrier in organized baseball. Scholars explored Robinson's role as a social activist after his playing career was over, reexamined the press coverage he received, and analyzed the prominent role of Jews in the struggle to break major league baseball's color line. Arnold Rampersad, the author of a two-volume life of Langston Hughes, contributed to this growing literature with what will probably be the most definitive Robinson biography. With Rachel Robinson's full cooperation, Rampersad had access to most of her personal letters and the archives at the Jackie Robinson Foundation.[20]

It is impossible to overestimate Robinson's importance not only as a gifted athlete who excelled in this country's national pastime during his era, but also as a political and social activist in the broader American society. His pioneering effort to break baseball's color barrier coincided with what the historian Manning Marable described as blacks making "decisive cracks in the citadel of white supremacy." Several prominent African Americans were appointed to key political positions that included Irvin C. Mollison, a black attorney, as an associate judge of the U.S. Customs Court; Charles S. Johnson, a black sociologist, appointed to the U.S. State Department position; and Ralph J. Bunche, who was appointed to the Anglo-American Caribbean position in the State Department. Several African American athletes began to make inroads in their respective sports that included Kenny Washington, Marion Motley, and Bill Willis in football and Chuck Cooper and Earl Lloyd in basketball. Early integration efforts indicate that black athletes embodied what can best be described as the "Jackie Robinson model." The few black athletes who entered the white sports world capitalized on their opportunities by striving for athletic excellence on the playing field. Concurrently, they accommodated to the social mores—particularly in the South—off the field, resulting in them, in some cases, being segregated from the rest of their teammates. This dual existence resulted in black athletes eventually gaining acceptance among their teammates, but not necessarily on the college campuses they resided on or in the cities in which professional athletes lived.[21]

This dual athletic existence undoubtedly fueled Robinson's desire to break down existing racial barriers to political, economic, and social equality. His efforts as a fund-raiser for the NAACP coincided with what historians August Meier and John Bracey referred to as a "revolution in expectations" among American blacks. A new sense of urgency to dismantle barriers to racial equality emerged, resulting in an outpouring of nonviolent direct action that, by the early 1960s, came to characterize this most recent phase of the civil rights movement. At times, Robinson's zeal to break down barriers to racial equality led to controversy. Raising funds for civil rights groups like the Southern Christian Leadership Conference (SCLC) strained his relationship with NAACP executive director Roy Wilkins. When Robinson was elected to the Hall of Fame in 1962, he staged a testimonial dinner for Martin Luther King Jr. and the SCLC's voter registration project in the South. Wilkins, invited to be an "honorary chairman" of the event, was furious. Aside from the loss of income to the SCLC, Wilkins was upset with Robinson for allowing King's group to take credit for voter registration efforts that in no way matched those of the NAACP. Considering that one of the NAACP's main focuses was voter registration at this time—particularly since President John F. Kennedy's administration was in full support of this effort—Wilkins's outrage was predictable.[22]

Yet Jackie Robinson's role as a social activist was an anomaly. On the one hand, he was a staunch assimilationist who sought the ultimate goal of integration into mainstream American society. He attempted to use his prestige and the example of his career to "open doors" for the NAACP and other civil rights organizations and to simultaneously build bridges to the white establishment. Robinson specifically appealed to establishment figures he knew, primarily politicians, who, according to Robinson, had shown sensitivity to civil rights issues. His support for Republican politicians like Richard Nixon, however, cost him some prestige with the African American public. More important, his support for Republican candidates conflicted with his central objective—the elimination of racial barriers as a means of group advancement. For example, Nixon's interest in civil rights and the black vote seemed frail next to his hunger for southern white support. The result was a tortuous campaign in which his denunciations of the "radical" Democratic platform sounded much louder than his general praise for progress in race relations.

On the other hand, Robinson's rhetoric was closer to a cultural black nationalist. His economic philosophy called for the creation of independent, self-sufficient black business enterprises and encouragement of black entrepreneurial endeavors. Robinson asserted that "blacks ought to become producers, manufacturing developers, and creators of business [and] providers of jobs." He added, "In addition to the economic security we could build with green power, we could use economic means to reinforce black power." Robinson reinforced his "green power" argument with a statement by Malcolm X, whom he disagreed with for many years. Referring to some college students who were fighting to be served in a Jim Crow restaurant, Malcolm wanted not only the cup of coffee, but also the cup and saucer, the counter, the store, and the land on which the restaurant existed.[23]

Robinson became involved in several ventures that exemplified his procapitalist stance. He was named co-chairman and director of the Manhattan-based Hamilton Life Insurance Company, which had $527 million worth of policies in force throughout the United States. His aim was to open a string of agencies in black neighborhoods to provide policies at reasonable rates. He asked other black athletes like Joe Louis, Sugar Ray Robinson, Hank Aaron, and Elston Howard to become partners in local Hamilton agencies, making the rounds with salesmen "to open the doors" of opportunity for African Americans. He continued to serve as a political aide for Governor Nelson Rockefeller. Toward the end of his life, he was involved with a construction firm that planned to build apartment houses in ghetto areas.

However, Hamilton Life Insurance proved to be a bad investment. Robinson invested $25,000 of his own money, most of which he never recovered. By 1967, the insurance company was $800,000 in debt. The following year, the Securities and Exchange Commission suspended over-the-counter trading in Hamilton stock. By March 1968, the state superintendent of insurance barred it from writing new policies.

Robinson also recognized the significance of fostering a new sense of racial pride and self-confidence. While he opposed total separation from mainstream America, he still acknowledged the necessity for blacks to stand apart and develop themselves independently. According to Robinson, blacks needed to establish their own sense of identity and the development of economic unity in order to build an independent power base to compete with whites on a level playing field. These accomplishments would allow blacks to negotiate from strength and self-respect rather than from a position of weakness. Malcolm X reinforced this notion. Speaking at a public rally in June 1964, Malcolm asserted that "we must recapture our heritage and our identity if we are to liberate ourselves from the bounds of white supremacy."[24]

Within this context, Robinson was a complex figure, admirable in many ways and paradoxical in others. This is what makes him so interesting to study, because his strengths and weaknesses exemplified the age that produced him. It was an age when the efforts to speed up the dismantling of racial barriers to equality ran high, but also an age when the progress to eliminate these obstacles occurred at a snail's pace, leading to calls of "Black Power" and the total separation of blacks from whites. No one performed better on the diamond under pressure than did Jackie Robinson. Yet no one was so naïve to think that celebrity status alone was sufficient enough to build bridges for individual blacks and civil rights organizations to the seat of corporate and political power. This combination of optimism and naïveté shaped his era and made Jackie Robinson the important man that he was. His is a story that teaches us what it means to be a pioneer, a social activist, and an exceptional high-performance athlete in America.

III The Fight for Civil Rights through Athletic Performance, Persuasion, and Protest

The integration of American sport following Jackie Robinson's entry into Major League baseball was a difficult and slow and uneven process. There were a number of sports that were especially resistant to integration and continue to be so to this very day. Tennis, swimming, golf, and other sports associated with private clubs and characterized by close informal contact between men and women both on the playing field and off have been very slow to desegregate. The sports that have seen more rapid integration have typically been those in which winning and commercial interests served as a stimulus to recruit the best players regardless of race or ethnicity. A disproportionate number of African American athletes have found their way into professional basketball and football as well as other revenue-generating sports at the intercollegiate level of competition.

Irrespective of the sports in which they have participated since Branch Rickey launched his noble experiment, African American athletes have experienced various forms of racial discrimination and inequality. Those African American athletes in the vanguard of the integration process during the 1950s and 1960s were confronted with humiliating discriminatory practices, including racial taunts from opponents and segregated accommodations in housing, transportation, and eating establishments. These more blatant forms of discrimination would gradually be eliminated as a result of relatively more liberalized attitudes toward race and civil rights legislation. In today's world African American athletes are still exposed to insensitivity and deep-seated stereotypical notions about the connections between race and both athletic and academic performance, but the more obvious forms of racial inequality are now found off the playing field and in the coaching profession as well as in the front offices of intercollegiate athletic departments and board rooms of professional sports franchises.

African Americans have, with some notable exceptions, been largely excluded from coaching, managerial, and other powerful administrative positions in sport.

Two of the more talented and important athletes of the second half of the twentieth century were Althea Gibson and Wilma Rudolph. Although they achieved fame in different sports and were quite opposite in temperament and personality, Gibson and Rudolph were similar in that they both hailed from the South, attended historically black colleges, and garnered worldwide athletic fame that resulted in their election to the International Women's Sports Hall of Fame in 1980. Gibson, born in Silver, South Carolina, became a legend in the African American community by capturing ten straight American Tennis Association (ATA) National Championships. In 1956 she became the first African American to win a grand-slam title by capturing the French Open. The following year she captured the Wimbledon and United States Lawn Tennis Association National Championships and in 1958 repeated the feat by once again winning both tournaments. In 1963 she launched her professional career in golf by joining the Ladies Professional Golf Association tour. Although never capturing a professional tournament in a nearly fifteen-year career, Gibson performed admirably on the tour with her best finish being a second-place tie in the 1970 Immke Buick Open in Columbus, Ohio.

In her essay "'Jackie Robinson without the Charm': The Challenges of Being Althea Gibson," Mary Jo Festle describes how difficult life was for Gibson and places the career of the great tennis champion in the context of other women athletes and the racial realities of both sport and the larger American society. Although Gibson spent her formative years in Harlem with her mother and abusive father, she eventually found a modicum of normalcy and the first real family she had ever known when as a teenager she moved in with Dr. Hubert Eaton and his wife in Wilmington, North Carolina. Festle speculates that this tough and disruptive childhood of Gibson perhaps helps explain her "notoriously difficult personality." Variously described as arrogant, aloof, insecure, moody, temperamental, tactless, and uncommunicative, Gibson seemingly had confrontations with almost everyone she encountered during her career. Gibson's difficult personality was combined with a reluctance to serve as a representative of her race. She wanted to be recognized for her athletic skills with the color of her skin being irrelevant to her success and was, to paraphrase from a passage in one of her autobiographies, unlike Jackie Robinson in that she shied away from a "role as a Negro battling for equality."

Rudolph's athletic career was decidedly shorter than Gibson's, but no less significant. Like Jesse Owens's great performance in Berlin in 1936, Rudolph was largely defined by one Olympiad. In the 1960 Games in Rome, the graceful track star from Tennessee State became the first American woman to win three gold medals by capturing the 100 meters, 200 meters, and 4 x 100 meter relay. Her dominating performance in Rome was made that much more appealing by virtue of the fact that she came from a poor family with twenty-two children, was diagnosed with polio and contracted scarlet fever and two bouts of pneumonia during her first two years of life, and wore a leg brace until the age of twelve. In essence, Rudolph's life was a classic success story recounted in her own 1977 autobiography and subsequent Hollywood movie.

Wayne Wilson, in his essay "Wilma Rudolph: The Making of an Olympic Icon," points out that Rudolph's meteoric rise to stardom resulted from a number of factors. Her extraordinary athleticism and the fact she was the first American woman to capture three gold medals in Olympic competition was a major factor in her star power. Another factor was her sheer physical beauty. Still another factor, at least in the United States, was that Rudolph's victories were against Soviet Union and Eastern European athletes during the cold war period. In essence, her triumphs took on symbolic importance because of the ideological warfare between the East and West during the 1950s and 1960s.

Tellingly, Rudolph was similar to Althea Gibson in that she generally avoided bringing attention to herself by speaking out on larger racial issues and civil rights. Her marginal status as a woman athlete combined with the nature of her personality precluded her more active involvement in the black power struggle and civil rights movement of the late 1960s and early 1970s. She was also similar to other African American women athletes in that she was not encouraged to participate alongside her male counterparts in protesting racial inequality in sport and the larger American society. For all intents and purposes, the much written about black athletic revolt of this period was a male athletic revolt as much as anything else. Confronted by racial discrimination, challenged by a caste system that allowed them few opportunities to display their masculinity, and having their honor challenged by more radical members of the African American community necessitated that African American male athletes consciously exert both their sense of racial pride and manhood by pushing African American female athletes into the background and not actively seeking their participation in the struggle for equal rights on the playing field and in the country more generally.

Three men who helped lead the black athletic revolt through both their words and actions were Bill Russell, Jim Brown, and Muhammad Ali. Russell, the great center who led the University of San Francisco to two NCAA championships and the Boston Celtics to eleven NBA championships, was one of the unquestioned leaders of the revolt. In her essay "Bill Russell: Pioneer and Champion of the Sixties," Maureen Smith makes clear that Russell was a man of enormous conviction and intelligence. He inspired younger African American athletes by refusing to acquiesce to the white power structure and speaking out passionately about black pride. Unlike any African American athlete before him and with great effect, Russell articulated the frustrations of many in the African American community and passionately voiced how proud he was to be a black man in American culture and sharing in the problem of those of his race. He "truly was and is a symbolic figure," writes Smith, "in the crusade for progress and justice in American sport and society."

Jim Brown, considered by many to be the greatest running back in NFL history, was of the same ilk as Russell, except with a bit more edge and defiance. He was always outspoken about the racial inequities in American society, whether it was during his nine-year professional football career or during his years as a Hollywood actor or during the recent past when he has worked to eliminate gang violence. This outspokenness combined with his history of physical assaults, notes Tom Jable in "Jim Brown: Superlative Athlete, Screen Star, Social Activist," resulted in much criticism of Brown and his problems with the law. At the same time, writes Jable, Brown has done much good, working diligently to improve the economic conditions of the African American community and assist troubled youth in becoming productive members of society. Brown has, in turn, been highly critical of many contemporary black athletes for their seeming lack of interest in improving the lives of members of the African American community. To Brown, many athletes of today, including Michael Jordan, Charles Barkley, and Tiger Woods, are more interested in accumulating money than helping those less fortunate than themselves.

Muhammad Ali, even more so than Bill Russell or Jim Brown, became the athlete most closely identified with the civil rights movement. Noncontroversial early in his career, everything changed in 1964 when Ali announced his membership in the Nation of Islam and then later refused military service on account of his religious beliefs. To many, Ali's pronouncements were alternately viewed as terrifying, treacherous, and un-American. To others, Ali's pronouncements brought him admiration and respect for his courageous stand and convictions. He served, among other things, as the inspiration for Harry Edwards and the African American athletes who led the proposed boycott of the 1968 Olympic Games in Mexico City. Ultimately, the sheer passage of time, the changing nature of the Nation of Islam, improved race relations in American society, and a host of other societal factors brought Ali near mythical status and an unparalleled place in the public consciousness that perhaps culminated most visibly in his lighting of the Olympic flame in Atlanta in 1996.

Gerald Early makes clear, however, that Ali was an extremely complex man who possessed many strengths, but also many weaknesses. In his essay "Muhammad Ali: Flawed Rebel with a Cause," Early contends that Ali changed the way people thought of black athletes. Very confident and boastful, Ali "made white America more aware" of Islam and black militancy while at once coming "to represent racial pride, strong religious principles, and youthful exuberance." But he also came to represent, says Early, something less positive. He never did anything to improve the lives of those in the boxing profession. Not a particularly smart or astute man outside the ring, Ali denigrated his opponents (especially black opponents), exhibiting "a lack of sportsmanship that was hardly excused by the need for a big gate." He was also a hypocrite, regularly violating the tenets of his religion, yet refusing to acknowledge that he ever did so.

The life of Arthur Ashe differed markedly from Ali, Jim Brown, and Bill Russell. The Richmond native and UCLA graduate realized his fame in tennis, a traditionally white upper-class sport most closely associated with suburban country clubs. He captured the prestigious U.S. Open singles title in 1968, the coveted Wimbledon singles title in 1975, and was captain and a member of several winning Davis Cup teams. Ashe was equally successful off the court. He fought valiantly to improve the education of African American youth, actively protested the apartheid policies in South Africa, and became a spokesperson for AIDS after he was stricken with the illness. Ashe was also a prolific writer, penning three coauthored autobiographical accounts of his life and career, and publishing a book on the history of African American involvement in sport.

In his essay "'The Quiet Militant': Arthur Ashe and Black Athletic Activism," Damion Thomas describes the struggle Ashe experienced in trying to reconcile the simultaneous demands made upon him by the tennis establishment, black power movement, and more conservative civil rights movement. Self described as "intensely independent" and a "reconciler rather than a divider of persons," the highly intelligent and soft-spoken Ashe faced criticism from some black athletes for not speaking out more boldly against racial inequities in sport and the larger American society. Black athletes of the period, including the likes of Tommie Smith, Lew Alcindor, and others, viewed individual athletic achievements as inadequate to break down the walls of racial discrimination. Ashe ultimately responded to demands to be more socially active and to help improve the conditions of members of his race, but in accordance with his value system that had been nurtured as a young child growing up in the segregated South and as a participant in one of the world's most elitist sports. One of the most notable examples of this approach, writes Thomas, was Ashe's much publicized involvement in the fight against apartheid in South Africa, a fight that brought him much respect and secured his reputation as a great humanitarian.

11 "Jackie Robinson without the Charm"

The Challenges of Being Althea Gibson

MARY JO FESTLE

In her 1958 autobiography, international women's tennis champion Althea Gibson recalled a telling incident from her childhood. A classmate known for being big and tough kept provoking her, pulling her hair, and ignoring requests to leave her alone. Finally Gibson had enough and said she would meet the girl outside after school. Word spread that there was going to be a fight, so a crowd gathered to hear them curse each other and prepare for battle. After the girl called her a "pig-tailed bitch," Gibson punched her rival in the face "so hard she just fell like a lump. Honest to God," she recalled, "she was out cold. Everybody backed away from me and just stared at me, and I turned around like I was Joe Louis and walked on home."[1]

This relatively minor incident foreshadowed some important aspects of Althea Gibson's life. It demonstrated her willingness to take on a challenge, which she did repeatedly in her seventy-six years, occasionally biting off more than she could chew. The story also hinted at the rough childhood that helped shape her fiercely independent and sometimes difficult personality. The fight illustrated both her athletic ability and propensity to engage in behavior considered unfeminine, while the reference to Joe Louis indicated her awareness of the popular boxing champ and race hero to whom she would later be compared when she grew up. Gibson would find the role of pioneering race representative such an unwelcome burden, though, that one journalist called her "Jackie Robinson without charm."[2] Althea Gibson was the first African American to play in and win the United States Lawn Tennis Association (USLTA) national championship and the ladies' championship at Wimbledon, and her achievements were as significant as those of men like Louis and Robinson, even if she was never as beloved by either blacks or whites. Gibson's life was a

Althea Gibson poses for the camera in 1956, the same year she became the first African American to capture a grand-slam tennis title by winning the French Open. *(Library of Congress)*

difficult one, and the obstacles she faced were enormous. She brought a few of them upon herself, but most resulted from the multiple levels of discrimination she suffered in the midcentury context, as a female in an athletic world that marginalized women, a working-class woman trying to break into an elitist sport, and a black woman in a racist nation, world, and sport. Although race, class, and gender combined to level repeated blows, she rolled with the punches.

Born August 25, 1927, in Silver, South Carolina, Althea Gibson was the child of sharecroppers Daniel and Annie Gibson, who like many southern blacks looked to the North for a more rewarding way of life. When she was one year old, Althea was sent to live with her mother's sister in New York with the plan that her parents would eventually join her. Later Althea lived at least a few years with another aunt in Philadelphia. Perhaps a decade passed before her whole immediate family—father, mother, Althea, three sisters, and a brother—lived together in New York, where her father worked as a garage attendant. By then, young Althea disliked school and played hooky frequently. She claimed she was "mischievous" (occasionally shoplifting and fighting) but didn't get into any "real trouble." She loved going to the movies, hanging out at the pool hall, bowling, and playing "paddle tennis,"[3] stickball, and softball. Her basketball club played contests up to four times a week, and she excelled because of her height (approximately 5 feet, 10½ inches) and her natural athletic ability. When she dropped out of school, Gibson worked odds jobs or lived on an allowance given by some "ladies from the Welfare Department." Eschewing dresses and skirts for slacks, she termed herself "the wildest tomboy you ever saw" who "didn't like people telling me what to do."[4]

Gibson's toughness was shaped by both her neighborhood and her family. She described Harlem as a "mean place to grow up in," a place where a kid had to prove herself by fighting to keep from being considered an "easy mark."[5] She encountered violence at home, too, including "some terrible whippings" for repeatedly running away. After one time when she hadn't been home a couple nights in a row, her father greeted her arrival with a powerful punch to her face. On at least one occasion, she went to a police station and reported that she was afraid to go home because her father was going to beat her up; after the police called her parents and she returned home, she got beaten for having gone to the police. At least twice she went to the Society for Prevention of Cruelty to Children, showing its officials big red welts on her back that came from her father's strap. She stayed there some nights, considering the dormitory far better than home, where "somebody was always yelling at me or, worse, hitting me."[6] In what seems to have been the classic response of an abused child, Gibson did not criticize her father for these beatings in her autobiography; in fact, she said that she loved him, that he was actually a patient man simply trying to teach her right from wrong, and that she deserved the beatings because of her misbehavior.[7] It's suggestive, though, that Gibson left home permanently as soon as possible and that her parents made relatively few appearances in her public discussions about her life. Later in her teens, when she lived with Dr. Hubert Eaton in Wilmington, North Carolina, she discovered what she termed "the first real family life I had ever known," and she called Dr. Eaton "Dad" and his wife, "Mom."[8] Gibson's parents gave their permission for Althea to stay with the Eatons, but after that, had no further contact with the Eatons. When Althea eventually graduated from Florida A and M College, the Eatons were the only "family" who attended the ceremony. Years after Gibson had been playing important national and international tournaments, including some in New York, her birth parents had never seen her play tennis.

While analyzing someone's psychology based on published accounts is necessarily speculative, it seems likely that a violent and abusive childhood, disruptions in family life, and growing up on the streets of a tough neighborhood go a long way toward explaining Gibson's notoriously difficult personality. One sportswriter said the adjectives most commonly used to describe Gibson were "arrogant," "moody," "temperamental," "tactless," and "aloof."[9] Even those closest to her agreed with those characterizations. One of her best friends on the tour, British player Angela Buxton, said that Gibson gave the impression of being "cold, unapproachable, assertive, and domineering." Her coach recognized that she had personality problems, including becoming uncommunicative and deeply depressed. Another friend observed that as a young woman, Gibson was unhappy, insecure, and prone to pull into herself.[10] Gibson acknowledged most of these traits. Although a certain swagger could help intimidate opponents, she knew it could be problematic as well, referring later in life to cockiness as "that old devil of mine" and to a "swelled head" as her "nemesis."[11] To many observers it seemed that the arrogance was actually a smokescreen for a lack of confidence. Later, Gibson said that showing off was a defense mechanism that she had adopted early in life. As for being aloof, she admitted that not allowing people to get close to her was a "fault" and attributed it to growing up suspicious and withdrawn, a loner wary about trusting any part of herself to anyone. Surely her fiercely independent streak served her well in her efforts to be a pioneer, but such independence could be double-edged: throughout her life, she suffered from depression and loneliness.

Although it might be expected that a tough and independent tomboy would gravitate toward sports, being a female athlete was difficult in the 1950s. Serious female athletes certainly existed, but they were still considered unusual. After all, sports required traits that were not associated with femininity, including assertiveness, aggressiveness, intensity, competitiveness, the desire to excel, physical exertion, and strength. An athlete frequently sweated and grimaced and rarely looked pretty in the conventional sense. Participation in sports was assumed to help boys develop into men, meaning that girls who competed risked being turned into men as well. A lack of resources—in terms of teams, funding, coaching, and facilities—contributed to the relatively small numbers of serious female athletes in the 1950s, but the ideology that sports was "unfeminine" was probably the most powerful inhibitor. Aware of the connotations of "masculine" female athletes as abnormal, immoral, uncouth, sexually promiscuous, or lesbian, females themselves chose not to participate and people rarely encouraged them to. Sportswriters ignored or ridiculed female athletes; school administrators said they wanted to produce homemakers, not athletes; other men said, "We like our women beautiful and feminine. We don't want to marry Amazons."[12] In the postwar period, women were no longer encouraged to be the independent, skilled workers needed during the war; now they were supposed to return home to traditional roles as helpmates and submissive mothers. It is not surprising, then, that females who wanted to participate in sports felt they had to adopt "apologetic behaviors," such as wearing hyper-feminine apparel and makeup, playing by special "girls' rules," hosting teas after "play days" instead of competitive intercollegiate contests, and reassuring reporters that they truly were "normal" women who didn't take sports too seriously and who wanted to get married.[13]

It was surprising, then, that any women in the postwar period had the nerve to challenge norms and participate in sports, but many did. There were barnstorming basketball teams, local bowling and softball leagues, and heartfelt intramural contests in schools. A handful of colleges awarded athletic scholarships, tennis and golf clubs offered occasional ladies' days, and some cities held AAU track meets. Probably the one common factor explaining how all these girls and women had the nerve to defy convention was that they had some sort of community support. That support might have come from employer or newspaper sponsorship, neighborhood pride, ethnic or religious organizations, the lesbian community, a YMCA or police department, or a dedicated parent. Some have argued that the African American community was more accepting of female athletes than the white middle class because black women, who historically required enormous emotional strength and needed to work outside the home, had a less restrictive definition of femininity.[14] Hopeful that adulation for athletes might benefit the whole race and that integration in sports might spread to other arenas, some black newspapers embraced female star athletes, and a few black colleges offered athletic scholarships to them. However, athletic success for black women could cut the opposite way, reinforcing disparaging stereotypes of black women as less feminine than white women.[15]

Understandably then, the black community was not unanimous in its attitude toward female athletes. A generation of girls in Baltimore, for example, grew up hearing comments like those of the *Baltimore Afro-American* sportswriter who said, "The girl who is too athletic is on the wrong track to becoming a wife. Men want feminine women."[16] One historian believes that the division among blacks cut primarily along class lines: that the middle class doubted that athleticism was compatible with femininity, while working-class and rural women enthusiastically embraced sports.[17] In that vein, in 1940 the National Association of College Women (just like its white counterpart) urged black women's colleges to eliminate intercollegiate athletics for women. Nevertheless, some saw positive potential in women's sports, including the respected physical educator Edwin B. Henderson, who acknowledged the fear that black women athletes would "lose some of their charm," but asserted that "so long as women of other races and other nations engage in these sports with no proven evidence of detriment, our girls have reason and right to compete." For him, racial achievement trumped gender concerns, since "victory in physical contests . . . helped kill off the Nazi-inspired doctrine of inferiority."[18] Hoping to win acceptance as both athletes and "normal" women, black athletes, coaches, teams, and organizations exhibited various kinds of apologetic behavior. Tennessee State's track coach Ed Temple, for example, tried to counteract masculine stereotypes by insisting on a strict dress code for his athletes and telling the press, "None of my girls have any trouble getting boyfriends. I tell them they are young ladies first, track girls second."[19] Similarly, the American Tennis Association held an annual "Miss ATA" contest honoring the most popular and pretty tennis competitors, complete with crown, evening gown, flowers, and dance.

Althea Gibson suffered the usual tribulations of the female athlete. In high school she wanted more opportunities than were offered girls, so she practiced with the football and baseball teams. As a result, she remembered, her classmates "looked at me like I was a freak," which "used to hurt me real bad."[20] Later, when she began to receive attention for her tennis, the press coverage often used gendered terms. "Right from the start," declared *Time* magazine, "Althea grimly set her lips and set out to play a man's game." Referring to her by her first name when it spoke of the male champ by his last name, the article also said she ranged the court "like a restless panther" and served "with unladylike gusto."[21] Of course, top women tennis players were used to snubs. They often had to play on the back courts, and they received less attention from the press. The attention they did receive often insulted them, and virtually every champion heard references to her "masculine" strokes as though she were the first female player ever to be strong. The fact that Gibson was tall, had a powerful serve, and played a serve and volley style of game provided additional reasons to refer to her "man's game." Media coverage also implied that she was overly serious and determined. One columnist for the *Baltimore Afro-American* actually attributed Gibson's difficult personality to the inherent contradiction in being female and an athlete:

> Gibson became not only the best girl athlete in her community, but as good as most of the boys as well. In one respect, this is good. All kids like to excel in sports. But in another, it isn't so good. When girls are able to play "boys'" sports well and better than the boys,

> they acquire "tomboy" labels. In later life the "tomboy" finds herself victimized by complexes. Miss Gibson is no exception. She has a way of going into her hard shell and refusing to come out of it.[22]

If all female athletes faced certain common problems in midcentury, things were somewhat better for tennis players because of the sport's upper-class reputation. Played first in the United States in the late nineteenth century by people who could afford to build private courts or belong to country clubs with finely manicured grass courts, the game had elaborate unwritten rules for gracious behavior both on the court and off. As one champion put it, a player had to "learn the book of social etiquette backwards."[23] Over time the construction of public courts opened the game up somewhat, but in 1950 a small elitist group still exerted tight control over the United States Lawn Tennis Association, and due to class even some white players felt uncomfortable and unaccepted in tennis circles. Although this exclusiveness could prove difficult, it also had its benefits. Those who were accepted could count on the hospitality of wealthy tennis patrons in their travels. Another benefit was that the game was considered appropriate for women. This more feminine reputation probably resulted from both its upper-class history and the fact that it was an individual and noncontact sport. Women played from the game's beginning, padding about the court in their long dresses and corsets, lightly tapping the ball. Even at midcentury, the stereotypical female player was "a nice girl who used the game like she used the foxtrot—as a social skill."[24] Aware of this proper reputation, many parents urged their athletically minded daughters to channel their competitive instincts away from other sports and toward tennis. The ritzy West Side Tennis Club in Forest Hills, New York, was the site of the annual USLTA national championship and a place where "the polite plunk of tennis balls, the whisper of sneakers on trim grass courts, the tinkle of ice in frost-beaded glasses still recall[ed] the long-gone white-flannel days of the courts."[25] As one might imagine, the social distance between Forest Hills and Gibson's neighborhood in Harlem was much further than the actual subway ride. When Gibson was first introduced to tennis, she found the elaborate rules silly, and therefore she regularly insulted her opponents.[26] After a while, however, she began to understand "that you could walk out on the court like a lady, all dressed up in immaculate white, be polite to everybody, and still play like a tiger and beat the liver and lights out of the ball."[27] That adaptation would be necessary if Gibson were ever to be allowed into invitation-only tournaments.

If the elitist nature of the sport made it far more difficult for a working-class player to be invited, it also was one reason many African Americans were eager to be included. College students and professionals were among the blacks who embraced the sport in the late nineteenth century. Snubbed by white-owned venues, they built their own courts and clubs and in 1916 organized the American Tennis Association (ATA). By midcentury, there were about 150 black tennis clubs in the nation, and the ATA hosted over thirty annual events, including a national championship. Encouraged by the changing political atmosphere and improvements for black male athletes in sports like major league baseball, professional football, and basketball in the postwar period, the ATA leaders had high hopes for the integration of tennis and began behind-the-scenes conversations about allowing ATA players into a USLTA tournament. However, Althea Gibson's potential entry into the USLTA represented much more than just another sport in the growing list of integrated sports, not only because Gibson was female, but also because of all that tennis represented. Tennis's reputation as appropriate for women was much better than that of basketball; indeed, many black colleges had eliminated basketball and other sports for women while retaining tennis.[28] Tennis was also more attractive for women than track and field, as *Ebony* magazine noted when it observed track did not "carry the glamour of tennis."[29] Nor was tennis brutish and primitive like men's boxing, nor as democratic as baseball. Indeed, tennis was appealing precisely because it was elitist. Entering integrated tournaments and clubs would allow whites to meet middle-class blacks who would counteract the stereotype that all blacks were poor, uneducated, and uncouth. In turn, those gracious blacks might influence the wealthy and educated whites who ruled tennis and the wider world. *Ebony* stated it well: by making good in this "snobbish" society, Althea Gibson could reach "over the masses to win the support of the few who frequently influence the masses."[30]

If she'd "made it," Gibson asserted, it was "half because I was game to a wicked amount of punishment along the way and half because there were an awful lot of people who cared enough to help me."[31] Indeed, many hands helped her along the path to stardom, including the

Police Athletic League supervisor who encouraged her to try tennis and the club pro at Harlem's Cosmopolitan Club, where she received free lessons, rackets, and membership. At the ATA national women's singles championship in 1946, Gibson impressed ATA officials and two tennis patrons in particular, Dr. Hubert A. Eaton and Dr. Robert W. Johnson. "Knowing that the Jim Crow signs on the tennis courts of the world had to come down sooner or later and that a strong black contender should be waiting in the wings," Eaton recalled, "Dr. Johnson and I began to plan Althea's future."[32] They hatched a scheme by which Gibson would spend the school year with the Eaton family in Wilmington, North Carolina, catching up on the education she'd missed out on, and during the summers she'd travel with Johnson, who shuttled promising players to ATA tournaments. Friends "Sugar" Ray and Edna Robinson encouraged Gibson to seize the opportunity. Middle-class southern life proved to be difficult (she wasn't permitted to visit pool halls, for example), and segregated movie theaters infuriated her, but Gibson adjusted. Having some "difficulty taking Harlem out of Althea," Eaton tried to teach her lessons in both tennis and self-discipline, and his wife tried to make her more feminine by making her wear dresses, straighten her hair, and use lipstick.[33] After taking three years to finish high school, Gibson won an athletic scholarship to Florida A and M College. The college had no women's tennis team, but she practiced with the men's team, starred on the women's basketball team, and regularly won ATA championships. "For what it was worth," Gibson recalled, "I was the best woman player in Negro tennis."[34]

Getting the chance to play against the best white players, though, would require even more help. After much lobbying by ATA officials, the USLTA opened its door a crack. In March 1948, Reginald Weir, a thirty-eight-year-old doctor and the top ATA male player, broke the color line at the U.S. Indoor Championships. Then Gibson was allowed into a couple of tournaments in 1949 and 1950, but not into the prestigious National Championships, supposedly because she had not proven herself in the lead-up grass-court tournaments. The problem was that the lead-up tournaments were in the hands of local (and racist) private clubs who had discretion over who was invited. "Miss Gibson is over a very cunningly-wrought barrel," wrote Alice Marble, a white former women's champion, giving tennis authorities the very public push they needed.[35] In her July 1950 letter to *American Lawn Tennis* magazine, Marble castigated tennis officials. "If tennis is a game for ladies and gentlemen, it's also time we acted a little more like gentlepeople and less like sanctimonious hypocrites." Marble's appeal embarrassed the USLTA, and shortly thereafter, Gibson was allowed to compete at the Eastern Grass Court Championship. Her performance there and in subsequent weeks convinced USLTA officials that she deserved an invitation to the National Championships at Forest Hills, New York.

Gibson made quite a splash at Forest Hills in 1950. She won her first-round match easily, the only controversy being that the match had been scheduled for a small remote court that couldn't possibly accommodate all the interested spectators. In the second round, Gibson faced reigning Wimbledon champ Louise Brough. Gibson's nerves showed in the first set, which she lost. In the second set, Gibson found her powerful serve and volley and won. A closely matched third set saw the two players trading the lead, with Gibson on the brink of victory when a thunderstorm interrupted play. After a bolt of lightning struck down one of the stone eagles resting on the stadium, many believed that traditions were truly toppling. When play resumed the next day, though, a rested Brough defeated a nervous Gibson.

Although she narrowly lost the match at Forest Hills, Gibson won a national reputation as a race pioneer. "Obviously, they all felt that what I had done was important not just to me but to all Negroes,"[36] she observed after a parade of fans and a 100-piece marching band greeted her return to Florida A and M. The *New York Amsterdam News* agreed.

> When Althea Gibson walked out on the court in Forest Hills Monday, she did so with the knowledge that millions of Americans, black and white, were rooting for her and hoping that, like Jackie Robinson, she would hit that ball and place it where the opposing racqueteer happened not to be. . . . Like Joe Louis, awaiting his chance at the title in 1937, she was a symbol of hope and a race group's faith in the unpredictable future.[37]

Seeing her as the next Jackie Robinson, black communities rallied around her cause. In Detroit, for example, a group raised $770 for her expenses. Joe Louis himself donated a round-trip airline ticket to London, where the next year she would become the first black player to compete at

Wimbledon. A syndicated sportswriter called her the most impressive black athlete of 1950. "First of her race to compete on the tennis courts of snobbish Forest Hills," he wrote, she had "moral strength that far transcended the physical powers" of the world's strongest man.[38] Never mentioning her difficult personality in the early 1950s, the black press portrayed her very positively. The *Pittsburgh Courier* said she had "an abundance of personal charm" and that she "handled herself well." An article in the *Chicago Defender* described her as modest, gracious, and a "lady off the court."[39]

While her debut in integrated tennis was impressive, over the next few years Gibson did not advance as fast as she hoped. For one thing, instead of opening the door wide for African American players at all USLTA tournaments, the white-run organization instead decided to permit only the top male and female ATA players into its national championships. This quota arrangement—a separate but unequal sort of tokenism—allowed USLTA-affiliated private clubs to exclude black players if they wished and denied black players the year-round competition necessary to be world-class players. Gibson's individual results were disappointing as well. Perhaps because she lacked topflight competition and coaching or perhaps because she was not ready to handle the pressure, she did not seem to play her best when it mattered most. In the mid-1950s, her national ranking was actually dropping instead of rising, and one black publication called her "the biggest disappointment in tennis."[40] Discouraged, she considered quitting the sport.

At this crucial moment in her career, Gibson's race actually worked to her advantage. The U.S. State Department was sponsoring cultural "goodwill tours" in a cold war effort to persuade developing countries of the superiority of American democratic capitalism. Gibson fit the bill perfectly as a talented participant who could demonstrate that bad publicity about American racism was simply propaganda and that despite legalized segregation and incidents like the murder of Emmett Till, American blacks had the chance to succeed. Invited to play in a series of tennis exhibitions throughout Asia in the winter of 1955–56, Gibson understood the government's goal and didn't mind helping achieve it. She jumped at the opportunity to be paid for traveling around the world and enjoying months of steady competition in the company of three other top players. Both her game and her confidence improved dramatically as a result of the tour. After she finished her official duties, she remained abroad another six months, winning the French championship and sixteen out of eighteen tournaments she entered. When in 1956 she paired with Angela Buxton to win the women's doubles title at Wimbledon, she was on the brink of reaching her potential.

It was in 1957 that Gibson put it all together. Now accustomed to winning tournaments, she was a wiser, more experienced player, less likely to fold under pressure and brandishing more consistent strokes. At Wimbledon in 1957, she sailed through the early singles rounds, and in typically confident fashion, predicted that in a match against British player Christine Truman, she'd "gobble her up."[41] In the final round of play, she defeated Californian Darlene Hard easily, in less than an hour. "At last! At last!" she cried. After the victory at this most prestigious of events, Gibson was feted like never before. At the Wimbledon ball, she danced with the men's champ, sang for the crowd, and thanked her friends, coaches, the ATA, the USLTA, and Drs. Johnson and Eaton. She seemed to enjoy every minute of the celebration, including shaking hands with the Queen and receiving congratulatory messages from admirers, including President Dwight Eisenhower. She returned home to a hero's welcome: a ticker-tape parade down Broadway, a medallion presented by the mayor at city hall, and a celebration in her old neighborhood. Everyone—New Yorkers, Americans, journalists, blacks and whites—lauded her achievement. The sports columnist for the *Baltimore Afro-American* called her win at Wimbledon "the greatest triumph a colored athlete has accomplished in my time."[42] After Wimbledon, Gibson went to Forest Hills and finally won the U.S. national women's singles championship there as well, resulting in even more honors. As the number-one player in the world, Gibson consistently excelled. In the following year, she successfully defended both her Wimbledon and Forest Hills titles.

Being the black tennis champion proved to be a mixed blessing, however. Discrimination might surface at any time. It wasn't the verbal or physical abuse that Jackie Robinson suffered, but there were places—even in the North—where she couldn't stay at the same place as the other players. There was a restaurant that tried to undermine a luncheon intended to honor her. There was the year she wasn't asked to play on the American Davis Cup team, even though she thought she deserved the bid. Her matches were sometimes relegated to side courts that champions didn't usually play on. There was "cool" treatment from spectators in many cities. Whether that was due to her personality or race it will never be known for sure, but one reporter overheard a spectator saying scornfully, "Joe Louis became a champ. And what happened? Nigger boxers came out from every stone. Same thing if Gibson walks away from here with a tennis pot."[43] Beyond clearly discriminatory treatment was the experience of being a novelty. She tired of being the only black player in the locker rooms, the first in many country clubs. Some people were patronizing while others were noticeably uncomfortable because they'd never known a black person. Her astonished roommate on the goodwill tour had never seen anything like how Gibson took care of her hair. Whether because of her aloofness, her race, her class, or some combination of factors, she never really fit in on the tour. In addition, she missed being around other blacks. She was lonely, and it was hard to always have her guard up.

Another unexpected disappointment was her treatment in many black newspapers. While the black press certainly lauded her *achievements,* less frequently did it praise *her.* In some papers, she claimed, she was "uncomfortably close to Public Enemy No. 1."[44] Beginning in 1956, negative stories abounded. After Russ Cowans of the *Chicago Defender* called her "ungracious as a stubborn jackass" and "the most arrogant athlete it has been my displeasure to meet," other papers began debating her personality.[45] Earlier in the decade, the black press had referred to Gibson's personal charm and character if they had commented at all about her personality, so why the change? It is possible that Gibson herself changed, since one article said she was "giving herself airs since her phenomenal contests throughout the world" and another that she'd "turned into a prima donna."[46] It may have been that in the crush of eager journalists, Gibson was not paying sufficient attention to the black journalists who had followed her career closely for years. Indeed, the immediate impetus for the "stubborn jackass" story was an incident at a tournament in Chicago where she rudely brushed off some black reporters. It may also have just been unlucky timing for Gibson. One journalist said that for many years the black press had treated black star athletes with kid gloves, as though they were beyond censure, but in the mid-1950s they'd decided to criticize black athletes when they said or did negative things.[47] Perhaps this new approach meant the black press would no longer ignore Gibson's difficult personality. Another possibility—the one Gibson believed—was that the black press turned on her because she did not sufficiently use her fame to advance the cause of integration.

Whatever the actual reasons for their criticism, it is certainly true that Gibson struggled with the expectations of being a race representative. She agreed with the observation that while Jackie Robinson "thrived on his role as a Negro battling for equality," she shied away from it.[48] Even as a young player at the Cosmopolitan Club, she resented club members' hypersensitivity about etiquette, and the pressure to behave properly magnified when she was on the national and international stage. "It was a strain, always trying to say and do the right thing, so that I wouldn't give people the wrong idea of what Negroes were like."[49] Gibson felt as though she were on display every minute. Articles about her in both the black and white press invariably mentioned her race, but she didn't want to have race on her mind all the time; she wanted to be considered "just another tennis player, not a Negro tennis player."[50] Her logic made sense—as she said, nobody referred to the race of white players—and her desire was understandable. Basically, she was a woman who wanted nothing more than to win in sports, and ideally race should have been irrelevant. At that point in history, however, her desire to be considered simply an athlete was impossible. As one black columnist put it, "She represents 16 million of her people in the field of tennis. Therefore she is obligated as a goodwill ambassador. Maybe she doesn't like the role, but it's hers automatically . . . and she's stuck with it."[51] Her reluctance to embrace this role became increasingly evident. She told reporters that she was going to concentrate on playing just for herself. "I tried to feel my responsibilities to Negroes, but that was a burden on my shoulders. If I did this or that, would they like it? Perhaps it contributed to my troubles in tennis. Now I'm playing tennis to please me, not them."[52] This desire allowed her to feel free, and it would not have been criticized in a white athlete, but it offended many of her fans. Black newspapers more frequently portrayed her as selfish and rude, and implied she was disloyal, unappreciative, and thought herself superior to others.

Her specific political approach may have also been part of the problem. In public statements made while abroad, she didn't criticize discrimination as strongly as she might have. "Sure we have a problem in the States, as every country has its problems," *Time* magazine quoted her. "But it's a problem that's solving itself, I believe."[53] She seemed overly optimistic about the possibility of blacks achieving equal treatment without protest and advocacy. "I feel that if I am a worthy person, and if I have something worth while to contribute, I will be accepted on my own merits." For that reason, she said,

> I do not beat the drums for any special cause, not even the cause of the Negro in the United States. . . . This doesn't mean that I'm opposed to the fight for integration of the schools or other movements like that. It simply means that in my own career I try to steer clear of political involvements and make my way as Althea Gibson, private individual.[54]

Although in her youth Gibson didn't mind defying conventions, in her prime Gibson was unwilling to rock the boat politically: she downplayed racial problems in the United States, stayed mum about racism she encountered from players, and never criticized the USLTA.

Gibson did try to defend herself against the criticism, though. After returning home from Wimbledon, she explained, she had been fatigued from months of international competition, was overwhelmed by the requests for interviews, and had intended to treat all reporters with respect. She said that although it wasn't her primary purpose, obviously she was happy if her success helped other blacks. She also suggested the expectations of her were unfair:

> Having to contend with crowds hostile to me because of my color, with newspapermen demanding twice as much of me as they did of anybody else because my color made me newsworthy, and even with powerful governments seeking to use me as an instrument of national policy because of my color, seemed to me to be more than anybody should have to bear.[55]

A few others spoke out on her behalf, saying that she was not obligated to be at the beck and call of reporters, that her critics didn't know the real her or understand the impossible expectations suddenly thrust upon her, or that people were jealous of her success. Undoubtedly Gibson's mistrustful nature did not help matters. She suspected that people who suddenly came out of the woodwork and acted friendly actually wanted to take advantage of her.[56] While it's difficult to sort out the degree to which her problems with the black press were caused by her politics or by her personality, there's no doubt that the role of "Negro tennis champion" was far less pleasurable to Gibson than that of "tennis champion."

If her years as Wimbledon and Forest Hills champ were somewhat difficult, in retrospect they were a high point. "I may be Queen of Tennis right now," she declared in 1958, "but I reign over an empty bank account."[57] Indeed, the very best female tennis stars in the 1950s were lucky if they could barely get by on the limited amount of money amateurs were permitted to accept for their expenses; most relied on parents, husbands, or part-time jobs. As a thirty-one-year-old single woman, Gibson was tired of depending on others for financial assistance and wanted to earn enough money for nice things and an apartment of her own. So after she won Forest Hills for the second time in 1958, she retired from amateur tennis, trusting that she could cash in on professional opportunities—either as a touring professional tennis player, an endorser of products, a teaching professional, or a musician. Unfortunately, she'd been overly optimistic about the offers, which turned out to be few and limited. She made a little money publishing her life story and received a decent income touring professionally one year, playing exhibition matches before Harlem Globetrotters games. The next year she made the unwise decision to organize her own tour, and the resulting failure lost over $20,000, putting her deep in debt for years. She made occasional appearances on behalf of the Ward Baking Company, but that contract lasted only a few years, and no other endorsement offers were forthcoming. No country club invited her to be a club professional, and touring opportunities for female pros in the early 1960s were rare. Therefore she could make no money from tennis, and neither was she, as a former amateur, permitted to compete in amateur tournaments like Wimbledon. Long having been a music lover, she recorded an album, "Althea Gibson Sings," but she had overestimated her ability, and that career idea flopped. She also tried acting, getting a small role as a maid to a southern belle in a John Wayne movie. Even if she had been a good actress, though, Hollywood rarely offered decent roles to African American women in those years. After these disappointments, Gibson felt lonely, empty, humiliated, and "bereft of purpose."[58] Finally, she tried to capitalize on her athletic ability in one of the few ways a woman could in the mid-1960s: on the women's professional golf tour. This effort brought daunting obstacles. Again she would be trying to break into an elitist and often racist sport, one played at country clubs that would occasionally refuse to allow her in their dressing rooms. In addition, as a latecomer to golf she had a lot of catching up to do. Gibson's golf swing was powerful, but she needed to refine her strokes and develop a full game. It took a few years before she was good enough to qualify for the tour, and even once she made it, her winnings as a mid-level player were never enough to cover her expenses.[59] For a woman who craved independence, relying on loans from friends and the bank in order to pursue her vocation was a difficult pill to swallow.

Because her identity was intertwined with her career ambitions, Gibson was destined to suffer much personal frustration. The title of her 1958 autobiography laid out her main life goal: "I Always Wanted to Be Somebody." It's not clear, however, precisely what she meant by "being somebody."[60] Sometimes it seemed to mean fame, other times earning good money, and sometimes self-reliance. Yet it also seemed to say something more subtle and basic about establishing a personal identity. These goals were both ambiguous and very difficult to achieve, leading to depression and a negative self-image. In the years after retiring from amateur tennis, she viewed herself as "someone who was *once* somebody," suggesting she was at best a "former somebody" and at worst, nobody. Gibson was fairly private about her personal life, so it is difficult to assess her quality of life, but there were disappointments there as well. She married at age thirty-eight to William Darben, a trusted friend whom she had held at arm's length for many years because there "just wasn't any spark between us"; they divorced after ten years, following difficulty creating a settled home and mutual accusations of infidelity. Later she married her former coach, Sydney Lewellyn, a marriage that surprised her friends who suspected Lewellyn's motives; that marriage also ended in divorce.[61] In her early sixties, Gibson found herself alone again. She was also unconnected to the tennis world, and with some reason, she felt underappreciated. Gibson's later life was spent ill and impoverished as a virtual recluse.[62] She'd suffered a stroke, had high blood pressure, and lost a great deal of weight. Depressed about her health and her inability to pay her bills, she considered suicide.[63] Her former doubles partner Angela Buxton rallied Gibson and people in the tennis world, who raised money on Gibson's behalf. Articles came out reminding people of Gibson's accomplishments and how she'd paved the way for the Williams sisters. Before she died in September 2003, Gibson lived to enjoy some of the tributes, but, true to form, struggled to accept help from others.

If Gibson's life was marked by disappointments and struggles, it also should be remembered for its extraordinary achievements. Althea Gibson was a dropout who went back to high school and then earned a college degree. A sharecropper's daughter, she ended up traveling the world and representing her country. A runaway who had a violent childhood, she ended up being honored by a mayor, a queen, and a president. The Associated Press named her Female Athlete of the Year in 1957. Gibson was the ATA women's national champion ten times, the first black woman to play in a USLTA-sanctioned tournament, and the first black person invited to compete at Wimbledon and many other tournaments. She won first place in singles both at Wimbledon and the U.S. national championships on two occasions and captured numerous important doubles titles. One tennis observer declared that "no player overcame more to become a champion than Althea Gibson."[64] In total, she amassed eleven "major championships" and undoubtedly would have won more with the coaching and opportunities enjoyed by more privileged players. She also would have won more championships and earned more money if she'd been lucky enough to play in the "open era" of tennis when amateurs and professionals were permitted to play against one another. Indeed, if she'd been born later, she could have easily made an excellent living as a professional golfer or basketball player as well. In a number of ways, then, Gibson was ahead of her time. She was a woman who wanted to make sports her career in an era that offered few such opportunities, a determined streetfighter in a sport not yet comfortable with the masses, and an African American athlete who wanted to be perceived simply as an athlete, not as a race representative. If Gibson was unlucky in some ways, she was luckier than ATA champions from earlier eras such as Isadore Channels, Ora Washington, Lula Ballard, and Flora Lomax, and countless other women, both black and white, who had the drive and skill to be stars but whose names are now lost to us. If we can't be sure that Gibson found happiness or fulfilled her childhood dream to "be somebody," we can remember her as a pioneer, if a sometimes reluctant one, and as a champion.

Wilma Rudolph receiving the World Trophy from Bill Shroeder at the 1961 Los Angeles Invitational Indoor Track Meet. *(Photo by Cecil Charles Spiller)*

12 Wilma Rudolph

The Making of an Olympic Icon

WAYNE WILSON

Track athlete Wilma Rudolph is best remembered for her participation in the 1960 Rome Olympic Games, where she won three gold medals in the 100 meters, 200 meters and 4 x 100-meter relay. Rudolph was one of the most-publicized stars of the Rome Games. Her celebrity at the games grew out of a number of factors, including her visibility as the first female African American Olympic star, her role as symbol of American athletic success during the cold war, the influence of television, and a remarkable personal story of overcoming adversity. Rudolph competed at a world-class level for six years, but occupied the limelight as an athlete for only about two years, between 1960 and 1962. Her impact during that brief period, however, was such that she became an icon of American sport whose legacy is closely associated with the rise to prominence of African American athletes from the 1960s forward and with the expansion of sport opportunities for women.

Rudolph was born on June 23, 1940, and reared in Clarksville, Tennessee. She was the sixth of her mother and father's eight children. Rudolph's father had had fourteen other children by a previous marriage, but most of those children were adults and did not live with Rudolph when she was growing up. Both parents' educations ended before finishing elementary school. Rudolph's father was a railroad worker, who also picked up other odd jobs when he could. Her mother was a maid, who cleaned white peoples' homes. Rudolph estimated that when she was a young girl her parents' combined income never rose above $2,500 a year.

The Rudolph family was by all accounts a stable one. The parents were strict, religious, and involved in their children's lives. The large family regularly came together for special occasions. Rudolph remembered Christmas as an especially exciting time of year when the extended family would gather and exchange gifts.

Rudolph was born prematurely, weighing four and a half pounds at birth. Throughout her early childhood, she suffered a variety of ailments including measles, chickenpox, whooping cough, and mumps. Rudolph had double pneumonia twice, had scarlet fever, and was unusually susceptible to colds that lingered for weeks. When Rudolph was four, it became apparent that she had a serious problem with one of her legs. Accounts of the precise nature and cause of the problem vary. Rudolph described her leg as being crooked and her foot as turning inward. She wrote that her mother sometimes told her that she had been born with polio. Other accounts maintain that Rudolph contracted polio at age four, causing a partial paralysis of the leg.[1]

Doctors fitted Rudolph, at age five, with a steel leg brace that she wore for the next six years. For Rudolph, the experience of wearing the brace was psychologically devastating. She yearned to be accepted as "normal." She cited the taunts she endured from other children as a motivating factor in her drive to excel in sports. The leg problem kept Rudolph out of school in kindergarten. For four years, between the ages of six and ten, Rudolph received physical therapy at Meharry Medical College, an African American medical center in Nashville. The round trip from Clarksville was about one hundred miles. Rudolph made the trip once and sometimes twice a week in the back of a segregated bus accompanied by her mother on her days off from work. The physical therapy regimen included exercise, traction, and massage.

The therapy gradually yielded results. Eventually, Rudolph learned to walk around the house without the brace. Her first public outing without the aid of the brace was a Sunday visit to church when she was nine and a half. She continued to wear the brace sporadically, as well as a specially designed shoe, until she was twelve. By the time she was twelve and entering seventh grade, Rudolph felt completely healthy for the first time in her life.

In *Wilma,* her 1977 autobiography, Rudolph described herself as a child who was conscious of the racial inequities of her hometown: "I remember I was six, maybe, and I said to myself, 'There's something not right about all this. White folks got all the luxury, and we black folks got the dirty work.'" *Wilma* recounted in some detail Rudolph's memories of racism in Clarksville. She described, rather disapprovingly, the strategy of accommodation practiced daily by adult African Americans in Clarksville as they negotiated the racial landscape. She wrote that the constant humiliation and degradation of black citizens she witnessed growing up inevitably led to a loss of self-esteem by African Americans. Her childhood perception of white people was that they were all "mean and evil."[2]

Rudolph's formal athletic career began in basketball. She began playing in pick-up games the summer before seventh grade and joined the school team that winter. For the next three years, under the leadership of Coach Clinton Gray, Rudolph was a reserve who rarely played in games. She became a starter in tenth grade. Her Burt High School team won the conference championship that year and went to the second round of the state tournament.[3]

At the end of Rudolph's eighth-grade basketball season, Gray formed a girls' track team. Gray did not possess a technical knowledge of the sport, but the team gave the girls an opportunity to run and stay fit. The track team, in its first year, participated in "play days" rather than formal meets. In ninth grade, though, the team began entering meets, with Rudolph winning every race she entered.

A critical event in Rudolph's development as a track athlete was her attendance at an annual summer camp for female sprinters run by Coach Ed Temple at Tennessee State University. Temple and Tennessee State were to play a pivotal role in Rudolph's life. Tennessee State was founded in 1912 in Nashville as a normal school for African Americans. It became a four-year institution authorized to grant bachelor's degrees in 1922, and awarded its first graduate degree in 1941.[4] The school formally organized a women's track team in 1946. Two Tennessee State women made the 1948 United States Olympic track and field team. Audrey Patterson won a bronze medal in the 200-meter race. Emma Reed competed in the long jump and high jump.

Temple, who also taught sociology at the school, became the assistant women's coach in 1950 and the head coach in 1953. The year he became head coach, Temple began offering a summer training camp. He invited young African American runners from around the United States to the one-month camp. Participants had to pay travel costs, but

Tennessee State covered all other expenses. The camp was an invaluable learning experience for young sprinters and proved to be an effective recruiting vehicle for the university. Nearly 90 percent of the high school runners invited to the camp eventually enrolled at Tennessee State, whose women's track team was known as the Tigerbelles.

Sources provide conflicting information on whether Rudolph attended the camp for the first time in 1955 or 1956. In either case, she performed well enough at the 1956 camp that Temple put her on the Tigerbelles team that traveled to Philadelphia to compete in the national championships. Despite being awed by her first visit to a big city, Rudolph had an outstanding meet. In the junior division, she finished second in the 75-yard event (after setting a national record in the semifinal) and ran on the victorious 300-yard relay team. Competing in the senior division, she took second in the 200-meter event and ran on the winning Tennessee State 400-meter relay team. She also had the opportunity to meet Jackie Robinson, who had reintegrated major league baseball in 1947. Robinson encouraged her to continue running. It was, wrote Rudolph, "The first time in my life I had a black person I could look up to as a real hero."[5]

A week after the nationals in Philadelphia, Temple and his athletes traveled to Washington, D.C., for the 1956 United States Olympic trials. Rudolph qualified for the Olympic team by placing second in the 200-meter event, recording a time identical to that of first-place finisher Mae Faggs. Rudolph and Faggs were selected for the 400-meter relay team, along with Margaret Mathews and Isabelle Daniels. All four relay runners were Tigerbelles.

The 1956 Olympic Games, staged in Melbourne, Australia, marked Rudolph's first international competition and her first opportunity to travel abroad. The 1956 Olympic experience was a mixed one for Rudolph. She was impressed by the travel and the camaraderie of athletes at the games, but the games also underscored the obstacles of race and class. En route to Melbourne, the team stopped in Hawaii for a brief layover. Rudolph was amazed by the tropical beauty, but was depressed by an event that occurred as she and her Tigerbelles teammates were sightseeing in Honolulu. A white woman, seeing Rudolph and three other black athletes on the sidewalk, made a point of crossing to the other side of the street. Once in Melbourne, Rudolph was struck by the disparity in the quality of running shoes owned by Australian women and their American counterparts. The Australians had high-quality lightweight shoes. Betty Cuthbert, one of the Australian sprinters, offered to take Rudolph to the shoemaker. Faggs offered to loan her money, but Rudolph had to decline the offer knowing neither she nor her parents could afford the thirty-dollar price tag.

The Melbourne Games were a showcase for the talents of the Australian women runners. The Australians won gold in each of the four women's track events, the 100 meters, 200 meters, 4 x 100-meter relay, and the 80-meter hurdles. In the three individual events, they took six of the nine total medals. Rudolph's success in 1956 was more modest. In the 200-meter race, Rudolph did not make it past the opening round of qualifying, finishing third in her heat. In the 4 x 100-meter relay, however, Rudolph and her teammates fared better. The Australians, as expected, won the relay, setting a world record of 44.5 seconds. The United States team finished third, to take the bronze medal.

So, at age sixteen, Rudolph returned home to Clarksville as an Olympic medallist. She began her junior year of high school as an established star in both basketball and track. With Rudolph averaging thirty-five points a game, Burt High School won the state basketball championship.

In her senior year, following a preseason medical examination for the basketball team, Rudolph discovered that she was pregnant. The father was her classmate and boyfriend, Robert Eldridge, a football and basketball player at Burt. The news traumatized Rudolph. She worried that the news would crush her parents and would cost her spot at Tennessee State. Eventually, Rudolph told her parents. They were supportive, as was Coach Temple. Temple visited the Rudolph household and, despite his rule against accepting mothers on his track team, told Rudolph that she would be allowed to join the Tigerbelles after high school graduation.

Achieving success as a world-class athlete is difficult under any circumstance. Doing so as an unwed teenage mother in 1950s Tennessee was even more challenging. The additional responsibilities and family tensions created by raising a baby were central realities of Rudolph's life as she emerged as an international sport star. Yet, 1960s press accounts of Rudolph never mentioned the child. Even some pieces written many years after 1960 ignored the topic. More than one account referred to her senior year as a period when she was "unwell" or in poor health. Whether this resulted from a lack of knowledge on the part of writers, or the tendency toward hagiography that characterized many of the stories about Rudolph is unclear. It was Rudolph herself, in *Wilma,* who dealt most forthrightly with the topic.

Rudolph entered Tennessee State in 1958. As a freshman her immediate athletic goal was to be accepted by her teammates. The 1960 Olympic trials were still nearly two years away. Coach Temple, who already had transformed Rudolph's life, became an even more important influence.

As a man who coached women and took women's sport seriously, Temple was an anomaly. He was devoted to his work with the track team, putting in long days, using poor facilities, and receiving little pay from the university for being a coach. He expected a high level of commitment from his athletes and sought to exert control over most aspects of their lives. Asked to describe Temple's attitude regarding track athletes and campus life at Tennessee State, one anonymous Tigerbelle replied, "No smoking, no late hours, no intramurals, no car riding, and no alcohol." Said another, "When we were not participating in track we were in class."[6] Coach Temple and his wife, Charlie B. Temple, essentially assumed the role of surrogate parents. On one occasion, Temple presumed to tell a reporter whom he thought would make a good husband for Rudolph.

Like many coaches, administrators, and athletes in women's sport, Temple felt obligated to counter the belief that athletic participation was not an acceptable feminine activity. Toward that end he encouraged his athletes to act and dress in concert with traditional gender mores. His motto was "ladies first, then Tigerbelles." As one athlete put it, "We were always aware that we were on display, and off the track we dressed and acted like young ladies."[7]

Rudolph was comfortable in the environment created by Temple. She won three national sprint titles as a freshman in 1959. Following her sophomore year, Rudolph set a world record in the 200, and went to the 1960 Olympic trials in Abilene, Texas, as the favorite in the sprints. She won both the 100- and 200-meter events. Three other Tigerbelles, Martha Hudson, Barbara Jones, and Lucinda Williams, also made the team. The four Tennessee State students composed the 4 x 100-meter relay team.

Being on the relay team meant that Rudolph would have an opportunity to compete in three events at the 1960 Rome Olympic Games. Rudolph's medal hopes got an added boost when Temple was named the United States coach for women's track and field.

Rudolph traveled to Rome well positioned to succeed. She was the defending national champion in the sprints and world record holder at 200 meters. She was surrounded by familiar teammates as well as by the coach who had trained her since high school. Three days before her first race in Rome, however, Rudolph twisted her ankle while jogging. Temple ordered her to rest. The ankle recovered. In the 100-meter semifinal, Rudolph ran 11.3, equaling the world record. She won the 100-meter final, winning by a wide margin over the second-place finisher, Dorothy Hyman of Great Britain. Her time in the final was 11.0 seconds, but it was wind-aided and therefore did not count as a world record. Rudolph went on to set an Olympic record in the first round of qualifying for the 200 meters. In the 200 final, she won gold by 0.4 seconds.

The 4 x 100-meter relay was the most exciting of Rudolph's victories. The United States had set a world record in the semifinal and entered the final as the favorite. Running the anchor leg, Rudolph mishandled the baton exchange from teammate Barbara Jones and found herself behind the German team. She closed the gap and finished 0.3 seconds ahead of the Germans to take the gold. It was the first time the United States women's team had won the Olympic 4 x 100-meter event.

Rudolph's triumphs at the Rome Games made her an overnight celebrity. She captured the imagination of the press and public alike. After the games, Rudolph and her Tigerbelles teammates remained in Europe to run in several meets, including the Empire Games in London. Rudolph was the center of attention wherever the team traveled. *Sports Illustrated* reported, "She tore up Rome, then Greece, England, Holland and Germany. In Cologne it took mounted police to keep back her admirers; in Wuppertal, police dogs. In Berlin her public stole her shoes, surrounded her bus (she boarded it in bare feet) and beat on it with their fists to make her wave. Autograph hunters jostled her wherever she went, and she was deluged with letters, gifts, telegrams, and pleas that she stay where she was or come to a dozen cities where she wasn't." Visiting New York a few months later, to compete in the Millrose Games, Rudolph was besieged by the press and the public. As the *New York Times* described it, "Some merely want her autograph or opinion; others her hand in marriage. The rest want her to give speeches hundreds of miles from wherever she happens to be at the moment, or hire her for jobs in which she has no particular interest."[8]

Rudolph's sudden rise to fame was spontaneous rather than manufactured. Her celebrity did not result from a premeditated advertising campaign or a calculated pregames decision by media to focus on her. Several factors contributed to the attention she received. Obviously, she was an outstanding athlete. No other American woman had ever won three gold medals in Olympic track and field in a single game. She was a physically striking presence. At nearly six feet tall, Rudolph was usually the tallest woman on the track. And, her running style was fluid and graceful.

Rudolph's success competing against athletes from the Soviet Union and Eastern Europe in the midst of the cold war undoubtedly contributed to her public acclaim in the United States. The American media, as well as political leaders, framed the Olympic Games of the late 1950s and the 1960s as confrontations between the United States and communist bloc nations. In 1964 Attorney General Robert Kennedy wrote in *Sports Illustrated*, "Part of a nation's prestige in the cold war is won in the Olympic Games . . . Nations use the scoreboard of sports as a visible measuring stick to prove their superiority."[9] Rudolph went head-to-head against Soviet athletes in all three finals at Rome and against Polish athletes in two. Her victories thus were symbolically important in the ideological contest between the United States and the Soviet Union. The drama of Rudolph's success was further heightened by the disappointing performance of American male athletes in earlier track and field events. In particular, high jumper John Thomas, thought by many to be unbeatable, failed to win gold, finishing third behind two jumpers from the Soviet Union.

The fact that Rudolph was black also was a central, if not always acknowledged, aspect of her celebrity. Among African Americans her accomplishments in Rome quickly established Rudolph as a leading sports figure worthy of public celebration. The European press referred to her blackness and African heritage without apparent reservation. The French and Italian press dubbed her *La Perle Noire* (the Black Pearl), *La Gazzelle Noire,* and *La Gazèlla Nera* (the Black Gazelle). The white

American press soon repeated the Black Gazelle nickname. Quoting the European press was a way for the white American writers to allude to Rudolph's race without taking full responsibility for the reference or its implications.[10]

Stories about Rudolph in the white-dominated press rarely made explicit mention of race. The three articles on Rudolph that appeared in *Sports Illustrated* in 1960 were typical.[11] The word "black" appeared only in reference to the nicknames used by the European press. The word "Negro" never was used. The journalistic narrative offered by the white press presented a sanitized, if not romanticized, version of Rudolph's life. What resulted often was a caricature, albeit a sympathetic one, of southern blacks. Rudolph, her family and teammates, as well as most of her coaches and teachers, were presented accurately as poor, hardworking, and religious. Stories about Rudolph left no doubt that she had overcome physical and social barriers. However, because writers so assiduously avoided the issue of race, the media construction of Rudolph never fully captured the true nature or extent of the social obstacles that she faced and never explored their root causes. Consequently, white Americans could celebrate the gold medals Rudolph won as a member of the United States team without fully confronting the reality of her status as an African American.

The Rome Games continued a trend, well under way in 1952 and 1956, toward an increasing black presence on the United States Olympic team. In 1960, a majority of women on the American track and field team were black. African American women won all four of the United States' medals in women's track and field. Seven of the ten boxers on the United States team were black. Led by Cassius Clay, later to become Muhammad Ali, American boxers took four medals in 1960. Each of the four boxers was African American. African Americans made up about a third of the men's track and field team. They won ten medals in individual events. Two black runners were on the gold-medal 4 x 400-meter relay team. The most-publicized man on the United States track team was Rafer Johnson, an African American. Johnson carried the American flag during the Opening Ceremony and narrowly defeated UCLA teammate C. K. Yang of Taiwan in dramatic fashion to earn the mythical title of "World's Greatest Athlete." Oscar Robertson was one of three African Americans on the victorious men's basketball team.

Predominantly white publications of the day ignored, or failed to recognize, the significance of the prominence of African American athletes at Rome. The growing importance of African Americans to the United States in international sport competition, a development that ultimately would lead to efforts to organize an African American athletes' boycott of the 1968 Mexico City Olympic Games, was treated as a nonissue in major American newspapers and magazines. By contrast, the *Baltimore Afro-American* in its year-end roundup of significant events ranked "the stellar performance of colored athletes at the Olympics—the winning of three gold medals by Wilma Rudolph" as the sixth most significant story of 1960, inside or outside of sport.[12]

Another key to Rudolph's popularity may have been the fact that neither the press construction of Rudolph nor Rudolph herself seriously challenged the established gender order. Press stories framed Rudolph within the prevailing gender ideology of the day. Reporters praised not only Rudolph's athletic talents, but also her physical appearance, her seemingly docile personality, and her heterosexuality. At the same time, writers avoided any mention of her child born out of wedlock. Rudolph was portrayed as pretty, sweet, and eager to become a wife. Tex Maule of *Sports Illustrated* waxed rhapsodic. His initial Rome report called her a "delightfully graceful, pretty girl." In a subsequent Olympic report, Maule consistently referred to male athletes by their last names, while referring to Rudolph with the more diminutive first name, "Wilma." Wilma was "America's lovely girl sprinter." Wilma was a "quiet girl" with "long bronze legs." Wilma dated fellow sprinter Ray Norton. Barbara Heilman, in a *Sports Illustrated* feature article on Rudolph and Temple, published two months after the Rome Games, wrote, "Her manners are a natural delicacy and sweetness as true as good weather." Her physical appearance suggested "a duchess." Heilman devoted two paragraphs to the rumored romance between Rudolph and Norton, adding that Rudolph planned to be married to someone, be it Norton or someone else, within the year. (Rudolph and Norton did not marry.) Heilman was either unaware of or unwilling to acknowledge Rudolph's pregnancy, explaining instead, "she was too ill to run at all during the 1958 season." A *Los Angeles Times* story in January 1961 described her as "pert-nosed," "willowy," and "pretty, very feminine." The *Baltimore Afro-American* assured readers that she was "utterly feminine." Rudolph, for her part, also strove to project a conventional image. When asked in a 1961 press conference if she would consider racing against men, she demurred by saying, "I'm a young lady." In response to a related question, she added, "Do I think athletics help young women? Definitely. It doesn't make them masculine, if that's what you mean." A few weeks later, she told a reporter in New York that being an athlete "doesn't mean I'm a tomboy."[13]

Television enhanced the magnitude of Rudolph's celebrity and the speed by which it grew. Eurovision broadcast more than ninety hours of coverage to eighteen European nations. The Rome Olympics were the first summer games broadcast on American network television. CBS showed twenty hours of same-day coverage, spread over eighteen days. Most broadcasts took place during primetime evening hours. Being an Olympic star in the relatively uncomplicated media environment of 1960, with only three national television networks, meant being seen by a large percentage of the American viewing public.[14]

Rudolph was not fully prepared for the adulation that followed the Olympic Games. A number of sources have reported that at a press conference in Rome, Rudolph became overwhelmed by the crush of reporters and cameras and burst into tears. In *Wilma,* although Rudolph did not mention breaking down in tears, she did recall that after winning her third gold medal she was swamped by reporters and well-wishers. An American Olympic official who escorted her away from the crowd told her, "Wilma, life will never be the same for you again."[15]

Upon her return to the United States, Rudolph was feted far and wide. The governor of Tennessee and a marching band greeted her at the airport in Nashville. A few days later, the town of Clarksville staged a parade and banquet at the Clarksville Armory in honor of Rudolph. Rudolph later wrote that the Clarksville celebration was the first integrated civic event in the town's history. An elderly local white judge spoke at the banquet. Relying on the hoary metaphor of black and white piano keys making beautiful music together, the judge used the occasion to call for greater integration.[16]

Rudolph traveled the country during the next year and a half, attending events in her honor. In Washington, Rudolph, her mother, and Temple were invited to the White House, where they had a thirty-five-minute meeting with President John F. Kennedy. Although white politicians often took part in events celebrating Rudolph, activities involving

African American audiences usually made up a significant part of the itinerary. In cities such as Washington, D.C., Chicago, Detroit, Atlanta, and Philadelphia, Tennessee State alumni and African American civic, business, and political groups organized many of the events in which Rudolph participated. "Wilma Rudolph Day," on January 13, 1962, in Baltimore was typical. A delegation of local African Americans, including Tennessee State alumni and Delta Sigma Theta Sorority members, met Rudolph at the airport. The first order of business was a meeting with the governor of Maryland, who made her an honorary citizen of the state. Then came a reception at the Baltimore City Hall. With civic, sports, and church officials in attendance, the mayor presented Rudolph with the key to the city. Following the meetings with politicians, Rudolph attended a luncheon with the president and trustees of Morgan State University. Next she accepted an award from a local African American newspaper. The day ended with Rudolph attending an indoor track meet as the guest of a local track club.

Rudolph's athletic career lasted just two years beyond the Rome Games. During that time, she remained the world's top sprinter, winning several national titles and setting a world record at 200 meters. As she contemplated her future, Rudolph concluded that she wanted to retire from running with her athletic reputation in tact. She believed that anything less than three gold medals at the 1964 Olympic Games would diminish the memory of her achievements in Rome. Rudolph raced for the last time at a dual meet with the Soviet Union at Stanford University on July 21, 1962. She won the 100 that day, and in her final event, before a crowd of 72,500, came from behind to lead the American team to victory in the relay.

Rudolph's success in 1960 and 1961 led to a variety of sports awards, including the United Press International Athlete of the Year (1960), the Helm's World Trophy Award (1960), the Sullivan Award as the year's outstanding amateur athlete (1961), and Associated Press Female Athlete of the Year (1960 and 1961).

The post-Olympic period of Rudolph's life, particularly her life after retiring from track and field, was characterized for many years by frustration during which Rudolph lamented her inability to translate celebrity into significant financial gain or to find employment that she found genuinely fulfilling. Rudolph believed that organizations and individuals too often offered her employment solely for the purpose of exploiting her hero status.

The year 1963 was an eventful one for Rudolph. She graduated from college with a degree in elementary education. The U.S. State Department sent her on a tour of West African nations. She later went to Japan with the Baptist Christian Athletes, on a tour organized by the evangelist Billy Graham. Shortly after that, she made a two-month trip to East Asia. After returning from Asia, Rudolph accepted two jobs in Clarksville, teaching second grade and coaching high school track. She actively participated in efforts to desegregate white-owned businesses in Clarksville. She was among three hundred African Americans who were turned away attempting to enter a local restaurant. Rudolph also married Robert Eldridge, the father of her first child.[17]

The teaching job soon left Rudolph dissatisfied. She complained about the school's conservatism, stating, "My idea of teaching was to bring new ideas into the classroom; after all, that's what I went to college for, to learn new ideas and methods. But they wanted to stay the same, no change, and they resisted everything I tried to do."[18] Rudolph remained at Cobb Elementary until the end of the 1964 school year and then resigned.

Her resignation from the school marked the beginning of an odyssey of new jobs and ever-changing domiciles that took Rudolph to Evansville, Indiana; Poland Springs, Maine; St. Louis, Detroit, and Europe. This was an unsettled time in Rudolph's life. Her husband was a student at Tennessee State during part of the period and later became seriously ill. Often acting as the family's sole source of income, Rudolph struggled to hold the family together and make ends meet. She reached what she called the "absolute low point of my life" in 1968.[19] On April 4, 1968, the same night that Martin Luther King was assassinated in Memphis, Tennessee, Rudolph and her children flew from Detroit to Nashville to attend the funeral of one of her aunts. She described the tension on the plane as incredible. In Nashville, while the family waited for a bus to Clarksville, a white man spat at Rudolph's children. Another passenger called the police, who arrested the man. The events of that day triggered a period of depression that Rudolph was unable to shake.

She confided in basketball player and 1956 Olympic teammate Bill Russell about her depression and her feeling "that nothing in my life had seemed to go right since 1960 and the Olympics." Russell suggested that she try a new start, living in California. Rudolph took the advice and moved to Los Angeles. She found work with the Watts Community Action Committee. Later she was hired by the UCLA Afro-American Culture Center, but felt unappreciated at the university. She moved on to a job working for Mayor Daley's Youth Foundation in Chicago. When a promised raise did not materialize Rudolph felt "betrayed and exploited" and resigned. Her next job took her to Charleston, West Virginia, where she helped raise money for a proposed track and field hall of fame. When that finished, Rudolph "was in debt again," and "decided there was no place to go but back home."[20]

Rudolph found a measure of peace living back in Clarksville with her family. A family, she said, "is a powerful thing." Reviewing her career in her autobiography, the woman who had traveled the world and met heads of state wrote, "here it is, over a decade and a half later, and I'm right back where I started, in Clarksville, Tennessee." Rudolph took pride in her athletic accomplishments and her college education, but regretted her inability to capitalize financially on her athletic career. As she put it, "I was strictly an amateur, in more ways than one." Despite the note of self-criticism in that statement, Rudolph also offered a broader critique of the American sport system of the mid-1970s, one informed by considerations of race, gender, and economics. Rudolph wrote, "The fact of the matter is that black women athletes are on the bottom rung of the ladder in American sports. Most of them are involved in track and field because that's the only sports (*sic*) still really open to them. How many black women golfers are there, or how many black women tennis players? When their track careers are over, no matter what they've accomplished in the Olympics, there is no place for them to go. They wind up drifting back to where they began, and nobody ever hears from them again . . . [When] you're a black woman athlete from the South . . . the doors to commercial success are pretty much closed to you."[21]

Rudolph came of age athletically at a time when track athletes made very little money in their sport and when the public viewed the Olympic movement as a bastion of idealism. Ironically, the amateur code of the early 1960s that prevented Rudolph the athlete from making the kind of income that top track athletes would make in later years also contributed to Rudolph's legacy by closely identifying her with an era of sport that much of the public and press perceived to be "pure." The perception of Rudolph as an embodiment of Olympic "ideals" helped elevate her to iconic status.[22]

The late 1970s marked a turning point in Rudolph's life. Her autobiography was published in 1977. The same year, NBC broadcast a made-for-television movie of her life, written and produced by Olympic documentarian Bud Greenspan. Rudolph founded a company called Wilma Unlimited. The company's main purpose was to schedule speaking engagements and other appearances for Rudolph.

In 1981, Rudolph moved to Indianapolis where she formed the Wilma Rudolph Foundation. The foundation provided sports opportunities and academic support to youngsters. There were more than one thousand young people in the program by the mid-1980s. While living in Indianapolis, Rudolph also took a job working at nearby DePauw University, in Greencastle, Indiana, as the women's track coach and an advisor to the university president on minority affairs.

Rudolph continued to accumulate honors and awards in the later part of her life. She was inducted into the Black Athletes Hall of Fame (1973), the National Track and Field Hall of Fame (1974), the International Sports Hall of Fame (1980), the Women's Sports Foundation Hall of Fame (1980), and the U.S. Olympic Hall of Fame (1983). Her awards included the Humanitarian of the Year Award of the Special Olympics (1985), the National Collegiate Athletic Association's Silver Anniversary Award (1987), the Jackie Robinson Image Award of the National Association for the Advancement of Colored People (1989), and the National Sports Award (1993).

Rudolph was diagnosed as having brain cancer in July 1994. She died on November 12, 1994, in Brentwood, Tennessee, surrounded by family members. She was fifty-four. Rudolph was survived by her four children and seven grandchildren. Leading figures from the world of track and field attended her memorial service in Nashville. Spectators lined Nashville streets as a motorcade made its way to the burial site in Clarksville and "drivers on Interstate 24 pulled over on the shoulders and left their vehicles. Some held their hands over their hearts as the procession passed." Commenting on Rudolph's significance, Olan Cassell, executive director of *USA Track & Field,* stated, "She was the greatest . . . the symbol of Wilma equals that of Jesse Owens."[23]

Bill Russell and his University of San Francisco teammates on a ferry headed to the 1955 NCAA Basketball Championships. Russell is on the far right wearing a hat and holding a raincoat. K. C. Jones, who would become Russell's longtime teammate on the Boston Celtics, is sixth from right with hands in pockets. *(Union Pacific Historical Collection)*

13 Bill Russell

Pioneer and Champion of the Sixties

MAUREEN M. SMITH

As the twentieth century came to a close, sports television channels and publications compiled their lists of the century's greatest athletes. Selecting athletes for their impact on both American sport and society, the sporting media at the millennium refocused our attention on some athletes whose days had passed but whose legacies were living on. Topping, or coming close to the top, of many of these lists was basketball great Bill Russell. Named "the greatest team player in history" by *Sports Illustrated,* Russell's team, the Boston Celtics, was named "greatest team of the twentieth century." HBO named Russell "the greatest winner of all time" and hall of fame coach John Wooden called him "the most important college player and pro player of all time."[1] ESPN had Russell at the number-eighteen spot on their SportsCentury list of the top one hundred North American athletes of the century. Thirty years after Russell had won his final NBA championship, sports fans were able to reflect on his accomplishments and appreciate the player who served as a "symbolic figure in the crusade" for civil rights.[2]

American sport during the civil rights era endured tremendous change in large part due to African American athletes whose success signified the shifting attitudes toward race in sport and the larger society. African American athletes, who in their early years were severally constrained by Jim Crow bigotry and had not fully benefited from the 1954 *Brown v. Board of Education* decision, integrated American sport with dignity, desire, and an immense amount of talent. Among these athletes, a few transformed their sport, as well as the cultural, social, and political landscape. Muhammad Ali is one such athlete; as a boxer, his involvement in the controversial Nation of Islam and his subsequent refusal to serve in the United States Army resulted in the loss of his heavyweight title. Russell, as a professional basketball player, provided a different image of an African American athlete. While he did speak out on controversial issues, none of his comments ever incited the kind of passionate feelings that Ali would kindle. Russell was not a "trashtalker," but a thoughtful philosopher, and by virtue of playing on a team, his livelihood was never threatened by his remarks or actions. He was not suspended, kicked off the team, or traded—instead he continued to perform at a high level throughout his career. He was too valuable to his team to punish for expressing his beliefs. Considered by author George Plimpton to be one of the most intriguing athletes of his generation, Russell contributed mightily to the Celtics dynasty and spoke out on issues of race, culture, and politics at a politically charged time in American history.[3] Unlike Ali, the reactions to Russell were less emotionally charged, though he did receive harsh criticism from the media for his outspokenness. Russell was one of the first African American athletes in a team sport to challenge the traditional stereotypes and expectations related to racial issues in sport. Moreover, Russell became the first African American to become a head coach in professional sports.

During his career as an athlete and coach, Russell changed the game of basketball and greatly impacted both American sport and society. His significance in the African American struggle for civil rights was largely due to his successful career in professional basketball. Thus, it is important and relevant to provide an overview of his playing career, with an emphasis on his college and professional accomplishments. Equally important are events in his childhood that provided Russell with varying perspectives on race, events that would serve as formative moments influencing his experiences in integrated sport.

William Felton Russell was born on February 12, 1934, and was raised in Monroe, Louisiana, for the first nine years of his life. Russell's family then moved to Oakland, California, where both parents, Mister Charlie and Katie, worked in the Oakland shipyards.[4] Russell's recollections of his parents' decision to move west indicate that as a young boy his instincts told him the move had something to do with two incidents that occurred in Louisiana that "permanently changed the direction" of his family.[5] One incident occurred when Russell's mother was yelled at by a policeman for dressing like a white woman, a pants outfit that Russell described as looking like a horse-riding suit. The other incident occurred when his father and a gas station attendant exchanged angry words and Russell's father walked toward the attendant with a tire iron in his hand. Witnessing the exchange, Russell remembered bursting with pride and wanting to cheer for his father except that his mother gave him a look that made him reconsider.[6] Raised on stories of Grandpa Russell fighting off the Klan, Russell was aware of racial violence, including lynching, from an early age. His experiences of growing up in the Deep South during the prewar 1930s and 1940s were influenced by "something deep and underlying—a disquieting factor," but Russell also said his return visits to Louisiana in the years following were equally significant.[7]

Both Russell parents were adamant that their two sons, Bill and his older brother Charlie, would receive educations. As such, Mister Charlie and Katie Russell decided to limit the size of the Russell family to ensure better opportunities for their sons. Russell's father explained their philosophy to him, saying, "We didn't want a house full of half-hungry children. You can't run hungry. You can't learn nothing hungry. You can't even *think good* hungry." Russell's mother had given him the middle name of Felton, after the president of Southern University, Felton Clark, and the couple started contributing to insurance policies in 1935 that would mature into college funds.[8] Russell's mother died without explanation when he was twelve years old, an event that left him shattered and devastated. He found refuge in the Oakland Public Library.

Reading provided the young Russell with sanctuary during his junior high school years. At this point in his young life, Russell was either not participating in organized sport, or did not consider it important enough to discuss in either of his autobiographies.[9] He recalled reading the story of Henri Christophe and the Citadel in one of his favorite books, *Complete Marvels of the World* by Richard Halliburton. Russell loved the story of Christophe, a slave who took part in a revolt and then became the emperor of Haiti, the first free black country in the Western Hemisphere. The story of Christophe and the construction of the Citadel inspired Russell, and he identified the slave-turned-emperor as one of his early heroes.[10] Russell had a wakeup call when he nearly failed eighth grade, an event he recalls as "humiliating," but which helped him to focus on school. Unable to make a sports team, Russell went out for the band.[11]

Russell's early basketball career began as the sixteenth player on his high school junior varsity team, and he shared the fifteenth uniform with a teammate rotating every other game. Still growing into his body, Russell played on the varsity team at McClymonds High School in Oakland, California, his junior and senior years.[12] Despite the success of his high school team, losing only three games in his two-year varsity career, Russell was not the cornerstone of the team's success. He considered himself "mediocre at best" and an "easily forgettable high-school player."[13] In a six-team league, Russell was not even named to one of the three all-league teams.

Interestingly enough, upon graduation Russell played with the California High School All-Stars on a tour of the Pacific Northwest. Despite not earning all-star status during the season, Russell was able to go on the trip because he had graduated in January; his selection to the team was largely due to his availability rather than his talent. He credits this all-star experience for helping him develop as a player, both his physical skills and his mentality as an athlete. Upon returning to Oakland following the tour, Russell applied to become an apprentice sheet-metal worker at the San Francisco Naval Shipyards.[14] After starting at the shipyards, Russell was offered a scholarship to play at the University of San Francisco (USF). Russell was surprised that he was "selected at a time when blacks were simply not given scholarships to prestigious four-year colleges." He was not, however, the only African American on the Dons; teammate KC Jones was also attending on a scholarship and would later become Russell's teammate on the Boston Celtics. In the early 1950s, Russell recalled that UCLA had been the most progressive university in the west in regard to the recruitment of African American athletes, but also acknowledged that many of these players had to first play at a junior college to prove their character. He wrote later of his realization:

> I was getting a straight pass. It did not occur to me that it happened because I was so good a prospect. Basketball was play; college was serious . . . I thought of college ball the same way I thought of high school—as an extracurricular activity—so I didn't draw as strong a correlation between my athletic skills and my college opportunity as I would now. For me, the benefit of the scholarship was entirely the chance to be in college.[15]

Russell played four years of basketball at San Francisco. He also earned a letter as a high jumper on the track and field team.[16] During his three years on the varsity basketball team, Russell, along with KC Jones, helped USF become one of the most exciting and successful college teams in the 1950s. In his debut with the Dons against Cal, Berkeley, Russell scored twenty-three points and collected thirteen rebounds, prompting the *San Francisco Chronicle* to compare his defense to covering "the backboard on rebounds like flypaper." USF beat Cal 51–33 and went on to a 14–7 record in 1953–54.[17] The next season Russell and the Dons lost their third game of the season to UCLA 47–40 and then embarked on a 55-game winning streak, including two national titles, beating defending champion LaSalle for the 1955 title and Iowa in 1956. Russell was a three-year letter winner under hall of fame coach Phil Woolpert and was named All-America and USA Player of the Year as a senior in 1956. Other accolades included winning the NCAA Most Outstanding Player Award in 1955. At the conclusion of the 1955 season, NCAA officials doubled the width of the foul lane from six to twelve feet, in what became known as the "Russell rule," because Russell had been so dominant as a rebounder and defensive player.[18] When the Dons beat Iowa 83–71 for their second NCAA title and fifty-fifth consecutive win, *Time* magazine said Russell "spent most of his time dancing in the air like a joyous giraffe and slapping Hawkeye shots out of basket range."[19] In seventy-nine college games, Russell scored 1,636 points (20.7 ppg) and grabbed 1,606 rebounds (20.3 rpg). At a time when offense garnered the praise and attention, Russell's agile defensive play began to provide evidence that the defensive aspect of basketball was equally important.

After his college career, Russell was named to the 1956 U.S. Olympic basketball team. Despite the rumors that had President Eisenhower telling the young Russell, "We need you for our next Olympic team," Russell recounted in later years that there was no such request from the president and that he made the decision to play for the United States in Melbourne, Australia.[20] The U.S. team won the gold medal, winning eight games in the tournament with an average margin of fifty-three points, still an Olympic record.

Three weeks after helping the United States win the Olympic gold, Russell made his professional debut with the Celtics, scoring six points and grabbing sixteen rebounds in twenty-one minutes of play. Though he had originally been drafted by the St. Louis Hawks, Red Auerbach traded Ed Macauley and Cliff Hagan to the Hawks to acquire Russell, who signed a $19,500 contract for his rookie season.[21] Harry Edwards speculated that Russell's rights were traded from the Hawks to the Celtics "largely because it was felt that St. Louis wasn't ready for a black basketball player."[22] Chuck Cooper had integrated the Celtics in 1950 as their first African American player, but was no longer with the team when Russell arrived in Boston six years later.[23] Russell believed that some fans and players would judge him based on his race and considered that he had two strikes against him: he was a "6–10 giant" and "a Negro," a combination he thought "provided the bigots with plenty of material for sly jokes."[24] *Sports Illustrated* viewed his debut in professional basketball with more optimism, noting that Russell was coming in on a "tidal wave of nationwide publicity following his triumphs at San Francisco and with the Olympic basketball team" and in Boston newspapers the rookie was already being hailed as a "conquering hero" before ever putting on a uniform. Predictions had the Celtics winning the NBA championship in Russell's first year.[25]

The predictions rang true and as a rookie Russell played in forty-eight games in 1956–57, the first championship season for the Celtics. The next year, Russell was injured in the playoffs and the Celtics were unable to defend their title. With a healthy Russell, the Celtics reclaimed the NBA title in 1959, the first of eight consecutive titles for the team.

Russell's athletic career allowed him to showcase his talents while also providing him with the unique opportunity to share his thoughts on important societal issues. As his athletic profile increased, so did his opportunities to speak his mind. By virtue of being an African American professional athlete, Russell was often sought out to discuss racial matters related to both sport and American society. When he was not asked for his opinions, Russell offered them anyway.[26] Playing college basketball in California in the 1950s was a much different experience than many of his future NBA peers would face in the slowly desegregating universities in the South in the 1960s. Equally significant, playing professional basketball in Boston, a racially divided city and the last city to desegregate in major league baseball, presented another opportunity for Russell to be a pioneer in American sport. Russell was miserable in Boston due to the racial climate and, despite his success on the court, was never beloved by a city that by all accounts should have welcomed him with open arms for the success he helped cultivate in the Boston Garden.[27] Boston's racial problems were structural, and sport was simply one more arena where the racial lines were drawn with Russell being a tragic casualty.

While Russell was becoming a dominant player in professional basketball, several incidents occurred in the first several years of his career that reveal the insidious ways that race and racism impacted him, other African American players, and the game.[28] After completing his rookie season, Russell was overlooked for the Rookie of the Year Award, which went to his teammate Tom Heinsohn. Russell felt slighted, reflecting in his 1966 autobiography, "They said it was because I came in December. Some guys said I was robbed. Some laughed. I figured Heinsohn was a great player. But I hurt inside."[29] A further slight that bothered him even more was when sportswriters failed to name him to the all-NBA team, despite Russell being chosen as the Most Valuable Player that year. Of the sportswriters' action, Russell commented, "They had to trip all over themselves to leave me out, putting three white forwards on the team and no center at all. What ingenuity, and what a trivial place for prejudice!"[30] In Russell's second season, he was featured in a *Sports Illustrated* article, "The Man Who Must Be Different." The article began, "Bill Russell is desperately sensitive about his height and about being a Negro. About being taller than a world of smaller men and standing out in a world of white men. At the same time, he is aggressively proud of both."[31]

Racial segregation in professional basketball was still very much an issue in the late 1950s. Several incidents illustrate some of the problems Russell and his African American teammates and opponents faced in southern cities. In 1958 the Celtics played an exhibition game in Charlotte, North Carolina. Assured by Coach Red Auerbach that Chuck Cooper had previously been able to play in Charlotte without racial incident, Russell and his teammate Sam Jones were surprised to find that they were housed in a different hotel than their white teammates. After the game, Russell told a sportswriter who commented that the Celtics seemed to have fun playing the game, "I'll tell you the unfunniest thing that ever happened to me. That was playing in this crummy town. I'll never play here again." Wire services picked up the quote and Auerbach issued a statement saying that Russell's comment did not represent the entire team. Similar incidents had occurred in Marion, Indiana, where Russell, KC Jones, and white teammate Carl Braun were not able to eat at a restaurant.[32] After the 1958 playoffs, Russell traveled with an all-star squad to Dallas where the African American players were told they would be "treated as much like Americans as anyone else," only to be told that they would be staying at a separate hotel. At that point, Russell left Dallas and did not play in the game.[33] At a 1961 preseason exhibition game against the St. Louis Hawks in Lexington, Kentucky, four African American players on the Celtics, excluding Russell, were refused service at a hotel coffeeshop. Despite Auerbach's attempts to convince them to stay, the African American players on the Celtics, as well as their counterparts on the Hawks, left Lexington and did not play in the game.[34] Russell and his teammates effectually staged a boycott at a time when the practice was just beginning to be used in the fight for civil rights. That Russell and his teammates would use such a practice at that time was a testament to their principles and willingness to use their athletic talent as a bargaining tool. Russell offered his perspective on segregated facilities to the press. "For a great number of years colored athletes and entertainers put up with these conditions because we figured they'd see we were nice people mostly . . . I'm not insulted by it. I'm just embarrassed. I'm of the opinion that some people can't insult me. But it was the greatest mistake we ever made, because as long as you go along with it, everybody assumes it's the *status quo*. The way I feel about it, if I can't eat, I can't entertain."[35]

Russell believed there was a quota system in the NBA and commented to the media that there was "an unwritten law of pro basketball that no team should have more than two Negroes—three at the most—because in the opinion of the owners it would be bad for a draw at the gate—and money, not heart, rules pro sports."[36] The practice of playing a specified number of African American players at the same time became an issue because of the increasing number of African Americans in the sport. As the Celtics added African American players to its roster, it became an issue that Russell continually discussed in the media, though he made clear that "the game was changing drastically and more and more Negro stars were being acknowledged."[37] The rumored quota increased to 50 percent a team, and Russell commented, "In order for any sport to be really successful, two or three of the top guys have to be white. Most sports, even these days are looking for the White Hope."[38]

A life-altering experience for Russell occurred in 1959 when he went on a State Department goodwill tour of Africa, armed with basketballs and films of the Celtics.[39] The State Department sponsored a number of trips that had African American athletes traveling to other countries to serve as evidence of American racial progress. African American athletes, as well as African American entertainers, were intended on these trips to be viewed as exemplars of success, including tennis champion Althea Gibson.[40] It is ironic that Russell would be used as an example of how well African Americans were treated in the United States when so much of what he expressed about this period of his life seemed to contradict the intent of the State Department's mission. These contradictions in Russell's experiences reveal the tumultuous social and personal times he was living through. The trip was a defining moment for Russell, who felt "confronted with the deep emotional feeling of returning to a homeland." After returning to the United States, Russell was asked about his trip, his subsequent investments in Liberia, and comments he made related to Africa being his ancestral homeland. Of the reception he received, Russell proclaimed that he had "found a place where I was welcome because I was black instead of in spite of being black."[41]

When Russell was asked if he planned to move to Africa, a reporter misunderstood his response and the story led to rumors of Russell being a Black Muslim, although he was not and did not indicate that he was moving to Africa.[42] These incidents in the first few years of Russell's entrance into the NBA serve as markers along the trail of desegregation in professional basketball, but also indicate the shifting racial attitudes of American society. As more and more African American players integrated basketball, their increasing numbers forced changes in preseason facilities, hotel accommodations, and the quota system.

As Russell entered the 1960s, he became part of a storied rivalry that propelled the NBA into its next phase—a phase where two individual players, Russell and Wilt Chamberlain, and one team, the Boston Celtics, would dominate the game, and a phase that ushered in African American players at an increasing rate. Throughout his career, Russell's rivalry with Chamberlain, who played for the Philadelphia Warriors, produced memorable games.[43] In their first matchup on November 7, 1959, Russell pulled down an amazing thirty-five rebounds, and Boston was victorious by a score of 115–106. Their rivalry defined basketball in the 1960s. Though Chamberlain won several scoring titles, Russell and the Celtics won a majority of the championships. Russell and Chamberlain met in the playoffs eight times, with Russell and the Celtics emerging victorious seven times. Of their relationship, Russell wrote, "Wilt Chamberlain and I carried on a friendship the entire time we played basketball together, even though the newspapers portrayed us as mortal enemies. There's a certain amount of show business in professional basketball, and the two of us were a promoter's dream. The sportswriters flogged their feverish imaginations . . . I can't think of any two players in a team sport who have been cast as antagonists and as personifications of various theories more than Wilt and I were."[44] Russell has credited Chamberlain for helping him negotiate his own contract with the Celtics. When Chamberlain signed a $100,000 contract in 1965, Russell indicated to the Celtics he was considering retirement. The Celtics responded by raising their $75,000 contract offer to $100,001, making him the highest-paid player in the game.[45] Over the duration of their eleven-year rivalry, Russell was outscored and outrebounded by his rival, but his Celtics beat Chamberlain's team eighty-six times and lost fifty-seven, with Russell winning nine titles to Chamberlain's one.

Russell, who once had 51 rebounds in a game against Syracuse in 1960, led the NBA in rebounding five times and grabbed 21,620 rebounds (second all-time) and averaged 15.1 ppg and 22.5 rpg for his career. He and Chamberlain are the only two players to have more than 50 rebounds in one game. Russell grabbed 40 or more rebounds in seven games of his career. He led the NBA in rebounding in his first three seasons (19.6, 22.7, 23.0) and five times overall. He scored 14,522 points (15.1 ppg) in his career and averaged 16.2 ppg in 165 playoff games.[46]

Sports Illustrated began to respect the defensive skills Russell brought to the game while admitting that "putting the ball through the hoop . . . is still the most spectacular piece of business on the court." Russell's greatness could not even be properly measured because at the time "no official records are kept on the things Russell does better than any other man before him, things which few players ever thought of doing. These are acts of *defense*."[47] Russell expressed his philosophy of the game he came to dominate.

> The psychology of defense is not blocking a shot or stealing a pass or getting the ball away. The psychology is to make the offensive team deviate from their normal habits. This is a game of habits, and the player with the most consistent habits is the best. What I try to do on defense is make the offensive man do not what *he* wants but what *I* want . . . In my modest opinion, shooting is of

> relatively little importance in a player's overall game . . . You learn the offensive aspects of the game long before you learn there even are defensive aspects. Defense is hard work because it is unnatural. Defense is a science . . . You have to fight the natural tendencies and do things naturally that aren't natural.[48]

Throughout his career, Russell came to dominate an offensive game as a defensive player. According to his coach, Red Auerbach, "Russell has had the biggest impact on the game of anyone in the last 10 years because he has instituted a new defensive weapon—that of the blocked shot. He has popularized the weapon to combat the aggressive, running-type game. He is by far the greatest center ever to play the game."[49]

During Russell's thirteen-year playing career with the Celtics, he won eleven NBA championships (1957, 1959–66, 1968–69) and was named NBA Most Valuable Player five times (1958, 1961–63, 1965). A twelve-time All-Star (1958–69), and the game's MVP in 1963 after tallying 19 points and 24 rebounds, Russell was named to the All-NBA First Team three times (1959, 1963, 1965) and All-NBA Second Team eight times (1958, 1960–62, 1964, 1966–68). He was declared the Greatest Player in the History of the NBA by the Professional Basketball Writers Association of America (1980), named "Sportsman of the Year" by *Sports Illustrated* (1968), and the *Sporting News* Athlete of the Decade in 1970. He is the Celtics all-time rebounder (21,620, 22.5 rpg in 963 games; second in history) and holds several NBA records including single-game for most rebounds in a half (32, vs. Philadelphia on November 16, 1957), career playoff record for most rebounds (4,104, 24.9 rpg) in 165 games, NBA Finals record for highest rebound per game average (29.5 rpg, 1959) and by a rookie (22.9 rpg, 1957), NBA Finals single-game record for most free throws attempted in one half (15, April 11, 1961, vs. St. Louis); most rebounds (40, March 29, 1960, vs. St. Louis and April 18, 1962, vs. Los Angeles); most rebounds by a rookie (32, April 13, 1967, vs. St. Louis); and most rebounds in a quarter (19, April 18, 1962, vs. Los Angeles). Russell's legacy in the game has been honored numerous times, including being named to the NBA Twenty-fifth Anniversary All-Time Team in 1970, the NBA Thirty-fifth Anniversary All-Time Team in 1980, and the NBA Fiftieth Anniversary All-Time Team in 1996. His jersey number 6 was retired by the Celtics.

At the beginning of the 1966 season, the Celtics named Russell to succeed Red Auerbach, making him the first ever African American NBA head coach. Upon his hiring, *Time* magazine offered an assessment of the Celtics' bold move, stating "the simple fact that he is a Negro is enough to ensure that Bill Russell will be a controversial coach. Russell would be controversial in any color. Often arrogant, usually angry, always outspoken, he is a born boat rocker—'all hung up,' in the words of his close friend and archrival, Wilt Chamberlain." The magazine provided further evidence of Russell's racial thinking when they noted that he named his daughter Kenyatta after the president of Kenya. As head coach of the Celtics, Russell was paid an additional $25,000 beyond his playing contract worth $100,001.[50]

Russell served as player/coach from 1966 to 1969 and led Boston to the 1968 and 1969 NBA titles. His coaching career, however, was not nearly as illustrious as his playing career, despite winning two championships with the Celtics as a player/coach. In addition to serving as player/coach of the Celtics for three seasons (1966–69), Russell coached the Seattle Supersonics (1973–77) to the Western Conference semifinals in 1976, and completed his coaching career with a brief stint with the Sacramento Kings (1987–88). Overall, he compiled a 341–290 record (.540) in eight seasons as a head coach in the NBA.[51] After his retirement from coaching, Russell noted the profound changes that had taken place in basketball since his rookie year.

> As a rookie, in 1957, I was the only black player on the Boston Celtics, and I was excluded from almost everything except practice and the games. Exactly twenty years later I was coach and general manager of the Seattle Supersonics, which had only two *white* players on the team—and they were excluded from almost everything but practice and the games. The black players left them out of meals, conversations, parties and anything else that makes a lonely road trip bearable. I told the blacks how unfair this was, and they made a token effort to change, but they said the white players were just too different. In basketball, it only took twenty years to go from the outhouse to the in-crowd.[52]

One thing that always separated Russell from the in-crowd was actually something of his own doing—something over which he had complete control, but consciously chose to do as a statement—the wearing of a beard. Russell wore a beard during his rookie season (1956–57), allowed his teammate Tom Heinsohn to shave it off after the Celtics title win, and then grew the beard back. The beard became symbolic of the ways Russell would be confronted and how he himself would confront race throughout his career. In a 1963 feature article in *Sports Illustrated,* Gilbert Rogin described Russell as an "angry, dissatisfied and aloof man of uncommon principle, and is no less remarkable as a person than he is as an athlete . . . he has deliberately set himself further apart by being one of the few professional athletes to wear a beard." Russell, in the article, wonders why he wears the beard and answers his own question. "It's part of this thing—I've always fought so hard to be different and I am different without even trying, and maybe it's just my own little revolution." Russell went on to say that he had made the effort to conform by shaving it once and did not consider the opinion of the Celtics management in the decision to grow the beard. He even admitted that his beard was "a very childish thing, in the sense of defiance," and that his decision to continue to wear a beard was to let people know that he was an "individual, who thinks for himself, and is opinionated."[53] In his first autobiography, *Go Up for Glory,* Russell's version of the beard issue implied his desire to simply be different. He noted that people had commented on the beard throughout his career and that at the time it was a "*cause celebre* of the NBA." He remembered people saying, "He could be a nice guy. Why doesn't he shave that beard?" Russell could never figure out what the beard had to do with his being a nice guy.[54] Thirteen years later in his second autobiography, *Second Wind: Memoirs of an Opinionated Man,* Russell saw the beard as his means of practicing freedom and how the practice of such freedom irritated others. He recalled that "in 1959 the NBA owners met to vote on a rule banning facial hair on the court. The reason was me; I'd grown a beard—not much of a one, but noticeable. Then Wilt grew one, and the league was faced with the first two hairy athletes in modern professional sports. The reaction couldn't have been any worse if we had taken up arson as a hobby."[55] The beard stayed on Russell's face throughout his playing and coaching career.

Russell's two autobiographies and the articles he wrote and was featured in for *Sports Illustrated* represent varying perspectives on his life as an African American, the role race played in his sporting career, and his status as a famous African American athlete. He represented "the Negro athlete" of the 1960s—"he does not incite to riot, but neither does he scrape or bow." Writers praised him as the best player in the world, while simultaneously considering him a "contemporary Negro: impatient, skeptical and at times weary of the white man's world."[56] Over time, he went from referring to himself as colored to Negro to becoming black, though sportswriters did not make the shift as quickly. Harry Edwards credits Russell's *Go Up for Glory,* written with William McSweeny, as one of the "first publicly acknowledged indications that a revolt by black athletes was imminent." Edwards's assessment was that Russell was "unwilling to communicate the same old tired clichés, glittering generalities, and distortions," and the autobiography "attempted to put the real sacrifices a famous black athlete endures and the rewards he receives in proper perspective." Russell's approach, moreover, "represented a radical departure from the fun-and-games, win-some-lose-some style of autobiography typically ghost-written for Negro and white sports stars."[57] Russell's second autobiography, coauthored with Taylor Branch, expanded on many of the stories Russell introduced in his first book, with more details and reflection on his experiences, as well as the changes in the game and American society over time.

Russell did not limit his comments to professional basketball, though being a professional athlete afforded him a platform from which to share his ideas about more significant issues. As indicated by Gilbert Rogin in his 1963 *Sports Illustrated* article, Russell struggled with his role as an African American athlete in a society fraught with racial conflict. Russell believed he had not made any worthy contributions to society and that playing professional basketball was "the most shallow thing in the world." Rogin observed that Russell "has made certain judgments that seem to him so correct and obvious that he is not afraid to enunciate them: basketball, or any other sport, is, at bottom, frivolous, and the imposition of being a Negro at this moment in history is an obligation that cannot be met on the floor of the Boston Garden. Where and how he can fulfill it Russell does not yet know."[58] In the same article, Russell offered his views on the struggles faced by African Americans in society at large. "The basic problem in Negro America is the destruction of race pride. One could say we have been victims of psychological warfare . . . With what we've had to work with we've done a pretty good job of surviving . . . I think it would be so much greater if everyone had an equal opportunity in every field."[59] Russell understood that his position as a professional athlete allowed him to address societal issues in a way that others could not. He was able to articulate his racial beliefs in magazines marketed to a largely white audience and took such opportunities to educate the masses on what he considered the pressing issues of the day.

> There used to be a lot of emphasis on the first Negro to do this, the first Negro to do that. It's unimportant who's the first or who's the last. The important thing is—how many? The rest is tokenism. When Thurgood Marshall was made a judge it made me feel real good, because he never attempted to disassociate himself, like some educated Negroes. Some Negroes live in a twilight zone, closing themselves off into a small, white society. The Negro world doesn't concern them. I feel sorry for them—to an extent. Education is the acquiring of the ability to think for oneself; anyone can get through college on memory courses. If a Negro judge says, "I don't think of myself as a Negro, just as a competent judge," he's not facing life the way it is in our society.[60]

When asked which athletes he admired, Russell listed four—Ted Williams, Jackie Robinson, Sonny Liston, and Floyd Patterson—and commented that "Some Negro athletes don't show me much. I'm disappointed in them. They are politicians in the sense of saying the right things all the time."[61] Russell recalled the early 1960s as one of loneliness and frustration; the "glow had left basketball" and he wanted to "help change the world, and was looking for a way to do it. The black revolution was beginning, and many other tides were turning."[62] Russell attended the March on Washington and considered it "the greatest thrill and proudest moment in his life."[63] At the request of Charlie Evers, brother of Medgar Evers, Russell went to Jackson, Mississippi, one summer to conduct basketball clinics.[64] He also moved into a white neighborhood in Reading, Massachusetts, and explained his decision to do so by stating, "I want the best kind of life, the best kind of schools, the best kind of police protection for my family. In our culture, the best is in the white neighborhoods. You don't find it in the Negro areas because they don't get full support of city government."[65] In 1967, Russell was one of ten African American athletes to meet with Muhammad Ali in Cleveland to discuss Ali's draft status, a sign of his stature and influence in the community of African American athletes and professional athletics as a whole. Russell followed with an article about the meeting in *Sports Illustrated* and his own reactions to Ali's decision, the Muslim religion, and the Vietnam War.[66]

After his playing days were over, Russell reflected on the changing racial landscape in professional basketball. "Racism on the part of the audience can still be mean and nasty, but owners and coaches can't afford it if they want to win. Inside sports, racism has become subtle. It lingers on in the attitudes of certain coaches and managers who have strange ideas about, for example, where a black man should play."[67] When *Sports Illustrated* published a piece in 1971 that attributed the success of black athletes to innate physical skills, Russell rebuked the magazine and their findings, which reinforced the stereotypes Russell had faced during his career. Responding to the magazine, he wrote, "To *Sports Illustrated,* however, it made perfect sense to say that blacks' prominence in sports must be caused either by physical or mental factors. It's doubtful that the mental one ever occurred to them, so they were stuck with the idea that we blacks win because we have long limbs and loose joints."[68]

In *Second Wind,* Russell candidly discussed his induction into the Basketball Hall of Fame. The hall of fame selected their first members in 1959 and Russell viewed himself as a "contemporary and an observer of its creation." In 1975, he was chosen by the hall's selection committee as the "first individual black player." Upon the announcement, Russell issued a statement saying that he preferred not to be inducted "for personal reasons." Russell explained in his book that when William Mokray, a statistician for the Celtics who had been inducted into the hall in 1965, published his *Basketball Stars of 1962,* he failed to mention Russell's name, despite Russell's dominance and MVP season. He had also been snubbed by Mokray on earlier occasions. Russell also disagreed with the membership of University of Kentucky coach Adolph Rupp, and "did not want to be associated with him or anybody else of his racial views." In essence, Russell did not respect the hall of fame, did not agree that some of the members belonged (such as Mokray and Rupp), did not feel their standards were high enough, and believed it was a political and self-serving institution.[69] Despite his statement declining the induction, the hall of fame enshrined Russell on April 28, 1975, though he was not in attendance. According to the Naismith Hall of Fame's biography of Russell, his legacy is "defense wins championships." Russell "initiated a defensive mentality that remains a focal part of championship basketball at every level" and according to the game's most prestigious institution "was the greatest defensive center in the history of basketball."[70]

Russell's legacy in basketball continues to be his defensive genius and abilities that have secured his place as one of the top players in the history of the game. Moreover, his membership in the unrivaled dynasty of the Boston Celtics of the late 1950s and throughout the 1960s ensure that he will not only be remembered for his individual accomplishments, but also for his commitment to teamwork and victory. It was Russell's storied membership with the Celtics that led him to pen his third book, *Russell Rules: 11 Lessons on Leadership from the Twentieth Century's Greatest Winner* in 2001. Unlike his two autobiographies, Russell frames his latest book around the concept of Celtic pride and eleven lessons that led to his success, and could be used by any reader in their pursuit of excellence in whatever field they choose. While Russell shares many of the same stories of his early life and playing career, there is a decidedly nonconfrontational tone throughout. Race is not mentioned and this version of his life and his successes are viewed through a seemingly colorblind lens, which is more reflective of the times perhaps rather than the man. At the start of the twenty-first century, the sporting world congratulates itself on the meritocracy of the playing field and the embracing of African American athletes by all sport fans. Russell's shift in his third book fits neatly into this "new attitude," just as his first two autobiographies were written more for an audience concerned with civil rights and a changing American society.

Russell played during an era that matched him with an equal rival, Wilt Chamberlain, and he was one of the most domineering players of the early 1960s, pioneering a path for other players of his race. While hundreds of African Americans have benefited from the trail blazed by Russell, few have been able to match his abilities and skills.[71] Some observers point out that other players have surpassed his statistical accomplishments, but no other player has achieved Russell's level of success—the statistics and NBA championships in combination. Fewer still have emerged as men able to articulate their positions related to the cultural, political, racial, and social issues of their respective time periods. Though Russell risked a great deal when he spoke out on important societal issues, the risk did not impede him from being involved in controversial activities, such as traveling to Africa, hosting clinics in Mississippi, or advising Muhammad Ali about military service. A player and man of principles, Bill Russell truly was and is a symbolic figure in the crusade for progress and justice in American sport and society.

Jimmy Brown sitting on the Cleveland Browns bench during a game in 1958. *(Getty Images)*

14 Jim Brown

Superlative Athlete, Screen Star, Social Activist

J. THOMAS JABLE

Athlete par excellence, football icon, movie star, social activist just begin to describe the broad and diverse characteristics that make up the complex personality of Jim Brown. As a football player, he had no equal; as an actor, he brought an African American action character to the movie screen; and as a champion of social justice, he reached deep into the African American community with economic aid and personal self-help. Yet beneath his signature African tiara, Jim Brown is a highly complex individual: an athlete whom most consider to have been the best of all time, a pioneer film star whose interracial love scenes transcended racial boundaries, a powerful voice of the African American people that relentlessly pursued racial equality and economic prosperity for the black community, and a sometimes angry and distraught person with a history of physical assault charges.

Brown's most recent foray with the law ended in a six-month jail sentence in 2002, the result of an argument with his wife that led to his breaking out her car windows. Brown protested what he considered to be an unjust sentence by refusing to take food for twenty-seven days. In four months he was set free, but during that time he was placed in lockdown for twenty-three hours of each day. Spending all but an hour each day in virtual solitude for four months and carrying out a hunger fast on top of that required enormous will power, discipline, determination, commitment, and self-confidence, all of which Brown possesses. This essay examines the nature of this unique and perplexing person as he confronted the challenges and obstacles of being a black man in American society. And in doing so, it attempts to unravel some of the complexities shrouding Jim Brown, providing perhaps greater insight to this marvel of an athlete, actor, and activist whose life began nearly seventy years ago on an island off the Georgia coast.

Born on St. Simons Island in 1936, Jim Brown spent the first eight years of his life in a segregated African American community where church and family were the focal points. During those early years, he was reared by his great-grandmother due to his father's abandonment two weeks after his birth and his mother's migration to Manhasset Long Island when he was two years old. He joined his mother up north in 1944 when his great-grandmother died. Life in integrated Manhasset was a much different experience for the young Brown than it had been on St. Simons. In his new environment Brown found himself involved in a bevy of fistfights provoked by his new schoolmates. Already an experienced and crafty fighter, Brown eventually established a reputation that led to his becoming president and warlord of a local gang, the Gaylords. Had it not been for athletics and a half dozen coaches and educators, Brown says he probably would have been a "career gangster." His high school football coach, Ed Walsh, was an early savior. Walsh gave Brown confidence, direction, and guidance, in shielding him from trouble. Brown was the consummate high school athlete, lettering in football, basketball, baseball, track and field, and lacrosse. During his senior year, he averaged 14.9 yards per carry on the gridiron and thirty-eight points a game on the basketball court. In addition to his athletic exploits, Brown was active in student government. He declined the nomination for student government president because he thought the office should go to a scholar with an enviable academic record. Instead, he was elected chief justice of the student court.[1]

When it came time for college, Brown wound up at Syracuse University, due to the efforts of Kenneth Malloy, a local attorney and former Syracuse lacrosse player, who befriended Brown. Malloy took a keen interest in Brown when he began to shine as an athlete during his adolescent years, over time earning Brown's trust as an advisor and confidant. Although Syracuse was not one of the forty-five colleges that offered Brown an athletic grant-in-aid to play football, Malloy crafted a plan to deliver Brown to Syracuse. First he convinced the university and the athletic department to admit Brown sans scholarship; then, unbeknownst to Brown, he raised sufficient monies from local businessmen in Manhassat to cover Brown's tuition and expenses for the fall semester, believing that once Brown demonstrated his athleticism on the gridiron, the university would ante up the requisite financial support.

When the spring semester arrived, the university did not respond as expected with an athletic scholarship for Brown, forcing Malloy and Manhassat citizens to dig deeper into their pockets to keep him at Syracuse. More menacing, though, were a series of events that frustrated Brown, nearly causing him to leave the university. His first shock came on the football field when the freshman coach, keenly aware of Brown's talent as a running back, tried to convert him to an end because the varsity needed receivers, a move that Brown rejected. Next, he began to feel the fangs of discrimination when his meal plan and living arrangements were different from the rest of the players on the football team. The university quartered him with freshman nonathletes in renovated World War II army Quonset huts some three miles away from campus and assigned him to a general dining hall, denying him of nutritious meals enjoyed by white athletes at the football training table. Further insult came when coaches, administrators, and even some players constantly reminded Brown to avoid becoming another "Avatus Stone," a former Syracuse black athlete who courted white coeds. Agonizing over the discrimination he faced and his coaches' unwillingness or inability to recognize his true athletic talent, Brown planned to leave Syracuse. Only the intervention of Malloy and Manhassat schools superintendent Dr. Raymond Collins convinced Brown to finish out the year. If things did not work out by then, they both promised to help Brown transfer to Ohio State, which had recruited him heavily and would use him as a running back.[2]

During the spring semester Brown played on the freshman basketball team. Both he and Vinnie Cohen, an African American player from Brooklyn, broke the school's freshman scoring record—Cohen did it as a starter, Brown as a reserve. When the weather broke, Brown joined the track team where he found an ally in Coach Bob Grieve, who recognized his talent and respected his persona. Brown found more solace when he joined the lacrosse team under Coach Roy Simmons, who also doubled as an assistant football coach. Meanwhile, the university came through with Brown's athletic grant-in-aid, giving head football coach Ben Schwartzwalder a reason to convert Brown to a receiver. But Brown steadfastly refused. The coach eventually acquiesced and penciled him in as the fifth-string running back. In the fall Brown quickly moved up, and by season's end, he was the team's starting running back. In his sophomore year, Brown was the top rebounder and second leading scorer on the basketball team, statistics he compiled as the sixth man through the team's first ten games. After that he cracked the starting lineup. The rest of Brown's athletic career at Syracuse is legion. He lettered in four sports, won All-American honors in football and lacrosse, set a national record at the time when he scored forty-three points in a football game against Colgate (six touchdowns and seven kicked extra points), and tied for the national scoring championship in lacrosse. In one of his last athletic performances, he led Syracuse to a doubleheader sweep over Army in track and field and lacrosse, scoring thirteen points for the track team and then switching uniforms to preserve an undefeated season for the lacrosse team.[3] Upon graduating from Syracuse, Brown took his talent to the professional level where he had a superlative career.

The Cleveland Browns selected Brown as their first draft choice in 1957. Most analysts regard him as the best running back ever, for in his short nine-year career he led the NFL in rushing eight times, running for 12,312 yards, an average of 104 yards per game and 5.2 yards per carry. He led the Browns to the 1964 NFL Championship and won the league's Most Valuable Player Awards in 1958 and 1965. He is the only person in the College Football, Pro Football, and Lacrosse Halls of Fame.

With Cleveland, Brown was the class of the NFL. As a running back, he had no equal. "For mercurial speed, airy nimbleness, and explosive violence in one package of undistilled evil, there is no other like Mr. Brown," wrote Red Smith, the Pulitzer Prize–winning sports columnist.[4] In spite of Paul Brown's authoritarian, rigid, and inflexible coaching, Brown ran the ball effectively, but he became increasingly frustrated because he did not have the latitude to improvise on the playing field and thus use his talent to the best of his ability. Things changed dramatically in 1963 when the Browns hired Blanton Collier as head coach. Collier, unlike his predecessor, solicited input from players, which assuaged Brown's frustrations. Now with freedom to improvise, Brown carried the ball to an NFL rushing record at that time of 1,863 yards.

He also was an astute and serious student of the game. He knew all the plays as well as the quarterback. Before games Brown would meditate, visualizing the holes he would run through, the cuts he would make, and the tacklers he would knock down as he scampered into the end zone. On evenings before road games, while most of the players took in a movie or enjoyed an evening of leisure, Brown would gather with his two primary blockers—John Wooten and Dick Schafrath—to discuss their opponents' vulnerability and design their own game strategy unbeknownst to their coaches. During these sessions, the trio worked on "attitude plays" that gave them a feeling of confidence that they could beat anybody. "Jimmy [Brown] . . . was the key to everything," recounted Schafrath, "I think he brought everybody to a higher level. I certainly played at a higher level because he was a great player, and he inspired me to do better." Reflecting on Brown's running prowess and on-field moxie, Wooten said that he has "seen them all [O. J. Simpson, Walter Payton, Emmit Smith, Barry Sanders] and there's not one runner . . . that you can compare to Jim Brown. . . . None of them had the power and strength and the speed and ability to analyze things and see things as he did."[5]

As much as Brown enjoyed playing football, his acting career hastened his departure from the game. As fate would have it, inclement weather in England during the summer of 1966 delayed production of Brown's second film, *The Dirty Dozen.* Unable to return to Cleveland in time for the opening of training camp, Brown requested permission to come in late. Art Modell, Cleveland Browns owner, denied Brown's request and threatened to fine him for every day he was late. At that point, Brown submitted his resignation from football, leaving the game, the glory, and his legacy on the football field as he jumped into a new career.

Brown ventured into movies in 1964 by happenstance. While in Los Angeles for the 1964 Pro Bowl, he received an invitation from 20th Century Fox to audition for a role in a movie. Never having acted before, Brown was somewhat reluctant, but, nevertheless, agreed to a screen test. He read the part well and landed a role in *Rio Conchos* (1964), a post–Civil War western in which Brown played an ex-army-officer-turned-cowboy. His second role came in *The Dirty Dozen* (1967), a film in which twelve misfits carry out a dangerous mission in destroying a German stronghold during World War II. Brown, cast in a strong supporting role, was a finalist for the Best Supporting Actor nomination that year.[6]

Perhaps the most celebrated and controversial film of his Hollywood career was *One Hundred Rifles* (1969) co-starring Raquel Welch and Burt Reynolds. Here, Brown broke through racial barriers and tackled taboos in becoming the first black to make a love scene with a white woman. Controversy and confusion erupted on the set while they were making the film in Spain. But even before the filming began, Brown introspectively had no desire to make a pass at Welch. "Raquel was nice. I liked her, everything was cool," he wrote in a 1989 *Ebony Magazine* feature, but "I was not particularly interested in her. I like my woman slim, with small breasts. Raquel was a small woman, yet she *looked* big. She had ample hips, large breasts, those big teeth. She was not my physical type." At one point Brown and Welch stopped speaking to each other. Everyone thought the silence was over a romantic spat, but Brown revealed it was the result of his refusal to support Welch when producers hired their own photographer to promote the film rather than use the one recommended by Welch's husband who, at the time, was also her promoter.[7]

When it came time to shoot the love scene, Brown was instructed to act "sex-starved" and to rip off Welch's blouse. "We began the scene and I started slowly, with sensitivity, suddenly pawing at Raquel's clothes," Brown recalled. "Her bosoms were exposed. I was kissing her and holding her and she became incredibly sexy to me. She wasn't lying on the bed being submissive. She was wild, defiant; she kissed me with her lips, her teeth; it became a sexual contest of who would conquer who in that bed." After watching the first take during a break, Brown realized that Welch preferred to have her face toward the camera. He obliged by moving his face to her side, giving her full access to the camera. "While I was over on the side, I kissed Raquel's ear," Brown continued, "and her body jumped. I stuck my tongue in softly. Raquel started heating up, so did the scene." During the next break, Welch asked Brown to keep his tongue out of her ear because she thought it messed up her makeup.[8]

Welch's memory of that incident had a different tone. "I had never had an actor do the things Jim did," Welch reflected. Then as she pointed to the left side of her face in Spike Lee's documentary, *Jim Brown: All-American,* Welch recalled, "I'm getting a squeegee on this side of my face. I thought, what is this crap! Nobody does this as a real actor! It's a guy thing and here he is . . . he's the gladiator and he's in the arena and he's acting out all these male fantasies—physical prowess. This is his idea of how he has to win in this arena, too."[9]

Two years after making *The Dirty Dozen,* Brown moved to California, purchasing a home in the Hollywood Hills, high above Sunset Boulevard.

He soon became a "certified regular" at The Candy Store, a local hangout of screen giants, Frank Sinatra, Dean Martin, Clint Eastwood, Tony Curtis, and a host of others. Brown hung out with Freddy Williamson and Timmy Brown. "Each group had its territory," Brown related, and "everyone respected that. We mingled, but mostly we'd be dealing with the high octane ladies."[10]

As Brown circulated among the Hollywood in-crowd, he became increasingly aware of the illusionary impact of movie roles. Not one to mince words, Brown made harsh comments about certain actors who "are so into being Macho, they've become cartoon characters." Robert Conrad inflated his shoulders, Tom Jones padded his crotch, and Sylvester Stallone could not leave the Rambo persona on the movie set. John Wayne, too, tried to play the tough guy image in real life. He acted like he could "whip anybody's a——," but in reality "there were 2 million guys," according to Brown, "who could kick John Wayne's a—— every day of the week. Deep inside, John probably knew it, too. So he played the image." "I look at guys like that, their affectations," related Brown, "what I see is weakness. I see self-doubting. A guy who is tough, for real, doesn't need to wear a neon sign."[11]

Brown credited the civil rights movement, the liberalism of the 1960s, and Hollywood's desire to bring a new dimension to the movie screen—a tough black action figure in leading roles—for his early success as a film star. He gave African Americans a new look on the screen. In his first four years in Hollywood, Brown made eight films, but then in the 1970s, racial barriers that Brown had successfully transcended quickly sprang up again. For Brown, film work was hard to find. Producers either changed their minds about casting Brown in a movie role or they stopped calling him altogether. Then, too, the 1968 incident in which Brown allegedly threw one of his girlfriends off a second-story balcony generated massive national publicity and reduced his popularity. But more than that, Brown believes his political activism turned off Hollywood in much the same way that America, a half century earlier, turned its back on Paul Robeson for his unflinching opposition to racial discrimination and social inequality. In fact, Brown looked upon Robeson as a historical hero and martyr who displayed great courage in standing up to all forms of institutionalized racism. Like Robeson, Brown, too, stood peerless in clamoring for racial equality. Though he eschewed Black Muslim ideology, Brown's relationships with Malcolm X and Louis Farrakhan caused filmmakers to perceive him as militant. Consequently, his movie career declined. At best he got some intermittent work with maverick producers.[12] In all Brown appeared in thirty-two films.

Flowing from Brown's movie career was an ill-fated joint venture with Richard Pryor—Indigo Productions. With Brown at the helm, Indigo's purpose was to enable African Americans to produce films about African Americans. Coca-Cola and other corporations contributed $40 million to get the production company started. But the enterprise failed because Jim Brown could not make things happen. According to Ross Greenberg, president of HBO sports, "Hollywood was not ready for black ownership. Even though they were giving Pryor a check, they were doing it really for Pryor to make his own films. I think [Brown] struggled with that for many years." Brown, however, felt double-crossed. Pryor was one of the few individuals Brown says who really hurt him. Brown had worked tirelessly with Pryor to help the rising movie star overcome his addiction to drugs, and then he devoted countless hours to Pryor's recovery and rehabilitation from the severe scalp and facial burns he endured in his self-immolation suicide attempt. Upon his recovery, Pryor asked Brown to give back his company. Brown obliged and Indigo disintegrated.[13] Though Hollywood heightened Brown's visibility, it was during his football career that the athlete-turned-actor began directing his energies toward social issues and the black community.

In 1966 Brown beckoned African American athletes to join him in forming the Negro Industrial and Economic Union, later the Black Economic Union, to bring economic relief to the black community. Some of the athletes who participated were Brig Owens and Jim Snowden of the Redskins; Irv Cross of the Eagles; Ray May, Jim Shorter, and Roy Jefferson of the Steelers; and Erich Barnes, Leroy Kelly, and Sidney Williams of the Browns. Following its motto, *"produce, achieve and prosper,"* BEU helped young blacks with a good idea to "get financing for that idea, then . . . technical knowledge to turn that idea into a business." BEU opened eight offices across the country, most of which were directed by a professional athlete. To help achieve its goals, the organization received more than $1 million in grant money from the Ford Foundation. According to Brown, "The result was wonderful: we started [over 400] businesses across America owned and operated by blacks." Brown clearly understood the importance of economics for survival and growth in the United States. He even chastised black leaders for their failure to emphasize the spirit of capitalism. "Because once I have money in America," Brown wrote, "if I work with *other* blacks who have money, I can get power. Then I don't have to run around asking anyone for anything."[14]

One of the early projects undertaken by the BEU in 1970 was the adoption of Marshall County in Mississippi where hunger and poverty strained the black community. Responding to pleas for help from local black leaders, Brown and sixteen BEU members, all black NFL players, visited Holly Springs, the county seat, to get a first-hand look at the conditions there. In adopting Marshall County, Brown offered a three-pronged offensive. They would begin with a Food First program that would send food and clothing there immediately for distribution to the needy as determined by the local leadership. Next they would tap into government programs already in existence for food, medicine, and financing farm development and small business ventures. Lastly, the BEU would request other black organizations of whatever type—political, economic, religious, social—to adopt other counties with similar conditions. In a follow-up Food First Drive held in Boulder, Colorado, Jim Brown and the BEU collected four truckloads of food and clothing and nearly $10,000 for Marshall County. Some Mississippians, however, were not pleased with Brown's benevolence. The governor, John Bell Williams, and the Holly Springs mayor, Sam Cooperwood, vehemently protested the BEU's incursion into their territory, claiming that "Jim Brown and a group of black militants had spent 'a couple of hours' in Holly Springs and took 'propaganda photos' in 'two or three selected places.'" Even the editor of Marshall County's weekly newspaper joined the protest when he offered a $100 reward to anyone who could confirm an actual starvation death in the county.[15]

Violence and crime in urban centers made it difficult, if not impossible, for BEU and Brown to reach young black males in the inner city, so Brown decided to attack this problem from a different direction. During the 1980s Brown worked with Coor's Golden Door and Barriers, two programs that helped ex-convicts find work and move back into society's mainstream. He also worked with the Vital Issues Project for six years and Jobs Plus, which fostered life-management skills and self-esteem for prisoners and the disenfranchised. Brown's experiences with those self-help and humanitarian organizations provided him with the knowledge and communication skills necessary to establish his own broad-based program to rehabilitate prisoners, gang members, and other underprivileged individuals.

Brown founded Amer-I-Can in 1988 to reach out to gang members and prisoners with the intent of rejuvenating their lives by teaching them personal management and conflict resolution skills. The program's Life Management Skills curriculum "is designed to empower individuals to take charge of their lives and achieve their full potential." The philosophy behind the training curriculum is "to change an individual's attitude from 'I-Can't to I-Can.'" Since 1989 the Amer-I-Can Program in California alone has trained more than 25,000 adult and juvenile inmates in more than thirty of the state's correctional institutions. Brown, himself, brokered a peace between two rival gangs in Los Angeles, the Bloods and the Crips. In resolving the dispute, Brown rejuvenated the Crips' prime leader, Rudolph "Rockhead" Johnson, who now serves as a board member for Amer-I-Can.[16]

Brown believes his Amer-I-Can program "could be the most important movement in the last 200 years." Emphasizing that success comes from viable life-management skills that include setting reasonable goals and controlling emotions, Brown stated in a 1991 *Newsweek* interview, "A lot of us take such things for granted. Some people have never been taught things like wearing a tie for a job interview and not beating up the guy next to you on the job over a slight disagreement. Those principles lead, little by little, to breaking the cycle of poverty and despair." In reaching out chiefly to young black males, Brown declared, "These are guys who have been in and out of prison so much that people say they've been lost forever, hopeless cases. But I've found them to be grateful for the love and acceptance we've shown them." Moreover, Brown continued, "most of these guys are just looking for a way off the streets. But they're warriors, and so you've got to give them something else, something positive to fight for. That's where my program comes in." To bring in revenue, Brown markets the program to prison officials, school administrators, and media outlets. He sees additional money flowing in from "franchising the idea to black activists who will then try to obtain funding for the program in their own communities."[17]

Amer-I-Can programs have spread to sixteen states. On the east coast Sahid Watson operates the Amer-I-Can Academy, Inc., of Trenton, New Jersey, where students learn how to construct resumes, develop strategies for earning their high school diplomas, and focus on setting goals for future employment opportunities. Watson's academy also serves eighteen juvenile and adult correctional institutions in New Jersey. At eleven schools in Rhode Island, nearly three thousand students have completed the training program since 1997. Among the trainees who have completed the program, disciplinary incidents declined by 55 percent, absenteeism decreased by 25 percent, and GPA's rose 18 percent. Although Amer-I-Can programs had operated in Buffalo, New York, in the early 1990s, gang violence and gangland murders in recent years have risen sharply in that city to a point where police officials attributed three-fourths of the thirty-four homicides in 2004 to gang-related activities. This prompted law enforcement officials, community leaders, and civic officeholders to summon Brown for help. Brown spent two days in Buffalo, meeting with gang members, elected officials and community leaders, police officers, and local residents. He told all of the groups that "police action is not the long-term solution. Financial investment needs to occur in poor neighborhoods so that residents have alternatives to lives of crime. The point is you fight crime and make investments in the community through education and rehabilitation."[18]

In 1993 Brown incorporated as a nonprofit organization the Amer-I-Can Foundation for Social Change in order to provide Amer-I-Can services to individuals and communities that could not afford them due to insufficient finances. The foundation's primary objective is "to bring about peace and social change" by reaching out to youth and young adults through community enrichment projects and human development programs, such as neighborhood clean-ups, assistance for the elderly, and participation in sports and other local functions. The foundation depends largely upon donations and grants for its support. With a generous donation from the Nissan Motor Company in 1997, the foundation and Nissan created the Amer-I-Can Peace Plan. Operating under the premise that the safety and security of residents must precede any social or economic development, the Peace Plan calls for community-based units, comprised mostly of local youth, to identify safe neighborhoods or to help create them. More recently, CMS Sports and Entertainment of Las Vegas has given the foundation a $3 million grant, and Rhinotek, a California computer products firm, has agreed to enter into a partnership with young people involved in Amer-I-Can programs.[19]

Although his programs have touched thousands in the black community, Brown believes it will take a unified effort by today's black superstars to make a significant dent in reducing poverty, crime, and violence in black communities across America. On the basis of his experiences with BEU and Amer-I-Can, Brown is convinced that two hundred of today's top black athletes coming together for a common cause could create vast and lasting changes. "If they came together, they could raise millions of dollars from the government, millions of dollars from the public," Brown reasoned. "They could have a tremendous impact on the schools. But they have to do it collectively. Everyone does it individually now."[20]

He chides modern-day athletes for their insensitivity. He has been especially critical of Michael Jordan, Charles Barkley, and Tiger Woods. They have the wealth to plow back into programs for disadvantaged black youth, but have yet to direct some of their resources there. Jordan and Woods have huge endorsement deals with Nike and former Georgetown basketball coach John Thompson sits on Nike's board of directors. Chastising all three, Brown declared that "Nike was getting more from Jordan and Woods and Thompson than any of them gave directly to the black community." Moreover, Brown sees today's athletes as complacent because "once they establish themselves, the money comes, the commercials come. That's what they care about. That's how they judge their success. By the money." No doubt, "it's a sad state of being," Brown lamented, "because if today's athletes had the passion to utilize their intelligence and their resources, they could make tremendous gains into the negative aspect of society." Upon hearing a current athlete refer to the NFL as a slave master, Brown had this response: "What you have is a know-nothing, do-nothing generation talking about the slave master. The slaves in this modern era makes [*sic*] millions of dollars. They have great promotional value. They—a lot of them are black—they neglect the black community, they do nothing collectively, do not understand the political arena and they complain about somebody being a slave master, but they hire mainly white and Jewish lawyers, which is cool. The agents handle their investment dollars, which does not go to the black community."[21]

Brown has been equally critical of Magic Johnson and Warren Moon, both of whom have the resources to pump some of their earnings back into the black community. But his invective for O. J. Simpson, whom he has called a "phony," was the most severe. "Your greatest hero of all, O. J. Simpson, turned the system into a spin," Brown asserted. The Simpson murder trial made "the worst of everything in our system come out because it tried to make a guy a hero who wasn't a hero." "There was confusion" following the trial, Brown stated, "because the African-American community was trying to get behind his cause. But he doesn't care about that community."[22]

In addition to his gallant efforts to raise the quality of life in the black community, Brown has worked fervently to conquer the racial mountain of injustice. Living under the cloud of segregation on St. Simons, Brown experienced racial discrimination early in life when he learned that he could not swim at the island's beautifully maintained beach reserved for "whites only" and that "coloreds" had to drink from a separate water fountain. African Americans did not deal with white people in that island community, which actually strengthened bonds within the black family, giving the children a sense of security and belonging. Brown attributes his spirit and attitude to those early years on St. Simons.

Moving to Manhassat opened Brown's eyes to another dimension as the white folks there interacted with him and gave him respect. But then when he arrived at Syracuse, he "ran chin first into overt racism. Someone had changed all the rules, forgotten [*sic*] to tell me," wrote Brown in his 1989 autobiography, *Out of Bounds,* "most people don't like discussing racism. It embarrasses many people." He stressed his desire to live a *natural* life which as a black American Brown was unable to do because in his own words, "I have to monitor almost everything I do. I must be careful of how I look, where I look, my body language. If I don't act the way a black man is Supposed To, I'll make the people around me embarrassed, injure their feelings, or generate their anger. I will create a Racial Situation." Neither fame nor fortune has exempted Jim Brown from the scepter of racism. "I am affected by it any time I see a black person who's not receiving an even shake," Brown remarked, "I don't have to go hungry to feel for the man with an empty belly. . . . People say, Yes, the white man has his foot up your ass. Be patient, be understanding. . . . Give him another two hundred years. Let him ease it out. I say, No. Take it out. Now."[23]

Brown, as a professional football player, was "very conscious of the civil-rights movement and very active in . . . the movement for dignity, equality and justice." "In fact, it superseded my interest in sports," Brown admitted. "Sports gave me the opportunity to help the cause. So I did." He leaped into action by taking the lead in supporting Muhammad Ali, who not only suffered blatant discrimination but also was stripped of his heavyweight crown when he refused induction into the United States Army. To marshal support for the dethroned champion, Brown summoned to Cleveland America's top black athletes at the time—Bill Russell, Kareem Abdul-Jabbar, Willie Davis, John Wooten, and others. He wanted the athletes to hear Ali's rationale for opposing military service in person and then to decide whether or not they could support him. Ali's religious convictions were clear and his sincerity was forthright. The athletes agreed to stand behind him. Brown reiterated Ali's position as a conscientious objector to the press corps. Years later, Brown would write: "Ali is one of the bravest individuals I have ever known. They tested him, threatened him, denied him what he loved, yet he never gave in. Other than Jackie Robinson, has there ever been a sports figure more important than Ali?"[24]

Brown argued in *Off My Chest,* his first autobiography published in 1964, that racism is an outgrowth of the white man's refusal or inability to understand the black man. Because the white man has more resources and more opportunities than does a black man, the white man has little concern about the "desire that thrives in a black man's heart." Though freedom, equality, and opportunity for the African American are passé in the white mind, Brown admonished the white man in the early 1960s to "start trying to understand [the black man]," because his "mood is explosive." The white man had no conception of the depth of the black protest back then, nor did he "realize that the Black Muslims' basic attitude toward whites is shared by almost 99 percent of the Negro population." Brown joined the moderate NAACP rather than radical Black Muslims, yet he announced that he was "all for the Black Muslims. We need every possible element going for us, whether it be a radical sect, a CORE picket line, or a team of NAACP lawyers arguing in court."[25]

A quarter century later in 1989, Brown, in his second autobiography, described the conception of "racism" as elusive, confusing, and often contradictory. The problem arises because "most white folks have no education when it comes to black folks, no meaningful exposure. What they have is TV. What they see there about blacks is ninety-five percent negative." Television, reference books, authority figures "spew derogatory, stereotypical information. That is powerful medicine. No wonder people get mixed up," concluded Brown.[26]

Now in 2004 Brown admits "the question of race in America is different than it was 15 years ago. And often, equality isn't as much about race as it is about who is richer and who is more educated." The wealthy and the educated have the power and "getting people with power to reach out is difficult." Whites still have power and position and some unquestionably are racist. "But never since the times of slavery has there been a time when there weren't white families reaching out," a tempered Brown proclaimed. "During the slave period, there were free houses for slaves owned by whites. The NAACP was created by a white woman. Branch Rickey was as important as Jackie Robinson. Throughout our Amer-I-Can program you'll find people in different races doing all they can do. There are special people who fight for the right thing."[27]

As noble and as forthright as Brown has been in promoting social justice and racial equality, over the years he has had some difficulty in controlling his anger and dealing with women. Since 1965 he has had to weather six physical assault charges, including one alleged rape. In none of the cases, however, was he convicted. A jury found Brown innocent of assault and battery in the 1965 incident in which he supposedly forced an eighteen-year-old to have sex with him after feeding her whisky. Four years later, Brown was acquitted of assaulting a man who wound up on the hood of his own car following a traffic accident. Then in 1978 he was fined five hundred dollars and incarcerated for a day after slugging his golfing partner. In 1985 he was charged with rape, sexual battery, and assault, but all charges were dropped when his accuser's testimony proved to be inconsistent. The following year he spent three hours in jail for allegedly beating his twenty-one-year-old fiancée whom he accused of flirting. The most notorious incident, however, occurred in 1968 when Brown and his girlfriend got into a stormy argument that culminated with the police finding a semiconscious Eva Maria Bohn-Chinn lying beneath a second-story balcony with an injured arm. Brown insists that Bonn-Chinn, in trying to protect Brown, fell as she attempted to evade the police who had been called to quell the disturbance. Bonn-Chinn's recollection of the incident is vague. She's really not sure what happened, but she is certain she did not jump. Brown, however, denies ever throwing anyone off of a balcony.[28]

Jim Brown makes no bones about his unorthodox attitude toward women. He readily admits that he is "not a one woman man." He likes his women young—late teens, early twenties. "Physically, from the standpoint of nature, a young woman is fabulous," Brown opined. "Everything is peaking. The breasts are firm, the thighs are taut, the buttocks are tight. Physically, between a young girl and an old one, there is no contest." He sometimes flaunts his own sexuality. "If a fine woman offers me her sexual charms," Brown wrote in his 1989 autobiography, "chances are I'll accept. I don't want to be lying on my death bed, doing the big summation, thinking about all those women I *didn't* get to have." During the 1960s when sexual freedom commanded center stage, especially in California, Brown and his followers held orgies at his Hollywood Hills home. He called them "Creative Orgies" in which they brought in women "who would never even consider going to an orgy," no prostitutes, no swingers. "You might make love to three girls in one night," Brown recounted, "and you might see others making love around you. But it was never vulgar or done with disrespect."[29]

Yet for all the orgies, drop-in nude socials, and other free swinging affairs that Brown hosted at his Hollywood mansion, he often threw sanitized parties for teenagers—one night it might be black kids from South Central Los Angeles, on another it might be a group of whites from Pacific Palisades. Brown insisted that his "parties for kids [were] always straight." While there may have been some "sexual undercurrents," not uncommon among teenagers, there never was any sex. In his autobiography, Brown described what he considered to be the most meaningful party he ever hosted. At the time he was playing golf with black gang members, he had agreed to allow the Miss Black California pageant entries to rehearse at his pool, and he was friendly with a group of white youths that he knew at the beach. One night he invited all three groups to his home. Jammed into his house, deck and patio were three disparate groups that wanted nothing to do with one another. But once he blasted out "Family Affair," by Sly Stone from his rooftop speakers, people started mixing and dancing. "It was the funniest looking shit on earth," Brown recalled. "Young white girls from the beach dancing with black gangster guys, and white beach boys were dancing with these pretty, poised black girls. There was no sex, no drugs, just the most harmonious, outgoing party I've ever had. End of night, these people were beaming, saying it was the finest party they'd ever been to."[30]

Although Brown could create instances of harmony among youth, his ideology of sex and love made it difficult, if not impossible, to develop an enduring, compatible relationship with a woman. Matrimony, at least for most of his life, was not in the offing. He did marry a Syracuse co-ed, fathered three children, and then divorced. He yearns for the comfort of women, but has not fostered lasting relationships. Describing his inability or unwillingness to enter into long-term relationships, Brown wrote, "sometimes I get the urge when I'm in a 'relationship,' I may love my woman, but I see another girl, I feel that heat. I will tell her upfront what kind of man I am. I'll say, 'I care about you. You're my baby. But there are times when I'm like a freak. It's a physical need that I have. I won't lie to you or run around behind your back. This is who I am. Can you accept that?'" Most women obviously can't, which inhibits the probability of establishing long-term relationships. In this vein, Brown admits that he is a "sexual hypocrite." "I want to be truly liberated. It's logical. It's fair. And I'm not," clamored Brown. "I want to freak when I want to, but I don't want my woman to. I want her to be something I'm not willing to be."[31]

In 1997 Brown entered into marriage a second time, to Latifa Monique Gunthrop, nearly forty years his junior. They have two children, Aris, a two-and-a-half-year-old boy, and Morgan, a twelve-month-old girl. The final scene in Spike Lee's documentary shows Jim Brown cradling his son, six months old at the time, in his arms. The scene coveys the image of a proud and content father who yearns to be a bonafide, full-time parent this time around. His children from his prior marriage have claimed their father was distant and hardly knew them, not unlike the relationship Brown had with is own father. But then, Brown, too, acknowledges his shortcomings as a husband and father with this oft-repeated phrase: "Don't have role models, have goal models. Only God is a role model." In dealing with children, Brown declared, "You've got to explain to them all human beings have positive and negative [attributes]. Don't bring me a total human being, say that's your role model and then find out that person has negatives."[32]

Overcoming the negatives is precisely what Brown must do as he approaches the age of seventy in order to be an engaged, full-time parent and a loyal faithful husband. It will take a stellar effort on his part to make his current relationship endure. But already there have been some rough spots. Following an argument with Monique on June 15, 1999, Brown took out his anger on his wife's car by smashing out the windows with a shovel. Brown's rampage prompted Monique to run to a neighbor's house and call 911. She made it clear to the operator that Brown had not physically assaulted her, but did acknowledge that she had been the victim of domestic abuse in the past. When the operator heard that, she immediately sent law enforcement officials to Brown's residence. Police arrested Brown, charging him with vandalism and making terrorist threats (in California spousal abuse combined with vandalism is considered an act of terror). On January 6, 2000, a jury acquitted Brown of terrorism, but found him guilty of vandalism. Judge Dale S. Fischer sentenced Brown to three years' probation, a year of counseling for anger management, an eighteen-hundred-dollar fine, and a choice of forty hours on a work crew or four hundred hours of community service. Brown refused the counseling and community service, saying he did not need counseling and community service was below his dignity. As a consequence, the judge sentenced Brown to six months in prison for his offenses.[33]

Jim Brown began serving his sentence in the Ventura County Correctional Facility on March 12, 2002. Immediately, he made nationwide headlines by going on a hunger strike (which he termed "spiritual cleansing") for the purpose of demonstrating to the world the injustice of his incarceration. Refusing food and taking only water, Brown proclaimed, "I'm fasting. I'm on a spiritual fast. That way I am setting the terms of my imprisonment." In refusing Judge Fischer's sentence, Brown likened himself to Nelson Mandela, whom he admired for his brave stance against South Africa's apartheid policy. "I took a position against a judge who did me wrong, who gave me a sentence that is totally out of whack," quipped Brown in his denunciation of Fischer. "I'm here on principle. I stood up to her and said I would fight her, and if I lose I will go to jail. I'm serving the time as an honorable person." Brown thought Fischer's actions were particularly vindictive because he had asked for her removal from his case on the grounds that she was a defendant in a legal malpractice case and sold stocks in violation of the law. In spite of Brown's protest, Fischer refused to recuse herself.[34]

Brown served four months of his six-month sentence prior to being released in July of 2002. He was, however, forced to serve his time in lockdown, in which he spent twenty-three hours each day in isolation in a 6' x 14' cell. He was allowed out of his cell for one hour each day to exercise. Prison officials called it "administration isolation" because of Brown's celebrity status. They feared Brown might organize a protest that could lead to an uprising or that inmates might harm him. Brown described the lockdown as "exceptional punishment" and self-serving because "administrative segregation" in Brown's view "takes away quite a few of your rights," but protects the prison (in this case the county) "from being liable for anything because nobody's going to touch you." Brown spent most of his time reading Scripture, American history, and civil rights history.

The *New York Amsterdam News,* a black newspaper, empathized with Brown and denounced his incarceration, while *USA Today* showed little sympathy in casting Brown as a self-proclaimed victim with a history of domestic abuse. The *Amsterdam News* considered Brown's incarceration "a direct result of what many have called a seemingly vindictive judge and opportunistic Los Angeles mayor." The L.A. district attorney had no plans to indict Brown and since Monique did not press charges, there would have been no case. However, Los Angeles mayoral candidate James Hahn, who was serving as the city's attorney at the time of Brown's arraignment, pursued the prosecution of Brown, which kept the candidate's name in the headlines leading up to his election as mayor. The New York paper was particularly harsh on Judge Fischer, pointing out her appellate court conviction for selling stocks illegally and then losing a plea to California's chief justice for a rehearing. All this plus her involvement in a legal malpractice case during her prosecution of Brown, along with dozens of others, did not carry enough weight to disqualify her from handling Brown's case. When Fischer issued her sentence of Brown, "courtroom observers couldn't believe the harsh penalty for a first-time misdemeanor charge." Furthermore, Rock Johnson, one of Brown's Amer-I-Can administrators, described the case as a joke, for Brown had "vandalized his own car." Thrusting Brown in a positive spotlight, the *Amsterdam News* concluded that "Brown has been doing community service across this nation for over 35 years. Now a Los Angeles County judge has him serving jail time on questionable charges."[35]

Jon Saraceno of *USA Today* viewed Brown's plight much differently.

"He is in jail by choice," wrote Saraceno, "which is rather ironic because it may be the cosmic retribution he deserves, given his misogynistic, violent history. Brown says he has repented to God, but . . . he insists his confinement is due to a corrupt judicial system racially stacked against African-Americans." Brown thought Judge Fischer's sentence was a sham, calling it "mean-spirited and vicious." The reporter then accused Brown of using a "cowardly defense—his wife's menstrual cycle—to explain his violent outbursts." "The only time (we) ever have an argument is during that period," Brown stated, "it happens to be a fact in our lives that we have struggled with PMS." But it is not about the safety of women, Brown argued, "it's about (the courts) making a political point. I can deal with any persecution or prosecution," and because Brown maintained that he is a victim of "society's institutionalized racism," he missed a great opportunity to turn a "liability into an asset." He should be preaching "personal responsibility and self-control," core tenets of Brown's "long-standing activism." "Instead, he chooses to hide behind '60s-style militant rhetoric and black-power salutes, railing against the 'evils of government.' He is out of step with society, black and white. He is missing the message of selflessness he has preached over the decades. Choosing jail was not a selfless act by a wronged man but the epitome of self-absorption and martyrdom." Saraceno believes that "Brown had become politically irrelevant, despite his good works aimed at empowering African-Americans. He now has a platform. . . . The spotlight of incarceration has illuminated that Jim Brown is not yet the man he wants us to believe he is."[36]

Throughout most of his adult years, Jim Brown has had a platform and the spotlight for promoting his beliefs and causes. At this stage of his life, he is hardly seeking more glory or newfound adulation. Nor is he trying to show America that he is something he is not, for on more than one occasion Brown's plea to his followers has been "don't take me as a role model. Take what you can use and leave the rest."[37]

Without question, Jim Brown has been a magnificent athlete, an unflappable, though mediocre at best, actor, and an influential social activist and provocateur of racial justice. As one who experienced and understood the pain of discrimination, Brown resented the label of "a second-class person," a discriminatory classification that he endured and resisted throughout his life. Elaborating on the racism, Brown said that he "fought to do everything . . . to never accept it, [and] worked to help a lot of other people from being under that psychologically debilitating thing."[38] Brown matured and changed as he passed through various stages of his life, and so, too, did his views on racism and discrimination—from naïveté as a young adult to abrasive confrontation in his prime as an athlete and actor to tempered protest in his later years. His positions on race, more or less, reflected that of his heroes during certain phases of his life. From Robeson he adopted resistance and confrontation, and from Mandela he accepted the notion of the pacifist protest.

Clearly, Jim Brown made a difference in whatever he did—on the athletic field or movie screen or in the social arena. He was always out in front as a leader. As a star athlete, he felt obligated to assume leading roles in speaking out for freedom, equality, dignity, and justice in America. Not only did he preach those tenets, but he also played an active role in helping the black community to grow economically because he equated freedom and equality with sound economic growth and stability. He brought capitalism to the black community through his Black Economic Union, but then he moved to attack inner-city poverty by getting at the root of crime and violence by rehabilitating the "incorrigibles" through his Amer-I-Can program that reaches out to gang members, prisoners, and the disenfranchised. Brown has proclaimed success in each of those areas and rightly so, for his charisma attracted followers.

On the flip side, however, he has had a history of physical assaults (mostly against women). How does one explain that behavior. We needn't even try. Jim Brown, like all mortals, has some flaws—one of them happens to be difficulty in handling anger. He appears to be getting a handle on the anger, or at least he seems to be directing it toward inanimate objects like cars rather than humans.

The complexity of Jim Brown is indecipherable. But Brown is really no different than most human beings with his quirks, oddities, and idiosyncrasies. "You can't figure him out," remarked James Box, a one-time felon whom Brown had resurrected. "Just accept him for what he is. You'll go crazy trying to figure him out."[39] Nevertheless, Brown is a bold, stand-up guy who is not afraid to admit his attraction for young women, his open expression of his sexuality, and his love for life and pleasure. He moved from stardom on the football field to leading roles in movies, to clarion advocate of racial justice, to purveyor of economic growth in the black community without skipping a beat. In spite of his shortcoming with anger management, Jim Brown, in Spike Lee's words, is indeed an All-American.

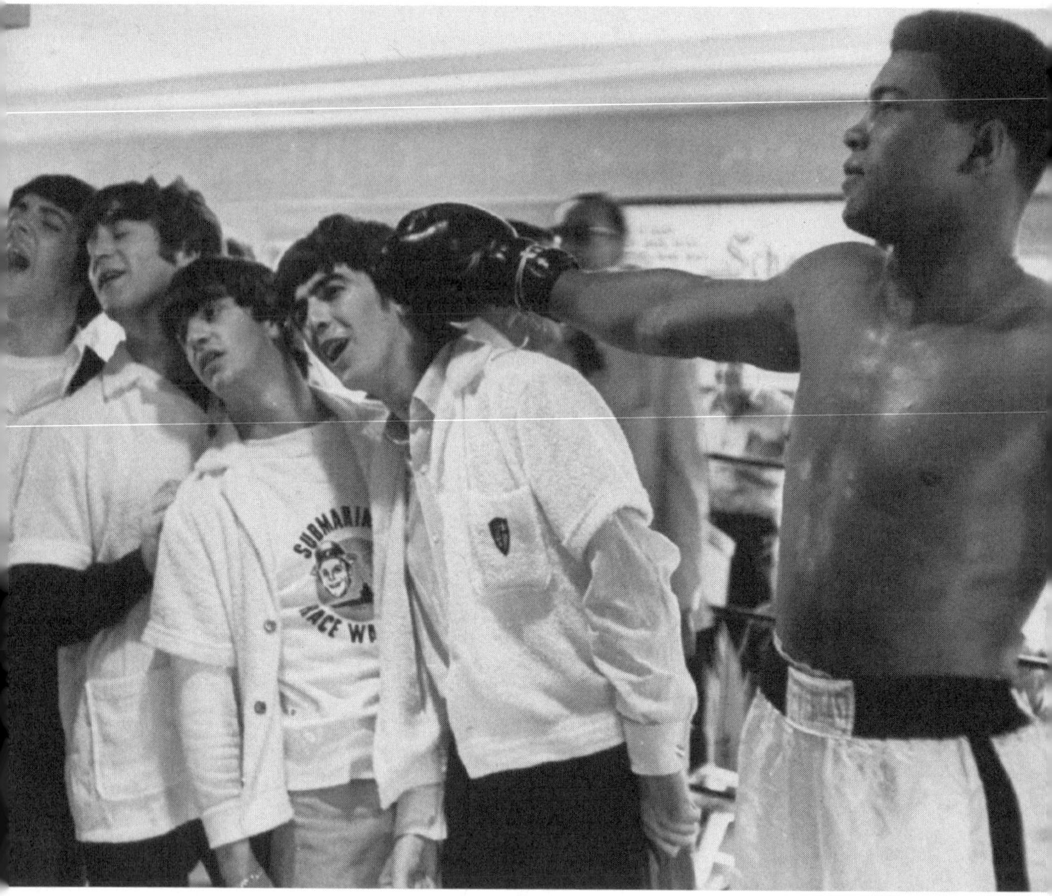

Muhammad Ali taking mock shot at the Beatles on February 18, 1964, in Miami. A week later Ali would defeat Sonny Liston to become the heavyweight champion and shortly thereafter announcing to the public he was a member of the Nation of Islam. *(Getty Images)*

15

Muhammad Ali

Flawed Rebel with a Cause

GERALD EARLY

There have been few athletes in the history of American amateur or professional sports that had either the fame or the cultural impact of heavyweight boxing champion Muhammad Ali. Certainly no other athlete so defined the era of the 1960s and 1970s, an era that gave us strikes and collective bargaining in major league baseball, saw blacks grow to dominate professional and college basketball and football, witnessed murder at the Olympics, experienced the creation and merger of several sports leagues, produced the rise of women's athletics, and saw television become a major force in presenting sports to the public and, exceeding newspapers, a significant mechanism in interpreting sports to their fans. Various individual sports stars emerged during these decades, from Wilt Chamberlain and Bill Russell to Joe Namath and O. J. Simpson, from Jack Nicklaus and Billie Jean King to A. J. Foyt and Bob Gibson. Yet somehow Muhammad Ali seemed to tower over all the other sports figures of his time. In the turbulent period of the Vietnam War and the civil rights movement and the protest cultures that both spawned, the urban riots, Watergate and the downfall of an American president, the rise of mainstream audiences for hardcore pornography and the erosion of that audience for the American western, Muhammad Ali affected several of the social and political changes that occurred during his young adulthood as he seemed to be a product of them.

Muhammad Ali was born Cassius Marcellus Clay Jr. on January 17, 1942, in Louisville, Kentucky. He was the older of two brothers. His father, Cassius Clay Sr., was a sign painter and something of a frustrated artist and his mother, Odessa Grady Clay, was a domestic. "He was a good boy," Clay Sr. said about his son. "Both them boys, him and his brother, were good boys growing up. They didn't give us any trouble. They were church boys, because my wife brought them to church every Sunday."[1] Clay Sr., who painted many murals for churches around Louisville, taught both his sons his trade, probably expecting them to follow in his footsteps. Clay's mother said she thought her young son was a special child, but of course it is hard to know whether she actually felt this way when he was a boy or only in hindsight after he had become famous.

Young Clay began to take boxing lessons in October 1954 at the age of twelve because someone had stolen his bicycle and he was determined to exact revenge against the perpetrators. He never discovered who stole his bike, but he did blossom as a young fighter, taking instruction from Louisville policeman Joe Martin. His brother, Rudolph Arnette Clay (Rudolph Valentino Clay in some sources, later Rahaman Ali), also took up boxing but, lacking his brother's talent, never became a significant presence in the sport. He eventually became part of his brother's circle of hangers-on, assistants, sycophants, hustlers, and Muslim strongmen who surrounded him in his glory days like a miasma. Perhaps some form of sibling rivalry inspired Cassius; his relationship with his brother was not always easy to understand.

Clay became a gym rat, feeling that he could succeed in boxing as he never could in school. Although he showed no special ability in his first few years, he was extraordinarily determined. "Cassius Clay," Joe Martin said, "when he first began coming around, looked no better or worse than the majority. . . . He was just ordinary, and I doubt whether any scout would have thought much of him in his first year." But, Martin went on, "He was a kid willing to make the sacrifices necessary to achieve something worthwhile in sports. I realized that it was almost impossible to discourage him. He was easily the hardest worker of any kid I ever taught."[2]

Cassius was a mediocre student, graduating from Central High School with a D- average, ranking 376 out of a class of 391. Clay could barely read and write, and although his high school progress report[3] showed his intelligence as average, on official IQ tests, he actually recorded below-average intelligence. It was clear that a combination of temperament, natural inclination, and little aptitude signaled that he was not likely to succeed in any profession that would require attaining a great deal of education or a high degree of literacy—another reason, therefore, that he threw himself into boxing. There were, moreover, models in the sport to inspire him. It was the era after the great Joe Louis, but there was Jersey Joe Walcott and Ezzard Charles and the magnificent middleweight Sugar Ray Robinson, who became Clay's idol. There was also the young black hero of the 1952 Helsinki Olympic Games, Floyd Patterson, who would, in later years, become Ali's nemesis and, oddly, one of his few public supporters in the sport when he was denied a license to fight in the late 1960s because of his conviction for violation of the Selective Service Act. Indeed, for young Clay, who was a first-generation child of television, boxing, the medium's most-televised sport, was a constant presence, a classroom both in the gym but also electronically with weekly programs like *Friday Night Fights.*

Cassius eventually became one of the most impressive amateur boxers in the country, winning six Kentucky Golden Gloves championships. He became the national Amateur Athletic Union (AAU) champion in 1959 and 1960 and won a gold medal as a light-heavyweight in the 1960 Rome Olympics, although he almost didn't go because he was afraid to fly on an airplane. At this point, Clay was already famous, having been occasionally televised locally as an amateur, and, of course, having been on national television during the Olympics. He enormously enjoyed the attention. One point of dispute has been what happened to Clay's gold medal: in his autobiography, *The Greatest: My Own Story,* Clay claims to have thrown it in the Ohio River after he returned from the Olympics and experienced racist treatment in his hometown: he was refused a meal at a restaurant and chased by a gang of white motorcyclists. This has been vigorously disputed by some who say this incident never happened.[4] While in Rome, Clay was asked about the American race situation by a reporter from the Soviet Union, to whom he replied: "Tell your readers we've got qualified people working on that problem, and I'm not worried about the outcome. To me, the U.S.A. is still the best country in the world, counting yours. It may be hard to get something to eat sometimes, but anyhow I ain't fighting alligators and living in a mud hut."[5] Clay had begun visiting the temples of the Nation of Islam in 1959, so it may be safe to say that while he was intrigued by the group at this stage, the Muslims did not seem to have made an impression upon his political views. That would come later.

Clay's boyish good looks, his outgoing personality, combined with the gimmicks of his poetry and his good-natured bragging, sustained his fame after the Olympics, as he received a great deal more media attention than most amateur fighters. He turned professional immediately after returning from Rome and was managed by a syndicate of eleven Louisville businessmen led by William Faversham. At first, he was placed under the guidance of light-heavyweight champion Archie Moore, but the two men could not get along. Clay resented Moore's advice and training regimen. He returned to Louisville from Moore's camp in California and was taken on by trainer Angelo Dundee. Skillfully guided by the wily Dundee, a highly experienced boxing man, who did not try to change Clay's unorthodox style, which had always infuriated most of the old heads of boxing, Clay, like most highly touted young fighters, won all of his early fights against either second- or third-rate opponents or noted fighters whose skills had deteriorated like Archie Moore, his short-lived tutor, whom he knocked out in four rounds on November 15, 1962, in Los Angeles. His most difficult fight of this "contender" stage was against Doug Jones, in which Clay won a ten-round decision on May 13, 1963, in New York, although many at ringside thought he lost the fight. Clay's relationship with Dundee was different from that of most between a boxer and a trainer: Dundee never spoke for Clay, never scripted his answers with the press, never advised him in any way in his personal life, never, in fact, seemed to advise him about boxing itself; Clay always spoke for himself, never through an intermediary, and he seemed never to take advice from anyone, not even Drew "Bundini" Brown, who was probably closer to Clay as a trainer throughout his career than Dundee was. Clay, in fact, throughout his entire career, always gave the impression that he trained himself, that he managed himself, that he created himself. He, thus, gave the impression that he had more power as a boxer than any previous fighter ever had in the sport. In fame and public reach, in creating his own persona and voicing his own views, this was certainly true. It was not true in his relation to the commercial powers that ran the sport. He was, in that regard, as controlled as any other fighter in the history of the sport. To be sure, with his constant bragging, his poetry, and his zany antics, he won a national following, even appearing briefly in the 1962 film version of Rod Serling's *Requiem for a Heavyweight*.

At six-feet-three and over two hundred pounds, Clay astonished sportswriters with his hand and foot speed, his reluctance ever to take a punch to the body or to fight in close, his ability to defend himself while holding his hands at his waist, and his insistence on avoiding punches by moving his head backward instead of moving to the side. Clay modeled much of his style after his idol, welterweight and middleweight champion Sugar Ray Robinson. But it seemed an inappropriate style for a heavyweight and a style that Archie Moore thought would only prolong his fights, much to Clay's detriment in the long run. He thought Clay was big enough and strong enough to knock out his opponents quickly, and he intended to teach Clay how to do that. One of the reasons the men fell out was that Clay was resistant to learning to fight in that way. But no heavyweight before Clay ever possessed such speed, quickness, or grace. He could succeed with the style he had because of his physical gifts and his ring savvy. "People said I held my hands too low and did other things wrong, but when I was young, my defense was my legs. My style in the ring was to keep my distance, don't get too close, stay just out of range, get in just enough to punch, and get out."[6] Clay attracted a great many people to boxing who would normally have had little interest in it simply because they were enthralled with the lyricism of his style.

On February 25, 1964, in Miami, Clay fought as a heavy underdog (7 to 1) for the heavyweight title against Charles Sonny Liston, an ex-convict who grew up in rural Arkansas among twenty-four brothers and sisters (he served time in prison in Jefferson City, Missouri, for armed robbery), who was thought by many to be virtually invincible because of his devastating one-round knockouts of former champion Floyd Patterson, the last heavyweight champion to weigh under two hundred pounds. He beat Patterson on September 25, 1962, to win the championship, a fight he had a difficult time getting because he was an ex-convict, and a fight that most of the public wanted to see him lose. He retained the title when he beat Patterson again on July 22, 1963. So few thought that the bragging Clay had a chance that rumors circulated that he would not even show up for the fight. Most thought the young fighter had no punch, no chin, and would hardly be able to withstand the hard-punching Liston. Clay, for his part, had been harassing Liston during most of the period before the fight, taunting him by calling him "the Bear" (a word for Liston he borrowed from Patterson's trainer Cus D'Amato) and "ugly," banging on Liston's front door in the early morning hours, demanding that he fight him then and there. It was unclear how afraid Clay might actually have been of Liston; fear plays an important part in the psychological makeup of a fighter, and most fighters enter the ring with some fear of both their opponents and of failing, of being physically punished. Liston once slapped a taunting Clay in the face in a Las Vegas casino and sent him meekly on his way.[7] The weigh-in ceremony the morning of the fight was part theater of the absurd, part screwball comedy, and part, no doubt, Clay trying to work up his courage against a formidable opponent. (After all, as a professional fighter, Clay knew very well how well Liston could fight, and he had no reason to believe that Liston would do anything less than his best.) At the weigh-in, Clay, wearing a robe that said "Bear Hunting," seemed as if he wanted to attack Liston, and gave the appearance of being completely out of control. It was, apparently, all an act on Clay's part to gain a psychological edge over his opponent. But yet it is unlikely that this greatly affected Liston, unless it was to make him overconfident. But Liston was already convinced that Clay was afraid of him.

What was more ominous, from the perspective of the fight's promoters and most of the general public, were rumors coming out of Miami that Clay was being seen with Malcolm X, the charismatic minister of the Nation of Islam, probably the most feared and misunderstood religious cult of the time and certainly one of the most militant black organizations to emerge since the Great Depression. Clay had already joined the controversial group but he did not announce this until after the fight with Liston, in part because he did not want the fight canceled because of his religious conversion and in part because the Muslims did not want to be overly embarrassed by his defeat, which nearly all in the organization thought would happen, including the NOI's leader, Elijah Muhammad. Indeed, Muhammad himself was not very pleased with having Clay as a member. He thought very little of prizefighters (dumb guys who participated in a politically incorrect sport) and was particularly unimpressed with Clay's antics, quite out of keeping with the somber, stern demeanor of the group. Clay was not fully aware at the time how little the Muslim leadership thought of him and how little confidence they had in his abilities to beat Liston. Malcolm X, however, was confident that Clay would win, convincing the young boxer that the fight was a jihad, a symbolic war that was both political and religious between the crescent and the cross or between the black man who was for his people and the black man who represented white interests, a psychological device that Clay nearly always, and his opponents occasionally, particularly Floyd Patterson, were to use to dramatize virtually all the major fights of his career, turning them into contesting forms of black political propaganda. Some of Clay's denigration of his opponents was distinctly not funny, not illuminating, not fair, and, as his career went along, seemed to become especially tiresome by the middle 1970s.

Clay stunned the sporting world by defeating the aging Liston fairly easily in seven rounds. After the fight, Clay announced that he had not only joined the Nation of Islam but that he had a new name, Muhammad Ali. The response from the boxing establishment, the sporting press, and the white public generally was hostile, even vitriolic. The NOI was largely seen, mistakenly so, as an antiwhite hate group, something on the order of the Ku Klux Klan, with its beliefs in complete racial separation, white racial inferiority, and Allah's ultimate descent into human history to right all racial wrongs, ending in a massive, supernaturally induced, white genocide. Although there had been a few black jazz musicians who had converted to Islam, such as Ahmad Jamal, Art Blakey, and Dakota Staton (they were not members of the Nation of Islam), most of the public, either black or white, knew little about the religion and the NOI's highly racialized distortion of the religion diminished further what little understanding most Americans had. Never was an athlete so pilloried by the public as Ali was. Most sports journalists ridiculed his religion and refused to call him by his new name. Former champion Floyd Patterson went on a personal crusade against the NOI in his fight against Ali on November 22, 1965, which Patterson lost, in part because he simply lacked the skills, and in part because he injured his back and was virtually unable to throw a meaningful punch in the fight. Patterson was particularly outraged that Ali would condemn America as he did and that he would permit himself to be taken over by the Muslims. (Ali fired his white syndicate, and Herbert Muhammad, one of Elijah Muhammad's sons, became his manager.) Patterson later became one of the few fighters to defend Ali publicly during his years of exile, but it must be remembered that Patterson was one of the most thoughtful men ever to enter the ring; he understood the nature of his profession and agonized over it far more than Ali did, simply because he was a far more introspective man. In any case, no black athlete since the reign of Jack Johnson (1908–15), the first black heavyweight champion, so enraged most whites, and more than a few blacks, with his opinions and the way he chose to live his life.

After winning his rematch with Sonny Liston in Lewiston, Maine, on May 25, 1965, in a bizarre first-round knockout caused by a punch no one saw thrown, just two months after Malcolm X was gunned down in Harlem by members of the NOI, Ali, probably one of the most unpopular fighters in history, spent most of the next year abroad, beating George Chuvalo in Toronto, Henry Cooper in London, and Karl Mildenberger in Germany. He also defeated Ernie Terrell in Houston, one of his few American fights during this period. (Liston claimed later that he took a dive in the fight because the Muslims threatened to murder him if he didn't. Apparently, Liston feared the Muslims even more than the mob, for whom he allegedly took a dive in the first fight, and for whom he worked for a good portion of his adult life. It is unclear whether Liston's story is true and most knowable boxing people believe Ali won the fights or had the skills to beat Liston, even if the fights were not entirely legitimate. But it is certain that the Nation of Islam was a frightening group to many people for good reason, and it was known that several of the mosques were heavily involved in organized crime in the black communities where they were located. So, Liston's story cannot be dismissed out of hand.)[8]

While Ali was abroad, the Selective Service changed his draft status from 1-Y (unfit for military service because of his low score on army intelligence tests; in high school, Ali only scored an 83 on standardized intelligence tests, which means that he had a score that was about one standard deviation below average intelligence) to 1-A (qualified for induction). Many saw this change as a direct response to intense negative public opinion concerning Ali's political views. In fact, after the August 1964 Gulf of Tonkin incident that produced the Gulf of Tonkin Resolution that gave President Johnson broad powers to escalate the war in Vietnam without an official declaration of war from the Congress, the passing score on the army intelligence tests was lowered, so that many other men besides Ali were affected. Ali refused to serve in the military on the grounds that it violated his religious beliefs. Elijah Muhammad, leader of the NOI, had served time in prison during World War II for refusing to serve in the armed services and for sympathizing with the Japanese. (There was greater, and misplaced, sympathy for the Japanese among many blacks during the 1930s and into World War II because they were a "colored" nation standing up to European and white American power.) Wallace

Muhammad, son of Elijah, also served time for refusing military service. Yet it was unclear how Ali saw himself as being exempted from service: Islam is not a pacifist religion, and Muslims have served in the American military. Ali himself made his money in a violent profession where it was possible he could permanently maim or kill an opponent, so he lived by no personal principal of pacifism like, say, Bayard Rustin or people associated with the Peace or War Resisters Movement. He claimed to be a Muslim preacher, one of his claims for exemption, yet he was never formally put in charge of any mosque, nor regularly preached for the Muslims anywhere. He never had the status in the organization that Malcolm X had and was never referred to, as Malcolm was, as a minister. Part of his claim of exemption was also that there were no blacks on his local draft board at the time his change in status occurred, and thus it was not a reflection of the local community. It must be understood that during the 1960s, most men had served in the military and thought it was something that everyone should be willing to do. Most veterans of the Korean War and World War II were alive and actively shaped American public opinion at the time. These men could not understand why Ali would be opposed to serving in the military, why he was unpatriotic, and how this had anything to do with his race. Joe Louis had served honorably during World War II. Why not Ali now? If anything, despite racism, and entrenched segregation before the Korean War, the military was largely seen as an attractive career by many black men. But blacks had had a troubled history with the military and many were not eager to serve. Some felt that society itself was stacked against them so that serving in the military was virtually the only option they had, short of a life on the margins of the criminal world. For his part, Ali was afraid to join the military because he thought he might be killed by some overly patriotic white (a not unrealistic possibility as Ali's opposition to military service and his membership in the NOI had stirred up plenty of racial hatred in an age when there was a great deal of violence committed against public figures). He also saw the war in racial terms and was not convinced that he should risk his life to fight for whites, as he saw it, against "colored" people (the Vietnamese) who had done nothing to him or anything to his country, as far as he could discern. The Vietnam War was seen as a race war by the American left and by many younger, more militant blacks. Naturally, the refusal to serve on the part of such a prominent and charismatic black person was bound to affect other young blacks, at least, to make people look upon resistance of this sort as something heroic, something principled.

In June 1967, Ali was convicted in federal court of violation of the Selective Service Act and sentenced to five years in prison and fined ten thousand dollars. He was immediately stripped of his boxing title and every state athletic commission stripped him of his boxing license. For the next three and one-half years, Ali, free on bond while appealing his case (which he eventually won unanimously on appeal to the U.S. Supreme Court on a technicality on June 28, 1971), was prohibited from boxing. He spoke on college campuses (because he needed the money, although his conservative views about race, sex, and morality were often met with skepticism, if not outright disapproval), became a darling of the antiwar movement because he was, as was often pointed out, sacrificing the best years of his athletic life for his beliefs (but so were athletes who had chosen to fight in wars and who had to endure the rigors of combat to boot), and inspired other black athletes such as Harry Edwards, who tried to organize a black boycott of the 1968 Mexico City Olympics. Medal-winning track stars Tommie Smith and John Carlos gave a clenched-fist salute during the playing of the National Anthem at those games and were promptly sent home.

In 1970, with public opinion strongly against the Vietnam War, and aided by growing black political power in several southern state governments, Ali was given a license to fight in Georgia, something made possible by the very civil rights movement's push for integration, that, as a Black Muslim, he condemned. He returned to the ring on October 26 and defeated journeyman Jerry Quarry in three rounds. Although he was still a brilliant fighter, the long layoff had eroded his skills to some degree. He took more punishment in the ring when he returned than before. This was to have dire consequences for him as he grew older.

Ali had his biggest, most competitive and commercially successful, fights in the 1970s. On March 8, 1971, he lost to undefeated Philadelphian Joe Frazier, Ali's archrival and the man he most ridiculed throughout his career, in a close fifteen-round decision at Madison Square Garden in what was the richest, most-publicized sporting event in American history. The fight was so brutal that both men were hospitalized after, Frazier for several weeks. It was Ali's first defeat. He won the North American Boxing

Federation title, a significant but lesser honor than the world's championship, in July 1971. He lost again in March 1973 against ex-marine Ken Norton in a twelve-round decision where Ali's jaw was broken late in the fight, not in the second round as Ali claimed, as virtually no fighter could have fought twelve rounds with a broken jaw. (It was said that Ali slept with two women the night before this fight.[9] It was during Ali's return to the ring in the 1970s that his womanizing grew legendary.) Ali regained his North American Boxing Federation title from Norton in a highly disputed twelve-round decision six months later. On January 28, 1974, he fought Frazier again at Madison Square Garden. It was a nontitle match as Frazier had lost his title to George Foreman on January 22, 1973, in Kingston, Jamaica. This time Ali won a close twelve-round decision. Ali finally regained the title in Kinshasa, Zaire, on October 30, 1974, when he knocked out Foreman in the eighth round of a fight where he was a decided underdog, most of the public thinking that Ali, at thirty-two, had passed his prime. Foreman, a gold medallist at the 1968 Olympic Games, where he, in contrast to Smith and Carlos's clenched-fist salute, carried small American flags around the ring when he won his medal, was a fearsome fighter who had easily beaten all of his opponents including Frazier and Ken Norton, both of whom gave Ali a tough time. Why Zairian dictator Sese Seko Mobutu bankrolled the fight (the fighters split ten million dollars, the biggest payday ever for a fight) is unclear, but one of the people who talked him into it was Don King, who emerged from this fight as a major promoter of big-time boxing matches. In the fight in Zaire, Ali used a technique he called "Rope-a-Dope," where he leaned against the ropes and permitted Foreman to punch away at him, which, punctuated by Ali's punishing flurries at the end of the round, eventually fatigued the heavy-fisted younger champion. Ali was to use this in later fights, when he was too lazy to train, and thus take increasingly more punishment in the ring. He also used this technique during training as well.

After regaining the title, Ali was lionized in the United States and enjoyed incredible popularity around the world. He became not only the most famous American Muslim but the most famous Muslim anywhere and was the most photographed and publicized black man in history. He appeared in a film version of his life—*The Greatest* (1977)—based on his 1975 autobiography that was edited by Toni Morrison, joining Jackie Robinson and Joe Louis as black athletes who starred in versions of their life stories on the screen. Ali also appeared on television programs and commercials. He even beat Superman in a special 1978 oversized issue of the DC comic. Part of this adulation and acceptance stemmed from the fact there was a general shift in attitude on the part of white sportswriters and the white public; in many instances, different sportswriters were covering Ali now than were doing so in the early days of his career and they were far more sympathetic to him. Also, Ali himself tended to be less doctrinaire in his political and religious views as he grew older. And he was always gregarious and funny, something that lessened some of the white public's venom against him even when he was most demonized. Sometimes, his denigration of black opponents and his bragging seemed shrill and tasteless, as if he himself had grown weary of the act. He eventually embraced Wallace D. Muhammad's more ecumenical form of Islam when the NOI split into two factions following the death of Elijah Muhammad in 1975.

On September 30, 1975, Ali fought Joe Frazier once again, this time in Manila, the Philippines, in what was probably the most brutal of the three hard bouts the two men fought. Ali won when Frazier was unable to come out for the fifteenth and final round in a fight where both men took terrific punishment and where Ali himself was unable to come out for the fifteenth round, either. Frazier simply did not know this. Many found the beatings that both men administered to be so savage that it was thought that neither should fight again. Both did, much to the regret of many who knew the fight game well and much to their regret in the end. Each man had totally depleted the other in this fight. Frazier fought only two more times. Ali fought ten more times, including very tough bouts against Jimmy Young and Earnie Shavers, among others. He had to continue to fight to support his huge entourage and because he craved the adulation and attention.

On February 15, 1978, an out-of-shape, uninspired Ali, deciding to create the "Rocky" story in real life, fought a young ex-marine and Olympic champion from St. Louis named Leon Spinks, who had had only seven professional fights. Ali lost his title for the third time in his career. Ali, however, managed to regain his title by beating Spinks easily on September 15 of the same year.

In 1979, weary of the ring wars, his reflexes shot, his legs gone, his appetite for competition slaked, Ali retired from the ring, only to do what so many great, aged champions do against the better judgment of everyone who knows them: come back. On October 2, 1980, Ali, with his hair dyed black and his body streamlined by diuretics, unsuccessfully challenged heavyweight champion and former sparring partner Larry Holmes, enduring a horrible beating over ten rounds. His next fight was a ten-round decision loss to Trevor Berbick on December 11 of the following year, a fight Ali took because he was still not convinced that he was no longer able to fight competitively. After the Berbick fight, Ali retired for good, with a professional record of fifty-six wins, thirty-seven by knockout, and five losses. He was elected to the Boxing Hall of Fame in 1987.

Even before his retirement from the ring, Ali's speech was becoming more slurred. This was noticed even at the time of the third fight with Frazier. In his fight against Holmes, Ali not only seemed old but sick, unhealthy. After retirement, he seemed to age rapidly, moving slowly, speaking with a thick tongue that was almost incomprehensible. He also suffered bouts of palsy. There is some debate as to whether Ali has Parkinson's disease or a Parkinson-like deterioration of his neurological system. Was this caused by the punishment he took in the ring in the later years of his career? It can certainly be safely said that his condition was surely aggravated by his ring career. Ali had a tendency to bring out the best in his opponents—that is to say, that his opponents often fought the best fights of their careers against him. This meant that Ali fought many hard fights, particularly when he returned to boxing in the 1970s. What is amazing about Ali is not that he finally succumbed to the cruelty of his trade but that he lasted as long as he did, over twenty years as a professional fighter. Today, although Ali leads a very active life, doing magic tricks, signing autographs, giving out copies of the Koran, traveling and appearing at various public events, including, most famously, the lighting of the Olympic flame in Atlanta at the 1996 Games in Atlanta, he walks slowly and rarely talks.

Ali's private life was turbulent. He has been married four times: Sonji Roi (1964–65), whom he divorced because she would not follow his Muslim beliefs and because the Muslims themselves never liked her; Belinda Boyd Ali (1967–76), who was reared a Muslim and was supportive of Ali during his exile years, probably the strongest of his wives; Veronica Porsche Ali (1977–86), who was probably the most beautiful of his wives and least compatible with him; and his current wife, Lonnie Ali, whom he knew as a girl in Louisville, and whom he married in 1986. He also had numerous affairs when he was younger, including having a teenage mistress who gave birth to a daughter. He has a total of nine children, including one adopted son.

Interest in Ali has been rekindled in recent years thanks to the Academy-Award–winning documentary *When We Were Kings* (1996) and *Ali,* a Hollywood feature film about the boxer's life starring Will Smith, which was released in 2001. The latter film did poorly at the box office, possibly because Ali does not mean as much to young people today as he does to people who are in their forties and fifties. And films are largely marketed to young people. The film was also a bit incoherent as a narrative, almost assuming that the viewer was already familiar with the story of Ali's life. Books continue to be written about him, and he has probably been the subject of more photographic books than any athlete in the twentieth century, including Benedikt Taschen and Howard Bingham's *GOAT: A Tribute to Muhammad Ali* (2004) (Greatest of All Time), a giant limited edition that weighs seventy-five pounds and costs three thousand dollars.

It is impossible to overestimate Ali's importance not only as a gifted athlete who dominated his sport for nearly two decades and helped to make sports generally a multimillion-dollar television enterprise, but as a religious and political presence in American popular culture. He changed the way both the public and the press related to black athletes. He also was a singularly different type of black personality to emerge at his time: the trash-talking, swaggering black athlete who defies the world to shut him up, to humble him. One can see Ali's descendants in figures like Terrell Owens, Ray Lewis, and Barry Bonds. Ali understood athletics as a form of showmanship and as a form of self-promotion. Ali clearly made white America more aware not only of Islam but of black militancy as a change in attitude. He made himself the first true world's champion by fighting abroad more than any other heavyweight champion had until that point, and having a following in countries that most Americans had never heard of. Ali clearly symbolized in the 1960s and 1970s the fact that blacks were now redefining their relationship with whites as blacks were also redefining themselves. Ali came to represent racial pride, strong religious principles, and youthful exuberance.

But he also represented something else as well, less positive. He gave us the athlete as petulant adolescent, as self-absorbed dramatist. Remember, Ali never once in his career ever did anything on behalf of the people in his profession. He never tried to organize boxers into a union or even mention that they needed one, which they did and still do. At the height of his fame, he had the influence at least to make the public think seriously about boxers having a union, about ways to make the profession better. But as he said, "I don't know anything about fightin', really. Only about *me* fightin'."[10] He may have given old fighters money or a job in his camp but this was largely his playing the typical champion's role of the padrone, the lavish, paternal lord. It did nothing for the profession as a whole. Ali may have sacrificed for his beliefs, but he was no Curt Flood. His denigration of his opponents, especially his black opponents (he almost never insulted his white opponents to the same degree), showed a lack of sportsmanship that was hardly excused by the need for a big gate. Ali was not only terribly overbearing but remarkably superficial. He was not a smart man or a particularly astute one outside of the ring. Most of what he said when he was being political was largely Black Muslim dogma, recited with the fervor that one can hear from any Jehovah's Witness or Child of God. Only the times he lived in and the fact that he was strikingly handsome made people take what he said seriously. He had the assurance and confidence of his dogma, which is what made him appear to have a livelier mind than he actually possessed. It is difficult to say whether he stayed in the Nation because he actually believed or because he was afraid of the group and that he might wind up like his good friend in the early 1970s, Major Coxson, who was murdered with his entire family in his Camden, New Jersey, home in what appeared to be a signature Nation of Islam hit. He had infinitely more courage standing up to the government than to the Muslims, probably because the government was an easier, less-frightening opponent. Ali was also a hypocrite, as he rarely practiced what he supposedly believed. He violated a number of tenets of his faith, even as he professed that he didn't. That hardly distinguishes him from most people of faith. But just as there was something heroic and grand about Ali, there has always been something faintly fraudulent about him as well: a man who got used by the Muslims, by the sport of boxing, by corporate powers of America, and by his own ego. How could anyone trust the judgment of a man who didn't have the sense to get out of his dangerous profession before it maimed him irreparably?

On balance, Ali was a complex figure, admirable in many ways, but weak and unappealing in others. This is what makes him such a fascinating person to think about and study, for his strengths and weaknesses so much mirror the age that produced him. It was an age of black pride, resistance, and heroic engagement but also an age of self-indulgence, immaturity, and dishonesty. No one performed better in the ring under pressure; no one seemed to have squandered his chances as much outside of it until Mike Tyson came along. Ali thought being a Muslim would allow him to resist the worst moral excesses of the age of "do your own thing," but it didn't, in the end. It only made it possible for him to mask his excesses from the public a bit longer than most boxing champions do. This blend of transcendence and failure, almost perfectly contoured to his era and, taken together, so much larger than life, is what makes Muhammad Ali the important, the extraordinary man that he is, a man whose story teaches and will continue to teach us all about what it means to be a celebrity and an exceptional high-performance athlete in America.

16 "The Quiet Militant"

Arthur Ashe and Black Athletic Activism

DAMION THOMAS

Arthur Ashe, the first African American male to win the U.S. Open, the Wimbledon Open, the Australian Open, and the NCAA's men's tennis singles championship enjoyed an outstanding tennis career. Nonetheless, his three grand-slam tournament victories do not warrant Ashe being mentioned alongside the all-time tennis greats, including such players as Jimmy Connors, Pete Sampras, and Bill Tilden. Ashe was certainly not the best tennis player of all-time; in fact, he was not even the best tennis player of his generation. His influence and social relevance, however, transcends and outdistances his accomplishments on the court. His work as a social activist and staunch defense of traditional tennis etiquette has garnered him a place in the American pantheon of heroes that is reserved for only the most important historical figures.[1] Throughout his career, Ashe maintained that he did not want his tennis victories to be his "culminating moment." This work illustrates how Ashe's tennis success gave him a social platform that he and others attempted to define. The seemingly contradictory description of Ashe as a "quiet militant" encapsulates the difficult position that Ashe encountered as reactionaries and radicals demanded that he serve as an exemplar and advocate of their values. Ashe came to prominence as the civil rights movement was increasingly challenged by a more rhetorically aggressive black power movement. Ashe, who thought of himself as "intensely independent," often struggled with the competing demands that were made of him by the elitist tennis establishment, the conservative civil rights movement, and the abrasive black power movement.

Tennis and golf were the preferred sports at country clubs in the United States during the late nineteenth century. Invented in England in

Arthur Ashe holding up his trophy after capturing the 1975 title at Wimbledon. *(Getty Images)*

1873, lawn tennis reached the United States the following year. Tennis's incubation in the elitist country-club setting illustrates the class divisions sports helped maintain in industrial America. The exclusive nature of tennis as a sport for the white, upper-class gentry helped reinforce Victorian notions of manhood based upon honor, respectability, civilization, sportsmanship, and emotional control. With tennis came the ability to maintain a balance between competition and social courtesy, and it became a symbol of the conduct and decorum that encapsulated Victorian values. Consequently, as the nineteenth century progressed, tennis increasingly became a means to provide moral and gentlemanly training.[2]

In *Manliness & Civilization: A Cultural History of Gender and Race in the United States, 1880–1917,* Gail Bederman argues that Victorian codes of manliness in the middle and late nineteenth century were based upon elite men's ability to control "powerful masculine passions through strong character and a powerful will." By basing Anglo-American manliness on notions of self-restraint, strong character, and honorable high-mindedness, white Americans argued that they were the "apex of civilization, the greatest achievement of human evolution, progress, and history." The idea that white men were able to display self-restraint by controlling their impulses served as rationale for their supposed responsibility and duty to protect, guide, and control those social groups deemed weaker than white men by Social Darwinist philosophers: women, children, and other races. Therefore, Victorian notions of manhood were designed to justify institutions of privilege and structural inequality.[3]

Emotional control and deference were the two principle virtues that governed Victorian notions of manhood. As Linda Young has argued, "Discipline of the emotions through concealment of feelings was integral to gentility." Men who were able to present themselves as calm and emotionally consistent were deemed to be the products of "good breeding," which suggested that one was trustworthy and reliable. As the *Illustrated Manners Book,* written to a male audience in 1855, suggested, "Command yourself, the man who is liable to fits passion; who cannot control his temper, but is subject to ungovernable excitements of any kind, is always a danger. The first element of a gentlemanly dignity is self-control." Emotional restraint meant that both excessive negative and positive emotional displays of anger and joy were unacceptable.[4]

This is true of tennis, where displaying a temper or excessive jubilation were both seen as transgressions of tennis culture, which mandated that players remain unemotional.

Arthur Ashe, born in Richmond, Virginia, in 1943 to Arthur Ashe Sr. and Matte Cordell, had been socialized into this tradition of deference and emotional control by his mentor Dr. Robert Johnson. Dr. Johnson was trained at Meharry Medical College, a historically black medical school, and subsequently established a private practice in Lynchburg, Virginia. He became an avid tennis player and an influential figure in the American Tennis Association (ATA), the African American counterpart to the United States Lawn Tennis Association (USLTA). Dr. Johnson committed his life to the development of African American tennis players "to storm the walls of tennis" as a means to counteract racist notions that African Americans did not possess the skills to compete at the elite levels of finesse sports. Dr. Johnson taught Ashe and his other protégés the lessons that dominated the socialization of young, middle-class African American boys in the segregated South: be clean and neat, work hard, demonstrate impeccable manners, and do not cause trouble. On the tennis court, Dr. Johnson taught his protégés that their behavior had to be beyond reproach—no racquet throwing, no hollering, and no expression of discontent with the decisions made by officials.[5] Hence, Dr. Johnson taught his pupils the strokes and strategies of tennis competition as well as the etiquette and bourgeois values of the sport.

Dr. Johnson advocated the need for respect and courtesy toward all tennis competitors. While "respect" and "courtesy" did not necessarily translate into victories on the court, they were designed to win support for larger objectives: to challenge assumptions of African American inferiority and to promote widespread desegregation and integration. For example, while changing sides between sets, Ashe was instructed to retrieve all of the balls, give them to his opponent, and to greet the opposition with "a warm smile." Furthermore, during the earlier rounds of junior tennis tournaments it was common for the competitors to act as the line judges in their matches. In these circumstances, Dr. Johnson required his students to play opponents shots that were out two inches or less and to give any reasonably close call to his opponents. Aware that tournament directors would use any excuse to exclude African American participants, Dr. Johnson taught his athletes to embody the code of

Victorian sportsmanship with such rigidity that their judgment would never be questioned.[6] Even after he was well established, Ashe continued to exemplify the sportsman's code that dominated tennis's early culture and his racial socialization, even as others began to defy, ridicule, and challenge tennis protocol.

According to one tennis historian, E. Digby Baltzell, the "reign of rampant rudeness" in tennis began when Arthur Ashe lost the five-set 1972 U.S. Open Men's final to Ilie "Nasty" Nastase of Romania after Nastase was able to rattle him with unsportsmanlike behavior. Ashe published a *Washington Post* article that describes Nastase as a brilliant player who could delight the crowd with his fantastic shot-making ability, but also his charisma and charm. Because of his tremendous talent, tennis fans were able to overlook Nastase's outrageous antics because he provided pizzazz to a sport that was still beholden to its gentlemanly traditions. However, by the time that Jimmy Connors lost to Ashe in the 1975 Wimbledon final, Nastase's antics no longer seemed to be the product of a spontaneous response to a perceived injustice, but rather, tactical emotional outbursts designed to rattle his opponents in order to gain a competitive advantage. When Nastase was in danger of losing an important match, his outbursts were formulaic: first he started disputing a few calls, then he stalled as a means to unsettle his opponent, sometimes he would hit an "errant" hard shot toward a linesman, while grinning impishly, as a tactical means to attempt to frustrate his opponents and intimidate officials. For example, in a closely contested contest with Ashe in Stockholm in 1975, Nastase faked his serve four times. The normally unflappable Ashe walked off the court to protest Nastase's unsportsmanlike conduct, in a contest that has become known as the "Great Double Defeat." However, because of his considerable talent and theatrics, Nastase became a leading draw in the tennis world.[7] Undoubtedly, Nastase's success, despite his temper, helped pave the way for other temperamental players such as Jimmy Connors and John McEnroe.

During the 1974 tennis tournament season, Connors joined the professional tour and his two victories over Ken Rosewall at Wimbledon and in the U.S. Open placed him at the top of the tennis world, but he seemed to enjoy maintaining a defiant opposition to the traditional and gentlemanly nature of tennis. For example, at a critical moment in a match with Corrado Barazutti, Barazutti disputed a call. Connors ran to Barazutti's side of the net and ended the dispute by rubbing out the ball mark in question with his toe. Connors most blatant snub occurred at the 1977 Wimbledon Championship, where he refused to join the parade of former champions before the Queen on Center Court. Years later, Connors confessed, "I was an animal early in my career . . . It was like I had rabies. I've bitten a lot of people along the way and that was the way I wanted it."[8]

Connors and Nastase were involved in one of the ugliest moments in tennis history. In 1977, Nastase and Connors played two highly publicized exhibition matches involving almost $650,000 in prize money at the Cerro Mar Hotel in Puerto Rico and at Caesars Place in Las Vegas. The day before the match in Puerto Rico, Nastase's hometown, Bucharest, Romania, suffered the worst earthquake in Romania's history. One of Nastase's longtime friends called Nastase's manager from Brussels, Germany, and informed him of the tragedy. All of the telephone lines to Bucharest were down. Consequently, it could not be determined whether Nastase's family was safe. Nastase's wife, Dominque, kept the bad news from him because his match with Connors was scheduled for later that afternoon. When Connors and Nastase appeared for the prematch warmup, Connors shouted across the net to Nastase, "Hey buddy, you'd better call Bucharest. You might not have a house anymore."[9] Connors despicable antics reveal the extent to which the gentlemanly code of honor had eroded.

Perhaps the most temperamental player during the 1970s and 1980s was John McEnroe. During the 1980 French Open, he called an official a "fucking French frog fag," and shouted to the French fans, "I hate this country." While McEnroe's on court behavior was antithetical to tennis traditions, his failure to show up at the traditional champion's dinner and ball after he won the men's Wimbledon championship "was unprecedented in its rudeness." All previous Wimbledon champions had been made honorary members of the prestigious All-England Club, but McEnroe was refused this honor after he did not attend the champion's dinner.[10]

On July 5, 1975, Ashe and Connors walked on to Centre Court to play the first all-American men's final match at the prestigious Wimbledon tournament since 1947. Ashe was the sentimental favorite for many in the tennis establishment because the Ashe-Connors Wimbledon final was billed as a battle between tennis's gentlemanly past and its rude future. In this symbolic battle Ashe was depicted as a symbol of tennis's sportsmanly nature, while Connors symbolized "tantrum tennis." Ashe had developed a reputation as a gentleman, while Connors was cast as the antihero: offensive, brash, and threatening. Ashe personified the aristocratic, amateur code of gentility in which the sport was founded. Connors symbolized the decline of manners and sportsmanship that characterized many of the leading players in the late 1970s.[11]

As the sixth seed, Ashe had struggled throughout the tournament. He needed four sets to defeat Bob Hewitt, Graham Stilwell, and an injured Bjorn Borg. In his semifinal match, Ashe lost a fourth-set tie breaker, before he came back to defeat Tony Roche in the decisive fifth set. Because Ashe had lost fourteen of his previous nineteen finals appearances entering 1975, most experts did not believe he had a realistic chance of defeating Connors.[12] Connors had developed an air of invisibility and looked unbeatable in the early rounds: the defending Wimbledon champion and number-one ranked player in the world had not lost a set during the tournament before his match with Ashe. During 1974, Connors first full year on the tour, he set an Open record by winning 96 percent of his matches: 99 of 103 singles contests, including Wimbledon, the Australian Open, the U.S. Open, and twelve additional tournaments. Furthermore, Connors had won all three of the previous meetings between him and Ashe, including two straight-set victories. Entering the match as a 3–20 favorite, Connors haughtily predicted that it would be "just another day at the office."[13]

In one of the greatest matches in tennis history, Ashe shocked the tennis world by winning the first nine games of the match, cruising to a 6–0 victory in the first set and a 6–1 victory in the second set, before Connors won the third set, 7–5. After Connors built a 3–0 lead in the fourth set, Ashe rallied and won the set, 6–4. Ashe was able to defeat Connors by playing a completely different style than he was accustomed to playing. Ashe was a noted power player who had a propensity to always go for the spectacular shot. *Tennis USA* characterized Ashe's playing style as "Ramblin' and gamblin'." Or as one commentator suggested, Ashe "had an attacking, confrontational game, highlighted by a hard serve and a tendency to take chances despite low odds for success . . . his tennis game was positively flamboyant." When he was able to get his risky shots to fall, his game was awe-inspiring. However, because he did not allow much room for error, he frequently was not able to continue to make near-impossible shots throughout important matches. Aware that he did not have the ability to defeat Connors without playing a flawless match, Ashe decided to adopt a radically different playing style.[14]

Consulting with his friends and tennis professionals, Ashe devised a style specifically designed to frustrate Connors. The basis of Ashe's strategy was to disrupt the flow of the match by hitting "junk"—chip shots, dink shots, and lobs. By keeping his shots low or high, changing their speed and hitting the ball at Connors to deny him crosscourt angles, Ashe was able to keep Connors off-balance. Ashe replaced his "slashing winners" and "do-or-die" strategy with "delicately placed" chip shots and graceful groundstrokes. The player known for his unapologetic tendency to hit wild shots at inopportune moments in key matches gave a "four-set lesson on pinpoint placement." Later, Ashe provided an apt comparison with his tactical approach when he likened his "chip-and-dink" strategy with Muhammad Ali's "rope-a-dope" strategy in his fight with George Foreman. Both were able to keep their opponents off-guard and confused by competing in an unorthodox fashion and seizing opportunities. Ashe's Wimbledon victory was the highlight of the 1975 tour, and he finished the year ranked number one by the United States Tennis Association (USTA), *Tennis* magazine, and *World Tennis* magazine.[15]

After his Wimbledon victory, Ashe's significance as an exemplar of traditional gentlemanly tennis values increased. E. Digby Baltzell, the late emeritus professor of history and sociology at the University of Pennsylvania and a leading authority on tennis and the White Anglo-Saxon Protestant (WASP) establishment, characterized Ashe as a "Virginia gentleman in the very best moral and mannerly meaning of that term." It is interesting that Baltzell began his important book, *Sporting Gentlemen,* with a discussion of two black men—C. L. R. James and Arthur Ashe—who embodied, exemplified, and even symbolized the values associated with two upper-class, elite white sports: cricket and tennis. In his seminal text, *Beyond a Boundary,* James stated that he learned the high-minded values of Victorian Britain through cricket: "I never cheated . . . I never argued with the umpire, I never jeered at a defeated opponent . . . My defeats and disappointments I took as stoically as I could . . . this code became the moral framework of my existence."[16] James' values have become known as the "cricket code."

"Arthur Ashe, a cultivated black man," claimed Baltzell, "was the last best example of the gentlemanly values of amateur tennis." Baltzell described Ashe as "a black lieutenant in the Army Reserves stationed at West Point, who, by natural instinct, parental training, and education," was able to personify the values of the Victorian gentleman and sportsman. By mentioning Ashe's army commission as an officer, he associates Ashe with the long-standing notions of honor that are reflected in military service. Certainly, Ashe's social etiquette was influenced by his education at the University of California at Los Angeles (UCLA) and by his dad, who was a strict disciplinarian. However, it is unclear why Baltzell chose "natural instinct" as a means to discuss Ashe's adherence to gentlemanly principles. By stressing "natural instinct" over other terms such as "social conditioning" or "racial pioneering," Baltzell downplays the racial and class significance of the Victorian moral code that dominated tennis: a moral code that was originally conceived in the nineteenth century and designed to prove the superiority of white men. It is not surprising that black men would be the athletes who would most closely adhere to the code of conduct. Punishment for violations of social mores was much more likely to be heaped upon those considered socially inferior than on the leading classes of American society.[17]

"I have tried to do what I thought was right and appropriate, and sometimes the effort to do right, and above all not to do wrong, led me to inaction," Ashe wrote in his memoir, *Days of Grace.* Ashe's revelation is crucial because it suggests that as a racial pioneer, he focused on not making a mistake. Given the teaching that he had received from Dr. Johnson about the political danger of violating rules of social engagement, it is not surprising that Ashe would assume a very conservative posture. Aware of the implications of his transgressions, he maintained that he was mild mannered because "if I angered anyone, people could shut doors . . . and I knew how hard Dr. Johnson worked to pry those doors open."[18]

Although the moral suasionist strategy adopted by Ashe predated the 1944 publication of Gunnar Myrdal's *American Dilemma,* in the post–World War II world Myrdal's work became the basis for postwar black-white collaboration. Myrdal's study argued that the inconsistencies between democratic ideals and racial prejudice greatly troubled Americans. He remained adamant that white America's sincere desire to live up to democratic and Christian principles would be the preeminent force driving reform. The Swedish economist had faith that the United States would make the right decision when he issued his oft-quoted challenge: "America is free to choose whether the Negro shall remain her liability or become her opportunity." Charles Thompson, the dean of the Howard University faculty and collaborator with Myrdal on the study, said that whether *An American Dilemma's* thesis was right or wrong, it supplied the rationale for civil rights organizations to adopt offensive strategies, rather than defensive postures.[19]

With its publication, Myrdal's study became, arguably, the most important book published on race relations since Harriet Beecher Stowe's *Uncle Tom's Cabin.* In a *Saturday Review* critique of the book, Robert S. Lynd, the noted writer, called Myrdal's work "the most penetrating and important book on contemporary American civilization that has ever been written." More pointedly, Ralph Ellison declared that the work destroyed the respectability of racism. Harry McPherson, an advisor to President Lyndon B. Johnson, said that Myrdal's ideas supplied "a kind of background music for the civil rights effort."[20] Undoubtedly, the moral suasionistic perspective employed in *An American Dilemma* reflected the nonviolent approach of the civil rights movement.

A major component of Ashe's acceptance was the fact that he did not frequently offer harsh criticisms of American race relations, and often seemed deferential. For example, Ashe admitted that he had resisted the notion that he should pressure southern tennis tournaments that would not allow him to compete. He argued that he was not going to get "militant" because he was "the only player shut out. When more Negroes want to play in Southern tournaments, and have the skill to be worth watching, then maybe I'll go along with an organized protest if one is needed." The conservative nature of his course of action is evinced by his downplaying the importance of his right to compete because he was the lone victim. Secondly, by arguing that African American players have to display skills "worth watching," he is arguing for a gradualist approach, one based upon having a critical mass of very good African American players. Lastly, after stating the preconditions for him to take a political stance, he still remained ambiguous regarding his potential involvement, by stating that after the preconditions were met, "maybe" he would participate in an organized protest. According to Ashe, his plan was consistent with Dr. Johnson's philosophy to develop good players, then "sit back and wait for Southerners to realize their own mistake in barring them."[21]

As a twenty-four-year-old tennis phenomenon, Ashe published his first autobiography, *Advantage Ashe,* in 1967, in which he takes a very conservative stance in opposition to the civil rights movement. Ashe maintained that he had "learned to blend into the background" rather than to participate in social protests. While he expressed admiration for Dr. Martin Luther King, he was critical of civil rights tactics. Rather than marching and protesting, Ashe asserted that the "best chance [for African Americans] to advance is to get himself an education somehow and prove his worth as an individual." Parroting the arguments advocated by white conservatives, Ashe concluded that African Americans were trying to "ram ourselves down people's throats." At one point Ashe explicitly remarked, "I'm not a marcher. I'm not a sign carrier." Ashe argued that "quiet negotiation and slow infiltration" were the most promising measures for African Americans, because African Americans would "never advance far by force, because we're outnumbered ten to one."[22]

Early in his career, Ashe assumed a deferential posture, and reporters and other influential whites lauded him as an example of racial transcendence. For example, Bud Collins, a sports reporter, who was a leading tennis journalist and friend of Ashe's, once wrote in the mid-1970s that "despite a few early indignities while growing up black in segregated Virginia, he didn't have a hard time. Anything but . . . most people in tennis have fallen over themselves to do things for him."[23] What is interesting about Collins's comments is that they were contained in a review of Ashe's book, *Arthur Ashe: Portrait in Motion.* Collins's analysis illustrates the degree to which many used Ashe's mild-mannered analytical and dispassionate approach, coupled with his tennis success, to minimize the realities of racial oppression in the United States.

As the civil rights movement gave way to the black power movement, the social strategies that had governed African American social activism came under attack. In their highly influential text, *Black Rage,* the psychiatrists William Grier and Price Cobbs described the "paradigmatic black man." Because African American males have had to be very conscious about offending white America, black men have had to "play it cool": be passive, nonassertive, and nonaggressive. The politics of "playing it cool" meant that African Americans males had to always present a serene exterior in the face of injustice perpetrated by whites, as was required of Ashe. Southern African Americans were painfully aware that aggression against whites would be cause for swift punishment. A central virtue of the "paradigmatic man" was his ingratiating and compliant manner, thus for many whites this became the standard by which all African Americans are measured. Because of his reputation as "unflappable" and "ultra-relaxed," Ashe became for many whites the embodiment of the perfect integrated black man.[24]

During the 1960s, black power advocates would criticize the Myrdalian notion that the "American Negro problem is a problem in the heart of America . . . It is there that the decisive struggle goes on." Rather than appealing to White America's heart, most black power advocates sought to gain cultural, economic, political, and social power. In *Black Power: The Politics of Liberation in America,* Stokely Carmichael and Charles Hamilton maintained that African Americans should not base their social engagement upon the idea that there was a moral dilemma that motivated white America. *Black Power* rejected the idea that African Americans could form viable coalitions with white Americans because "coalitions between the strong and the weak lead to a preservation of the hierarchical structure." They argued that relying upon national sentiment placed African Americans in a beggar's role, and mistakenly believed that African Americans could "bow . . . its way to a position of power."[25]

Ashe acknowledged that as black power advocates challenged the leadership of Dr. King, "blacks like me found it difficult to choose a position." Nonetheless, he realized that the "status quo would not do." As Ashe prepared to make his political debut, he was the subject of a January 28, 1968, article in the *New York Times,* which detailed his preparation for his first public, political speech. "Poverty is one-half laziness," "Everything yields to diligence," and "NO VIOLENCE" were several of the notes that Ashe had scattered on his desk at the U.S. military academy in New York, where he was serving a two-year tour of duty as a systems analyst. Ashe was asked by Reverend Jefferson Rogers, the pastor of the Church of the Redeemer in Washington, D.C., to speak about the role of the black athlete in the civil rights movement. "People shouldn't have to tell me to do these things," Ashe said with a tinge of embarrassment, because he did not become involved in civil rights until he was approached by Reverend Rogers and others.[26]

Until his initial speech, Ashe had made clear his desire to avoid direct political involvement and was content to let his tennis racquet "do the talking." When asked about the shift, he said, "I guess I'm becoming more and more militant." The *New York Times* writer Neil Amdur reported that Ashe made this statement with a serious expression before he began to grin at its implications. Amdur further downplayed Ashe's remark when he noted that "Ashe's 'militancy' is subtle."[27] Transcripts of the speech are not available, but Ashe's later recollections of the speech, as well as an article published in the *Washington Post* the following day, suggest that the contents were more conservative than militant.

His foray into public speaking was not an unequivocal success. The main thrust of his remarks was that African American athletes must make a commitment to the black community and work to transform it. There is a conservative undertone to Ashe's description of Jim Brown's organization, the Negro Industrial and Economic Union, as a "network of do-it-yourselfers." The tennis star went on to assert that "there is a lot we can do and we don't because we're lazy. This may be brutal, but poverty is half laziness." While the "bootstraps" mentality is grounded in a long tradition of self-help initiatives advocated by African American leaders, Ashe's statements suggested that structural barriers were no longer overwhelming and that African Americans should succeed "no matter what the odds." This is a perspective shared by many black conservatives. While the contents of the speech were not militant, Ashe was aware that he would be chastised by the military for the "political" nature of his words. Indeed, he was later warned by the military not to give any more speeches. Accepting the rebuke as a "way of paying dues to the cause," he maintained that the speech at the Church of the Redeemer was transformative. "In the sixties," Ashe acknowledged, "I had done nothing but play tennis and enjoy life. The seventies would be different."[28]

Several months later, on September 9, 1968, Ashe became the first African American and the first American since 1955 to win the prestigious tennis tournament at Forest Hills. This was the first year that the tournament, renamed the U.S. Open, had allowed amateurs to compete with professionals. Of the six Open tournaments that inaugural year, Ashe was the only male amateur to capture a singles title. His victory over Tom Okker in the finals was his twenty-fifth consecutive singles win, and guaranteed that he would be the number-one ranked amateur player in the U.S.[29]

When Ashe was asked about his twenty-five-match winning streak, he said that he was motivated by the goals of the African American athletes who were then endorsing a boycott of the Mexico City Olympic Games. Ashe said that he had thought about quitting the Davis Cup team and boycotting the U.S. Open, but decided that a better alternative was to win in order to create a platform. "People don't listen to losers," Ashe said. "Now, whenever I say something, people listen." Shortly after his victory, *Ebony* magazine anointed him as "the ranking young black sports idol." The U.S. Open champion stated that his newfound status as a civil rights spokesman was a major factor in his success because after he began asserting himself "off the court," he found the confidence to assert himself as a tennis player.[30]

"The Icy Elegance of Arthur Ashe," published just after his U.S. Open victory, was the title of arguably the most significant article written about Ashe during his playing career. The *Life* magazine cover story featured Ashe's oft-repeated statement: "What I like most about myself is my demeanor. I'm seldom ruffled." Describing Ashe's "detachment" as an important means of identification that had the ability to heighten his celebrity, there is a decidedly political undertone to the discussion of his "icy elegance." Even as Ashe tried to assume a more assertive public persona, the press turned his reputation as mild mannered into a virtue because of the symbolic importance of his "cool" demeanor when juxtaposed against the aggressive posturing of Muhammad Ali, John Carlos, and Tommie Smith. More comfortable with the silent and integrationist bent, reporters lionized Ashe's restraint. Reporters continued to express admiration for Ashe and his accomodationist perspective. For example, Arthur Daley celebrated Ashe in contradictory terms when he said that Ashe's "militancy is the quiet kind." Whites were more comfortable with what *Black Enterprise* termed, Ashe's "refined revolution," in which Ashe maintained that "I don't argue. I don't take stands." Ashe began to reflect on why he was so "acceptable" to white society and concluded that his detached approach did mean that he was not a threat to the elitist values of tennis or to the dominant racial order.[31]

Nonetheless, Ashe's social engagement made him part of a larger shift in the consciousness of African American athletes best exemplified by the title of Harry Edwards's important book, *The Revolt of the Black Athlete.* By 1968, a major shift had taken place in the athletic landscape. When Ashe won the U.S. Open, approximately one-half of all professional basketball players were African American. Additionally, roughly one-third of all professional football players and one-fourth of all professional baseball players were African Americans. Between 1954 and 1964, African American athletes had won seven of eleven National League batting championships and led the league in home runs eight of those years. As African Americans became more visible in athletics, their mere presence ceased to be a positive, progressive racial force. Their success did not have the same symbolic meaning. The black athlete increasingly became "part of the status quo, the expected, the taken for granted.[32] Consequently, the "silent symbol model" of athletic behavior exhibited by Jesse Owens and Joe Louis was now interpreted by a new generation of black athletes headed by Tommie Smith, Harry Edwards, and Lew Alcindor as hindering racial advancement and as a form of legitimization of existing racial inequalities.

Adopting what he believed was a "more militant" perspective, Ashe acknowledged that he was moving beyond his long-standing belief that he would simply accomplish as much as he could individually, which would have positioned him as an "example" of African American success. Ashe became actively involved in the National Urban League, of which he said, "We don't scream; I guess we'd be classified as moderates, but we get the job done." Referring to his newfound commitment to social action, Ashe proclaimed, "I know that I'm not the favorite of a lot of people in the black community. I'll be the first to admit that I arrived late. I've got a backlog of unpaid dues."[33]

Ashe maintained that he had spoken with Stokely Carmichael several times in the late 1960s and that he was inspired by Carmichael's "raw courage." Nonetheless, Ashe asserted that black power rhetoric "clashed violently" with some of his core principles: love of peace, moderation, and religion. Ashe maintained that "intrinsically, I disapprove of what black militants do." Dismissing them as "chic" and "fashionable" he maintained that their influence upon race relations was not in the best interest of African American people.[34]

Ashe's increased desire to become more politically involved, coupled with the growing oppositional stance advocated by many black power leaders, placed Ashe in an important quandary: how to become more politically involved, while advocating a social philosophy that was losing popularity among many black activists. Ashe found a compromise social issue: the antiapartheid movement in South Africa.

Given Ashe's reticence to become actively involved in the civil rights movement in the United States and his displeasure with black power, it is surprising, yet understandable why Ashe would move to the forefront of the fight to bring international pressure against South African apartheid. When Ashe became actively involved in the antiapartheid movement in 1969, it was not a major issue in the United States. The United Nations had not voted to impose social and cultural sanctions against South Africa. Not until the bloody Soweto Uprising in 1976 did condemnation of South African apartheid became a major international issue. Ashe's decision to lead the charge against apartheid was "conscious" and political. Ashe has said publicly that his involvement in South African apartheid was motivated by his lack of involvement in the civil rights movement. However, by the time that Ashe decided to become politically active in 1968, the tactics of the civil rights movement had given way to the confrontational rhetoric of the black power movement. As the black power movement increasingly called for African American athletes to assume more aggressive and assertive roles in the struggle to alleviate the oppression of African Americans, Ashe felt compelled to take action. As someone who was committed to the values and methods of the civil rights movement, Ashe tried to use South Africa as a means to respond to the imperative to be socially active, but in a manner that was consistent with his value system that had been influenced by growing up in the segregated South and in the tennis world.[35]

Because Ashe considered himself to be a "reconciler rather than a divider of persons," he was more drawn to the example of Andrew Young, whom he described as a "conciliator committed to the cause, someone who could haggle, bargain, and compromise with whites." By taking the lead in the antiapartheid movement in the United States, Ashe sought to help control the agenda and tactical methods. For example, he frequently met with executives from corporations with investments in South Africa, including IBM and Ford Motor Company. He asserted that his method of trying to negotiate was "dignified, maintained his credibility, and did not shut doors."[36]

One of the fundamental assumptions that drove the civil rights movement was the notion that equal protection of constitutional rights would afford African Americans equal opportunity to acquire wealth, stature, and prosperity. However, civil rights laws alone could not sufficiently mitigate the effects of past discrimination: economic disparity and lingering prejudice. Having achieved equal protection under the law with the passage of the 1964 Civil Rights Bill and the Voting Rights Bill in 1965, Dr. Martin Luther King and other advocates attempted to shift the civil rights movement in the direction of the eradication of poverty and urban blight. Despite King's and others' attempts, many white liberal reformers suggested that the removal of legal restrictions meant that the United States was no longer a nation plagued by racism. The widespread belief was that now merit, rather than race, would determine each individual's life chances.

Many liberal reformers were content to leave untouched basic features of the American system that had traditionally left African Americans in a subordinate, marginal economic position. The removal of the legal impediments led Americans to assert that the market and civil society would fully integrate African Americans in a relatively quick period. The equalization of laws, rules, and norms meant that individual African Americans would be able to rise or fall according to their ability and initiative. However, black folk began to affirm that although legal restrictions had been removed, racism remained institutionalized and visibly demonstrated by urban poverty, limited educational opportunities, and restrictive hiring practices, thus hindering the upward mobility of most African Americans.

Within this context, Ashe's engagement with the antiapartheid movement held tremendous symbolism. Because many Americans believed that the civil rights movement had eradicated racism, continued African American unrest and discontentment caused resentment among many white Americans. Because many Americans thought of racism as individual acts of prejudice and discrimination, they were unable to grasp black power–era arguments that suggested that racism remained institutionalized in this country and curtailed the social and economic advancement of most African Americans. Therefore, when Ashe, who suffered a tragic death from AIDS in 1993, began to privilege involvement in the antiapartheid campaign, his actions seemed to suggest that the social problems in the United States had been successfully eradicated. It is in this context that many people came to lionize Ashe as a humanitarian, but have demonized and been very critical of black power advocates who called into question the fundamental ideas of the social reform movement in the United States.

Ashe's story is similar to other athletic trailblazers like Joe Louis, Jesse Owens, and Jackie Robinson who extended the range of opportunities that were available for hardworking and talented African Americans, who challenged racist assumptions about African American inferiority while excelling in a white-dominated profession. Jackie Robinson's success proved that African Americans could compete on the same athletic level as whites, but the agreement that he and Branch Rickey reached was that he would have to be deferential and unwavering in his emotional restraint. As Maureen Smith has suggested, Jackie Robinson's willingness to "endure racial harassment provided the nation with an acceptable and ideal image of an African American athlete."[37] Initially, Ashe was beholden to the tradition that Jackie Robinson represented. However, as the demands placed on African American athletes in the late 1960s changed, Ashe found himself caught in a quandary. By examining Ashe's thoughts about the civil rights movement, black power, and the tennis establishment, we can see the complexity of the decision making that confronted him and others who attempted to come to grips with the changing social and political landscape in the late 1960s.

IV Race, Sport, and Celebrity Culture

Arthur Ashe and many of his contemporaries not only realized untold fame and a forum for speaking out on larger societal issues, but a degree of financial independence as well. They did not realize, however, the incredibly large amount of money and corporate sponsorship that have marked the careers of Michael Jordan, Tiger Woods, and Venus and Serena Williams. These four individuals, taking advantage of the new celebrity culture and the global economic market, have parlayed their successes in sport into multimillion-dollar business deals that athletes of yesteryear could only have dreamed of. Jordan, the University of North Carolina, Chicago Bulls, and Washington Wizard's basketball great, is perhaps the most influential athletic pitchman in history, selling everything from Nike shoes, McDonald's hamburgers, Gatorade, and Hanes underwear. Making an estimated $40 million a year at one time for product endorsements, Jordan is also involved in the restaurant business and serves on the corporate boards of Oakley and Diving Interventures.

Douglas Hartmann, in his "Bound by Blackness or Above It? Michael Jordan and the Paradoxes of Post–Civil Rights American Race Relations," provides an analysis of Jordan's role as an icon and the "race neutral discourse that surrounded and defined him." Although bound by race in many ways, says Hartmann, Jordan was far less constrained than those African American athletes who preceded him, seemingly able to transcend the stigma of being black and profit from his celebrity status as the world's greatest basketball player. This apparent ability to overcome race and realize unprecedented success has been interpreted in many different ways, some observers believing that it was an indication of racial progress in sport and the larger American society. Other observers, most notably academicians interested in sport and racial issues, contend that Jordan's apparent ability to overcome race is merely an anomaly and that his success has diverted attention from the racial discrimination and deep-seated stereotypes that still exist in American society. Still others suggest that Jordan's extraordinary success was actually a result of his race, people attracted to and fascinated by his blackness.

The apparent ability to overcome race was just as true for Tiger Woods as it was for Michael Jordan. As Steven Pope explains in "'Race,' Family, and Nation: The Significance of Tiger Woods in American Culture," Woods has, at least for middle-class white golf fans, "transcended, if not negated, racial issues altogether." And like Jordan, Woods does not talk about race, avoids speaking out on social or political issues, and has made an extraordinary amount of money through endorsements. He nets approximately $54 million a year through his work with such corporations as Nike, American Express, Buick, Rolex, and Titlest. He complements his endorsement deals with highly publicized philanthropic work. Woods has put the "icing on the cake of his celebrity image" by means of his work with disadvantaged children. Through the Tiger Woods Foundation (established with his father, Earl, in 1996), Woods has introduced the game of golf to literally hundreds of underprivileged children. Interestingly enough, Pope cogently observes, Woods has provided more opportunities for underprivileged children to play golf by surrounding "himself with the very corporate institutions and 'players' that have served as the bulwarks of the establishment and system of privilege for upper-class America."

Like Woods and Jordan, Venus and Serena Williams, between them winners of all the major tennis championships, have netted millions through various endorsement deals. Appealing to advertisers because of their background growing up on public courts in Compton, California, and their enormous success in the sport, the Williams sisters have carved out careers played out on the world stage and in front of major media markets. Unfortunately, the Williams sisters have been on the receiving end of much criticism, tennis opponents and others contending that they are aloof, conceited, and noncommunicative. Although reluctant to claim that this criticism is based on race, the Williams sisters have made it clear that they believe racial prejudice still exists in the white-dominated sport of tennis.

The dimensions of racism surrounding the Williams sisters is the focus of Pierre and Ellen Rodgers's "'Ghetto Cinderellas': Venus and

Serena Williams and the Discourse of Racism." Utilizing elements of rhetorical ideology, the Rodgerses examine the discursive language of racism confronted by Venus and Serena and how the two sisters dealt with both blatant and implicit forms of discrimination. One of the most troubling examples of racialized attitudes being communicated in verbal discourse was what took place at the highly publicized 2001 tennis tournament in Indian Wells, California. Spectators, livid at Venus's last-minute withdrawal from her semifinal match with Serena, booed widely and hurled angry racial epithets at both sisters and their controversial father, Richard, who was suspected of orchestrating events. In customary fashion, Venus and Serena, although most directly affected by the racial slurs, allowed their father to publicly respond to the incident. "I think Indian Wells," said Richard Williams, "disgraced America."

Michael Jordan going up for a dunk in a 1995 game at the Fleet Center in Boston. *(Lipofsky.com)*

17 Bound by Blackness or Above It?

Michael Jordan and the Paradoxes of Post–Civil Rights American Race Relations

DOUGLAS HARTMANN

If there is one thing the modern sports world does exceptionally well, it is produce cultural icons: individuals whose personalities and performances are larger-than-life and, as such, take on meaning and significance far beyond the bounds of their athletic excellence.[1] And in the final decade of the twentieth century no sports star was more of an icon in the United States (if not the world)—no athlete more representative of collective hopes and dreams and ambivalences, more reflective of cultural trends and social transformations—than Michael Jordan. Scholars and journalists have generated myriad facts and figures to demonstrate Jordan's iconic status but sport sociologists Mary MacDonald and David Andrews provide one of the most provocative: just prior to the turn of the millennium, a California-based market research company claimed that a photograph of the back of Jordan's head was more identifiable among American shoppers than the faces of Bill Clinton, Newt Gingrich, or Jesus Christ.[2]

As an icon, Jordan represented—or, perhaps more frequently and precisely, was made to represent—many different things to many different people. For many, Jordan stood as an All-American original, one of those rare, extraordinary figures whose creativity, resilience, competitiveness, and unparalleled success embodied all the best of American individualism. Others focused less on his nationality and saw instead, as Kenneth Dutton has put it, a "Greek hero figure," whose virtues and accomplishments represented "the highest realization of human potential." For his part, the award-winning journalist David Halberstam portrayed Jordan as a "one-man corporate conglomerate" who helped transform the National Basketball Association from a niche-market, subcultural curiosity into a full-fledged popular cultural force, thus ushering in a new era of global sport, the Americanization of world culture, and the continued worldwide expansion of capitalism, commodification, and marketing. Indeed, most recent scholarly writings on Jordan have been about his celebrity, his advertising clout, his role in global commerce and licensing—all of which continue to resonate today, well after Jordan's third retirement from the game he dominated and in many ways transcended.[3]

There can be no doubt that Jordan's racial identity, his skin color, his African American heritage, have been at the center of all this. As one of the most prominent and successful African American figures in a society still obsessed with race and marked by both persistent racial inequalities and resilient antiblack attitudes, it could hardly have been otherwise. But while the "fact of Michael Jordan's blackness" (in David Andrews's memorable phrase) is impossible to deny, just exactly what the iconic Jordan signals about late-twentieth-century American race relations is not easy to pinpoint.

Part of the problem is that Jordan himself almost never talked publicly about race (or, for that matter, about any other political or publicly contentious topics). In addition, the racial meanings swirling around and often foisted upon Jordan were, as we will see, multifaceted, complex, and contradictory—some positive and optimistic, others far more skeptical.[4] But the biggest challenge in specifying Michael Jordan's racial meaning and symbolism in late-twentieth-century American culture is that most of the meanings imputed to him and his career were rarely explicit; rather, Jordan's racial significance was conveyed in subtle, coded ways, by inference and implicit comparison, by what was not said more than what was said.

This ostensible silence can be interpreted in two basic but very different ways. On the one hand, the fact that Jordan's skin color is only rarely mentioned can be seen as a positive development, evidence that he overcame the stigma of being black and the constraints of racism. Many proponents of this optimistic interpretation—which dominates public thought and talk—go much further to suggest that Jordan's ability to overcome race is indicative of racial progress in sport and even the whole of society at the end of the twentieth century. Jordan, in this view, is an illustration of the progress and accomplishments of the post–civil rights era, a member of the first generation of African Americans not bound by extreme segregation, stereotyping, and exploitation. On the other hand, most sport scholars and race experts have been very critical. To the extent that Jordan can be said to have overcome his skin color, these critics tend to think of him as an exceptional case, one whose extraordinary individual accomplishments have tended to deflect attention away from persistent racial hierarchies and stereotypes, or even worse have served as an excuse for others to relax prematurely in the push for racial equality and integration. Many of these critics take Jordan himself to task for not having done more to advocate for racial change. Others go so far as to suggest that Jordan's phenomenal popularity and prominence were achieved not *in spite of* his race but largely *because of* it—that far from overcoming racism Jordan and his career have been bound by his blackness and thus reproductive dominant racial images and attitudes albeit in subtler, more covert forms than ever before.

Powerful though it might be, the temptation to choose between these two alternative visions must be avoided if Michael Jordan's racial meaning and significance is to be comprehended. Both are necessary. Freed of the most onerous personal and material constraints of racism in many respects, Jordan—particularly the public Jordan—was still bound by race in other, more subtle and insidious ways. Indeed, it is precisely this bipolar experience and these dueling social visions that make Jordan such an exemplary and revealing icon of the accomplishments, possibilities, and contradictions of post–civil rights American race relations.[5]

The popular perception—fueled by a 1990s Nike marketing campaign that played off the fact that Jordan was cut from the varsity basketball team in his sophomore year of high school—is that Michael Jordan burst out of nowhere in the middle of the 1980s with a triumvirate of spectacular performances on each of basketball's biggest stages: his buzzer-beating shot to win the NCAA national championship for the North Carolina Tar Heels in 1982, his standout play on the gold-medal winning 1984 U.S. Olympic team, and finally his spectacular 1985 rookie season on the lowly Chicago Bulls. Jordan's flair for the dramatic notwithstanding, this characterization is not entirely accurate. Even before he had entered college, as David Halberstam has chronicled, Jordan had already established an extremely large reputation and high set of expectations within basketball circles by his senior year in high school—hence, his recruitment by one of the top college basketball programs in the country.[6] However, it is true that these feats propelled Jordan from the sports pages into the broader public culture and consciousness. What is also (and more importantly) beyond dispute is that the various contradictory elements of Jordan's racial imagery and implication began to take shape here in the national spotlight.

Reading through the accounts of Jordan's breakout performances today, one is struck by two main characteristics. First and by now most familiar is how infrequently Jordan's race was talked about or even directly referenced. The bulk of the coverage and commentary is about his remarkable performances and his individual athletic brilliance—qualities we now know as legendary. Race is almost never mentioned, not even as an adjective. The simple fact of *not* being automatically labeled and identified in racial terms is an obvious indicator of historic racial change; yet it is dangerous to assume that this development was entirely positive without evaluating how this color-blind, race-neutral framing was interpreted by American audiences. The self-satisfied, celebratory nature of commentaries and profiles of this young superstar certainly gave the impression that Jordan's success on the court had much larger and more progressive meaning. And on those rare instances when race was mentioned, it was typically to insist that Jordan had overcome its constraints or that his success served to validate and dignify his people. Such positive if often implicit interpretations—the second striking feature of the initial coverage—have clearly become the norm in the years since. They are at the core of Halberstam's widely acclaimed *Playing for Keeps: Michael Jordan and the World He Made.*

Halberstam doesn't go to great lengths to discuss Jordan's racial significance in this book; quite the contrary, he pays almost no attention to it. You can count on two hands the number of times race is mentioned or discussed explicitly—either for Jordan or anyone else or any other theme in the book—in the 430 pages of the text. In the epilogue Halberstam explains that he downplayed Jordan's racial significance deliberately, on the grounds that Jordan was "not one of those men like Jack Johnson, Paul Robeson, Jackie Robinson, Muhammad Ali, or Arthur Ashe whose own complicated lives and painful struggles against long-established prejudices and racial barriers revealed a great deal not merely about sports but about the history of race in America." Jordan was not, in short, a racial pioneer, nor did he make a powerful challenge to the white establishment. In an early discussion of Jordan's parents, James and Delores, Halberstam describes Michael as among that first generation of African American children, post–civil rights babies, who were "neither blinded nor burdened by race." Indeed, in Halberstam's view, "precious little had been denied [Jordan] because of race."[7]

There is a good deal of truth to this depiction. Born in Brooklyn on February 17, 1963, Michael Jeffrey Jordan led an almost idyllic childhood growing up in Wilmington, North Carolina. His parents, James and Delores, were reputable career folks who held stable, integrated jobs—his mother as a bank teller, his father at a General Electric factory where he started as a mechanic and eventually moved into management. His father's air force pension provided the family of seven (Michael was the fourth of five children) the luxury of a third income and a solidly middle- if not upper-middle-class lifestyle. Like his four siblings, Michael attended integrated schools and had white friends as well as black ones. His childhood was marked by normal rivalries with his brothers (especially his older brother Larry), high parental expectations (of mobility and success from his mother, dedication and self-discipline from his father), and lots of athletics. He played and excelled at all sports all seasons, pitching two no-hitters for his little league regional tournament team in 1975 and playing quarterback on his junior high football team. Like other young African Americans of his generation, Michael Jordan obviously had more opportunities, higher expectations, and faced fewer social barriers and stresses than ever before in American history.

At the same time, this color-blind, race-neutral narrative—especially when coupled with unqualified references to racial progress in America—makes it easy to ignore or discount the barriers of residential segregation, economic and educational inequities, and persistent antiblack stereotypes that African Americans continued to face in the post–civil rights period.[8] Even in the athletic realm, exploitation persisted and discrimination and prejudice remained problematic, especially in terms of coaching, management, and ownership.[9] Surely Jordan witnessed and even experienced these ongoing challenges, even if his parents insisted he "treat everyone the same" and that "the less [the family] paid attention to race the less it would be factored in against them."[10] But the real issue here is not whether (or to what extent) Jordan himself faced racial constraints, or even how aware he was of such larger sociological realities. Rather, the most important issue is the conclusions about race relations that mainstream, majority-white audiences would have drawn when one of the few African American men they felt some connection to was portrayed in glowing, race-less terms. Too often this formula has served either to deflect attention away from the more general, persistent problems of race in America or, even worse, to legitimate the racial status quo by making it seem as if there are no barriers standing in the way of African American opportunity, assimilation, and mobility.

A more basic problem with uncritical color-blind accounts is that they simply don't square with the ways in which race figured in the earliest public portrayals of the young superstar. Reading more closely, these initial treatments pay inordinate attention to Jordan's body, his natural ability, the pure physicality of his game. Consider, for example, this description of his play on the gold-medal–winning 1984 Olympic team from a national correspondent: "The flashiest men's player was Jordan, the 6 ft. 6 in. University of North Carolina senior who has won six awards designating him America's best collegian. Born to dunk, he penetrated the zone defenses of opponents to slam at least one goal in each of the eight games."[11] The key phrases in this very typical depiction are "flashiest" and "born to dunk." Jordan, to be certain, was blessed with an exceptional physical talent, and his tenacious, slashing style of play fit his corporeal skills perfectly. But there were other aspects of his game that were truly exceptional as well: his extraordinary work ethic, his psychological toughness and mental acuity, his unrelenting defensive play, his absolute and unquenchable will to win, and his ability to adapt and change his game depending upon his health (and later, age). Eventually these qualities and characteristics would come to the fore of public understandings of Jordan's game (aided by Halberstam's wonderful portrayal), but they were not the focus in the beginning. Rather, the initial emphasis played off of old stereotypes about the natural athleticism and inherent physicality of black men—stereotypes which not only stripped African American athletes like Jordan of their humanity but that also (because of persistent mind-body dualisms in the West) reinforced racial differences as essential and implied mental inferiority or even moral deficiency.[12]

The Nike company, which rode Jordan's popularity to unprecedented profit and market domination, also made Jordan's physical aura the focal point of its original "Air Jordan" marketing campaign. Their first advertising spot, aired in 1985, featured Jordan executing a dunk in slow motion on an urban playground with the screams of jet engines accelerating for takeoff in the background, with the words "Who said a man wasn't meant to fly?" printed on the screen. In addition to focusing on his body, the otherwise incongruous juxtaposition of Jordan soaring (with the planes) above an outdoor, inner-city playground court highlights another way in which Jordan's blackness was initially marked and conveyed—by situating him and his style of play in inner-city America, a space culturally imagined as African American. And in stark contrast to its usual sociological functions, Jordan's blackness was fascinating and exciting, an object of mainstream, white middle-class desire and consumption.[13]

The connections between basketball and blackness in American culture are deep and multifaceted, as the cultural critic Nelson George discussed in his classic book *Elevating the Game,* which depicts basketball as having a distinctive African American male aesthetic. In fact, according to David Andrews, the history of basketball is almost always imagined as an evolutionary chain whose modern lineage begins with the emergence of African American players like Elgin Baylor, Connie Hawkins, and Julius Erving and ultimately culminating with "the supreme basketball being, Michael Jordan."[14] Indeed, when Jordan was compared with his contemporaries, they were invariably African American. The cultural and historical dynamics of this lineage are far more complicated than can possibly be covered in this particular essay.[15] Context, for example, is crucial. The blackness that Baylor and Hawkins represented in the 1950s and 1960s was far different, in both form and function, from that embodied by players in Jordan's era in the aftermath of the civil rights movement. In fact, the single most defining feature of the post–civil rights basketball landscape may be that by the 1980s African American players were so dominant in the sport that their struggle was not integration but dealing with the unique opportunities and tensions presented by what a taxi-cab driver once described to me as overintegration. But no matter what was or wasn't said about race, simply playing a sport so thoroughly associated with blackness in the United States ensured that Jordan as athlete, icon, and commodity form would be marked as African American (though even this wasn't left to chance by early advertising campaigns).

Of course, it wasn't long before the public Jordan began to shed these more traditional racial markers and take on the more individualized and apparently race-less public personae he inhabits today. In their recent fiftieth anniversary edition, *Sports Illustrated* recalled an event that encapsulates the image, a September 1985 press conference to announce Jordan's endorsement deal with Coca-Cola. At some point, Jordan was asked whether he preferred Coke Classic or the new formula the company was then promoting as a replacement. Because the company was experiencing a public backlash against the proposed change (it was eventually abandoned in one of the most notorious flops in American business history), the question put Jordan in perilous territory. His now-legendary response was simple and, according to *SI,* pure "genius": "Coke is coke," he said matter-of-factly. "Both taste great." "Bland but not boring, evasive without being a lie, almost charming," this answer (which the magazine ranks as the fourth most important "tipping point" in the last half century of sports) made Michael Jordan into "Mr. Middle America despite his dark skin color." Jordan emerged as "the nonthreatening black man whites would accept as one of their own" and in the process "helped white America discover other black men they could trust: Bill Cosby, Denzel Washington, Colin Powell." "Do you ever hear anybody talking about Tiger Woods and race?" the magazine rhetorically asks. "You may credit Coke, Jordan, and his deft answer to a personal question for that."[16]

Here we see all the elements that corporations ranging from McDonalds and Wheaties to Chevrolet and Hanes wanted to represent them and their products: Jordan's easy smile and off-court presence, his winning personality, his sense of style and obvious personal charisma, as well as the grandiose implications of leaving race completely behind. And it is not incidental that *Sports Illustrated* chose to commemorate a corporate venue rather than an athletic one. Jordan continued to show dramatic progress as an NBA player throughout the 1980s, winning a series of scoring titles and then being named the MVP of the league for the first time in 1988 and defensive player of the year that same season. (And this isn't even to mention how his playing style revolutionized the game on the court and in the public mind—not only in terms of bringing an emphasis on high-flying dunks but also in terms of the kind of defense opposing teams employed in an effort to slow Jordan down. Recall, here, Detroit Piston's coach Charles Daly's infamous "Jordan

Rules" defense.) But the lack of success of his team, the Bulls, raised questions about how much of a team player Jordan was, how much he improved those around him, and about the mark he would ultimately leave on basketball history. In athletic terms, the late 1980s marked a period of frustration and disappointment for Jordan, a fierce competitor who was never satisfied with losing no matter what the game or how low the stakes. As a corporate pitchman and media celebrity, however, Jordan's success was unparalleled and unqualified. According to Jordan's agent David Falk, his client embodied "Norman Rockwell values but with a contemporary flair." Much as Jordan the basketball superstar seemed to defy the laws of physics, Jordan-the-name-brand appeared to transcend all the usual social labels and stereotypes with the unique force of his personality and athletic brilliance. As Falk put it, "He's the first modern crossover in team sports. We think he transcends race, transcends basketball."[17]

Though he wasn't actually the first to lay claim to being a crossover, colorless cultural icon (that distinction would fall to O. J. Simpson[18]), the role was still relatively novel and reflective of African American advances of the post–civil rights era, and Jordan took it to unprecedented heights. The rhetoric of what David Andrews called the "All-American, transcendental Jordan" became a recurring theme among astute social observers and cultural critics. The novelist John Edgar Wideman has said that Jordan "escapes gravity" and "makes us rise above our obsession with race" because he leaps the great divide between races and classes by being a down-to-earth, middle-class, and apolitical hero." Even Harry Edwards, the sociologist who built his career and national reputation on pointing out racial injustice in the sports world, used that language. He talked to David Halberstam about Jordan "representing the highest level of human achievement, on the order of Ghandi, Einstein, or Michelangelo," maintaining that if he were in charge of introducing an alien being "to the epitome of human potential, creativity, perseverance and spirit, I would introduce that alien life to Michael Jordan." The idea of the transcendental Jordan may have received its most elaborate and erudite expression in the work of the famed Harvard social scientist Orlando Patterson. In the third and final volume of his massive trilogy on American race relations, Patterson used Jordan, whom he described as "America's only living man-god," as the centerpiece of his argument that in the post–civil rights era African American sports figures and entertainers have become America's primary "Dionysian figures"—individuals who not only cross boundaries but dissolve them, pointing the way to fuller, more complex understandings of self, citizenship, culture, and civilization.[19]

Not everyone saw it this way. The cultural sociologist David Andrews argued that Jordan's "carefully engineered" public image was not an example of racial transcendence—that is, of overcoming race and racism—but rather of racial displacement and disavowal.[20] On the one hand, Andrews lamented how Jordan's "prototypical, simulated Reaganite hard body" was "lauded by the popular media for being living proof of the existence of an open class structure, racial tolerance, economic mobility, the sanctity of individualism, and the availability of the American dream for black Americans."[21] On the other, he also insisted that the idealized and ostensibly race-less Jordan—especially the Jordan who appeared with Mars Blackmon in the memorable Nike ads done by director Spike Lee—was actually situated in opposition to other, presumably problematic African Americans: namely, the masses of black folks who were believed to be failing and thereby threatening to American social stability. Thus, in Andrews's view, Jordan's All-American identity didn't transcend his race but was predicated precisely on it, on the idealized, assimilated type of blackness he represented, presented, and embodied. It is what race scholars have talked about as "enlightened racism," where stereotypes about the deep cultural differences and deficiencies of the African American masses ("bad blacks" as one recent critic says) are reinforced and reproduced precisely in celebrating individual African Americans ("good" blacks) believed to have repudiated and overcome these traits and characteristics. There is no better, more appropriate illustration of this dyad of blackness that Michael Jordan was bound up than C. L. Cole's brilliant analysis of the Nike Corporation's "PLAY" movement and its use of Jordan in the marketing campaign that accompanied it.[22]

The Nike campaign was the product of a splashy, well-publicized "Youth Fitness Summit" held in Washington, D.C., in 1993, which, in response to the decline of public facilities for recreation and sport in urban areas, was an attempt to create a movement and network of organizations and agencies that would secure every child's "right to play." Nike's "public-service style advertisements" were obviously intended to serve as "expressions of Nike's conscience and its overlapping commitment to and investment in America" (p. 380). And they did so with a broad, universalist defense of children and of sport as a means of appropriate socialization that set up the company (and by extension Jordan) as an alternative to the conservative "policing and punishment scenarios" being played out elsewhere in the United States PLAY offered, in other words, a kinder, gentler, more inclusive America—one that realized the rights of all American children regardless of cultural differences such as race, class, gender, or religion.

But there was, according to Cole, an implicit racial component to PLAY's public appeal. When it came to how African American young people were represented in the campaign, the narrative shifted slightly but significantly. "Whereas sport and physical activity are used to shore up America's bourgeois fantasy of childhood fun and play for White middle-class youth, sport and physical activity function to regulate, discipline, and police already deviant [black] bodies in urban areas." This is revealed *not* in what the advertising campaign says, Cole claims, but in what it doesn't say, in its absences and its silences—and this is where Jordan, as narrator/host of the spot, played the crucial role.

"What if there were no sports?" Jordan's disembodied voice famously intones in the first ad. "What if there were no teams? What if there were no dreams?" Cole insists there is a subtle racial subtext—a threat of general disorder and social deterioration—underlying these questions. What is implied, in Cole's view, is that without sports African American youth are "at risk" for crime, disposed to disorder, and inclined to risky behavior. This subtext is made manifest in the advertisement's closing sequence where Jordan is, finally, pictured on the screen. In Cole's view, the image of Michael Jordan, an athlete who despite all of his crossover appeal is still unmistakably a black man, signals the racial logic and threat underlying and justifying the PLAY movement. It reminds us, more specifically, that without sports we would not only lose the chance for future Michael Jordans, we would likely be left with all of the problems associated with blackness and risk itself: gangs, crime, drugs, violence, and so forth. "If we did not imagine Jordan in the space of sport, where would we imagine him?" Cole asks, mimicking the ad. Who, in other words, do we imagine him turning out to be?

Thus, Cole concludes, the Jordan-featured PLAY movement "appears to break from popular discourses on crime . . . in actuality, however, it only makes sense in relation to and in fact depends upon these racialized discourses, this imagined sense of "what/who we understand to be America's urban problems and how race is made to matter and not matter in the national imagination."

So where did Michael-Jordan-the-person, the human being with a family and a private life and views all his own, fit into this? This is not an easy question to answer—not just because Jordan did not talk often about his personal politics or his views on race but because everything he thought about and talked about and did was so carefully packaged and performed. The Michael Jordan that the public knew (and that we know today) was very literally not an individual but an icon, a product of media representations, public relations, and marketing campaigns. The public was afforded a few glimpses of Michael Jordan the person early in his career (for example, Bob Greene's two-part biography) but these were few and far between, and one has to wonder to what extent these, too, were part of a public relations campaign. Even Halberstam, despite initial assurances from Jordan's agent David Falk, was unable to interview Jordan personally for his mammoth treatment.[23] It is for good reason that Ellis Cashmore has called Jordan "the most controlled athlete in history";[24] indeed, this is why this essay so far has been more of a cultural history than a biography proper (and thus rather unlike many of the other contributions to this volume).

Public relations and media packaging is obviously a well-accepted aspect of life for popular athletes, movie stars, political leaders, and all manner of public figures in our celebrity-infatuated society. And the most famous black athletes of the twentieth century—Joe Louis, Jesse Owens, and especially Jackie Robinson, for examples—have been among the most carefully marketed and tightly controlled figures in American history. What is unique about Jordan's case, however, is the degree to which Michael Jordan himself was actively and self-consciously involved in the making of his image, his career, and his public personae. Observers and reporters who spent time around Jordan—even those who were critical of him—almost universally marveled at his maturity, his poise and self-confidence, his control. Jordan always seemed to be comfortable and in control. Even more remarkable was the extent to which Jordan shaped and reshaped and transformed those individuals and institutions he was around—whether it was the game of basketball, the NBA, corporate marketing strategies, or Hollywood movies. In this respect David Halberstam's subtitle could not be more appropriate: that the world Michael Jordan inhabited was very much a world of his own making. Jordan was not your typical athlete but rather one of those rare individuals—not just in sport history—who shaped the world around him even as it shaped him.

Jordan's active and self-conscious engagement is important for two reasons. In the first place, because no black athlete in history, perhaps no athlete in history, exercised a comparable degree of control in shaping his or her image and in profiting from that image. Jordan is a truly historic figure in this respect. The second reason Jordan's exceptional involvement and understanding is significant brings us back to the question of race and his ostensibly color-blind, race-neutral image. The point is this: given how much input and awareness Jordan had in shaping his public image, there is no reason to think that things would have been any different when it came to issues of race. He had to be aware of himself as a black man and have some sense of all the irony and contradiction that his success involved, his apparent color blindness no less than anything else. The fact that Jordan did not talk about race publicly should not be taken as evidence of a lack of understanding but rather a deliberate choice on the part of a very successful, self-conscious African American man.

This is necessarily somewhat of a conjecture, but it is not completely without foundation. When he signed his first professional sports contracts and endorsement deals, Jordan and his associates very deliberately rejected appeals that would have typecast him or niche-marketed him for African American audiences. Jordan's understanding of his personal identity and its relationship to broader racial stereotypes took further shape in an incident that took place in his first NBA All-Star game in 1985. Jordan showed up for the event decked out in a full-length fur coat and lots of fancy jewelry. It was, he told Bob Greene several years after the fact, how he thought NBA stars were supposed to dress and act. Jordan quickly realized he felt neither comfortable nor accepted in the get-up and began to adopt the more toned-down, mainstream style that would become his trademark.[25]

This was obviously not the racial role, identity, or vision his critics would have liked. Accommodating and even apologetic, Jordan's centrist sensibilities were, as we have seen, expressed in abstract, universalistic terms full of class-inflected racial undertone and implication. And his complicity with the unfettered market, commodification, consumption, and the pursuit of personal wealth was beyond question. Still, it is important not to push these criticisms too far. For one thing, there is no reason that athletes should be held up to scrutiny and standards of political involvement that apply to no one else in society (though admittedly Jordan did bring this on himself at times as, for example, when he intimated support for certain liberal causes but then declined to publicly support an African American candidate trying to unseat conservative North Carolina senator Jesse Helms).

Connected with this, the opportunities for meaningful racial resistance and change through professional sports in the United States were (and remain) far more limited than critics often imagine. The economic and institutional demands of big-business, globalized sport are almost overwhelming, as Helen Page's study of the experience of Jordan's onetime Bulls teammate Craig Hodges illustrates. Despite being one of the top three point shooters in the league, Hodges found himself quickly (if quietly) bounced out of the league after making some modest public comments on racial issues. Even the most personal, stylized aspects of player dress and on-court celebratory behaviors are policed through racialized codes of conduct and sportsmanship.[26] Just as important (if often overlooked) are the cultural conceptions of sport that define its role and the appropriate role of athletes in social life—the notion that sports needs to be protected from the perceived corruption of politics; the fact that most Americans experience sports as being deeply meaningful but ultimately trivial; worn dumb-jock stereotypes. These cultural structures make it difficult for athletes to be open and upfront about their social views, and almost impossible for mainstream audiences to accept them when they do. Indeed, taken together these social and cultural forces dictate that most of the social meaning and significance conveyed through athletes in the sports media is constituted via image, body language, and style.[27]

This context and these limitations should make us mindful of the racial significance and self-consciousness of Jordan's dress and demeanor and discourse, both on the court and off it. Indeed, my guess is that Jordan saw himself as one of those figures who pushed for racial change by working within the system, creating opportunities for others, constructing new alternative images of blackness, and breaking down traditional prejudices and stereotypes. It is what the historian Kevin Gaines has called "racial uplift" or "self-help ideology," a tradition that traces its roots back to Booker T. Washington through E. Franklin Frazier and the NAACP up to Bill Cosby. "Believing that the improvement of African American's material and moral condition through self-help would diminish white racism," Gaines has written, advocates have "sought to rehabilitate the race's image by embodying respectability enacted through an ethos of service to the masses," thereby incorporating African Americans into the ostensibly universal narrative of Western progress, civilization, and citizenship.[28] "African American uplift" is not a radical approach but neither is it entirely apolitical; in certain circles, in fact, there is no more reasonable point of view and program to champion.

However informed and aware Jordan may have been about this vision, nowhere does he more clearly reflect the paradoxical, conflicted state of post–civil rights American race relations than in this color-blind, race-neutral discourse, and nowhere does he play a more prominent role in setting in relief its tensions, contradictions, and possibilities.

One of Jordan's greatest gifts, as both an ad-man and an athlete (and perhaps even as a racial icon), was impeccable timing. Even if he might have wanted it to come sooner, Jordan's first NBA championship with the Chicago Bulls in 1991 probably couldn't have been better scripted by a Hollywood screenwriter. After a half decade of mounting expectations and bitter disappointments, the title not only provided dramatic confirmation of Jordan's basketball greatness, it propelled him to even greater, unforeseen heights of popularity and stardom. Indeed, if it is possible to pinpoint the moment in which Jordan's crossover status was consolidated and he emerged as a truly larger-than-life cultural icon—not just Air Jordan but "His Airness," not Michael Jordan but "MJ" or just plain "Michael"—this first NBA championship would have to be it. Reporters covering the Jordan phenomenon grasped for metaphors and parallels to capture and convey his popularity: Elvis Presley, the Beatles, movie stars, war heroes. But in many ways Jordan was in a league all his own.

Predictably, however, this popularity came with a price. The more fame and fortune Jordan experienced, the less he was able to enjoy the regular, ordinary aspects of daily life that the rest of us take for granted. He couldn't do his own shopping, go out for dinner, go to a movie, or even leave his hotel room without getting mobbed. Fans would do virtually anything to get his autograph, or even just his attention. Signs saying "Michael Jordan for President" began popping up at arenas across the league. Jordan was quickly becoming a prisoner of his own popularity, and the more the team won, the worse it got. Jordan continued to cultivate his public image but increasingly his trademark smile was reserved for television appearances and commercials. Forget (for the moment) the question of whether Jordan was bound by race, Michael Jordan was bound by being "Michael Jordan." It got so bad in the early 1990s that Jordan confided to Chicago writer Bob Greene that the basketball court was the only place he really felt free, where he could be his uncontained, fully realized self.

> The basketball court for me, during a game, is the most peaceful place I can imagine. I truly feel less pressure there than anyplace I go. On the basketball court I worry about nothing. When I'm out there, no one can bother me. Being out there is one of the most private parts of my life. Being on the court is very much like meditation for me. If something is on my mind, I can think about it on the court. If my wife and I had a disagreement at home, I know that if we have a game that night, I'll be out there on the court by myself for a few hours and by the time I get home again at the end of the evening, all of that will have passed.[29]

These sentiments are remarkable not only because they show how captive to and controlled by his public personae Jordan was. They also reflect that rare and remarkable synthesis of discipline, focus, and creativity we associate with real genius. Set in the context of African American sports history, one also can't help but contrast the freedom Jordan felt in the athletic arena with the tremendous racial burden previous generations of African American athletes carried with them into the athletic arena. Every bout Joe Louis fought, for example, was for the credit of his race. The proud and otherwise defiant Jackie Robinson was under orders not to argue or protest and was thus unable to respond to the racial taunts and slurs of opposing fans and players.[30] While Jordan had plenty of other responsibilities and obligations, his experience of sport as a site of release and achievement, a genuine "field of play," signals at least one more respect in which race relations had progressed, at least within the world of sport.

This uncompromising focus and freedom also help to account for one of the many memorable emotional moments of Jordan's career: his post-game celebration after the Bulls' first championship. Upon realizing what he and his teammates had finally accomplished (he had also been named MVP of the finals), Jordan fell to his knees in the locker room, in tears, cradling the championship trophy all to himself. It was a rare, unguarded moment of personal fulfillment for the very public Jordan (and may even have helped to usher in a new era of emotionality and masculinity in American sporting culture).

But the championship only intensified the pressures and public scrutiny on Jordan. Even as he and his Bulls remained at the top of the league the following season, substantial public criticism of Jordan arose for the first time during the 1991–92 campaign. It came from many angles: Jordan was rebuked for failing to attend a White House ceremony where President Bush honored the Bulls' championship; he was taken to task (by Chicago sportswriter Stan Smith in *The Jordan Rules*) for his hyper-competitive, win-at-all-costs nature, and castigated for gambling large sums of money in golf. His public image also took a hit when he declined to immediately accept the invitation to play for the 1992 U.S. Olympic team, and then for wrangling with the NBA and Olympic authorities over the commercial rights to his likeness and his obligation to wear athletic apparel that bore the label of Nike's chief competitor Reebok during the games.[31] Air Jordan, in short, was being brought back down to earth.

Popular backlash against erstwhile athletic heroes and celebrities is a regular and predictable feature of the modern mass media and its tabloid industry, especially in democratic societies where the best and the brightest typically provoke deep anxieties about our idealized visions of equality, universality, and shared humanity.[32] But what was unique and largely unexpected in Jordan's case (especially in light of his erstwhile colorlessness) was the appearance of racial undercurrents and overtones in the coverage and commentary. Increasingly, as David Andrews has documented, Jordan was described as being either defiant and ungrateful, or prone to selfish, irresponsible, and self-destructive behavior—tropes that have been used to marginalize and contain successful black men throughout American history.

Aided by another NBA championship in 1992 and his starring role on the "Dream Team" that won gold in Barcelona that summer, Jordan and his handlers weathered the initial storm of criticism pretty well and the racial aspects remained fairly isolated and under the radar. But that would not last. A new, more intensive round of attacks on Jordan's character and credibility took shape less than one year later when reporters broke the story that Jordan had been gambling in Atlantic City in the wee hours of the morning on the eve of Game 2 of the Bulls' 1993 Eastern Conference Final series against the New York Knicks. These reports were followed by intensive media scrutiny and speculation where Jordan was clearly and often deliberately linked with all of the racially inscribed deviance and pathology believed to be associated with the NBA: not just gambling, but drinking and drug use, gang associations, sexual promiscuity. All of a sudden, Jordan's race-less-ness was disappearing and he was being transformed from the "good" black athlete to one of the bad ones. If there is ever any doubt about Jordan's public image being bound with blackness, one need only look back to these commentaries (documented by David Andrews and others) to confirm.

The re-appearance of race in the context of Jordan's supposed transgressions was not, in fact, unprecedented. When Magic Johnson divulged that he had contracted the HIV virus from illicit sexual encounters, for example, he was quickly and unceremoniously transformed into being "just another black guy" in the national media. And the re-racialization process kicked into full gear when the original crossover icon O. J. Simpson was accused of the double murders of Nicole Brown and Ronald Goldman.[33] In many ways, these reactions reflect the ambivalence that black male success, in all arenas but especially athletic ones, provokes in white America: that, on the one hand, it generates deep fascination, admiration, and desire, but on the other, also produces a simultaneous fear and resentment. Predictable though it was, Jordan had done nothing wrong and certainly committed no crimes. Even more troubling, the racialized public reaction actually intensified when a heinous crime was committed against him and his family later in August. It was perhaps the most troubling event in Jordan's personal life: the disappearance and, as it turned out, murder of his father, James.

Connie Chung framed the story for the nation on the *CBS Evening News:* "Triumph. Turmoil. And now, tragedy. Michael Jordan has seen it all this year. Today police in North Carolina confirmed the worst fears about the basketball star's missing father. James Jordan shot to death. Killer and motive unknown." The subsequent film segment reported on Michael's devastation and went on to comment, "Authorities have not said whether they will consider the possibility the killing might be connected to the family's gambling activities." "In one fell swoop," as Andrews put it, "[these] less-than-subtle inferences provided the viewing public with a seemingly compelling rationale for the murder; one which clearly implicated Michael Jordan, without any direct reference to him." With a picture of the elder Jordan in the backdrop, Chung's concluding reference to his son's career made the racial subtext of the story uncomfortably clear: "Jordan's murder adds another bitter twist to the darker side of an American success story."[34]

Jordan's fall from grace as an American icon was mercifully shortlived. The negative, racialized images began to abate with the arrest and conviction of his father's murderers, one of them an African American male who was made to bear the brunt of what Andrews described as "the accusatory and racist vectors of the popular media" that had initially landed on Michael. Jordan's surprise retirement from the game that had made him and that he had helped to remake—prompted, according to reports, by his father's death and his frustration over media treatment—further accelerated the rehabilitation process. It was viewed as an occasion of national mourning and loss, and prompted the celebration (and vindication) of an All-American life. The syndicated columnist Ira Berkow's comments illustrate: "His wholesome image, his broad smile and his basketball achievements made him the embodiment of the American dream." Even President Clinton got into the act: "We may never see another like him again. We will miss him—here and all around America, in every small-town backyard and paved city lot where kids play one-on-one and dream of being like Mike."[35] And then there was

Jordan's foray into professional baseball, his decision to join a minor league baseball team in an attempt to play the game that was his first athletic love at the highest possible level. Baseball's historic reputation as the national pastime; Jordan's unlikely dream and the lengths he was willing to chase it; the fact that he was obviously not in it for the money (unlike major leaguers, then in the middle of the most contentious labor dispute in the history of American sports); that despite all of his best efforts he wasn't even particularly good at the game—these were all factors that once again endeared Jordan to the America public, and promoters were quick to capitalize on them, spinning out entire marketing campaigns on Jordan's "baseball odyssey" as well as a series of coffee table and self-help books on Jordan's personal philosophy about life.[36] With their emphasis on the abstract, universal virtues and values Jordan was said to represent, these texts were almost gloriously free of even the subtlest references to race and racism.

Yet even in these moments of apparent transcendence, race was never far from the surface. During Jordan's self-imposed hiatus from basketball, journalists wrote numerous stories and commentaries about the perceived decline of the NBA and basketball in general, focusing especially on the deviance and delinquency and disobedience associated with the new generation of African American stars. Players like Dennis Rodman, Chris Webber, Derrick Coleman, Isaiah Rider, and eventually Allen Iverson were lumped together as "slammin', jammin', no jump-shooting, fundamentally unsound kids who have bought into NBA's and Madison Avenue's shallow MTV-generated marketing of the game. People with no soul for the essence of the game turned the poetry into gangster rap." The thrust of many of these commentaries was that the league's discipline problem mirrored the problems of society, and that Jordan represented the "good" black athlete against which these young black stars were imagined. As a December 1994 *Inside Sports* cover story asked: "Why Can't Shaq Be Like Mike?"[37]

Never does Jordan's awareness and acceptance of his paradoxical racial identity and role emerge more clearly than upon his dramatic return to the NBA in 1995. Employing color-blind language that appealed implicitly to uplift notions of racial respectability, he told CNN: "I really felt that I wanted to instill some positive things back to the game. You know, there's a lot of negative things that have been happening to the game, and I guess in terms of me coming back, I come back with the notion of, you know, Magic Johnson and the Larry Birds and the Dr. Js—all those guys who paved the road for a lot of the young guys. And the young guys are not taking care of their responsibilities in terms of maintaining that love for the game, you know, and not let it waste to where it's so business-oriented that the integrity of the game's going to be at stake."[38]

This perspective would take him to three more NBA championships, another celebrated retirement, his own corporate division at Nike, partial ownership and a management role in an NBA franchise, an unlikely (and surprisingly successful) third comeback with the Washington Wizards, and continuing commercial popularity and endorsement success. In recent years—in the wake of his less-than-Jordanesque play for the Wizards, his eventual dis-association with the Washington franchise, the uneven fortunes of the Nike corporation with which he is so closely associated—Jordan has been less visible and iconic than in the decade of his glory. Much of that was probably inevitable and predictable. My guess—if I am allowed to play prognosticator for a moment—is that this decline will be temporary, that with his (imminent) enshrinement in the Basketball Hall of Fame Jordan will once again come back into the public consciousness and have his athletic reputation returned to his iconic status. History, in other words, will be kind to Jordan.

What is less certain are the racial implications of all this, the racial meaning and significance Michael Jordan will hold in his post-athletic years. Part of the uncertainty here has to do with the unpredictable future of race relations in America. It also has to do with Jordan himself—what he chooses to do with his time and popularity in the years to come. Will he retreat from public life? Will he continue in his ostensibly apolitical, color-blind ways? Or will he develop the courage and audacity to try to use his fame and fortune to broader social and political ends, if not with the politics of a Bill Russell or Muhammad Ali, then perhaps with the intelligence and passion and grace of a Jackie Robinson or Arthur Ashe. If the verdict is still out on these questions that is because the story of Michael Jordan, his life history, is still far from over. But there is no doubt that his future will be tied up with the fate of the paradoxical, color-blind idealism that Jordan represented so proudly and so consistently through his basketball career.

Recent studies of racial images and representations in sport have been very critical of sport's dominant color-blind discourse and the ways in which it can displace, marginalize, and even legitimate the deeply problematic racial status quo.[39] This is appropriate. It is crucial to establish that racism and racial inequalities persist (both in sport and in society) and to consider how this discourse is complicit with insidious racial stereotypes and injustices. Jordan's career provides us a rare opportunity to analyze this discourse, understand its depths, and evaluate its relationship to broader structural and institutional realities. At the same time, we should not forget that while color blindness and race neutrality offer deeply flawed depictions of contemporary racial realities, they present for many Americans—white and black alike—very real and meaningful ideals to strive for, standards to try to live up to. And this, too, Jordan represented. In this respect, John Wideman is onto something when he calls Jordan "the truest prophet of what might be possible" for the future of race in America.[40]

David Wiggins has written of the "double consciousness" of African American athletes, their awareness of being both black and American.[41] The very notion of a double (or split) consciousness almost invariably signals the problems and pathology of race in America. But, borrowed as it is from W. E. B. Du Bois, this bifocal vision should also suggest a sense of critical possibility and promise, a lens onto alternative visions of race and the larger, mainstream society. I would like to think that Jordan cultivated some measure of this double-ness during his athletic career, and even to imagine that he will find a time and a place and a vehicle to act on that in coming years. But whether or not that turns out to be the case, let us be clear that Michael Jordan inhabited and embodied a complex, paradoxical racial space—a space that, if we can understand it properly, can not only help us grasp the challenges (and significance) of being an African American athlete but also and perhaps more importantly begin to cultivate a double consciousness of our own—a consciousness that is at once attentive to both racial progress and stasis, to new possibilities and long-standing limitations, and especially to the ways in which we might aspire to color blindness even as we must nevertheless remain deeply and diligently conscious of color. In an essentially conservative, consensual culture, such a bifocal vision is difficult to cultivate, but nothing, in my view, could be more essential for understanding and acting to confront the complexities of race in contemporary America, especially those propagated in and through sports.

Tiger Woods celebrating a birdie putt on the seventeenth green during the final round of the 2004 Wachovia Championship in Charlotte, North Carolina. *(Getty Images)*

18 "Race," Family, and Nation

The Significance of Tiger Woods in American Culture

S. W. POPE

In his brief lifetime of less than thirty years, Eldrick "Tiger" Woods has been called "the Greatest," "the Chosen One," "sport's messiah," and a "savior" for people of color. As a proud father, Earl Woods has extolled the attributes of his son. Speaking with hyperbolic gusto, Woods Sr. proclaimed that Tiger "has already transcended the game of golf. He is a world figure, not just a world golf figure. He has transcended athletics already[1] . . . He will do more than any other man in history to change the course of humanity . . . The world will be a better place to live in . . . by virtue of his existence . . . and his presence."[2] As if such a prophesy was not grandiose enough, Woods Sr. (who claimed that he "was personally selected by God himself . . . to nurture this young man") alleged that his son could have an even greater humanitarian influence than Mandela, Gandhi, or the Buddha given that Tiger "has a larger forum than any of them . . . Because he's qualified through his ethnicity to accomplish miracles . . . There's no limit because he has guidance . . . The world is just getting a taste of his power."[3]

The twenty-four-year-old son had been a professional golfer for a mere three years at the time of the father's public statements. During those three years, however, Woods's accomplishments evoked comparisons with the legendary Jack Nicklaus. On paper, Tiger confirmed the celebratory discourse: at twenty-four, Nicklaus had won three majors, twelve tournaments, had a scoring average of 69.9, and had an inflation-adjusted $1.6 million; whereas Tiger had won four majors and twenty-one tournaments, had a 67.7 average, and had $17 million in winnings.[4] By 2000, Tiger's sporting accomplishments had fuelled an insatiable media frenzy of unprecedented televised tournament ratings, newsstand sales, a phenomenal increase in Nike golf merchandise, and public opinion poll findings. According to one June 2000 Gallup poll, 88 percent of Americans looked upon Tiger more favorably than any other athlete—*ever.*[5]

The cascading pronouncements of golfing greatness were not without foundation. During his first full season on the PGA tour, Woods won six of twenty-five events with a record $2,066,833 in earnings. He won the 1997 Masters by a record 18 under par and a 12-stroke margin of victory; in 2000 he won the U.S. Open by a record 15 strokes. Tiger became the fifth golfer after Gene Sarazen, Ben Hogan, Gary Player, and Jack Nicklaus (and the first in thirty-four years) to have taken all of pro golf's grand-slam titles (which he simultaneously held after his win at the 2001 Masters). Woods is the youngest player to have won all four of golf's major tournaments—the Masters, the U.S. Open, the PGA Championship, and the British Open (with a 19-under 269, a record at St. Andrews and the lowest score ever in relation to par at a major tournament). He holds the all-time scoring record in three of these majors and shares the record in another. In 1998, at the age of twenty-one, he became the youngest player in history (by eight years) to be ranked number one in the world after finishing in the top five eight times that year. He remained the world's number one until September 2004, but reclaimed the title spot six months later by winning the Ford Championship at Doral in March 2005.

Unlike most athletes (and virtually all African American athletes) Woods's ascension to the heights of popular adulation was not launched solely from his *professional* successes. The details and tropes of Tiger's rise to stardom were emplotted by the media since his infancy in the late 1970s. Millions of Americans have watched Tiger "grow up." His rise to becoming one of the most recognized sport celebrities has been widely chronicled over the past decade and have become household knowledge. This was no accident. "National intimacy was encoded and enacted through these re-contextualized media clips of child-Woods . . . sutured together and re-circulated to provide evidence of an America collectively anticipating a sporting, cultural, and economic phenomenon in the making," sociologists Cheryl Cole and David Andrews argue provocatively. Through this carefully managed media epic story, Woods was "positioned and confirmed as America's son; [and] relatedly, *Woods personal achievements were easily translated into national accomplishments*" (my emphasis) so as to "corroborate the fantasy of a conflict-free and color-blind America."[6]

Thus, documenting the biographical details of a young, contemporary celebrity is an intellectual endeavor beset with the well-established tropes and meta-narratives. In the case of young Tiger, most of the discourse (and heretofore published biographical works that tend toward hagiography) is thoroughly encoded, as Cole and Andrews theorize, with elements of race, family, and nation such that Woods serves as "an 'antidote' to the anxieties weighing down America (and 'the world') at the end of the [twentieth] century."[7] Young Woods's ascendancy coincided with what the historian Robin Kelley termed a post-nostalgic generation for African Americans. Although there remains an interest in the struggle for racial equality in sport (e.g., the legacy of the Negro Leagues, Jessie Owens's achievements at the 1936 Olympics, Joe Louis's boxing exploits, Jackie Robinson's integration of major league in 1947), American collective memory of golf history is so selective that few people know much about the game's black pioneers prior to Woods. As such, Woods became the defunct "pioneer" for integrating the long-standing white-dominated sport of golf. Yet, with even a cursory survey of the longer history of African American achievements in professional golf, one finds other, "forgotten" pioneers in this sport.

One hundred years before Woods joined the Professional Golf Association (PGA) tour, the African American golfer John Shippen Jr.—who taught golf at the Shinnecock golf course in Long Island, New York—competed in a 36-hole U.S. Open held in Southampton, New York, in 1896. The tournament was marred by Jim Crow laws during the very year of the pivotal *Plessy v. Ferguson* case decided by the U.S. Supreme Court which codified the notion of "separate but equal" conditions for blacks and whites. Several white golfers threatened to boycott the tournament so as not to participate in a racially mixed competition. Shippen and Oscar Bunn, a Shinnecock Native Indian, were grudgingly allowed to play when then United States Golf Association (USGA) president Theodore Havermyer informed the field that "we are going to play this thing today even if Shippen and Bunn are the only people in it." Shippen finished a respectable fifth with ten dollars in winnings. As a club pro and a greenkeeper at the nation's first black country club, Shady Rest in New Jersey, for the next thirty years, he played in six subsequent U.S. Open tournaments—the final one, in 1913, marked the last appearance by a black golfer until Theodore "Teddy" Rhodes competed in Nashville, Tennessee, in 1948.[8] One year after Jackie Robinson broke the major league baseball color barrier as a second baseman for the Brooklyn Dodgers, Rhodes, Bill Spiller, and Madison Gunther filed a civil lawsuit against the PGA for its Jim Crow practices, but the governing body did not formally drop the "Caucasians-only" clause from its constitution until 1961.[9] Barred from the PGA tour and "white" country clubs, a group of golf-playing physicians from Washington, D.C., tired of Jim Crow rules in their home city (which forced them to travel to New England each summer to play) formed the United Golfers Association (UGA).[10] The UGA organized black-only tournaments for over fifty years and attracted celebrity golfers, including jazz singer Billy Eckstine, baseball legend Jackie Robinson, footballer Jim Brown, boxer Joe Louis, and various other celebrity athletes who popularized the circuit. As a champion playing at the margins, Rhodes died in relative obscurity at the age of fifty-three after winning over 150 tournaments on the "unofficial" black tours organized under the auspices of the UGA.[11]

Charlie Sifford was the first African American golfer to receive full PGA Tour status in March 1960. After winning five consecutive National Negro Championships between 1952 and 1956, Sifford bridged two eras by winning the PGA-sanctioned Long Beach Open in 1957 to become the first black golfer to win a major PGA tournament.[12] Sifford emerged during an era when black golfers dominated the caddying at all-white country clubs—a racialized situation within which black golfers, like Sifford, exploited their access to the links and mastered the game. As Sifford recalled in his autobiography, "I found out I could smack a golf ball and make it go straight and far . . . And once I learned that, nothing was going to stop me from playing the game and getting better."[13]

During the 1970s and 1980s, Lee Elder and Calvin Peete were the leading black golfers on the PGA tour. Elder became the first African American golfer to compete in the Masters Tournament in 1975, and in 1979, he became the first African American to represent the United States on a Ryder Cup team. Peete, who swung a golf club for the first time at age twenty-three, won eleven PGA tour events during the 1980s until the effects of a neurological disease began to take a toll on his game.[14]

In short, Woods was not the first successful "black" golfer—others had blazed a trail and tradition that had been forgotten by even avid golf fans. Rather, Woods, America's newest multicultural sports celebrity, burst onto the scene at a fortuitous historical moment, as sportswriter John Feinstein notes, during which time "no sport needed a black superstar more than golf . . . because no sport has had more of a racist image than golf."[15]

The well-known "Tiger Woods Story" follows the "rapid rise" variant of a well-established "golden success" sporting narrative. For the "new kids on the block" (like Woods), according to the sport sociologist Gary Whannel, the story is a "celebration of youthful success and attention to newness is part of the neophiliac character of the culture" narrated in the following pattern: triumph—childhood—early prowess—first successes—advancement—successes—triumph.[16] In this regard, the Tiger Woods's story does not depart significantly from a long-established narrative tradition within sports writing.

Eldrick was born on December 30, 1975, to Earl and Kultida Woods. He was exposed to his future life's work while, as a toddler sitting in a high chair, he watched his father practice golf swings in the family's southern California garage. By his first birthday, Tiger tried to imitate his father's swing with a sawed-off club; by two, Tiger accompanied Earl to a nearby driving range and the Navy Golf Club in Cypress, California; by three, Tiger gave a putting demonstration on the popular, nationally televised Michael Douglas variety show—alongside Hollywood legends Bob Hope and James Stewart (thereafter, he competed and won a ten and under nine-hole tournament). Sportscaster and former pro football player Jim Hill predicted that the "young man is going to be to golf what Jimmy Connors and Chris Evert are to tennis." As a four-year-old, Woods shot a 48 over nine holes at his home Navy Golf Club course.

The child prodigy developed under the tutelage of his mentor and lifelong promoter, Earl Woods, who was born in Manhattan, Kansas, during the Great Depression. Earl was the youngest of six children of a father who worked as a brick mason and gardener and a college-educated mother who worked as a housemaid—both of whom died by the time he was a teenager.[17] As a fan of Negro League baseball (especially the Homestead Grays), Earl attended a predominately white high school and played catcher on an otherwise all-white American Legion team during which time he achieved All-State honors. Upon graduation, he attended Kansas State University and became the first black baseball player in the Big Twelve Conference where he experienced the racist culture that transcended the supposedly meritocratic playing fields of late 1950s America.

Earl Woods's life and worldview were transformed during his military service in Vietnam. Lieutenant Colonel Earl Dennison Woods served in Vietnam from February 12, 1962, to February 24, 1963.[18] As a career military man, the thirty-five-year-old Woods made a second tour as a Green Beret in Vietnam from August 15, 1970, to August 13, 1971, and for unspecified acts of bravery, he was awarded the Vietnamese Silver Star.[19] It was during this second tour of duty that Earl served as an advisor to the deputy chief of the Binh Thuan Province, Colonel Vuong Phong—a close personal friend whom Earl had nicknamed "Tiger" (in whose memory he nicknamed his youngest son, Eldrick).[20] While in Vietnam, Earl met Ku Tida Punsawad (Tida)—a woman from Thai, Chinese, and Caucasian parentage whose family in Bangkok owned a tin mine and a fleet of Bangkok city buses. Earl and Tida married in 1969. Earl retired from the army with the rank of colonel in 1974, and he and Tida moved from New York and settled in southern California.

Their son, Eldrick, would be their lifelong project. "Eldrick" was a name fashioned by Tida—starting with "E" for Earl and ending in K for Kultida—but from the second day in the maternity ward he was unofficially rechristened "Tiger." According to Earl, "Tiger was raised as an Asian child, not as an American." Under Tida's influence, "Tiger was taught to respect his parents and other adults, to rely on his instincts and feelings, to be unselfish and generous . . . These are all tenets of Asian philosophy and culture." Although one would imagine that Earl, as a career military man, would have exerted the strong disciplinary influence, according to Tiger, his father never spanked him because "Mom [a petite Buddhist] beat the hell out of my ass. I've still got the handprints," Tiger remembered much later. "Mom isn't the sentimentalist Dad is; she doesn't cry." Tida confirmed this: "Old man is soft. He cry. He forgive people. Not me. I don't forgive anybody."[21] As the disciplinarian in the family, Tida used golf as an incentive—Tiger was forbidden to hit practice balls until he had finished his homework.[22]

Earl and Tida brought their respective talents to Project Tiger. The two created an incredibly stable home life—"almost freakish for a close-of-the-millennium California child" as *Sports Illustrated* writer Gary Smith characterized it—the same two parents, same house all his twenty years, the same best friends (and, allegedly, Tiger never once had a babysitter).[23] In the process, Earl and Tida made substantial personal and financial sacrifices.[24]

At age forty-two, Earl took up golf and became a scratch player five years later. On evenings after dinner, he hit balls into a garage net, while the infant son watched from his high chair. Young Tiger was captivated by the motion, and one day, according to Earl, he clutched a baby-sized plastic club and executed an imitation of his father's swing. Tiger made that first swing left-handed—a mirror image of his right-handed role model. A few days later, he stepped around the ball, correctly reversed his grip, and made an equally precocious swing from the opposite side. At that moment, Earl realized he was the steward of an extraordinary talent. As a toddler, according to Earl, Tiger was able to identify the swing flaws of adult players; and before he could count to ten, Earl claims his son could tell on any golf hole, where each member of a foursome stood in relation to par.[25]

Such skills were honed through rigorous daily practice. On some days, "Pop would drop me off at Heartwell Golf Course on his way to work" (as a contract administrator and materials manager at McDonnell Douglas, a military contractor in Huntington Beach, California), where-after Tiger would play eighteen holes and then work on his short game until Earl retrieved him. Rather than the result of a controlling father, Tiger usually initiated the daily ritual. "I would call Pop at work to ask if I could practice with him. He would always pause for a second or two—keeping me in suspense—but he always said yes," Tiger recalled. "In his own way he was teaching me initiative. You see, he never pushed me to play. Whether I practiced or played was always my idea. He was instrumental in helping me develop the drive to achieve . . . golf for me was an apparent attempt to emulate the person I looked up to more than anyone else: my father . . . I was very eager to learn as much as I could about the game that had so thoroughly captivated my father."[26] Writer David Owen wonders whether "Tiger didn't in some sense 'create' his parents as much as they created him. From the moment he climbed down from that high chair, he seems to have been phenomenally well equipped—temperamentally, emotionally, intellectually—to exploit the physical gift that he was born with. Is it outlandish to wonder whether part of his genius didn't lie in an ability to inspire his parents to conduct their lives in perfect harmony with his ambition?"[27]

Although many athletically gifted children dream and aspire to greatness, few have exuded the level of confidence that Woods did from an early age. In one piece of family film footage, a smiling, young Tiger spoke to the camera: "I want to win all the big tournaments—the major ones—and I hope to play well when I get older, and beat all the pros." Tiger proved that such aspirations weren't merely a pipe dream when, as an eight-year-old, he came from behind to win the Optimist International Junior Championship in San Diego—a tournament he won four more times during the following six years. Yet, at a seminal 1984 tournament wherein he established this characteristic confidence, "knowing that I could play this game against a high level of players," he recalled "and from then on I felt like I could compete against the best players anywhere around the world." Tiger first beat his father by a single stroke, with a score of 71, when he was eleven. That same summer Tiger entered thirty-three junior tournaments and won them all.[28]

Woods's success in the junior championships caused the national sports media to take note of the young golfer's achievements. *Sports Illustrated,* in particular, played a major role in the familiarization of Woods, as Tiger first appeared in the "Face in the Crowd" section of the magazine on September 24, 1990. As the youngest champion in the history of the U.S. Junior Amateur in 1991, *Sports Illustrated* published its first profile of Woods in March 1991 when Tiger was a fifteen-year-old high school freshman.[29] As Michael Mac Cambridge wrote in his history of the magazine, perhaps it was because *Sports Illustrated* "covered golf so thoroughly in its Golf Plus supplement [that] the magazine recognized Woods's significance and spoke with a special authority about his impact on the sport." Between 1992 and 1996, Woods almost single-handedly popularized American amateur golf by winning the U.S. Junior National Championship in 1992 and 1993 and the U.S. Amateur Championship in 1994 and 1995. As a freshman at Stanford University, Woods was named an NCAA First Team All-American and tied for forty-first place in his first Master's tournament (the only amateur to make the cut that year). In 1996, Tiger became the first golfer in history to win three consecutive

U.S. Amateur titles. He also won the NCAA individual men's championship during his second collegiate season.

Woods's golfing prowess during his late teenage years was bolstered by his coach—a talented, traveling professional golfer, Butch Harmon, contracted by Earl in 1993 to take his seventeen-year-old son to the next level (as well as a navy doctor, Captain Jay Brunza, who worked as Woods's sports psychologist since Tiger was thirteen). As a teaching pro who had dreamed of this opportunity of working with that "once-in-a-lifetime dream guy"—Harmon agreed with two stipulations—that he wouldn't charge a dime until Tiger turned pro (thereafter, he would send a hefty invoice for services rendered) and two, that Earl could not interfere with the instructional process.[30] "There was a question as to whether all that energy could be harnessed without being lost . . . whether everything Tiger had could be toned down and at the same time kept," Harmon recalled, but instinctively surmised that " I really wanted a shot at this." Tiger was in close telephone contact with Harmon during the unprecedented three consecutive U.S. Amateur championships. As golf journalist Tom Callahan explained, "the shorthand they developed wasn't far from a code. Before long, they were finishing each other's sentences . . . For the two years Tiger was at Stanford, they kept mailbags warm with videotapes relayed back and forth. Recording every lesson he gave Tiger, Butch combined streams of these images with TV grabs into a montage that was equal parts battle plan and ballet."[31] Harmon served as Tiger's coach until 2002.[32]

During a two-year stint as a student at Stanford University, Woods emerged as an adult golfer. Although he admitted—perhaps nostalgically—several years after his departure from Stanford that he missed college life ("Just hanging around, drinking beer, talking half the night, getting in a little trouble, being with people my own age"[33]) by most accounts Woods was not particularly disposed to being a typical university student-athlete. According to his coach, Wally Goodwin, Woods did not show any propensity to bond closely with the other golfers on the Stanford team nor did he demonstrate much interest in being "one of the guys." For Tiger, there was always a detached relationship with his teammates. As a *New York Times* writer discerned, "It's not that Woods can't be a generous team-mate . . . [it] is that he is not going to be easily shoved off course by anyone, whether it's his team-mates, his coach, the press . . . or even the frequently excessive enthusiasms of his beloved old man." As a twenty-year-old, Woods declared that "I'm the one who is sort of creating all this. And I'm the one who has to handle it."[34] As he said just after becoming a professional, "golfwise, there was nothing left for me in college."[35]

Woods's realization that he was destined for much bigger and better things fundamentally influenced his relationship with the larger world. His intensely driven, individualistic ethos drove him to adopt an aloof attitude toward the media—a development that has been duly corroborated by several prominent golf journalists. The distinguished golf writer Tom Callahan noted that Tiger is generally "unavailable" and difficult to land for a scheduled interview. According to *Sports Illustrated* contributor John Garrity, when people asked "what's Tiger like?" he was forced to admit "I don't know." Tiger is so focused that "he has no personal empathy for others," Garrity discerns, "if you're in his field of vision he looks like he's never seen you before." Even John Feinstein, arguably the most prominent American sports journalist of his generation, noted how Woods was "not very dynamic off the course" and that "Tiger gives you that big smile and ten minutes later you look down and there's nothing in your notebook." Woods became skilled at saying nothing of substance at an early stage of his career, which may be interpreted as a survival mechanism or quiescence about things personal (and potentially controversial) or both. Curt Sampson wondered why Tiger should "speak for himself when Nike and others paid him so much to speak for them." Woods's relationship with the sports media has been a subject of debate and controversy.[36]

The 1996 and 1997 seasons marked a watershed in both Woods's career and his ascendancy as a sport celebrity of international renown. During the first eight months of 1996 Woods became the first golfer in history to win three consecutive U.S. Amateur titles. He also won the NCAA individual men's championship and competed as an amateur in the Master's and the U.S. Open. On August 27, he decided to leave Stanford to become a professional and finished (tied for) sixtieth in the Greater Milwaukee Open—which netted him a check for the modest sum of $2,544. The following week, at the Bell Canadian Open, he finished eleventh; the week after that, fifth; the week after, third. At his fifth pro stop, the Las Vegas Invitational, Woods shot 64 and won a one-hole playoff against Davis Love III for his first victory on the PGA tour. In all, the new pro earned $790,594 in his maiden year on the tour. In 1997, Woods won his first major championship, the Masters, by an unprecedented twelve strokes to become the youngest ever winner of the tournament.

As important as Woods's accomplishments on the links were observers' more subjective assessments. Tom Callahan noted that "every week you'd look at him and he'd appear to be a full year older." *Sports Illustrated* writer Gary Van Sickle proclaimed, "Golf, as we know it, is over. It came to an end on a chamber of commerce Sunday evening in Las Vegas when Tiger Woods went for the upgrade: He's not just a promising young Tour pro anymore, he's an era . . . Golf may never be the same." Commenting upon the meaning of Woods's victory in Las Vegas, John Garrity wrote: "It has been said that a camel will pass through the eye of a needle before the winner of the Disney World-Magic Kingdom Classic makes the cover of *Sports Illustrated*. Tiger Woods accomplished the latter feat in October 1996, when he won his second Tour event in eight weeks as a pro and then landed, for the first time, smack on *SI's* glossy face."[37]

The effusive accolades and hyperbolic predictions were not restricted to salivating sportswriters pursuing the latest athletic demigod. In a letter to an editor postmarked "Sarasota, FL," an anonymous fan and lifelong golfer who watched the 1997 Masters confessed to being in "a state of depression," believing that "we just experienced the beginning of its [golf] demise as we have known it." Tiger Woods has, according to the writer,

> made a mockery of one of our most challenging and exciting tournaments . . . I fear that TV ratings will ultimately decline, since many of us real golfers are not interested in simply watching Tiger mechanically bring good courses to their knees. Just for the record, my sadness has nothing to do with the color of his skin; but rather, my fear that he has ruined the last of the dignified sports.[38]

As with most doomsday predictions, the author could not imagine the potentially transformative effects of young Tiger's accomplishments for the future of sport. The same cannot be said for the CEO of Nike, Phil Knight. As one whose material interests is inextricably tied to emerging trends and personalities in the American (and global) sports marketplace, Knight saw in Woods's devastating attack on the Masters as a gift from the marketing gods. Upon turning professional, Tiger signed with the International Management Group (IMG)—the world's most prestigious sports marketing firm. IMG had courted the teenage Woods with such dogged determination that they had given Earl Woods a paid position as a "talent scout" for the American Junior Golf Association several years earlier. IMG's developmental efforts were not wasted. Earl Woods delivered the goods and IMG negotiated a $40 million five year sponsorship contract with Nike, which anticipated that the young star would "resuscitate their stagnant golf division and, in so doing, significantly bolster the company's overall profits," which would be "measured in terms of the diversification and expansion of the market for golf-related products and services both within the United States and abroad."[39]

Unbeknownst to the sporting public, Nike had crafted a major advertising campaign to be launched after the conclusion of the Greater Milwaukee Open. The company's creative team provided Woods with the opening words for his first press conference as a professional tour player. On August 28, 1996, Woods casually intoned "I guess, hello world" to the throng of journalists and photographers. "The *faux* spontaneity of this carefully scripted sound-byte"[40] became evident the following day when Nike formally launched its first television advertising campaign entitled "Hello World," which integrated clips of Woods's earlier golf highlights with the accompanying text:

> Hello world.
> I shot in the 70s when I was 8.
> I shot in the 60s when I was 12.
> I won the US Junior Amateur when I was 15.
> Hello world.
> I played the Nissan Open when I was 16.
> Hello world.
> I won the US Amateur when I was 18.
> I played in the Masters when I was 19.
> I am the only man to win three consecutive US Amateur titles.
> Hello world.
> There are still courses in the US I am not allowed to play because of the color of my skin.

Hello world.
I've heard I am not ready for you.
Are you ready for me?

This Nike spot was filmed during a lunch break at which time Woods had spontaneously bounced a ball on the face of a sand wedge. "I've been doing this since I was pretty young (maybe six or seven years old), out of boredom," Tiger recalled. "At the shoot that day," Nike's Kel Devlin remembered, "we'd throw him a ball from ten feet away and he'd catch it on the clubface." So, a new commercial was drawn, music composed. Tiger was instructed to improvise with ball and club for thirty seconds. On the fourth and final take, Tiger bounced the ball to eye level, behind his back, between his legs—forty-nine times. When the director whispered "five seconds," Devlin recalled that "Woods turned sideways, flipped the ball waist high and slammed it out of the air straight down the middle" of the fairway.[41]

The Nike commercial was a professionally orchestrated cultural statement. "By highlighting Woods' energy, skill, and earned successes, and then deliberately confronting America with a 'racial dilemma,'" Cole and Andrews argue, "America's ideals of color-blindedness and proper citizenship were . . . frankly violated and questioned by an obviously 'black' or African American athlete."[42] As such, Nike's "Hello World" campaign engaged and negotiated the problems of racism in a palatable fashion. Tiger became "an eminently safe symbol for the celebration of a self-congratulatory patriotism imbued with notions of anti-affirmative action meritocracy."[43] On the American Broadcasting Company's popular news show *Nightline*, sportswriter John Feinstein noted, controversially, the way in which Nike was marketing Woods as "a black player, not just a talented player . . . [which] tells you that all this money that's being thrown in his direction has as much to do with the color of his skin and his ability to be a role model as it does with golf."[44]

Although the "Hello World" campaign forged a cozy relationship between the young star and Nike, the duo was excoriated by various writers and commentators for the stridency of the message. Nike (re)learned that confrontational politics and bold social statements were not the best method of selling shoes. "Tiger seemed to learn a lesson" as well, according to the sociologist and activist Richard Lapchick. "It is the one that I wish he and other athletes had not learned: no more political issues," as Lapchick stated the case, and Woods "has been silent since then because of what happened early in his career."[45] While this perspective attributes Woods's quiescence to learned behavior about commercial imperatives, other critics are less sympathetic. Golf journalist Curt Sampson quotes at length a fellow "well-known journalist who requested anonymity":

> He's exceeded everyone's expectations on the golf course, but in terms of social contributions, he's disappointing. Tiger has established this pattern of insularity. He follows his friend Michael Jordan, who disappeared on the Nike sweatshop issue. Has Tiger ever taken a stand? He gets a pass because four days a year he does a clinic for the TWF and his time's worth a lot. We don't know what he thinks. Or if he thinks.[46]

On one level, Woods and Nike were an unlikely combination. At the time of signing Woods to a lucrative contract, Nike was not particularly interested in golf. Woods, as a model son, accompanied his mother to a Buddhist temple and made gifts of rice, sugar, and salt to the monks in a symbolic renunciation of material goods throughout his youth.[47] In an early interview with *Sports Illustrated* contributor Gary Smith, Woods declared, "I like Buddhism because it's a whole way of being and living . . . based on discipline and respect and personal responsibility. I like Asian culture better than ours because of that. Asians are much more disciplined than we are." Yet, perhaps sensing the cultural contradictions of a new celebrity in a hyper-commercialized culture, Woods vacillated. "I believe in Buddhism. Not every aspect, but most of it. So I take bits and pieces . . . I can enjoy material things, but that doesn't mean I need them. It doesn't matter to me whether I live in a place like this"—the golf club in his hand makes a sweep of an Orlando, Florida, villa—"or in a shack. I'd be fine in a shack, as long as I could play some golf. I'll do the commercials for Nike and for Titleist, but there won't be much more than that. I have no desire to be the king of endorsement money."[48]

As a young, albeit savvy and articulate, athlete Woods wrestled with his professed ethnic identity. In a letter to the King, Majesty of Thailand, he declared, "Although I am an American citizen my heart is Thai."[49] As a boy who was raised in a mostly white, middle-class world, as a university student, Tiger delineated his differences with his father about race. For Earl, golf and race cannot be separated. For Tiger, golf is all that matters. "I told him straight out when he was a little boy," Earl says, "that in America, if you have a drop of black blood in you, you're black."[50] But Tiger, in spite of his Thai, Chinese, American Indian, and African American heritage came to consider himself a multicultural young man (and coined a word to describe his ethnic/racial makeup—"Cablinasian" —to denote Caucasian, black, American Indian, and Asian). "It's a familiar pattern," Peter de Jonge writes, "the father determined to do everything he can to prevent his son from being tainted by the prejudice he has to deal with, and doing such a good job that the son doesn't see what all the fuss is about."[51]

Such textual, autobiographical, and ideological issues were largely lost on an American public that was utterly infatuated with Woods the "black," multicultural young golfer whose story evoked "self-evident proof of the existence of a color-blind meritocracy," as Cole and Andrews write, "a popular icon from whom the American populace could derive a sense of intimacy, pride, and reassurance."[52]

Yet a handful of critical commentators, such as sportswriter John Feinstein, wryly noted that "it has been said in the past that when an athlete puts a corporate logo on his body or his equipment, he sells off a piece of his soul. If that is the case, Tiger Woods has very little soul left to work with, because almost everything he owns—from cap to shoes, golf bag to golf balls, even his free time—has been sold. In the corporate world the term is 'golden handcuffs.'"[53] Sportswriter Christine Brennan was even more pointed in her assessment of the nation's apolitical hero and darling of the corporate world. "Every time he [Woods] has been presented with a chance to make a social comment," she writes, "he has turned and walked the other way . . . He's all . . . about corporate acquiescence and playing it safe on the sponsor's dime."[54]

Whether or not Woods was originally a thoughtful, progressive-minded (Buddhist) young athlete who was lured by Mammon or just another apolitical, narcissistic, money-grubbing athlete, the first $100 million Nike deal sealed his fate as sport's king of endorsement money. In rapid succession, Tiger signed substantial deals: $30 million over five years with General Motors; $30 million over five years with EA Sports;

$45 million over five years with Upper Deck; $20 million over five years with Disney; $25 million over five years with Asahi Beverages; $26 million over five years with American Express; $40 million over five years with Buick;[55] $10 million over five years with TLC Laser Eye Centers; $7 million over five years with Tag Heuer; as well as other sponsorship deals with Wheaties, Coca-Cola, and *Golf Digest*. By comparison, his earnings on the course seem less impressive, although his purses around the world in 2000 alone amounted to $11,034,530—about double that of Jack Nicklaus's career golf earnings.[56]

In 1997, Earl Woods published his first of several books, *Training a Tiger,* which given the timing of its release, became a national bestseller. As the most influential narrator of the Tiger Woods story, Earl's instructional tome, directed explicitly toward parents, pushed all the right buttons about family, individual responsibility, diligence / hard work, success, divine guidance, and the fundamentals of golf, which, supposedly, applied to the game of life. Tiger, the ever-dutiful son, wrote the Foreword, wherein he paid tribute to how the lessons and life experiences imparted by his father underpinned his success as a golfer.

Earl wrote of how he came to golf following his own father's love of sport (baseball): "By the time he [Tiger] was born, I was nearly a scratch player, so God's game plan was already in effect . . . The Almighty entrusted this precocious child to me. He is orchestrating this entire scenario and has a plan to utilize Tiger to make an impact on the world. I don't know what it is, but I sincerely believe it will be spiritual and humanitarian and will transcend the game of golf." Generalizing on this personal experience, Woods Sr. maintained that golf provides an excellent vehicle for "developing closer ties with your children, teaching them to perform and function effectively . . . And if you as parents can teach your children to love and respect the game of golf, they will inevitably learn all these associated lessons about life. This book is my way of giving back to a game that has given me so much."[57]

The text engaged the key topics found in most instructional manuals on grip, swing, putting, the short game, mental preparation, tournament preparation, and the like but with a generous number of young Tiger and father-and-son photos. The book's conclusion shamelessly included an excerpt from Earl's next book—*Playing Through: On Making a Champion in Golf and Life,* published the following year (1998) by

HarperCollins—wherein he reiterated the refrain that "the game of golf can be a metaphor for life."[58] "Tiger and I certainly do not profess to have all the answers, but I hope that our story will inspire people of all ages to rise to every occasion and to turn obstacles into opportunities," Earl preached. Bringing his platitudes to a marketing-oriented conclusion, Woods noted how "life will always be a work in progress filled with unexpected twists and turns, and new joys and new challenges. But one thing is for certain: Tiger and I are determined to keep *playing through*."[59]

In 2001, after the culmination of the most legendary single season in golf history, Tiger followed his father into the world of publishing with *How I Play Golf: A Master Class with the World's Greatest Golfer.* This time it was Earl's turn to write the Foreword to his son's book. With the memories and emotions of his son's most recent Masters victory still effervescent, the father noted how "Tiger has been a teacher his entire life. I know he has taught me things . . . I hope this work will unlock the door to a wonderful game for those who share in his passion for it. Within its pages you will find wisdom, guidance, technical tips and pure instruction. Listen to Tiger's heart. It is speaking to you. I trust that you will get the message."[60] If the established reputation of golf's first father was somehow inadequate to establish the world's best golfer as a credible teacher of the game's fundamentals, the editors of *Golf Digest* crafted a Preface wherein they confessed to approaching Tiger for such a book in 1997 and how, four years later, they had (curiously) underestimated the twenty-one-year-old champion's knowledge of the game's mechanics and strategy. "The first research session with him was a revelation," the editors confessed, "his grasp of the fundamentals was complete. His understanding of cause and effect in the full swing was astonishing and would grow even richer through time. What's more, his explanations were expansive, articulate, and ordered perfectly. He quickly displayed a knack for phrasing his advice in a way that embraced the widest range of golfers possible."[61] Surely such sober statements were intended to bolster the book's aspirations of eclipsing Jack Nicklaus's instructional classic, *Golf My Way* (which has sold over two million copies since it was first published in 1974).

Within the pages of this impeccably illustrated instructional book, Woods (unlike Nicklaus) summarily lapsed into the dominant discourses of family, nation, individual responsibility, meritocracy, and sport as a metaphor of life. In the book's opening chapter, Tiger notes that "the difference between golf and most other sports is that anyone of average intelligence and coordination can learn to play it well. It requires a commitment to being the best that you can be." He proceeds to acknowledge his father, whose "greatest advice to me was to always be myself. I pass that along to you as the first lesson in this book, which I wrote not as a panacea but as the ultimate tribute to Mom and Pop's ideal of caring and sharing."[62] After a thorough review of the fundamentals of the swing, putting, "escaping the sand," playing the fairways, strength-training, psychology, and the like, Woods returned to the well-established themes that underpinned his celebrity identity within American culture:

> There is no greater joy in this game than being able to give back. I love working with kids, helping them achieve their dreams, whether in golf or life. I owe a debt of gratitude to a lot of people who helped me attain my dreams, and I'm determined to help others . . . By positively influencing others, I believe I can make a difference . . . In the big picture what truly matters is the lives we touch. That is how we measure our legacy. I measure mine in the warmth of those [childrens'] smiles. My parents have been the biggest influence in my life. They taught me to give of myself, my time, talent, and, most of all, my love. I have never forgotten those early lessons of life. I hope you won't forget the lessons you've learned from the pages of this book. I love this game because it has loved me. I love it because it has allowed me to give you the best of me. And that is the most fun of all.[63]

One of the enduring appeals of Woods's public persona is his dedication to less-advantaged, minority children. For an elite golfer from a diverse ethnic background, a well-publicized philanthropic mission is the icing on the cake of his celebrity image. In a December 1996 interview on the Golf Channel, the twenty-one-year-old golfer, on the cusp of stardom during the coming year, declared that "golf is a great game, why limit it to just a few, when it can by enjoyed by all?" proclaimed that "one of my main goals is to make golf look like America." It was not clear, though, what "making golf look like America" entailed or how such an ambiguous goal could be pursued.

Woods's implicit strategy would presumably evolve from *his* personal philanthropic work. Upon turning pro in 1996, Woods (and his father, Earl) created the Tiger Woods Foundation with an initial $500,000 donation to provide the necessary venture capital. With the creation of the First Tee project (funded by the PGA, the USGA, the LPGA, and the Augusta National) Tiger sounded his main intention for establishing the Tiger Woods Foundation: "I want basically to give kids in the inner city—in any city really—the chance to play a beautiful game."[64] To affect such goals Woods turned to his high-powered corporate contacts to serve on the board of directors and raise millions of dollars for the foundation. The board of directors is headed by Earl Woods (president) and is staffed by representatives of the Target Corporation, Avis Ford, American Express, IMG, Coca-Cola, ETW Corporation, as well as an energy products company, and finally an attorney from a major law firm. Joining the board are Diamond and Silver sponsors of the foundation, which include Buick, Countrywide (lending), Dole, *Golf Digest,* Nike Golf, Sherwood Country Club (in Los Angeles), American Golf, Asahi Soft Drinks, Netjets, IMG, Titleist, Wheaties, and Upper Deck.[65] In short, while Woods may wish to change the demographics and public access to golf, he has surrounded himself with the very corporate institutions and "players" that have served as the bulwarks of the establishment and system of privilege for upper-class America.

Presenting the foundation with the well-known personal storylines (that harkened back to the didactic, "American Dream"–encoded writing of Horatio Alger Jr. of an earlier era), Woods addresses visitors to the TWF corporate website as "Dear Friends":

> When I was younger, my Dad encouraged me to change the world. He taught me that anything is possible and he showed me how to use my talents to reach my goals. Golf has been good to me, but the lessons I've learned transcended the game. I'm now trying to pass these lessons on and show kids how they can be applied to every aspect of life. Do your best. Play fairly. Embrace every activity with integrity, honesty and discipline. Be responsible for your actions. And above all, have fun.

Substantiating that his words were, indeed, tinged with irony (for a solely juvenile audience), Woods appealed to the importance of "parental responsibility" with seamless precision—declaring himself as a "role model who embraces the responsibility of influencing others positively." Appealing to adults (all the while), Woods asks "help me teach kids that if they dream big enough, miracles can happen . . . With your help, I believe we can make a difference in the lives of children across the world."[66]

The foundation's logo—comprised of eyes, columns, the globe, the "T," the base, and the color red—collectively symbolize Woods's self-declared (and well-known) personal traits and worldviews. The TWF seeks to "empower young people to reach their highest potential by initiating and supporting community-based programs that promote the health, education and welfare of all of America's children." The TWF provides funding to community-based groups in the areas of education, youth development, parenting, and family health and welfare through a range of grants, scholarships, benefactor programs, and sponsored programs (e.g., junior golf clinics, an annual public concert—the Tiger Jam—and the Target World Challenge).[67] Between 1997 and 2004, the TWF funded $2.8 million in grants to a wide range of private, community, and municipal organizations with increased funding in successive years.[68]

The newest initiative of the foundation is the Tiger Woods Learning Center to be located in Orange County, California—a 35,000-square-foot campus situated on a twenty-three-acre golf teaching facility (designed by Woods and famed course architect Tom Fazio) will represent "an innovative facility designed to open the minds of children through advanced educational programs and an introduction to the game of golf."[69] Launched eight years after the creation of the TWF, the $25 million project was begun with a $5 million dollar donation by Woods; thereafter, all subsequent contributions would be used evenly for construction and operational expenses. The development campaign provides a two-tiered appeal for "Founding Partners"—major gifts in the range of $500,000 to $2.5 million (with attractive naming opportunities) and "Supporting Partners" for logo and name identification via marketing and public relations visibility in the $10,000 to $100,000 range.

Courting corporate and well-heeled private sponsors, the TWF website invites contributors "to make a difference in the lives of countless underserved youth through your generous support" for the TWLC "a place for countless children to achieve their individual dreams" built on hallowed grounds "the very ground where Tiger got his start as a golfer." The Learning Center's educational approach "combines use of the latest technology, one-on-one tutoring, athletic programs and personal enrichment all provided by outstanding local educators who will work year round to ensure each child's success." In an appeal to corporate benefactors, the TWLC notes the "approximately $60 billion a year in productivity lost due to a workforce lacking in basic skills" and extols the "limitless possibilities of education" in helping young people "develop healthier relationships and social skills, resulting in lower incidences of drug-use, violence and pregnancy." Students will "achieve success in ways they never thought possible—all while having fun!"[70] And, presumably, future students will learn about character and good games within a totally corporatized environment (as Founding Partners will be able to brand the auditorium, media resource center, personal enrichment center, student lounge, golf shop, café, board room, computer lab, and tutoring classrooms with their own identities).

The TWF mission is invariably presented by the adoring corporate media as a benevolent gesture, rather than as a shrewd financial planning decision. One gets a different mental picture of Woods as CEO of Eldrick Tiger Woods Inc., with a reported $80 million in endorsements from Nike, American Express, Titleist, Buick, the All Star Café—sitting atop a multimillion-dollar financial empire—than Woods as founder of the Tiger Woods Foundation. As such, the foundation has received glowing praise within media, golfing, and philanthropic circles as the selfless efforts of a young athlete giving back and making positive changes for race and opportunity—a classic liberal story. Woods's much-celebrated community efforts beyond the links have brought acclaim to the TWF as a pioneering enterprise to introduce golf to disadvantaged, inner-city young people. Representative of this coverage, on the eve of a TWF clinic in June 2000, a journalist noted the conspicuous number of African Americans queuing at Denver's Park Hill Club awaiting the arrival of Woods—not only "the best golfer on the planet" but the "athletic Pied Piper of our time, crossing generations, races and genders" who, according to the coordinator of the event, has "made it OK (for blacks) to play golf." The event was "geared to reach out to minority and inner-city children and invite them into what has stubbornly been a white man's game." Noting the doubling increase in African American golfers as a result of Woods ("like a volcano, Woods' impact was explosive at first"), but buried deep within the long feature article, was a reference to various forerunners—the Multicultural Golf Association and the National Minority Golf Foundation—in the mission of introducing inner-city youth to the game.[71]

Eclipsed by Tigermania, the Multicultural Golf Association of America Inc. (MGAA), the African American Golf Association (AAGA), and the National Minority Golf Foundation (NMGF) were already established in the early 1990s to promote golf for disadvantaged youth of color. Yet, unlike the TWF, these other organizations did not restrict their work to developing and educating youth; but implemented a broader-based, activist agenda for increasing the visibility of minorities within the wider golf industry. The NMGF champions the need for greater multicultural diversity within the golf industry by "promoting golf careers to create an awareness of the value of golf as a business tool." Organized in 1991 under similar auspices of the TWF, the MGAA's vision has transcended the rhetoric of the "limitless possibilities of education" and "character development through sport" and "family values" to envision how, according to president Barbara Douglas, the "finish line . . . is when you can no longer name the minorities employed in the golf industry, when you walk into an NCAA golf event and the minorities are just a matter of course, or when you look at the PGA Tour and don't think about how few minorities are in it."[72]

Few would-be critics or skeptics would publicly question Tiger's commitment to children or making the world of golf "look more like America." Asked about the social conscience of contemporary athletes, football legend Jim Brown told *SI*'s Don Yaeger that Tiger was focused solely on golf. "I'm not talking about teaching black kids to golf and get to country clubs," Brown differentiated. "Come on! That's wonderful to do, but Tiger makes enough money that he could change many more things that are important to black kids than learning to golf."[73] In spite of his father's well-known predictions that Tiger would do historically significant things outside of golf, Woods was asked in mid-2002 by a Canadian journalist, "Do you have great goals away from the sport?" To which Woods responded, "For my foundation, yes, but that's about it."[74]

Between 2002 and 2005 there was a notable shift in the discourse about Woods—away from the breathless infatuation with "America's Son" and resonant multicultural symbol toward a consideration as to whether or not Tiger had slipped from atop his pedestal. The key topic of conversation surrounding professional golf tournaments once was "how did Tiger do?" Yet, in recent years this certainty of success was momentarily eclipsed by commentaries and speculations about Woods's apparent "slump" of winning majors or his eminent decline. Is he washed-up? Has he become just another player? Had he altered his swing? Had his switch from Titleist to Nike balls and clubs affected his driving accuracy? Had his romance and recent marriage to Swedish model Elin Nordegren taken a toll on his game? Had other competitors simply leveled the field? Is his head still in the game? Has the Tiger era ended? Was he destined for an early retirement?[75]

During the 2003–04 seasons speculations by television golf savants were rife on all fronts, but the primary debate was on Woods's swing (led notably by Johnny Miller, Peter Kostis, and Curtis Strange). Woods responded publicly with a tone of annoyance and disbelief. "Am I tired of it? Yeah," Woods said during a June 15, 2004, interview. "A lot of times they don't have an understanding of what I'm trying to work on, or what I'm working on, or what they conceive is a nice golf swing. Everyone's opinion of a nice golf swing is different . . . I think that's where you have to step out of the box sometimes, which these guys don't . . . They watch one golf shot and they analyze, like when they take out a shot I hit in 2000 and compare it to a shot I hit this year."[76] The surge of play by the likes of Ernie Els, Vijay Singh, and Phil Mickelson alongside of Woods's statements that "I've always said I'll never play golf when my best is not good enough to win" (and Earl Woods's newest predictions that "I forsee that he [Tiger] will make his largest contribution in the philanthropic area and humanitarian-type efforts. It will dwarf anything he has accomplished in golf")[77] only fuelled doubt about Woods's future as darling of the golf establishment. Gone was Woods's cloak of invincibility. Even Woods (while not explicitly taking credit for elevating the game) confessed that "the guys are working harder. The equipment has gotten better. The guys are in better shape now. Their techniques are better. They're working more hours on the range, as well as in the gym. It's just a matter of time before those guys were going to take it up another notch, and they have."[78]

The critics' musings reached a crescendo by late 2004—a year that even most doomsayers could not have foretold—one that saw Woods without even a single stroke-play tournament win on the U.S. tour (during which time he finished 182nd in driving accuracy). When the European team easily swept the Ryder Cup (by a record margin) from the much-touted but dismal play of the American squad on their home turf at Oakland Hills, sportswriters focused on the chilly relationship ("the coolness between the two is the Tour's most open secret")[79] between Woods and Phil Mickelson as a contributing factor. British sportswriter David Davies characterized Woods's Ryder Cup record as "unthinkable." In his *Guardian* commentary ("Easy Ryders and Toothless Tigers"), Davies took Woods to task:

> For a man who professes to love both pressure and matchplay, to have scored only eight points in 20 matches is downright poor and his inability to surrender control of himself to the team ethic is apparent and costly. Woods hates the hoopla that goes on around the Ryder Cup and sulks because it means he cannot eat when he wants to, exercise when he wants to, practice when he wants to or play with whom he wants to.[80]

The Woods-Mickelson relationship proved to be a publicity boost for the Ford Championship at Doral in March 2005. Mickelson, buoyant after his 2004 Masters victory (and an impressive early 2005 start) was touted as "not only Ford's highest-profile endorser but also Woods' perfect foil" for the "Dual at Doral." Tied at 23 under par going to the seventeenth green, the electric atmosphere of the thirty-five thousand spectators ensured that the final round, according to *Sports Illustrated,* "provided the most stirring duet in recent memory and bespoke a new level of parity among the world's top players with the Players Championship and the Masters looming."[81] Woods defeated Mickelson with a thirty-foot putt on the seventeenth to finish with a 24-under 264—a tournament record at Doral—and received a $990,000 victory check en route to regaining his number-one spot atop the international rankings.

Less than one month later, Woods bested Chris DiMarco in a sudden-death playoff at Augusta to win his fourth Masters with a 12-under performance. His birdie chip shot on the sixteenth hole—immediately described as "a defining moment in Masters history"[82]—was the critical juncture of an otherwise "up-and-down" day for Woods. As one of the most heralded traditions in golf, the previous year's champion, Phil

Mickelson, presented the green jacket and helped slip it onto the shoulders of the 2005 winner (Woods's fourth such green blazer).

The least disputed "legacy" of Woods in the early twenty-first century was the way in which his stellar play forced the world's leading golfers to reevaluate their own respective levels of talent. For the first time, perhaps, in modern golf history, one individual surged to such a plateau as to challenge all his peers to elevate their physical and mental skills to a substantively higher level than was previously thought attainable. Woods's legendary achievements between 1997 and 2001 dramatically elevated the PGA Tour to the mainstream of American sport and thereby, heightened the challenge of all leading golfers to "chase Tiger." This sudden boon netted record television ratings and tournament purses. Prize money on the PGA Tour in 1996 (Woods's first year as a professional) was just over $69 million; by 2001 it had almost tripled to $180 million—largely due to the growth in television revenues hinged largely upon Woods's participation. In addition to raising the financial stakes, Woods transformed golf's public image from a conservative, suburban image replete with saddle shoes, frumpy clothing, cigars, and miniature electric cars to a more chic, trans-class activity for popular consumption.

Woods's significance as an exemplar of the dominant American notions of race, family, and national identity is, however, more contested.[83] In terms of the "racial mountain," "black America" has been (and continues to be) of two minds about Tiger Woods. "There's a tug of war over him," writes the popular African American journalist Clarence Page, "and sometimes the tug of war is inside the same people. On the one hand, they want to embrace Tiger as their hero. On the other hand, they want to reject his belief that he doesn't belong to just one group"[84] as when Woods has stated publicly that "I feel fortunate, and equally proud, to be both African American and Asian. It does not make a difference to me. The bottom line is that I am an American . . . and proud of it."[85] Yet, in spite of Woods's professed multicultural identity, writer David Owen's observation of a group of young African American players at an Oklahoma TWF clinic revealed that Woods's appeal had everything to do with race. "The color of his skin was the bridge they were crossing into the game," Owen writes. For these black teenagers,

Woods represents a "fearless conqueror of the world"—a guy "who looks like me—if he can do it, I can do it."[86]

For middle-class white fans, a major part of Woods's appeal is that he seems to have transcended, if not negated, "racial issues" altogether. After all, as this dominant discourse maintains, "he's just Tiger, the best golfer in the world." In his 2001 essay in the quintessential conservative magazine, *National Review,* Jay Nordlinger noted how "sixty-year-old white chief executive officers with their own personal jets were as excited as ten-year-old kids would be about having a chance to see Woods in person." Their excitement was "genuine, and, to the extent that such a thing is possible, it was color-blind," according to Nordlinger. "When white golfers do think about Woods' racial background, it's often with a sense of relief: his dominance feels like an act of forgiveness, as though in a single spectacular career he could make up for the game's ugly past all by himself." As proof of this assertion, he cites Woods's penultimate statement on the "race" issue—"that ethnic background and / or composition should not make a difference. It does NOT make a difference to me. The bottom line is that I am an American . . . and proud of it! That is who I am and what I am."[87]

Less explicitly conservative voices sang a similar, complementary refrain. For over one hundred years, "golf in America has stood as a potent symbol of exclusion and racial intolerance," David Owen wrote in his biography, *The Chosen One.* "It is still overwhelmingly a white man's game, but Woods has cracked it to the core, and there is no doubt that when he eventually retires he will leave the game in a very different condition from the one in which he found it."[88] As one of the most influential narrators of Woods entitled his controversial *Sports Illustrated* expose, "The Chosen One" five years earlier, Gary Smith maintained that "when we swallow Tiger Woods, the yellow-black-red-white man, we swallow . . . hope in the American experiment, in the pell-mell jumbling of genes. We swallow the belief that the face of the future is not necessarily a bitter or bewildered face; that it might even, one day, be something like Tiger Woods's face: handsome and smiling and ready to kick all comers' asses."[89] Smith crafted what a decade in hindsight was a revealing glimpse into the allegedly "color-blind" mentality of post-historical, imperial America.

Within such a worldview, Eldrick "Tiger" Woods stands as a sporting hero for a variegated, often-polarized American society. He is the perfect icon for a white world—"black," handsome, athletic, well spoken, and respectable, with a clear commitment to the Protestant work ethic. Woods is the inheritor of a racialized lineage stretching in the popular imagination from Jesse Owens to Carl Lewis as a symbol of white liberal hopes of integration (and, in the most recent conservative-dominated discourse, Woods's achievements nullify affirmative action and the longer historical poignancy of the civil rights movement). Emerging at a critical historical moment in the nation's history, had Woods not existed, it would have been necessary for the media sports industry to have invented him (which of course, in many respects, they did).[90] In short, Woods is an ideal postmodern sports hero who represents and embodies multiple national narratives in late-twentieth- to early-twenty-first-century American culture.[91]

Venus and Serena Williams celebrating a victory in a doubles match at Wimbledon in 2003. *(Getty Images)*

19 "Ghetto Cinderellas"

Venus and Serena Williams and the Discourse of Racism

R. PIERRE RODGERS AND ELLEN B. DROGIN RODGERS

Communication scholar James Andrews notes that "rhetoric grows out of events that a speaker wants us to see as important." Further, "historical and political events and trends can force certain issues into our consciousness; the situation can make it *imperative* that we somehow come to grips with issues."[1] Chronicling the rise of African American tennis superstars Venus and Serena Williams might well be an exercise in myth-building: "By now, the unlikely story of the Williams family has been repeated so often that it has the ring of an urban legend—which, one might argue, it essentially is."[2]

Much has been made of the Williams sisters' upbringing in Compton, an urban area in southern California notorious for its crime and gang activity.[3] In fact, part of the urban legend regarding their formative years is that Venus and Serena had "to dodge bullets while practicing on the debris-strewn courts" of Compton.[4] But this much is known about the sisters: they rose from relative obscurity to the heights of the tennis world.[5] Dubbed "ghetto Cinderellas"[6] by their outspoken father and coach, Richard, Venus and Serena currently hold lifetime career singles rankings of 4 and 16, respectively, by the Sony Ericsson Women's Tennis Association (WTA).[7]

The fourth and fifth daughters of Richard Williams and Oracene Price, Venus Ebony Starr Williams was born on June 17, 1980, in Lynwood, California; sister Serena was born fifteen months later on September 26, 1981, in Saginaw, Michigan. Both Venus and Serena were initially home-schooled, raised as devout Jehovah's Witnesses (in their mother's faith), and coached early and intensely by their father. These tennis prodigies (and best friends) displayed extraordinary talent at a very young age, each playing in their first tournament at four years old. In 1991, the family moved to Florida so that Venus (and subsequently Serena) could take advantage of tennis training camp opportunities. While neither sister competed in junior tournaments as a teenager, each began professional play in the WTA at age fourteen. The sisters have accomplished a great deal in their relatively short history. Venus was the first unseeded player to reach the finals at the U.S. Open.[8] Three years later, in 2000, "her first win in a Grand Slam event . . . occurred when she became the first African American since Althea Gibson to win the All-England Ladies' Singles Championship at Wimbledon."[9] Younger sister Serena was actually the first Williams sister to win a Grand Slam event, the 1999 U.S. Open. Ironically, she defeated Venus en route to the title—besting Martina Hingis for the trophy.[10] Together, the sisters combined for doubles titles at Wimbledon in 1999 and at the U.S. Open in 2000. They also won Olympic gold that year in doubles.[11] Venus and Serena have fifty-eight WTA singles titles between them and eleven doubles championships. Both have similarly been ranked number one in career-high singles—Venus on February 25, 2002, and Serena on July 8, 2002.[12] When their father predicted such lofty heights for his daughters at ages ten and nine, respectively, he was met with skepticism. As Jon Wertheim recalls:

> [Richard Williams] announced that, good as Venus was, she wasn't even going to be the best player in the family. His younger daughter Serena had the build of an Olympic swimmer and she was every bit as athletic as Venus. Plus, he said gleefully, she was meaner. One day soon, Richard predicted, his daughters would rally the top ranking back and forth and play each other in Grand Slam finals. The tennis world laughed. This wasn't a tennis father from hell. This was a tennis father from outer space. . . . A few years later, Richard Williams was vindicated. Venus and Serena proved to be as good as advertised.[13]

Not only are the sisters similar in their physical makeup—Venus at six-feet-one; Serena at five-feet-eleven—their approach to the game is comparable. They are known for their confidence, power, athleticism, and dominance on the court. But there *are* differences between the two:

> Venus, who can serve a ball at 127 m.p.h., is actually less powerful than her sister. But she's faster, comes to the net more and chokes the court off from opponents, forcing them into more difficult shots. Serena's game is still raw; she tends to blast away from the baseline. When she's on, she's undefeatable. When she's not, the ball boys wear cups.[14]

As Serena jokingly sizes up their style of play:

> [She's taller,] I'm quicker. Like at the net, I'm really, really quick. But Venus can hit any ball. Venus is the type of player that will stab a person, draw back and stab, and draw until they eventually die. I would just shoot 'em, and then go about my business.[15]

Personably, "baby sister" Serena is considered more outgoing and emotional, while big sister Venus's "demeanor is typically calm and refined."[16]

Venus and Serena Williams have had their share of criticism from detractors. Specifically, locker-room talk centers on the impression they are arrogant, aloof, and antisocial with their tennis opponents. Additionally, they have achieved success in a sport that has been traditionally dominated by members of the white upper class. As Karen Duda reports, "while Venus and Serena have not been as vocal about the issue, they contend that racial prejudice still exists on the courts."[17] Such a belief resonates with what sport sociologist Jay Coakley deems the often-subtle racial ideology at work regarding sport performances.[18] Citing the success of Nordic and Swiss skiers, Coakley notes that emphasis is placed on cultural environs—cold weather and regional opportunities for youth to acquire and revel in such sport. "Whiteness" is dismissed as a reason for success:

> When athletes with black skin excel or fail at a certain sport, regardless of where they come from in the world, many people look for genetic explanations consistent with racial ideology. They seek to explain the successes and failures of black athletes in terms of natural or instinctive qualities or weaknesses, rather than experience, strategy, motivation, and intelligence. When the skin color of athletes is a shade of "dark," the discussion quickly turns to race-related questions, and people embark on searches for *the* physical traits possessed by *those* people, even when success clearly involves a combination of physical, psychological, and cognitive

> skills across different sports and even when the athletes come in different sizes and shapes and have racially mixed ancestries. In the process, there is a tendency for many people to ignore, discount, or understate the influence of social and cultural factors in the lives of people of color.[19]

What follows is a rhetorical analysis of the dimensions of racism associated with Venus and Serena Williams. Specifically, we use elements of *rhetorical ideology* to better understand the discursive language of racism encountered by the Williams sisters and how they addressed blatant and implied forms of discrimination.

"An ideology," explains rhetorical critic Sonja Foss, "usually permeates everything produced in that culture or group, so its rhetorical artifacts—its works of art, religious practices, and institutions, for example—embody, enact, and express that ideology."[20] Our application of rhetorical ideological criticism entails examination of disparate yet discrete units of analysis—newspaper accounts, popular and sports-related articles—to locate hints of a discourse of racism. Thus, we study perceptions of and, in some cases, responses to racism as experienced by Venus and Serena Williams.

Assuming that racism is a part of dominant ideology, it becomes crucial to identify racist discourse. Such discourse can be termed, as Stuart Hall[21] observes, overt and inferential racism. *Overt racism* occurs "when open and favourable [*sic*] coverage is given to arguments, positions and spokespersons who are in the business of elaborating an openly racist argument or view." Conversely, *inferential racism* deals with

> those apparently naturalised [*sic*] representations of events and situations relating to race, whether "factual" or "fictional," which have racist premises and propositions inscribed in them as a set of *unquestioned assumptions*. These enable racist statements to be formulated without ever bringing into awareness the racist predicates on which the statements are grounded . . . inferential racism is more widespread—and in many ways, more insidious [than overt racism] because it is largely *invisible* even to those who formulate the world on its terms.[22]

Instances of both types of racism can be found in the rhetorical artifacts relating to Venus and Serena Williams. Our discussion of overt and inferential racism is instructive in that we contend that the Williams sisters deal with everyday racism that is induced by jealousy and envy, primarily from tennis compatriots and spectators.[23] As the sociolinguistics expert Tuen van Dijk notes, "When White majority group members talk about ethnic out-groups, they do not merely express their personal beliefs and attitudes. In different senses of the term, they *reproduce* ethnic opinions of their in-group as a whole, such as shared stereotypes or prejudices and information they have heard or read from other sources."[24] Clearly, this racial reproduction can be verbal or nonverbal, direct or indirect. Of interest here, is the type of discourse used in referring to the Williams sisters. Racist attacks can be in the form of spoken epithets or insidious coded language. Sociologist Eduardo Bonilla-Silva comments:

> When people of color were property or regarded as secondary human beings, there was no reason to be concerned in talking about them. But the Civil Rights era shattered, among other things, the United States' norms about public discussions on race. Hence using words such as "nigger" and "Spic" and even saying things that sound or can be perceived as racist is deemed immoral.[25]

In examining racist discourse in conjunction with the Williams sisters, other difficulties come into play. On one hand, there are cases of unmistakable racial taunts against them. On the other, there exists verbalized jeering from sports "fans," expressing ephemeral or sustained displeasure with athletic performance. Instant fan reaction—deserved or unwarranted, expressing accolades or contempt—is something that comes with the territory for athletes at all levels. But when the athlete is a member of a minority group—racially and/or gendered—at what point does booing become a personal affront? When does it become a "racial" attack? The answers to these questions, if any exist, are beyond the scope of this chapter. However, we believe that an analysis of statements by and about Venus and Serena provides the potential for a rhetoric of racial ideology. In the complex of language, discourse, and racial oppression, it is vital to understand how racism, as Geneva Smitherman and Teun van Dijk explain, is discursively reproduced:

> Whether in informal or in institutional contexts, whether among the elite or the public at large, racial oppression becomes structural,

> rather than individual or incidental, when its conditions are shared by the dominant group. Reasons, motivations, goals, or interests must be communicated in the dominant group. They are linked with opinions and attitudes, and these also need expression, verbalization, and persuasive formulation in a variety of communicative contexts and in various types of talk and text. We find them in everyday storytelling as well as in news reports, in corporate meetings as well as in job interviews, in comics, in racial graffiti, in classroom talk and textbooks, in television comedies, in novels, and in many, many forms of communication and language use. In other words, the expression, enactment, and legitimation of racism in society takes place also, and sometimes predominantly, at a symbolic level.[26]

"There has been a tendency," Patricia Vertinsky and Gwendolyn Captain argue, "to neglect serious study and analysis of the black female since sport history has traditionally been gendered and until the last decade or so has focused upon masculinity and men's history to the exclusion of serious attention to women."[27] A perusal of the literature about Venus and Serena Williams appears to confirm Vertinsky and Captain's appraisal of the dearth of academic resources available. One notable exception is Nancy Spencer's article in the *Journal of Sport and Social Issues* that centers on the 2001 Indian Wells, California, tennis match where the two sisters, along with their father, were soundly booed and endured racial epithets.[28] Based on the "racialized events" that occurred at the California tournament, Spencer contends that white racism still exists; politically incorrect fictive accounts help "to explain the integral role played by myths in sustaining White racism, while obscuring how the terms of racism have shifted."[29]

A slightly different scholarly perspective on the Williams sisters is supplied by Delia Douglas in the *Sociology of Sport Online* journal.[30] Douglas maintains that mass-mediated treatments of the Williams sisters focus on their racialized "differences." Such mediated imagery has reported on their physical appearance, athletic style, and attitude. In sum, Douglas "considers some of the narratives that have been made available to us in an effort to understand how the various interpretive conflicts over portrayals of Venus and Serena on the tennis tour are tied to prevailing relations of race and gender (and class) power."[31]

While there may be limited scholarship on Venus and Serena

Williams, there are any number of books and articles about them in the popular press. Most of the books seem to follow a contention made by Vertinsky and Captain that "much of what has been written about black women in sport has been designed to document the selective achievements of high-achieving African American women such as Alice Coachman, Wilma Rudolph and Althea Gibson, often explaining their use of sport as a means of social mobility or as an expression of the 'natural' physicality or lack of femininity."[32] Indeed, a sampling of recent biographical works about the Williams sisters reveals a pattern of highlighting the humble, racialized upbringing of the two. Their success in the tennis world came about because of hard work and parental vision in spite of racial and class barriers. The innate, natural ability thesis is muted, but the rise in social mobility is well chronicled.

Interestingly, the glut of "we shall overcome" books are directed to juvenile reading audiences,[33] save for investigative works like Jon Wertheim's[34] *Venus Envy: Power Games, Teenage Vixens, and Million-Dollar Egos on the Women's Tennis Tour* and first-person tennis tell-all books like Dave Rineberg's[35] *Venus & Serena: My Seven Years as Hitting Coach for the Williams Sisters.* A representative offering by Glenn Stout is typical of the biographical, rags-to-riches success story:

> One summer morning in 1984, a father loaded his Volkswagen van for a special trip. He carefully placed seven milk crates full of tennis balls and several tennis rackets in the back of the van. Then he went back in the house and called for his four-year-old daughter. They were going to go somewhere special.
>
> The little girl eagerly followed him. She loved going places with her father. They drove from their modest Compton, California, home toward a nearby public park. They wound through the city streets, surrounded by depressing scenery. Compton, an inner-city community near Los Angeles, would be described by most people as a ghetto. The city is poor, and many residents of the mostly African-American and Hispanic community struggle to make ends meet. The buildings are run-down. Crime and poverty are rampant. While most residents are hard-working and law-abiding citizens, many live day-to-day, with little thought of the future.
>
> But the future was all the girl's father was thinking about. Several years before, he'd watched a tennis match on television.

> The winner, Virginia Ruzici, earned nearly thirty thousand dollars for winning the tournament. Richard Williams was impressed. Professional tennis players traveled the world, and the best made thousands of dollars playing one or two matches a day for three or four days every couple of weeks. Seeing that match had given him an idea.
>
> Now it was time to test that idea. Williams wanted his daughter to become a tennis player.[36]

After the author describes the abandoned tennis courts, strewn with broken bottle glass and graffiti, and frequented by "a few young men [lingering] on the sidelines, just hanging out," Stout discusses how patiently the father taught the girl to grip the racket and hit at the hundreds of tennis balls he lobbed to her. "When the crates were empty," Stout continues, "the two would gather up the loose balls, making a game of who could get the most balls in the crate, and start over."[37] When finished for the day, Stout concludes:

> The father and daughter gathered up the tennis balls, loaded them back into the van, and returned home.
>
> When they got out of the car, the man's other daughter, still several weeks shy of her third birthday, greeted them. She felt left out and was pouting. She hated being apart from her sister. The father explained to her that she'd soon be able to come along on trips to the park.
>
> The tennis careers of Venus and Serena Williams had begun.[38]

This account, with its simplistic narrative and romanticism, captures some of the mythic constructions of race and class found in the discourse of racial ideology regarding Venus and Serena Williams. If, as rhetorical scholar Edwin Black asserts, "discourses contain tokens of their authors,"[39] then a reading of statements by and about the Williams sisters and their tennis social world may reveal insights about the persistence of racism in sports and society at large.

Communication critic Mark McPhail observes that the "language with which racial interaction is constructed sustains a discriminatory discourse, premised upon assumptions of negative difference, that continues to separate individuals from each other in both attitude and action."[40] When discussing the Williams sisters, it is informative the sort of world view that is created via statements about and by them. As the subjects of racialized sports commentary, it may be, as Rachel Cepeda writes, "what Venus and Serena don't say is often just as revealing as what they do."[41] Clearly, the constructed discourse can be examined at blatant and subtle levels.

Perhaps the most overt verbal evidence of racism against the Williams sisters occurred in March 2001 at a tennis tournament in Indian Wells, California.[42] The match was hyped because of the possibility that Venus and Serena would meet in the semifinals. The possibility remained just that, when elder sister Venus withdrew only a few minutes before the match was slated to begin, "because of [tendonitis] in her right knee."[43] Spectators were livid at Venus's withdrawal, suspecting it had been orchestrated by their controversial father and coach, Richard Williams: "The episode fueled long-held suspicions that the outcome of matches between the sisters [is] predetermined by their father."[44]

Simmering fan displeasure and hostility spilled over into the championship match two days later between Serena and Kim Clijsters: "Sounding more like a cynical boxing crowd than the usual polite tennis gathering, the fans' booing built to a crescendo when Serena was introduced. As Richard and Venus Williams took their seats, they also drew loud boos."[45] The boos were, in fact, accompanied by angry racial epithets. As Richard Williams recalled:

> When Venus and I were walking down the stairs to our seats, people kept calling me nigger. . . .
>
> One guy said, "I wish it was '75; we'd skin you alive." That's when I stopped and walked toward that way. Then I realized that (my) best bet was to handle the situation nonviolently. I had trouble holding back the tears. I think Indian Wells disgraced America.[46]

In an interview with *The Final Call,* Williams noted that the name-calling "was a wake-up call for me." The racial incident did not come as a shock, however: "I am not surprised that racism is alive and well. What disappointed me was that I reacted angrily."[47] He continues:

> The reality is that many whites believe that we should be happy that they allowed us in the gate to play, and that we should shut up and entertain them. And if we don't entertain them, then we should go home. That was my wake-up call.[48]

What is interesting about the racist tirade is how the use of *nigger* involved all three members of the Williams family: sister Venus, who withdrew from the match; father Richard, who accompanied Venus to the finals; and sister Serena, who played in the championship match by default. The racial epithets served as a blanket indictment of both the Williams trio and African Americans in society at large. The inappropriate language effectively vilified Serena Williams, and her sister and father by association.

Racist language alternated with a mixture of boos and cheers for Serena and opponent Clijsters, respectively:

> Clijsters, a 17-year-old from Belgium, was cheered when she was introduced and during the match. The majority of the fans yelled their approval and applauded Clijsters' good shots, giving her a standing ovation when she won the first set.
>
> There were more boos when Williams won the second, but cheers were mixed in with the boos when she won the match.
>
> Many of the same fans were in the crowd that had awaited the Williams sisters' semifinal on Thursday night, and booed then when it was announced that Venus had withdrawn.[49]

Clijsters was an unwitting beneficiary of the crowd's cheering, as it no doubt helped her have early success in the final against Serena.[50] Serena herself did not blame Clijsters for the unfortunate situation: "I'm sure it threw her off too. She's a really nice girl, and I get along with her very well. But she was young too. I ended up winning the match."[51]

The blatant use of racial epithets to express displeasure may operate as a linguistic device for the dominant racial ideology. Having the insensitive n-word hurled in public, even in an age of political correctness, is undeniably offensive. In the case of the Williams sisters, their rhetorical responses were necessarily reactive and defensive. For father Richard Williams, "All I could think of was my child out on that court by herself in front of all these ignorant people. If I were Venus or Serena, I'd never play Indian Wells again."[52] Williams, in fact, was the key person to voice objections regarding racist language and mistreatment. As *Newsweek* reported, "Not about to sit back and take the heat for the uprising at Indian Wells, Williams turned the tables and accused the crowd of racism."[53] His accusatory remarks, while arguably justified, did nothing to quell his brash, outspoken reputation. On his image,

Williams says, "I'm seen as a problem because I don't lay down and kiss arse [*sic*], and I don't look up to no-one."[54]

Although Serena and Venus Williams were most directly affected by the racial slurs, they strategically allowed their father to be the spokesman for the Indian Wells incident. Both sisters dismissed the incident while standing up for their father. Said Venus:

> He has a great influence on me. . . . He has given me everything that I have right now or else I would be somewhere struggling in college. Maybe lots of bad things could have happened to me. So I am very, very thankful and I have nothing bad to say against him because he loves me. He wants the best for me and has done everything he can for me . . . he would give me his right arm.
>
> People are afraid to face the reality. . . . No one wants to see bad things, no one wants to see the dark side. They want to be happy and I don't blame them for that. But we've got to face our fears and meet any problem head on that we might have in America.[55]

And Serena, the winner at Indian Wells, opined:

> When they gave me the mike, I said, "I would like to just thank everybody who supported me. And if you didn't, I love you anyway and I'll see you next time." Later, I almost started to cry in the interview room. I thought: That's ridiculous; you don't need to be crying. Do like your mom, she's mean. My dad was very proud of me. He [said I had] the heart of a champion.[56]

At least for the Williams sisters, their discourse regarding Indian Wells was nuanced. Especially in Venus's statement, we have an acknowledgment of the problems of race. In a magazine article about the sisters published four years *before* the Indian Wells controversy, journalist Sally Jenkins wrote, "The truth is that there is racism in tennis, and it has been directed at the Williamses, although it has rarely been explicit."[57]

In sum, the overt racial epithets directed at Venus and Serena Williams, along with their father, demonstrate the pervasiveness of negative, racialized attitudes communicated in verbal discourse. Perhaps not all of the Indian Wells spectators were guilty of booing or racial taunting. One fan commented, "Usually it's a very polite crowd. I've never seen anything like it."[58] Charles Pasarell, Indian Wells tournament director, expressed embarrassment for Serena and the crowd: "If Richard says someone yelled something, maybe they did, but I know that's not Indian Wells people."[59] And it is highly unlikely that blacks were among those uttering racial slurs.[60] Still, it can be reasoned that some spectator reactions are inherently antisocial in nature; since crowd behavior at sporting events can run from the innocuous to the obnoxious: "the reactions spectators have to other spectators is a major factor contributing to the excitement, the arousal, and ultimately the entertainment value that result[s] from sports spectatorship."[61]

While there may exist a sense of disgust over the Williams sisters' perceived on- and off-court arrogance and dominance, this sentiment may be due, in part, to Richard Williams. Radio sports talk-show host Larry Hardesty reveals, "Many of our callers said they felt things would be fine for the Williams sisters if their father would stop yelling racism, step back and just let them play tennis. What I believe Richard Williams sees is that the more the girls win, the more people hate them."[62] Whether this disdain emanates from the sisters' winning ways, their father's invective, or a combination of the two is debatable. But the interplay between daughters and father is unquestioned. As a former women's tennis tour player explains, "They're good girls, but they often get overshadowed by their father and his antics. . . . People project their dislike for him onto them, and that's a difficult place for them to be."[63]

If Indian Wells represented the most obvious use of negative discourse, then perhaps the most common type of racist language associated with Venus and Serena Williams is indirect in nature. "It has been conveyed," observes Jenkins:

> by innuendo and insinuation, and in a subtle disproportion in the way people respond to them, alternating between vitriol and over-congratulation. "People talk about how smart and articulate Venus is," says their attorney Kevin Davis, "as if it's surprising. Why? Because judgments are already made. People don't expect her to be able to talk."[64]

This brand of subtle racism is embedded in the discourse used to describe the Williams sisters as well. Such "semantic moves" work as "strategically managed relations between propositions"[65] in the speech-act context. At least two covert racial communicative patterns emerge: sports commentators' discourse and dismissive language used by fellow opponents on the professional tennis circuit.

Descriptive language can influence audience perceptions of athletes: "[I]f the press or sports commentary merely brings the focus of the sports contest 'up close and personal' . . . , this will have little, if any, impact on the enjoyment of a contest unless this personalization heightens the drama of the contest in some way."[66] It follows that media "chatter"—in print, over the air, on the screen—can influence our perceptions of sporting events and also sports performers. Media sports commentary may involve racialized terminology[67] or gender-biased language.[68] The very descriptors employed by commentators are based on the notion of sport as commodity. Note Margaret Carlisle Duncan and Barry Brummett:

> Televised sport creates fetishes by commodifying athletes and their actions, that is, by treating the material of sports as goods to be closely examined, appraised, and assessed. Commentators discourse calls attention to key features of plays in instant replay. Commentators recite the athletes' personal statistics such as height, weight, batting averages, and free-throw percentages. Color commentary fills the nonaction time with evaluations of the performances and with information about the athletes. The commentators' discourse encourages us to think of the athletes and their movements as objects with specific, measurable, and desirable values; the look this discourse encourages is therefore appreciative, evaluative, and covetous.[69]

If Duncan and Brummett are correct, then those things said about an athlete's performance can reveal discourse bias—by gender or by race. We would argue that the influence of language also expresses negative or covert cues about values and race. This focus on language is vital because of "the possibility that the public discourse concerning racial prejudice has led to a substitution from overt to covert expressions of prejudice in the general public."[70] So, what have commentators said about the Williams sisters?

One subject of media commentary deals with lingering suspicions of match-fixing by Richard Williams. When journalists have anticipated a spirited competition in a Venus-Serena match, more often than not, the level of play has been less than spectacular.[71] Concerning the few times Venus and Serena have played each other, a piece in the online *Sports Illustrated* noted, "the quality of their five showdowns as professionals, all heavily hyped, has been uniformly poor."[72] And "alas, Venus and Serena rarely enter the same tournament. One sister or the other has missed three of the last seven Grand Slam events, partially because they're prone to injury. . . . They compound suspicions with coy comments on the subject."[73] Such remarks typify the unanswered questions about the veracity of the sisters' claims. As *ESPN.com* journalist Greg Garber opines: "They are notoriously slow starters. But there are signs that their tennis lives could stand, well, a little more tennis and a lot less life."[74] The Williams sisters have made no secret that they plan post-tennis careers in fashion, interior design, and acting; in fact, they "didn't want to wait until after they stopped playing tennis to start careers in design."[75] Between their endorsement deals and life-after-tennis endeavors, Garber's comment suggests a lack of commitment to or appreciation of the sport. While the discourse is not explicitly racial, it does evoke stereotypic impressions of African Americans being "strong but physically fragile."[76] To their skeptics, Venus offered this pointed advice: "I just want to say to all of my fans not to believe everything you read. . . . Serena and I are great competitors, fierce competitors. We have no fear playing each other."[77]

Beyond the innuendoes, sports commentators have weighed in on the play of Venus and Serena Williams. "Some contend," says Peter Noel, "that the alleged arrogance displayed by Venus and Serena extends to the homegrown style that defines the sisters' game. This truly upsets the white tennis experts."[78] John McEnroe, formerly top-ranked men's tennis-player-turned-announcer, has complained about the Williams sisters and their apparent lack of court decorum and deference for the game. As he wrote in a London newspaper, "What they have achieved is great, but they have no respect for anyone in the game."[79] There is irony in this admonishment of the sisters, as McEnroe's interpretation no doubt reflects his own playing days and his own bratty, bad boy reputation. In the *New Yorker,* he was quoted as saying that "a lot of male college kids and members of the seniors' tour could beat the sisters."[80] His comments are based on a perception of arrogance exhibited by Venus and Serena. What is interpreted as arrogance, however, may be a black female survival strategy for public display—a "mask" as a sign of resistance to racial and gender oppression.[81] Further, McEnroe's discourse can be read as an attempt to stay relevant in the sports world. Serena Williams speaks to the announcer's opinions:

> I don't talk about John McEnroe. He says things [about us] so he can be in the press, because his good time is over. If that's what you have to do to make it, stab and break someone else's back . . . hey, I'm not sure it's going to bless you.[82]

Semi-retired and longtime top-ranked women's player Martina Navratilova has similarly leveled criticism against Venus and Serena about their attitude toward the sport. Referring to their character, according to Douglas, "points to the unspoken, but ever present tension between relations of gender, race and sexuality."[83] Navratilova's discourse echoes this lack-of-commitment-to-tennis theme. Venus and Serena are "cheating the game and themselves,"[84] according to Navratilova. Speaking to their supposed and previous image of power and dominance, she told the *London Evening Standard:*

> [Playing competitive tennis] needs to be a full-time deal because it takes a long time to build up confidence and so little time to shatter it. Players used to go on court against either sister hoping they were not going to make a fool of themselves. Now even lower-ranked women know they can hang in there and get a respectable score. The better players know they can win, and that levels the playing field a tremendous amount. The aura of invincibility which the Williams sisters used to have has gone.[85]

Additionally, Navratilova has attacked the sisters' character: "They have made excuses and not given credit to their opponents. They're afraid to show any kind of humility. Humble doesn't mean you're weak."[86] Again, this ex-jock commentary about the Williams sisters appears to be based on a perception of arrogance. Although racism is not an explicit indictment, the subtext may be, as Jenkins observes, "that no white player would have received such a raft of criticism for being different from—or the same as—everybody else."[87] The on- and off-court mask of aloofness and brashness that Venus and Serena demonstrate speak to the point that "top players are rarely sociable in the locker room."[88] The fact that they happen to be black *and* female alludes to their racial and gender realities. When the sisters choose to respond to criticism from commentators, their rhetoric is typically matter-of-fact. For instance, note how Venus defends her "multi-tasking"—tennis and interior design: "People seem to expect that because you're an athlete you have no right to focus on anything else. But you are who you are. You don't say, 'I have a job, so I can't be anyone else.' I'm preparing for life, not just for a sport. I do me off the court."[89] In short, what characterizes Venus and Serena's discourse when it comes to "experts" is their seeming indifference. "You have to listen to what we say and any other statements that people make are just their opinions," surmises Venus.[90] Similarly, Serena explains that "people are entitled to their own opinions."[91]

If their responses to expert "opinions" reflect structured indifference, then a similar pattern emerges when discussing WTA tour opponents. Venus and Serena consistently contend with a tide of comments, brimming with tales of envy and jealousy. In a post-match press conference at the 1997 U.S. Open, Irina Spirlea blurted, "She thinks she's *the* fucking Venus Williams."[92] Her frustration was partially due to a ballyhooed chest-bumping incident during a court changeover. Racial controversy aside, Venus won the match. Other players have chimed in on the sisters' aloofness. Monica Seles offered this anecdote: "I said hi to her once and she didn't say it back."[93] Lindsay Davenport, "who is popular in the locker room, observed that Venus refused to smile back at her."[94] When Serena complained of stomach illness as a factor in her 2001 quarterfinals loss at Wimbledon, David Steele offered this editorial:

> It started not with esteemed medical expert Jennifer Capriati and well-renowned gastroenterologist Lindsay Davenport, but with the whispers around the All-England Club. They spread across the ocean almost immediately, to columnists, anchors, talk-show hosts and callers who weren't even awake to see the match, who watch about 20 minutes of tennis each year, and who can't really tell you apart from your sister Venus.
>
> Within hours, it was no longer speculation, it was fact: Serena made up this whole upset-stomach thing. She quit, and she made up a weak excuse for her late collapse. That's how she's always been, you know.
>
> And how did those who later sheepishly acknowledged Serena's illness rationalize their change of opinion? Well, she brought the second-guessing on herself, for having a father who acts too outrageous for our tastes.[95]

The rhetoric of "playa haters"[96] is based on an external state of affairs. To find ways of rationalizing their own subpar play or simply being beaten by the Williamses, the language of these rivals reverts to verbal qualifiers, focusing on the sisters' mean-spiritedness and antisocial behavior.

A final example of *playa hating* is instructive; it comes from Czech-born, Swiss-raised rival, Martina Hingis. A common opponent of both sisters, Hingis has a particular aversion for Venus. "They are perfect foils," observes Wertheim, "and their differences play out beautifully and dramatically on the court."[97] Tellingly, "there is plenty of personal animus between them—despite their attempts to downplay it publicly."[98] Out of this backdrop, however, Hingis has expressed a kind of jealousy infused with racial assertions: "Being black only helps them. . . . Many times they get sponsors because they are black. And they have had a lot of advantages because they can always say, 'It's racism.' They can always come back and say, 'Because we are this color, things happen.'"[99] Her jealousy is based on the numerous product endorsements the Williams sisters command.[100] Not only did she verbalize resentment of the sisters' commercial tie-ins, she called the sisters' claims of racism following the Indian Wells tournament "nonsense." Hingis went on to say that Venus and Serena had a tour advantage because "they can always say it's racism or something like that, and it's not the case at all. . . . I could say, yeah, I am only surrounded by Americans. . . . I could say it's racism against me. The public is there, the crowds and the fans are usually for the Americans if I play in this country. So like I am standing alone up there as the only European."[101] Bill Rhoden points out Hingis's misplaced anger confused *racism* with *nationalism*.[102] Still, Hingis's comments can be read as a type of reverse racism, a strategic retreat for supposedly color-blind whites.[103]

In terms of responding to her opponents, Venus claims, "People criticize me as being arrogant. . . . Maybe because I'm a little smarter than the others. Maybe it's because when they ask me a silly question, I refuse to answer it and make myself look foolish."[104] Her sister speaks to the matter of envy:

> Maybe people are jealous—down to the bone. You can't be successful being jealous of people. You have to actually go out and do something about it, not just give up. I didn't get jealous [when

> people were beating me]. I went out and I worked hard. Nothing is given in this business. I work hard for everything. People are jealous? I don't care, really. Better for me.[105]

Thus, the discourse of Venus and Serena is not necessarily reactive. Indeed, if they choose to respond at all to the jealousies of their rivals, the rejoinder is dismissive. It is as if they have other, more pressing things with which to be concerned; player complaints are trivialized.

"Rhetorical criticism, as a hermeneutical endeavor," as wryly observed by Edwin Black, "exerts a chronic temptation to circularity, so that the most fastidious analysis may end simply by reaffirming the convictions with which it began. Often, the only question asked at the threshold of a rhetorical critique is a form of rhetorical question: Will I find confirmed in the discourse that I examine the presuppositions with which I examine it? The question, like a rhetorical question, has its answer already etched within it."[106] In our analysis of the discourse of Venus and Serena Williams, we presupposed that their worldview is based on racial identity. As oratory, broadly defined, we might say that their rhetoric is "grounded in the experience of being Black in America, an element of the rhetorical scene that seems to cross the situational divides of religion, class, occupation, ideology, or issue."[107] Their experiences as sports figures must necessarily reflect the centrality of race, gender, and family influence. Being highly touted players brings with it admiration and notoriety—admiration from African Americans, women, and the general public; notoriety from sports pundits, jealous opponents, and those who negatively view the achievements of minority group members. Because everyday "talk" can reveal communicative clues about attitude and perspective, it is insightful to examine discourse for impressions about the interrelationship of race, sport, and ideology.

The rhetoric of Venus and Serena Williams relies little on the things they do and say; rather, it is a dismissive, strategic perspective based on the sometimes erroneous impressions that people have about them. Make no mistake—the perceptions of others are largely based on mediated verbal and visual imagery. As Peter Noel writes:

> Although they are idolized by many African Americans, backhanded bad-mouthing of the broad-shouldered, long-legged, and attractive Williams sisters is not uncommon among the blueblood cabals, who

> imply in their running commentary that poor Venus and Serena just seem out of place in the lily-white world of professional tennis. They criticize the sisters' game (the way they rush the net—only souped-up niggers could be that good, suggesting that Venus and Serena should be tested for steroids and other performance-enhancing drugs); their walk (a ghettoized swagger is unbecoming); their attitude (too moody, withdrawn); their nappy tresses (the colorful beads are deemed "childish"); even their clothing (too FuBu, and Serena is much too obsessed with the color purple); and, of course, their parents (overprotective, amateur psychologists).[108]

At once, the Williams sisters represent enigmas regarding race, appropriateness, and stereotypes. It is out of this context that the two construct their discourse—sometimes orally, sometimes in writing, and sometimes by not saying a word. Much like racism can be obvious or implied, their reproduced discourse has a basis in racial identity and can be both reactive and symbolic.

Rhetorical analysis can reveal subtleties of language; by locating patterns and tendencies, we can come to a better understanding of a speaker's persuasive motivations and choices. In the case of the Williams sisters, the trick is to "get past all of the surface crap," as Jenkins suggests:

> If you can't, all you will get is the surface image, Venus and Serena, a couple of media-wise, so-called "Cinderellas of the ghetto" playing on all your assumptions and laughing at your expense. You will never get down to what is really important about them, to their anger, their ambivalence and their irreverence as they expose the dry rot in one of the most elitist sports on earth.[109]

Perhaps our focus on the discourse of racism and the continuing story of Venus and Serena Williams is but a first step in getting beneath that elusive veneer.

NOTES

1 Jimmy Winkfield: The "Black Maestro" of the Racetrack, by Susan Hamburger

1. Ed Hotaling, *Wink: The Incredible Life and Epic Journey of Jimmy Winkfield* (Camden, ME: McGraw-Hill, 2005), 11.

2. *Thoroughbred Record,* February 21, 1959.

3. Hotaling, *Wink,* 7, 20–22.

4. Elisha Warfield Kelly, "Our Horses and Jockeys Abroad," *Munsey's Magazine* 24 (December 1900): 354.

5. Roy Terrell, "Around the World in 80 Years," *Sports Illustrated,* May 8, 1961, 73.

6. Terrell, "Around the World in 80 Years," 73.

7. Hotaling, *Wink,* 225.

8. *Goodwin's Annual Official Turf Guide Adopted and Used by All Jockey Clubs and Racing Associations in the United States and Canada* (New York: Goodwin Bros., 1900); *Goodwin's Annual Official Turf Guide,* 1901; *Goodwin's Annual Official Turf Guide,* 1902.

9. Edward Hotaling, *The Great Black Jockeys: The Lives and Times of the Men Who Dominated America's First National Sport* (Rocklin, CA: Forum, 1999), 315.

10. Terrell, "Around the World in 80 Years," 73.

11. Neil Schmidt, "Black Jockey's Journey Spanned Different Worlds," *Cincinnati Enquirer,* April 29, 2004. http://www.enquirer.com/editions/2002/04/29/spt_black_jockeys.html (Accessed September 12, 2004).

12. Susan Hamburger, "Horse Racing," in *African Americans in Sports,* ed. David K. Wiggins (Armonk, NY: M. E. Sharpe, 2004), 159–60; Hotaling, *Wink,* 37–38.

13. Hotaling, *The Great Black Jockeys,* 313.

14. Jim Bolus, "The Black Riders," *Courier-Journal & Times Magazine,* April 27, 1975, 19.

15. Hotaling, *The Great Black Jockeys,* 325.

16. Hotaling, *Wink,* 89–90.

17. In 1909 Kentucky, New York, and Maryland withstood the "reform" movement that abolished horse racing in California, Tennessee, Arkansas, and Louisiana. http://www.kentuckyderby.com/ (accessed February 4, 2005); Mary Simon, *Racing through the Century: The Story of Thoroughbred Racing in America* (Irvine, CA: Bowtie, 2002), 30, 38.

18. "Jockey Winkfield Did Well in Russia This Year," *Courier-Journal,* December 11, 1904, sec. 3, 6.

19. The Associated Press was founded in 1848 (http://www.ap.org/pages/about/history/history.html [accessed January 25, 2005]); UPI was founded in 1907 by E. W. Scripps as the United Press (UP). It became known as UPI when the UP merged with the International News Service in 1958, which was founded in 1909 by William Randolph Hearst (http://about.upi.com/company/

[accessed January 25, 2005]). Not until 1945 did UPI launch an all-sports wire (http://about.upi.com/company/milestones/1941 [accessed January 25, 2005]).

20. Schmidt, "Black Jockey's Journey."

21. Terrell, "Around the World in 80 Years," 81.

22. Hotaling, *Wink,* 140, 147; Schmidt, "Black Jockey's Journey."

23. Terrell, "Around the World in 80 Years," 82.

24. Hotaling, *Wink,* 162–69.

25. Hotaling, *Wink,* 113, 135, 139.

26. Hotaling, *Wink,* 174, 199, 212, 217, 219, 231, 251, 258.

27. Terrell, "Around the World in 80 Years," 86.

28. Hotaling, *Wink,* 215, 217, 227; Schmidt, "Black Jockey's Journey."

29. Terrell, "Around the World in 80 Years," 72.

30. Hotaling, *Wink,* 250, 254, 258, 259, 262, 263, 265, 269, 273–74, 278, 279, 280, 283, 284, 285.

31. Hotaling, *Wink,* 200, 269.

32. Schmidt, "Black Jockey's Journey"; *New York Times,* March 25, 1974, 34.

33. *New York Times,* March 25, 1974, 34.

34. "The Museum Celebrates Jockey Jimmy Winkfield," Kentucky Derby Museum WWW page http://www.derbymuseum.org/news/wink03.html (accessed September 12, 2004).

35. "Class of 2004 Inducted into Hall of Fame," NTRA WWW page <http://www.ntra.com/news.asp?type=news&id=12007> (accessed September 12, 2004).

2 Marshall "Major" Taylor: The Fastest Bicycle Rider in the World, by Andrew Ritchie

1. *Worcester Spy,* April 29, 1900.

2. The full story of Major Taylor's life is told in Andrew Ritchie, *Major Taylor: The Extraordinary Career of a Champion Bicycle Racer* (Baltimore: Johns Hopkins University Press, 1996). Major Taylor's autobiography is *The Fastest Bicycle Rider in the World* (Worcester, MA: Wormley Publishing, 1928).

3. The League of American Wheelmen was constituted on May 30, 1880. From its inception, the League saw the organization and promotion of bicycle racing as one of its primary tasks and a Racing Board was created, which sanctioned race meetings and participated in the classification of amateur and professional riders. Within such a large national organization, with its rotating national committee and decentralized state-run local divisions, there was plenty of room for disagreement, and the annual League conventions were hotbeds of wrangling and intrigue. The role of the powerful bicycle industry and its tendency to lure amateur riders toward professionalism within an organization that struggled to uphold amateur ideals was one constant source of tension. Who was and was not an amateur was a question constantly at issue in American bicycle racing, just as it was across the Atlantic in Great Britain. In the United States, the question of membership and race was another controversial issue, debated and voted on at the League conventions in the 1890s. As the League

grew, in the southern states as well as on the East Coast, in the Midwest, and on the Pacific Coast, who should be accepted for League membership was contested. And during these years the organization was most actively debating its "white only" rule when Major Taylor began to win important races on America's bicycle racing tracks.

4. The "six-day race," which began in the high-wheel period, was organized to overcome the disapproval of holding sporting events on Sundays, since the racing could start at midnight on Sunday, and finish at midnight the next Saturday. It was a test of endurance, and a chance for promoters to earn money at the box office over a prolonged period. It could also be held indoors in the winter.

5. For a detailed examination of the introduction of this "white only" rule into the League of American Wheelmen, see Andrew Ritchie, "The League of American Wheelmen, Major Taylor, and the 'Color Question' in the 1890s," in *Ethnicity, Sport, Identity: Struggles for Status,* ed. J. A. Mangan and Andrew Ritchie (London: Frank Cass, 2004).

6. *Fort Wayne News* (Indiana), April 23, 1898. Taylor's institutional affiliations were additionally complicated by the creation in the late 1890s of the National Cycling Association, a rival professional organization to the LAW, which was prepared to grant Major Taylor a license to race.

7. The white riders were Nat and Frank Butler, Burns Pierce, and Eddie McDuffie. Although the team existed only for this one event, this was the earliest integrated team in American bicycle racing, and a very early example of an integrated team in any sport. See Ritchie, *Major Taylor,* 69–70. Reported in *Bearings,* July 29, 1897.

8. *New York Sun,* September 18, 1897.

9. *Worcester Telegram,* September 20, 1897.

10. *Bicycling World,* October 1, 1897; also "Choked Taylor—Police Had to Interfere at Taunton—Becker Pulled the Major from His Bicycle," *Boston Globe,* September 24, 1897.

11. Unidentified newspaper clipping in Taylor scrapbook, Indianapolis Historical Museum.

12. *Worcester Telegram,* report from late July 1898, newspaper clipping in Taylor scrapbook, Indianapolis Historical Museum.

13. *Worcester Telegram,* September 18, 1897.

14. *New York Morning Telegraph,* undated clipping in Major Taylor scrapbook, Indianapolis Historical Society.

15. *Syracuse Telegram,* May 27, 1899.

16. Unidentified newspaper in Taylor scrapbook.

17. Unidentified newspaper in Taylor scrapbook.

18. Unidentified newspaper in Taylor scrapbook.

19. *Worcester Spy,* March 4, 1901.

20. *Le Vélo,* January 27, 1901.

21. *Le Vélo,* May 17, 1901.

22. "Le Nègre," *Le Vélo,* May 14, 1901. The racist implications and overtones of such an examination should, of course, be recognized in light of the then-ongoing and global anthropological and scientific study of alleged primitive peoples. The actual report of this incident has yet to be found.

23. Quoted in *Cycle Age,* April 18, 1901.

24. *La Vie au Grand Air,* May 4, 1901.

25. *Worcester Telegram,* July 22, 1901.

26. *Cycle Age,* July 18, 1901.

27. Taylor, *The Fastest Bicycle Rider,* "Foreword."

28. *Chicago Defender,* June 24, 1932 (city edition), July 2, 1932 (national edition).

29. The group that organized this unusual re-interment was called the Bicycle Racing Stars of the Nineteenth Century. About one hundred people were present at the ceremony, including runner Ralph Metcalfe (world record holder in 1932, also ran with Jesse Owens at the 1936 Olympics), Duke Slater, Bobby Anderson, Mel Walker, John Brooks, Claude Young, and Leroy Winbush. Also present, remarkably, was Tom Hay, of the Hay and Willits bicycle shop in Indianapolis, who fifty-six years earlier had dangled the medal in front of the young Taylor in 1892 and thus given him the incentive to win his first race.

30. Taylor, *The Fastest Bicycle Rider,* "Foreword."

31. Christopher Sinsabaugh, *Who, Me? 40 Years of Automobile History* (Detroit, MI: Arnold-Powers, 1940).

32. Taylor, *The Fastest Bicycle Rider,* 409 and 422.

3 The Strange Career of William Henry Lewis, by Gregory Bond

1. For Ashley Lewis in the army, see William H. Lewis, *The Negro as a Citizen* (New York: American Missionary Association, c. 1911), 2. Ashley served as a private in the First Regiment of the United States Colored Cavalry; see *Compiled Service Records of Volunteer Union Soldiers who Served in the United States Colored Troops* (Washington, DC: National Archives and Record Administration), microfilm roll 54. Lewis household information is from the 1870 United States Census, Virginia, Norfolk County, Washington Township; and 1880 United States Census, Virginia, Norfolk County, Portsmouth, Second Ward.

2. Booker T. Washington, "William Henry Lewis," *American Magazine,* June 1913, 34. In subsequent notes, I use the abbreviations BTW and WHL for Washington's and Lewis's names.

3. Edgar Toppin and Lucious Edwards, *Loyal Sons and Daughters: Virginia State University, 1882–1992* (Norfolk: Virginia Sate University, 1992), ch. 2. The state legislature stripped the school of its collegiate programs in 1902 and rechristened the institution the Virginia Normal and Industrial Institute.

4. For biographical information on John Mercer Langston, see William F. Cheek and Aimee Lee Cheek, *John Mercer Langston and the Fight for Black Freedom, 1829–65* (Urbana: University of Illinois Press, 1989); William F. Cheek, "A Negro Runs for Congress: John Mercer Langston and the Virginia Campaign of 1888," *Journal of Negro History* 52 (January 1967): 14–34.

5. For biographical information on William T .S. Jackson, see Harold Wade Jr., *Black Men of Amherst* (Amherst, MA: Amherst University Press, 1976), 23–27; and "Jackson, William Tecumseh Sherman," *Who's Who of the Colored Race,* Vol. 1, ed. Frank Lincoln Mather (Chicago, Illinois, 1915), 151.

6. Toppin and Edwards, *Loyal Sons and Daughters,* 19 and 62. Toppin and Edwards do not indicate the length of the students' suspension, but Langston resented the insult and assisted his protégés in leaving the Virginia school.

7. For Senator Hoar's support of Lewis and Jackson, see Edwin Henderson, *The Negro in Sports,* rev. ed. (Washington, DC: Associated Publishers, 1949), 6; and *Topeka Plaindealer,* August 9, 1912, 1.

8. Roscoe Simmons, "The Untold Story," *Chicago Daily Tribune,* November 28, 1948, S5; and WHL, "The Amherst Idea" [Class Oration], *Amherst Student,* June 18, 1892, 260–61, as quoted in Wade, *Black Men of Amherst,* 115–19.

9. Wade, *Black Men of Amherst,* 15.

10. *The Olio* [Amherst College Annual Yearbook] (Amherst College, 1893), 26; "Amherst College: Three Afro-Americans in Graduating Class," *Detroit Plaindealer,* July 15, 1892, 8; and *New York Tribune,* December 1891, as quoted in *Cleveland Gazette,* December 26, 1891, 1.

11. The centre rush (as it was originally spelled) is analogous to the position of center in modern football, but in the days before the neutral zone there was an even greater emphasis on quickness and agility. Lewis himself described the position as "one requiring painstaking hard work [and] admitting of very little glory." WHL, *A Primer of College Foot Ball* (New York: Harper and Brothers, 1896), 70.

12. Fisher played for Beloit in 1889 and occasionally for a few more seasons; see Daniel Green, "Beloit College Defeated UW," *Beloit Daily News,* November 23, 2001.

13. "Harvard Defeats Amherst," *New York Times*, October 1, 1891, 2.

14. "Collegians at Football," *New York Times,* November 13, 1889, 1; "Football Game at Amherst," *New York Times,* November 20, 1890, 5; and "An Ambulance Was Necessary," *Chicago Daily Tribune,* November 12, 1891, 7.

15. "Amherst College," *New York Times,* December 21, 1890, 11.

16. David Gerber, *Black Ohio and the Color Line, 1860–1915* (Chicago: University of Illinois Press, 1976), 50–51, 59.

17. As quoted in Robert A. Bellinger, *The Hope of the Race: African Americans in White Colleges and Universities, 1890–1915* (PhD dissertation, Boston University, 2000), 100.

18. Lewis's speech is reproduced in Wade, *Black Men of Amherst,* 115–19. All quotations derived from this reprint.

19. Simmons, *The Untold Story,* S5.

20. "Foot-Ball," *Harvard Crimson,* October 17, 1892, 1.

21. William T. Bull, "Why Yale Will Win," *Chicago Tribune,* November 13, 1892, 14.

22. David R. Robinson, "Harvard's Great Rusher," *Cleveland Gazette,* November 26, 1892, 1.

23. *Harper's Weekly,* December 10, 1892, 1199.

24. "Of the Harvard Yale Game," *Boston Herald,* November 24, 1961.

25. Roscoe Simmons, "The Untold Story," *Chicago Daily Tribune,* December 5, 1948, page SW21.

26. *Boston Globe* quoted in Ocania Chalk, *Black College Sport* (New York: Dodd, Mead and Company, 1976), 148; and "Football," *Harvard Crimson,* October 30, 1893, 1.

27. *Boston Globe* quoted in Chalk, *Black College Sport,* 149.

28. *Harper's Weekly,* December 30, 1893, 1262–63.

29. Walter Camp, "The 11 Greatest Football Players of America," *The Independent* 57, no. 2916 (October 20, 1904), 952–53.

30. *Boston Globe,* November 21, 1929, as quoted in Henderson, *The Negro in Sports,* 102; "All-Time Team Brings Rebuff in Ivy League," *Chicago Daily Tribune,* April 13, 1951, C1.

31. Harvard, Penn, and several New England schools adopted uniform eligibility requirements. Lewis ran afoul of three of the new rules: "No post-graduate student shall play. No graduates of any other college shall play. No student shall play for more than four years." *Harper's Weekly,* January 20, 1894.

32. Harold Kaese, "Bill Lewis, Great Negro Center, Recalls Day He Captained Harvard vs. Penn in '93," *Boston Globe,* November 28, 1948, 35; "Harvard Happenings," *Sporting Life,* September 29, 1894, 9.

33. *Sporting Life,* November 4, 1893, 6; *Sporting Life,* September 22, 1894, 9; and *Outing,* November 1900, 235.

34. *Boston Globe,* November 21, 1929, as quoted in Henderson, *The Negro in Sports,* 102.

35. Morris A. Bealle, *History of Harvard Football* (Washington, DC: Columbia Publishing Company, 1948), 396.

36. WHL, *A Primer of College Football.* Walter Camp, *Spalding's Official Foot Ball Guide, 1904* (New York: American Sports Publishing Company, 1904). WHL, "Making a Football Team," *Outing,* November 1902, 221–29. Lewis also was a central figure in the rules committee of 1906 that reformed the game to make it less violent. His primary suggestion was the neutral zone between the two opposing teams. See for example, "Harvard on Football," *Washington Post,* January 10, 1906, 9.

37. "Haughton Will Coach Cornell Kickers," *New York Times,* September 29, 1899, 8; "Gossip of the Gridiron," *Washington Post,* October 1, 1899, 23; "Gridiron Gossip," *Washington Post,* October 3, 1899, 9; and "Harvard's off for the Fray," *New York Times,* November 3, 1899, 4.

38. Kaese, "Bill Lewis, Great Negro Center," 35; "How Lewis Got the Place," *Washington Post,* January 17, 1903, 6.

39. *Harvard University Athletic Committee Minutes,* Vol. I (6/15/1882–6/15/1908), Harvard University Archives. See: 1/10/1901, 404; 5/7/1902, 424; 12/21/1903, 504; 10/8/1904, 507; 11/1/1904, 508. For more on Lewis's coaching, see Ronald A. Smith, *Big Time Football at Harvard, 1905* (Chicago: University of Illinois Press, 1994), *passim.*

40. "Lewis' Great Work," *AME Zion Quarterly Review* 10 (October–December 1900): 63–64, as quoted in David K. Wiggins and Patrick B. Miller, *The Unlevel Playing Field: A Documentary History of the African-American Experience in Sport* (Chicago: University of Illinois Press, 2003), 71–73.

41. *Cleveland Gazette,* November 24, 1900, 1.

42. "Communication," *Harvard Crimson,* May 26, 1893, 1. The authors of the letter were Bernard W. Tafford, Joseph D. Upton, Bernard G. Waters, and Frank W. Hallowell. *Harvard Crimson,* May 26, 1893, 2.

43. "The Color Line," *Boston Post,* May 27, 1893, 4; *Boston Evening Record,* May 26, 1893, 2.

44. "Harvard to a Man with Him," *Boston Globe,* May 26, 1893, 3.

45. Kazuteru Omori, "Race Neutral Individualism and Resurgence of the Color

Line: Massachusetts Civil Rights Legislation, 1855–1895," *Journal of American Ethnic History* 22 (Fall 2002): 39–40. See also: "Lewis' Case," *Boston Evening Record,* May 26, 1893, 1.

46. "A Cambridge Barber Has a Fine to Pay," *New York Times,* June 28, 1895, 3.

47. Emmet Jay Scott and Lyman Beecher Stowe, *Booker T. Washington, Builder of a Civilization* (Garden City, NY: Doubleday and Company, 1916), 314.

48. Louis R. Harlan, et al., editors, *BTW Papers*, Vol. 5 (Chicago: University of Illinois Press, 1976), 94.

49. Letter from President Seelye, as quoted in WHL, *The Negro as a Citizen*, 3–4.

50. Theodore Roosevelt to WHL, July 26, 1900, in Elting Morison, ed., *The Letters of Theodore Roosevelt,* Vol. 2 (Cambridge, MA: Harvard University Press, 1951), 1364–65.

51. Maxwell Bloomfield, "Lewis, William Henry," *American National Biography,* Vol. 13, ed. John A. Garraty and Mark C. Carnes (New York: Oxford University Press, 1999), 613. For a description of a White House meeting between Lewis and Roosevelt, see *BTW Papers*, Vol. 6, 614–15.

52. BTW to WHL, October 1, 1901, as quoted in Scott and Stowe, *Booker T. Washington*, 316. See also WHL to BTW, October 14, 1901, *BTW Papers*, Vol. 6, 242.

53. See for example, WHL to BTW, December 29, 1902, *BTW Papers,* Vol. 6, 614; and WHL to BTW, April 3, 1909, *BTW Papers,* Vol. 10, 85.

54. Stephen R. Fox, *The Guardian of Boston: William Monroe Trotter* (New York: Atheneum, 1970), 49–58.

55. WHL, "Ohio and Emancipation," *Colored American Magazine* 17, no. 5 (November 1909): 262–63.

56. John Daniels, *In Freedom's Birthplace: A Study of the Boston Negroes* (Boston: Houghton Mifflin Company, 1914), 128–29.

57. WHL, "Booker T. Washington—A Lover of His Fellow-Men," *Negro Orators and Their Orations*, ed. Carter G. Woodson (New York: Russell and Russell, 1969), 600–01.

58. Fox, *The Guardian of Boston*, 56; *Boston Guardian,* January 30, 1904, 1; *Boston Guardian,* March 12, 1904, 4; *Boston Guardian,* August 1, 1903, 4.

59. *Boston Guardian*, as quoted in "Disgraces His Race," *Washington Colored American,* January 11, 1902, 4.

60. "Lawyer Brown's Race Defence," *Boston Guardian,* October 26, 1907, 4.

61. WHL, "Warning against Theodore Roosevelt," as quoted in Leslie H. Fishel and Benjamin Quarles, editors, *The Negro American: A Documentary History* (New York: William Morrow and Company, 1968), 388.

62. *Boston Guardian,* February 29, 1908, 2.

63. WHL to BTW, April 3, 1909, *BTW Papers,* Vol. 10, 85–86.

64. Louis R. Harlan, *Booker T. Washington: The Wizard of Tuskegee, 1901–1915* (New York: Oxford University Press, 1983), 76. WHL to BTW, July 2, 1909, *BTW Papers,* Vol. 10, 141. See also Mark R. Schneider, *Boston Confronts Jim Crow, 1890–1920* (Boston: Northeastern University Press, 1997), 197–202.

65. "Taft Silent on Lewis," *Washington Post,* October 29, 1910, 3; "Taft Appoints Lewis," *Washington Post,* March 3, 1911, 3; and "All Ready for Lewis," *Washington Post,* March 21, 1911, 4.

66. "Would Oust Lewis," *Washington Post,* March 1, 1912, 1; and "The Color Line at the Bar," *The Nation,* 94, no. 2447 (May 23, 1912), 590–10.

67. In the midst of the controversy it evolved that two other African Americans—including Bostonian Butler Wilson—had quietly joined the ABA in recent years. The organization came to the same solution for all three lawyers.

68. *Boston Guardian,* October 1902, as quoted in *Indianapolis Freeman,* November 15, 1902, 4.

69. See Loren Miller, *The Petitioners: The Story of the Supreme Court of the United States and the Negro* (New York: Pantheon Books, 1966), 252–54.

70. Fox, *The Guardian of Boston,* 188–201.

71. "Leader of Negroes to Work for Davis," *New York Times,* August 31, 1924, E1; and "Trend in the West for Hoover Victory, Leaders Tell Him," *New York Times,* September 16, 1928, 1.

72. WHL, *The Negro as a Citizen,* 6 and 8. WHL, "Address of William H. Lewis . . . Before the Massachusetts House of Representatives," *Negro Orators and Their Orations,* ed. Carter G. Woodson (New York: Russell and Russell, 1969), 571.

73. John M. Carroll, *Fritz Pollard: Pioneer in Racial Advancement* (Chicago: University of Illinois Press, 1992), 52–55.

74. Kaese, "Bill Lewis," 35.

75. *Time,* January 10, 1949, 80; and "W. H. Lewis Is Dead," *New York Times,* January 2, 1949, 60.

76. C. Vann Woodward, *The Strange Career of Jim Crow,* 2nd rev. ed. (New York: Oxford University Press, 1966), 33.

4 Jack Johnson and the Quest for Racial Respect, by Gerald R. Gems

1. Randy Roberts, *Papa Jack: Jack Johnson and the Era of White Hopes* (New York: Free Press, 1983), 3, has established that his given name was Arthur John Johnson. He carried the nickname "Lil' Arthur" thereafter. For a recent account of Johnson's life, see Geoffrey C. Ward, *Unforgivable Blackness: The Rise and Fall of Jack Johnson* (New York: Alfred A. Knopf, 2004).

2. Roberts, *Papa Jack,* 6–8.

3. Roberts, *Papa Jack,* 9–12.

4. Jack Johnson, *Jack Johnson Is a Dandy: An Autobiography* (New York: Chelsea House, 1969), 21.

5. Roberts, *Papa Jack,* 9, 23–24; A. S. "Doc" Young, "Was Jack Johnson Boxing's Greatest Champ," *Ebony* 18:3 (January 1963): 67–74.

6. Roberts, *Papa Jack,* 13–16.

7. *New Orleans Times-Democrat,* September 7, 1892, 1; September 8, 1892, 4.

8. Corbett had previously fought a draw with the great black heavyweight Peter Jackson; but upon defeating Sullivan for the title in 1892 he upheld the restriction. Jeffries, too, had contested with blacks before his title reign. See Jeffrey Sammons, *Beyond the Ring: The Role of Boxing in American Society* (Urbana: University of Illinois Press, 1988), 34–36; and David K. Wiggins, "Peter Jackson and the Elusive

Heavyweight Championship: A Black Athlete's Struggle against the Late Nineteenth-Century Color-Line," *Journal of Sport History* 12 (Summer 1985): 143–68, on the plight of black boxers during the era.

9. Roberts, *Papa Jack,* 29; Al-Tony Gilmore, *Bad Nigger! The National Impact of Jack Johnson* (Port Washington, NY: Kennikat Press, 1975), 13–18; Nat Fleischer, *Black Dynamite: The Story of the Negro in the Prize Ring from 1782 to 1938* (New York: C. J. O'Brien, 1939), vol. 5:5.

10. Roberts, *Papa Jack,* 49–50.

11. Roberts, *Papa Jack,* 54–67; Johnson, *Jack Johnson Is a Dandy,* 53.

12. Roberts, *Papa Jack,* 81–84.

13. Roberts, *Papa Jack,* xiii, 115–20; *Chicago Tribune,* July 3, 1910, pt. 3:3.

14. *Chicago Tribune,* July 1, 1910, 13; July 2, 1910, 11; July 3, 1910, pt. 3:1, pt. 3:3; July 4, 1910, 1, 11. The *Chicago Defender,* an African American newspaper, predicted a Johnson victory, July 2, 1910, 1.

15. *Chicago Tribune,* July 4, 1910, 1.

16. *Chicago Tribune,* July 1, 1910, 13; July 2, 1910, 11; July 4, 1910, 10; July 5, 1910, 1; pt. 2:25.

17. *Chicago Tribune,* July 5, 1910, 1.

18. *Chicago Defender,* July 23, 1910, 2; July 30, 1910, 3; *Chicago Tribune,* July 4, 1910, 10; July 5, 1910, 1, 4; Roberts, *Papa Jack,* 113.

19. David K. Wiggins and Patrick B. Miller, *The Unlevel Playing Field: A Documentary History of the African American Experience in Sport* (Urbana: University of Illinois Press, 2003), 77–82.

20. *Chicago Defender,* July 30, 1910, 3 (quote); Roberts, *Papa Jack,* 86–88, 115–30; Chicago Historical Society (CHS), Boxing Scrapbooks, vol. 15, clippings, 1910–1911, on assassination attempts. Finis Farr, "Jeff, it's up to you!" *American Heritage* (February 1964): 64–77; Farr, *Black Champion,* 107; Johnson, *Jack Johnson Is a Dandy,* 66–68. See *Chicago Defender,* July 23, 1910, 2, on legal problems, and September 4, 1912, 1, 7; September 21, 1912, 1, on suicide.

21. For extensive coverage on Johnson in the Austrian press, see *Illustr. Osterr Sportblatt,* VII: 2 (January 7, 1911): 11–12; VII:12 (March 18, 1911): 10, on racial "war"; VII:14, n.p.; VII:22 (May 25, 1911): 11–12; VII:46 (November 11, 1911): 10; VII:48 (November 25, 1911): 16; VII:50 (December 9, 1911): 14–16, on boxing films in Germany. My thanks to Dr. Gertrud Pfister for calling my attention to the European coverage and providing the translations.

22. CHS, Boxing Scrapbooks, vol. 16 (1912), July 4, 1912, clippings; Roberts, *Papa Jack,* 130–38.

23. *Chicago Defender,* September 14, 1912, 7; Roberts, *Papa Jack,* 139; Johnson, *Jack Johnson Is a Dandy,* 66–68.

24. *Chicago Defender,* October 26, 1912, 1, 6 (quote).

25. *Chicago Defender,* October 26, 1912, 1.

26. *Chicago Defender,* October 26, 1912, 1; Roberts, *Papa Jack,* 138–66; Gilmore, *Bad Nigger!* 99–113.

27. Roberts, *Papa Jack,* 132, 167–89, indicates a fine of $1,000 plus $740 in court costs; but Johnson also lost the confiscated necklace valued as high as $6,000.

28. *Chicago Tribune* , April 6, 1915, 12; Johnson, *Jack Johnson Is a Dandy,* 89–100; Farr, *Black Champion,* 155; Gilmore, *Bad Nigger!* 134–35.

29. *Chicago Tribune,* April 6, 1915, 13.

30. *Chicago Tribune,* April 6, 1915, 12.

31. *Chicago Tribune,* April 6, 1915, 12.

32. *Chicago Tribune,* April 6, 1915, 13.

33. *Chicago Tribune,* April 6, 1915, 12; *Chicago Defender,* April 24, 1915, 7; Roberts, *Papa Jack,* 197–205; Johnson, *Jack Johnson is a Dandy,* 102; Farr, *Black Champion,* 164–165; Gilmore, *Bad Nigger!* 137.

34. *Chicago Tribune,* April 6, 1915, 12 (quote), 13.

35. Roberts, *Papa Jack,* 204–5; Farr, *Black Champion,* 167–70; Johnson, *Jack Johnson Is a Dandy,* 103.

36. Johnson, *Jack Johnson Is a Dandy,* 103–10; Roberts, *Papa Jack,* 205–10.

37. Johnson, *Jack Johnson Is a Dandy,* 111–21, 128; Roberts, *Papa Jack,* 210–14.

38. Johnson, *Jack Johnson Is a Dandy,* 229; Roberts, *Papa Jack,* 221–23; Farr, *Black Champion,* 183, 188; Young, "Was Jack Johnson Boxing's Greatest Champ?" 68–72; Sammons, *Beyond the Ring,* 123.

39. Young, "Was Jack Johnson Boxing's Greatest Champ?"; Fleischer, *Black Dynamite,* 7; Cleaver cited in Gilmore, *Bad Nigger!* 25.

40. Young, "Was Jack Johnson Boxing's Greatest Champ?"; Fleischer, *Black Dynamite,* 7; Cleaver cited in Gilmore, *Bad Nigger!* 25.

41. Sammons, *Beyond the Ring,* 46.

42. See John M. Carroll, *Fritz Pollard: Pioneer in Racial Advancement* (Urbana: University of Illinois Press, 1992); and Martin Bauml Duberman, *Paul Robeson: A Biography* (New York: Ballantine Books, 1989).

5 Ora Washington: The First Black Female Star, by Pamela Grundy

1. See *Philadelphia Tribune* April 9, 1931, 11; March 10, 1932, 10; July 24, 1930, 10. Washington's tennis achievements in particular were regularly chronicled in most of the nation's major black papers. Many of the articles cited here were shared with me by Rita Liberti, whose pioneering research into black women's basketball was essential to this project.

2. Denise Dennis, *A Century of Greatness, 1900–1999: The Urban League of Philadelphia's Tribute to the Outstanding African-American Philadelphians of the Twentieth Century* (Philadelphia: Urban League of Philadelphia, 2002), 189.

3. J. Bernard Childs interview by Pamela Grundy, July 31, 2003, telephone; J. Bernard Childs interview by Pamela Grundy, October 4, 2003, Bowling Green, Va., in Grundy's possession. Most of this essay's descriptions of Washington family history are drawn from these conversations with Childs, the son of Washington's older sister, Lenora. Much research, however, remains to be done. The *Philadelphia Tribune* published an obituary on June 5, 1971, 2.

4. Marshall Wingfield, *A History of Caroline County Virginia from Its Formation in 1727 to 1924* (Baltimore: Clearfield Company, 1997), 34–35; 167.

5. Childs interviews.

6. J. Douglas Smith, *Managing White Supremacy: Race, Politics, and Citizenship in Jim Crow Virginia* (Chapel Hill: University of North Carolina Press, 2002), 22–30. On her Social Security account number application, submitted in 1943, Washington listed her birth date as January 16, 1899. Application for Social Security Account Number 183204110, April 28, 1943.

7. U.S. Census of the Population, Carolina County, Va., 1910, E.D. 17, 5.

8. U.S. Census of the Population, Philadelphia County, Penn., 1920, E.D. 632, 8.

9. Charles Ashley Hardy, "Race and Opportunity: Black Philadelphia during the Era of the Great Migration, 1916–1930" (Ph.D. diss., Temple University, 1989), 15–16, 41–46, 53–59, 219–21.

10. Hardy, "Race and Opportunity," 445–46.

11. For an account of early black men's basketball, see Bob Kuska, *Hot Potato: How Washington and New York Gave Birth to Black Basketball and Changed America's Game Forever* (Charlottesville: University of Virginia Press, 2004). For a history of the Hilldale club, see Neil Lanctot, *Fair Dealing and Clean Playing: The Hilldale Club and the Development of Black Professional Baseball, 1910–1932* (Jefferson, NC: McFarland Company, 1994). A description of the early years of the ATA can be found in Edwin Bancroft Henderson, *The Negro In Sports*, rev. ed. (Washington, DC: Associated Publishers, 1949), 174–85.

12. Report of Branch Secretary, April 1919, Folder 11, Box 25, Young Women's Christian Association of Germantown collection, Urban Archives, Temple University. For a detailed description of Y activities, see Stephanie Yvette Felix, "Committed to Their Own: African American Women Leaders in the YWCA of Germantown, Philadelphia, Pennsylvania, 1870–1970" (Ph.D. diss., Temple University, 1999), 123–29.

13. Young, *Negro Firsts in Sports*, 194; Childs interviews.

14. *Philadelphia Tribune*, September 13, 1924, 10; *Chicago Defender*, August 29, 1925, 2–8. For a full list of the ATA champions over the years, see Arthur R. Ashe Jr., *A Hard Road to Glory: A History of the African-American Athlete, 1919–1945*, vol. 2., 443–63.

15. Annual Report of Branch Secretary, 1925, and Report of Branch Secretary, September 1925. Both in Folder 11, Box 25, YWCA of Germantown collection.

16. Young, *Negro Firsts in Sports*, 195.

17. *Philadelphia Tribune*, August 29, 1929, 10. The 1930 U.S. Census recorded Washington as living in Chicago. U.S. Census of the Population, Cook County, Ill., 1930, E.D. 16–186, 15.

18. Young, *Negro Firsts in Sports*, 195; Amaleta Moore and Ruth Glover Mullen interview by Pamela Grundy, October 7, 2003, West Cape May, N.J., located at Southern Historical Collection, Wilson Library, University of North Carolina, Chapel Hill; Lewis Hill interview by Pamela Grundy, July 31, 2003, telephone; *Chicago Defender*, March 14, 1931.

19. Young, *Negro Firsts in Sports*, 195. For efforts to integrate the USLTA, see Ashe, *A Hard Road to Glory*, 60–64.

20. For analysis of black community attitudes toward women's sports, see Pamela Grundy and Susan Shackelford, *Shattering the Glass: A History of American Women's Basketball* (New York: New Press, 2005), and Rita Liberti, "We Were Ladies, We Just Played Like Boys: African-American Womanhood and Competitive Basketball at

Bennett College, 1928–1942," in *Sport and the Color Line: Black Athletes and Race Relations in Twentieth-Century America,* ed. Patrick B. Miller and David K. Wiggins (New York: Routledge, 2004), 81–99.

21. *Philadelphia Tribune,* April 9, 1931, 11.

22. The Hornets' amicable break with the Y is described in Branch Secretary Report, October 1931, Folder 13, Box 25, Germantown YWCA collection. The transformation of the Quick Steppers, along with an account of Patterson's athletic career, can be found in Henderson, *The Negro in Sports,* 211–15. Some of the dates in that account are inaccurate. Otto Briggs's outstanding career with the Hilldale baseball club is described in Lanctot, *Fair Dealing and Clean Playing.*

23. *Philadelphia Tribune,* January 14, 1932, 11.

24. *Philadelphia Tribune,* February 11, 1932, 11.

25. *Philadelphia Tribune,* March 17, 1932, 11.

26. *Philadelphia Tribune,* April 7, 1932, 10. In the absence of a tournament to determine a national champion, prominent teams generally claimed their titles on the basis of overall records and opponents defeated.

27. *Philadelphia Tribune,* February 25, 1932, 11; March 10, 1932, 10; March 17, 1932, 10.

28. *Philadelphia Tribune,* November 10, 1932, 10.

29. The game at Asbury Park, N.J., is described in *Chicago Defender,* April 29, 1933, 9.

30. *Greensboro Daily News,* March 9, 1934, 12.

31. Amaleta Moore and Ruth Glover Mullen interview by Rita Liberti, July 30, 1995, West Cape May, N.J., in Liberti's possession.

32. Moore and Mullen interview by Pamela Grundy; Lucille Townsend interview by Rita Liberti, Richmond, Va., August 6, 1995, in Liberti's possession.

33. *Atlanta Daily World,* January 31, 1938, 5.

34. *Philadelphia Tribune,* August 29, 1936, 14.

35. *Baltimore Afro-American,* August 5, 1939, 21; *Philadelphia Tribune,* September 6, 1934, 9; July 26, 1934, 12.

36. Young, *Negro Firsts in Sports,* 197.

37. *Pittsburgh Courier,* January 21, 1939, 15.

38. *Baltimore Afro-American,* August 5, 1939, 21.

39. *Baltimore Afro-American,* August 5, 1939, 21.

40. Childs interviews. For descriptions of changes in black women's basketball, see Grundy and Shackelford, *Shattering the Glass.* Accounts of the Tribunes' play periodically mention white teams. One white rival that received particular attention was the Leavittsburg Athletic Club, led by Susie Spoonseller, which played the Tribunes in Ohio and made at least one trip to Philadelphia. See *Philadelphia Tribune,* January 26, 1933, 10; March 29, 1934, 10; and *Chicago Defender,* February 4, 1933, 8. Another rival was the Buckstown Quintette of Buckstown, Pennsylvania. See *Atlanta Daily World,* February 25, 1938, 5.

41. Childs interview, July 31, 2003. Intriguingly, Childs noted that Washington periodically went to New York to visit a white female friend she had met through basketball.

42. Young, *Negrō Firsts in Sports,* 195.

6 Satchel Paige's Struggle for Selfhood in the Era of Jim Crow, by Donald Spivey

1. Verification of Birth Record for Leroy Page, July 7, 1906; Issued February 5, 1954, Office of Vital Statistics, County Health Department, Mobile, Alabama.

2. Leroy Satchel Paige as told to David Lipman, *Maybe I'll Pitch Forever: A Great Baseball Player Tells the Hilarious Story behind the Legend* (Lincoln: University of Nebraska Press, 1993 rept.), 16.

3. Paige and Lipman, *Maybe I'll Pitch Forever,* 32.

4. William Dismukes, "Ye Olde Stove League," *Pittsburgh Courier,* January 5, 1929, 4, sec. 3.

5. Leroy Satchel Paige as told to Hal Lebovitz, *Pitchin' Man* (Westport, CT: Meckler Publishing, 1948; rept. 1992), 31–32; see Mark Ribowsky, *Don't Look Back: Satchel Paige in the Shadows of Baseball* (New York: Simon and Schuster, 1994), 53–54.

6. Cited in Rob Ruck, *Sandlot Seasons: Sport in Black Pittsburgh* (Urbana: University of Illinois Press, 1987), 154. See also Donn Rogosin, *Invisible Men: Life in Baseball's Negro Leagues* (New York: Kodansha Publishers, 1983), 45, 53–55.

7. Larry Lester, *Black Baseball's National Showcase: The East-West All-Star Game, 1933–1953* (Lincoln: University of Nebraska Press, 2001), 6–10, 15.

8. *Pittsburgh Courier,* September 1, 1934, 4.

9. See Robert Gregory, *Diz: The Story of Dizzy Dean and Baseball during the Great Depression* (New York: Viking Penguin, 1992), 242.

10. Lebovitz, *Pitchin' Man,* 53–60; Paige and Lipman, *Maybe I'll Pitch Forever,* 115–27.

11. Lebovitz, *Pitchin' Man,* 53–60; Paige and Lipman, *Maybe I'll Pitch Forever,* 115–27.

12. For further discussion along these lines, see "Major Baseball Bar Drove Paige to Cuba," *Chicago Defender,* May 29, 1937, 13; "Baseball War Brews over Satchell Paige As Two Teams Claim His Services," *Pittsburgh Courier,* June 1, 1940, 17; *Invisible Men: Life in Baseball's Negro Leagues,* 96–110 and passim; Buck O'Neil, *I Was Right on Time: My Journey from the Negro Leagues to the Majors* (New York: Fireside, 1996), 100–23.

13. Richard Donovan, "The Fabulous Satchel Paige," in *Satchel Page Collection,* Baseball Hall of Fame Library, Cooperstown, New York, 350–52.

14. See for example, "A Concurrent Resolution Congratulating Satchel Paige on his Election to the Baseball Hall of Fame, House Concurrent Resolution No. 3032, Forty-Second Legislative Assembly, State of North Dakota, Capitol in City of Bismarck, on Tuesday, the fifth day of January, one thousand nine hundred and seventy-one," in *Satchel Paige Collection,* Baseball Hall of Fame, Cooperstown, New York; "Why Doesn't Baseball Put Paige in Front of Hall?" *Newsday,* February 5, 1971; Joe O' Day, Associated Press, "Death Finally Catches Satchel Paige," June 9, 1982."

7 Jesse Owens: Leading Man in Modern American Tales of Racial Progress and Limits, by Mark Dyreson

1. *Olympische Spiele* (Leni Riefenstahl-Produktion, 1936–1938).

2. For histories of the scientific quest to assign athletic prowess on the basis of race, see David K. Wiggins, "'Great Speed But Little Stamina': The Historical Debate over Black Athletic Superiority," *Journal of Sport History* 16 (Summer 1989): 158–85; Patrick B. Miller, "The Anatomy of Scientific Racism: Racialist Responses to Black Athletic Achievement," *Journal of Sport History* 25 (Spring 1998): 119–51; and Mark Dyreson, "American Ideas about Race and Olympic Races from the 1890s to the 1950s: Shattering Myths or Reinforcing Scientific Racism?" *Journal of Sport History* 28 (Summer 2001): 173–215. See also John Hoberman, *Darwin's Athletes: How Sport Has Damaged Black America and Preserved the Myth of Race* (Boston: Houghton Mifflin, 1997). Hoberman's work has been somewhat controversial. For an introduction to the debate, see Jeffrey T. Sammons, "A Proportional and Measured Response to the Provocation That Is Darwin's Athletes, *Journal of Sport History* 24 (Fall 1997): 378–88; and John Hoberman, "How Not to Misread *Darwin's Athletes:* A Response to Jeffrey Sammons," *Journal of Sport History* 24 (Fall 1997): 389–96.

3. Harry Edwards invented the term "athletic plantation" in Harry Edwards, *The Revolt of the Black Athlete* (New York: Free Press, 1969).

4. A classic and extremely well crafted example is Michael Oriard, "Muhammad Ali: The Hero in the Age of Mass Media," in *Muhammad Ali: The People's Champion,* ed. Elliott Gorn (Urbana: University of Illinois Press, 1995).

5. Certainly Owens appears in a multiplicity of texts. A standard American history textbook claims Owens "confounded Nazi racial theories." Paul S. Boyer, Clifford E. Clark Jr., Joseph Kett, Neal Salisbury, Harvard Sitkoff, and Nancy Woloch, *The Enduring Vision,* 2nd ed. (Lexington, MA: D. C. Heath, 1993), 888. Film and documentary examples abound. See, for instance, "One Hundred Years of Olympic Glory," produced by Turner Home Entertainment (Atlanta: Turner Home Entertainment, 1996); *The Journey of the African-American Athlete* (New York: HBO Home Video, 1996); "To Be Somebody," part 6 of *The Great Depression,* produced by WGBH-TV, Boston (Alexandria, VA: PBS Video, 1993); *The Jesse Owens Story* (Los Angeles: Paramount, 1984). For Owens's place in African American studies, see J. Patrick Lewis, *Freedom Like Sunlight: Praise songs for Black Americans* (Mankato, MN: Creative Editions, 2000); Roger A. Hammer, *African America: Heralding a Heritage* (Golden Valley, MN: The Place in the Woods, 1992). Owens has also inspired a raft of juvenile biographies, including Patricia and Fredrick McKissack, *Jesse Owens: Olympic Star,* rev. ed. (Berkeley Heights, NJ: Enslow Publishers, 2001); Wayne Coffey, *Jesse Owens* (Woodbridge, CT: Blackbirch Press, 1992); David Adler, *A Picture Book of Jesse Owens* (New York: Holiday House, 1992); William R. Sanford and Carl R. Green, *Jesse Owens* (New York: Crestwood House, 1992).

6. "Owens Still Sets a Swift Pace," *New York Times,* November 22, 1964, sec. S, 8.

7. William J. Baker, *Jesse Owens: An American Life* (New York: Free Press, 1986).

8. Indeed the major film biography of Owens is the television miniseries entitled *The Jesse Owens Story* (1984).

9. Baker's *Jesse Owens* remains the outstanding biography. Owens himself crafted a series of autobiographies with Paul Neimark. Jesse Owens, with Paul Neimark, *The Jesse Owens Story* (New York: Putnam's, 1970); Jesse Owens, with Paul Neimark, *Blackthink: My Life as Black Man and White Man* (New York: William Morrow, 1970); Jesse Owens, with Paul Neimark, *I Have Changed* (New York: William Morrow, 1972); Jesse Owens, with Paul Neimark, *Jesse: A Spiritual Autobiography* (Plainfield, NJ: Logos International, 1978); Jesse Owens, with Paul Neimark, *Jesse, The Man Who Outran Hitler* (New York: Ballantine Books, 1978). An interesting hodgepodge of biographical tidbits can be found in Rhussus L. Perry, "Jesse Owens," American Life Histories: Manuscripts from the Federal Writers' Project, 1936–1940, Library of Congress Archives, Washington, DC. See also, Larry Snyder, "My Boy Jesse," *Saturday Evening Post,* November 7, 1937, 14–15 and 97–101; "Don Newcombe and Jesse Owens Featured in 'Sport,'" Negro History Bulletin, 17 (April 1954): 150.

10. Nicholas Lemann, *The Promised Land: The Great Black Migration and How It Changed America* (New York: Knopf, 1991). On how the great migration altered American sport, see especially Jules Tygiel, *Baseball's Great Experiment,* rev. ed. (New York: Oxford University Press, 1997); Chris Mead, *Champion: Joe Louis, Black Hero in White America* (New York: C. Scribner's Sons, 1985); Thomas R. Hietala, *The Fight of the Century: Jack Johnson, Joe Louis, and the Struggle for Racial Equality* (Armonk, NY: M. E. Sharpe, 2002); Arthur Ashe, *A Hard Road to Glory: A History of the African American Athlete, 1919–1945* (New York: Amistad, 1993).

11. Baker, *Jesse Owens, 5–32*; Kenneth L. Kusmer, *A Ghetto Takes Shape: Black Cleveland, 1870–1930* (Urbana: University of Illinois Press, 1976); Carol Poh Miller and Robert Wheeler, *Cleveland: A Concise History, 1796–1996,* 2nd ed. (Bloomington: Indiana University Press, 1997).

12. Baker, *Jesse Owens,* 17–32; Owens, *The Jesse Owens Story;* Owens, *Jesse, The Man Who Outran Hitler.*

13. Baker, *Jesse Owens,* 17–32.

14. Charles H. Williams, "Negro Athletes in the Tenth Olympiad," *Southern Workman* 61 (November 1932): 449–60; Elmer A. Carter, "The Negro in College Athletics," *Journal of Negro Life* 11 (July 1933): 208–19. For histories of racial dynamics at the 1932 Olympic Games, see Mark Dyreson, "Marketing National Identity: The Olympic Games of 1932 and American Culture," *Olympika: The International Journal of Olympic Studies* 4 (1995): 23–48; David Welky, "U.S. Journalism and the 1932 Olympics," *Journal of Sport History* 24 (Spring 1997): 24–49; Eriko Yamamoto, "Cheers for Japanese Athletes: The 1932 Los Angeles Olympics and the Japanese American Community," *Pacific Historical Review* 69 (August 2000): 399–429.

15. Baker, *Jesse Owens,* 33–53; Owens, *The Jesse Owens Story;* Owens, *Jesse, The Man Who Outran Hitler.*

16. Baker, *Jesse Owens,* 33–53.

17. "Owens Sets Three World's Track Marks," *Chicago Defender,* June 1, 1935, sec. 2, 13; "Colored Mercuries Wear Spikes Instead of Winged Shoes," *News-Week* 6 (July 20, 1935): 2627.

18. "Jesse Owens Sidesteps a 'Balm' Suit," *Chicago Defender,* July 6, 1935, sec. 2, 13.

19. Baker, *Jesse Owens,* 54–72.

20. "Jesse Owens' Pro Charge Is Held Up," *Chicago Defender,* July 24, 1935, sec. 2, 14; Baker, *Jesse Owens,* 54–72.

21. William Penn, "Eastern Sports Dope," *Chicago Defender,* January 11, 1936, sec. 2, 13.

22. On the boycott controversies, see Arnd Krüger and William Murray, *The Nazi Olympics: Sport, Politics and Appeasement in the 1930s,* rev. ed. (Urbana: University of Illinois Press, 2003), and Richard Mandell, *The Nazi Olympics* (New York: Macmillan, 1971).

23. Baker, *Jesse Owens,* 65–66.

24. David K. Wiggins, "The 1936 Olympic Games in Berlin: The Response of America's Black Press," *Research Quarterly for Exercise and Sport* 54 (September 1983): 278–92.

25. Unsent letter from Walter White, Secretary of the NAACP, to Jesse Owens, December 4, 1935, NAACP Collection, Library of Congress Manuscript Division, Washington, DC.

26. *Amsterdam News,* August 23, 1936, reprinted in The Committee on Fair Play, 1936.

27. Jack Lippert, "Olympics in Hitlerland," *Scholastic Magazine* 27 (November 16, 1935): 26–27.

28. Herbert Wycliffe Baumgarder, "Measuring Negro Self-Respect," *Journal of Negro Education* 4 (October 1935): 490–99. The oddly phrased survey question read: "That Paul Robeson, Fritz Pollard, Duke Slater, Eddie Tolan, DeHart Hubbard, Jesse Owens and other Negroes have been outstanding in athletics proves that Negroes are better athletes than white people."

29. "Joe Louis and Jesse Owens," *Crisis* 42 (August 1935): 241.

30. "Captain Jesse Owens," *Chicago Defender,* June 15, 1935, sec. 2, 13; "Topics of the Week," Cartoon, "Ohio State Proves Its Right to Be Called a Great School," *Chicago Defender,* June 15, 1935, sec. 2, 16.

31. "Winter Olympics on Deck," *Literary Digest* 120 (December 14, 1935): 39.

32. "Topics of the Times: Some Olympic Performers," *New York Times,* July 14, 1936, sec. 1, 18; "Trials and Tryouts," *Time* 8 (July 20, 1936): 50–54; "Olympics: Record Holders and Champions Too Slow to Qualify," *News-Week* 8 (July 18, 1936): 30–31; "Olympic Trials," *Nation* 143 (July 18, 1936): 62.

33. One reason for the change was the aggressive politicking of the University of Southern California coach to ensure that his athletes were on the relay team. Anti-Semitism clearly played a role as well. Owens's role in the controversy remains clouded in mystery. Ralph Metcalfe and Frank Wyckoff, who also ran on the relay team, later insinuated that Owens had caused the changes in a selfish quest for four gold medals. Glickman defended Owens and recalled that the Ohio State star had openly lobbied the coaches to keep the two Jewish sprinters on the team. Marty Glickman, with Stan Isaacs, *The Fastest Kid on the Block: The Marty Glickman Story* (Syracuse, NY: Syracuse University Press, 1996), 8–35; Baker, *Jesse Owens,* 89–108.

34. "Non Aryan Victors in Nazi Olympics," *Literary Digest* 122 (August 29, 1936): 33–34; "Olympic Games (Cont'd)," *Time* 28 (August 24, 1936): 56–60; Arthur J. Daley, "Owens Captures Olympic Title," *New York Times,* August 4, 1936, 1, 23; John Kieran, "Sports of the Times: There He Goes Again!" *New York Times,* August 5, 1936, 26.

35. Baker, *Jesse Owens,* 89–91; Allen Guttmann, *The Games Must Go On: Avery Brundage and the Olympic Movement* (New York: Columbia University Press, 1984),

78–79; Richard D. Mandell, *The Nazi Olympics* (New York: Macmillan, 1971), 227–29.

36. "Olympic Games (Cont'd)," *Time* 28 (August 17, 1936): 37–40.

37. "Olympics: Germany, Unofficial World Champions; U.S. Second," *News-Week* 8 (August 22, 1936): 20–21.

38. On how Owens was interpreted by the contemporary media, see Wiggins, "The 1936 Olympic Games in Berlin," 278–92; and D. A. Kass, "The Issue of Racism at the 1936 Olympics," *Journal of Sport History* 3 (Winter 1976): 223–35.

39. "Negro University Seeks Owens as Track Coach," *New York Times*, August 14, 1936, 21.

40. "Owens to Become Stage Performer," *New York Times*, August 30, 1936, sec. 5, 1–2; Baker, *Jesse Owens*, 109–28.

41. "Cleveland to Stage Parade," *New York Times*, August 25, 1936, 25; "Cheering Thousands Greet Owens in Demonstrations at Cleveland," *New York Times*, August 26, 1936, 27; "Owens Honored in Columbus," *New York Times*, August 29, 1936, 9.

42. "City to Greet Olympians, *New York Times*, August 15, 1936, 8; "City Plans Parade for Olympic Team," *New York Times*, August 22, 1936, 15; Arthur J. Daley, "U.S. Olympic Team Returns Tonight," *New York Times*, August 28, 1936, 11; Arthur J. Daley, "Olympians Staying as Guests of City," *New York Times*, August 30, 1936, sec. 5, 1–2; "Olympic Victors Parade Here Today," *New York Times*, September 3, 1936, 23; "Olympic Stars Get Welcome of City," *New York Times*, September 4, 1936, 21.

43. "Olympic Stars Get Welcome of City," 21.

44. "Olympic Stars Get Welcome of City," 21.

45. Oswald Garrison Villard, "Issues and Men," *Nation* 143 (August 15, 1936): 185.

46. Arthur Raper, "The South Strains toward Decency," *North American Review* 243 (Spring 1937): 109.

47. "Letters to the Sports Editor," *New York Times*, August 15, 1936, 10.

48. See, for instance, Jon Entine, *Taboo: Why Black Athletes Dominate Sports and Why We Are Afraid to Talk about* It (New York: Public Affairs, 2000).

49. Dyreson, "American Ideas about Race and Olympic Races," 173–215; Wiggins, "'Great Speed But Little Stamina,'" 158–85; Miller, "The Anatomy of Scientific Racism," 119–51; Hoberman, *Darwin's Athletes*.

50. Cleveland *Call and Post*, September 17, 1936, as cited in Baker, *Jesse Owens*, 129.

51. "Forkins, Manager of Owens, Plans Quick Action Regarding Two Offers, *New York Times*, September 3, 1936, 29; Snyder, "My Boy Jesse," 14–15 and 97–101.

52. Arthur J. Daley, "Will Not Turn Pro, Jesse Owens Says," *New York Times*, September 13, 1936, sec. S, 1; "Requests Removal of Ban on Owens," *New York Times*, September 15, 1936, 42; "Owens Ineligible, Track Meet Is Off," *New York Times*, September 16, 1936, 32.

53. Baker, *Jesse Owens*, 129–45.

54. William E. Leuchtenburg, *The FDR Years: On Roosevelt and His Legacy* (New York: Columbia University Press, 1995); T. H. Watkins, *The Great Depression: America in the 1930s* (Boston: Little, Brown, 1993); Harvard Sitkoff, *A New Deal for Blacks: The Emergence of Civil Rights as a National Issue* (New York: Oxford University Press, 1978).

55. "XI Olympics: James Cleveland Owen's Name Led All the Rest," *News-Week*, August 15, 1936, 23–26; "Home Sought for Owens," *New York Times*, August 22, 1936, 15; Snyder, "My Boy Jesse," 14–15 and 97–101; Baker, *Jesse Owens*, 129–45.

56. "Owens Will Talk in Landon Drive," *New York Times,* September 3, 1936, 10; James A. Hagerty, "Landon to Invade Maine," *New York Times,* September 9, 1936, 1; James A. Hagerty, "18 Landon Talks Set for Trip East," *New York Times,* September 10, 1936, 2; "Billed by Both Parties, Owens Needs New Speed," *New York Times,* September 27, 1936, 2; "Jesse Owens Extols Landon," *New York Times,* September 29, 1936, 23; "Gov. Landon's Chicago Address Attacking New Deal Expenditures," *New York Times,* October 10, 1936, 8; John Kieran, "Sports of the Times: A Little Campaign Literature," *New York Times,* October 25, 1936, sec. S., 2; Baker, *Jesse Owens,* 132–38.

57. "Owens Is Named No. 1 Star of the Year," *New York Times,* December 15, 1936, 32.

58. "Ten on Final List for Sullivan Award," *New York Times,* December 5, 1936, 11; "Morris Captures Sullivan Award," *New York Times,* December 31, 1936, 10; "News 'Funny' to Owens," *New York Times,* December 31, 1936, 10.

59. John R. Tunis, *Democracy and Sport* (New York: A. S. Barnes, 1941), 27–28. Tunis quoted from Paul Gallico, *Farewell to Sport* (New York: Knopf, 1938), 299.

60. Baker, *Jesse Owens,* 146–62.

61. Baker, *Jesse Owens,* 146–62.

62. For an interesting interpretation of Weismuller's film career, see Paul Gallico's chapter on the swimmer in *The Golden People* (Garden City, NJ: Doubleday, 1965), 219–34.

63. Sandra Kimberly Hall and Greg Ambrose, *Memories of Duke: The Legend Comes to Life* (Honolulu: Bess, 1995); Joseph L. Brennan, *The Life Story of Hawai'i's Duke Kahanamoku* (Honolulu: Ku Pa'a Publishing. 1994). For an excellent interpretation of Kahanamoku's role in American ideas about race, see James Nendel, "A New Hawaiian Monarchy: The Media Representations of Duke Kahanamoku, 1911–1912," forthcoming in the *Journal of Sport History.*

64. Baker, *Jesse Owens,* 146–62.

65. Even before his turn on the screen as Tarzan Johnny Weissmuller shared swimming time with alligators. In 1929 he appeared in Florida aquacades with fellow Olympians Peter de Jardines and Helen Meany along with reptile wrangler "Alligator Al" and his animals. John Kieran, "Sports of the Times," *New York Times,* March 2, 1929, 19.

66. "Jesse Owens Presents Eleven-Room House to Parents, Who Were Once on Plantation," *New York Times,* December 2, 1936, 39; "Jesse Owens Bankrupt," *New York Times,* May 6, 1939; Baker, *Jesse Owens,* 146–62.

67. "Owens in Civilian Defense Job," *New York Times,* January 11, 1942, sec. S, 3; "Jesse Owens Joins OCD Staff," *New York Times,* February 7, 1942, 30; "Owens Is Placed in 1-A," *New York Times,* March 11, 1944, 18; Baker, *Jesse Owens,* 163–81.

68. Baker, *Jesse Owens,* 163–202.

69. "Jesse Owens First among Track Aces," *New York Times,* January 27, 1950, 39.

70. Baker, *Jesse Owens,* 163–81.

71. "Seventy-five Thousand in Berlin Hail Jesse Owens," *New York Times,* August 23, 1951, 37; "End Tour of 14 Nations: Globetrotters, Owens Return after 'Selling America,'" *New York Times,* August 26, 1951, sec. S, 7.

72. "A Famous Athlete's Diplomatic Debut," *Life,* October 31, 1955, 49–50; "Jesse Owens in New Delhi," *New York Times,* October 4, 1955, 46; "Ex-'Fastest Man' a Speedy U.S. Aide," *New York Times,* October 5, 1955, 4.

73. "Olympic Athletes Feted at Dinner," *New York Times,* October 13, 1954, 35; "Olympic 'Gloom' Decried by Owens," *New York Times,* December 2, 1954, 45; Kenneth I. Brown, "Jesse Owens Commended," *New York Times,* November 3, 1955, 30; "Owens Reaches Melbourne," *New York Times,* November 16, 1956, 41; "Brundage Praises Preparations for Olympics," *New York Times,* November 17, 1956, 25; Allison Danzig, "Hero of 1936 on Scene," *New York Times,* November 17, 1956, 25.

74. "Ex-Bar Leader Will Help Nixon," *New York Times,* August 22, 1960, 12; "Jesse Owens Fights Charge of U.S. Income Tax Evasion," *New York Times,* November 24, 1965, 27; "Owens Gets Fine for Tax Evasion," *New York Times,* February 2, 1966, 27; Baker, *Jesse Owens,* 182–202.

75. *Jesse Owens Returns to Berlin;* "Owens Still Sets a Swift Pace," *New York Times,* November 22, 1964, sec. S, 8; Jack Gould, "TV: At Long Last," *New York Times,* March 30, 1968, 67.

76. Rufus E. Clement, "Racial Integration in the Field of Sports," *Journal of Negro Education* 23 (Summer 1954): 222–30.

77. "Segregation and Sport," *New York Times,* November 30, 1958, sec. E, 8. See also "'Race,' and 'Performance,'" *New York Times,* July 22, 1956, sec. E, 8.

78. Owens, with Paul Neimark, *The Jesse Owens Story* (New York: Putnam's, 1970); Owens, with Paul Neimark, *Jesse: A Spiritual Autobiography;* Owens, with Paul Neimark, *Jesse, The Man Who Outran Hitler;* Baker, *Jesse Owens,* 203–20.

79. Steve Cady, "Owens Recalls 1936 Sprinter's Ordeal," *New York Times,* October 17, 1968, 59.

80. Two recent studies provide excellent analysis of the controversies and protests surrounding the Mexico City Games. Amy Bass, *Not the Triumph But the Struggle: The 1968 Olympics and the Making of the Black Athlete* (Minneapolis: University of Minnesota Press, 2002); Douglas Hartmann, *Race, Culture, and the Revolt of the Black Athlete: The 1968 Olympic Protests and Their Aftermath* (Chicago: University of Chicago Press, 2003). Vincent Matthews, with Neil Amdur, *My Race Be Won* (New York: Charterhouse, 1974).

81. "Negroes Divided on Olympics Ban," *New York Times,* November 26, 1967, sec. S, 12; Matthews, *My Race Be Won.*

82. Willie Mays and Rafer Johnson were also featured for a time onto this wall of shame. Arnold Hano, "The Black Rebel Who 'Whitelists' the Olympics," *New York Times Sunday Magazine,* May 12, 1968, 32–40.

83. Jesse Owens, "My Life as a Black Man," *Reader's Digest,* May 1970, 126–31.

84. Jesse Owens, with Paul Neimark, *Blackthink: My Life as Black Man and White Man,* 50–51.

85. Jesse Owens, with Paul Neimark, *I Have Changed.* See also, Jesse Owens, "How I Learned Marching Is Sometimes More Important than Running," *Sepia,* December 1974, 26–29.

86. Baker, *Jesse Owens,* 221–37.

87. For an insightful tour of Lincoln's political philosophies, see J. David Greenstone, *The Lincoln Persuasion: Remaking American Liberalism* (Princeton, NJ: Princeton University Press, 1993).

88. On Washington's complexities, see Kevern Verney, *The Art of the Possible: Booker T. Washington and Black Leadership in the United States, 1881–1925* (New York: Routledge, 2001).

89. Among the better reads are Hank Aaron, with Lonnie Wheeler, *I Had a*

Hammer: The Hank Aaron Story (New York: HarperCollins, 1991); Kareem Abdul-Jabbar and Peter Knobler, *Giant Steps: The Autobiography of Kareem Abdul-Jabbar* (New York: Bantam, 1985); Muhammad Ali, with Richard Durham, *The Greatest: My Own Story* (New York: Random House, 1975); Arthur Ashe, with Frank Deford, *Portrait in Motion* (Boston: Houghton Mifflin, 1975); Jim Brown, with Steve Delsohn, *Out of Bounds* (New York: Kensington, 1989); Althea Gibson, *I Always Wanted to Be Somebody* (New York: Harper, 1958); Jack Johnson, *Jack Johnson Is a Dandy: An Autobiography* (New York: Chelsea House, 1969); Rafer Johnson, with Philip Goldberg, *The Best That I Can Be: An Autobiography* (New York: Random House, 1998); Jackie Joyner-Kersee and Sonja Steptoe, *A Kind of Grace: The Autobiography of the World's Greatest Female Athlete* (New York: Warner Books, 1997); Joe Louis, with Edna and Art Rust Jr., *Joe Louis: My Life* (New York: Harcourt Brace Jovanovich, 1978); Matthews, *My Race Be Won;* Jackie Robinson, with Alfred Duckett, *I Never Had It Made* (New York: Putnam, 1972); Dennis Rodman, with Tim Keown, *Bad as I Wanna Be* (New York: Delacorte, 1996); Wilma Rudolph, *Wilma* (New York: New American Library, 1977); Bill Russell and Taylor Branch, *Second Wind: Memoirs of an Opinionated Man* (New York: Random House, 1974); Chet Walker, with Chris Messenger, *Long Time Coming: A Black Athlete's Coming-of-Age in America* (New York: Grove, 1995).

90. Oriard, "Muhammad Ali: The Hero in the Age of Mass Media." See also David Zang's chapter on Ali in *SportsWars: Athletes in the Age of Aquarius* (Fayetteville: University of Arkansas Press, 2001), 96–118.

8 Joe Louis, Boxing, and American Culture, by Anthony O. Edmonds

1. Donald McRae, *Heroes without a Country: America's Betrayal of Joe Louis and Jesse Owens* (New York: HarperCollins, 2002), 179. Johnson actually challenged Louis to a three-round fight in late 1936. Louis declined. The historian Donald McRae speculates that Johnson's attitude stemmed in part from jealousy of another black fighter who seemed to be deeply respected by most whites and blacks alike. Because Johnson was almost universally despised by whites, including boxing officials and promoters who had drawn a firm color line in the heavyweight division, Louis's people wanted no hint of an association between the two black fighters.

2. David Remnick, *King of the World: Muhammad Ali and the Rise of an American Hero* (New York: Vintage Books, 1999), 228. While Louis had publicly ignored Johnson, Ali struck back at Louis, calling the Brown Bomber "an Uncle Tom" who fought mainly "bums." Ali claimed that if he had fought such fighters "today in Madison Square Garden, they'd boo them out of the ring" (229).

3. The boxing historian Ted Carroll, for example, concludes that although it "was possible" that Clay would have beaten Louis in a bout that lasted the full fifteen rounds, it was difficult to imagine Ali avoiding the Brown Bomber's devastating punches that long. See Monte D. Cox, "How Joe Louis Would Have Beaten Muhammad Ali," http://coxcorner.tripod.com/alilouis.htm, (accessed December 28, 2004).

4. Anthony O. Edmonds, *Joe Louis* (Grand Rapids: Eerdmans, 1973), 7. I rely a good deal on this account of Louis's image, as well as on later works that have

expanded and sometimes differed with what I concluded. Especially important are Chris Mead, *Champion: Joe Louis, Black Hero in White America* (New York: Charles Scribner's Sons, 1985); Jeff Sammons, *Beyond the Ring: The Role of Boxing in American Society* (Urbana: University of Illinois Press, 1988); and McRae, *Heroes without a Country,* cited above. Although some, like the historian David Wiggins, might argue with some justice that a biography should "explore Louis' character, motivation, features and mannerisms, strengths and weaknesses, and conflicts, a brief interpretive essay like this one must focus on the more essential and historically important. See David K. Wiggins, review *Champion: Joe Louis, Black Hero in White America* by Chris Mead, *Journal of Sport History* 13 (Winter 1986): 274.

5. Edmonds, *Joe Louis,* 26.

6. Joe Louis Barrow Jr. and Barbara Munder, *Joe Louis: Fifty Years an American Hero* (New York: McGraw-Hill, 1988), 26.

7. Joe Louis, *My Life Story* (New York: Duell, Sloan & Pearce, 1947), 33.

8. Roxborough's advise appears in Alexander J. Young Jr., "Joe Louis, Symbol" (unpublished Ph.D. dissertation, University of Maryland, 1968), 16.

9. Mead, *Champion,* 50. Sportswriters of the period were excessively fond of alternative nicknames for their subjects. Almost all of the ones applied to Louis referred to his race. Mead collected a veritable plethora of these purple phrases, including "the sepia slugger," "the mahogany maimer," "the sable cyclone," "the saffron sandman," "the chocolate chopper," and, in the lone allusion to a white man, "the tan Tarzan of thump." The most popular Louis sobriquet was "Brown Bomber," followed by "Dark Destroyer" (Mead, *Champion,* 51–52).

10. Edmonds, *Joe Louis,* 52.

11. Edmonds, *Joe Louis,* 35.

12. Young, "Joe Louis, Symbol," 3.

13. Edmonds, *Joe Louis,* 63. According to the historian Jeffrey Sammons, this comment was fairly typical of the reaction of the southern press to Louis's rise. To be sure, there was some out and out hostility to Louis. In 1935, journalist William McKeefe of the *New Orleans Times-Picayune,* for example, "condemned the Brown Bomber's victory over [Primo] Carnera as bad for boxing." In 1936, he also "hailed [Max] Schmeling's victory as a vindication of white supremacy," as it ended "the reign of terror in heavyweight boxing." Similarly, according to the historian Al-Tony Gilmore, some southern members of the U.S. Senate actually broke into cheers on hearing of Schmeling's victory (Al-Tony Gilmore, "The Myth, Legend, and Folklore of Joe Louis: The Impression of Sport on Society," *South Atlantic Quarterly* 82, no. 3 [Summer 1983]: 265). But, according to Sammons, most of the southern press displayed a "reserved reaction," even after Louis defeated Jimmy Braddock for the championship. Louis had managed to behave himself, the fight did not take place on southern soil, and black southerners' reaction to Louis's victory was itself "humble and restrained." In other words, Joe Louis, urged to do so by his backers, showed "a willingness to fulfill white expectations" (Sammons, *Beyond the Ring,* 102, 108, 113, 112). Or perhaps more accurately, Joe Louis did not become their worst nightmare—another Jack Johnson.

14. Edmonds, *Joe Louis,* 64.

15. Edmonds, *Joe Louis,* 66.

16. Edmonds, *Joe Louis,* 66. According to Donald McRae, Louis in fact was "seeing" white women, including actress Lana Turner and skater Sonja Henie, although the liaisons were so discreet that the press and the public were never aware of them. He also had an affair with black singer Lena Horne, which also stayed below the public radar screen (McRae, *Heroes without a Country,* 222).

17. Edward van Every, *Joe Louis: Man and Super Fighter* (New York: Frederick A. Stokes Co., 1936), 74.

18. Edmonds, *Joe Louis,* 93.

19. Edmonds, *Joe Louis,* 94.

20. Edmonds, *Joe Louis,* 94–95.

21. Edmonds, *Joe Louis,* 95, 96.

22. Lil Johnson, "Winner Joe," http://heptune.com/winnerjo.htm (accessed December 30, 2004).

23. David Margolick, "'Joe Louis: An American Hero': A New CD Includes Songs Inspired by and Athlete," http://www. race matters.org/joelouisongs.htm (accessed December 30 2004), 3.

24. Margolick, "'Joe Louis: An American Hero.'"

25. Margolick, "'Joe Louis: An American Hero.'"Bill Gaither sang about the second Schmeling fight: "If I had a million dollars I would have bet every dime on Joe." Had he done so, of course he "would be a rich man this very day/And I wouldn't have to worry no more" (ibid.). This is an especially poignant and ironic fantasy, since only a very few African Americans at that time had such a sum to wager.

26. Edmonds, *Joe Louis,* 98.

27. David Margolick, *Beyond Glory: Joe Louis vs. Max Schmeling, and a World on the Brink* (New York: Alfred A. Knopf, 2005), 126. Margolick makes a strong case that Martin Luther King Jr. wildly exaggerated this incident. King wrote that a black convict was being put to death in the gas chamber, and "As the pellet dropped into the container and gas curled upward, through the microphone came these words: 'Save me, Joe Louis. Save me, Joe Louis. Save me, Joe Louis.'" King concluded that in the young victim's mind, "Joe Louis would care because he was a Negro [and] . . . could do something because he was a fighter" (Martin Luther King, Jr., *Why We Can't Wait* [New York: Signet, 1964], 110–11).

28. Edmonds, *Joe Louis,* 99.

29. Mead, *Champion,* 201.

30. Mead, *Champion,* 196.

31. Edmonds, *Joe Louis,* 78.

32. Edmonds, *Joe Louis,* 79. Interestingly, according to the historian William H. Wiggins, white cartoonists' portrayal of Louis became less stereotypical in the wake of this fight. He was portrayed more as a human male who happened to be black than as the large-lipped, big-eyed, watermelon-eating portrait earlier prominent. See William H. Wiggins Jr., "Boxing's Sambo Twins: Racial Stereotypes in Jack Johnson and Joe Louis Cartoons, 1908–1938," *Journal of Sport History* 15, no. 3 (Winter 1988): 242–54.

33. *Milwaukee Journal,* June 23, 1938, Michigan Historical Collections—Joe Louis Scrapbooks, University of Michigan, Ann Arbor, Michigan (hereinafter cited at MHC-JLS).

34. Edmonds, *Joe Louis,* 82.

35. Unidentified newspaper article, MHC-JLS.

36. May Bordeaux Edmonds, interview by Anthony O. Edmonds, June 1972. Some American journalists tried to downplay the international significance of the fight. Frank Graham of the *New York Sun,* for example, pointed out that Schmeling "was not responsible for the rape of Austria [or] the persecution of the Jews." Rather, he was "simply a German prizefighter . . . entitled to an even break" (Edmonds, *Joe Louis,* 83). But the vast majority of Americans apparently saw the fight as political and racial melodrama.

37. Edmonds, *Joe Louis,* 84.

38. Edmonds, *Joe Louis,* 86.

39. Edmonds, *Joe Louis,* 100.

40. It could be argued that the ease with which an increasing number of black athletes have climbed that mountain over the past seven decades is indeed a double-edged sword. We have to confront a paradox: without Joe Louis, perhaps no Jackie Robinson, no Bobby Bonds, and the list goes on. But by helping to open this small door, through which only a very few can ever squeeze, Louis and his accomplishment may have inadvertently helped close—or make unappealing—other doors that a myriad of young African Americans might have negotiated. Of course it would be terribly reductionist to somehow blame Joe Louis for this conundrum. But maybe it would have been a better world had that young man in the Mississippi gas chamber all those years ago been comfortable screaming: "Help me, Dr. Louis. Help me, Judge Louis." Or even, "Help me, Professor Louis."

41. Dominic J. Capeci Jr. and Martha Wilkerson, "Multifarious Hero: Joe Louis, American Society, and Race Relations during World Crisis, 1935–1945," *Journal of Sport History* 10, no. 3 (Winter 1983): 24.

42. Remnick, *King of the World,* 229.

43. Mead, *Champion,* 293.

44. Remnick, *King of the World,* 229.

9 Alice Coachman: Quiet Champion of the 1940s, by Jennifer H. Lansbury

1. Louise Mead Tricard, *American Women's Track and Field: A History, 1895 through 1980* (Jefferson, NC: MacFarland & Company, 1985), 251–305. Placing Coachman's numbers into context is complicated. Coachman's rival Stella Walsh holds the number-one ranking. Upon Walsh's death in 1980, however, medical examiners performing her autopsy discovered that she had male sexual organs. No sophisticated chromosome test ever concluded that she was male, and the record books remain unchanged. See Michael D. Davis, *Black American Women in Olympic Track and Field* (Jefferson, NC: McFarland & Company, 1992), 158, 161. Moreover, there is the issue of comparing Coachman with the athletes that have competed since. No one has approached her national championship numbers, but athletes today compete more regularly on the international scale than Coachman did. Comparing the two typical meet schedules is difficult. Suffice it to say that the number of national titles that Coachman held places her among the top female track and field athletes of all time.

2. For example, see John A. Kirk, *Redefining the Color Line: Black Activism in Little Rock, Arkansas, 1940–1970* (Gainesville: University Press of Florida, 2002); Greta de Jong, *A Different Day: African American Struggles for Justice in Rural Louisiana, 1900–1970* (Chapel Hill: University of North Carolina Press, 2002); Patrick J. Gilpin and Marybeth Gasman, *Charles S. Johnson: Leadership beyond the Veil in the Age of Jim Crow* (Albany: State University of New York Press, 2003); Carol Anderson, *Eyes off the Prize: The United Nations and the African American Struggle for Human Rights, 1944–1955* (Cambridge: Cambridge University Press, 2003); Peter C. Murray, *Methodists and the Crucible of Race, 1930–1975* (Columbia: University of Missouri Press, 2004); Mark R. Schneider, *"We Return Fighting": The Civil Rights Movement in the Jazz Age* (Boston: Northeastern University Press, 2002); The Documentary Institute of the University of Florida, *Freedom Never Dies: The Legacy of Harry T. Moore* (Berkeley: University of California Extension Center for Media and Independent Learning, 2000), videorecording; and Steven Hahn, *A Nation under Our Feet: Black Political Struggles in the Rural South from Slavery to the Great Migration* (Cambridge: Belknap Press of Harvard University Press, 2003).

3. The Documentary Institute of the University of Florida, *Freedom Never Dies: The Legacy of Harry T. Moore* (Berkeley: University of California Extension Center for Media and Independent Learning, 2000), videorecording.

4. Lawrence P. Scott and William M. Womack Sr., *Double V: The Civil Rights Struggle of the Tuskegee Airmen* (East Lansing: Michigan State University Press, 1994), 1–2.

5. Ed Decker, "Alice Coachman," in *Contemporary Black Biography: Profiles from the International Black Community,* 32 vols., ed. Shirelle Phelps (Detroit: Gale Research, 1992), 18:28–29.

6. Susan Cahn, "'Cinderellas' of Sport: Black Women in Track and Field," in *Coming on Strong: Gender and Sexuality in Twentieth-Century Women's Sports* (New York: Free Press, 1994), 114–15.

7. Cahn, "'Cinderellas' of Sport," 116–17, 121.

8. Decker, *Contemporary Black Biography,* 18:29.

9. Decker, *Contemporary Black Biography,* 18:29.

10. Alice Coachman Davis, interview by author, tape recording, Tuskegee, Al., February 10, 2003.

11. Decker, *Contemporary Black Biography,* 18:29.

12. Coachman interview, February 10, 2003.

13. Coachman interview, February 10, 2003.

14. Coachman interview, February 10, 2003.

15. *Baltimore Afro-American,* July 7, 1945, 18.

16. Trichard, *American Women's Track and Field,* 251–84. The twenty-three were personal titles; as part of the Tigerettes, Coachman also earned eight team titles.

17. Coachman interview, February 10, 2003.

18. Coachman interview, February 10, 2003.

19. Trichard, *American Women's Track and Field,* 243–322. Tuskegee also held the national indoor title for three of these years. Most of the years during this time period the indoor national championships were not held.

20. Coachman interview, February 10, 2003; *Baltimore Afro-American,* July 13, 1940, 19.

21. *Baltimore Afro-American,* July 13, 1940, 19.

22. Jennifer H. Lansbury, "'The Tuskegee Flash' and 'The Slender Harlem Stroker': Black Women Athletes on the Margin," *Journal of Sport History* 28 (Summer 2001): 240.

23. Coachman interview, February 10, 2003.

24. Louis R. Harlan, "Booker T. Washington and the Politics of Accommodation," in *Black Leaders of the Twentieth Century,* ed. John Hope Franklin and August Meier (Urbana: University of Illinois Press, 1982), 3–4; Coachman interview, February 10, 2003.

25. Coachman interview, February 10, 2003.

26. Harlan, "Booker T. Washington and the Politics of Accommodation," in *Black Leaders of the Twentieth Century,* ed. Franklin and Meier, 4–6.

27. Coachman interview, February 10, 2003.

28. *Albany Herald,* July 25, 1948, sec. B, 2.

29. *Baltimore Afro-American,* July 24, 1948, 7.

30. *Baltimore Afro-American,* July 24, 1948, 7.African American sports legend Edwin B. Henderson's column in the edition of the *Afro-American* featuring a picture of the women's team was entitled, "Bronze Athletes Hold Margin in Olympics." Henderson notes, with interest: "Now that the Tuskegee and other colored girls have come through to take all but three or four of the 11 berths on the girls' track team, America will have to depend on us in this area."

31. Lansbury, "Tuskegee Flash," 238. While the white press virtually ignored women's track and field during the 1930s and 1940s, the black press routinely gave the sport one- and two-page spreads in the sports section, complete with photographs. African American sportswriters' efforts to feminize the athletes through articles like the peanut oil story, however, served to diminish the talent and hard work these cinder stars brought to their sport.

32. For example, see *Albany Herald,* July 1, 1945, 12; August 5, 1946, 8; and June 30, 1947, 8.

33. *Albany Herald,* July 25, 1948, sec. B, 2.

34. For example, see *Chicago Tribune,* July 1, 1945, sec. 2, 4; *New York Times,* July 9, 1944, sec. 3, 1; *New York Times,* August 5, 1946, 27.

35. "Spec" Towns of August, Georgia, won Olympic gold for the hurdles in 1936. *Atlanta Constitution,* August 8, 1948, sec. B, 11.

36. The *Albany Herald* has also given Coachman the headline when they printed the United Press release on the Olympic trials two weeks before: "Alice Coachman, Albany Negro Star, Betters Record, Makes Olympic Team." See *Albany Herald,* July 13, 1948, 9.

37. Coachman interview, February 10, 2003.

38. Blankers-Koen dominated the 1948 Games in women's track and field, coming away with four gold medals.

39. Coachman interview, February 10, 2003. Coachman was not the only one embarrassed by the American women's track and field performance. The black press had high hopes before the Olympic Games began believing that the female African American cinder stars would come away with multiple medals, as described in note 29, and they did not hide their disappointment when most of the athletes didn't even qualify for the finals in their event. A *Baltimore Afro-American* sportswriter summarized the

women's track and field competition with a byline entitled, "Didn't Do So Well," observing how the U.S. team was nervous and up against some serious competition but, nonetheless, gained some valuable experience. *Baltimore Afro-American,* August 14, 1948, 8. Likewise, the Chicago Defender ran an article during their 1948 Olympic coverage entitled, "Negroes in 1936 Olympics Had Much Better Record." *Chicago Defender,* August 21, 1948, 11.

40. *Chicago Tribune,* August 8, 1948, 4.

41. Coachman interview, February 10, 2003.

42. *Albany Herald,* September 2, 1948, 1.

43. Front page articles of Coachman's win and ensuing plans to honor her appeared in the *Albany Herald* on the following dates: August 8, 1948; August 10, 1948; August 26, 1948;August 30, 1948; September 1, 1948; and September 2, 1948.

44. Scott and Womack, *Double V,* 1–2, 20.

45. For a good overview of the impact of the cold war on the African American civil rights movement, see Mary L. Dudziak, *Cold War, Civil Rights: Race and the Image of American Democracy* (Princeton, NJ: Princeton University Press, 2000), especially the introduction, 3–17.

46. *Chicago Tribune,* August 8, 1948, 4.

47. Coachman was a natural to endorse the soft drink. Even today, she remembers how a nice, cold Coca-Cola was one of the few things she wanted after winning the gold medal in London. Coachman interview, February 10, 2003.

48. Helen Nash, "Fw: Alice Coachman ads for Coca-Cola," 23 September 2004, personal email (September 24, 2004).

49. Coachman interview, February 10, 2003.

50. While Coachman would like for her Olympic accomplishment to be remembered, to this day she downplays her athletic ability in favor of several of her teammates at Tuskegee. In particular, she still considers Lula Hymes, one of the senior girls Coachman looked up to when she first joined the famous track team, a better sprinter. During my interview with her, Coachman graciously wanted to speak about the other talented women who helped make Tuskegee a track and field powerhouse during those years. Yet the timing was in Coachman's favor, and she was the one who found herself on the world stage in 1948.

10 Jackie Robinson: Racial Pioneer and Athlete Extraordinaire in an Era of Change, by Michael E. Lomax

1. Arnold Rampersad, *Jackie Robinson: A Biography* (New York: Alfred A. Knopf, 1997), 43.

2. Jules Tygiel, *Baseball's Great Experiment: Jackie Robinson and His Legacy* (New York: Oxford University Press, 1983), 60.

3. Rampersad, *Jackie,* 134–35.

4. Rampersad, *Jackie,* 131.

5. Rampersad, *Jackie,* 135.

6. Jackie Robinson, with Alfred Duckett, *I Never Had It Made* (Hopewell, NJ: Ecco Press, 1995), 11.

7. Rampersad, *Jackie,* 168.

8. Rampersad, *Jackie,* 191.

9. Tygiel, *Baseball's Great Experiment,* 63.

10. Tygiel, *Baseball's Great Experiment,* 63–64.

11. Tygiel, *Baseball's Great Experiment,* 121. Rampersad, *Jackie,* 265.

12. Rampersad, *Jackie,* 271.

13. Rampersad, *Jackie,* 288–89.

14. Mann's comment in David Falkner, *Great Time Coming: The Life of Jackie Robinson, from Baseball to Birmingham* (New York: Simon and Schuster, 1995), 163.

15. Harold Parrott, *The Lords of Baseball* (New York: Praeger, 1976), 194.

16. Robinson, with Alfred Duckett, *I Never Had It Made,* 59.

17. Tygiel, *Baseball's Great Experiment,* 193, 195.

18. Martin Duberman, *Paul Robeson* (New York: Alfred A. Knopf, 1988), 360.

19. Robinson, with Alfred Duckett, *I Never Had It Made.*

20. Rampersad, *Jackie Robinson.* Additional scholarly accounts in the 1990s include Steven K. Wisensale, "The Political Wars of Jackie Robinson," *Nine: Journal of Baseball History and Social Perspectives* 1 (1993): 18–28; Anthony R. Pratkanis and Marlene Turner, "The Year Cool Papa Bell Lost the Batting Title: Mr. Branch Rickey and Mr. Jackie Robinson's Plea for Affirmative Action," *Nine: Journal of Baseball History and Social Perspectives* 2 (1994): 260–76; "Nine Principles of Successful Affirmative Action: Mr. Branch Rickey, Mr. Jackie Robinson, and the Integration of Baseball," *Nine: Journal of Baseball History and Social Perspectives* 2 (Fall 1994): 36–65; John Vernon, "Beyond the Box Score: Jackie Robinson, Civil Rights Crusader," *Negro History Bulletin* 58 (October–December 1995): 15–22; Michael E. Lomax, "'I Never Had It Made' Revisited: The Political, Economic, and Social Ideology of Jackie Robinson," *Afro-Americans in New York Life and History* 23 (January 1999): 39–60; Jules Tygiel, *The Jackie Robinson Reader: Perspective on an American Hero* (New York: Plume, 1997); *Extra Bases: Reflections on Jackie Robinson, Race, and Baseball History* (Lincoln: University of Nebraska Press, 2002); "Jackie Robinson: 'A Lone Negro' in Major League Baseball," in *Sport and the Color Line: Black Athletes and Race Relations in Twentieth-Century America,* ed. Patrick B. Miller and David K. Wiggins (New York: Routledge, 2004), 167–90; Joseph Dorinson, "Paul Robeson and Jackie Robinson: Athletes and Activists at Armageddon," *Pennsylvania History* 66 (Winter 1999): 17–26; Michael Berenbaum, "Jackie and Campy: Ethnicity in the 1950s," *Jewish Journal* (April 18–24, 1997): 29, 31, 47; Arthur Diamond, *The Importance of Jackie Robinson* (San Diego: Lucent Books, 1992); Joseph Dorinson and Joram Warmund, eds., *Jackie Robinson: Race, Sports and the American Dream* (Armonk, NY: M. E. Sharpe, 1998). Richard Ian Kimball analyzes the reception Robinson received from the local press in Indianapolis in "Beyond the 'Great Experiment': Integrated Baseball Comes to Indianapolis," *Journal of Sport History* 26 (Spring 1999): 142–62. Chris Lamb, *Blackout: The Untold Story of Jackie Robinson's First Spring Training* (Lincoln: University of Nebraska Press, 2004); "'I Never Want to Take Another Trip Like This One': Jackie Robinson's Journey to Integrate Baseball," *Journal of Sport History* 24 (Summer 1997): 177–91; Chris Lamb and Glen Bleske, "Democracy on the Field: The Black Press Takes on White Baseball,"

Journalism History 24 (Summer 1998): 51–59. Stephen H. Norwood and Harold Brackman, "Going to Bat for Jackie Robinson: The Jewish Role in Breaking Baseball's Color Line," *Journal of Sport History* 26 (Spring 1999): 115–41. Henry D. Fetter, "The Party Line and the Color Line: The American Communist Party, the *Daily Worker,* and Jackie Robinson," *Journal of Sport History* 28 (Fall 2001): 375–402.

21. Manning Marable, *Race, Reform, and Rebellion: The Second Reconstruction in Black America, 1945–1982* (Jackson: University Press of Mississippi, 1984), 15–16.

22. August Meier and John Bracey, "The NAACP as a Reform Movement, 1909–1965," *Journal of Southern History* 59 (February 1993): 26–27.

23. Robinson, with Alfred Duckett, *I Never Had It Made,* 166–67.

24. Malcolm X quote in William Van DeBurg, *New Day in Babylon: The Black Power Movement and American Culture, 1965–1975* (Chicago: University of Chicago Press, 1992), 5, 22.

11 "Jackie Robinson without the Charm": The Challenges of Being Althea Gibson, by Mary Jo Festle

1. Althea Gibson, and edited by Edward E. Fitzgerald, *I Always Wanted to Be Somebody* (New York: Harper and Brothers, 1958), 13.

2. Josh Greenfeld, "Althea against the World," in *Sport, Sport, Sport: True Stories of Great Athletes and Great Human Beings,* ed. John Lowell Pratt (New York: Franklin Watts, 1960), 64.

3. Paddle tennis was a street version of tennis different from lawn tennis in its wooden paddle, ball, and rules.

4. Gibson, *I Always Wanted to Be Somebody,* 25, 1, 15, 6.

5. Gibson, *I Always Wanted to Be Somebody,* 11–12.

6. Gibson, *I Always Wanted to Be Somebody,* 8, 20–21.

7. Gibson, *I Always Wanted to Be Somebody,* 20–21, 11. Her brother confirmed the violence in Frances Clayton Gray and Yanick Rice Lamb, *Born to Win: The Authorized Biography of Althea Gibson* (Hoboken, NJ: Wiley, 2004), 18–19.

8. Gibson, *I Always Wanted to Be Somebody,* 44; Eaton, *Every Man Should Try* (Wilmington, NC: Bonaparte Press, 1984), 30–34; "Althea's Odyssey," *Life,* July 2, 1956, 88.

9. Greenfeld, "Althea against the World," 64.

10. Buxton quoted in Gibson, *I Always Wanted to Be Somebody,* 160; "Althea's Greatest, Says Her Coach," *Birmingham Post-Herald,* June 7, 1956; Edna Robinson quoted in "That Gibson Girl," *Time,* August 26, 1957, 45.

11. Althea Gibson with Richard Curtis, *So Much to Live For* (New York: Putnam's Sons, 1968), 18, 65; Gibson, *I Always Wanted to Be Somebody,* 160; Billie Jean King with Cynthia Starr, *We Have Come a Long Way,* (New York: McGraw-Hill), 95.

12. Mary Jo Festle, *Playing Nice: Politics and Apologies in Women's Sports* (New York: Columbia University Press, 1996), 43.

13. Festle, *Playing Nice,* 15, 43–50.

14. Susan Cahn, "'Cinderellas' of Sport—Black Women in Track and Field," in

Sport and the Color Line; Black Athletes and Race Relations in Twentieth-Century America, ed. Patrick B. Miller and David K. Wiggins (New York: Routledge, 2004), 215–26.

15. Cahn, "'Cinderellas' of Sport," 212; Patricia Vertinsky and Gwendolyn Captain, "More Myth than History: American Culture and Representations of the Black Female Athletic Ability," *Journal of Sport History* 25, no. 3 (Fall 1998): 532–61, point out that acceptance of the strong powerful black woman paradoxically also means accepting such negative stereotypes as emasculating matriarch and erotic sex object. They see great danger in the notion that sports should come "naturally" to black women.

16. Rita Liberti, "We Were Ladies, We Just Played Like Boys," in *Sport and the Color Line,* ed. Miller and Wiggins, 91.

17. Cindy Himes Gissendanner, "African-American Women and Competitive Sport, 1920–1940," in *Women, Sport, and Culture,* ed. Susan Birrell and Cheryl L. Cole (Champaign, IL: Human Kinetics, 1994), 89.

18. Edwin B. Henderson, "Negro Women in Sports," *Negro History Bulletin* (December 1951): 55.

19. Cahn, "'Cinderellas' of Sport," 225; "Mrs. Bethune Will Crown Tennis Queen," *Chicago Defender,* August 22, 1953, 24.

20. Gibson, *I Always Wanted to Be Somebody,* 48–49.

21. "The Power Game," *Time,* July 15, 1957, 61; Festle, *Playing Nice,* 53–71.

22. Vertinsky and Captain, "More Myth than History," 540.

23. Quoted in Caryl Phillips, ed., *The Right Set: A Tennis Anthology* (New York: Vintage Books, 1999), 96.

24. Bruce Schoenfeld, *The Match: Althea Gibson and Angela Buxton* (New York: Amistad, 2004), 57.

25. "That Gibson Girl," *Time,* August 26, 1957, 44.

26. Instead of graciously complimenting an opponent who defeated her, Gibson might say nothing or boast that she would beat her next time. Schoenfeld, *The Match,* 69.

27. Gibson, *I Always Wanted to Be Somebody,* 29.

28. Gissendanner, "African-American Women and Competitive Sport," 87.

29. "Fastest Women in the World," *Ebony,* June 1955, 22–32.

30. "Althea Has Finally Arrived," *Ebony,* August 1956, 35–38. White papers noted the class significance as well. The *New York Post* said a "Harlem urchin discovered by Negroes, nurtured by Negroes, trained by Negroes, educated by Negroes" became "the best in the world in 'the game for ladies and gentlemen.'" Quoted in Jennifer H. Lansbury, "'The Tuskegee Flash' and 'the Slender Harlem Stroker': Black Women Athletes on the Margin," *Journal of Sport History* 28, no. 2 (Summer 2001): 247.

31. Gibson, *I Always Wanted to Be Somebody,* 2.

32. Hubert A. Eaton, *Every Man Should Try* (Wilmington, NC: Bonaparte Press, 1984), 27; "Whirlwind" Johnson was a former college football player living in Lynchburg, Virginia.

33. "That Gibson Girl," *Time,* August 26, 1957, 56; Eaton, *Every Man Should Try,* 31–32, 36.

34. Gibson, *I Always Wanted to Be Somebody,* 50.

35. Quoted in Schoenfeld, *The Match,* 61–62.

36. Gibson, *I Always Wanted to Be Somebody,* 61.

37. "Althea's Big Climb," *New York Amsterdam News,* September 2, 1950.

38. Alvin Moses, "Review of 1950 Sports Year," *Oklahoma Black Dispatch,* December 30, 1950.

39. James Edmond Boyack,"Handles Herself Well in Women's Nat'l," *Pittsburgh Courier,* September 9, 1950; Wendell Smith's Sports Beat, *Pittsburgh Courier,* July 29, 1950; "President Gore, Coach Gaither Welcome Althea Gibson on Her Return," *Nashville Globe,* October 13, 1950; "Althea Gibson Looks Forward to Bid to Compete in Nationals This Summer," *Chicago Defender,* June 17, 1950.

40. Gibson, *I Always Wanted to Be Somebody,* 80–87.

41. "The Power Game," *Time,* July 15, 1956, 61.

42. Lansbury, "Tuskegee Flash," 246.

43. Quoted in Gibson, *I Always Wanted to Be Somebody,* 116; Schoenfeld has a good discussion of her personality and spectator response to it; *The Match,* 23.

44. Gibson, *I Always Wanted to Be Somebody,* 159.

45. Russ Cowans, "Sports Writers Sour on Althea, But She's Still Champ," *Chicago Defender,* July 27, 1957, 1; Russ Cowans, "Russ' Corner; She Should Be Told," *Chicago Defender,* July 27, 1957, 17; Gray and Lamb, *Born to Win,* 107–8.

46. "Althea Not As Talkative As She Was on 1951 Net Tour," *Chicago Defender,* July 7, 1956; and "Miss Gibson Bitter in Cup Score," *Baltimore Afro-American,* August 17, 1957.

47. Marion E. Jackson, "Sports of the World," *Atlanta World,* April 27, 1955. Jackson was upset with Major League Baseball players who no longer had time for the black press and seemed scornful of their roots.

48. Gibson, *I Always Wanted to Be Somebody,* 158; Jennifer H. Lansbury has accumulated evidence and agrees with Gibson's assessment. Lansbury, "'The Tuskegee Flash' and 'the Slender Harlem Stroker.'"

49. Gibson, *I Always Wanted to Be Somebody,* 105.

50. Kennett Love, "Althea Is at Home Abroad on Tennis Court," *New York Times,* June 24, 1956; Gibson, *I Always Wanted to Be Somebody,* 158.

51. Robert M. Ratcliffe, "Behind the Headlines: Althea and the Press," *Pittsburgh Courier,* August 31, 1957, 5.

52. "That Gibson Girl," *Time,* August 26, 1957, 48.

53. "That Gibson Girl," 46; see also Gray and Lamb, *Born to Win,* 128–30.

54. Gibson, *I Always Wanted to Be Somebody,* 61–62; "That Gibson Girl," 46.

55. Gibson, *I Always Wanted to Be Somebody,* 118; Sam Lacy, "From A to Z: Althea," *Baltimore Afro-American,* September 14, 1957, 13; "Miss Gibson Bitter in Cup Score," *Baltimore Afro-American,* August 17, 1957, 13.

56. See, for example, "Fay Says," *Chicago Defender,* July 14, 1956, 13; H. B. Webber, "Miss Gibson Impressive in N.J. Exhibition Match; Disputes 'High-Hat' Charge," *Norfolk Journal and Guide,* August 17, 1957; Ratcliffe, "Behind the Headlines: Althea and the Press;" and "Althea Gibson Not As Talkative Now As She Was on 1951 Net Tour," *Chicago Defender,* July 7, 1956.

57. Gibson, *So Much to Live For,* 18–19.

58. Gibson, *So Much to Live For,* 92.

59. Schoenfeld, *The Match,* 265; Gibson, *So Much to Live For,* 134–35.

60. This interpretation is based on language from Gibson's two autobiographies, especially *So Much to Live For,* 91–94, 156, and *I Always Wanted to Be Somebody,* 25, 176.

61. Gibson, *I Always Wanted to Be Somebody,* 79; Schoenfeld provides unique information about Gibson's personal life in *The Match,* 266–67, 282. He said some of Gibson's friends thought he married her in order to gain citizenship. Schoenfeld's book appears to be well researched, but has no specific references or endnotes, so it's difficult to check his sources. He also says that there were rumors about Gibson's sexual orientation. Gray and Lamb reported that Gibson's friends thought Lewellyn was mainly out to take advantage of Gibson's fame and money; *Born to Win,* 169–70.

62. As Lansbury points out, one measure of a person's fame is books about her life. Late in the twentieth century the main books about Gibson were by Gibson herself, plus a couple of juvenile books. With regard to Gibson's illness, Schoenfeld quotes a former doctor of hers as saying her stroke was the result of venereal disease lying dormant for many years; *The Match,* 282. Her reclusive lifestyle was observed in Howie Evans, "Althea Gibson Was a Role Model for the Ages," *New York Amsterdam News,* October 2, 2003, Howard Chua-Eoan and Charlotte Faltermayer, "The Woman Who Was Somebody," *Time Australia* 36, September 8, 1997, 80.

63. Schoenfeld, *The Match,* 1–7, 285; Gray and Lamb, *Born to Win,* 204–6.

64. Bud Collins, *Total Tennis: The Ultimate Tennis Encyclopedia* (Toronto: Sport Media Publishing, Inc., 2003), 671–72.

12 Wilma Rudolph: The Making of an Olympic Icon, by Wayne Wilson

1. Most sources state that Rudolph's left leg was afflicted; others say it was the right leg. Rudolph's autobiography gives two versions, stating first that the problem was with the left leg. Later references, though, refer to the right leg. There are, in fact, a number of discrepancies among sources regarding details of Rudolph's life. The disputed points include the number of children in her family, her birth order, her birthplace, the age at which she began wearing a brace, the age at which she abandoned walking aids, the year she first attended Ed Temple's Tennessee State University sprinter camps and details of her competitive career. Unless persuaded by primary or compelling secondary evidence to the contrary, I have relied on the autobiography as the authoritative source. That said, it should be noted that the autobiography does contain errors.

2. Wilma Rudolph, with Martin Ralbovsky, *Wilma: The Story of Wilma Rudolph* (New York: New American Library, 1977), 8, 11.

3. The term "state tournament" is something of a misnomer. Interscholastic competition in Tennessee was racially segregated when Rudolph was in high school. Therefore, in so-called state tournaments or state championships, black schools played only other black schools, and white schools competed only against white schools.

4. The university's official name until 1968 was Tennessee Agricultural & Industrial State University. The name Tennessee State University, however, was used well before that time. At the 1956 Olympic trials, both Rudolph and teammate Mae Faggs wore uniforms that read, "Tenn. State University."

5. Rudolph, *Wilma,* 79.

6. Vivian Bernice Lee Adkins, "The Development of Negro Female Olympic Talent" (Doctor of Physical Education diss., Indiana University, 1967), 157.

7. Adkins, "The Development of Negro Female Olympic Talent," 182.

8. Barbara Heilman, "Wilma and Ed," *Sports Illustrated,* November 14, 1960, 48; Robert L. Teague, "Everyone Has Wilma Rudolph on the Run," *New York Times,* February 4, 1961, 11.

9. Robert F. Kennedy, "A Bold Proposal for American Sport," *Sports Illustrated,* July 27, 1964, 13.

10. As Amy Bass has written in *Not the Triumph but the Struggle: The 1968 Olympics and the Making of the Black Athlete* (Minneapolis: University of Minnesota, 2002), 404, the nickname referring to an animal, however well intended, reinforced the "inference that black athletic ability is as natural as that of the delicate African deer." Rudolph's attitude regarding the Gazelle appellation was ambiguous, or perhaps it changed over time. In *Wilma,* 150, she wrote that she had told President Kennedy that she did not like the nickname. Many years later, though, she told an interviewer, "They called me the 'Black Gazelle' in Rome, and I thought it was wonderful. I didn't find it offensive at all." See Lyn Votava, "Ahead of Their Time," *Runner's World,* June 1993, 51.

11. See Tex Maule, "Citius! Altius! Fortius!" *Sports Illustrated,* September 12, 1960, 17–24; Tex Maule, "The Most Exciting Five Minutes," *Sports Illustrated,* September 19, 1960, 20–27; Heilman, "Wilma and Ed," 47–58.

12. "The Top Ten Stories," *Baltimore Afro-American,* December 27, 1960, http://www.paperofrecord.com.

13. Tex Maule, "Citius! Altius! Fortius!" 22; Maule, "The Most Exciting Five Minutes," 24–25; Heilman, "Wilma and Ed," 48–49; Jeanne Hoffman, "Speedy Wilma Rudolph Not Interested in Racing Men," *Los Angeles Times,* January 19, 1961, C1; Lula Jones Garrett, "Baltimoreans Put Out Welcome Mat for Olympic Star Wilma Rudolph," *Baltimore Afro-American,* January 20, 1962, 10, http://www.paperofrecord.com; Teague, "Everyone Has Wilma Rudolph on the Run," 10.

14. "Fifty Years of Olympic Broadcasting," *Marketing Matters,* Summer 1994, 7. CBS achieved same-day coverage by flying videotape from Rome to New York. From the airport in New York, technicians relayed the footage to CBS master control at Grand Central Station for national broadcast. See Joseph Michalak, "CBS Plans Same-Day Telecasts of Rome Olympic Games," *New York Times,* August 21, 1960, X11.

15. Rudolph, *Wilma,* 136.

16. Some sources claim that Rudolph refused to participate in the Clarksville ceremonies unless they were integrated. Her autobiography does not mention such an ultimatum.

17. Eldridge was Rudolph's second husband. She married a fellow Tennessee State athlete named William Ward, on October 14, 1961. They separated after seven months. Rudolph filed for divorce in early 1963.

18. Rudolph, *Wilma,* 158.

19. Rudolph, *Wilma,* 162.

20. Rudolph, *Wilma,* 162, 165. Between the King assassination and Rudolph's hiring at UCLA, a leftist Italian newspaper reported that Rudolph was indigent, had relinquished control of her children, and had pawned her Olympic medals. The con-

servative daily, *Il Tempo,* responded by flying her to Rome for a press conference. Rudolph denied selling her medals. She stated that she was temporarily jobless, but only "because I won't take a job for any salary lower than what I think I'm worth." Asked her opinion on a variety of racial issues, Rudolph stated, "I can't think of one Negro who hasn't had trouble because of skin color." She voiced support for "all black leaders" in the United States and described herself as "not nonviolent." She also expressed approval of the clench-fist salute by Tommie Smith and John Carlos at the 1968 Mexico City Olympic Games. See Alfred Friendly Jr., "Wilma Rudolph Denies Selling Medals," *New York Times,* March 26, 1969, 54.

21. Friendly Jr., "Wilma Rudolph Denies Selling Medals," 165–68.

22. Never was the nostalgia for the early Sixties more evident than during NBC's Olympic coverage of August 4, 1996 (Day 17, Show 48). On the final Sunday of the Atlanta Games, the network broadcast, without commercial interruption, a special forty-six-minute film titled "The Wonders of Rome." The Emmy-winning film focused on five athletes, Wilma Rudolph, Cassius Clay, Rafer Johnson, Oscar Robertson, and Jerry West, who starred in the 1960 Games. These athletes, according to NBC, were "kids in a feel-good time," taking part in the "last Games of innocence." Unsullied by steroids and unaffected by a desire for "instant riches," Rudolph and her teammates were the "purest that an athlete can be." They considered it an "honor and a privilege" to compete in the Rome Games, an environment NBC called a "sporting paradise."

23. William Rhoden, "The End of a Winding Road," *New York Times,* November 19, 1994, 31; Athelia Knight, "Olympic Track Star Wilma Rudolph Dies," *Washington Post,* November 13, 1994, D5.

13 Bill Russell: Pioneer and Champion of the 60s, by Maureen M. Smith

1. Bill Russell with Alan Hilburg and David Falkner, *Russell Rules:11 Lessons on Leadership from the Twentieth-Century's Greatest Winner* (New York: New American Library, 2001), 4–5.

2. David K. Wiggins and Patrick B. Miller, *The Unlevel Playing Field: A Documentary History of the African American Experience in Sport* (Urbana: University of Illinois Press, 2003), 3.

3. Thomas Hauser, *Muhammad Ali: His Life and Times* (New York: Simon and Schuster, 1991), 282.

4. Russell's parents move west to work in the Oakland shipyards was part of a larger migration of African Americans heading to work in California. See Marilynn S. Johnson, *The Second Gold Rush: Oakland and the East Bay in World War II* (Berkeley and Los Angeles: University of California Press, 1993). Russell has authored two autobiographies; the first, *Go Up for Glory,* as told to William McSweeny in 1966, and the second, *Second Wind: Memoirs of an Opinionated Man,* with Taylor Branch in 1979.

5. Bill Russell and Taylor Branch, *Second Wind: The Memoirs of an Opinionated Man* (New York: Random House, 1979), 24.

6. Russell and Branch, *Second Wind,* 24–27.

7. Bill Russell as told to William McSweeny, *Go Up for Glory* (New York: Coward-McCann, 1966), 13.

8. Russell and Branch, *Second Wind,* 30.

9. He writes one sentence about playing basketball when he first moved to Oakland. See Russell, *Go Up for Glory,* 17.

10. Russell and Branch, *Second Wind,* 36–38.

11. Russell, *Go Up for Glory,* 24.

12. McClymonds High School in Oakland has produced a number of professional athletes. One of Russell's basketball teammates was Frank Robinson, who later starred in Major League Baseball and would become the first African American manager in the Major Leagues. Vada Pinson was also a baseball player at McClymonds High School while Russell was at the school. Major leaguer and reserve clause challenger Curt Flood graduated from McClymonds High. For more on athletics at McClymonds High School, see "High School of Champions: McClymonds of Oakland, California," *Ebony,* April 18, 1965, 25–28.

13. Russell and Branch, *Second Wind,* 61.

14. Russell and Branch, *Second Wind,* 74.

15. Russell and Branch, *Second Wind,* 78.

16. Russell high jumped 6 feet 9 1/4 inches and ran the 440 in 49.5 for the USF track team. Of his track experience, Russell said, "I didn't think I was very good, but I found I could see all the great athletes from a good seat. It was sheer enjoyment, even more as a spectator than as a participant." See Gilbert Rogin, "'We're Grown Men Playing a Child's Game,'" *Sports Illustrated,* November 18, 1963, 88.

17. Jeff Faraudo, "Russell's Defense Turned USF into an NCAA Power in 1950s," *Oakland Tribune* (March 15, 2004), online edition.

18. Arthur Ashe, *A Hard Road to Glory: A History of the African-American Athlete since 1946* (New York: Warner Books, 1988), 68. Also see Russell's account of the rule change in *Go Up for Glory,* 44.

19. "Not Muscle, Just Russell," *Time,* April 2, 1956, 56.

20. *Ebony,* April 1956, 52, as cited in Ashe, *A Hard Road to Glory: A History of the African-American Athlete since 1946*), 53. Russell dismisses this story in *Go Up for Glory,* 47–48. Russell met Eisenhower at a physical fitness luncheon held in Washington, DC. He was the college basketball representative. Meeting the president was a "tremendous thrill" for Russell. See Bill Russell as told to Al Hirshberg, "I Was a 6' 9" Babe in the Woods," *Saturday Evening Post,* January 18, 1958, 25.

21. Russell, *Go Up for Glory,* 55.

22. Thomas Hauser, *Muhammad Ali,* 450.

23. For more on the integration of the NBA, see Ron Thomas, *They Cleared the Lane: The NBA's Black Pioneers* (Lincoln: University of Nebraska Press, 2002).

24. Russell, *Go Up for Glory,* 70–71.

25. Jeremiah Tax, "The Man Who Must Be Different," *Sports Illustrated,* February 3, 1958, 31.

26. See Bill Russell as told to Al Hirshberg, "I Was a 6' 9" Babe in the Woods," *Saturday Evening Post,* January 18, 1958; Jeremiah Tax, "The Man Who Must Be Different," *Sports Illustrated,* February 3, 1958; Gilbert Rogin, "We're Grown Men Playing a Child's Game,'" *Sports Illustrated,* November 18, 1963; Bill Russell with Tex Maule, "'I am not worried about Ali,'" *Sports Illustrated,* June 19, 1967, 18–21.

27. For more on Russell's experiences living and playing in Boston, see Howard Bryant, *Shut Out: A Story of Race and Baseball in Boston* (New York: Routledge, 2002).

28. Arthur Ashe categorizes the time period of the 1950s to the 1959–60 season as the "Breaking In" years, and 1960 to 1973 as the "Wilt Chamberlain and Bill Russell reign"; see Ashe, *A Hard Road to Glory,* 65.

29. Russell, *Go Up for Glory,* 165. Russell's rookie season statistics: 48 games, 706 points, 19.6 rebounds per game, 1.8 assists per game, and 14.7 points per game. Heinsohn's rookie seasons statistics: 72 games, 1,163 points, 9.8 rebounds per game, 1.6 assists per game, and 16.2 points per game. See Alex Sachare (ed.), *The Official NBA Basketball Encyclopedia,* 2nd ed. (New York: NBA Properties, 1989).

30. Russell and Branch, *Second Wind,* 187.

31. Tax, "The Man Who Must Be Different," 29.

32. Russell, *Go Up for Glory,* 113–14.

33. Russell, *Go Up for Glory,* 116.

34. Russell, *Go Up for Glory,* 117–19.

35. Edward Linn, "I Owe the Public Nothing," *Saturday Evening Post,* January 18, 1964, 62.

36. Russell, *Go Up for Glory,* 75.

37. Russell, *Go Up for Glory,* 93.

38. Linn, "I Owe the Public Nothing," 60.

39. Russell and Branch, *Second Wind,* 88.

40. For more on the use of African American athletes on State Department tours, see Damion Thomas, "The 'Good Negroes': African-American Athletes and the Cultural Cold War, 1945–1968" (Unpublished diss., University of California, Los Angeles, 2002). The State Department also produced a number of films that served similar purposes. Athletes highlighted in the films included Rafer Johnson, Wilma Rudolph, and Althea Gibson. For more on the films, see Melinda M. Schwenk, "'Negro Stars' and the USIA's Portrait of Democracy," *Race, Gender & Class* 8 (2001).

41. Gilbert Rogin, "'We're Grown Men Playing a Child's Game,'" *Sports Illustrated,* November 18, 1963, 82.

42. Russell, *Go Up for Glory,* 194–96.

43. For more on Wilt Chamberlain, see Wilt Chamberlain, *Who's Running the Asylum? Inside the Insane World of Sports Today* (San Diego: International Promotions/ Promotion Publishing, 1997); Robert A. Cherry, *Wilt: Larger Than Life* (Chicago: Triumph Books, 2004); Wayne Lynch, *Season of the 76ers: Wilt Chamberlain and the 1967 NBA Champion 76ers* (New York: Thomas Dunne Books, 2002).

44. Russell and Branch, *Second Wind: The Memoirs of an Opinionated Man,* 158.

45. Russell, *Go Up for Glory,* 137.

46. Alex Sachare (ed.), *The Official NBA Basketball Encyclopedia.*

47. Tax, "The Man Who Must Be Different," 29.

48. Rogin, "'We're Grown Men Playing a Child's Game,'" 75.

49. Rogin, "'We're Grown Men Playing a Child's Game,'" 75. For more on Red Auerbach, see Red Auerbach and John Feinstein, Let Me Tell You a Story: A Lifetime in the Game (New York: Little, Brown, 2004); Arnold Auerbach, Red Auerbach: Winning the Hard Way (New York: Little, Brown, 1966); Arnold Auerbach, Red Auerbach: An Autobiography (New York: Putnam, 1977); and Red Auerbach, On and Off the Court (New York: Bantam, 1986).

50. "All the Credentials," *Time,* April 29, 1965, 104–5. In his first autobiography, *Go Up for Glory,* 215, Russell offered another explanation for naming his daughter Kenyatta. "I named her Kenyatta because it means 'Burning Spear' and because it will always remind her of the beauty of Africa and the beauty of the noble race from which she descended." Also see "Ol' Massa Russell," *Nation,* March 1, 1965, 211.

51. Russell's coaching record with each team.

52. Russell and Branch, *Second Wind,* 188.

53. Rogin, "'We're Grown Men Playing a Child's Game,'" 77.

54. Russell, *Go Up for Glory,* 153.

55. Russell and Branch, *Second Wind,* 200–201.

56. Linn, "I Owe the Public Nothing," 60.

57. Harry Edwards, *The Revolt of the Black Athlete* (New York: Free Press, 1969), 39–40.

58. Rogin, "'We're Grown Men Playing a Child's Game,'" 74.

59. Rogin, "'We're Grown Men Playing a Child's Game,'" 85.

60. Rogin, "'We're Grown Men Playing a Child's Game,'" 80.

61. Rogin, "'We're Grown Men Playing a Child's Game,'" 82.

62. Russell and Branch, *Second Wind,* 182.

63. Linn, "I Owe the Public Nothing," 61.

64. Russell, *Go Up for Glory,* 210, states it was July 1963; Russell and Branch, *Second Wind,* 184, states it was the summer of 1964.

65. Russell, *Go Up for Glory,* 171.

66. Bill Russell with Tex Maule, "'I am not worried about Ali,'" *Sports Illustrated,* June 19, 1967, 18–21.

67. Russell and Branch, *Second Wind,* 102.

68. Russell and Branch, *Second Wind,* 175.

69. Russell, *Second Wind,* 210–14.

70. Naismith Hall of Fame web site; http://www.hoophall.com.

71. When ESPN named Russell as the #18 Greatest Athlete of the 20th Century, he was the fourth basketball player listed—after Michael Jordan (#1), Wilt Chamberlain (#13), and Magic Johnson (#17).

14 Jim Brown: Superlative Athlete, Screen Star, Social Activist, by J. Thomas Jable

1. Jimmy Brown with Myron Cope, *Off My Chest* (Garden City, NY: Doubleday and Company, 1964), 97–112.

2. Brown, *Off My Chest,* 113–24.

3. Brown, *Off My Chest,* 123–40.

4. Brown, *Off My Chest,* vii.

5. *The Plain Dealer* (Cleveland), [online], September 5, 2004. Available: LexisNexis, September 15, 2004; Spike Lee, *Jim Brown All-American,* DVD video (Home Box Office, 2004).

6. Jim Brown, "Jim Brown on Life and Love in Hollywood," *Ebony,* December 1989, 62–66.

7. Brown, "Life and Love in Hollywood."

8. Brown, "Life and Love in Hollywood."

9. Lee, *Jim Brown All-American.*

10. Brown, "Life and Love in Hollywood," 62–66.

11. Brown, "Life and Love in Hollywood."

12. Brown, "Life and Love in Hollywood"; *New York Times,* December 12, 1995.

13. *The Hollywood Reporter* [online], December 11, 2002. Available: LexisNexis, December 8, 2004; Lee, *Jim BrownAll-American.*

14. Jim Brown with Steve Delsohn, *Out of Bounds* (New York: Zebra Books; Kensington Publishing, 1989), 58–59.

15. Charles Gillespie, "Jim Brown Comes to Mississippi," *Nation* 211, no. 8 (September 21, 1970): 236–43.

16. Amer-I-Can (November 12, 2004), *Amer-I-Can Program* [online]. Available: http://www.amer-i-can.org (November 12, 2004).

17. C. Leerhsen, "Going Like Gangbusters," *Newsweek* [online], June 17, 1991, 58–59. Available: Academic Search Premier, August 31, 2004.

18. *Christian Science Monitor* [online], January 19, 1996. Available: Academic Search Premier, August 31, 2004; *Providence Journal* [online], June 5, 2004. Available: LexisNexis, August 30, 2004; *Buffalo News* [online], August 12, 13, 20, 2004. Available: LexisNexis, August 30, 2004.

19. Amer-I-Can (November 12, 2004), *Amer-I-Can Foundation* [online]. Available: http:// www.amer-i-can.org (November 14, 2004).

20. *Plain Dealer* (Cleveland), September 5, 2004.

21. *New York Times,* April 19, 1998; *Denver Post* [online], September 7, 2003. Available: LexisNexis, August 30, 2004.

22. *New York Times,* December 12, 1995.

23. Brown, *Out of Bounds,* 46–47.

24. Steve Rushin, "The Long, Hard Run," *Sports Illustrated* [online], August 16, 1994, 55–62. Available: Academic Search Premier, August 31, 2004; Brown, *Out of Bounds,* 190–92.

25. Brown, *Off My Chest,* 165–67.

26. Brown, *Out of Bounds,* 47–48.

27. *Providence Journal,* June 5, 2004.

28. ESPN (October 17, 2004), *Jim Brown Was Hard to Bring Down* [online]. Available: http://espn.go.com/classics/biography/s/Brown _Jim.html; Lee, *Jim Brown All-American; New York Times,* June 11, 1968.

29. Brown, *Out of Bounds,* 118, 125.

30. Brown, *Out of Bounds,* 124–25.

31. Brown, *Out of Bounds,* 131.

32. *Plain Dealer* (Cleveland), September 5, 2004; *Hartford Courant,* June 24, 2004.

33. *New York Amsterdam News,* April 4, 10, 2002; *USA Today* [online], April 10, 2002. Available: Academic Search Premier, August 21, 2004; Jason Zengerle, "Inexcusable," *New Republic* 221, no. 10 (September 6, 1999): 15–16.

34. *New York Times,* March 28, 2002; Don Yeager and Jim Brown, "Prisoner of Conscience," *Sports Illustrated* [online], April 15, 2002, 54–57. Available: Academic Search Premier, August 31, 2004; *Amsterdam News,* April 4,10, 2002.

35. *Amsterdam News,* April 4, 10, 2002.

36. *USA Today,* April 10, 2002.

37. *Atlanta Journal Constitution* [online], December 11, 2002. Available: LexisNexis, December 8, 2004.

38. *Denver Post,* September 7, 2003.

39. *Plain Dealer* (Cleveland), September 5, 2004.

15 Muhammad Ali: Flawed Rebel with a Cause, by Gerald Early

1. Thomas Hauser, *Muhammad Ali: His Life and Times* (New York: Simon and Schuster, 1991), 15.

2. Hauser, *Muhammad Ali,* 19.

3. Hauser, *Muhammad Ali,* 22–23.

4. David Remnick, *King of the World: Muhammad Ali and the Rise of an American Hero* (New York: Random House, 1998), 89, 90–91.

5. Remnick, *King of the World,* 103–4.

6. Hauser, *Muhammad Ali,* 42.

7. Remnick, *King of the World,* 74.

8. Nick Tosches, *The Devil and Sonny Liston* (Boston: Little, Brown, 2000), 201–7, 220–25. Mark Kram, *The Ghosts of Manila: The Fateful Blood Feud between Muhammad Ali and Joe Frazier* (New York: HarperCollins, 2001), 118–22.

9. Mark Kram, *The Ghosts of Manila,* 151, 153–54.

10. Mark Kram, *The Ghosts of Manila,* 16, emphasis Ali's.

16 "The Quiet Militant": Arthur Ashe and Black Athletic Activism, by Damion Thomas

1. S. L. Price, "Arthur Ashe," *Sports Illustrated,* September 19, 1994; Margo Jefferson, "On the Court, In the World," *New York Times,* June 13, 1993.

2. Steven Riess, *Sport in Industrial America, 1850–1920* (New York: Harlan Davidson, 1995), 53–55; Kenny Moore, "He Did All He Could," *Sports Illustrated,* February 15, 1993; Paul Fein, *Tennis Confidential: Today's Greatest Players, Matches, Controversies* (New York: Brassey's, 2002), 143; E. Digby Baltzell, *Sporting Gentlemen* (New York: Free Press, 1995), 17–19, 31.

3. Gail Bederman, *Manliness and Civilization: A Cultural History of Gender and Race in the United States, 1880–1917* (Chicago: University of Chicago Press, 1996), xi, 11–12, 18; John F. Kasson, *Rudeness and Civility: Manners in Nineteenth-Century Urban America* (New York: Hill and Wang Press, 1991), 3.

4. Linda Young, *Middle-Class Culture in the Nineteenth Century: America, Australia, and Britain* (New York: Macmillan, 2003), 23, 83–84; Kasson, *Rudeness and Civility,* 148; Arthur Ashe, *Advantage Ashe* (New York: Coward-McCann Press, 1967), 81.

5. John McPhee, *Levels of the Game* (New York: Farrar, Straus and Giroux, 1969), 24, 27, 42; Mary Huzinec, "Man of Grace and Glory," *People Weekly,* February 1993, 66–72; Jay Jennings, "Arthur Ashe: Lessons from a Noble Life," *Biography,* May 1998, 72; Louie Robinson, "A Crown for King Arthur," *Ebony,* November 1968, 64–66.

6. McPhee, *Levels of the Game,* 28–29; Arthur Ashe with Frank Deford, *Arthur Ashe: Portrait in Motion* (New York: Carroll & Graf Publishers, 1975), 225; Jennings, "Arthur Ashe," 72; Baltzell, *Sporting Gentlemen,* 9; Arthur Ashe with Neil Amdur, *Off the Court* (New York: New American Library, 1982), 42.

7. Baltzell, *Sporting Gentlemen,* 348; Dave Hirshey, "The Rise and Fall and Rise of Ilie Nastaste," *Tennis USA,* January 1976, 14–17; Arthur Ashe, "Brashness Was Started by Nastaste: Connors, McEnroe Carry It to Top," *Washington Post,* February 4, 1979; Al Barkow, "The Man Who Has to Win," *Tennis USA,* January 1978, 24–27.

8. Baltzell, *Sporting Gentlemen,* 352–53; Barkow, "The Man Who Has to Win," 24–27; Richard Evans, *Open Tennis, 1968–1988: The Players, the Politics, the Pressures, the Passions, and the Great Matches* (New York: Stephen Greene Press, 1989), 129.

9. Baltzell, *Sporting Gentlemen,* 354.

10. Connors's and McEnroe's status as the leading American tennis players was exemplified by their dominance of the U.S. Open: for seven years, 1978–1984, only Connors or McEnroe won the men's U.S. Open championship. Connors won in 1978, 1982, and 1983, and McEnroe hoisted the championship trophy in 1979, 1980, 1981, and 1984. Connors's and McEnroe's dominance made their outburst highly visible. Baltzell, *Sporting Gentlemen,* 363–68.

11. Evans, *Open Tennis, 1968–1988,* 132–34.

12. "Connors Is Top Choice at Wimbledon Tourney," *New York Times,* June 22, 1975; Joe Jares, "A Centre Court Case," *Sports Illustrated,* July 14, 1975, 12–14; Fein, *Tennis Confidential,* 276.

13. Ashe, *Off the Court,* 167; Evans, *Open Tennis, 1968–1988,* 129; Fred Tupper, "Ashe Topples Connors for Crown at Wimbledon," *New York Times,* July 6, 1975; Arthur Ashe with Arnold Rampersad, *Days of Grace* (New York: Ballantine Press, 1994), 6; Fein, *Tennis Confidential,* 276; "Upset at Wimbledon," *Time,* July 14, 1975, 42.

14. Dave Anderson, "Tennis in Cold Blood," *New York Times,* July 6, 1975; "U.S. Top Ten," *Tennis USA,* February 1977, 30–31; Jennings, "Arthur Ashe," 72; Evans, *Open Tennis, 1968–1988,* 131.

15. This clash between Connors and Ashe became a grudge match because two weeks before the beginning of the Wimbledon tournament Connors filed a $5 million libel suit against Ashe. In a private letter to some members of the Association of Tennis Professionals (ATP) Ashe criticized Connors as "seemingly unpatriotic" because Connors repeatedly turned down invitations to compete as a member of the U.S. Davis Cup team. As they entered Centre Court together, Ashe wore his blue Davis Cup warm-up jacket with "USA" in red letters as a means to emphasize the distinctions and disagreements between the two athletes. Additionally, Connors had previously filed three lawsuits against the ATP, of which Ashe was the president. Anderson, "Tennis in Cold Blood"; Arthur Ashe, "Catching Connors in the Stretch," *Sports Illustrated,* July 21, 1975, 20–21; H. W. Winn, "From Wimbledon to Forest Hills—A Summer to Remember," *New Yorker,* August 1975, 32–36; Evans, *Open Tennis,*

1968–1988, 133, 135; Paul Witteman, "A Man of Fire and Grace," *Time,* February 15, 1993; Charles Friedman, "Ashe Rated Number One at Net, Connors Second," *New York Times,* January 18, 1976; Jennings, "Arthur Ashe," 72–75; "Tennis in Cold Blood;" Jares, "A Centre Court Case," 12–14.

16. Baltzell, *Sporting Gentlemen,* 4–5, 8; Fein, *Tennis Confidential,* 143.

17. Baltzell, *Sporting Gentlemen,* 218, 232; Kasson, *Rudeness and Civility,* 180.

18. Ashe, *Days of Grace,* 124; Ashe, *Advantage Ashe,* 100.

19. David Southern, *Gunnar Myrdal and Black-White Relations: The Use and Abuse of an American Dilemma, 1944–1969* (Baton Rouge: Louisiana State University Press, 1987), 177, 200–201, 55, 92.

20. Southern, *Gunnar Myrdal and Black-White Relations,* xiii, 94, 187, 226.

21. Ashe, *Advantage Ashe,* 90.

22. Ashe, *Advantage Ashe,* 90; McPhee, *Levels of the Game,* 143.

23. Bud Collins, "Tennis Star of Many Faces," *New York Times,* May 25, 1975.

24. William Grier and Price Cobb, *Black Rage* (New York: Wipf & Stock Publishers, 2000), 59–68; Bill Becker, "Ashe Is Approaching Top Stardom in Tennis," *New York Times,* August 15, 1965; Frank Deford, "An Understudy Takes Charge," *Sports Illustrated,* August 9, 1965, 18–19; McPhee, *Levels of the Game,* 7.

25. Stokely Carmichael and Charles V. Hamilton, *Black Power: The Politics of Liberation in America* (New York: Vintage Books, 1967), 51, 60, 77.

26. Ashe, *Off the Court,* 102; Neil Amdur, "Ashe, Net Pro of Future, Prepares Civil Rights Talk," *New York Times,* January 28, 1968.

27. "Ashe, Net Pro of Future, Prepares Civil Rights Talk."

28. Mark Asher, "'Me Power' Can Combat Ghetto Attitude," *Washington Post,* March 11, 1968; Ashe, *Off the Court,* 102–3.

29. Neil Amdur, "Ashe Beats Lutz in Five Sets for U.S. Amateur Tennis Title," *New York Times,* August 26, 1968; "No Love Set," *New York Times,* August 29, 1968; Dave Anderson, "Ashe Beats Okker to Win Tennis Open," *New York Times,* September 10, 1968.

30. "The Icy Elegance of Arthur Ashe," *Life,* September 20, 1968.

31. "The Icy Elegance of Arthur Ashe"; Arthur Daley, "What's in a Name?" *New York Times,* March 21, 1969; Matthew Scott, "Ashe Reaches the End of His Road to Glory," *Black Enterprise,* April 1993, 16; Ashe, *Advantage Ashe,* 101; Frank Deford, "Lessons from a Friend," *Newsweek,* February 2, 1993; Arthur Ashe, "First Sign of Decline, Color Discovered; Color Convenient Scapegoat," *Washington Post,* March 17, 1979.

32. Maureen Smith, "Identity and Citizenship: African American Athletes, Sport, and the Freedom Struggles of the 1960s" (PhD Diss., Ohio State University, 1998), 12; Douglas Hartmann, *Race, Culture, and the Revolt of the Black Athlete: The 1968 Olympic Protests and Their Aftermath* (Chicago: University of Chicago Press, 2003), 135–37; Harry Edwards, "Why Negroes Should Boycott Whitey's Olympics," *Saturday Evening Post,* March 9, 1968.

33. McPhee, *Levels of the Game,* 146; Dave Anderson, "Gift of One Hundred GM Shares Worth $8,900 Keeps Arthur Smiling!" *New York Times,* October 28, 1968; "Icy Elegance of Arthur Ashe."

34. McPhee, *Levels of the Game,* 144; Ashe, *Days of Grace,* 115, 145.

35. Ashe, *Days of Grace,* 107–9.

36. Ashe, *Days of Grace,* 156; Ashe, *Off the Court,* 156, 89; Ashe, *Portrait in Motion,* 151–52.

37. Smith, "Identity and Citizenship," 7.

17 Bound by Blackness or Above It? Michael Jordan and the Paradoxes of Post–Civil Rights American Race Relations, by Douglas Hartmann

1. Special thanks to my nine-year-old son, Benjamin, who read and reported on several "juvenile" biographies of Jordan for me and prepared a timeline that allowed me to catch some otherwise embarrassing factual mistakes.

My reading of Michael Jordan and his career in this essay as a cultural icon is inspired by C. L. R. James's seminal depiction of cricket as a "stage on which selected individuals played representative roles which were charged with social significance" (*Beyond a Boundary* [Durham, NC: Duke University Press, 1993], 66). It is what I have previously described as a "dramaturgical approach" to the analysis of sport and its racial significance wherein athletes and athletic contests display in microcosm broader social patterns, processes, and tension ("What Can We Learn from Sport if We Take Sport Seriously as a Racial Force? Lessons from C. L. R. James's *Beyond a Boundary,*" *Ethnic and Racial Studies* (May 2003): 451–83; see also Joseph Gusfield, "Sports as Story: Form and Content in Agonistic Games," Conference Proceedings, The First International Conference on the Olympics and East/West and South/North Cultural Exchange in the World System (1987), Seoul, Korea; and, for exemplary applications: Gerald Early, "Performance and Reality: Race, Sports, and the Modern World," *Nation,* August 10/17, 1998: 11–20; and Susan Birrell and Mary G. McDonald, *Reading Sport* (Boston: Northeastern University Press, 2000).

This essay is also informed by the burgeoning literature on sports celebrity, and several classic works on sports heroes. On the former, see David L. Andrews and Steven J. Jackson, eds., *Sport Stars: The Cultural Politics of Sporting Celebrity* (London: Routledge, 2001); Anthony Baker and Todd Boyd, eds., *Out of Bounds: Sports, Media, and the Politics of Identity* (Bloomington: Indiana University Press, 1997); D. Rowe, *Popular Cultures: Rock Music, Sport, and the Politics of Pleasure* (London: Sage Publications, 1995); and Gary Whannel, "Individual Stars and Collective Identities in Media Sport," in *Sport, Popular Culture and Identity,* ed. M. Roche (Aachen: Meyer and Meyer Verlag, 1998), 23–36. On the latter: Michael Oriard, *Dreaming of Heroes: American Sports Fiction, 1868–1980* (Chicago: Nelson Hall, 1982); Robert Holt, J. A. Mangan, and P. Lanfranchi, eds., *European Heroes: Myth, Identity, Sport* (London: Frank Cass, 1996); William J. Goode, *The Celebration of Heroes: Prestige as a System of Control* (Chicago: University of Chicago Press, 1978); see also William L. Van Deburg, *Black Camelot: African-American Culture Heroes in Their Times, 1960–1980* (Chicago: University of Chicago Press, 1997).

2. Mary G. McDonald and David L. Andrews, "Michael Jordan and Postmodern Celebrityhood," in Andrews and Jackson, *Sport Stars,* 20–35.

3. Kenneth R. Dutton, *The Perfectible Body: The Western Ideal of Male Physical Development* (New York: Continuum Books, 1995), 63; David Halberstam, *Playing for Keeps: Michael Jordan and the World He Made* (New York: Broadway Books, 2000). Most recent scholarly analyses of Jordan have focused on economics and media: see, for examples: Douglas Kellner, "The Sports Spectacle, Michael Jordan, and Nike," in *Sport and the Color Line: Black Athletes and Race Relations in Twentieth-Century America,* ed. Patrick B. Miller and David K. Wiggins (New York: Routledge, 2004), 305–26; Walter LaFeber, *Michael Jordan and the New Global Capitalism* (New York: W. W. Norton and Company, 1999); G. Maharaj, "Talking Trash: Late Capitalism, Black (Re)productivity, and Professional Basketball," in *Cultural Politics: Vol. 16, Sport Cult,* ed. R. Martin and T. Miller (Minneapolis: University of Minnesota Press, 1999), 227–40; Mary G. McDonald, "Michael Jordan's Family Values: Marketing, Meaning, and Post-Reagan America," *Sociology of Sport Journal* 13, no. 4 (1996): 344–65. Many of these and others are collected in David L. Andrews, ed., *Michael Jordan, Inc.: Corporate Sport, Media Culture, and Late Modern America* (Albany, NY: SUNY Press, 2003).

4. Probably the most well known and rightly influential scholarly works on Jordan's racial meaning and symbolism come from David L. Andrews; see especially: "The Fact(s) of Michael Jordan's Blackness: Excavating a Floating Racial Signifier," *Sociology of Sport Journal* 13, no. 2 (1996): 125–58, and "Excavating Michael Jordan: Notes on a Critical Pedagogy of Sporting Representation," in *Sport and Postmodern Times,* ed. Genevieve Rail (Albany, NY: SUNY Press, 1998), 185–220. Indeed, Andrews's conception of Jordan's mediated cultural identity as a "floating racial signifier"—a "complex narrative incorporating many of the historically grounded racial codes that continue to structure the racial format of the United States" ("The Fact(s) of Michael Jordan's Blackness," 125)—has been foundational for my understanding of the racial dimensions of Jordan's iconography. While I rely heavily on his research throughout this chapter, I do not employ Andrews's terminology directly because I mean to focus more on the color-blind, race-neutral discourse within and through which the various racial meanings, both positive and negative, are forged in the public culture and consciousness.

5. These alternately celebratory and critical readings of Michael Jordan mirror and reproduce a larger, more general dynamic about race and sport that I have analyzed previously; see "Rethinking the Relationships between Sport and Race in American Culture: Golden Ghettos and Contested Terrain," *Sociology of Sport Journal* 17 (2000): 229–53. As I discussed in that context, the critical impulse and scholarly temptation is to side with the academic interpretations which (not incidentally) have been among the very best and most influential works produced in the sociology of sport in the past decade. That said, I believe it is a mistake to dismiss the more popular, optimistic accounts out of hand, if only because they constitute a potential avenue for contestation and change absent the conventional scholarly critiques.

6. See, Halberstam, *Playing for Keeps,* 57–72. This essay is informed, first of all, by the countless magazine and newspaper articles, television profiles, sports books, and the like that I have consumed (mostly as a sports fan) over the years. In addition to the scholarly articles cited throughout the piece, I also draw upon numerous biographies and popular histories, including Bob Greene, *Hang Time: Days and Dreams with Michael Jordan* (New York: Doubleday, 1992); Mitchell Krugel, *Michael Jordan and One Last Shot: The Story of Michael Jordan's Comeback* (New York: St. Martin's, 2002); Stan Smith,

The Jordan Rules (New York: Pocket, 1993). That said, I should make clear that I have made no attempt to systematically collect or analyze these documents and sources at this point.

7. Halberstam, *Playing for Keeps,* 18, 416.

8. African American inequalities in the 1980s and early 1990s were well documented by sociologists of the period. On residential segregation, see Douglas S. Massey and Nancy Denton, *American Apartheid: Segregation and the Making of the Underclass* (Cambridge: Harvard University Press, 1993); on economic and education disparities: William Julius Wilson, *The Truly Disadvantaged: The Inner City, the Underclass, and Public Policy* (Chicago: University of Chicago Press, 1987); and on persistent anti-Black prejudices: Joe R. Feagin, "The Continuing Significance of Racism," *American Sociological Review* 56, no. 1 (1991): 101–16. For a study emphasizing the accomplishments of African Americans in the post–Civil Rights era, see Abigail Thernstrom and Stephan Thernstrom, *America in Black and White* (New York: Simon and Schuster, 1997).

9. For a contemporaneous review that details the literature on discrimination in sport, see James H. Frey and D. Stanley Eitzen, "Sport and Society," *Annual Review of Sociology* 17 (August 1991): 503–22.

10. Halberstam, *Playing for Keeps,* 18.

11. Quoted in Andrews, "The Fact(s) of Michael Jordan's Blackness," 135.

12. For a sociological study, see Pamela Wonsek, "College Basketball on Television: A Study of Racism in the Media," *Media, Culture & Society* 14 (1992): 449–61. Scholars have consistently and systematically criticized the belief that black athletic achievement stems from natural/physiological factors insisting instead upon social, cultural, and historical explanations. Probably the most well known and certainly most controversial treatment is John Hoberman, *Darwin's Athletes: How Sport Has Damaged Black America and Preserved the Myth of Race* (Boston: Houghton Mifflin, 1997), which drew upon the pioneering work of Harry Edwards, "The Sources of Black Athletic Superiority," *Black Scholar* 3 (November 1971): 32–41. Other key scholarly works include Laurel R. Davis, "The Articulation of Difference: White Preoccupation with the Question of Racially Linked Genetic Differences among Athletes," *Sociology of Sport Journal* 7 (June 1990): 179–87; Patrick B. Miller, "The Anatomy of Scientific Racism: Racialist Responses to Black Athletic Achievement," in *Sport and the Color Line: Black Athletes and Race Relations in Twentieth Century America,* ed. Patrick Miller and David K. Wiggins (New York: Routledge, 2004); Gary Sailes, "The Myth of Black Sports Supremacy," *Journal of Black Studies* 21 (June 1991): 480–87; and David K. Wiggins, "Great Speed but Little Stamina': The Historical Debate over Black Athletic Superiority," *Journal of Sport History* 16 (Summer 1989): 158–85.

13. See Michael Eric Dyson, "Be Like Mike? Michael Jordan and the Pedagogy of Desire," in *Reflecting Black: African-American Cultural Criticism* (Minneapolis: University of Minnesota Press, 1993), 64–75.

14. Andrews, "The Fact(s) of Michael Jordan's Blackness," 136. Nelson George, *Elevating the Game: The History and Aesthetics of Black Men in Basketball* (New York: HarperCollins, 1992). The groundwork for this popular conception was laid in the 1970s with the publication of such contemporary bestsellers as Pete Axthelm's *The City Game: Basketball from the Garden to the Playgrounds* (New York: Penguin, 1970) and Rick Telander's *Heaven Is a Playground* (New York: Simon and Schuster, 1976), but the

social and historical roots are far deeper as discussed by Gena Caponi-Tabery, "Jump for Joy: Jump Blues, Dance, and Basketball in 1930s African America," in *Sports Matters: Race, Recreation and Culture,* ed. John Bloom and Michael Nevin Willard (New York: New York University Press, 2002), 39–74. In recent years scholars and cultural critics have offered up a number of additional commentaries that capture the power of the sport as experienced and understood within the African American community. These include Todd Boyd and Kenneth L. Shropshire, eds., *Basketball Jones: America above the Rim* (New York: New York University Press, 2000); Robin D. G. Kelley, "Playing for Keeps: Pleasure and Profit on the Postindustrial Playground," in *The House That Race Built,* ed. Wahneema Lubiano (New York: Pantheon, 1997), 195–231; and John Edgar Wideman, *Hoop Roots: Basketball, Race, and Love* (New York: Houghton Mifflin, 2001). See also David Shields, *Black Planet: Race during an NBA Season* (New York: Three Rivers Press, 1999).

15. On the one hand, basketball is clearly an avenue of prominence and mobility for African Americans, individually and taken as a whole. More than this, the popularity of this distinctive subcultural form provides a mode of interaction and exchange with black America that white America participates in, and has often stood as an alternative to the bland, uninspiring (and uninspired) middle-class culture and lifestyle. Yet as these characteristics are so often romanticized and commodified, black basketball can, on the other hand, also become a source of exploitation and mystification, a cultural form which capital not only profits from but which serves to exaggerate racial differences and to blind the white majority to the injustices and inequalities that continue to be associated with being black in contemporary America. In addition to Dyson ("Be Like Mike?"), see Todd Boyd, *Young, Black, Rich, and Famous: The Rise of the NBA, the Hip Hop Invasion, and the Transformation of American Culture* (New York: Doubleday, 2003); for historical studies that lay the groundwork for these ideas, see George Fredrickson, *The Black Image in the White Mind* (New York: Harper and Row, 1971); and Eric Lott, *Love and Theft: Blackface Minstrelsy and the American Working Class* (New York: Oxford University Press, 1993).

16. *Sports Illustrated,* September 27, 2004, 127.

17. *Sports Illustrated,* "In an Orbit All His Own," November 9, 1987, 82–92.

18. See Leola Johnson and David Roediger, "Hertz Don't It? Becoming Colorless and Staying Black in the Crossover," in *Reading Sport: Critical Essays on Power and Representation,* ed. Susan Birrell and Mary G. McDonald (Boston: Northeastern University Press, 2000), 40–73.

19. John Edgar Wideman, "Michael Jordan Leaps the Great Divide," *Esquire* (November 1990): 140–45, 210–16. Edwards is quoted in Halberstam, *Playing for Keeps,* 9; Orlando Patterson, "American Dionysus: Images of Afro-American Men at the Dawn of the Twenty-First Century," in *Rituals of Blood: Consequences of Slavery in Two American Centuries* (New York: Basic Books, 1998), 233–80.

20. Johnson and Roediger ("Hertz Don't It?") make a similar argument for O. J. Simpson focusing on the football star's ability to set himself and his blackness up in opposition to the more radical and outspoken athletes of his era.

21. Andrews, "The Fact(s) of Michael Jordan's Blackness," 138. Here it should be pointed out that Patterson ("American Dionyssus") did not argue that Jordan was race-less; quite the contrary, he insisted that his race was crucial to Jordan's cultural role because his racial background marked Jordan as "different enough to commit the

outrage of crossing, but close enough not to overturn the moral order by so doing." It was a role that Patterson says would have been impossible for African American men to play until recent years, after the civil rights movement ensured that black men were no longer confined to symbolically embodying the quintessential Other.

22. Cheryl L. Cole, "American Jordan: P.L.A.Y., Consensus, and Punishment," *Sociology of Sport Journal* 13, no. 4 (1996): 366–97. I read this article as the culmination of a series of articles Cole and her coauthors produced exploring the ways in which racial difference and deviance are constructed in and through sport media, including Cheryl L. Cole and David L. Andrews, "'Look—It's NBA Showtime!' Visions of Race in the Popular Imaginary," *Cultural Studies Annual* 1 (1996): 141–81.

23. Although the interview never materialized, Halberstam appears to harbor no grudges about it. Indeed, he says: "Michael never tried to block my access to important people who were close to him and who checked with him as to whether it was okay to go ahead and talk" (*Playing for Keeps*, 429–30). It is also worth noting that Halberstam had interviewed Jordan for one of the stories *Sports Illustrated* commissioned when it named him Sportsman of the Year in January 1992 and recalled the encounter very positively.

24. Ellis Cashmore, *Tyson: Nurture of the Beast* (Cambridge, UK: Polity, 2005), 112.

25. Greene, *Hang Time*, 133.

26. Helen Page, "'Black Male' Imagery and Media Containment of African American Men," *American Anthropologist* 99, no. 1 (1997): 99–111; Vernon Andrews, "African American Player Codes on Celebration, Taunting, and Sportsmanlike Conduct," in *African Americans in Sport*, ed. Gary Sailes (New Brunswick, NJ: Transaction Press, 1998), 145–80; "Black Bodies—White Control: The Contested Terrain of Sportsmanlike Conduct," *Journal of African American Men* 2, no. 1 (1996): 33–59.

27. I develop these points at some length in my study of the movement that is probably the most famous and exceptional example of African American athletic activism in U.S. history. *Race, Culture, and the Revolt of the Black Athlete: The 1968 African American Olympic Protests and Their Aftermath* (Chicago: University of Chicago Press, 2003), see especially chapters 3 and 5. See also Amy Bass, *Not the Triumph but the Struggle: The 1968 Olympics and the Making of the Black Athlete* (Minneapolis: University of Minnesota Press, 2002). For more general theoretical treatments of race, resistance, and sport, see Ben Carrington, "Sport, Masculinity, and Black Cultural Resistance," *Journal of Sport and Social Issues* (Summer 1998): 275–98; and my 2003 piece on C. L. R. James ("What Can We Learn from Sport if We Take Sport Seriously as a Racial Force?").

28. Kenneth K. Gaines, *Uplifting the Race: Black Leadership, Politics, and Culture in the Twentieth Century* (Chapel Hill: University of North Carolina Press, 1996), xiv.

29. Greene, *Hang Time*, 163.

30. It is easy to assume that this on-court freedom and release automatically translates to higher degrees of achievement and success for African American athletes as it did for Jordan; however, I am not convinced that this is always and necessarily the case. Indeed, I have suggested that the pressure to succeed for their race may have actually impelled African American track and field athletes of the late 1960s to great heights and times than they had ever known before (Hartmann, *Race, Culture, and the Revolt of the Black Athlete*, 130, and ch. 5).

31. Andrews, "The Fact(s) of Michael Jordan's Blackness," 143.

32. See John J. MacAloon, "Double Visions: Olympic Games and American Culture," in *The Olympic Games in Transition,* ed. Jeffrey O. Segrave and Donald Chu (Champaign, IL: Human Kinetics Books, 1987), 279–94.

33. On Johnson, see Cheryl L. Cole and Harry Denny III, "Visualizing Deviance in Post-Reagan America: Magic Johnson, AIDS, and the Promiscuous World of Professional Sport," *Critical Sociology* 20, no. 3 (1994): 123–47; for the Simpson case, Johnson and Roediger, "Hertz Don't It?" For a more general related treatment, see Brian Wilson, "'Good Blacks' and 'Bad Blacks': Media Construction of African-American Athletes in Canadian Basketball," *International Review for the Sociology of Sport* 32, no. 2 (1997): 177–89.

34. Andrews, "The Fact(s) of Michael Jordan's Blackness," 146. For more on the links between white fear and white desire as they converge on the black male body, see Dyson, "Be Like Mike?"; Henry Giroux, *Disturbing Pleasures: Learning Popular Culture* (New York: Routledge, 1994); George Lipsitz, *The Possessive Investment in Whiteness* (Philadelphia: Temple University Press, 1998), ch. 5 and 6); and Kobena Mercer, *Welcome to the Jungle: New Positions in Black Cultural Studies* (London: Routledge, 1994), 178–79.

35. Quotes and analysis from Andrews, "The Fact(s) of Michael Jordan's Blackness," 147.

36. See, for examples, M. Vancil, ed., *I Can't Accept Not Trying: Michael Jordan on the Pursuit of Excellence* (San Francisco: HarperCollins, 1994); *Rare Air: Michael on Michael* (San Francisco: HarperCollins, 1993).

37. Andrews, "The Fact(s) of Michael Jordan's Blackness," 150.

38. CNN interview, March 19, 1995, quoted in Andrews, "The Fact(s) of Michael Jordan's Blackness."

39. For representative examples, see David J. Leonard, "The Next M. J. or the Next O. J.? Kobe Bryant, Race, and the Absurdity of Colorblind Rhetoric," *Journal of Sport and Social Issues* (August 2004): 284–313; and Glyn Hughes, "Managing Black Guys: Representation, Corporate Culture, and the NBA," *Sociology of Sport Journal* 21, no. 2 (2004): 163–84; and Henry Yu, "How Tiger Woods Lost His Stripes: Post-National American Studies as a History of Race, Migration, and the Commodification of Culture," in *Post-Nationalist American Studies,* ed. John C. Rowe (Berkeley and Los Angeles: University of California Press, 2000). I put a great deal of emphasis on this individualist, meritocratic discourse in my own work on the 1968 Olympic protests (*Race, Culture, and the Revolt of the Black Athlete,* see especially chapter 3, 60–92).

Much of the critique of colorblindness came out of critical legal theory: Cf. Kimberle W. Crenshaw, "Color-Blind Dreams and Racial Nightmares: Reconfiguring Racism in the Post–Civil Rights Era," in *Birth of a Nation 'hood: Gaze, Script, and Spectacle in the O. J. Simpson Case,* ed. Toni Morrison (New York: Random House, 1997), 97–168; Neil Gotanda, "A Critique of 'Our Constitution is Color-Blind,'" *Stanford Law Review* 44, no. 1 (1991): 28–30. The whole notion of colorblindness has been the subject of a good deal of sociological work in recent years as well. See for example: Eduardo Bonilla-Silva, *White Supremacy and Racism in the Post–Civil Rights Era* (Boulder, CO: Lynne Reinner Publishers, 2001); Eduardo Bonilla-Silva and Tyrone Forman, "'I'm Not a Racist but . . . ': Mapping White College Students Racial Ideology in the U.S.A.," *Discourse and Society* 11, no. 1 (2000): 53–85; Michael K. Brown, Martin Carnoy, Elliot Currie, Troy Duster, David B. Oppenheimer, Marjorie M. Schultz, and David Wellman,

White-Washing Race: The Myth of a Color-Blind Society (Berkeley and Los Angeles: University of California Press, 2003); L. G. Carr, *Colorblind Racism* (Thousand Oaks, CA: Sage Publications, 1997); Amanda E. Lewis, "'What Group?' Studying Whites and Whiteness in the Era of 'Color-Blindness,'" *Sociological Theory* 22, no. 4 (2004): 623–46.

40. John Edgar Wideman, "Michael Jordan's Great Leap Forward," in *Signifyin(g), Sanctifyin', and Slam Dunking: A Reader in African American Expressive Culture,* ed. Gena Dagel Caponi (Amherst: University of Massachusetts Press, 1999), 389.

41. David K. Wiggins, "The Notion of Double-Consciousness and the Involvement of Black Athletes in American Sport," in *Ethnicity and Sport in North American History and Culture,* ed. George Eisen and David K. Wiggins (Westport, CT: Greenwood Press, 1994), 133–55.

18 "Race," Family, and Nation: The Significance of Tiger Woods in American Culture, by S. W. Pope

1. Earl Woods prophetic sentiments have been quoted in a variety of places. See, for example, David Owen, *The Chosen One: Tiger Woods and the Dilemma of Greatness* (New York: Simon and Schuster, 2001), 63.

2. Quoted in Gary Smith, "The Chosen One," *Sports Illustrated,* December 23, 1996, reprinted in Glenn Stout, ed., *Chasing Tiger: The Tiger Woods Reader* (Cambridge, MA: De Capo Press, 2002), 54.

3. Smith, "The Chosen One."

4. James Lawton, "The Greatest," *The Independent,* August 22, 2000, reprinted in Stout, *Chasing Tiger,* 167.

5. Lawton, "The Greatest," 3.

6. Cheryl L. Cole and David L. Andrews, "America's New Son: Tiger Woods and America's Multiculturalism," in *Sport Stars: The Cultural Politics of Sporting Celebrity,* ed. David L. Andrews and Steven J. Jackson (London: Routledge, 2001), 73–74.

7. Cole and Andrews, "America's New Son," 70. Sport sociologist Gary Whannel characterizes such "narrativisation" as the embodiment of power relations developed within "sets of production practices, framed by professional ideologies, within the context of institutional structures." See Gary Whannel, *Media Sport Stars: Masculinities and Moralities* (London: Routledge, 2002), 173. Whannel astutely theorizes this process in terms of "narrativisation" and "reinscription"—a process "whereby star biographies are constantly rewritten in the 'continuous present'—their lives are interpreted according to the dominant concerns at the time of writing." According to Whannel, all we ever have are "layers of discourse—and stars can only be 'known' through media representation." See *Media Sports Stars,* especially 56–60.

8. "Teeing Off: History of Blacks in Golf," *Black Enterprise* 25, no. 2 (1994): 69; see also Peter Aviles, "Who Was John Shippen, and Why Should We Care?" *Black Athlete Sports Network,* http://www.blackathletesportsnetwork.net/golf/golf060902.html.

9. The boxer, Joe Louis, played in a PGA-sanctioned event in San Diego, California, in 1952 and was a notable exception to the PGA's "Caucasians-only" clause.

10. Arthur Ashe Jr., *A Hard Road to Glory: A History of the African-American Athlete 1919–1945* (New York: Warner Books, 1988), 66.

11. http://www.jimcrowhistory.org/scripts/imcrow/sports.cgi?sport=golf; and "Teeing Off," 70.

12. Sifford later won two other PGA tournaments in 1967 and 1969.

13. See Sifford's autobiographical account, Charlie Sifford, with James Gallo, *Just Let Me Play: The Story of Charlie Sifford, the First Black PGA Golfer* (Latham, NY: British American Publishing, 1992).

14. For a recent perspective on Peete, see Pete McDaniel, "What Ever Happened to Calvin Peete?" *Golf Digest*, April 1, 2005.

15. John Feinstein, *The First Coming: Tiger Woods, Master or Martyr* (New York: Ballantine Books, 1998), 22.

16. Whannel, *Media Sports Stars*, 60.

17. Earl Woods, *Training a Tiger: Raising a Winner in Golf and Life* (New York: HarperCollins, 1997), xiii–xvi.

18. See the chapter "Marriages and Mulligans," in Woods's autobiography, Earl Woods, *Playing Through: Straight Talk on Hard Work, Big Dreams, and Adventures with Tiger* (New York: HarperCollins, 1998). I've yet to encounter any discussion or exposé of either Earl's or Tiger's relationship with the former's other three children.

19. Tom Callahan, *In Search of Tiger* (New York: Mainstream Publishing, 2004), 30.

20. For more on Woods's search for Nguyen Phong, see Callahan, *In Search of Tiger*, 11–26.

21. Callahan, *In Search of Tiger*, 203.

22. Owen, *The Chosen One*, 81.

23. Smith, "The Chosen One," 68–69.

24. They did not take a vacation together for twenty years. For the spare dollars needed to transport Tiger to tournaments, Earl estimates that the family's annual travel expenses during Tiger's junior golf years amounted to as much as $30,000/year—financed through a succession of home equity loans. Earl and Tida's sacrifices took a toll on the marriage—they have lived apart for several years now. According to Smith, "There may be no animosity between them, but there doesn't seem to be much warmth, either. Maybe raising Tiger wore both of them out." Smith, "The Chosen One," 83–84.

25. Smith, "The Chosen One," 59.

26. Tiger's words from the Foreword to Earl Woods, *Training a Tiger*, xi–xii; and Tiger Woods (with the editors of *Golf Digest*), *How I Play Golf: A Master Class with the World's Greatest Golfer* (New York: Little, Brown and Company, 2001), 295.

27. Owen, *The Chosen One*, 88–89.

28. Owen, *The Chosen One*, 65.

29. John Garrity, ed., *Tiger Woods: The Making of a Champion* (New York: Fireside, 1997), 6—an edited collection of twenty pieces published on Woods in *Sports Illustrated* from 1992 to 1997.

30. Rather than receiving a salary during the early years, Harmon cashed in on advertising himself as Woods's coach to promote books, videos, golf schools—and to teach celebrities.

31. Harmon quoted in Callahan, *In Search of Tiger*, 77.

32. From 2002 to 2004, Woods, without Coach Harmon, did not win a major tournament.

33. Callahan, *In Search of Tiger*, 56.

34. Peter de Jonge, "A Zone of His Own," *New York Times Magazine*, February 5, 1995, reprinted in Stout, *Chasing Tiger*, 26–27.

35. Smith, "The Chosen One," 64.

36. Feinstein, *The First Coming*; Curt Sampson, *Chasing Tiger* (New York: Atria Books, 2002), 246. Feinstein's relationship with Woods got off to a rocky start after Feinstein wrote a 1996 article for *Newsweek* ("Tiger by the Tail")—wherein he drew parallels between Earl Woods and Stefano Capriati (two pushy fathers—building their lives around their child becoming a star—trying to capitalize on their children's wealth and prestige). According to Owen, Tiger no longer gives individual interviews to print reporters, except on rare occasions, and then only briefly. He does not sign golf balls. Reporters grumble about having to live with restricted access; the first two paragraphs of *Sports Illustrated*'s cover story about Tiger's 2000 U.S. Open victory concerned not the tournament but Woods's refusal to be interviewed on the practice tee by reporters from competing television networks. Owen claims that although sportswriters complain about being frozen out—when they get the opportunities to ask questions in press interview rooms—they cover the same tired ground again and again. See Owen, *The Chosen One*, 141.

37. Garrity, *Tiger Woods*, 66.

38. Callahan, *In Search of Tiger*, 39; the Van Sickle and Garrity quotes are from Stout, *Chasing Tiger*, 87, 89, 66; Callahan, *In Search of Tiger*, 219.

39. Cole and Andrews, "America's New Son," 74. Although golf is the smallest division within Nike, it's also the fastest growing one—sporting astronomical increases in the sales of balls, bags, shoes, and apparel (due, in large part, to Woods).

40. Cole and Andrews, "America's New Son," 75.

41. Titlelist thought it looked too much like a golf ball commercial—the beginning of the Nike golf ball business, see Callahan, *In Search of Tiger*, 139–40.

42. Cole and Andrews, "America's New Son," 80.

43. Cole and Andrews, "America's New Son," 81.

44. John Feinstein's statement was presented on the nationally televised news show, *Nightline* (hosted by Ted Koppel), September 2, 1996.

45. Lapchick quoted in Kelly Candaele and Peter Drier, "Where Are the Jocks for Justice?" *Nation*, June 28, 2004.

46. Sampson, *Chasing Tiger*, 246.

47. This information comes from Smith's "The Chosen One" essay published in 1996 at the early stage of Woods's career. The author has not verified whether or not Woods continues to revere such religious icons.

48. Smith, *"The Chosen One,"* 73–74.

49. Callahan, *In Search of Tiger*, 201.

50. De Jonge, "A Zone of His Own," 23.

51. De Jonge, "A Zone of His Own," *23*.

52. Andrews and Cole, "America's New Son," 78–79.

53. Feinstein, *The First Coming*, 15. Feinstein was especially critical of the "Team Tiger" insatiable pursuit of endorsement money and special guest appearance fees. According to him, Woods's management company, IMG, ruthlessly milked the star's newly acquired celebrity status above and beyond what was reasonable in terms of their client's financial or athletic well-being. See Feinstein, *The First Coming*, especially 50–52. Feinstein's polemic concludes with a critique of Woods as an independent

operator. "If there is one thing in his life that Tiger cannot own outright, it is his dream. He has to share that. He shares it with a father, who honestly believes that he is responsible for Tiger's greatness. He shares it with a management company that sees him as a money machine that must be pumped dry before he escapes. He shares it with corporate sponsors who expect time, charm, and victories in return for their millions. And he shares it with a public that wants him to be the sweet, sensitive guy it sees in his commercials and is shocked and dismayed when he turns out to be a twenty-two-year-old who tells dirty jokes, stamps his foot when he doesn't get his way, and stalks angrily off golf courses when he shoots," 74.

54. Christine Brennan, "Time for Tiger to Meet Father's Expectations," *USA Today,* June 14, 2001.

55. Sampson noted wryly on the credibility of this endorsement, "a young man earning $50 million a year wouldn't likely drive a Buick—clearly the company hopes its proximity to Tiger will rub some jazz on its stodgy reputation"; Sampson, *Chasing Tiger,* 210.

56. Callahan, *In Search of Tiger,* 144–45. For more on Tiger's endorsement deals, see Sampson, *Chasing Tiger,* 202–12. Within eight years of statements about the virtues of Buddhism and living a less materialistic life, Woods sued Christensen Shipyards, Ltd.—the manufacturer of his 150-foot yacht (named "Privacy") in late 2004 for an alleged breach of confidentiality in Woods's contract to purchase the boat.

57. Woods, *Training a Tiger,* xxi.

58. Woods, *Training a Tiger,* 209.

59. Woods, *Training a Tiger,* 215.

60. Woods, *How I Play Golf,* 11.

61. Woods, *How I Play Golf,* 8.

62. Woods, *How I Play Golf,* 13.

63. Woods, *How I Play Golf, 310.*

64. Sampson, *Chasing Tiger,* 46.

65. See the TWF website at http://www.tigerwoodsfoundation.org/aboutTWF.

66. TWF website at http://www.tigerwoodsfoundation.org/aboutTWF.

67. TWF website at http://www.tigerwoodsfoundation.org/aboutTWF.

68. For a complete list of the Foundation's grants, see http://www.tigerwoods-foundation.org/charity/benevolence.

69. See http://www.Tigerwoods.com/TWLC.

70. See http://www.Tigerwoods.com/TWLC.

71. John Branch, "Woods Part of Crusade: Minority Golf Numbers Growing," *Gazette,* June 7, 2000, http://www.texnews.com/tiger/part0607.html.

72. http://www.nmgf.org/who.html; http://www.mgaa.com/about.html; Douglas quoted in Branch, "Woods Part of Crusade," http://www.texnews.com/tiger/part0607.html.

73. Don Yeager, "Prisoner of Conscience," *Sports Illustrated,* April 15, 2002, 56.

74. *Maclean's,* June 10, 2002, 50.

75. For representative speculations, see Ed Sherman, "Tiger's Head Still in the Game," *Chicago Tribune,* http://sports.yahoo.golfserv.com/gdc/news/article.asp?id=24440; and Jerry Potter, "Woods Turns to New Club for Old Results," *USA Today,* July 14, 2004.

76. Dave Anderson, "Woods Says TV Critics Should Think Outside the Box," *New York Times*, June 16, 2004.

77. Quotes from Ann Oldenburg, "Tiger Driven to Help Kids," *USA Today*, June 31, 2004.

78. Woods quoted in Aaron J. Lopez, "Els' Climb to the Top Puts Pressure on Tiger," *Rocky Mountain News*, http://sports.yahoo.golfserv.com/gdc/news/article.asp?id=25573.

79. Chris Lewis, "The Dual at Doral," *Sports Illustrated*, March 14, 2005, 53.

80. David Davies, "Easy Ryders and Toothless Tigers," *Guardian*, November 23, 2004, 27.

81. Lewis, "The Dual at Doral."

82. See PGA website coverage, http://www.pga.com/tournaments/Masters/2005/index.cfm.

83. For a discussion of the problematical nature of "race" in American sport, see S. W. Pope, "De-Centering 'Race' and (Re)presenting 'Black' Performance in Sport History," *Deconstructing Sport History: The Postmodern Challenge,* ed. Murray Phillips (New York: State University of New York Press, 2005). For an analysis of sport and the construction of early-twentieth-century American sporting culture, see Pope, *Patriotic Games: Sporting Traditions in the American Imagination, 1876–1926* (New York: Oxford University Press, 1997); and Alan Barnier, *Sport, Nationalism, and Globalization: European and American Perspectives* (Albany, NY: SUNY Press, 2001).

84. Page quoted in Callahan, *In Search of Tiger,* 151.

85. Woods quoted in Joe Concannon, "Fore! It's Tiger Time," *Boston Globe*, October 24, 1996.

86. Owen, *The Chosen One,* 193–95.

87. Jay Nordlinger, "Tiger Time: The Wonder of an American Hero," *National Review*, April 30, 2001, reprinted in Stout, *Chasing Tiger,* 193.

88. Owen, *The Chosen One,* 177.

89. Smith, "The Chosen One," 81.

90. Whannel, *Media Sports Stars,* 177.

91. For a more elaborate discussion of this characterization, see also Cole and Andrews, "America's New Son," 72–73.

19 "Ghetto Cinderellas": Venus and Serena Williams and the Discourse of Racism, by R. Pierre Rodgers and Ellen B. Drogin Rodgers

1. James R. Andrews, *The Practice of Rhetorical Criticism,* 2nd ed. (New York: Longman, 1990), 17.

2. L. Jon Wertheim, *Venus Envy: Power Games, Teenage Vixens, and Million-Dollar Egos on the Women's Tennis Tour* (New York: Perennial, 2002), 70.

3. Compton received notoriety from the controversial, hard-core hip-hop album, "Straight Outta Compton," by N.W.A. See the entry for *Straight Outta Compton* in the online *Rap Dictionary,* http://rapdict.org/Straight_Outta_Compton. For an insightful analysis of the decline of the suburb, see Josh Sides, "Straight into Compton:

American Dreams, Urban Nightmares and the Metamorphosis of a Black Suburb," *American Quarterly* 56, no. 3 (2004): 583–605.

4. Nancy E. Spencer, "Sister Act VI: Venus and Serena Williams at Indian Wells: 'Sincere Fictions' and White Racism," *Journal of Sport & Social Issues* 28, no. 2 (2004): 125. The "legend" is also confirmed by Rachel Cepeda, "Courting Destiny," *Essence*, June 2001, 126.

5. Biographical information is drawn from Cepeda, "Courting Destiny," 124–26, 182–84, 192–93; Karen E. Duda, "Williams, Venus, and Williams, Serena," in *Current Biography Yearbook 2003*, ed. Clifford Thompson (New York: H. W. Wilson, 2003), 571–77; Robin Finn, "Defying Her Sport's Logic, a Tennis Prodigy Emerges," *New York Times*, September 7, 1997, http://www.proquest.com; Angela Lumpkin, "Serena Williams," in *African Americans in Sports, vol. 2*, ed. David K. Wiggins (Armonk, NY: Shaupe Reference, 2004), 406–7; Sally Jenkins, "Double Trouble," *Women's Sports & Fitness*, November/December 1998, 102–5, 144, 149; Peter Noel, "Fear of the Williams Sisters: Venus and Serena Battle Charges of Arrogance and the Myth of the Superbred Black Athlete," *Village Voice*, November 18, 2000, http://villagevoice.com/news/0045,noel,19639,1.html; "Serena Williams (USA)" [Player Profile], Sony Ericsson WTA, http://www.wtatour.com/players/playerprofiles/playerbio.asp?PlayerID=230234; "Venus Williams (USA)" [Player Profile], Sony Ericsson WTA, http://www.wtatour.com/players/playerprofiles/playerbio.asp?PlayerID=230220; Maureen M. Smith, "Williams, Venus, and Serena Williams," in *African American Lives*, ed. Henry Louis Gates Jr. and Evelyn Brooks Higginbotham (New York: Oxford University Press, 2004), 898–99; and Wertheim, *Venus Envy*.

6. Finn, "Defying," par. 12; Jenkins, "Double Trouble," 103; and Spencer, "Sister Act VI," 125.

7. Sony Ericsson WTA Career Singles Rankings, http://www.wtatour.com/rankings/singles_numeric.asp.

8. Jenkins, "Double Trouble," 105.

9. Lumpkin, "Venus Williams," 407.

10. Duda, "Williams, Venus, and Williams, Serena," 573.

11. Smith, "Williams, Venus, and Serena Williams," 898–99.

12. "Serena Williams (USA)" [Player Profile]; and "Venus Williams (USA)" [Player Profile].

13. Wertheim, *Venus Envy*, 73–74.

14. Joel Stein, "The Power Game," *Time*, September 3, 2001, par. 5, http://www.proquest.com.

15. Quoted in Roy S. Johnson, "Sister Slam," *Savoy*, November 2002, 56.

16. Duda, "Williams, Venus, and Williams, Serena," 575.

17. Duda, "Williams, Venus, and Williams, Serena," 575.

18. Jay Coakley, *Sports in Society: Issues and Controversies*, 8th ed. (Boston: McGraw-Hill, 2004), 290–91.

19. Coakley, *Sports in Society*, 291.

20. Sonja K. Foss, *Rhetorical Criticism: Exploration and Practice*, 2nd ed. (Prospect Heights, IL: Waveland, 1996), 291. A similar perspective to rhetorical ideology is presented by Malcolm O. Sillars and Bruce E. Gronbeck, *Communication Criticism: Rhetoric, Social Codes, Cultural Studies* (Prospect Heights, IL: Waveland, 2001), 261–79.

21. Stuart Hall, "The Whites of Their Eyes: Racist Ideologies and the Media," in

The Media Reader, ed. M. Alvardo and J. O. Thompson (London: BFI, 1990), 12–13, quoted in Rod Brookes, *Representing Sport* (London: Arnold, 2002), 111–12.

22. Hall, "The Whites of Their Eyes," 112.

23. In Derrick Bell's *Faces at the Bottom of the Well: The Permanence of Racism* (New York: Basic Books, 1992), 175, he notes "the very absence of signs of discrimination creates an atmosphere of racial neutrality and encourages whites to believe that racism is a thing of the past." Everyday racism in language is addressed by Geneva Smitherman and Tuen A. van Dijk in "Introduction: Words That Hurt," in *Discourse and Discrimination,* ed. Geneva Smitherman and Tuen A. van Dijk (Detroit: Wayne State University Press, 1988), 11–22. For a broad account of the Williams sisters' experiences with racism and jealousy within the Women's Tennis Association, see Wertheim, *Venus Envy.*

24. Teun A. van Dijk, *Communicating Racism: Ethnic Prejudice in Thought and Talk* (Newbury Park, CA: Sage Publications, 1987), 23.

25. Eduardo Bonilla-Silva, *Racism without Racists: Color-Blind Racism and the Persistence of Racial Inequality in the United States* (Lanham, MD: Rowman and Littlefield, 2003), 54–55.

26. Smitherman and van Dijk, "Introduction," 17.

27. Patricia Vertinsky and Gwendolyn Captain, "More Myth than History: American Culture and Representation of the Black Female's Athletic Ability," *Journal of Sport History* 25, no. 3 (1998): 538–39.

28. Spencer, "Sister Act VI," 115–35.

29. Spencer, "Sister Act VI," 117.

30. Delia D. Douglas, "To Be Young, Gifted, Black, and Female: A Meditation on the Cultural Politics at Play in Representations of Venus and Serena Williams," *Sociology of Sport Online* 5, no. 2 (2002): http://physed.otago.ac.nz/sosol/v5i2/v5i2_3.html.

31. Douglas, "To Be Young, Gifted, Black, and Female," par. 1.3.

32. Vertinsky and Captain, "More Myth than History," 540.

33. See for example, Mary Hall, *Serena and Venus Williams* (New York: Children's Press, 2003); Roxanne Dorrie, *Venus and Serena Williams: The Smashing Sisters* (Bloomington, MN: Red Brick Learning, 2004); Glenn Stout, *On the Court with . . . Venus and Serena Williams* (Boston: Little, Brown, 2002); Mike Wilson, *The Williams Sisters: Venus and Serena* (London: Hodden & Stoughton, 2002); Terri Morgan, *Venus and Serena Williams: Grand Slam Sisters* (Minneapolis: Lerner Sports, 2001); Mark Stewart, *Venus & Serena: Sisters in Arms* (Brookfield, CT: Millbrook, 2000); and Bill Gutman, *Venus & Serena: The Grand Slam Sisters* (New York: Scholastic, 2001). The books listed are illustrative of variations on a familiar theme; how many ways can "Venus" and "Serena" be rearranged in a title? Or alternating between "and" and an ampersand?

34. Wertheim, *Venus Envy.*

35. Dave Rineberg, *Venus & Serena: My Seven Years as Hitting Coach for the Williams Sisters* (Hollywood, FL: F. Fell, 2001).

36. Stout, *On the Court with . . . Venus and Serena Williams,* 1–2.

37. Stout, *On the Court with . . . Venus and Serena Williams,* 3.

38. Stout, *On the Court with . . . Venus and Serena Williams,* 4.

39. Edwin Black, "The Second Persona," in *Readings in Rhetorical Criticism,* 2nd ed., ed. Carl R. Burgchardt (State College, PA: Strata, 2000), 191.

40. Mark Lawrence McPhail, *The Rhetoric of Racism Revisited: Reparations or Separation?* (Lanham, MD: Rowman and Littlefield, 2002), 58.

41. Cepeda, "Courting Destiny," 126.

42. Historical accounts of the incident are drawn from Allison Samuels, "Life with Father," *Newsweek,* July 2, 2001, http://www.proquest.com; "Unpopular: Williams Booed after Indian Wells Win," *Sports Illustrated,* March 17, 2001, http://sportsillustrated.cnn.com/tennis/news/2001/03/17/williams_win_ap/; Greg Garber, "Are Williams Sisters All Business on the Court?" *ESPN.com,* March 30, 2001, http://espn.go.com/tennis/s/2001/0320/1158645.html; William C. Rhoden, "Tennis, Race, and Much More," *New York Times,* March 30, 2001, http://www.proquest.com; "Richard Williams Laments His Tennis Star Daughters Are Subjected to Racial Slurs; Denies Rigging Their Matches," *Jet,* April 9, 2001, 51; Saeed Shabazz, "Race and Sports: Father of Serena and Venus Williams Denounces Racial Epithets," *Final Call,* April 10, 2001, http://www.finalcall.com/national/williams04–10–2001.htm; Spencer, "Sister Act VI," 115–116; "Unfazed: Williams Sisters Sign Endorsement, Shrug Off Controversy," *Sports Illustrated,* March 22, 2001, http://sportsillustrated.cnn.com/tennis/news/2001/03/22/williams_ap/; and "Avoiding the Issue: Sisters Venus, Serena Are Reluctant Rivals on the Court," *Sports Illustrated,* March 24, 2001, http://sportsillustrated.cnn.com/tennis/news/2001/03/24/williams_rivalry_ap/.

43. Garber, "Are Williams Sisters All Business on the Court," par. 5.

44. "Unfazed," par. 4.

45. "Unpopular," par. 9.

46. "Richard Williams Laments," 51.

47. Shabazz, "Race and Sports," par. 3.

48. Shabazz, "Race and Sports,"par. 4.

49. "Unpopular," par. 11–13.

50. See Spencer, "Sister Act VI," 116; "Unpopular," par. 2.

51. Johnson, "Sister Slam," 54.

52. "Richard Williams Laments," 51.

53. Samuels, "Life with Father," par. 2.

54. Quoted in Sheila Watson, "'I Do Not Kiss Arse': Tennis Aces' Dad Richard Williams Praises Daughters Venus and Serena and Dismisses Jealous Critics," *The Voice,* July 2, 2001, par. 7, http://www.proquest.com.

55. Quoted in Shabazz, "Race and Sports," par. 8–9.

56. Quoted in Johnson, "Sister Slam," 54.

57. Jenkins, "Double Trouble," 105. Indian Wells was not the only venue for boos. Playing for the first time in the Australian Open in 2003, again against Kim Clijsters, Serena developed painful and bleeding foot blisters. She called for a number of injury time-outs to be re-bandaged. While the television audience was aware of this, the spectators were not. So she was jeered by the fans, thinking she was attempting to stem the rally of her opponent. See Christopher Clarey, "For Williams Sisters, Are Racism and Sexism in the Crowd?" *International Herald Tribune,* January 27, 2003, http://www.iht.com/articles/2003/01/27/mom_ed3_.php.

58. Quoted in "Unpopular," par. 10.

59. Quoted in Doug Smith, "Williams' Father Says Booing Racially Motivated," *USA Today,* March 26, 2001, par. 7, http://www.usatoday.com/sports/tennis/stories/2001–03–26-williams.htm.

60. See Ralph Wiley, "The Eye of the Beholder," *ESPN.com: Page 2,* March 29, 2001, par. 4, http://espn.go.com/page2/s/wiley/010329.html.

61. John E. Hocking, "Sports and Spectators: Intra-audience Effects," *Journal of Communication* 32, no. 1 (1982): 100–101.

62. Quoted in Shabazz, "Race and Sports," par. 14.

63. Quoted in Samuels, "Life with Father," par. 8.

64. Jenkins, "Double Trouble," 105.

65. van Dijk, *Communicating Racism,* 86. See also Bonilla-Silva, *Racism Without Racists,* 57.

66. Jennings Bryant, Dan Brown, Paul W. Comisky, and Dolf Zillman, "Sports and Spectators: Commentary and Appreciation," *Journal of Communication* 32, no. 1 (1982): 117–18.

67. See, for example, Raymond E. Rainville and Edward McCormick, "Extent of Covert Racial Prejudice in Pro Football Announcers' Speech," *Journalism Quarterly* 54, no. 1 (1977).

68. See Christy Halbert and Melissa Latimer, "'Battling' Gendered Language: An Analysis of the Language Used by Sports Commentators in a Televised Coed Tennis Competition," *Sociology of Sport Journal* 11, no. 3 (1994); and Susan Tyler Eastman and Andrew C. Billings, "Sportscasting and Sports Reporting: The Power of Gender Bias," *Journal of Sport & Social Issues* 24, no. 2 (2000).

69. Margaret Carlisle Duncan and Barry Brummett, "Types and Sources of Spectating Pleasure in Televised Sports," *Sociology of Sport Journal* 6, no. 3 (1989): 199–200. For an extended look at the interplay of race, gender, and sports commodification, see Brookes, *Representing Sport,* chapters 5 and 6.

70. Rainville and McCormick, "Extent of Covert Racial Prejudice," 20.

71. See Gary Shelton, "Just Between Them," *St. Petersburg Times,* July 5, 2002, http://www.sptimes.com/2002/07/05/Columns/Just_between_them.shtml; "Avoiding the Issue," par. 5–13; Tim Adams, "What Planet Is She On?" *Observer,* June 9, 2002, http://observer.guardian.co.uk/osm/story/0,6903,727737,00.html; and "[Profiles of L. L. Cool J, Venus and Serena Williams]," *CNN People in the News,* Cable News Network, September 18, 2004.

72. "Avoiding the Issue," par. 12.

73. "Avoiding the Issue," par. 14–15.

74. Garber, "Are Williams Sisters All Business on the Court?" par. 7.

75. Melody K. Hoffman, "The Williams Sisters: How They Inspire Each Other to Score in Tennis, Design and Life," *Jet,* December 20, 2004, 58. Also see Kevin Chappell, "Richard Williams: Venus and Serena's Father Whips the Pros and Makes His Family No. 1 in Tennis," *Ebony,* June 2000; "The Williams Sisters," *E! True Hollywood Stories,* E! Entertainment Television, May 23, 2004.

76. Jon Entine, *Taboo: Why Black Athletes Dominate Sports and Why We're Afraid to Talk about It* (New York: PublicAffairs, 2000), 152. A similar concern about Serena Williams is made by David Steele, "The Bug of Racism Now Attacks Serena," *San Francisco Chronicle,* July 6, 2001, http://sfgate.com/cgi-bin/article.cgi?file=/chronicle/archive/2001/07/06/SP218394.DTL.

77. Quoted in "Unfazed," par. 5.

78. Noel, "Fear of the Williams Sisters," par. 15.

79. Quoted in Noel, "Fear of the Williams Sisters," par. 7.

80. Noel, "Fear of the Williams Sisters," par. 8.

81. Douglas, "To Be Young," par. 7.3. See also Cepeda, "Courting Destiny."

82. Quoted in Johnson, "Sister Slam," 56.

83. Douglas, "To Be Young," par. 6.5. Also see Raven Tyler, "Crossing the Color Line with New Faces in Tennis," *Philadelphia Tribune,* September 7, 2001, par. 6, http://proquest.com.

84. Quoted in Bruce Jenkins, "Venus, Serena: Brash, Mold-Breaking, Intriguing," *San Francisco Chronicle,* July 7, 2001, par. 3, http://www.sfgate.com/cgi-bin/article.cgi?f=/chronicle/archive/2001/07/07/SP147732.DTL.

85. Quoted in "Navratilova Accuses Serena, Venus," *Mid Day,* June 18, 2004, par. 5–8, http://web.mid-day.com/sports/international/2004/june/85966.htm.

86. Stein, "The Power Game," par. 15.

87. Jenkins, "Double Trouble," 105.

88. Jenkins, "Double Trouble," 105.

89. Quoted in "Navratilova Accuses Serena, Venus," par. 14.

90. Quoted in "Navratilova Accuses Serena, Venus,"par. 13.

91. Quoted in Cepeda, "Courting Destiny," 184.

92. Quoted in "The Williams Sisters," *E! True Hollywood Stories.* Also see Jenkins, "Double Trouble," 105.

93. Quoted in Jenkins, "Double Trouble," 105.

94. Quoted in Jenkins, "Double Trouble," 105.

95. Steele, "The Bug of Racism," par. 5–7.

96. A *player* (or *playa*) *hater* is defined in the online *Rap Dictionary,* http://rapdict.org/Player_hater, as "one who despises or speaks ill of another player because he does not have any game of his own."

97. Wertheim, *Venus Envy,* 168.

98. Wertheim, *Venus Envy,* 169.

99. Quoted in Stein, "The Power Game," par. 13.

100. See Tyler, "Crossing the Color Line"; and Spencer, "Sister Act VI."

101. Quoted in Rhoden, "Tennis, Race, and Much More," par. 6–8.

102. Quoted in Rhoden, "Tennis, Race, and Much More," par. 6–8.

103. See Bonilla-Silva, *Racism without Racists,* 4. Law professor Kimberle Williams Crenshaw makes a similar contention. Echoing the politics of affirmative action, she notes that when blacks do well in an unexpected arena traditionally dominated by whites, there is a tendency to find a way to explain the "unfair advantage" that blacks have. *The Tavis Smiley Show,* National Public Radio, August 30, 2002, http://www.npr.org/features/feature.php?wfId=1149163.

104. Quoted in Stein, "The Power Game," par. 1.

105. Quoted in Johnson, "Sister Slam," 56.

106. Edwin Black, *Rhetorical Questions: Studies of Public Discourse* (Chicago: University of Chicago Press, 1992), 1.

107. Richard W. Leeman, "Introduction," in *African-American Orators: A Bio-Critical Sourcebook,* ed. Richard W. Leeman (Westport, CT: Greenwood Press, 1996), xvii.

108. Noel, "Fear of the Williams Sisters," par. 4.

109. Jenkins, "Double Trouble," 103.

BIBLIOGRAPHICAL NOTE

The athletes profiled in this book all realized great success in their respective sports and gained national, and in some cases, international acclaim for their exploits. They have not, however, received an equal amount of attention from either academicians or more popular writers. Some of them have had their lives and careers recounted in a seemingly endless number of articles and books. Others have hardly received any attention and the result is that their athletic accomplishments have been largely forgotten and lost to historical memory. The reason for the disparity in the amount of attention given to these athletes is complex and not always easily understood, but it certainly had something to do with the sport in which they participated, whether they spent most of their careers competing behind segregated walls, and whether their athletic successes were combined with a willingness to speak out on larger societal issues and took place either during world conflict or in connection with the new global economic market.

Jimmy Winkfield, Marshall "Major" Taylor, and William Henry Lewis, the first three athletes profiled, have all received relatively scant attention. Winkfield, who has always been overshadowed by another great black jockey, Isaac Murphy, has recently been accorded the recognition he deserves. He was one of the fifteen athletes included in Henry Louis Gates and Cornel West, *The African-American Century: How Black Americans Have Shaped Our Country* (2000). Even more details about Winkfield's life and career are provided in Edward Hotaling, *The Great Black Jockeys: The Lives and Times of the Men Who Dominated America's First National Sport* (1999) and *Wink: The Incredible Life and Epic Journey of Jimmy Winkfield* (2005). Information on Marshall "Major" Taylor can be gleaned from his modestly titled autobiography, *Fastest Bicycle Rider in the World* (1928). The only biography of Taylor is Andrew Ritchie's nicely researched, informative, and insightful *Major Taylor: The Extraordinary Career of a Champion Bicycle Racer* (1996). Readers interested in William Henry Lewis will have to search far and wide for information about the great football player, coach, lawyer, and politician because he has yet to have a biographer. Some information about him, however, can be found in such diverse sources as Ronald Smith, *Big Time Football at Harvard, 1905: The Diary of Coach Bill Reid* (1994); David K. Wiggins and Patrick B. Miller, *The Unlevel Playing Field: A Documentary History of the African American Athlete* (2003); Edwin B. Henderson, *The Negro in Sports* (1939); Harold Wade Jr., *Black Men of Amherst* (1976); Ocania Chalk's, *Black College Sport* (1976); and Arthur Ashe, *A Hard Road to Glory* (1988).

Readers interested in Jack Johnson have plenty of sources to consult. The controversial heavyweight champion penned his autobiography *Jack Johnson Is a Dandy,* which is, as many historians have pointed out, an interesting mix of fact and fiction. Various aspects of Johnson's life can be gleaned from such articles as Richard Broome's "The Australian Reaction to Jack Johnson, Black Pugilist, 1907–09," in Richard Cashman and Michael McKerman's, eds., *Sports in History: The Making of Modern Sporting History* (1979), 343–63; Al-Tony Gilmore's "Jack Johnson and White Women: The National Impact," *Journal of Negro History* 58 (1973): 18–38; Raymond Wilson's "Another White Hope Bites the Dust: The Jack Johnson-Jim Flynn Heavyweight Fight of 1912," *Montana: The Magazine of History* 29 (1979): 30–39; and William H. Wiggins's "Jack Johnson as Bad Nigger: The Folklore of His Life," *Black Scholar* (1971): 4–19. Perhaps the most insightful work on Johnson is still Randy Roberts, *Papa Jack: Jack Johnson and the Era of White Hopes* (1983). Roberts's book is fascinating to read and astutely ties Johnson's career to larger racial issues and the sport of boxing. Other biographies of Johnson include Finis Farr, *Black Champion: The Life and Times of Jack Johnson* (1965); Danzil Batchelor, *Jack Johnson and His Times* (1956); Robert H. deCoy, *The Big Black Fire* (1969); Al-Tony Gilmore, *Bad Nigger! The National Impact of Jack Johnson;* and Geoffrey C. Ward, *Unforgivable Blackness: The Rise and Fall of Jack Johnson* (2004). Additional information on Johnson can be gathered from Gail Bederman's *Manliness and Civilization: A Cultural History of Gender and Race in the United States, 1880–1917* (1995); Thomas Hietala's dual biography, *The Fight of the Century: Jack Johnson, Joe Louis, and the Struggle for Racial Equality* (2002), and such works on boxing and black life as Jeffrey Sammons, *Beyond the Ring: The Role of Boxing in American Society* (1988); Alexander Johnson, *Ten and Out! The Complete Story of the Prize Ring in America* (1947); John D. McCallum, *The Heavyweight Boxing Championship: A History* (1974); Nat Fleischer, *Fifty Years at Ringside* (1958); John Lardner, *White Hopes and Other Tigers* (1951); Lawrence Levine, *Black Culture and Black Consciousness: Afro-American Folk Thought from Slavery to Freedom* (1977); and James Weldon Johnson, *Along This Way* (1933).

The African American female athletes profiled here have generally received less coverage than their male counterparts, particularly those who spent the majority of their careers participating in segregated sport during the inter-war years. In fact, as Jennifer Lansbury and other historians have made clear, African American women athletes have typically been the subject of more children's literature than serious scholarly studies. Unfortunately, Ora Washington has not even received this much. She has not, as far as I know, been the focus of any scholarly studies, but only part of larger works dealing with African American participation in sport. Examples of these works are Rita Liberti's "We Were Ladies, We Just Played Like Boys: African-American Womanhood and Competitive Basketball at Bennett College, 1928–1942," *Journal of Sport History* 26 (1999): 567–84; A. S. "Doc" Young's *Negro Firsts in Sports* (1963); Edwin B. Henderson's *The Negro in Sports* (1949); and Arthur Ashe's *A Hard Road to Glory* (1988).

Alice Coachman, Althea Gibson, and Wilma Rudolph have all received more scholarly attention than Washington. This is largely a result of the fact that these three athletes were part of the integration of sport in the post–World War II era and that they realized some of their greatest triumphs on the international stage. Very good information and insightful commentary about Coachman and Gibson can be found in Jennifer Lansbury's "The 'Tuskegee Flash' and 'The Slender Harlem Stroker': Black Women Athletes on the Margin," *Journal of Sport History* 2 (2001): 233–52. Insights into Gibson's life and career can be gleaned from her autobiographies: Althea Gibson, and edited by Edward E. Fitzgerald, *I Always Wanted to Be Somebody* (1958), and Althea Gibson with Richard Curtis, *So Much to Live For* (1968). The story of Gibson's friendship with another tennis player Angela Buxton is nicely covered in Bruce Schoenfeld's *The Match: Althea Gibson and Angela Buxton* (2004). Both Coachman and Rudolph are discussed in Cindy Himes Gissendanner, "African-American Women and Competitive Sport, 1920–1960," in Susan Birrell and Cheryl Cole's, eds., *Women, Sport, and Culture* (1994), 81–92; idem., "African American Women Olympians: The Impact of Race, Gender, and Class Ideologies, 1932–1968," *Research Quarterly for Exercise and Sport* 67 (1996): 172–82; Susan K. Cahn's, *Coming on Strong: Gender and Sexuality in Twentieth-Century Women's Sport* (1994); and Michael D. Davis, *Black American Women in Olympic Track and Field* (1992). Additional information on Rudolph can be found in her autobiography, Wilma Rudolph with Martin Ralbovsky, *Wilma: The Story of Wilma Rudolph* (1977).

Satchel Paige, interestingly enough, has never been the subject of a scholarly biography. Much of the information we have on the great baseball star comes from his autobiography, Leroy (Satchel) Paige, as told to David Lipman, *Maybe I'll Pitch Forever: A Great Baseball Player Tells the Hilarious Story behind the Legend* (1962) and a host of popular biographies and books on the history of Negro League baseball. Two popular biographies that add good information on Paige are John B. Holway's *Josh and Satch* (1991) and Mark Ribowsky's *Don't Look Back: Satchel Paige in the Shadows of Baseball* (1994). The following books on the history of Negro League baseball are particularly good in their treatment of Paige: Janet Bruce, *The Kansas City Monarchs: Champions of Black Baseball* (1985); Phil Dixon and Patrick J. Hannigan, *The Negro Baseball Leagues: A Photographic Essay* (1992); Donn Rogosin, *Invisible Men: Life in Baseball's Negro Leagues* (1987); Brad Snyder, *Beyond the Shadow of the Senators: The Untold Story of the Homestead Grays and the Integration of Baseball* (2003); and Neil Lanctot, *Negro League Baseball: The Rise and Ruin of a Black Institution* (2004).

The writings on Jesse Owens and Joe Louis are voluminous. The definitive work on Owens still remains William J. Baker's *Jesse Owens: An American Life* (1986). Extremely well written, nicely researched, and informative, the book chronicles Owens's life with great passion from his earliest days in Alabama up through his death from lung cancer in 1980. Some important, yet sometimes strange, insights into Owens can be gleaned from the five autobiographies he wrote with Paul Neimark, *The Jesse Owens Story* (1970); *Blackthink: My Life as Black Man and White Man* (1970); *I Have Changed* (1972); *Jesse: A Spiritual Autobiography* (1978); and *Jesse: The Man Who Outran Hitler* (1978). In addition to his autobiographies, much can be learned about Owens through the many articles and books written on the 1936 Olympic Games as well as the debate over race and athletic prowess. A few of the most significant of these works are David K. Wiggins, "'Great Speed but Little Stamina': The Historical Debate over Black Athletic Superiority," *Journal of Sport History* 16 (1989): 158–85; Patrick B. Miller, "The Anatomy of Scientific Racism: Racialist Responses to Black Athletic Achievement," *Journal of Sport History* 25 (1998): 119–51; Mark Dyreson, "American Ideas about Race and Olympic Races from the 1890s to the 1950s: Shattering Myths or Reinforcing Scientific Racism?" *Journal of Sport History* 28 (2001): 173–215; David K. Wiggins, "The 1936 Olympic Games in Berlin: The Response of America's Black Press," *Research Quarterly for Exercise and Sport* 54 (1983): 278–92; Arnd Kruger and William Murray's, *The Nazi Olympics: Sport, Politics, and Appeasement in the 1930s* (2003); Richard Mandell's, *The Nazi Olympics* (1971); and Marty Glickman with Stan Isaacs, *The Fastest Kid on the Block: The Marty Glickman Story* (1996).

The writings on Joe Louis have been even more extensive than those on Owens. The great heavyweight champion has been the subject of literally hundreds of articles and books that have analyzed everything from his early years in Detroit and the beginning of his boxing career to his historic bouts with Max Schmeling and troubles with the government over back taxes. Donald McRae has written a highly interesting dual biography of Louis and Owens, *Heroes without a Country: America's Betrayal of Joe Louis and Jesse Owens* (2002). Three solid biographies of Louis are Chris Mead's *Champion—Joe Louis: Black Hero in White America* (1985); Richard Bak's *Joe Louis: The Great Black Hope* (1996); and Anthony O. Edmonds's *Joe Louis* (1973). Louis's much publicized and emotionally charged fights with Max Schmeling have drawn much attention from scholars. Especially good is Lewis Erenberg's *The Greatest Fight of Our Generation: Louis vs. Schmeling* (2006), but other important works on the topic are Anthony O. Edmonds, "Second Louis-Schmeling Fight: Sport, Symbol, and Culture," *Journal of Popular Culture* 7 (1973): 42–50; and David Margolick, *Beyond Glory: Joe Louis vs. Max Schmeling and a World on the Brink* (2005). Important interpretive articles that examine Louis in the context of American race relations are Jeffrey T. Sammons, "Boxing as a Reflection of Society: The Southern Reaction to Joe Louis," *Journal of Popular Culture* 16 (1983): 23–33; Al-Tony Gilmore, "The Myth, Legend, and Folklore of Joe Louis: The Impressions of Sport on Society," *South Atlantic Quarterly* 82 (1983): 256–68; Dominic J. Capeci Jr. and Martha Wilkerson, "Multifarious Hero: Joe Louis, American Society, and Race Relations during World Crisis, 1935–1945," *Journal of Sport History* 10 (1983): 5–25; and William H. Wiggins, "Boxing's Sambo Twins: Racial Stereotypes in Jack Johnson and Joe Louis Newspaper Cartoons, 1908 to 1938," *Journal of Sport History* 15

(1988): 242–54. Anyone interested in finding out how beloved and admired Louis was in the black community would do well to read the work of African American writers and intellectuals who followed the ring triumphs of the legendary heavyweight champion. Of this genre, the observations of Louis made by Maya Angelou in her acclaimed *I Know Why the Caged Bird Sings* (1993) and by Richard Wright in "Joe Louis Uncovers Dynamite," *New Masses* 17 (1935), and "High Tide in Harlem: Joe Louis as a Symbol of Freedom," *New Masses* (1938): 18–20, are particularly powerful and poignant. Additional information about Louis can be gleaned from his autobiography *My Life* written by Edna and Art Rust Jr. Individuals searching for research materials on all facets of Louis's career should consult the reference book by Lenwood G. Davis, *Joe Louis: A Bibliography of Articles, Books, Pamphlets, Records, and Archival Material* (1983).

The literature on Jackie Robinson is extensive and often very good. His autobiography with Alfred Duckett, *I Never Had It Made* (1972), is one of the better memoirs written by an African American athlete. Jules Tygiel's *Baseball's Great Experiment: Jackie Robinson and His Legacy* is still the most thorough and cogent analysis of Robinson and the integration process in Major League baseball. Tygiel followed his landmark study with two other major works on Robinson, *Extra Bases: Reflections on Jackie Robinson, Race, and Baseball History* (2002) and *The Jackie Robinson Reader: Perspectives on an American Hero* (1997). Arnold Rampersad's *Jackie Robinson: A Biography* is an excellent biography that covers in great detail Robinson's life and career. Having access to personal letters and other primary materials not available to previous scholars, Rampersad provides an intimate portrait of Robinson and his family and other close friends and associates. In addition to the aforementioned works, there are a plethora of articles and books that provide insights into different elements of Robinson's life, including his experience in spring training, relationship to Paul Robeson, friendships he established with Branch Rickey and his teammates, and type of media coverage he received from both the black and white press. Some of the best known of these studies are Stephen H. Norwood and Harold Brackman, "Going to Bat for Jackie Robinson: The Jewish Role in Breaking Baseball's Color Line," *Journal of Sport History* 26 (1999): 115–41; Henry D. Fetter, "The Party Line and the Color Line: The American Communist Party," *Daily Worker,* and Jackie Robinson," *Journal of Sport History* 28 (2001): 375–402; Chris Lamb, "'I Never Want to Take Another Trip Like This One': Jackie Robinson's Journey to Integrate Baseball," *Journal of Sport History* 24 (1997): 177–91; Michael E. Lomax, "'I Never Had It Made' Revisited: The Political, Economic, and Social Ideology of Jackie Robinson," *Afro-Americans in New York Life and History* 23 (1999): 39–60; William Simons, "Jackie Robinson and the American Mind: Journalistic Perceptions of the Reintegration of Baseball," *Journal of Sport History* 12 (1985): 39–64; Ronald A. Smith, "The Paul Robeson–Jackie Robinson Saga and a Political Collision," *Journal of Sport History* 6 (1979): 5–27; Joseph Dorinson and Soram Warmund, eds., *Jackie Robinson: Race, Sports, and the American Dream* (2002); Gerald Early, "American Integration, Black Heroism, and the Meaning of Jackie Robinson," *Chronicles of Higher Education* (May 23, 1997), B4–B5; and Anthony R. Pretkanis and Marlena Turner, "Nine Principles of Successful Affirmative Action: Mr. Branch Rickey, Mr. Jackie Robinson, and the Integration of Baseball," *Nine: Journal of Baseball History and Social Perspectives* 2 (1994): 36–65.

The scholarly literature on Bill Russell, Jim Brown, and Arthur Ashe is rather scant considering their contributions to sport and the larger civil rights struggle. None of them yet has a serious biographer. In fact, other than the recent book by John Taylor, *The Rivalry: Bill Russell, Wilt Chamberlain, and the Golden Age of Basketball* (2006), and a smattering of more popular works, much of what we know about the three legendary athletes is derived from the highly interesting and thought-provoking autobiographies they have written. Russell's autobiography with William McSweeney, *Go Up for Glory* (1966), was an enormously influential book and decidedly different from anything else previously written by an African American athlete in that it talked seriously about both sport and race in American society. He would follow eight years later with the thoughtful and refreshingly frank autobiography with Taylor Branch, *Second Wind: The Memoirs of an Opinionated Man* (1974). Jim Brown would pen two very honest and, in some ways, very strident memoirs with Myron Cope, *Off My Chest* (1964), and with Steve Delsohn, *Out of Bounds* (1989). Arthur Ashe wrote three autobiographies, with Frank DeFord, *Portrait in Motion* (1975), with Neil Amdur, *Off the Court* (1981), and with Arnold Rampersad, *Days of Grace* (1993). Of these three autobiographies, *Days of Grace* is perhaps the most intriguing, candid, and poignant. Ashe describes, among other things, his involvement in the Davis Cup, his assessments of his fellow tour players, his relationship with his wife and daughter, his participation in the struggle against apartheid, and his losing battle with AIDS.

Muhammad Ali has been the focus of many works, some of them more popular in nature and some of them more highly interpretive and scholarly. An especially interesting book on the controversial heavyweight champion is Thomas Hauser's *Muhammad Ali: His Life and Times* (1991). Hauser, author of the popular *Black Lights: Inside the World of Professional Boxing* (1986), crafted an insightful and highly interesting analysis of Ali through interviews with many of his closest friends and associates. David Remnick's *King of the World: Muhammad Ali and the Rise of a Hero* (1998) provides a thoughtful portrait of Ali and is especially good at placing him in the context of the boxing subculture and the larger American society. Elliott Gorn's edited *Muhammad Ali: The People's Champ* (1995) consists of seven essays originally given as presentations at a special conference on Ali sponsored by Miami University, Ohio. Well written and analytical, the essays are largely concerned with Ali as a cultural symbol and what role he served in American society. Like Joe Louis before him, Ali became a favorite topic of essayists, sportswriters, poets, musicians, and even other athletes. The writings of many of these individuals—including Norman Mailer, Jimmy Cannon, Joyce Carol Oates, Gay Talese, Jackie Robinson, George Plimpton, Tom Wolfe, Hunter Thompson, and Gordon Parks—make up Gerald Early's edited *The Muhammad Ali Reader* (1998). Early also writes eloquently about Ali in his *Tuxedo Junction: Essays on American Culture* (1989) and *The Culture of Bruising: Essays on Prizefighting, Literature, and Modern American Culture* (1994). Ali is also seemingly a part of every scholarly work devoted to African American involvement in sport, including more specialized studies such as Douglas Hartmann's *Race, Culture, and the Revolt of the Black Athlete: The 1968 Olympic Protests and Their Aftermath* (2003) and Amy Bass's *Not the Triumph but the Struggle: The 1968 Olympics and the Making of the Black Athlete* (2002). Readers interested in Ali, moreover, might want to take a look at his intriguing yet not entirely accurate autobiography with Richard Durham, *The Greatest: My Own Story* (1975).

The fascination that the world has with Michael Jordan and Tiger Woods is reflected in the many publications about their lives and careers.

There are a countless number of more popular articles, newspaper columns, juvenile literature, and biographies written on the two men. Scholars, too, have explored what the two athletes have meant to both white and African Americans and how they have been portrayed by the media in a world still marked by racialist thinking and fascinated by celebrity. Some of the best work regarding the symbolism of Jordan is in David L. Andrews, "The Fact(s) of Michael Jordan's Blackness: Excavating a Floating Racial Signifier," *Sociology of Sport Journal* 13 (1996): 125–58, and "Excavating Michael Jordan: Notes on a Critical Pedagogy of Sporting Representation" in Genevieve Rail, ed., *Sport and Postmodern Times* (1998): 185–220; and Mary G. McDonald and David L. Andrews, "Michael Jordan: Corporate Sport and Postmodern Celebrityhood," in David L. Andrews and Steven J. Jackson, eds., *Sport Stars: The Cultural Politics of Sporting Celebrity* (2001). Other important pieces on Jordan, many of which are concerned with economics and the media, are Mary G. McDonald, "Michael Jordan's Family Values: Marketing, Meaning, and Post-Reagan America," *Sociology of Sport Journal* 13 (1996): 344–65; Douglas Kellner, "The Sports Spectacle, Michael Jordan, and Nike," in Patrick B. Miller and David K. Wiggins, eds., *Sport and the Color Line: Black Athletes and Race Relations in Twentieth-Century America* (2004); David Halberstam, *Playing for Keeps: Michael Jordan and the World He Made* (2000); and Walter LaFeber, *Michael Jordan and the New Global Capitalism* (1999).

The work on Tiger Woods, while not as expansive as that devoted to Jordan, is generally informative and insightful. Some of our best sportswriters have taken their turn analyzing the meaning of Woods and his place in the history of golf and American sport. Those of particular interest are Gary Smith, "The Chosen One," in Glenn Stout, ed., *Chasing Tiger: The Tiger Woods Reader* (2002); John Feinstein, *The First Coming: Tiger Woods: Master or Martyr* (1998); and John Garrity, ed., *Tiger Woods: The Making of a Champion* (1997). The latter book is especially noteworthy in that it is a collection of twenty pieces previously published in *Sports Illustrated*. In addition to the selections penned by sportswriters, a few scholars have analyzed Woods from various vantage points. A particularly good piece is Cheryl L. Cole and David L. Andrews's, "America's New Son: Tiger Woods and America's Multiculturism," in David L. Andrews and Steven J. Jackson, eds., *Sports Stars: The Cultural Politics of Sporting Celebrity* (2001). Henry Yu has also added significantly to our understanding of Woods and larger issues of race and popular culture through a series of insightful essays that include "Tiger Woods Is Not the End of History, or Why Sex across the Color Line Will Not Save Us All," *American Historical Review* 108 (2003): 1406–14; "Tiger Woods at the Center of History: Looking Back at the Twentieth Century through the Lenses of Race, Sports, and Mass Consumption," in John Bloom and Michael Nevin Willard, eds., *Sports Matters: Race, Recreation, and Culture* (2002); and "How Tiger Lost His Stripes: Post-National American Studies as A History of Race, Migration and the Commodification of Culture," in John C. Rowe, ed., *Post-National American Studies* (2000).

Venus and Serena Williams have been the subjects of a score of writings. Like other African American women athletes, the two sisters have been the focus of a number of biographies intended for a juvenile audience. These include such works as Mark Stewart's *Venus & Serena: Sisters in Arms* (2000); Bill Gutman's *Venus & Serena: The Grand Slam Sisters* (2001); Glenn Stout's *On the Court with . . . Venus and Serena Williams* (2002); Roxanne Dorrie's *Venus & Serena Williams: The Smashing Sisters* (2004); and Mary Hall's *Serena and Venus Williams* (2003). The two sisters have also received an extraordinary amount of coverage in both the black and white press and some recent scholarly attention from academicians. Perhaps the best known of these works are Nancy E. Spencer's articles "Sister Act VI: Venus and Serena Williams at Indian Wells: 'Sincere Fictions' and White Racism," *Journal of Sport & Social Issues* 28 (2004): 115–35, and "From 'Child's Play' to 'Party Crasher': Venus Williams, Racism, and Professional Women's Tennis," in David L. Andrews and Steven J. Jackson, eds., *Sport Stars: The Cultural Politics of Sports Celebrity* (2001).

CONTRIBUTORS

GREGORY BOND is a doctoral candidate in American history at the University of Wisconsin. His dissertation is titled "Jim Crow at Play: Race, Manliness, and the Segregation of American Sports, 1876–1916." He has published essays in several anthologies as well as in the *Journal of Nebraska History.*

MARK DYRESON is associate professor of kinesiology and history at the Pennsylvania State University. He serves as president of the North American Society for Sport History and as the associate academic editor for the *International Journal of the History of Sport.* His research focuses primarily on the role of sport in shaping national, ethnic, and racial identities. Among his publications are *Making the American Team: Sport, Culture, and the Olympic Experience* and *Sport and American Society: Insularity, Exceptionalism, and "Imperialism"* (with J. A. Mangan). He has published several articles on sport and race in American culture in the *Journal of Sport History,* the *Journal of Contemporary History, Gateway Heritage, Proteus, Olympika,* and other journals.

GERALD EARLY is Merle Kling Professor of Modern Letters at Washington University, St. Louis. He is the editor and author of many books, including *This Is Where I Came In: Black America in the 1960s; The Sammy Davis, Jr. Reader; The Muhammad Ali Reader; Body Language: Writers on Sport; Lure and Loathing: Essays on Race, Identity, and the Ambivalence of Assimilation; The Culture of Bruising: Essays on Prizefighting, Literature, and Modern American Culture;* and *Tuxedo Junction.* He is currently finishing a book on Fisk University.

ANTHONY O. EDMONDS is George and Frances Ball Distinguished Professor of History at Ball State University. His research in sport history focuses on the cultural significance of prizefighting. He is the author of a biography of *Joe Louis* and has published articles on sport history in the *Journal of Popular Culture* and *Conspectus of History.* He has also written a history of the Vietnam War.

MARY JO FESTLE is a professor of history and director of the university-wide Honors Program at Elon University. Her research has focused on women's sports, civil rights, and the history of medicine. She is the author of *Playing Nice: Politics and Apologies in Women's Sports.*

GERALD R. GEMS is a professor of health and physical education at North Central College and past president of the North American Society for Sport History. He is the author of *Sports in North America: Sports Organized, 1880–1900; Windy City Wars: Labor, Leisure, and Sport in the Making of Chicago; For Pride, Profit, and Patriarchy: Football and the Incorporation of American Cultural Values; Viet Nam Vignettes: Tales of the Magnificent Bastards;* and *The American Crusade: Sport and American Imperialism.*

PAMELA GRUNDY is a historian who lives in Charlotte, North Carolina, where she pursues a variety of writing, teaching, and museum projects. Among her many publications are *You Always Think of Home: A Portrait of Clay County, Alabama; Learning to Win: Sport, Education, and Social Change in North Carolina, 1880–1970;* and *Shattering the Glass: The Remarkable History of Women's Basketball. Learning to Win* garnered both the Herbert Feis Award from the American Historical Association and the Outstanding Book Award from the North American Society for Sport History.

SUSAN HAMBURGER is the manuscripts cataloging librarian at the Pennsylvania State University. She is on the editorial board of the Society of American Archivists' journal, *American Archivist,* and her research interests include horse racing, African Americans, social history, the American Civil War, and archival topics. Among her publications are "On the Land for Life: Black Tenant Farmers on Tall Timbers Plantation," *Florida Historical Quarterly*; seventeen biographical essays in *American National Biography;* "We Take Care of Our Womenfolk: The Home for Needy Confederate Women in Richmond, Virginia," in *Before the New Deal: Southern Social Welfare History, 1830–1930;* four essays in *African Americans in Sports;* and eight essays in *Encyclopedia of New Jersey.*

DOUGLAS HARTMANN is associate professor of sociology at the University of Minnesota. He is the author of *Race, Culture, and the Revolt of the Black Athlete: The 1968 African American Olympic Protests and Their Aftermath*. He is currently completing a study of midnight basketball that explores the relationships among race, sports, and risk prevention in contemporary, neo-liberal public policy and popular culture.

J. THOMAS JABLE is a professor in the Department of Exercise and Movement Sciences and director of the Center for Research, College of Science and Health, at William Paterson University. He served as president of the North American Society for Sport History and as chair of the History Academy of the American Alliance for Health, Physical Education, Recreation, and Dance. He is coauthor (with Marilyn Buck and Patricia Floyd) of *Introduction to Physical Education and Sport* and coeditor of "The Modern Olympic Games: New Interpretations and Perspectives" (with David K. Wiggins), *Research Quarterly for Exercise and Sport*. He also produced a teleconference and a 240-minute videotape, "The Coloring of American Sport: Black and Latino Athletes in the Twentieth Century." Currently, he is serving as interim editor of the *Journal of Sport History*.

JENNIFER H. LANSBURY is a doctoral candidate at George Mason University, a former assistant for the *Journal of Social History*, and the recipient of the Department of History's 2000 Webber Outstanding Graduate Student Award. Her article, "'The Tuskegee Flash' and 'the Slender Harlem Stroker': Black Women Athletes on the Margin," received the 2001 Josephine Pacheco Award for an outstanding graduate paper and was subsequently published in the *Journal of Sport History*. She is currently at work on her dissertation, entitled "Champions Indeed: The Emergence of African American Women Athletes in American Society, 1930–1960."

MICHAEL E. LOMAX is an associate professor of health and sport studies at the University of Iowa. He has a particular interest in sport business, sport and entrepreneurship, and the critical cultural analysis of race and sport. He has published a number of essays on various aspects of sport and is the author of *Operating by Any Means Necessary: Black Baseball and Black Entrepreneurship in the National Pastime, 1860–1901.*

S. W. POPE is senior lecturer in history and program leader of American studies at the University of Lincoln (United Kingdom). He is the book series editor of "Sport and Popular Culture" for the University of Tennessee Press and a former section editor of the *Journal of Sport History.* Pope is the author of *Patriotic Games: Sporting Traditions in the American Imagination, 1876–1926;* and editor of *The New American Sport History: Recent Approaches and Perspectives.* Although his work had and continues to focus on sport and nationalism, he has recently contributed a chapter on sport and race: "Decentering 'Race' and (Re)presenting 'Black' Performance in Sport History: Basketball and Jazz in American Culture, 1920–1950," in Murray G. Phillips, ed., *Deconstructing Sport History: A Postmodern Analysis.*

ANDREW RITCHIE is a sport historian who lives in Berkeley, California, and specializes in the early history of the bicycle, from the point of view of competition, as regards the development of technology, and as an aspect of social history. He is the author of *King of the Road: An Illustrated History of Bicycle Technology* and *Major Taylor: The Extraordinary Career of a Champion Bicycle Racer.* Recently, he has been working on his doctoral dissertation, "Bicycle Racing: Sport, Technology, and Modernity, 1867–1903," a version of which will shortly be published by the Johns Hopkins University Press. He is a lifelong cyclist who enjoys endurance riding and touring in foreign countries.

ELLEN B. DROGIN RODGERS is an associate professor and director of the Center for Recreation and Tourism Research and Policy at George Mason University. Her research, publications, and teaching focus on Research Methodology, Demography, and the Social Psychology of Leisure. She is currently coeditor of the *Journal of Park and Recreation Administration* and has published numerous articles in the *Journal of Leisure Research,* the *Gerontologist, Journal of Experiential Education, Tourism Management,* and *Activities, Adaptation, and Aging* on factors constraining recreation participation of underrepresented and marginalized groups (women, seniors, African Americans, and individuals with disabilities).

R. PIERRE RODGERS is an associate professor of sport management in the School of Recreation, Health, and Tourism at George Mason University. He teaches courses in racial/gender issues in sport, sports communication, and rhetoric and public address. He is a former associate editor for *Communication Teacher.* His research appears in journals such as *World Communication, Psychological Reports,* and the *Journal of the Collegiate Forensic Association.* His research interests focus on the interrelationship between race, sport, popular culture, and communication.

MAUREEN M. SMITH is a professor in the Department of Kinesiology and Health Science at California State University, Sacramento. Her research in sport history has focused on the African American sport experience in the mid-twentieth century. Among her publications are "Muhammad Speaks and Muhammad Ali: Intersections of the Nation of Islam and Sport in the 1960s," in *With God on Their Side: Sport in the Service of Religion,* Tara Magdalinksi and Tim Chandler, eds., and "New Orleans, New Football League, and New Attitudes: The American Football League All-Star Game Boycott, January 1965," in a forthcoming anthology related to African Americans and post–World War II sport, edited by Michael E. Lomax.

DONALD SPIVEY is professor of history at the University of Miami. His field of study is late-nineteenth- and twentieth-century America, with specialization in African American history, sport, labor, music, and education. Among his many publications are *Fire from the Soul: A History of the African-American Struggle; The Politics of Miseducation: The Booker Washington Institute of Liberia;* and *Schooling for the New Slavery: Black Industrial Education, 1868–1915.* He is currently working on a biography of Leroy "Satchel" Paige.

DAMION THOMAS is an assistant professor in the African American Studies Program and the Department of Kinesiology at the University of Illinois-Urbana/Champaign. He completed a Ph.D in United States

History at the University of California, Los Angeles, in 2002. He is currently working on a book manuscript that focuses on U.S. government attempts to manipulate international perceptions of American race relations by sending African American athletes abroad on goodwill tours during the cold war.

WAYNE WILSON is vice president of research at the Amateur Athletic Foundation of Los Angeles, where he supervises research projects, website development, conference planning, and the foundation's sports library. Wilson, the author of several articles on the Olympic movement, was the executive producer and cowriter of the CD-ROM *An Olympic Journey: The Story of Women in the Olympic Games.* Since 1990, he has edited a series of research reports published by the Amateur Athletic Foundation on race, gender, and sports media. He also is the coeditor of *Doping in Elite Sport: The Politics of Drugs in the Olympic Movement.*

INDEX

DAVID K. WIGGINS is a professor and the director of the School of Recreation, Health and Tourism at George Mason University. He is a leading scholar on African American sport and the author of *Glory Bound: Black Athletes in a White America* (Syracuse University Press, 1997), editor of *Sport in America: From Wicked Amusement to National Obsession* (Human Kinetics Publishers, 1995), coeditor of *Ethnicity and Sport in North American History and Culture* (Greenwood Press, 1994), coauthor of *The Unlevel Playing Field: A Documentary History of the African American Experience in Sport* (University of Illinois Press, 2003), co-author of *African Americans in Sports* (M. E. Sharpe, 2004), and coeditor of *Sport and the Color Line: Black Athletes and Race Relations in Twentieth Century America* (Routledge, 2004).